Fighter Combat
TACTICS AND MANEUVERING

Fighter Combat
TACTICS AND MANEUVERING

By Robert L. Shaw

Naval Institute Press
Annapolis, Maryland

Library of Congress Cataloging-in-Publication Data
Shaw, Robert L., 1947-
  Fighter combat.

  Bibliography: p.
  Includes index.
  1. Fighter plane combat.   I. Title.
UG700.S5   1985   358.4′ 142   85-21452
ISBN 0-87021-059-9

Printed in the United States of America on acid-free paper ∞

12 11 10 9 8 7

Contents

Preface

As a young "nugget" naval aviator and aspiring fighter pilot I listened intently to my instructors, studied hard, did my best to apply what I had learned during airborne practice flights . . . and constantly got "hammered." After some period of enduring this humiliation I began asking embarrassing questions of my salty old instructors concerning what I assumed to be pretty basic tactical concepts. Probably the best answer I got was: "Oh, you're supposed to lose at this stage."

> We wanted a man of the caliber of Boelcke or Mannock or Mölders or Malan to explain the unknown and to clear our confused and apprehensive minds; but on this occasion the right senior officer was not present.
> Air Vice-Marshal J. E. "Johnnie" Johnson, RAF
> Leading RAF Ace in Europe, WW-II
> 38 Victories

Being a hard-to-please sort of guy, I have persisted in my dumb questions throughout what seems to be a rather long, but unillustrious, career as a fighter pilot. After a relatively short time, however, I came to a startling conclusion: Nobody seemed to have the answers I was looking for—or if they did, they weren't talking. In desperation I searched the literature, thinking that surely, in sixty years of fighter aviation, someone had written the answers down. What I found, mostly, were histories that covered periods of aerial combat with broad strokes and a superficial depth, histories whose authors, it often appeared, were working from newspaper accounts to find information on a subject about which they had little firsthand knowledge. There were also some personal histories written by successful (i.e., living) fighter pilots (or derived from interviews with these pilots), who recounted in detail some of their more interesting combat anecdotes. Aside from being fascinating to another fighter pilot, this latter class of work quite often actually covered tactics the pilots used and those employed by their opponents. Unfortunately, I soon discovered that these tactics varied greatly, and, amazingly, that all were sometimes successful but disastrous at other times. Although some of the more general concepts of air combat gleaned from such accounts seemed to be valid in modern warfare, many of the details were not. Each engagement appeared to be a little slice out of time which could never be repeated. The aircraft, the people, the weapons, the tactics, and the conditions all came together to form a result, and if the engagement had been repeated, even the next day, the outcome easily could have been reversed. Luck and chance seem to be very strong players in this game. Indeed, one of a fighter pilot's favorite expressions is "I'd rather be lucky than good any day."

> An excellent weapon and luck had been on my side. To be successful the best fighter pilot needs both.
>> Lt. General Adolph Galland
>> General of the Fighter Arm, Luftwaffe, 1941–45
>> 104 Victories

But my engineering background had taught me that somewhere there exists a neat mathematical solution to even the messiest of problems, so I continued to search for the basic "truths" that govern these events—or at least stack the odds one way or the other. Some of these principles do exist, and I hope most of them are included in this text. Much of what you will read here has been derived from personal flight experience, engineering analysis of fighter performance data, and "bar talk" with other fighter pilots. (It's amazing how smart a person becomes after a couple of beers.) If I have stolen anyone's favorite move or pet expression, please accept my apologies. I can assure you the theft was not intentional. It is impossible to be certain of the exact origins of impressions and opinions formed over many years. Neither do the tactics described here necessarily reflect the tactical doctrines of the air services of any nation. I have done my best to be as objective as possible on this controversial subject by discussing the pros and cons of several doctrines. No doctrine is perfect, and there will, no doubt, be "B.S." flags flown by some students and practitioners of this science. In this business there is certainly plenty of room for disagreement.

> Nothing is true in tactics.
>> Commander Randy "Duke" Cunningham, USN
>> 5 Victories, Vietnam Conflict

It has been my experience that nations, and even separate air arms within a given nation, differ in air combat tactics as widely as they do in other areas. In fact, they often disagree even on what constitutes a "tactical doctrine." For example, I have found that asking two U.S. pilots for their tactics in a given situation elicits three different answers. By contrast, it is my understanding that three Russian fighter pilots will all give the same answer. Probably neither of these extremes is optimum. Obviously, if you have only one tactic, it had better be the correct one; however, even if this is the case, there are disadvantages to inflexibility. Almost any tactic can be defeated if it is totally predictable, and dogma stifles innovation. Total flexibility is not ideal either, as it is difficult for the fighter pilot to become proficient if he is constantly changing his style and technique.

. . . a fighter pilot must be free to propose improvements [in tactics] or he will
get himself killed.
Commander Randy "Duke" Cunningham, USN

A few words might be in order to explain the title of this work, *Fighter Combat: Tactics and Maneuvering.* The subtitle may sound redundant, but actually many fighter tactics have very little to do with maneuvering. Although all the maneuvers described here have tactical applications, some are used more in practice than in actual combat, where anything more than a level turn feels exotic. *Air combat maneuvering* (ACM), therefore, has a connotation of "simulated" combat. *Fighter tactics* are more the "real thing." Both are covered here, and it may not be clear which is which. One clue is to look for phrases such as *uncontrolled conditions* or *unknown environment,* which are usually associated with combat fighter tactics.

I didn't turn with enemy pilots as a rule. I might make one turn—to see what the situation was—but not often. It was too risky.
General John C. Meyer
Vice-Chief of Staff, USAF
26 Victories, WW-II and Korean Conflict

Another term that requires definition is *fighter.* These days every military airplane jockey, whether he straps on a helo or a trash-hauling transport, thinks he's flying a fighter. *Fighter,* in this book, will mean an aircraft whose mission is destroying other airborne aircraft. Much has been made of the term *fighter-bomber,* which describes an aircraft that can perform both air-to-air and air-to-ground missions. Regardless of the designation, as long as that aircraft is assigned to drop things in the dirt, it's a *target,* not a fighter. Once it has jettisoned that air-to-mud stuff and goes looking for trouble, *then* it's a fighter. As a self-respecting fighter pilot, that's all I'll say on that subject.

There are only two types of aircraft—fighters and targets.
Major Doyle "Wahoo" Nicholson, USMC
Fighter Pilot

The word *tactics* also could use some clarification. Too often historians confuse this term with the term *strategy.* *Strategy* signifies pre-engagement planning for accomplishing rather large-scale goals. For instance, in the Battle of Britain, the English developed a strategy of using coordinated fighters and ground-based radar controllers as a defense against German bombers. The *tactics* of the fighters would have included their choice of attack formations, pre-attack positioning, attack speed, maneuvering to attain a firing position, and engagement/disengagement decision criteria. You will find that most of the literature which purports to deal with fighter tactics in actuality covers only strategy. This is probably because information on strategy is much more readily available and is easier for both the writer and the reader to comprehend, but such works are of little more than entertainment value to the practicing fighter pilot. Although strategic concepts are outlined here, the primary purpose of this text is to fill the current void of information and understanding associated with nitty-gritty air combat tactics.

> Bombing is often called "strategic" when we hit the enemy, and "tactical" when he hits us, and it is often difficult to know where one finishes and the other begins.
>
>   Air Vice-Marshal J. E. "Johnnie" Johnson, RAF

Throughout my research in this area, I often have come upon the theory that air combat has remained essentially unchanged since its advent in World War I. To a certain extent this is true. Obviously the laws of physics and geometry do not change very rapidly, so as long as fighter aircraft remain fixed-wing airplanes with air-breathing engines, there will be some continuity in combat tactics. The details of these tactics, however, are changing constantly. Although the total bag of available tactics probably has not been expanded appreciably since World War I, those tactics which will be successful vary with each new weapon, aircraft, and combat situation. Military planners often fail to account for this evolution, and consequently they fall into the old trap of training and equipping for the last war. The opposite also has been true, however. Probably the best example of this was seen in the 1950s and 1960s, when many fighters were designed and built without guns, since it seemed obvious that the tremendous speeds of these new aircraft would preclude the close-range turning engagement and that the new "wish-'em-dead" missiles being employed would make such dogfights unnecessary. The first large-scale combat with these aircraft and weapons proved this reasoning to be seriously flawed. Once again the predicted demise of the dogfight had been "greatly exaggerated."

> The most important thing is to have a flexible approach. . . . The truth is no one knows exactly what air fighting will be like in the future. We can't say anything will stay as it is, but we also can't be certain the future will conform to particular theories, which so often, between the wars, have proved wrong.
>
>   Brigadier General Robin Olds, USAF
>   16 Victories, WW-II and Vietnam Conflict

Along with tactics and aircraft, the fighter pilot also has changed. The crude "packing crates" and weapons of World War I demanded great physical dexterity and endurance, excellent marksmanship, good eyesight, and quick reflexes. Successful fighter pilots were, therefore, drawn largely from the ranks of athletes, hunters, sport flyers, horsemen, and race-car drivers. Although the same attributes and talents are still valuable today, modern fighters and weapons systems have shifted the emphasis somewhat more toward eyesight, manual dexterity, and the ability to think in combat, and away from marksmanship and reflexes. Flying today's fighter aircraft is much like playing a piccolo with each hand, while 3,000-psi hydraulic systems have reduced the requirements for great physical strength. Paradoxically, the faster speeds of modern fighters have actually slowed the pace of turning dogfights because of the resulting slower turn rates. World War I fighters usually could reverse course in less than five seconds, while today's fighters often require about triple that. More time provides greater opportunity for the pilot to think and plan during the engagement, and so reduces the reliance on reflex reactions to the opponent's maneuvering. Conversely, longer turn radii and greater weapons range have greatly increased the engagement distances between opposing fighters, making excellent eyesight even more critical. Simultaneously, guided weapons and computerized gunsights have reduced marksmanship requirements.

Aside from the physical qualities, however, aggressiveness, determination, patience, and a cool head seem to have distinguished the successful fighter pilot throughout the history of aerial combat. Although the purely physical attributes normally must be provided by nature, many of the mental and psychological qualities can be gained through experience. Particularly in modern air combat, the experience of an older pilot can outweigh the physical strength and quicker reflexes of youth, as long as the older pilot can maintain his eyesight, either naturally or by artificial means.

> Great pilots are made not born. . . . A man may possess good eyesight, sensitive hands, and perfect coordination, but the end product is only fashioned by steady coaching, much practice, and experience.
> Air Vice-Marshal J. E. "Johnnie" Johnson, RAF

Only one further point needs to be made at this time; this regarding the nature of air combat. Since so much in this business involves human action and reaction, there are few absolutes, so it is unwise to make unqualified statements about almost anything in the field. Inevitably someone will expose a legitimate exception to any proposed rule. Therefore, I adhere to the "never-say-never" philosophy. So, if you should note statements that include unqualified words such as *always* or *never,* please consider them to be oversights.

ACM has many of the qualities of boxing, chess, auto racing, and video gaming, with the ultimate reward for success or failure. It can be sweaty, exhausting, highly cerebral, and terrifying, and it requires great skill and reflexes. Herein lies its challenge and its fascination.

> Nothing makes a man more aware of his capabilities and of his limitations than those moments when he must push aside all the familiar defenses of ego and vanity, and accept reality by staring, with the fear that is normal to a man in combat, into the face of Death.
> Major Robert S. Johnson, USAAF
> 27 Victories, WW-II

Acknowledgments

Much of the credit for this book must go to my wife, Sue, whose patience and encouragement over the several years of this project have made it all possible.

Thanks to Mrs. Ann Jarrett, who devoted many of her valuable evenings and weekends to typing the manuscript, and to Greg High who did such a fine job preparing the numerous illustrations.

I also appreciate the many suggestions and the assistance, explanations, demonstrations, and good-natured ribbing provided by the air crews of Navy Reserve Fighter Squadron VF-301, based at NAS Miramar, California, with whom I served during my most serious years of research for, and preparation of, this text. If my work gets by them, I'll be content. There will be no tougher audience.

The quotes by Adolph Galland (p. 406), Robert S. Johnson (p. 28), David McCampbell (p. 106), John C. Meyer (p. xi), Robin Olds (pp. xii, 52, 67, 236, 254), George Preddy, Jr. (pp. 30, 341), and Erich Rudorffer (p. 9) are from *Fighter Tactics and Strategy, 1914–1970,* by Edward H. Sims. I am grateful to the author and to Harper and Row, and Aero Publishers, Inc., for allowing me to reproduce this material.

I wish to express sincere appreciation for permission to quote from the following works, as well:

Bishop, William A., *Winged Warfare.* ©1967 by Doubleday and Company, Inc., Garden City, NY.

Boyington, Gregory "Pappy," *Baa Baa Black Sheep.* ©1958, Wilson Press, Fresno, CA.

Caidin, Martin, *Fork-Tailed Devil: The P-38.* ©1971, Ballantine Books, NY. With permission of the author.

Cunningham, Randy, with Ethell, Jeff, *Fox Two: The Story of America's First Ace in Vietnam.* ©1984, Champlin Fighter Museum, Mesa, AZ.

Galland, Adolph, translated by M. Savill,*The First and the Last.* ©1954, 1982 by Holt Rinehart and Winston, NY. Reprinted by permission of Holt, Rinehart and Winston, Publishers, and Rosica Colin, Ltd.

Godfrey, John T., *The Look of Eagles.* ©1958 by Random House, Inc., NY. With permission of the publisher.

Hall, Grover C., Jr., *1000 Destroyed.* ©1978, Aero Publishers, Fallbrook, CA.

Higham, Robin, and Siddall, Abigail T., eds., *Flying Combat Aircraft of the USAAF-USAF.* ©1975 by the Air Force Historical Foundation, Manhattan, KS.

Johnson, J. E., *Full Circle.* ©1964 by J. E. Johnson. By permission of Hutchinson Publishing Group Limited.

Johnson, Robert S., with Caidin, Martin, *Thunderbolt!* ©1958, 1959, by Martin Caidin and Robert S. Johnson. With permission of the author.

McCudden, James T. B., *Flying Fury.* ©1968 by Stanley Ulanoff. With permission of Doubleday and Company, Inc., and Mrs. J. M. Benns.

Musashi, Miyamoto, *A Book of Five Rings,* trans. Victor Harris. ©1974, The Overlook Press, Woodstock, NY. With permission of The Overlook Press, Lewis Holloe Road, Woodstock, NY 12498 and Allison and Busby Ltd., London.

Rickenbacker, Eddie V., *Fighting the Flying Circus.* ©1965, Doubleday and Company, Inc., Garden City, NY.

Scott, Robert L., Jr., *God Is My Co-Pilot.* ©1943, 1971, Ballantine Books, NY.

Taylor, W. P., and Irvine, F. L., *History of the 148th Aero Squadron.* ©1957 by The Air Force Historical Foundation, Manhattan, KS.

Toliver, Raymond F., and Constable, Trevor J., *Horrido! (Fighter Aces of the Luftwaffe).* ©1968, 1977, by Raymond F. Toliver and Trevor J. Constable. New York: Bantam Books, 1979.

Abbreviations

AAA	anti-aircraft artillery
AAM	air-to-air missile
AC	aerodynamic center
ACM	air combat maneuvering
AIC	airborne intercept control
AOA	angle of attack
AON	angle off the nose
AOT	angle off the tail
ATA	antenna-train angle
BFM	basic fighter maneuver
BVR	beyond visual range
CAP	combat air patrol
C^3	command, control, and communications
CG	center of gravity
CW	continuous wave
DTG	degrees to go
ECCM	electronic counter-countermeasures
ECM	electronic countermeasures
EID	electronic identification
E_S	specific energy
EW	electronic warfare
FM	frequency modulation
FQ	forward quarter
G	acceleration in gravity units
GAF	German Air Force
GAI	ground-alert interceptor
GBL	gun-bore line
GCI	ground-controlled intercept
G_R	radial acceleration
H	altitude
H-M	altitude-Mach

HUD	heads-up display
IADS	integrated air-defense system
INS	inertial navigation system
IR	infrared
IRCCM	infrared counter-countermeasures
IRCM	infrared countermeasures
KFT	thousand feet
KIAS	knots indicated airspeed
KTAS	knots true airspeed
LCOS	lead-computing optical sight
L/D	lift-to-drag ratio
LOS	line of sight
M	Mach
MBC	main-beam clutter
M_{CR}	critical Mach
MSL	mean sea level
n	load factor
NM	nautical miles
PD	pulse-Doppler
PRF	pulse-repetition frequency
P_S	specific excess power
Q	dynamic pressure
RAF	Royal Air Force (British)
RFC	Royal Flying Corps (British)
ROE	rules of engagement
RQ	rear quarter
R_T	turn radius
RWR	radar-warning receiver
SAM	surface-to-air missile
SLC	side-lobe clutter
TAA	target-aspect angle
TCA	track-crossing angle
TOF	time of flight
TR	turn rate
T/W	thrust-to-weight ratio
USAAF	United States Army Air Force
USAF	United States Air Force
USAS	United States Air Service
USMC	United States Marine Corps
USN	United States Navy
USNR	United States Navy Reserve
V	velocity (true airspeed)
V_C	corner speed
VID	visual identification
VIFF	thrust vector in forward flight
V_S	stall speed at 1 G
V/STOL	vertical/short-takeoff or -landing
WW-I	World War One
WW-II	World War Two

Fighter Combat

TACTICS AND MANEUVERING

1

Fighter Weapons

Fighter aircraft exist to destroy other aircraft. The airplane itself may be considered only a weapons platform designed to bring the weapons system into position for firing. Fighter weapons have varied greatly over the years, and each weapon has had unique requirements for successful employment. The requirements might include effective ranges, aiming, relative position of fighter and target, or any number of other factors. All of the requirements of a particular weapon must be satisfied simultaneously in order for the weapon to be used successfully. Meeting these weapons-firing requirements, while frustrating those of the enemy, must therefore be the goal of all fighter tactics and maneuvering.

Before fighter tactics can be discussed effectively, an understanding of weapons systems must be developed, since these weapons are the driving forces behind tactics. This chapter discusses the major classes of weapons which have been used by and against fighter aircraft. Included in the discussion are operating characteristics, operating limitations, and countermeasures associated with these weapons.

Air-to-Air Guns

The most important thing in fighting was shooting, next the various tactics in coming into a fight and last of all flying ability itself.

Lt. Colonel W. A. "Billy" Bishop, RAF
Probably the leading RAF Ace of WW-I
72 Victories

The gun is by far the most widely used and important air-to-air weapon ever devised. The story of the adaptation of this weapon for aircraft use is very interesting and has been the subject of several other works, so it will only be treated in summary fashion here.

Aircraft guns may be classified as "fixed" or "flexible." Fixed guns are installed in a stationary position relative to the aircraft, usually are forward firing, and are aimed by pointing the entire fighter. Flexible guns, although fixed to the aircraft, may be aimed up, down, and from side to side by the operator to cover a certain field of fire, which may be in any direction relative to the aircraft. Such guns may be manually operated or installed in power turrets.

Fixed, forward-firing guns have many advantages for small, maneuverable fighters. Their installation is generally lighter and produces less drag, so they have less negative impact on performance. Flexible guns usually require a dedicated operator in addition to the pilot, which further adds to aircraft size and weight. Maneuvering relative to another aircraft is also much simpler when the opponent can be kept in front of the attacker, which essentially requires a forward field of fire. For these and other reasons, fixed forward-firing guns have been found to be superior for small, offensive aircraft (fighters), while flexible guns are generally preferred for the defense of larger, less maneuverable aircraft.

By trial and error, fighter armament in World War I progressed from personal side arms to flexible machine guns and, eventually, to fixed machine guns. The standard fighter at the end of this conflict had two .30-cal-class fixed forward-firing machine guns, which often were equipped with synchronizers to allow fire through the propeller disc.

The tremendous progress in aircraft performance during the 1920s and 1930s was in large measure the result of the intense interest generated by the many international speed competitions of those years. Aircraft structural methods were also revolutionized, as essentially all-metal construction became standard. These developments, as well as the lessons of World War I on the value of firepower, led to significantly increased fighter armament by the outbreak of World War II.

The reasoning behind these developments is fairly clear. First, increased aircraft performance allowed the weight of greater armament to be carried. Second, designers recognized that the higher closure rates resulting from faster aircraft speeds would, in general, lead to shorter firing times, so more destructive power was necessary in a shorter period of time. Third, metal aircraft, particularly the bombers, were much tougher targets, and increased performance enabled the planes to carry additional armor that could be used to protect vital areas of the aircraft (armor for World War I fighters sometimes was an iron stove lid in the pilot's seat).

These developments created a need for greater firepower, which could be achieved by more guns, larger projectiles, higher rates of fire, greater muzzle velocities, or explosive bullets. Some pairs of these factors, however, are related in such a way that neither member of the pair can be increased independently. Probably the most important of these relationships is that between projectile weight and rate of fire. In general, the greater the weight of the shell (including bullet, charge, and casing), the slower the rate of fire, owing primarily to the inertia of the heavier moving parts required to handle this ammunition. Obviously, depending on the gun technology at a given time, there should be an optimum balance between these two factors. As guns and ammunition are made lighter for a given projectile weight, the optimum balance shifts toward heavier bullets. Another factor in this equation involves target vulnerability. The greater rate of fire possible with smaller bullets results in an increased probability of registering a hit, but greater projectile weight generally leads to more target damage given that a hit occurs.

Some of the armament variations of the combatants during World War II can be explained by this factor. For instance, bombers generally are relatively large, poorly maneuvering aircraft that are fairly easy to hit but hard to destroy because of the armoring of vital areas and greater redundancy of important systems. Such a target best may be destroyed by fewer numbers of more destructive projectiles. The opposite may be true of smaller, highly maneuverable fighters, which are usually harder to hit.

The search for more destructive projectiles led to the development of the aircraft cannon. A cannon is essentially a gun that fires explosive bullets. In general, these explosive charges are armed by the firing acceleration of the shell, and they explode on contact with a target. Although some use was made of single-shot cannon in World War I, truly effective automatic cannon were developed between the wars. These were generally 20- to 40-mm weapons and had projectiles significantly larger than those of the .30- and .50-cal-class machine guns in common use, with correspondingly lower rates of fire. The cannon themselves were also larger and heavier, leading to further tradeoffs in usable aircraft space and in performance.

The many variations and exceptions of aircraft armament used in World War II cannot be discussed in detail here, but some general trends deserve mention. The firepower of the earlier fighters was invariably increased in later versions of the same aircraft, as well as in new fighters introduced during the war; increased projectile/target specialization also was apparent as the conflict progressed through its various stages. For instance, U.S. fighter designers, primarily concerned with German and Japanese fighter opposition, tended to stay with high rate-of-fire machine guns. The standard armament of the more important U.S. fighters (P-51, P-47, F4U, F6F) at war's end was six or eight .50-cal Browning machine guns. These were usually mounted in the wings, where there was more room and no requirement for synchronization, so that the full rate of fire could be developed. German designers generally employed a combination of cowl-mounted (often synchronized) and wing guns, and they tended to use cannon for more potency against the heavy bombers that were their prime concern. Late in the war the Me 262 (jet) and Me 163 (rocket) fighters, primarily used as bomber interceptors, employed four 30-mm cannon and/or 50-mm unguided rockets. Even larger guns were used successfully by both sides in an air-to-ground role, as were unguided rockets.

The advent of wing-mounted guns led to increased problems with bullet dispersion. When all guns were cowl mounted, they were simply boresighted to fire essentially straight ahead (the sight might be aligned to allow for the normal gravity drop of the bullets at a selected range). But when guns were spread out over much of the span of the wings, bullet dispersion became excessive, leaving large holes in the bullet pattern at some firing ranges. The "lethal bullet density" was increased by a method known as "harmonization," which generally involved using one of two techniques.

"Point harmonization" aligned the outboard guns slightly toward the aircraft centerline so that the bullets met at a point that was assumed to be the optimum combat firing range (normally 700 to 800 ft). This method resulted in maximum lethal density near this particular range, but led to wide dispersion at much longer ranges. Point harmonization was often preferred by the pilots who had the best marksmanship and were confident they could place this maximum density point on target.

For most pilots, another method, known as "pattern harmonization," yielded better results. This involved adjusting each gun individually slightly up, down, left, or right to produce a fairly uniform bullet pattern of a certain diameter at the harmonization range. Although maximum lethal density was not achieved in this manner, the average fighter pilot had a better chance of getting hits. The advantages of this method were much like those of a shotgun over those of a rifle. More lethal projectiles also favored this technique, as maximum density usually was not necessary.

Mounting guns such that their line of fire does not extend through the aircraft center of gravity (CG) introduces other problems. Particularly when wing-mounted guns are located large distances from the CG, failure of a gun to fire on one side can cause the aircraft to yaw significantly, greatly complicating aim. Aircraft designed with asymmetrical gun mounts often require some automatic aerodynamic control coordination, such as rudder deflection, to compensate for these effects.

The recoil action of heavy, rapid-fire guns can be considerable and can often cause significant speed loss for the firing aircraft. At slow speeds, especially under asymmetrical firing conditions, this recoil can cause a stall and subsequent loss of control.

With the advent of jet aircraft, one further complication has arisen to the mounting of guns. The gun gases produced must be exhausted in such a manner that they are not ingested by the engine, as this can cause compressor stalls and flameouts.

The next significant technical breakthrough in air-to-air guns appeared following World War II. This was a new cannon, modeled from an experimental German gun and built around a rotating cylinder similar to a "revolver" handgun. This design, known as the M39 in the United States, resulted in a great increase in rate of fire.

Even greater performance was obtained in the late 1950s with the introduction of the "Gatling-gun" cannon. Rather than a revolving cylinder, this weapon employed multiple rotating barrels. Designated the M61 in the United States, this gun could develop a tremendous rate of fire with less barrel overheating and erosion. Additionally, this gun was usually electrically, hydraulically, or pneumatically propelled; because it was not dependent on the residual energy of the expended round, problems associated with duds were eliminated.

During the 1950s and 1960s there was a definite trend away from the gun as the fighter's primary armament. The feeling was that the high speeds of jet fighters and the heavy armament of new bombers made the gun obsolete, particularly for night and all-weather missions. During this period many fighters were not equipped with guns at all; their air-to-air weapons package consisted entirely of unguided rockets, and then of guided missiles (which are discussed later in this chapter). This trend was reversed in the 1970s, after further combat experience had once again demonstrated the value of the gun and the limitations of some of the more exotic weapons.

Table 1-1 is a collection of statistics on many of the guns which have been important in American combat aircraft, and it is fairly representative of the armaments of other nations, as well. A good indication of the technological development of a gun is the weight of the projectiles that it can fire in one minute (assuming barrel limitations and ammunition supply allows). In this table weight of fire is measured by the factor W_F. Tremendous progress can easily be seen here by comparing the post–World War I Browning .30-cal M2 machine gun with the 20-mm M61 Gatling gun of the 1950s. Improvement in this area has been one of the leading factors in the lethality increase of airborne gun systems.

The lethality of a gun can be measured by multiplying the destructive power of its projectile and the number of hits. For nonexplosive bullets, destructive qualities are generally proportional to kinetic energy: half the mass of the projectile times the square of its velocity. To be more technically correct, the velocity used should be the relative impact velocity, but for comparison purposes, muzzle velocity will do. The factor F_L in Table 1-1, a measure of the lethality of the gun, is proportional to the kinetic energy of each projectile and the rate of fire.

F_L should be roughly indicative of the lethality of a nonexplosive bullet fired at the specified rate from a given gun. Cannon are a somewhat different case, since much of the lethality of these weapons is derived from their explosive shells. Therefore F_L is a fairly accurate relative assessment of the destructiveness of machine guns, but it underrates the cannon in comparison. Likewise, it can be used to compare cannon of the same projectile size, but it would slight larger guns in comparison with smaller ones.

Even with its limitations, F_L can give a qualitative feel for the incredible increase in fighter gun-system lethality over the years. For example, the combined F_L of the two .30-cal-class synchronized machine guns typical of fighters at the end of World War I would be on the order of $F_L = 2$, while the six wing-mounted .50-cal guns of the World War II P-51D fighter would rate about $F_L = 38$. In addition, a much better gunsight on the P-51 and many other fighters of its day greatly increased the probability that hits would be scored. A further lethality increase can be seen in the gun systems of some present-day fighters, such as the F-14, F-15, F-16, and F-18, which mount a single M61 Gatling gun. Ignoring the increased lethality of the explosive shell and even better gunsights, these aircraft would rate about $F_L = 145$. Such technological advances, combined with inherent

Table 1-1. American Aircraft Guns

Type	Operational Date	Bullet Weight (lbs)	Rate of Fire (rounds/min)	Weight of Fire W_F (lbs/min)	Muzzle Velocity V_M (ft/sec)	Lethality F_L ($W_F \times V_M^2 \times 10^{-8}$)
Machine Guns						
.30-cal M2	1929	.02	1,200	25	2,600	1.7
.50-cal M2	1933	.10	800	81	2,810	6.4
.50-cal M3	1947	.10	1,200	121	2,840	9.8
Cannon						
20-mm M2	1941	.30	650	196	2,850	15.9
20-mm M3	1944	.30	800	241	2,750	18.2
20-mm M39	1953	.22	1,500	332	3,330	36.8
20-mm M61	1957	.22	6,000	1,330	3,300	144.8
37-mm M4	1941	1.34	135	181	2,000	7.2

reliability, cost-effectiveness, simplicity, and flexibility in comparison with many other weapons systems, make the gun a formidable asset of the modern fighter.

Regardless of the lethality of a given gun system, it is of little value unless it can be brought to bear on the target. The fact that even the relatively benign systems of World War I were effective in their time demonstrates that lethality is certainly not the only factor, and probably not even the most important factor, in gun effectiveness. The ability to achieve a hit initially is probably more relevant. By this reasoning, a simple comparison of rates of fire among the various guns and gun installations is likely to be a better measure of their effectiveness, since this factor is more closely related to the probability of a hit. Lethality and target vulnerability are still important, however, since they determine the number of hits required for a kill. Additionally, for the guns to be placed in a reasonable firing position, aircraft peformance and pilot ability must be adequate. The location of this position is very much dependent on the effectiveness of the gunsight, as is discussed later.

Air-to-Air Gunnery Principles

The air-to-air gunnery problem is a difficult one; it involves hitting a moving target from a moving platform with projectiles that follow curved paths at varying speeds. This complicated problem can be better understood if each part of it is isolated in turn.

Most people who have fired a gun or an arrow or have thrown a rock at a stationary target realize that the projectile takes a finite length of time to reach that target. During this period the projectile is acted on by gravity, which causes it to curve downward. The longer the projectile time of flight (TOF), the farther the projectile drops. In the first second this gravity drop is about 16 ft. During its flight the projectile is also subjected to aerodynamic drag, which causes it to decelerate at a rate dependent on its shape, size, weight, and speed, as well as the density of the air. In general, the greater the muzzle velocity of a bullet, the shorter the TOF and the smaller the gravity drop at a given range. As range, and therefore TOF, increases, however, the rate of gravity drop also increases. Gravity drop may be negligible at very short ranges, but it becomes increasingly important as TOF increases.

This finite TOF also poses a problem if the target happens to be moving, since the target's position will change somewhat from firing of the projectile to its impact; thus lead is required for the projectile and target to arrive at the same point in space at the same instant. This will come as no surprise to anyone who has ever shot at flying birds or skeet. The lead required is roughly proportional to the crossing speed of the target, so if its track is directly toward or away from the shooter, no lead is necessary, but maximum lead is called for when the target's track is 90° to the line of sight (LOS) from shooter to target.

As shown in Figure 1-1, lead usually is described as a "lead angle." Lead angle is sensitive to target crossing speed and average bullet speed. Range is also a factor, since average bullet speed decreases with greater TOF. Lead angle is also dependent on the geometry of the firing situation because of the influence of this factor on target crossing speed and TOF. This geometry can be described as "target-aspect angle" (TAA), which is defined as the angle between the target's velocity vector (flight path) and the LOS betwen the target and shooter. When the target is moving directly toward the shooter, TAA is zero. The shooter would have a 180° TAA when he is situated directly behind the target, and a 90° TAA on the target's beam (i.e., "abeam" the target). As TAA varies, so does target crossing speed, changing the lead angle required.

> I had no system of shooting as such. It is definitely more in the feeling side of things that these skills develop. I was at the front five and a half years, and you just get a feeling for the right amount of lead.
>
> Lt. General Guenther Rall, GAF
> Third Leading Luftwaffe Ace, WW-II
> 275 Victories

To this point only nonmaneuvering targets (i.e., those traveling in a straight line at constant speed) have been discussed. To gain an appreciation of the effects of target maneuvering on lead angle, assume that the shooter is directly behind the target at the moment of firing, but before the bullet TOF the target begins a turn to left or right. If the shooter applied no lead angle (because target crossing speed was zero at the time of firing), the bullet might pass behind the target. The target's lateral acceleration (radial G) has generated an average crossing velocity that requires a lead correction. The amount of this lead correction is very sensitive to target G near nose or tail TAAs, but it is less dependent on target maneuver (and more dependent on target speed) near beam aspects when the target turns directly toward or away from the shooter.

Target movement and maneuver also affect range. If TOF, gravity drop, lead angle, etc., are calculated based on target range at the time of firing (position "1" in Figure 1-1), any movement or maneuver during projectile TOF could change the range, invalidating all calculations and causing a miss.

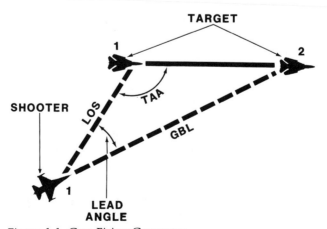

Figure 1-1. Gun-Firing Geometry

The final complication in air-to-air gunnery is the motion of the shooter aircraft itself. Accurate ballistics calculations depend on knowing the true velocity of the projectile as it leaves the barrel. The true airspeed of the shooter must be added to the muzzle velocity to determine launch speed. Shooter aircraft maneuvering will also have several important effects. For example, as the shooter maneuvers, the gun-bore line (GBL) may be displaced somewhat from the firing aircraft's direction of motion because of "angle of attack," sideslip, etc. (Angle of attack is discussed in the Appendix.) The actual trajectory at the instant the bullet leaves the muzzle will not, therefore, generally be aligned with the GBL. Motion imparted to the projectile by rotating barrels (Gatling gun), as well as aircraft flexing under maneuvering loads, may be factors. These and some other factors are usually grouped together under the term "trajectory jump," which includes any angular difference between the GBL and the initial trajectory.

Given all the foregoing factors that come into play, it's amazing that an air-to-air gun kill is ever recorded, especially when many of these factors are unknown quantities for the pilot. Little wonder that the most effective technique often is to "fill the windscreen with target and let 'er rip." Effective air-to-air gunsights have done much to aid the fighter pilot in this difficult task.

> As to gunnery passes, the best was when you dived with speed, made one pass, shot an opponent down quickly, and pulled back up. . . . The secret was to do the job in one pass; it could be from the side or from behind and I usually tried to open fire at about 150 feet.
>
> Major Erich Rudorffer, Luftwaffe
> Seventh Leading Ace, WW-II
> 222 Victories (13 on One Mission)

Tracer bullets, introduced during World War I, were also a great aid to the pilot, since he could see the trajectory of his bullet stream and make corrections. Small pyrotechnic charges located in the rear of tracer bullets burn during the TOF, making the projectile visible. Although this feature can be an aid in placing bullets on the target, the benefits can work both ways. The pilots of many target aircraft do not realize they are under attack until the first shots are fired. Any tracer that misses the target will definitely get the target pilot's attention and cause him to maneuver defensively. Without tracers, attacking pilot normally gets a few extra seconds' chance at a steady target, greatly increasing the probability of a kill. For this reason it is recommended that tracer ammunition be used only for gunnery practice, to allow the student to develop a feel for bullet trajectories and dispersion.

> Sometimes you miss with the first bullets and the tracers give you away.
> Colonel Francis S. "Gabby" Gabreski, USAAF
> Leading American Ace in Europe, WW-II
> 34.5 Victories, WW-II and Korean Conflict

The usual practice with tracers is to intersperse these rounds among the normal ammunition (every fifth bullet, for example), since rate of fire is usually such that several will be in the air simultaneously anyway. Since the ballistics of tracer ammunition generally varies slightly from the ballistics of the nontracer rounds, the trajectories also are likely to differ slightly, which can be misleading, especially when the pilot is firing at long range. Difficulties in depth perception can also make assessment of tracer trajectories ambiguous. With the advent of effective air-to-air gunsights, the disadvantages of tracers in combat probably began to outweigh the benefits.

> [The commanding officer] ordered the tracer ammo removed . . . I'll never forget the spectacular results we got. Our kill rate went up from 50 to 100 per cent.
>
> Colonel Charles W. King, USAF
> 5 Victories, WW-II

In the absence of an ammo-remaining indicator, tracers have been used to warn the pilot that his ammo is nearly spent. For this purpose, the last few rounds in the can might include some tracers. It doesn't take long for an observant enemy to pick up on this practice, however, and it may give him the advantage of knowing which fighters are low on ammo. Some other indicator of rounds remaining is, therefore, preferable.

Air-to-Air Gunsights

The earliest sights for air-to-air guns were of the fixed variety, most often consisting of a ring and bead, as illustrated in Figure 1-2. This arrangement usually included a ring or concentric rings with cross-braces located near the muzzle of the gun, and a vertical post located near the rear of the gun, closer to the pilot. (Sometimes these positions are reversed.) By moving his head so as to align the tip of the post (the bead) with the center of the ring, the pilot was sighting down the GBL. Since the size of the ring was known, as was generally the size of the target (wingspan is the most common measure used for target size), the relationship between the ring and the apparent target size varied with target range. This relationship provided a handy range-estimation method. For instance, the pilot might know that he was within the maximum effective range of his guns when the wing-

Figure 1-2. Ring-and-Bead
Sight

span of the enemy aircraft just extended over half the diameter of his sight ring. The ring was also a useful tool in estimating the required lead angle. For a nonmaneuvering target of a given speed at a known range, the lead angle required is roughly related to the TAA. If the target was flying directly toward or away from the shooter, only a small correction would be required for gravity drop. However, if the attack was made from a position off the target's flight path, some lead would be required. The pilot would generally have a set of thumb rules, learned from the experiences of other pilots in his squadron as well as his own, which related target position within the sight ring to TAA at a given range. For instance, if the target fills the sight ring at a 90° TAA, the shooter might place the target's nose tangent to the bottom of the inner sight ring, about as shown in Figure 1-2. Of course, further corrections might be required for gravity drop and maneuvering target or shooter aircraft, making "Kentucky windage" an important factor.

Shots that require great amounts of lead, generally as a result of large angles off the nose or tail of the target, are called "high-deflection" shots, and the art of hitting targets under these conditions is known as deflection shooting. Only the best marksmen mastered this art with fixed gunsights, and their scores generally reflected their proficiency.

One of the factors which must be understood when shooting with a sight such as the ring and bead is the effect of the pilot's head position. If the pilot moves his head forward, closer to the sight, the ring will appear larger and will cover a wider angular cone at a given range. This cone angle can be measured in degrees or, more commonly, in mils (1° = 17.5 mils). A mil represents the span of an object 1 ft in length when viewed from a distance of 1,000 ft. A target with a 35-ft wingspan would appear to span 2° (35 mils) at a range of 1,000 ft, and 1° at 2,000 ft. Therefore, changes in the apparent span of the sight ring caused by pilot head position can result in large errors in both range and lead-angle estimation. Some installations included headrests to assist the pilot in head positioning.

This problem was normally addressed by the fixed optical sights, some resembling telescopic rifle sights, which largely replaced the ring-and-bead variety between late World War I and early World War II. The optics of such a sight required a certain pilot head position for a view of the entire sight picture or a clear target image or some other inducement, and largely eliminated this variable. The earlier designs were in tubular form, but these were generally replaced before World War II by reflector sights. This optical sight was usually in the form of a circle, or sometimes several concentric circles, of light projected onto a "combining glass" through which the pilot sighted the target. The combining glass was transparent, but it still reflected the sight image so that the sight and target could be seen simultaneously. These sight images were normally focused near infinity so that both the target and the sight would be in sharp focus to the pilot. This also eliminated any apparent changes in the size of the sight ring with head position.

Once again, the angular span of the sight rings could be used for range and lead estimation. Some of these sights also had an adjustable feature, often bars of light on each side of the sight image, which could be moved toward or away from the center of the sight to represent the wingspan of various targets at maximum or optimum ranges. The center of these sights was usually shown as a spot or a cross of light called the "pipper."

Optical sights of this type represented only a very small advance over the original ring-and-bead variety. The fighter pilot needed more help, particularly with lead estimation for high-deflection shots. For some, this help arrived during World War II in the form of the gyroscopic lead-computing optical sight (LCOS). There are many variations of the LCOS, both in sight picture and sophistication, so a general discussion is called for.

The three basic components of the LCOS are a sight display unit, a gyroscopic sensing unit, and a computer. The attacking pilot tracks the target by attempting to hold the pipper steady on the center or some vulnerable portion of the target. Simultaneously, he constantly adjusts the sight picture to the wingspan of the target, often by turning an adjustable throttle grip, which, when the type of target or its wingspan has been selected prior to the attack, allows the computer to calculate target range. Any turning required by the attacking aircraft in order to track the target is sensed by the gyroscopes and is also sent to the computer. Once the angular rate of the target LOS and target range are known, the computer can calculate the required lead angle. The gyros can also sense the shooter's attitude and enable the computer to calculate the direction and magnitude of the gravity drop for the target's range.

All these corrections are displayed to the pilot by the sight unit, which causes the sight picture to move opposite to the direction of the LOS movement. In order to continue tracking the target, the pilot must adjust his aim in the proper direction for the lead correction. For example, if the computer determines that more lead is required, the pipper slides toward the target's tail, requiring the pilot to adjust his aim farther forward, thereby providing the necessary lead correction.

Such a sight system attempts to predict the future LOS to the target based on the present LOS and its angular rate of change. The time for which this future LOS position is predicted is the TOF of a bullet fired at the present time. The TOF, in turn, is dependent on the firing conditions (essentially shooter speed and altitude) and the distance the bullet must travel to reach the target. This distance must also be predicted, based on range at firing and the range rate of change (closure).

Obviously, there is a lot of predicting going on here. The fire-control computer must make these calculations based only on the quality of the information available to it. Since not only current values of various parameters (LOS, range, etc.), but also the rates of change in these parameters, may be used in the calculations, smoothness of the input information (i.e., smooth, steady tracking and smoothly changing range input) is essential to avoid large errors caused by false rate information. Each computer also requires a finite amount of time, known as "settling time," to make calculations based on new data inputs. Rapid changes in these inputs can cause large, erratic pipper movements during this settling time, making the sight unusable.

> You can have computer sights or anything you like, but I think you have to go to the enemy on the shortest distance and knock him down from point-blank range. You'll get him from in close. At long distance, it's questionable.
> Colonel Erich "Bubi" Hartmann, GAF
> World's Leading Ace, Luftwaffe
> 352 Victories, WW-II

A significant advancement in gunsight technology was the addition of automatic ranging information, usually provided by radar. Early systems used a fixed radar beam, with fairly wide-angle coverage, centered directly ahead of the fighter. Whenever a target (or anything else) was placed within its field of view and range coverage (usually on the order of one mile), this range-only radar would measure the distance to the target, indicate the range through the sight system, and send values of range and range rate to the gunsight computer. Radar-measured range and range-rate information is ordinarily much more accurate and smoother than manual input. In case of a radar malfunction, manual backup might be possible, or the computer might simply assume some nominal range and range rate.

Radar is discussed in much greater detail later in this chapter, but two of its limitations can be mentioned now in connection with gunsights. One of the problems with most designs is encountered when the radar is looking down at low altitudes, where "ground return" might obscure return from a relatively small target and render the radar ranging unusable. In addition, radars are susceptible to a wide variety of electronic countermeasures (ECM). Figure 1-3 is an illustration of a typical radar LCOS display.

A gunsight that causes the pipper to move around within the sight field of view (as opposed to a fixed sight) in response to the maneuvers of the shooter aircraft is sometimes referred to as a "disturbed-reticle" system. Within this broad category there are many variations. The type of LCOS which has been described attempts to predict the position of the target (LOS and range) at one TOF in the future and then displays a pipper that directs the pilot in providing the proper amount of lead. This type is known as a "director" or "predictor" sight. Besides all these difficult predictions, the accuracy of this system is also dependent on the target maintaining a fairly constant maneuver (the closer to a straight line at constant speed, the better) for at least one TOF after the prediction is completed.

Another mechanization of the disturbed-reticle LCOS might be called a "historical" or "real-time" sight. This system only predicts the bullet trajectory and "remembers" this trajectory until its TOF would be complete. It then displays a pipper that represents the point of impact of that bullet on a geometric plane at the target's present range. Such a gunsight tells the shooter what is happening at the present time to bullets fired one TOF in the past, thus the term *historical*. If the pipper is superimposed on the target, bullets should be passing through the target if the shooter was firing one TOF earlier.

This system has several advantages over the predictor method. One of these is that the only calculations involved are based on the most accurate information: bullet ballistics and the shooter aircraft's attitude and maneuvers. Another is that the information displayed by the pipper is real-time, and so is not dependent on future target maneuvers.

With a historical sight, the pilot must remember to open fire at least one TOF before the pipper appears to touch the target on the sight unit in order to get the maximum number of hits. Tracking can also be somewhat more difficult, since there is a lag of one TOF between movement of the shooter aircraft and a change in the pipper indication. The pilot has little immediate control of the pipper (just as he can't control the flight path of bullets after they are fired) for fine tracking corrections. Even with these shortcomings, however, sights based on this real-time technique generally show better results against maneuvering targets than do director sights.

Many variations of these two basic methods have been tried with some success. Often the differences are only in display formats, and sometimes combinations of the two computational techniques are used. Several clever prediction and estimation tricks that are often employed result in a need for much less computer sophistication than the full historical sight requires.

Undoubtedly the quest will continue for the "perfect" air-to-air gunsight, but there are practical limits to the attainable accuracy, in large measure because of manufacturing variations in ammunition which cause slight ballistics changes. Barrel vibrations during fire and other factors also have an effect. The practical accuracy of air-to-air guns at present, discounting sight errors, seems to be about 5 mils.

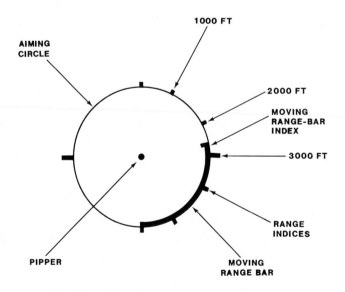

NOTE: MOVABLE RANGE BAR INDICATES TARGET RANGE
(IN THIS CASE ABOUT 2700 FT)

Figure 1-3. Typical Radar Lead-Computing Gunsight Display

Gun Employment

> When one has shot down one's first, second or third opponent, then one
> begins to find out how the trick is done.
>
> Baron Manfred von Richthofen
> Leading Ace of WW-I, German Air Service
> 80 Victories

In order to destroy a target with a gun system, the shooter must meet range, aiming, and firing-time requirements. Weapons-system range constraints usually involve both maximum- and minimum-range limits. Effective maximum range for air-to-air guns depends on many factors, including bullet ballistics, sight accuracy, fuzing requirements (cannon), dispersion, target vulnerability (including size), altitude, shooter and target speeds, and firing geometry. A reasonable effective maximum range for modern gun systems against fighter targets is about 3,000 ft.

Minimum range for a gun system is somewhat harder to define, being based primarily on the shooter's ability to avoid a collision with the target or the target debris. Closure, shooter maneuverability, deflection, and pilot reaction time are the primary factors here. Minimum range has generally increased with fighter speeds. At typical jet-fighter speeds in a maneuvering situation, 500 ft might be a reasonable minimum range.

Here is a firsthand account of just what a min-range gun shot is like. This passage is a description of Major John Godfrey's first victory; he was flying a P-47 over Europe, and the victim was a German Me 109.

> Breathlessly I watched the 109 in between the breaks in the clouds as I dove. At 12,000 feet I leveled off and watched him up ahead. In diving I had picked up speed, and now had hit 550 miles an hour. I was about 500 feet below him and closing fast. *Quick now, I've got time.* I checked all around, in back and above me, to insure that no other Jerries were doing the same to me. My speed was slackening off now, but I still had enough to pick up that extra 500 feet and position myself 200 yards dead astern. The 109 flew as straight as an arrow, with no weaving. As his plane filled my gun sight I pressed the tit. The results were incredible. No sooner did I feel the plane shudder as the machine guns went off, than a huge flame engulfed the 109, followed immediately by a black cloud of debris extending fifty feet in all directions in front of me. Instinctively I threw up my arm over my face and pulled back on the stick, expecting any minute that the wreckage would break my windshield.[1]

The aiming requirement is to point the guns so that the bullets hit the target. The techniques and difficulty of this task depend largely on the sight design and the firing geometry. In general, the GBL must be pointed in front of the target by the amount of the required lead angle, as previously discussed.

The required firing time is related to both the number of bullets hitting the target over a given period of time and the number of hits required for a kill. Required firing time is therefore dependent on the lethality of the gun system, dispersion, range, firing geometry, and target vulnerability.

For a kill to be registered, the available firing time must exceed the required firing time. Available firing time commences when the guns are properly aimed between maximum and minimum ranges, and it ends whenever range or aiming constraints cease to be satisfied. It is sensitive to the range at which proper aim is first achieved, closure, firing geometry, and relative aircraft performance capabilities.

There are two broad categories of air-to-air gun-firing situations: "tracking" shots and "snapshots." The tracking shot occurs when the pipper remains steady on the computed aim point for longer than the settling time of the sight. A snapshot, sometimes called "raking guns," refers to a situation when the pipper merely passes through the proper aim point, never stopping.

Tracking Shots. Steady tracking is usually necessary for a predictor gunsight to calculate an accurate lead angle, and therefore tracking greatly improves the chances of achieving a hit with this type of sight. Tracking also enhances the effectiveness of a fixed sight, since a relatively long firing time generally is required to find the proper aim point. Since the historical sight usually requires only that bullets be in the air at least one TOF in order to display their impact point accurately, tracking is not generally a requirement with this sight, but it may provide greater chances of a kill by increasing the firing time.

> Aerial gunnery is 90 percent instinct and 10 percent aim.
> Captain Frederick C. Libby, RFC
> First American to Shoot Down 5 Enemy Aircraft, WW-I
> 24 Victories (10 as Observer, 14 as Pilot)

The best firing technique depends on many factors and tradeoffs. The improved lethality of tracking must be assessed relative to the shooter's sight design and gun-system lethality. This assessment then must be weighed against the tactical situation. Tracking requires the shooter to concentrate on the target and fly a predictable flight path for a longer time. If the situation is such that other hostile aircraft may achieve a threatening position during this time, tracking may not be advisable. Closure is one of the major factors in available tracking time, and since the shooter's speed contributes to closure, decreased speed usually increases tracking time. Performance and maneuverability are also affected by speed, however, so such a speed reduction may not be desirable because of its effect on the shooter's offensive or defensive maneuvering potential following the shot. One other factor is the time required to achieve a position from which a tracking shot is practical. Because of the resulting presented target size, reduced closure, and required lead, the optimum firing position for tracking a maneuvering target is generally in the rear quarter (about 30° to 60° off the tail with a LCOS, 0° to 30° for fixed sights), near the target's vertical plane of symmetry. Achieving such a position on an evasive target can take a considerable amount of time, possibly more than is prudent in a hostile environment. Target defensive fire is also a consideration. Multi-crew aircraft, such as many bombers, may be well defended in the area where tracking is best.

I am not a good shot. Few of us are. To make up for this I hold my fire until I
have a shot of less than 20° deflection and until I'm within 300 yards. Good
discipline on this score can make up for a great deal.

Lt. Colonel John C. Meyer, USAAF

In order to track effectively with fixed guns, the pilot of the attacking
fighter needs to stop the relative angular motion between the pipper and
the target. This relative motion can be broken down into two components
when viewed through the shooter's gunsight: lateral motion and vertical
motion relative to the shooter's windscreen. When the shooter is located
in the target's plane of maneuver, target relative motion will appear to be
in a straight line, which greatly simplifies tracking. To maintain this
situation for any length of time, the shooter must establish a maneuver in
the same plane as the target. To accomplish this, the shooter first maneuvers to a position in the opponent's rear hemisphere, inside his turn. The
nose is placed to point well ahead of the target, and the aircraft attitude is
adjusted to approximate that of the target aircraft, that is, the shooter
aligns fuselages and matches bank angle. The shooter matches his turn
rate to the LOS rate of the opponent so that the target stays a constant
distance below the pipper. The target then might appear to move left or
right in relation to the shooter's nose. Small bank corrections are made in
the direction of this apparent motion, and the nose position and bank angle
are readjusted to center the target again below the pipper. This procedure is
repeated as necessary until the left/right drift of the target is removed,
while the turn rate is continually adjusted as required to keep the target at
the original distance below the pipper. Once all relative motion between
the target and the shooter's nose has been stopped, the shooter is established in the target's plane of maneuver, a position sometimes referred to
as "in the saddle." Although this sounds like a very involved process, it is
fairly natural, and with some practice a shooter can "saddle up" rather
quickly on a cooperative target.

Up to this point the gun-tracking technique is fairly independent of the
sight system, but now the sight begins to dictate the procedures. As the
desired firing range is approached with a fixed sight, the shooter relaxes his
turn slightly, allowing the target to fly up toward the pipper. When the
estimated lead angle is reached, firing commences. Because of the limited
accuracy of such a sight in a high-deflection situation, the usual procedure
is to fire a short burst (about one second) and check the flight path of the
tracers. The lead can be readjusted in small increments until hits are
achieved, and then a sustained burst can be fired until the target is destroyed, minimum range is reached, or tracking the target farther is impossible. Small adjustments will be required in lead angle and bank angle
throughout the firing pass to maintain correct pipper position. Generally
less lead is required as range decreases.

Go in close, and then when you think you are too close, go on in closer.

Major Thomas B. "Tommy" McGuire, USAAF
Second Leading U.S. Ace, WW-II
38 Victories

With a disturbed-reticle sight the pipper moves around in response to shooter-aircraft maneuvers, and its direction and the rate of movement are not always predictable. Because of this the pipper is not a suitable reference for shooter nose position while maneuvering into the saddle, and some fixed point on the sight or windscreen is normally used. The shooter must concentrate on the target rather than on the pipper during this procedure to avoid "chasing the pipper," which always seems to be moving the wrong way. Once in the saddle, where maneuvering is at a minimum, the pilot should find the pipper to be fairly steady, and he can fly the target smoothly toward the pipper while still concentrating on the target. With a real-time sight, the shooter needs to estimate the point when the pipper is one bullet TOF from the target. This is the earliest effective open-fire point, but firing may be delayed until the target is centered and held steady in the pipper. A director sight usually requires that the target be tracked steadily in the pipper until the computer's settling time for an accurate firing solution has passed.

> Good flying never killed [an enemy] yet.
> Major Edward "Mick" Mannock, RAF
> Probably Second Leading British Ace, WW-I
> 50–73 Victories

In addition to chasing the pipper, another common mistake made in this process is getting into the target's plane of turn too early. The opponent must be beaten first, and then shot. If the attacker saddles up well out of range, angle off the tail (AOT) of a hard-turning target will increase rapidly, with concurrent increases in LOS rate (increasing the shooter turn rate required to track) and closure (decreasing available firing time). The attack should be planned so that the firing position (preferably in the target's rear quarter) is achieved just as desired firing range is reached.

Closure must also be closely controlled. High closure is desirable at long range to shorten the attack time, which reduces the target's reaction time and limits the attacker's exposure to other hostile aircraft. But as firing range is approached, the rate of closure should be reduced to provide increased tracking time. Even if the attacker reduces his speed to somewhat less than that of the target, his position inside the target's turn and his nose position in front of the target will generally result in some closure. In order to maintain a continuous tracking position in the rear quarter of the turning target, the shooter would need to be slower than the target. The shooter also would be turning on a smaller radius than the target, with about the same turn rate. Such a situation is not always advisable in combat, since this lower speed may not allow the attacker the necessary maneuverability to reposition for another attack or to escape in the event he fails to destroy the target on the first attempt. Some speed advantage is usually preferable, which inevitably results in closure. Excessive speed, however, limits tracking time and usually increases the shooter's required G, making tracking more difficult and increasing the probability of gun jams.

Guns are like alcohol: valuable, useful, popular, and fun—but, without discretion, self-destructive to the user.

                                                                    Unknown

In making his guns approach, the shooter must also plan for the possibility of a missed shot. Approaching with high closure is conducive to overshooting the target, which may give the opponent an opportunity to reverse his turn and assume an offensive position. The shooter should also break off a gun attack whenever he is unable to maintain proper lead for the shot. Further turning in the target's plane of maneuver usually results in excessive loss of speed and often leads to an overshoot. Instead, the shooter can reposition for a second attack or disengage.

> Suddenly you go into a steep turn. Your Mach drops off. The MiG turns with you, and you let him gradually creep up and outturn you. At the critical moment you reverse your turn. The hydraulic controls [F-86] work beautifully. The MiG [-15] cannot turn as readily as you and is slung out to the side. When you pop your speed brakes, the MiG flashes by you. Quickly closing the brakes, you slide onto his tail and hammer him with your "50's."
> Colonel Harrison R. "Harry" Thyng, USAF
> 10 Victories, WW-II and Korean Conflict

Another typical error is not allowing sufficient excess lead in the saddle position. At long range, target LOS rate is relatively slow, making it easy to maintain excess lead. As the range closes, however, AOT, LOS rate, and required shooter G build steadily. In a rear-quarter attack on a turning target, AOT will usually increase to a maximum, stabilize, and then decrease again as minimum range is approached. Maximum G required by the shooter generally occurs soon after AOT begins to decrease. This maximum G is often greater than that of the target, particularly when the shooter has the usual speed advantage, and easily can exceed the shooter's turn-performance capabilities before he reaches minimum firing range. It is much more effective to allow, by stabilizing or slowing the rate of G increase, the target to fly up to the pipper as firing range is approached; this allows the target motion to take out the excess lead and is preferable to trying to "pull" the pipper up to the target from behind. Also, the excess G required to pull the pipper to the proper aim point can exceed the shooter's capabilities. Shooter G, particularly with a real-time gunsight, should be stable or constantly increasing during the attack for best pipper control.

> Pulling up into his blind spot I watched his plane grow larger and larger in my ring sight. But this German pilot was not content to fly straight and level. Before I could open fire, his plane slewed to the right, and seeing me on his tail he jerked back on the stick into the only defensive maneuver his plane could make. I banked my 47 over to the right and pulled back on the stick, striving to get him once more into my ring sight. This violent maneuver applied terrific G's to my body, and I started to black out as the blood rushed from my head. Fighting every second to overcome this blackness about me, I pulled back the stick, further and further, so that the enemy plane would just show at the bottom of my ring sight to allow for the correct deflection.

We were both flying in a tight circle. *Just a little more and I'll have him.* Pressing the tit I waited expectantly for the 109 to explode. *I've hit his wing.* A section two-feet long broke loose from the right wing as the machine guns cut like a machete through it. *Too low, a little more rudder and the bullets will find his cockpit.* I could see occasional strikes further up the wing, but it was too late. The 109, sensing that I was inside him on the turn, slunk into a nearby cloud. Straightening my plane I climbed over the top of the bank and poised on the other side, waiting for him to appear. But the 109 did not appear, and not wishing to tempt the gods of fate further, I pushed the stick forward, entered the protective cover of the clouds myself, and headed home.[2]

Snapshots. Although tracking shots may provide the highest probability of kill, they may not be tactically advisable, or even possible, in a given situation. Depending on the initial geometry, relative aircraft performance, and pilot ability, tracking may be impossible within the effective range of the gun system. A snapshot, however, may still be available and lethal.

Snapshots may be categorized by the shooter's G level during firing, ranging from zero to maximum load factor. For a low-G snapshot, the attacker first projects the target's flight path, and then he positions his pipper well in front along this path. The amount of lead taken depends on the target's maneuver, LOS rate, and time remaining before reaching firing range. Ideally the shooter positions the pipper and then flies a straight line while waiting for the target to fly through the aim point at firing range. As a practical matter some small corrections nearly always will be necessary as the firing point is approached. This technique usually results in very short firing times and is not highly effective except with very lethal gun systems or at relatively close range.

> I opened fire only when the whole windshield was black with the enemy . . . at minimum range . . . it doesn't matter what your angle is to him or whether you are in a turn or any other maneuver.
>
> Colonel Erich "Bubi" Hartmann, GAF

The high-G snapshot is "almost a tracking shot," and the same procedures generally apply, with the exception that somewhat more initial lead is usually taken than for the tracking shot. The shooter normally attempts to get into the target's plane of maneuver, as in tracking, but this is not a requirement, although it does make the task of bringing pipper and target together in firing range much simpler. The dynamics of this shot may be such that the shooter is never quite able to saddle up by stopping the apparent motion of the target relative to the pipper; but G is applied, possibly up to the shooter's maximum capability, to slow the relative motion to a minimum during the actual firing period. The slower this relative motion, the greater the exposure time to the bullet stream. A further advantage of being in the target's maneuver plane at firing time is the greater lethality that usually results. The most vulnerable area of an aircraft is usually the fuselage, and since a fuselage is generally longer than it is wide, maximum exposure time results if the pipper slides the length of the fuselage from nose to tail, rather than diagonally, as it does when the shooter is out of plane.

Most snapshots lie somewhere between the low-G and max-G varieties. The low-G snapshot generally requires more initial excess lead than the high-G snapshot or the tracking shot. If the required excess lead is very great and the shooter is located near the target's plane of turn, the shooter may have to place the target below his nose, out of sight, to establish this lead. Although this technique can be quite effective when it is mastered, it has several drawbacks. First, it is difficult to judge the proper amount of lead and exact plane of turn when the target is not visible for several seconds, so the technique requires much practice. Practicing blind lead turns is exceedingly dangerous. The pilot of the target aircraft may not see the attacker, and a slight miscalculation on the shooter's part or a small change in target G can result in a midair collision, which could ruin the entire day. Additionally, in combat, if the target pilot sees the attacker performing a blind lead turn, he can easily change his G or maneuver plane, ruining the shot and possibly causing the attacker to lose sight. This could provide the target with an opportunity to escape or even to reverse the roles.

> I'd hate to see an epitaph on a fighter pilot's tombstone that says, "I told you I needed training." . . . How do you train for the most dangerous game in the world by being as safe as possible? When you don't let a guy train because it's dangerous, you're saying, "Go fight those lions with your bare hands in that arena, because we can't teach you to learn how to use a spear. If we do, you might cut your finger while you're learning." And that's just about the same as murder.
>
> Colonel "Boots" Boothby, USAF
> Fighter Pilot

A better technique for providing large amounts of lead (when time is available) is to turn slightly out of plane. This should allow the attacker to maintain sight of the target just to one side of the nose. After the range has decreased substantially, the attacker can roll toward the target and pull the pipper back to its flight path. The shooter then can allow the target to fly through the pipper (low-G snapshot), or he can quickly roll back in the opposite direction to get into the target's plane of turn and attempt to slow the LOS rate (high-G snapshot). Although this method takes a little longer, it does not have the disadvantages of the in-plane technique.

The chances for success with a snapshot depend on many factors, but one of the most important is the gunsight. With a fixed sight, the shooter is almost committed to being near the target's plane of maneuver when firing. This greatly simplifies the left/right aiming problem that results from target maneuver. The shooter's marksmanship is still tested, however, by estimations of gravity drop, trajectory jump, etc., but these are greatly diminished at close range. Firing commences as the target approaches the computed aim point, and it should continue as long as the tracers show bullets passing forward of the target's tail and near its flight path.

> I liked the whole front of my windscreen to be full of the enemy aircraft when I fired.
>
> Colonel Erich "Bubi" Hartmann, GAF

The predictor LCOS is little better than a fixed sight in this environment, though it may provide gravity, jump, and other minor corrections. Its major advantage, as long as the shooter's maneuver is fairly constant for the settling time of the sight, is an accurate indication of the plane of the bullet stream (left/right reference relative to the shooter's windscreen), which must be estimated with the fixed sight. Because relative motion remains between the target and the pipper, however, lead correction (up/down relative to the shooter's windscreen) is usually inaccurate and must still be estimated. Computed lead is generally less than that required, by an amount that is proportional to the apparent LOS rate. For a reasonable chance of success with this type of sight, the shooter must get into the target's plane of turn early and establish considerable excess lead; stabilize his maneuver until the sight settles down; make small, smooth corrections to place the pipper on the target's flight path; and open fire well before the target reaches the pipper.

The historical type of LCOS is optimized for the snapshot, but it is not without problems. It is designed to show the location of bullets fired one TOF in the past, so theoretically its lead projection is accurate as long as bullets were indeed in the air one TOF previously. Settling time is generally not a problem with this sight since it is normally quite short and, except at very close range, usually expires before bullet TOF, eliminating its effect on the pipper display. These characteristics require only that the shooter somehow get the target and pipper to converge, and that he open fire at least one bullet TOF prior to convergence. Although theoretically this can be accomplished in any maneuver plane and with high LOS rates, hit and kill probability are still enhanced by low LOS rates and in-plane maneuvering.

> A good fighter pilot, like a good boxer, should have a knockout punch. . . . You will find one attack you prefer to all others. Work on it till you can do it to perfection . . . then use it whenever possible.
>
> Captain Reade Tilley, USAAF
> 7 Victories, WW-II

Air-to-air gunnery is one of the most difficult skills a fighter pilot can master. Regardless of the type of sight, consistent accuracy depends on total, intense concentration on the target. Whether attempting a tracking or a snapshot pass, the shooter must make minute, smooth aiming corrections while approaching the firing position. Usually such fine control can be achieved best with conventional controls by holding the stick firmly (but not squeezing out black juice) with both hands, resting the forearms or elbows on the knees or upper legs, and applying corrections with slight variations in finger and wrist pressure. Some positive back-pressure on the controls usually helps, but in very high-G situations the shooter may prefer to trim out excessive pressure to reduce fatigue. The aircraft should be flown as close to balanced flight as possible, since most sights do not correct for bullet curvature caused by the "Magnus effect" that results from a yaw angle. (This is the phenomenon that allows baseball pitchers to throw curves.) For ammunition conservation, short bursts (about one second) should be used until the shooter is fairly certain of his firing solution, then let 'er rip. "Hosepiping" tracers at a target with long bursts is generally ineffective and severely reduces ammunition endurance. Effective training in air-to-air gunnery techniques necessitates a gunsight camera for debrief purposes. Video cameras are ideal for this purpose since film-processing time is eliminated.

> I gained in experience with every plane shot down, and now was able to fire in a calm, deliberate manner. Each attack was made in a precise manner. Distance and deflection were carefully judged before firing. This is not something that comes by accident; only by experience can a pilot overcome feelings of panic. A thousand missions could be flown and be of no use if the pilot had not exchanged fire with the enemy.
>
> Major John T. Godfrey, USAAF
> 16.33 Victories, WW-II

Guns Defense

In discussing defenses against any weapon it is useful to look at the weapon as a system. Each component of this system must work effectively if it is to succeed in its mission. Defeating any one component will defeat the system, and the more subsystems degraded, the less the chances of system success. The components of a gun system are the gun and ammunition, the gun platform (aircraft), the sight, and the aircrewman firing the guns.

The gun/ammunition combination largely determines the maximum effective range of the system at various aspects about the target. Some of the factors involved are muzzle velocity, rate of fire, dispersion, bullet aerodynamics, and fuzing characteristics. Probably the best defense against a gun is to remain outside its effective range. This may be accomplished if the defending aircraft has speed capability greater than that of the attacker and the attacker is detected far enough away (depending on aspect and overtake) to allow the defender to turn away and outrun him. When this situation exists and the defender does not wish to engage, he can make a maximum-performance turn away from the attacker to place him as close to dead astern as possible, accelerate to maximum speed, and fly as straight a line as possible until he is no longer threatened. If the defender does not put the opponent close to the six o'clock position, the attacker may continue to close to guns range because of the geometry. Turning during the run-out (arcing) allows even a slower fighter to close the range by flying across the circle. Under some circumstances it may be desirable to keep the attacker in sight during this maneuver or to change the direction of the run-out after it has begun. To maintain sight and to reduce geometric closure to a minimum, the attacker should be kept near the defender's aft visibility limit. A series of small, hard turns can be made in the desired direction (allowing the attacker to be kept in sight), and each turn can be followed by a period of straight-line flight until the attacker drifts back to the aft visibility limit; this process can be repeated until the desired heading is reached. Sight can be maintained after this point by making a series of these small turns alternately left and right of the desired course. This technique is often called an "extension maneuver."

The next best thing to denying the attacker any shot at all is to deny him a good shot. This can be accomplished by complicating the task of any of the gun subsystems. Looking a little deeper into the requirements for a good gun shot will clarify the discussion that follows. Figure 1-4 is a representative guns "envelope," looking down on the target located in the center, which is heading toward the top of the page. It can be seen that the effective guns envelope is defined by the min-range boundary (primarily a function of closure) and the max-range boundary (primarily a function of gun/ammunition characteristics, dispersion, lethality, gunsight, closure, apparent target size, and vulnerability). Note that min-range is much greater in the target's forward hemisphere because of higher closure. Max-range is also generally greater in the forward hemisphere for the same reason. This relates to shorter bullet TOF, smaller dispersion radius, and greater bullet density on the target. Lethality is also improved in the forward hemisphere since greater bullet kinetic energy is provided by the closure. Maximum effective range increases in the target's beam because of larger apparent target size and better fuzing of the shells (cannon) resulting from a higher "grazing angle" with the target. Low grazing angles in the forward and rear quarters may allow shells to bounce off the target without penetrating or exploding.

As might be expected, within the overall effective envelope of the gun some areas are better than others. The tracking area is limited on the min-range side by the attacker's ability to turn fast enough to stop the target's LOS rate. In the case depicted, the target can be tracked slightly forward of the beam at long ranges. The forward limit is predicated on sufficient tracking time between max- and min-range to ensure destruc-

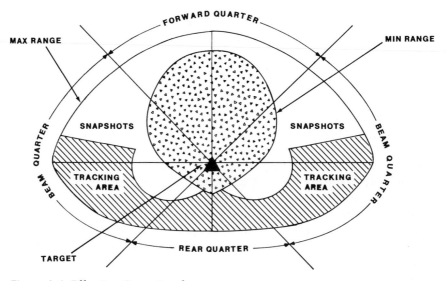

Figure 1-4. Effective Guns Envelope

tion of the target. As closure increases forward of the target's beam region, tracking time is reduced. Even within the tracking envelope there are many tradeoffs. When factors such as ease of tracking, closure, tracking time, and apparent target area are weighed, the optimum tracking region with a LCOS is generally found to be about 30° to 60° off the target's tail. Closer to the stern position may be better with fixed sights because of reduced deflection.

Although drawn in two dimensions, this envelope is actually three dimensional and would probably vary only slightly depending on the attacker's position relative to the target's plane of symmetry. The optimum LCOS tracking zone can be envisioned, therefore, as the volume between two cones extending rearward from the target's tail at about 30° and 60° angles, with appropriate max- and min-range limits. Outside the full tracking area as depicted, but still within effective range limits, is an area in which only snapshots are possible.

> As long as I look right into the muzzles, nothing can happen to me. Only if he pulls lead am I in danger.
>
>   Captain Hans-Joachim Marseille, Luftwaffe
>   158 Victories (17 in One Day), WW-II

If the attacker cannot be prevented from reaching effective guns range, the next priority is to keep him out of the tracking area, where kill probability is highest. This is accomplished most effectively by performing a maximum-performance "break" turn toward the attacker to rotate him into the forward hemisphere, generally the farther forward the better, since this also degrades his snapshot capabilities. The AOT is increased most rapidly by placing the attacker in the plane of the break turn, which is accomplished by first rolling to put the attacker near the vertical plane of the aircraft, i.e., along the centerline of the canopy. However, an in-plane turn by the defender solves many of the shooter's sighting problems and must be used judiciously. The in-plane turn should not be used once the shooter's range and nose position indicate that he may be about to open fire. This point must be assessed visually by the defender, and determining it requires practice. In most cases, with any deflection at all, the shooter's nose must be pointed ahead of the defender to be threatening. This should give the defender a view of the belly of the attacking aircraft. One notable exception to this rule is a fighter designed with guns that are canted slightly upward relative to the axis of the aircraft. Such a fighter may have proper lead when its nose appears to point directly at, or slightly behind, the defender.

> Watching carefully over your shoulder and judging the moment he will open fire, you turn your machine quickly so as to fly at right angles to him. His bullets will generally pass behind you during the maneuver.
>
>   Lt. Colonel W. A. "Billy" Bishop, RAF

The break turn does several things for the defender in conjunction with increasing AOT. High G and greater AOT increase the shooter's lead requirement. If he failed to allow adequate excess lead during his approach, he may not be able to generate it after the break. The resulting higher tracking G, shorter firing time, and increased min-range also make the attacker's job more difficult.

The following episode describes a successful guns defense begun just a little too late. Here John Godfrey is flying a P-47 and is attacked by an unseen Me 109.

> "Break, Purple Two, break!" It was too late, a 109 was right on my tail, and I heard the thunder of explosions as his cannon shells burst in my plane. Fiery red balls were passing on all sides of me. *Crunch*, I was hit in the wing. *Crunch*, one exploded in back of my armor plating, and chunks of shrapnel smashed against my instrument panel. It would be only a matter of seconds now. I had lost air speed, and even if I turned left or right, or dived, I would still, probably, not be able to escape him. But then I remembered sitting back in Eshott, listening to two RAF Battle of Britain pilots talking. Their words stuck in my memory: "The important thing is to do something. Make no movement gently, but be as violent as possible. Pull back on the stick and apply left rudder at the same time. It might rip the wings out of the plane, but if you're a goner anyway, what's the difference?"
>
> All this raced through my mind at the same time, no longer than it takes to blink an eyelash. I nearly pulled the control stick from its socket with my violent yank; at the same time I pushed with all the strength of a desperate man against the left rudder bar. The maneuver blacked me out.[3]

If the shooter is able to maintain his firing position, both range and lead, a continued break turn is no longer appropriate. Continuation of an in-plane turn past this point can result in sustained tracking or a very deadly in-plane snapshot. As the shooter regains his firing position the defender should roll quickly about 90° in either direction, using maximum-performance roll techniques, to throw the attacker rapidly out-of-plane. The defender then reapplies G to turn sharply in a plane perpendicular to that of the shooter. This second turn is continued until the shooter breaks off his attack for minimum range or no longer positions his nose for a shot. A slow roll toward the attacker is required to keep the shooter in the defender's horizontal plane, i.e., in the plane of the defender's wings, so that the perpendicular plane of maneuver is maintained throughout. The defender is actually performing a near "barrel roll," inscribing a circle around the shooter's aircraft. The attacker's closure will generally cause him to break off the attack or overshoot the defender's flight path well before the defender completes 360° of this maneuver. This tactic is illustrated in Figure 1-5.

At time "1" in this example the defender sees the attacker approaching from the right at about co-altitude and approximately 90° off the tail, apparently attempting to close to guns range. The defender quickly rolls right and breaks into the bogey in an attempt to increase AOT as much as possible. The attacker also rolls right and pulls to maintain his lead and begin the saddle-up process by maneuvering in the same plane as his target (in a level turn at the same altitude in this case) while continuing to close. At time "2" the defender judges by the attacker's range and nose position that he is about to open fire. A continued in-plane turn past this point could be fatal, since it offers the shooter a nice steady target to track.

Instead, the defender rolls farther right, almost to the inverted position, and pulls down hard. After this roll the defender will be looking at his opponent out the left side of the cockpit, near the left wingtip. The shooter is no longer in the target's plane of motion and must maneuver radically to reposition for the shot. In this case he also rolls inverted and tries to follow the target through its defensive maneuver. The defender continues to pull, and rolls slowly toward the bogey (i.e., left) in order to hold the attacker on the left wingtip. This technique continuously changes the target's plane of maneuver (spiral) and prevents the attacker from saddling-up. By time "3" the shooter can no longer follow the target through the maneuver; he loses the lead necessary for a shot and overshoots the defender's flight path.

Assuming the shooter's original plane of attack is nearly horizontal, this rolling out-of-plane maneuver will be initiated either nose-high or nose-low, as in Figure 1-5. The best choice depends on the tactical situation, but a turn toward the attacker's belly-side is probably tougher to counter. A nose-low maneuver, or a high-G barrel roll underneath, can result in considerable loss of altitude and is probably not wise at a low level. It does, however, have a gravity assist in its early stages and results in less speed loss during the maneuver, possibly providing better maneuverability for the defender. The high-G barrel roll over the top causes greater speed loss, which will increase the closure of an attacker in the rear hemisphere. If begun at too low a speed, however, it may leave the defender too slow and unmaneuverable on top, unable to avoid a close-range snapshot. Besides speed and altitude, the choice of nose-high or -low also depends on the

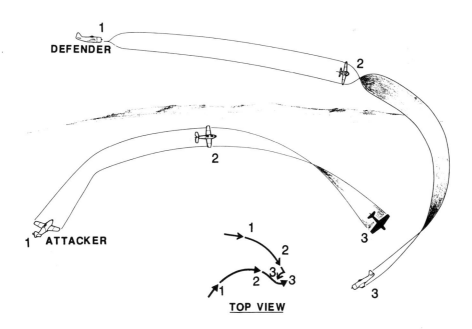

Figure 1-5. Guns-Defense Maneuvering

defender's intentions after he successfully defeats the attack. A nose-high turn usually results in a greater overshoot and may allow the defender to gain an offensive position by reversing back toward the attacker as the overshoot occurs. If the defender plans to disengage after defeating the attack, a nose-low barrel roll usually places him in a better position to begin a nose-low extension, as described earlier.

In some cases when an attacker is detected closing rapidly to guns range from the rear, defenders prefer to delay a break turn until the last possible instant, hoping that this break at close range will prevent the shooter from gaining enough lead for a snapshot and possibly cause an overshoot. Although this method can be effective, it cannot be recommended. Snapshots at high angle-off are relatively easy to defeat with out-of-plane "jinks." An attempt to avoid such a snapshot by delaying the break may give the attacker an even better shot if the break is misjudged, and it generally results in a more defensive situation for the defender after he beats the shooter's first pass.

One problem with out-of-plane maneuvers is that they require a good amount of angle off nose or tail to be effective. If the attacker is detected too late to generate AOT, or if he attacks from head-on, a turn in any direction is essentially an in-plane maneuver. When the shooter is located well to one side of the target (i.e., has a "beam aspect"), relative target motion and lead requirements are created by the target's speed, while relative motion head-on or tail-on must be generated by target G. The defender therefore must turn hard in any direction (using either positive G or negative G) long enough to change his flight path significantly, but not long enough to allow the shooter to correct his aim and track. If the defender can maintain sight of the attacker, he can estimate when the shooter has repositioned and again quickly change the plane of turn. If not, the defender must estimate the time for each new break based on what he knows of the attacker's sight system and maneuver capabilities. The clue he would like to avoid is the sight of tracers ripping by the cockpit. In either case, each jink should be made in a plane at least 90° from the direction of the previous jink. The pattern of jink planes must not be too predictable or the attacker, particularly if he is unseen, may position early for the next jink and wait for the defender to fly into his sight. The defender's roll rate and technique are of great importance in this maneuver. If the attacker has better roll performance, he may be able to track the defender from a stern position regardless of his evasive attempts.

> When he saw me behind he began to whip back and forth, left and right, as violently as he could. I followed, but it was hard to line him up for a shot. Finally, as we kept whipping back and forth, right and left, I began to shoot before he whipped and he had to fly through my fire.
>
> Major Robert S. Johnson, USAAF

This jinking procedure should be continued until the attack is terminated, usually either when the shooter closes to min-range or the defender opens to outside max-range. If the attacker already has closure and cannot be outrun, closure may be increased to hasten his passage through the firing zone by retarding power (or applying reverse thrust) and increasing drag (speedbrakes, etc.) while jinking. Once the attack has been defeated, a clean-up and max-power are normally in order for either reengagement or disengagement.

If little or no closure exists and the defender has the capability of outrunning the attacker, a slightly modified jinking procedure may be useful. Each jink can be continued until the defender has adequate rear-ward vision of the shooter, and might be followed by an unloaded accelera-tion until the shooter repositions for another shot. Another quick jink and straight-line acceleration should follow, with the periods of acceleration providing the defender with a quicker opening rate until he reaches max-range. Once again, the defender must have a roll-performance advantage if he is to have the luxury of any straight-line time. A detailed discussion of roll and acceleration techniques can be found in the Appendix.

The jink is also useful against a head-on shooter, but one or two jinks are usually sufficient to spoil this attack. Figure 1-4 shows that the effective head-on envelope is very narrow (if it exists at all), and high closure decreases firing time to only a flash. Of course, the best defense against head-on guns may be to fire first and let the other guy worry about defense. It is very difficult to aim while dodging tracers. Such a game of "chicken," however, is probably not advisable if the opponent has a more lethal gun system or a less vulnerable aircraft.

> About 3,000 yds. directly ahead of me, and at the same level, a [Me 109] was just completing a turn preparatory to reentering the fray. He saw me almost immediately and rolled out of his turn towards me so that a head-on attack became inevitable. Using both hands on the control column to steady the aircraft and thus keep my aim steady, I peered through the reflector sight at the rapidly closing enemy aircraft. We opened fire together, and immediately a hail of lead thudded into my Spitfire. One moment the Messerschmitt was a clearly defined shape, its wingspan nicely enclosed within the circle of my reflector sight, and the next it was on top of me, a terrifying blur which blotted out the sky ahead. Then we hit.[4]
>
> Group Captain Alan C. Deere, RAF
> 22.5 Victories, WW-II

Another effective tactic against a radar gunsight is chaff, the results of which are discussed later in this chapter. Briefly, chaff denies the shooter's gunsight accurate radar-range information, seriously degrading its per-formance. Chaff is particularly effective against range-only radars in the rear quarter, as well as against many tracking radars in beam aspects. Automatic electronic-countermeasures "black boxes" may also degrade sight performance. Another trick is to release something from the aircraft, such as drop tanks, bombs, or flares, which will tend to break the shooter's concentration and may require him to make an evasive maneuver to avoid collision.

> [The Japanese] are excellent stick-and-rudder men, but their weakness is that all their maneuvers are evenly co-ordinated. They make use of sharp turns

and aerobatic maneuvers, seldom using skids, slips, or violent uncoordinated maneuvers in their evasive tactics.

> Lt. Colonel Gerald R. Johnson, USAAF
> 22 Victories, WW-II

A technique that has proven to affect adversely the performance of attacking aircrewmen is the defender's use of unbalanced flight during evasive maneuvers. This is usually done by applying large amounts of rudder in one direction or the other to make the aircraft slip or skid while making turns, causing the defender's aircraft to point at an angle to its flight path. The shooter's saddling-up technique is based almost exclusively on his ability to judge the target's flight path, and he uses the target's attitude as a cue (aligning fuselages, matching bank angle, etc.). Such out-of-balance flight gives the shooter false visual cues that can be very disturbing as well as difficult to overcome. Unconventional control systems, such as direct-lift and direct-side-force controls, and pivoting jet exhaust nozzles that "decouple" aircraft attitude from its flight path (i.e., provide turn without bank or increased load factor without increased pitch) may have even more dramatic effects. Negative-G maneuvers are also very difficult to counter.

> If a pilot sees an enemy aircraft behind him in firing range he must take evasive action immediately. He slips and skids the ship as much as possible giving the [attacker] maximum deflection. It is a good idea to turn in the direction of friendly planes, so they can shoot or scare Jerry off your tail.
>
> Major George Preddy, Jr., USAAF
> 26.83 Victories, WW-II

One further useful defensive maneuver against a near dead-stern attack is a continuous rolling turn rather than a jinking series. This tactic is similar to the out-of-plane barrel roll described earlier, but because of the attacker's lack of AOT, the out-of-plane LOS rates generated are not usually as large. The defender pulls maximum G available while rolling rather rapidly in one direction, again inscribing a circle around the attacker's flight path. This maneuver may be started either nose-high or -low and is usually accompanied by uncoordinated flight techniques, power reduction, and drag increase as available in order to increase the attacker's closure. This tactic also may be referred to as a high-G barrel roll (underneath or over the top), and it is most effective when the attacker is at close range with high overtake. It is not recommended if the attacker enjoys a substantial turn advantage over the defender (either by design or by relative airspeeds) since, if the shooter can control his overtake, he may still be camped at the defender's six o'clock after completion of the maneuver.

A modification of this maneuver has also proven useful under some circumstances. When the attacker is near six o'clock with little closure and inferior roll and acceleration performance, the defender can use a continuous low-G barrel roll. The aircraft is rolled in one direction just fast enough to prevent the attacker from matching wing positions, and a small load factor is maintained to produce a spiraling, "corkscrew" flight path.

This maneuver spoils the attacker's aim until the defender can dive and accelerate out of range using full power.

The guns defense tactics described here are designed first to defeat the gun itself (extension maneuver to deny max-range), then to defeat the gun platform (break turn to deny a tracking position), and, finally, to defeat or complicate the tasks of the gunsight and the attacking pilot (out-of-plane barrel rolls and jinks). The objectives are first, to deny any shot, second, to deny a good shot opportunity, and third, to make even a poor shot as difficult as possible. As long as the defender has awareness, speed, and altitude for maneuvering, he can make the task of an attacking gunfighter almost impossible. These are by no means the only guns defense tactics, but they have proven extremely effective.

Guided Missiles

When discussing missiles in relation to air combat this section refers to the guided variety that change their flight paths in response to target maneuvers. Unguided rockets may be thought of as big bullets, and essentially the same tactics and techniques may be applied to these weapons as to guns. Guided missiles are broadly categorized according to their mission, which is generally stated in terms of their launching platform and intended target: air-to-air, air-to-surface, surface-to-surface, and surface-to-air. This section deals primarily with air-to-air missiles (AAMs), but much of the discussion is also relevant to other types, particularly surface-to-air missiles (SAMs).

Figure 1-6 is a depiction of a generic guided missile indicating the subsystems commonly associated with these weapons. Depending on the design, some of the functions of these subsystems may be assisted or even replaced by equipment located with the launching platform. The functions of all these subsystems, however, must be performed in some manner for success of the entire system.

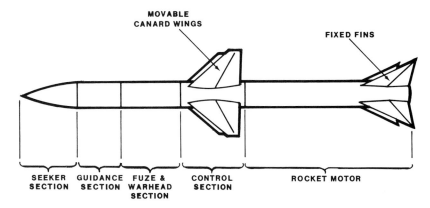

Figure 1-6. Typical Guided Missile

Missile Propulsion

The propulsion system of a missile may be of any type suitable for airborne vehicles, but because of the typically high speeds of their targets, AAMs and SAMs are generally rocket or jet powered. Rockets are usually preferred for shorter-range missiles, since rocket engines provide very high thrust-to-weight, generating great acceleration and high speeds during the short duration of the flight. Solid-fuel rockets are generally preferred because small engines of this type usually have higher thrust-to-weight, are simpler, and seldom require throttling.

As range requirements for the missile increase, so does the complexity of the motor design. Simply increasing the size of the rocket to provide greater endurance would cause the missile size and weight to grow rapidly, so more propulsive efficiency is required. For medium-range missiles this is sometimes accomplished by a solid-fuel rocket designed to produce two levels of thrust: an initial high-thrust booster and a longer-lasting, low-thrust sustainer. As the rocket grows in size to provide greater range, liquid-fuel designs become more competitive in thrust-to-weight while also providing convenient thrust control. Ramjet propulsion, however, is usually preferable to liquid-fuel rockets in this application as long as the missiles can remain within jet atmospheric limits. Often, particularly with SAMs, a solid rocket booster will be provided to assist the missile in initial acceleration to efficient ramjet operating speed.

Missile Control

The control system causes the missile to maneuver in response to inputs from the guidance system. Missiles are often controlled aerodynamically, like conventional aircraft, but they may also use thrust-vector control or an arrangement of fixed control jets. The aerodynamic controls of missiles vary little from aircraft controls. Since anti-air missiles are usually supersonic vehicles, they often use all-moving irreversible control surfaces. They also make frequent use of canard controls for improved maneuverability, as well as sophisticated autopilots to maintain stability. As with aircraft controls, missile aerodynamic controls are subject to the lift limitations of airfoils and the results of induced drag. Unlike fighters, however, missiles are seldom restricted to a limiting structural load factor, i.e., they generally operate at speeds below their corner velocities. (See the Appendix for a discussion of aerodynamics and performance.) Aerodynamically controlled missiles, therefore, often have their best turn performance at their highest speeds. With many rocket-powered missiles there is a short period of rocket thrust followed by "gliding," or unpowered flight, for the remainder of their operation. Maximum speed, minimum weight (due to fuel exhaustion), and therefore greatest maneuverability for this type of missile would generally occur near the time of motor burnout. One of the advantages of aerodynamic controls is that they can provide control during the gliding portion of the missile's flight.

Thrust-vector control is provided by altering the direction of the exhaust gases to change the thrust line. This may be accomplished by swiveling the nozzles, by installing deflector vanes in the exhaust, or by other means to cause the missile to pivot about its CG in a severe sideslip. The thrust is then vectored to stop the body rotation at the proper heading, and, finally, it is centered to send the missile off in the desired new direction. Such a system is highly unstable and requires an extremely fast and sophisticated autopilot, but it has the potential for great maneuverability, such as the ability to turn nearly square corners at low speed. One obvious disadvantage of thrust-vector control is that the motor must be burning, making it inoperable during a gliding flight segment. This would tend to make the missile bigger for a given range and may limit its application to fairly short-range weapons.

Most thrust-vector-controlled vehicles are inherently more maneuverable at very low speeds, since there is less inertia in the missile to be overcome by the thrust in producing a change in flight direction. There are many other factors involved, however, including vehicle weight, moment of inertia about the vehicle's CG, and CG location. These factors generally tend to increase maneuverability near the point of motor burnout, so such a missile should remain very agile throughout its powered flight. This type of control is quite useful for very high-altitude missiles, since, unlike aerodynamic controls, it is not dependent on the atmosphere.

Fixed control jets, arranged around the missile body to pivot the vehicle about its CG, are just another method of thrust-vector control; in this case the thrust line is changed by rotating the entire missile rather than just the nozzle or exhaust gases. A system of fixed control jets may be lighter than a straight thrust-vector control system, since no large actuators are required. Some maneuverability may be lost, however, since greater control power is usually available from the main engine, but maneuverability characteristics are essentially the same.

Almost any control system requires actuators of some sort for movement of control surfaces, nozzles, valves, etc. The power source and the design of these actuators also have an effect on the maneuverability of the missile. These power sources are usually pneumatic, electric, or hydraulic, or some combination thereof. Pneumatic power may be provided by bottles of compressed gas or by a gas generator. Such systems are lightweight and simple, but they are generally fairly slow in reacting, particularly when heavy control loads are involved, and they have a rather limited endurance. Pneumatic control systems, therefore, are usually found only in small, short-range missiles.

Electric actuators are generally faster than pneumatic ones. Also, since virtually all guided missiles already have electrical systems, electric actuators may simplify the missile by eliminating additional systems. Electric actuators, however, are expensive and tend to be heavy when great amounts of control power are required.

Hydraulic actuators usually provide the fastest reaction time of these three methods, and they can produce great control forces efficiently. Missile hydraulic systems may be either "open" or "closed." In an open system used hydraulic fluid is vented overboard. In a closed system the used fluid is returned to the reservoir for reuse.

Missile Guidance

The guidance system provides inputs to the missile control system, which in turn maneuvers the missile to intercept the target. Guidance for AAMs and SAMs can be classified as one of the following: preset, command, beam-rider, and homing.

Preset guidance means that a prelaunch determination is made of the missile-target intercept point in space. Prior to missile launch the guidance system is provided with this information and the trajectory to be followed (by dead reckoning, inertial, or some other form of navigation) to the missile's destination. Since this information cannot be changed after the missile is fired, any inherent system inaccuracy or postlaunch target maneuver may result in a wide miss. Preset guidance is therefore closely related to the unguided rocket, and it is applicable to the anti-air mission only in conjunction with very large warheads (nuclear) or as an initial guidance mode in combination with more accurate terminal guidance techniques.

Command guidance may be likened to classic remote control. During missile flight the positions of both the target and the missile are monitored at the launching platform, and commands are sent to the missile to fly a course that will result in target interception. Tracking of target and missile is usually accomplished by radar, through electro-optics (television), or by sight. Of these three methods, only radar generally provides target/missile range information sufficiently accurate to allow computing of a lead-intercept trajectory for the missile, but since two tracking radars are usually required, this technique largely has been limited to SAM systems. Without range data the missile is ordinarily guided along the LOS between the target and the launcher. This technique, known as "command-to-LOS," can be accomplished with no range information at all and is applicable to visual and electro-optical systems as well as to radar and combination systems.

The guidance instructions to the missile are generally transmitted by radio data link, which is susceptible to jamming, as are most radar trackers. Trailing wires (wires connecting the missile and the launch platform) have been used for transmitting guidance commands with much success in several short-range air-to-surface and surface-to-surface applications. Such a system is highly resistant to jamming, and was employed by the first AAM. This was a German X-4, designed and tested late in World War II for use by the Me 262 and Fw 190. The X-4 was a command-to-LOS trailing-wire system that was controlled manually by the launching pilot along the visual LOS to the target aircraft. Apparently it was never used operationally.

Beam-rider guidance is somewhat similar to command-to-LOS guidance, except that the missile guidance system is designed to seek and follow the center of the guidance beam automatically, without specific correction instructions from the launching platform. The guidance beam may be provided by a target-tracking radar, by electro-optics, or by a visual system. Like radar-enhanced command guidance systems, radar beam-rider systems are not limited to daylight, good-weather conditions, but they are more susceptible to electronic countermeasures than are electro-optical and visual trackers.

One problem with beam-rider systems, as with command-to-LOS, is that the missile must have high maneuverability in order to intercept an evasive target. As they approach the target, beam-rider missiles often must tighten their turns continually to keep up. At high speeds tight turns may exceed the missile's capabilities. Using two radars, one for target tracking and a second for missile tracking and guidance, can reduce this problem somewhat by providing a more efficient lead trajectory, but such systems are more complex and their use is generally limited to SAMs. Beam-rider guidance, however, is usually more accurate and faster-reacting than command guidance systems, and it can be quite effective against even evasive aircraft targets.

The most effective type of guidance against evasive targets is homing. Within this broad category are three subtypes: passive, semi-active, and active. The simplest of these, passive homing, relies on emissions given off by the target itself (e.g., sound, radio, radar, heat, light) for its guidance information. Semi-active homing systems guide on energy reflecting off the target. This energy, usually radar or laser, is provided by a source external to the missile, often the launching platform. For active homing guidance the missile itself illuminates and tracks the target.

Before examining these guidance systems in more detail it would be helpful to investigate variations in missile trajectories. Figure 1-7 illustrates some rather simplified missile trajectories where the speed of the missiles is constant (about 1.5 times the target speed) and the target flies a

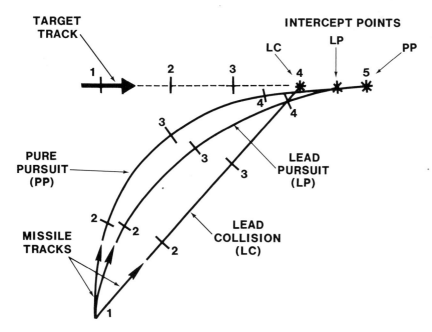

Figure 1-7. Pursuit Trajectories

straight path. The numbers along each trajectory denote time intervals after launch for ease in visualizing the geometry involved. The missiles are fired at time "1."

The missile following the "pure-pursuit" path keeps its nose (and its velocity vector) pointed directly at the target at all times, generating a curved flight path that ends in a tail-chase with the target and intercept at about point "5."

The "lead-pursuit" trajectory results from the missile leading the target somewhat, keeping its nose in front by a small amount. This is the trajectory that would be expected of a single-beam beam-rider or a command-to-LOS system where the launcher, missile, and target positions always lie in a straight line. This trajectory also terminates in a tail-chase, but the inherent lead of this system results in a slightly earlier intercept, between points "4" and "5."

The most efficient trajectory depicted here is the "lead collision," which is a straight line with an intercept near point "4." Such a path is possible for preset, command, or beam-rider guidance systems with separate tracking and guidance beams.

Homing guidance systems may be programmed to follow any of these trajectories to the target. Pure pursuit is probably the simplest course to follow since it requires a less sophisticated guidance computer. For heat seekers, pure pursuit has the added benefit of tending to keep the missile farther into the target's rear hemisphere, which aids in maintaining a good view of a jet aircraft's tailpipe. Pure pursuit has some serious problems, however. One is reduced maximum range under many circumstances, a result of the inefficient trajectory. Another is the great amount of maneuvering required when significant AOT exists as the missile nears a fast target. This requirement is accentuated if the target turns toward the missile, and the required maneuvering may easily exceed the weapon's turn capability.

Lead collision is probably the optimum missile trajectory, since it is generally the most efficient and ideally requires the least maneuvering. It does, however, require a more sophisticated guidance system.

A lead-pursuit course, in which the missile pulls some lead but not enough for a collision course, requires essentially the same guidance complexity in a homing system as lead collision and has nearly all the problems of pure pursuit. Thus, it is seldom used by homing systems, but it is quite common with beam-riders and command guidance. Another trajectory type, known as "lag pursuit," causes the missile to point its nose behind a moving target. Because of trajectory inefficiency it is not commonly used by missiles, but it may result of necessity if the missile is unable to make its intercept turn and overshoots the target's flight path.

Passive homing has become quite popular among AAM systems because of its simplicity and resultant reliability. The first AAM to score a kill in combat [1958] was the passive heat-seeking Sidewinder missile developed by the U.S. Navy. Since that time many versions of heat-seeking missiles have emerged worldwide. The high heat output of jet engines makes heat seekers especially effective, but to some extent they may also home on reciprocating engine exhaust. Because modern aircraft can travel at speeds comparable to or even faster than the speed of sound, acoustic homing tends to result in inefficient lag-pursuit trajectories and is seldom used. This method may, however, be very effective against slow, noisy aircraft such as helicopters.

Passive homing systems are often designed to follow pure-pursuit trajectories, since target LOS is usually the only input to the guidance system. It is possible, however, with only this information, to compute a lead-collision course by a process known as "proportional navigation." This involves turning the missile until a heading is found which stops the target's apparent LOS drift rate. By maintaining this constant lead angle, the missile will theoretically fly a straight path to intercept a non-maneuvering target. In actuality the lead required to stop the LOS drift rate depends on target speed and aspect, as well as missile speed (note: no range dependence). For a nonmaneuvering target (constant speed and TAA), the lead required for a proportional-navigation course varies with missile speed. Figure 1-8 illustrates the resultant flight path of a boost-glide missile initially launched directly at the target. Immediately at launch the missile senses the target drifting to the right of its nose and turns right to stop the LOS rate (apparent target drift across the horizon) by time "2," establishing an intercept course. At this point the missile is still accelerating and its speed advantage over the target is small, requiring a rather large lead angle. As the missile's speed continues to increase, however, it requires less lead to maintain the constant LOS, and it turns back toward the

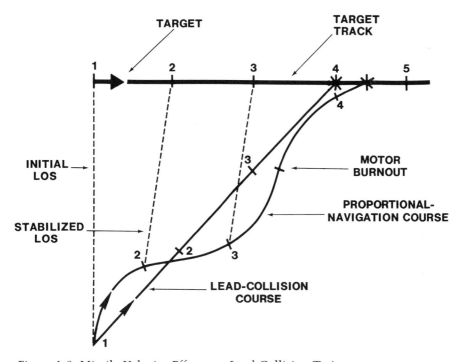

Figure 1-8. Missile Velocity Effects on Lead-Collision Trajectory

target to correct. After motor burnout the missile begins to decelerate and once again must increase its lead to complete the intercept. The ideal proportional-navigation course (or lead-collision course) for a constant-speed missile with about the same average speed is shown for reference. For a constant-speed missile, a proportional-navigation course is identical to a lead-collision trajectory against a nonmaneuvering target.

Proportional navigation assumes that the target is traveling in a straight line at any moment; should the target be maneuvering, constant lead-angle changes are required. The "perfect" lead-collision course is a straight path to the intercept point, but since the target is generally free to change its maneuver during the missile's flight, this intercept point is difficult to predict. It is usually not greatly advantageous for the missile to attempt to predict the impact point for maneuvering targets, so many "lead-collision" guidance systems actually use proportional-navigation principles.

One of the major drawbacks of passive homing is its dependence on a cooperative target that continues to emit the energy required for homing. Semi-active homing avoids this problem by having the missile home on reflected energy that is provided by another source, often the launch platform. The missile can derive LOS information from the reflected beam; or, by comparing the characteristics of the reflected beam with those of the same beam received directly from the guidance platform, it may also be able to compute target range, closure, and maneuver, for guidance and warhead-fuzing purposes. Although this guidance system provides capability against uncooperative targets, one of its major problems is greatly increased complexity, and added complexity usually results in reduced reliability. Essentially this technique requires two separate, properly operating tracking systems (one in the missile, the other in the launch platform) to be successful. Another serious drawback is the requirement for target illumination by the guidance platform throughout the missile TOF. This requirement makes the illuminator vulnerable to passive-homing weapons, and with airborne illuminators it often restricts the maneuvering options of the aircraft providing target illumination. As is explained later, predictable flight paths greatly increase vulnerability in air combat situations, and destruction of the illuminator effectively terminates its missile threat.

An active-homing system provides the source of illuminating energy in the missile itself. Although this method requires a more complex, a larger, and a more expensive missile, the total guidance system is no more involved than the semi-active system, and in some ways it is simpler and more reliable. It also gives the launching platform "launch-and-leave" capability, as do passive systems. One disadvantage, however, is the possibility of reduced target detection and tracking ranges. The maximum range of radar systems using a given power and level of technology is proportional to the area of the antenna. Since the missile is usually limited by size to carrying a smaller antenna than a launching aircraft or ground-based system can support, semi-active homing may provide greater maximum launch ranges than active homing.

The various forms of homing guidance generally offer improved capability against airborne targets, especially highly maneuverable targets. More efficient trajectories and better guidance accuracy in the critical terminal phase of the intercept are often available. Each guidance method, however, has some advantage over the others in certain situations, so combination systems are sometimes employed. An example is the use of preset or command guidance during the early portion of a long-range shot to get the missile close enough to the target to allow passive or active homing. Advances in solid-state electronics technology have made it practical to place more sophisticated guidance and sensor capability in small, lightweight missile packages.

Missile Seekers

The seeker system of a missile is responsible for sensing and tracking the target and providing the information necessary for performance of the guidance system. Preset and command guidance do not require a seeker in the missile, since the tracking function is accomplished by the launching/guidance platform. Beam-rider missiles usually have a receiver in the tail to collect information from the host guidance/tracking beam. Passive missiles generally require a sensor receiver in the nose, as do semi-active homers; but semi-active homers may also include a rear receiver for interception of information directly from the illuminating platform which can be compared to the reflected energy received by the forward sensor to derive additional guidance data. Active homers require both a transmitter and a receiver, generally located forward.

The maximum range of its seeker operation often limits the effective range of a missile system. Passive seekers have an inherent advantage here, because their received power is inversely proportional to the square of the target range, while the max-range of active and semi-active systems varies inversely with the fourth power. Several other factors also are involved. For passive systems these include the intensity of the target radiation in the direction of the sensor, the type of radiation (which determines the rate of signal attenuation by the atmosphere), and the seeker sensitivity. For active and semi-active systems maximum range depends on, in addition to transmitted power and receiver sensitivity, the reflective characteristics of the target relative to the type of illumination used. These reflective characteristics are usually sensitive to target size, and also to the target's construction material, shape, surface contours, and aspect, all of which may combine to increase or decrease reflectivity.

The most common passive seeker now in use is the heat seeker. This device contains a material (the detector) which is sensitive to heat (infrared—IR—radiation) that is produced primarily by the target's propulsion system. The detector is often cryogenically cooled to eliminate internally generated thermal "noise" and allow detection of even very small amounts of IR energy coming from an external source. The seeker must still have the capability to discriminate between target radiation and background radiation, however. Such differentiation is essential for all sensor systems, which normally require that the strength of the target signal exceed that of the background (i.e., the signal-to-noise ratio must be greater than one).

Background IR radiation is generated by the sun, by reflections off water, snow, etc., and also by clouds and hot terrain such as deserts. If the temperature of the background is within the band of sensitivity of the sensor material and is of sufficient intensity, it will be detected along with the target heat. When sensors are made sensitive to cooler targets for improved detection, the seeker becomes more susceptible to background noise also. This problem is partially resolved by designing the seeker to track only small, "point-source" radiations, usually associated with aircraft targets, rather than the broader areas of IR energy common to many background sources. In general, the seeker tends to track the most intense point-source target within its band of temperature sensitivity. The greater the background radiation within the band of temperature sensitivity of the seeker, the stronger the IR signal received from the target must be if it is to be detected and tracked. This fact may limit the detection range for a target of given IR intensity.

A hot object emits IR energy in a rather wide band of frequencies. As the object becomes hotter the radiated power increases very sharply (proportional to the fourth power of absolute temperature), and the frequency of the most intense IR radiation is shifted higher. The hot metal of jet tailpipes can be expected to emit IR energy of greater intensity and higher frequency than that of the hot exhaust gases, which begin to cool rapidly. Depending on the sensor material used, a heat-seeking missile may detect only the tailpipe, or it may also be sensitive to the cooler exhaust gas and even to the heat generated by air friction on a very fast aircraft. One disadvantage of tailpipe guidance is the likelihood that the hot metal may in some views be shielded by part of the aircraft structure. Hot exhaust gas is usually more difficult to shield, and this fact has led to heat seekers with "all-aspect" capability. However, the pilot of the target aircraft can reduce substantially the IR signature of his exhaust gases easier and faster (by power reduction) than he can his metal tailpipe, which tends to retain heat longer. The physical size of an exhaust plume may also cause problems for hot-gas seekers, as they may become "saturated" at close range. Rather sophisticated guidance techniques are required to cause such missiles to aim forward of the heat source in order to hit the target. Discrimination between this cooler target and the background radiation may also be a problem, as explained previously.

IR energy is absorbed and dissipated by water vapor, making heat seekers all but useless in clouds or rain. Even in relatively dry air this energy is attenuated more quickly than many other types of radiation, with the rate largely dependent on altitude and humidity. This characteristic makes heat seekers most compatible with short-range weapons.

Radar-guided missiles, using many of the guidance techniques discussed, are currently the most widely used all-weather AAMs. Besides weapons guidance, radars are also valuable for providing fighters with the information necessary to detect enemy aircraft at long range, at night, and in bad weather, so that they might be intercepted and attacked on advantageous terms. There are three types of radars which have application to fighter weapons: pulse, continuous wave, and pulse Doppler.

Pulse radars work by transmitting a burst of radio energy (pulse) and then receiving echoes of that pulse reflected off distant objects. If the antenna is highly directional, aiming the energy pulse almost entirely within a very narrow beam, the LOS to the target (azimuth and elevation) can be accurately determined. This narrow beam can be formed mechanically (parabolic-shaped antenna) or electronically (phased-array antenna). Also, since radio waves travel at a known speed, the time elapsed between transmittal of the pulse and receipt of the echo can be measured to derive target range.

Radar electronics requires many compromises. Desirable features include small size, light weight, long range, good range and angular accuracy (resolution), and short minimum range. Unfortunately, improvement in one area often leads to degradation in another. Light weight and small size are important characteristics for aircraft radars, and obtaining them usually requires relatively low-power, high-frequency units, which place limitations on range. The small size of practical antennas also results in wider beams, reducing angular resolution.

Range resolution is enhanced by shortening the duration of each pulse (pulse width) so that the complete echo of a near target is received before the first echo of a farther target arrives. Shortening the pulse width, however, reduces the average transmitted power of the radar, thereby lessening its maximum range. There are some electronic processing techniques which can largely overcome this problem, allowing longer pulse widths for greater range while maintaining range resolution, but minimum-range performance, which is also proportional to pulse width, usually must be sacrificed.

As the name implies, continuous-wave (CW) radars are not pulsed, they transmit continuously. This means that the antenna used for transmission cannot be used for reception, as with pulse radars, so multiple antennas are required. CW is used quite often for semi-active and beam-rider missile guidance, with the host platform transmitting and the missile seeker receiving the transmission and/or the reflected energy. For long-range shots the CW energy may be formed into a narrow beam and directed at the target by the host tracking system. For short-range firings a fixed, wide-angle antenna may be used to illuminate targets within its field of view.

CW radars generally measure target closing velocity by the Doppler principle, which most often is illustrated by the change in pitch (frequency) of the whistle on a passing train. While the train is approaching, one pitch is heard (higher than that actually produced by the whistle), and as the train passes the pitch seems to decrease to a lower frequency. Relative motion changes the frequency of sound waves or other waves such that closing velocity between the source of the transmission and the receiver causes an apparent frequency increase, while opening velocity causes a decrease. This frequency shift is proportional to the closure and offers a direct means of velocity measurement.

Since CW radars have no pulses that can be timed for range determination, another method is necessary. This is generally accomplished through a frequency-modulation (FM) technique. If the transmitter frequency is varied continuously up and down, the reflected wave will vary in the same manner. The peaks of the reflected wave, however, will be delayed (phase shifted) by a length of time proportional to the range between the receiver and the target. The accuracy of FM ranging is usually inversely proportional to target range (i.e., accuracy improves as range decreases), unlike pulse-ranging accuracy, which is fairly independent of range. So, although FM ranging can be very accurate over short distances, its accuracy is usually inferior to that of pulse technique at greater ranges.

The great advantage of CW over pulse radar is its much higher average transmitted power, since the transmitter does not have to turn off and wait for an echo. The pulse-ranging technique requires long listening periods between each pulse because of the time necessary for the pulse to reach a distant target and return. Such a radar is classified as having a low pulse-repetition frequency (low PRF). Low PRF results in less average power and fewer pulses of energy reaching the target per second, reducing range performance. Another method, known as high PRF, allows many pulses to be in the air at a given time and substitutes FM-ranging techniques for conventional pulse ranging. This results in greater average power and the long-range benefits of CW, while allowing the double use of a single antenna, as with pulse.

Pulse-Doppler radars are commonly of this high-PRF variety. They send out pulses of a very finely tuned (coherent) frequency and listen for returns of a different frequency, which would indicate Doppler effect from bouncing off a moving object. This technique offers the great advantage of being able to distinguish moving targets from stationary ones, such as the ground. Again, FM ranging normally is employed.

One of the most severe limitations of pulse radars is ground clutter, or reflections off the earth's surface. These reflections may be returns of the radar's main beam, or of any of the many weaker side lobes of energy radiated in all directions because of antenna imperfections and other factors. Clutter is seen by a receiver as noise, and the strength of the target return must exceed that of the noise by a given amount for target detection. When a target is close to the ground its return may lie within the main-beam clutter (MBC) of an illuminating radar. In this case the target will most likely be obscured by the noise created by the ground. Likewise, when the radar platform is near the ground, reflections from the side lobes generate noise in the receiver, even when the radar is looking up, requiring increased power in the target return before detection is possible, and reducing maximum range.

Doppler radars in moving aircraft also have problems with clutter, since returns off the ground reflect the host aircraft's own airspeed. Because this speed is known, however, MBC can be eliminated by "blanking out" returns of the approximate frequency associated with this closing velocity, so that the intensity of the clutter return will not overpower the receiver.

Of course, this technique also eliminates any returns from real targets having about the same closure, which includes those with beam aspects (approximately 90° TAA). MBC is less of a problem with high-altitude targets or when the radar is looking up at the target. By not blanking out the MBC, radar missiles may retain a capability under such conditions against targets with beam aspects.

Because Doppler radars only detect relative motion, targets flying in nearly the same direction at about the same speed as the host aircraft may not be detected either. Since side-lobe clutter (SLC) is associated with closing speeds equal to or less than the host aircraft's own airspeed, it too may be eliminated. But because this procedure would limit detectable targets to those with forward aspects, and SLC is usually fairly weak, this is generally not done. Doppler SLC does, however, limit detection ranges when the host aircraft is in the target's rear hemisphere. The amount of this degradation is largely dependent on the host aircraft's altitude.

Doppler's great advantage is in detecting targets with high closure (forward aspects), in which case clutter is not a problem even when the radar is looking down. This leads to radars with so-called "look-down" capability. A missile directed by such a system is said to have "shoot-down" capability. A given Doppler radar is limited, however, in the band of return frequencies it can detect. It is theoretically possible, therefore, for a target to be closing or opening too fast to be detected.

Besides detection problems, various types of missile seekers have other limitations. Most missiles that employ proportional-navigation techniques require a movable seeker to keep track of the target. Such seekers have physical stops in all directions, called gimbal limits, which restrict their field of view and therefore limit the amount of lead the missile may develop while the seeker points at the target. If the seeker bumps the gimbal limit, the missile usually loses its guidance capability. Such situations most often develop when the missile's speed advantage over the target is low and the target LOS rate is high. This may occur early in the missile's flight, before it has accelerated fully, with a high target LOS rate. It also becomes a problem near maximum range, when the missile has decelerated greatly and must pull more and more lead to maintain a stationary target LOS.

Although the gimbal limit may be bumped in a hard-turning intercept with a maneuvering target when the missile's turn capability cannot quite stop the target LOS drift, this situation more often leads to exceeding the seeker's tracking-rate limit. Missile seekers are usually gyro-stabilized to point along a fixed line in space, much like the needle of a magnetic compass. The body of the missile is then free to turn about the "fixed" seeker. Such motion causes little problem and generally is limited only by the missile's turn capability and the seeker's gimbal limits. If the seeker's LOS must be changed, however, because of changing target LOS, its gyro must be precessed. The rate at which this can be accomplished (known as the target's maximum gyro tracking rate) is limited, and it is often dependent on the target's signal-to-noise ratio.

Missile Fuzes

The purpose of a missile fuze system is to cause the detonation of the warhead at the time that produces the maximum target damage, while also ensuring the safety of the firing platform and personnel. Typically, a fuze is "armed" (made capable of causing warhead detonation) when it senses that firing has occurred and that safe separation from the firing platform has been achieved. The acceleration of the missile during motor burn may be used to start a timing mechanism for arming, or any number of other methods may be employed. Once a fuze is armed, another fuze function is required in order to detonate the warhead.

Fuzes can be classified as contact, time delay, command, and proximity. Contact fuzes were discussed previously in conjunction with explosive cannon projectiles. Nearly all anti-aircraft missiles have such a fuze, either alone or in combination with another type. Time-delay fuzes are preset before launch to explode at a given time that is calculated to place the missile in the vicinity of the target. This is a fuze commonly used by large-caliber anti-aircraft artillery, but seldom by missiles because of its lack of accuracy. Command fuzes are activated by radio command from the guidance platform when the tracking system indicates that the missile has reached its closest point of approach to the target. This method is most applicable to command-type guidance systems and generally requires relatively large warheads to be effective against airborne targets.

Proximity fuzes are probably the most effective fuzes against maneuvering aircraft; they come in many designs, including passive, semi-active, and active. Passive fuzes rely for their activation on a phenomenon associated with the target. This might be noise, heat, radio emissions, etc. Semi-active fuzes generally function on an interaction between the guidance system and the target, such as rapidly dropping Doppler frequency or high target LOS rates. An active fuze sends out some sort of signal and activates when it receives a reflection from the target. Popular designs include radio-proximity fuzes and laser fuzes. For maximum effectiveness the proximity fuze should be capable of detecting the target out to the maximum lethal radius of the warhead.

Because of the wide range of intercept conditions possible in engagements with aircraft targets, fuze design is one of the weakest links in missile systems. Proximity fuzes are usually tailored to the guidance trajectory of the missile, the most probable target, and the most likely intercept geometry. "Functional delays" are generally used for this purpose. For instance, if a missile is expected to approach the target from the rear with a relatively low closure, a fairly long functional delay might be incorporated to allow the missile to travel from the target's tailpipe area (where detection would presumably occur) to some point near the middle of the target, where an explosion would probably do the most damage. However, if this missile intercepted the target from the side or head-on, such a time delay might cause detonation past the target, resulting in little or no damage.

All-aspect missiles, because of their larger variety of possible intercept conditions, offer the greatest challenge to the fuze designer. One approach is sometimes called an "adaptive" fuze, which might alter fuze delays during the missile's flight based on projected intercept conditions calculated from guidance data. Such a fuze might also "aim" the warhead to cause maximum destructive effects on the target side of the missile at intercept.

Missile Warheads

The warheads used in AAMs are typically blast-fragmentation types, incendiary or explosive pellets, or expanding-rod types. Blast-fragmentation warheads are intended to cause damage through the combined effects of the explosive shock wave and high-velocity fragments (usually pieces of the warhead casing). Pellet designs are similar, except some of the fragments are actually small bomblets that explode or burn on contact with, or penetration of, the target. Because of the decreased air density at high altitude, the damage to airborne targets from blast effect alone is not usually great unless the missile actually hits the target, penetrates, and explodes inside. Fragments tend to spread out from the point of the explosion, rapidly losing killing power as miss distance increases. Explosive or incendiary pellets reduce this problem somewhat since a single hit can do more damage. The expanding-rod warhead also addresses this problem. It is comprised of many short lengths of steel rod placed side by side in an annular arrangement around the explosive material. The rods are welded together at alternate ends so that when detonation occurs they expand outward in a solid, continuous ring, much like an expanding watch band, until reaching their maximum radius. In theory this continuous rod is more likely to cut through control cables, hydraulic and fuel lines, and structural members than are individual fragments. In addition, the lethality of such a warhead should be maintained to greater distances, since the damaging fragments do not spread apart. In practice, however, such expanding rods often separate early in the explosion, leaving large gaps in the warhead coverage.

The lethality of a warhead depends largely on the amount of explosive material and the number and size of the fragments. Warheads should be designed with specific target types in mind, and they must complement the missile guidance and fuze design. Larger expected miss distances and imprecise fuzes require bigger warheads.

Fuzes must make allowance for the fact that the missile's forward velocity is imparted to the warhead fragments on detonation, so that as they expand they are also moving forward, forming a cone-shaped lethal volume ahead of the warhead detonation point. Warheads have been developed which can aim most of their fragments in the direction of the target based on fuze command. "Shaped charges" have been used to enhance target penetration, particularly with contact fuzes. Nuclear warheads also may be employed for special situations.

Missile Employment

Employment of AAMs involves satisfying the requirements of the particular missile in the given situation. Missiles are complicated systems comprised of many interdependent subsystems, each having limitations. All these limitations must be observed for a successful shot.

One method of visualizing the capabilities and limitations of a missile is to study its firing envelope. Figure 1-9 illustrates two such envelopes for a hypothetical Doppler-radar-homing AAM. One envelope is for a non-maneuvering target, and the other is for a target in a continuous level turn.

The nonmaneuvering envelope is a scale diagram looking down from above a target (the arrow) which is flying toward the top of the page. The various boundaries depicted illustrate the missile capabilities and limitations. Assume first of all that the shooter has obtained the required radar track on the target and has aimed the missile in the proper direction for launch.

The outermost boundary is the maximum aerodynamic, or "kinematic," range at which the missile is capable of guiding to within the lethal miss-distance of the target. This boundary reflects the capabilities of the missile propulsion, guidance, and control systems, as well as the speeds of the launching aircraft and target and the aspect (position relative to the target) from which the missile is launched. One of the most striking features of this boundary is the great difference in maximum range between forward-quarter and rear-quarter shots: here, about five to one. This obviously reflects the fact that the target is flying toward a missile fired in its forward quarter and is running away from a rear-quarter shot.

The seeker-limit line shows the tracking limit of the missile's radar seeker based on the reflectivity of this particular target. Remember that this reflectivity is a function of target size and other factors. Since missile radar antennas are necessarily small, their range is limited. In this case the seeker capability restricts the maximum forward-quarter firing range; but with a larger target, or at a lower altitude (where maximum aerodynamic range is reduced), it may not.

The narrow zones marked "look-up required" on both sides of the target are associated with ground clutter, the Doppler MBC previously discussed. Missiles required to look down on the target, especially at low altitude, from a beam aspect are likely to lose track of the target in the clutter. Looking up at the target reduces MBC and allows continuous track of the target.

The wider areas on either side of the target reflect the fuzing and warhead problems associated with beam-quarter target intercepts. The missile may guide to well within lethal distance, but the geometry of the intercept and the design of the fuze and the warhead may cause detonation to occur on the far side of the target, possible resulting in no damage. A missile launched from this area is not considered to have a high probability of success. The small area in the stern quarter near maximum-kinematic range is also the result of a fuze limitation. In this case there is insufficient missile closing velocity at target intercept for proper fuze functioning.

The inner boundary surrounding the target is the minimum-range limit. Depending on the aspect this may be the result of fuze-arming time, the missile's turning capability, guidance reaction time, or the seeker's gimbal limits or gyro-tracking rate.

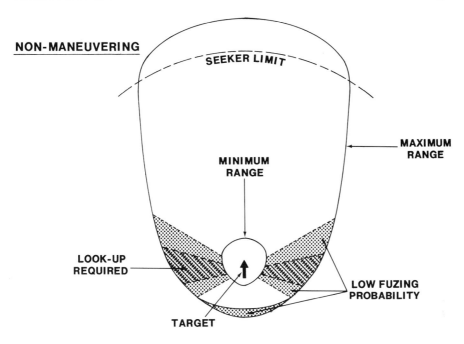

NON-MANEUVERING

SEEKER LIMIT

MAXIMUM RANGE

MINIMUM RANGE

LOOK-UP REQUIRED

LOW FUZING PROBABILITY

TARGET

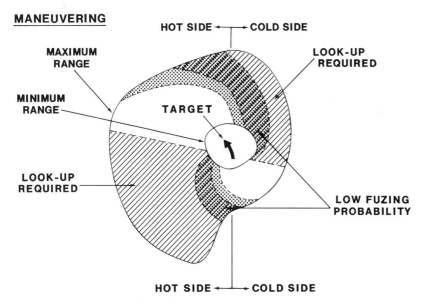

MANEUVERING

HOT SIDE ← → COLD SIDE

MAXIMUM RANGE

LOOK-UP REQUIRED

MINIMUM RANGE

TARGET

LOOK-UP REQUIRED

LOW FUZING PROBABILITY

HOT SIDE ← → COLD SIDE

Figure 1-9. Typical Missile Envelopes

The maneuvering envelope illustrates the same conditions, with the target still flying toward the top of the page, except this time the target begins a level left-hand turn just as the missile is launched and continues this turn throughout the missile TOF. The diagram is labelled "hot side" and "cold side" to define the target's direction of turn. The labels "inside the turn" or "outside the turn" also could have been used. These terms reflect initial conditions only (i.e., the instant of missile launch), as the cold and hot sides rotate with the target aircraft as it turns. An observer on the hot side of the turn at any point normally would be looking at the top of the target aircraft, while on the cold side he would have a belly view.

The maneuvering aerodynamic max-range envelope is highly asymmetrical, with the hot-side range being much greater than the range on the cold side, as the timing of the turn is such that the target essentially is flying out to meet missiles fired from its left side, and flying away from those initially coming from the right. By choosing the direction and rate of turn, the target can exert tremendous influence on this max-range envelope. The min-range boundary is also affected, expanding somewhat on the hot side, but not to as great an extent.

The regions of the envelope requiring look-up are greatly expanded in the maneuvering case. A missile fired from these regions would have to pass through the target's beam area before intercept could occur, greatly increasing the chances of losing target track in clutter, especially if it was looking down. These regions comprise a considerable portion of the entire kinematic envelope, particularly at longer ranges, and serve to emphasize the importance of look-up when employing this type of missile against maneuvering targets.

The fuze-limited regions are also increased somewhat in the maneuvering case. A missile launched in one of these regions would intercept the target at close to a beam aspect, either hot side or cold side, with low probability of warhead damage. Also note that all max-range limits have been reduced to below the seeker-sensitivity limit, so that restriction does not affect this case.

These envelopes are already confusing, but a full picture of the capabilities of this missile would require many such charts to cover a wide range of possible target maneuvers, shooter/target speeds, and altitudes. In addition, a single fighter may carry two or three different kinds of missiles, all with widely differing operating characteristics and envelopes. Envelope recognition, therefore, becomes one of the major difficulties in AAM employment. Even if the fighter pilot could draw each envelope from memory, how would he determine the vital parameters necessary to decide which envelope was valid (including target speed and turn rate) and his position within that envelope (including range and target aspect)?

Probably the most workable solution to this problem is to equip the fighter with a tracking radar system and a fire-control computer. Such systems can accurately assess and display to the pilot the missile's aerodynamic capabilities, and as many of the other limits as might be deemed desirable, almost instantaneously. Most modern fighters have such systems.

In order to make inputs to the fire-control computer it is necessary that the radar track, rather than just detect, the target. Automatic radar track-ing is possible using electronic methods that vary with the design of the particular radar system. The transition from radar detection to automatic track is called the "acquisition" or "lock-up" process. Depending on the sophistication of the radar, this too may be an automatic procedure requir-ing very little time or aircrew effort, or it may be a manual process of designating the target LOS and range or closing velocity so that the radar can determine which return is the desired target. Manual methods are generally adequate at longer ranges, when LOS rates are low, but once a fighter is engaged in a close-range swirling "dogfight" some automatic means of target acquisition is almost a necessity. The ability of Doppler radars to distinguish between moving airborne targets and ground clutter makes automatic acquisition systems more practical.

In some cases, however, a radar lock may not be available. If the missile (a heat seeker, for instance) does not require a host-aircraft radar lock for guidance information, then some other means of envelope recognition is necessary. Generally it is achieved by reducing the many envelopes to a very few, relatively simple "rules of thumb" which describe optimum firing zones for the missile under expected combat conditions of altitude, speed, target turn rate, etc. Pilots then must memorize these thumb rules, along with any special operating restrictions for the missile, such as requirements for look-up, acceptable load factor at launch, etc. In essence these rules of thumb provide the pilot with very simplified envelopes that give him a "ballpark idea" of his missile's capabilities. Of necessity, such simplifications will underestimate the weapon's true performance under some circumstances and be overly optimistic in others.

Once the envelope is known, recognition of the critical parameters becomes the problem. Often range and target aspect must be estimated visually, based on the apparent size and presented view of the target. Stadiametric ranging, the method by which gunsight mil dimensions are compared to the apparent size of a target of known size, was discussed in relation to air-to-air gun employment. This method may also be used with missiles, but because of the typically longer ranges of AAMs, where slight variations in apparent target size may equate to very great differences in distance, it is generally useful only at short range. A more widely used method involves the ability to discern various features of the target aircraft and equate this ability to approximate target range. For instance, at some range the target will appear to change from a mere black dot to something recognizable as an aircraft. A little closer, depending on aspect, its type may be apparent, then the canopy may become visible, followed by its markings and color scheme. Mastering such methods requires a great amount of practice, and at best this method results in rough approxima-tions. In tests of experienced fighter pilots estimating the range of familiar aircraft, it has been found that errors of 50 to 200 percent can be expected. The results will be even worse against unfamiliar target aircraft.

> We always underestimated our range.
>   Air Vice-Marshal J. E. "Johnnie" Johnson, RAF

Target aspect estimation presents a similar problem, with $\pm 30°$ accuracy being about the norm. The difficulty is compounded with hard-maneuvering targets, since missile envelopes are generally based on the direction of the target's velocity vector, not on its attitude, which is the only visual reference available to the attacking fighter pilot. These two references may vary widely with high target angle of attack (AOA), making visual estimation of target aspect more prone to error.

In addition to the restrictions imposed by their operating envelopes, AAMs also usually have aiming requirements. Since guided missiles can correct for some aiming error, the aiming restrictions for them are much looser than those for unguided weapons, but there are restrictions nevertheless. Some missiles, including many heat seekers, must be launched along the LOS in order to detect and guide on the target. Others may be launched with lead or lag, i.e., pointing ahead of or behind the target. A lag heading at launch is seldom beneficial for missile guidance since it requires a larger turn to establish a collision course and usually results in greater LOS rates. Lead heading can be quite helpful, however, particularly for min-range launches, by reducing the required missile maneuver. Fire-control computers often provide the pilot with an indication of the optimum lead heading, ideally allowing the missile to fly a straight path to target intercept. These inputs often make the assumption that the target is nonmaneuvering, and they may or may not account for the effect of the shooter's angle of attack on apparent lead heading, an effect that can be considerable during heavy maneuvering. AOA is a factor since missiles usually weathercock toward the relative wind immediately after launch.

Although each missile design has its own set of unique problems, most missiles are affected to a greater or lesser degree by difficulties in distinguishing the target from its background. Even though Doppler-radar guidance has largely eliminated the clutter obstacle for forward-hemisphere targets, the hypothetical maneuvering missile envelope demonstrates that limitations remain. The guidance performance of radar missiles is, in general, enhanced when the missile is looking up at a target with only sky in the background. Because of the effects of SLC, the performance of such missiles may also be degraded at low altitudes, even with look-up.

The effects of clutter are sometimes bewildering and difficult to predict. However, it usually can be said that the impact varies with the roughness of the earth's surface along the target LOS and the "grazing angle," or degree of look-down. Over land, particularly rough terrain, clutter is usually a greater factor than it is over water.

Background is also a serious problem for heat-seeking missiles, with the sun being the culprit, either directly or indirectly. The sun is much more intense than any target exhaust and will "capture" the missile seeker if the target LOS approaches too near at any point from launch to intercept. (Don't worry; nobody has hit it yet.) Reflections of the sun off water, snow, clouds, etc., can also cause problems. These produce a wide area of background IR noise, as opposed to a point source, reducing target acquisition ranges and degrading guidance through a decrease in signal-to-noise ratio. Look-down may have much the same effect, especially against hot desert backgrounds. As with radar missiles, a clear, blue sky is the optimum background for heat-seeking missile employment.

Besides the guidance problems already discussed, very low altitude employment of AAMs offers other difficulties. Most guidance and control systems cause the missile to oscillate some distance around the intended trajectory. At very low altitudes one of these corrections may result in ground impact. Fuzing can also be a concern, especially with active fuzes, since the surface may be mistaken for the target by the fuze, causing premature detonation. Ground clutter may have the same effect with Doppler-rate fuzes.

Extremely high altitudes also can cause problems for missiles, as the thin air reduces the maneuvering capability of aerodynamic controls and results in sloppy guidance.

The advent of AAMs having capability against targets with forward aspect, particularly semi-active AAMs, has increased the importance of a performance parameter known as "relative range." A missile fired at its maximum relative range results in target impact at the greatest distance from the launching aircraft. The shooter-to-target range at impact is often called "F-pole" or stand-off distance. When two missile-equipped fighters approach nearly head-on, the one with the greater F-pole generally has the advantage, since its missile would arrive on target first. In the case of semi-active missiles, which require target illumination by the launching aircraft, this also terminates any threat from the enemy's missile still in flight. Maximum stand-off distance occurs when the missile decelerates to the speed of the launching aircraft. After this point the shooter would begin to close on his own missile, decreasing the range at target impact.

Maximum relative range is generally somewhat less than the ultimate aerodynamic range, but a missile launched at this point will arrive on target first. So, depending on average missile speed, the aircraft firing first is not necessarily the winner of such a game of "chicken." However, a missile in the air has an uncanny ability to attract the attention of the pilot in the target aircraft, often causing him to forget all about launching his own weapon. Because of this psychological factor missiles are sometimes "fired for effect" even when the shooter knows there is little chance for success. The target's defensive reaction may place the shooter in a much more favorable position. In some cases it may be advantageous to fire one missile at maximum aerodynamic range, or even beyond, for effect, and follow it with another at maximum relative range. This is often possible with radar missiles, but a second heat seeker may conceivably guide on the tailpipe of the first one, limiting the usefulness of this tactic with heat-seeking missiles. Missiles of two different types are often fired together, since target defensive countermeasures employed against one may be ineffective against the other.

Increased stand-off distance is also valuable in that it may allow assessment of the results of the first missile and, if necessary, permit the firing of another before minimum range is reached. Under almost any imaginable circumstances, missiles with launch-and-leave capability are preferable to semi-active types with about equal range, since the former do not restrict the shooter's maneuver capability after launch.

Maximum F-pole normally can be increased by firing the missile at higher aircraft speed (which in turn increases the missile's velocity), and then slowing the launching fighter as much as practical, allowing the weapon to gain greater separation. The firing fighter may also be able to turn away from the target by some amount after launch, further increasing target range at missile intercept. Slowing down and turning away from a target in the forward hemisphere also tends to reduce the opponent's effective firing range.

Missile Defense

> Here come the SAMs! The trick is seeing the launch. You can see the steam. It goes straight up, turns more level, then the booster drops off. If it maintains a relatively stable position, it's coming for you and you're in trouble. You're eager to make a move but can't. If you dodge too fast it will turn and catch you; if you wait too late it will explode near enough to get you. What you do at the right moment is poke your nose down, go down as hard as you can, pull maybe three negative Gs up to 550 knots and once it follows you down, you go up as hard as you can. It can't follow that and goes under. In a two-minute period [the North Vietnamese] once shot thirty-eight SAMs at us.[5]
>
> Brigadier General Robin Olds, USAF

The philosophy of successful missile defense is parallel to guns defense, discussed earlier. First, prevent the missile from being launched at all. Failing this, attempt to present the shooter with the least favorable shot opportunity, and then endeavor to make the missile's task as difficult as possible by attacking the capabilities and limitations of its various subsystems. The more of these subsystems with degraded performance, the less the chance of a successful missile shot. Guided missiles are normally much more complicated than gun systems, and they have more subsystems to attack. Usually the firing ranges and projectile speeds involved also will result in greater TOF, allowing the defender more time to defeat the weapon.

In order to prevent a missile firing, it is necessary to deny the shooter his required launch parameters, usually including range, aspect, and aim. The ability to achieve this objective depends on knowledge of the threat weapon system, largely based on intelligence information and prior experience. The more the defender knows about his adversary's capabilities and limitations, the more effective can be his defensive tactics. Ideally, this knowledge should include launch envelopes such as those presented in Figure 1-9, as well as any other restrictions, such as aiming requirements, threat-aircraft radar capabilities, and expected tactics.

Once these factors are known, the defender is faced with the same problem he encounters in employing his own missiles; namely, envelope recognition. The task here is often made more difficult for two reasons: the defender does not always know the type of missile he is facing, and in defensive situations his own fire-control system may not be effective in assessing his position relative to the threat envelope.

Even allowing for these limitations, there are some basic tactics which are generally effective in reducing the size of the launch envelope for missiles within broad categories. Altitude probably has the greatest effect on missile range and effectiveness. In general, the range of both jet- and

rocket-powered vehicles increases when they are operating at higher altitudes. Although higher altitude reduces jet thrust, drag usually decreases
even faster, particularly for supersonic vehicles, up to about the level of the
tropopause. For rockets, thrust usually increases with higher altitude. This
in conjunction with lower drag results in significant improvement in range
with increasing altitude. Figure 1-10 gives an approximation of the effect of
altitude on a rocket-powered missile's maximum aerodynamic range
against a co-altitude target, using sea-level performance as a standard.
Similar variations can be expected in both rear- and forward-quarter
launches. Note that missile aerodynamic range increases dramatically
with altitude, particularly at the higher levels. Range at 20,000 ft above
mean sea level (MSL) can be expected to be about double the sea-level
value, with performance doubling again by 40,000 ft. For look-up or look-
down shots, range is closely related to the median altitude between the
shooter and the target. Look-down shots, however, are more likely to be
limited by factors other than aerodynamics.

When operating against fixed SAM sites, low altitudes can offer some
benefit. Earth curvature and terrain masking provided by hills, trees, etc.,
may limit target acquisition range even below aerodynamic range. Ground
clutter is also a problem for radar-controlled SAMs, but it can be reduced
by Doppler techniques and alternative optical guidance systems. When
considering very low altitude operations, the pilot must balance the benefits against mission objectives and the greater effectiveness of small arms,
anti-aircraft artillery (AAA), and very short range SAMs. Within their
operating envelopes most missiles can be expected to be more maneuverable at low altitude because of better aerodynamic control. Low-level
operations may also limit the usefulness of the fighter's own offensive
weapons system.

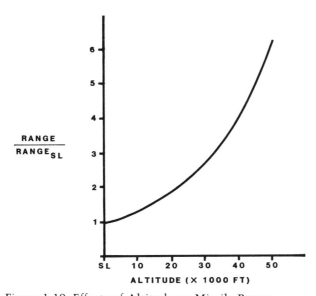

Figure 1-10. Effects of Altitude on Missile Range

Shooter and target speeds are critical elements in the aerodynamic range of missiles. Increasing the speed of both aircraft tends to reduce the range of rear-quarter missiles and increase forward-quarter range. Figure 1-11 shows typical range variations for co-speed shooter and target at various Mach numbers, using .4 M as a reference. For example, with both shooter and target aircraft at 1.0 M, forward-quarter missile range might increase by over 50 percent, and rear-quarter range might decrease more than 30 percent, as compared with the same shots when the aircraft speeds are .4 M. A target speed advantage over the shooter affects maximum aerodynamic range even further, with the percentage impact being very sensitive to the particular missile's average flight speed. The effect therefore varies widely from missile to missile, but typically a 100-knot target speed advantage (range increasing) decreases rear-quarter max-range 5 to 25 percent, with slower missiles suffering the greatest effect. Large target speed advantages can also cause acquisition difficulties for many Doppler-radar missiles fired from the rear.

In summary, the combined effects of low attitude, high speeds, and a target speed advantage can yield a dramatic reduction in the rear-quarter missile envelope. Greatest reductions in the forward quarter can be achieved by low-altitude, slow-speed operation.

Missile minimum kinematic range can also be influenced by target speed and altitude. Forward-quarter min-range is of greatest interest, since during close-in visual combat with all-aspect missiles this limit is often the most difficult to satisfy. In this instance high altitude and high speed serve to increase minimum forward-quarter range. This is because of the greater distance traveled by the target during the minimum fuze-arming time of the missile and the quicker guidance reactions required for high-

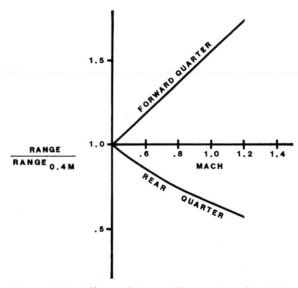

Figure 1-11. Effects of Target/Shooter Speed on Missile Range

speed targets. Higher altitudes tend to reduce missile maneuverability and increase reaction time.

Particularly with rear-quarter AAMs, but also to some extent with all-aspect missiles, a further benefit of a target speed advantage is the increased difficulty encountered by an unseen attacker in placing his aircraft within the envelope and satisfying his aiming requirements in the reduced time made available by a faster target. Especially with short-range rear-quarter weapons, for an attacker to have a reasonable chance of achieving a firing position on a nonmaneuvering target, he must be in an ideal position even before the target is detected visually.

Aircraft designers can decrease fighter vulnerability to missile attack by using many camouflage and suppression techniques. These include reducing the aircraft's radar reflectivity by using nonreflecting materials and radar-absorbing paint, when practical. Reflectivity is also sensitive to engine inlet design and placement, and to the physical size and shape of various aircraft parts. IR signatures can be suppressed by using special jet-nozzle designs, by monitoring exhaust placement, by using engines with cooler exhausts, and by adding chemicals to the exhaust. Even optical tracking can be made more difficult by using camouflage techniques that reduce the aircraft's contrast with the background.

Besides reducing the size of his vulnerable envelope, the target has other means of preventing a missile shot. Countering an attacker's attempts to satisfy his aiming requirements is a matter of generating LOS rates that exceed the shooter's turn capability. The techniques involved with this are discussed in much greater detail in the chapters on maneuvering.

> The weapon where the man is sitting in is always superior against the other.
>
> Colonel Erich "Bubi" Hartmann, GAF

Denying the attacker a favorable target aspect is also a function of maneuvering. This is one of the primary defenses against weapons with a limited-aspect capability, such as rear-quarter heat seekers. Obviously, such a defense is more difficult to accomplish against all-aspect missiles. Some aspects, however, are less favorable than others for almost any weapon. We have already discussed the problems encountered with Doppler-guided missiles and beam aspects, especially in look-down situations. Special limitations of particular weapons, such as this one, often may be exploited to prevent or degrade a shot. For example, power reductions and IR-masking techniques can be used at critical times to prevent or delay heat-seeking missile acquisition, and to degrade guidance after launch.

A special problem encountered by most radar tracking systems is known as glint. This is a phenomenon that may cause the radar to shift auto-track among several targets that have approximately the same range (pulse radars) or closing velocity (Doppler radars) and that are closely spaced along the LOS of the tracking beam. The radar may tend to lock on one target, then another, in a random, unpredictable manner. In the case of very large targets, the radar may shift lock from one part of the aircraft to another continuously. A missile relying on such a radar for guidance often will exhibit large, jerky course changes as it attempts to guide on different targets. These maneuvers tend to increase aerodynamic drag and reduce maximum range. As the missile approaches the terminal phase it may simply guide on a point near the centroid of the target mass, resulting in a wide miss on any individual target.

Passive seekers have a similar problem. When confronted with several hot tailpipes in close proximity, a heat seeker, for instance, may guide on the centroid of the target group based on the relative intensities of the various sources.

These limitations may be exploited for defensive purposes by large numbers of aircraft flying in carefully spaced formations, usually called "cells." This tactic is more effective against missiles with remote tracking platforms, such as command and beam-rider weapons, where the tracking radar is at greater range than the missile itself. A homing missile is less susceptible since, as it nears the target cell, its tracking beam encompasses fewer and fewer targets, possibly allowing the weapon to "cut one out of the pack."

Although such tactics may be very effective against selected threats under some conditions, many radar missile systems, particularly SAMs, have alternative optical tracking, which is not susceptible to glint. Highly maneuverable fighters usually have other defensive options which are more dependable and somewhat less nerve-racking for the pilots than flying straight-and-level and watching missiles whiz through their formations.

> No matter how many SAMs a pilot might defeat, he respected them. Each SAM call brought doubts of survival and numbing fear. They were never faced complacently.
>
> Commander Randy "Duke" Cunningham, USN

A broad classification of defensive techniques is known as electronic countermeasures. These methods can be subdivided into two categories: noise and deception. Noise jamming is an attempt to produce a strong signal that will overpower the target return when it is received by the enemy radar. The attacker ideally obtains a very strong return along the LOS to the target, but he cannot get range information, since the reflected pulse is overpowered and indistinguishable in the noise. Doppler radars are generally less susceptible to this technique, since they do not require pulse timing.

The effectiveness of noise jamming is related to the ratio of the jamming power received by the enemy radar to the strength of the target return. Since reflected target energy is much more sensitive to target range than is the received noise, this method is very effective at long distances, but as range decreases the radar return power increases at a faster rate, possibly allowing "burnthrough" and target detection. Noise is also more effective if it can be concentrated in a narrow beam at the enemy radar, rather than being radiated in all directions. The jamming may be done by the target itself, or by a "stand-off jammer," which attempts to conceal other aircraft with its noise. Noise jamming actually may allow the radar receiver to detect the target LOS at much greater than the normal range, but by denying range information, noise can prevent or delay missile launch, force some missiles into less efficient pursuit trajectories, and possibly degrade fuzing.

Deception jamming involves many techniques, including generation of false targets and causing radars to lose automatic track. False targets may be produced by delaying or altering the characteristics of the reflected radar energy, by chaff, or by decoys, which either enhance the radar's return energy or continuously transmit signals that may be mistaken for echoes, thereby causing missile guidance on the wrong target. Inability to auto-track may force less efficient manual tracking and may also degrade fuzing.

One of the earliest forms of ECM was chaff, generally large quantities of radar-reflective material (often small lengths of foil or wire, but also possibly gases) released into the air to produce false targets or large "clouds" of clutterlike noise. More than forty years after its first use in World War II, it is still among the simplest and most effective ECM techniques. Since the effects of chaff are much like those of ground clutter, Doppler radars, if affected at all, are usually deceived only in beam aspects, but missile fuzing may be vulnerable at any aspect. Doppler radars may also be deceived if the chaff is blown by a strong wind.

The most common form of infrared countermeasure (IRCM) is the decoy flare. When expelled by the target this flare presents a point source of IR energy, generally more intense than that of the target, which tends to attract a heat-seeking missile. IR deception is also possible by use of a pulsing heat source, which tends to confuse IR-missile seekers. In the future there may even be defensive laser systems that can be directed at the missile to saturate its seeker.

As micro-electronics technology makes it possible to place larger amounts of "intelligence" into small missile packages, these weapons are becoming "smarter." Given sufficient information-processing capability, electronic and infrared counter-countermeasures (ECCM and IRCCM) can be devised for almost any defensive deception techniques. Such CCMs are, however, more effective in some situations than in others. If enough is known about any particular CCM technique, methods can be found to defeat it.

The quantum advances in electronics over the past few years have made the air-combat environment, and most other battlefields, virtual electronic jungles. Few air combat engagements of the future can be expected to be totally free of electronic-warfare (EW) considerations. Unfortunately for fighter aircraft, which are inherently small in size, have limited aircrew numbers, and have high aircrew task loads, most defensive ECM must be highly automated. Except for the possibility of manual deployment of chaff, flares, or small decoys, fighter aircrew involvement in ECM must be limited essentially to turning the equipment on and off once during the mission.

So far this discussion has centered on how to avoid or delay missile shots; but what if, in spite of the defender's best efforts, he suddenly receives warning, either visually or through a radar warning receiver

(RWR), that an enemy missile is airborne, possibly intended for his air-craft? The pilot's first defensive reaction is dependent on the situation; namely, what type of warning he receives, the direction and range of the threat, and the particular type of weapon approaching him. RWRs usually give the pilot a good idea of the direction of the guidance platform and, often, a fairly good idea of the type of missile that has been launched, but they do not usually provide adequate information on the range of the threat. In addition, some weapons, particularly passive homers, may not be indicated at all by a RWR. IR or Doppler warning systems, however, may detect a missile's approach.

Visual detection of the missile, and possibly the launch platform, pro-vides probably the best early defense against this weapon. Such a sighting furnishes a reliable threat direction, often a good indication of range, and possibly knowledge of the type of weapon involved. Because of the small size of many AAMs (particularly when viewed from the head-on aspect), their great speed, and the often limited relative motion they generate, visual range estimation can be very difficult. Visual acquisition of the launching platform at the moment of firing usually provides a better reference. Intelligence, RWR indications, and identification of the launch platform may provide reliable threat classification. The more information the target pilot receives in a timely fashion, the more effectively he can defend.

> There is nothing, absolutely nothing, to describe what goes on inside a pilot's gut when he sees a SAM get airborne.
> Commander Randy "Duke" Cunningham, USN

If the defender receives any warning at all, it is usually a rough indica-tion of the threat direction by RWR or voice call. With only this informa-tion he is forced to assume a worst-case situation, i.e., imminent missile impact by an unknown weapon. Even so, he is usually far from helpless. Immediate employment of ECM, chaff, flares, and decoys is appropriate. Simultaneously a break (hard as possible) turn should be made, accompa-nied by a quick power reduction if any possibility of a heat seeker exists. There are several purposes for this break turn. One is to increase the LOS rate, making it more difficult for a missile to track and maneuver to an intercept. A second is to degrade seeker and guidance performance by rotating the heat source away from a rear-hemisphere IR missile or by gaining a beam aspect against a radar weapon. Attaining a beam aspect also may degrade fuze and/or warhead effectiveness. In addition, particularly when the threat has appeared in the rear hemisphere, the break turn allows the earliest visual acquisition of the missile and launch platform.

> Just as [my] missile left the rail the MiG [-21] executed a maximum G, tight turning, starboard break turn. He couldn't have seen me. Either his wingman called a break or his tail warning radar was working. I had an instantaneous plan view of him and he was really hauling. . . . The missile couldn't handle it, exploding out of lethal range.
> Commander Randy "Duke" Cunningham, USN

For forward- or rear-quarter threats, the effectiveness of a missile break depends on the target's G. Because of the usual large speed advantage of the missile over the target, a good rule of thumb is that the missile will require about five times the G capability of the target to complete a successful intercept. Although the LOS rate increase is primarily a function of target G, the time required to produce a beam aspect is dependent on target turn rate. Since the optimum instantaneous-turn-rate performance and maximum G of an aircraft are obtained near its corner velocity, it behooves the fighter aircrew to maintain at least this speed when in hostile airspace. (A discussion of turn performance can be found in the Appendix.) Faster speeds are usually not as injurious to turn performance as slower speeds, since deceleration is generally much quicker than acceleration in break-turn situations. Turn rate and radial G may also be enhanced by breaking downward, altitude permitting, to exploit the added G of gravity. Nose-down breaks have the additional advantages associated with lower altitudes and increased missile look-down. If a heat seeker is suspected, however, a break toward the sun or into a cloud might be the best move. Other defensive measures (i.e., chaff, flares, etc.) should be continued during the break turn as long as the threat may still exist, or until additional threat information is received.

The direction of the defensive break turn depends on the aspect of the threat, and usually should be in the closest direction to achieve a beam aspect. For rear-hemisphere missiles this generally means breaking toward the threat, and turning away from forward-hemisphere threats. For nearly head-on or tail-on threats, the break direction is the pilot's choice, with vertically nose-down usually preferable if that option is available. Particularly for forward-hemisphere threats, the optimum maneuver plane may have to be altered somewhat if the defender is to maintain sight of the missile.

If a threat is detected near a beam aspect, or if a break turn succeeds in producing a beam aspect before intercept, continuation of the break turn in the same plane is usually not advantageous, as this would tend to rotate the missile out of the beam region. In addition to the other possible problems already mentioned, the beam aspect presents the greatest LOS rate to the missile. One exception to this rule pertains if the threat is suspected of being a rear-hemisphere-limited heat-seeking weapon, in which case a continued turn toward the missile rotates it into the forward hemisphere, further degrading its chances of guidance.

Otherwise an out-of-plane break turn, similar to the maneuver described for guns defense (Figure 1-5), usually should be initiated against a missile in the beam region. This could mean an immediate upward or downward break on missile launch warning, or an approximate 90° change in the plane of a turn already commenced. For example, if the reaction to a rear-quarter threat had been a nose-low vertical turn (split-S) of about 90°, and indications were that the missile was then near the beam, an approximate 90° roll should be made, followed by a pull-up. This out-of-plane maneuver should be continued, while turning toward the missile (i.e., barrel-rolling around it) only fast enough to keep it in a beam aspect, until the threat has ended.

Missile range information, acquired either visually or by other means, as well as some indication of the type of weapon involved, can allow the defender a much more reasoned response. For instance, if the missile is detected near its forward-hemisphere maximum aerodynamic range, the target pilot may choose a hard turn away to place the threat in his rear quarter, accompanied by a dive and acceleration simply to outrun the reduced range capabilities of the weapon. Likewise, a max-range rear-hemisphere missile may be outrun by turning away to place it as close to dead astern as possible, diving and accelerating away. If any doubt exists as to the range capabilities of the weapon, the defender should maintain visual contact so that a last-second break turn can be accomplished as the missile approaches intercept.

Visual acquisition of the missile and its launch platform provides the defender with a wealth of valuable information. Since many missiles are of the boost-glide variety, with engines that produce large quantities of highly visible smoke or dust at launch, acquisition near the moment of firing may be critical. Weapons with smokeless engines are particularly difficult to spot visually, but even these usually produce a vapor contrail at high altitudes which can be seen for many miles.

Knowledge of the various threat weapons systems and visual sighting of the missile in flight usually can provide missile identification and an indication of the most effective defense. Missile smoke characteristics and the weapons available to a particular launch platform are two indications. The launch conditions themselves provide another. It can be assumed, for instance, that a weapon launched in the forward hemisphere has forward-hemisphere capability. If it does not, it normally will be of little danger even if the wrong identification is made. The missile's guidance trajectory offers another clue. A proportional-navigation weapon will attempt to gain lead and stabilize its position relative to the distant horizon. A beam-rider will appear to superimpose itself on the LOS to the guidance platform. A pure-pursuit missile will keep its nose pointed directly at the target and will appear to drift back along the horizon toward the rear of the defender's aircraft.

Watching the missile's flight path also can provide the defender with feedback on how well the weapon is performing. If a radical defensive maneuver is made and no missile correction is observed, the weapon is either ballistic or guiding on another aircraft in the flight. Missile trajectory response may be misleading, however. Once the weapon is at close range, defensive measures should be continued through the point of closest approach regardless of missile maneuver, since termination of such defenses could result in reduced miss distance and possible damage.

Visual acquisition of the missile provides other benefits, including knowledge of the weapon's plane of attack. The initial break turn against the missile usually should be made in this plane, since the generation of aspect and LOS rate is maximized in this manner. Timing is also important, as the effectiveness of maneuvers designed to produce large LOS rates varies with range. An out-of-plane maneuver performed too early will have little effect, while one begun late just may be too late. When in doubt, however, a slightly early response is usually preferable.

> Waiting for a proper moment to begin my evasion tactic was agonizing. Panic rose up in my throat, urging loss of reason. At the last moment I pulled up with eight Gs after breaking down and starboard. The missile couldn't take the turn, going off a thousand feet below.
>
> Commander Randy "Duke" Cunningham, USN

One example of the value of visual sighting and timing is a forward-quarter missile shot at relatively close range. Generally the rule is to turn away from such threats, but if the defender determines that intercept will occur before he can generate a beam aspect and commence an out-of-plane maneuver, another tactic may be preferable. A break turn toward the threat, actually pulling it across the target's nose, will require a large lead correction on the part of the missile. Depending on the missile's maneuver capabilities, such a correction may not be possible in the short time available because of high forward-quarter closure. If this tactic is used and the defender sees the missile correcting, presumably within sufficient time, a rapid reversal should be made back toward the missile, pulling it back across the nose from the other direction. If started soon after the missile begins its first correction, this reversal will often produce a wide overshoot in the direction of the initial break turn, since missile guidance corrections will lag target maneuvers and produce out-of-phase missile responses. A variation on this tactic is a rolling-turn maneuver that causes the target's nose to inscribe a circle around the missile (i.e., a barrel roll). Again, this move causes the missile to make continuous large lead corrections. This variation is usually most effective when the missile is 30° to 60° off the target's nose. Both tactics can be expected to produce best results against larger, less maneuverable missiles and at higher altitudes, where missile-control reaction time is usually increased.

Missile defense often requires instant analysis and rapid reactions. The tactics to be employed in any conceivable situation must be predetermined and practiced often so that they become automatic. Once the missile is launched, it is too late for leisurely development of a response.

Notes

1. John T. Godfrey, *The Look of Eagles*, pp. 79–80.
2. Ibid., p. 81.
3. Ibid., p. 85.
4. Alan C. Deere, *Nine Lives*, p. 90.
5. Edward H. Sims, *Fighter Tactics and Strategy, 1914–1970*, p. 245.

2

Basic Fighter Maneuvers

I fly close to my man, aim well and then of course he falls down.
Captain Oswald Boelcke
Probably the World's First Ace
German Air Service, WW-I

Basic fighter maneuvers (BFMs) are the building blocks of fighter tactics. They may be classified as primary maneuvers, which can be performed without regard to an adversary (e.g., accelerations, climbs, turns), and relative maneuvers, which must be described or performed in relation to another aircraft. The physics and techniques involved in most primary maneuvers are discussed in the Appendix and therefore are not covered here.

No guts, no glory. If you are going to shoot him down, you have to get in there and mix it up with him.
Major Frederick C. "Boots" Blesse, USAF
10 Victories, Korean Conflict

Pursuit Curves

Pursuit curves were discussed previously in relation to missile trajectories; they are equally relevant to fighter maneuvering. The three forms of pursuit—lead, pure, and lag—are technically defined by the orientation of the attacking aircraft's velocity vector ahead of, directly toward, or behind the target aircraft, respectively. Since the fighter pilot does not always have an indication of the precise direction of his velocity vector, his nose position is usually substituted as a reference. In maneuvering situations these two references (velocity vector and nose position) vary by the amount of the attacker's angle of attack and sideslip, which are generally not great enough to be of importance. So, what is called "pure pursuit," for instance, may actually involve a small amount of lag.

Lead Pursuit

A lead-pursuit path is followed by positioning the aircraft's nose ahead of the target, or "bogey," fighter. As discussed in the gun-employment section, the practical maximum lead when the attacker is maneuvering near the target's plane of turn is often limited by the attacker's over-the-nose visibility and the requirement that he maintain sight of the bogey. "Blind" lead turns may be appropriate under some circumstances, but they are inherently dangerous, both because of the possibility of a collision and because of the potential for losing sight of the bogey and allowing it to gain a more threatening position or to escape. Larger amounts of lead can often be generated by turning in a parallel plane with the target, so that sight may be maintained over the side of the attacker's nose.

The purpose of lead pursuit is primarily to increase closure on the target by use of geometry. The ideal lead angle for greatest closure depends on relative aircraft positions, relative speeds, and target maneuver. As with missiles, a proportional-navigation course usually maximizes closure, and can be estimated visually as the lead angle that causes the target to appear to remain stationary against the distant horizon. If the target's drift appears to be toward the attacker's nose, more lead is called for, and vice versa.

The lead-collision or lead-pursuit curve may even allow an attacker to close on a much faster target, particularly if that target turns toward the attacker at a rate that places the attacker at a large AOT.

Figure 2-1 depicts a fighter using lead pursuit to close on a faster target from a rear-hemisphere position. Note that in this example the target aircraft is turning toward the attacker, inscribing a rather large arc in the sky, while the attacker keeps his nose in front of the target's position and turns inside its flight path to close the range. The attacking fighter is not maintaining a perfect proportional-navigation (lead-collision) track in this case, since the LOS to the target is rotating throughout the maneuver, but

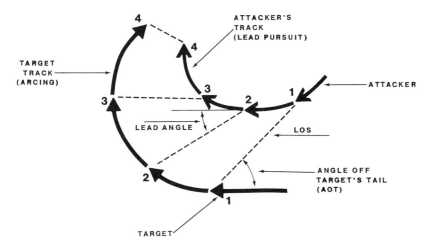

Figure 2-1. Effects of Arcing and Lead Pursuit

the combination of its position at high AOT and lead pursuit allows it to close the range continuously, even with inferior airspeed. In general, a fighter cannot maintain a lead-collision course from a position near the target's beam without equal or superior speed, but lead pursuit can provide closure at a reduced rate.

Two other points are worth mentioning about this example. It illustrates that, in using lead pursuit, the attacker must turn with a decreasing radius and increasing rate as he closes the range. Eventually he may have to turn much tighter and faster than the target in order to maintain lead pursuit. Also note that lead pursuit results in increasing AOT, thereby reducing the attacker's angular position advantage in the target's rear hemisphere.

Figure 2-2 depicts two possible defenses against a lead-pursuit maneuver performed by an attacker still out of firing parameters, one appropriate for a defender with a speed advantage (solid path), the other for a defender with a speed disadvantage (broken path). In the first case the defender turns away from the attacker to decrease AOT as much as practical, and then uses his superior speed to increase range by an extension maneuver as described earlier. This may allow him to disengage, or it may provide enough separation eventually to enable him to come back at the attacking fighter and meet it head-on, negating the attacker's angular position advantage. This option may not be appropriate against a missle-equipped attacker, since the turn-away could place the opponent within his firing envelope.

In the second case slower speed enables the defender to turn tightly enough to prevent the detrimental effects of arcing, and he meets the

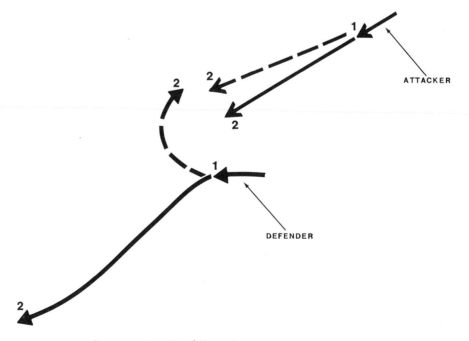

Figure 2-2. Defenses against Lead Pursuit

attacker with high AOT. It may not be possible for the defender to complete this option before a guns or missile defense maneuver is required, depending on the actual ranges and weapons involved. The attacker's angular position advantage may be reduced or eliminated in this manner if he can be met with high AOT.

Pure Pursuit

Holding the attacking aircraft's nose directly on the target also provides closure, unless the target has a significant speed advantage and AOT is very small. Although pure pursuit does not generate as much closure as lead pursuit under most conditions, neither does it cause AOT to increase as rapidly. In addition, pure pursuit presents the minimum frontal area of the attacking fighter to the target pilot, increasing the defender's visual problems.

> Months of preparation, one of those few opportunities, and the judgement of a split second are what makes some pilot an ace, while others think back on what they could have done.
>
> Colonel Gregory "Pappy" Boyington, USMC
> 28 Victories, WW-II

Lag Pursuit

In lag pursuit the attacker places his nose at an angle behind the target aircraft. This tactic is useful in slowing or stopping closure to maintain a desired separation from the target while simultaneously maintaining or decreasing AOT. Using lag pursuit, even a faster fighter can maintain a position in the rear hemisphere of a maneuvering target aircraft. Figure 2-3 illustrates the use of lag pursuit to attain a stabilized position in the rear hemisphere of a slower opponent. In this example the attacker finds

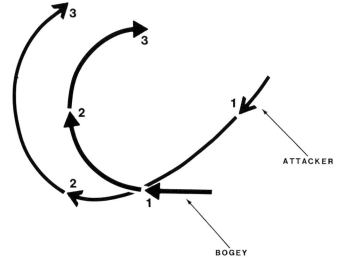

Figure 2-3. Lag Pursuit

himself on the inside of the target's turn at high AOT and presumably out of firing parameters. His turn capability will not allow him to pull enough lead for a gun snapshot (or perhaps he is equipped with rear-quarter missiles only). One option is to relax the turn, allowing the nose to drift to a point behind the bogey for lag pursuit. This reduced turn rate also offers the attacker a good opportunity to increase his energy by accelerating. (See the Appendix for a discussion of energy.) Eventually this fighter approaches the bogey's flight path and reinitiates a hard turn back toward the target, achieving a fairly stable position behind the bogey and outside its turn. This position, which affords the attacker a view of the underside of the hard-turning bogey, is termed "cold-side" lag.

As long as the fighter has a speed advantage over its opponent and can achieve the same turn rate, stabilized lag pursuit is possible in the bogey's rear hemisphere. However, there are several very strict constraints on combinations of range, relative speed, turn radii, and relative fighter positions which must be met for stabilized lag pursuit. All these parameters are very difficult to meet in practice, even with a cooperative target, so lag pursuit is generally a temporary state of affairs. Nevertheless, this tactic does allow a fighter to maintain a speed advantage over a maneuvering target while remaining in its rear hemisphere.

Lag also may make it very difficult for the bogey pilot to maintain sight of the attacker, particularly when the attacker is on the cold side or near the bogey's six o'clock (i.e., dead astern); this forces the defender to turn harder or to reverse his turn direction. If the attacker is equipped with an off-boresight weapon, one that can be fired at a target that is not directly ahead, there may be a shot opportunity regardless of the bogey's maneuver. If the bogey pilot cannot safely reverse without giving his attacker a shot opportunity, the continued turn occupies his attention and forces him to be predictable, making him easy pickings for a second fighter.

Likewise, however, an attacker is also predictable and vulnerable while performing prolonged lag pursuit. When using this tactic a pilot should attempt to gain a position from which a shot opportunity will be presented with his available weapons if the bogey reverses. Unless the attacker is gun equipped, lag, particularly cold-side lag, at close range with the nose well off the bogey may allow the bogey to reverse with impunity, possibly gaining an offensive position. At the very least this condition does not make the bogey predictable. It also may result in a difficult position from which to disengage should disengagement be necessary. Additionally, sustained lag pursuit can be very taxing physically to the attacking pilot, since his greater speed requires a higher load factor than that of his opponent.

Stabilized lag pursuit with its many constraints may not offer the optimum offensive position for the attacker considering his weapons system and relative maneuvering capabilities. It is usually desirable for the attacker to stabilize within the boundaries of his weapons envelope, possibly only having to satisfy aiming requirements for a valid shot. If the attacker can reach such a position even temporarily, especially if he is out of the defender's field of vision, the bogey pilot is forced to react in order to regain sight.

Effective defense against lag pursuit involves simply changing the defender's speed, turn direction, or G. For hot-side lag this generally means tightening the turn, sometimes with a gravity assist by turning nose-low. Cold-side lag is usually countered by a turn reversal, which places the attacker on the inside of the defender's turn in lead pursuit. Such a maneuver results in a rapid decrease in range and may actually cause the attacker to fly out in front of the defender, reversing the roles. This reversal is often more effective when performed nose-high, causing a reduction in the defender's forward velocity and increasing closure. Reversals are quite effective against missiles-only fighters, as these fighters will often quickly pass through the min-range missile boundary unless the lag geometry is just right. For gun-equipped fighters, however, a bogey reversal usually results in at least a snapshot opportunity for the attacker.

> Fighting spirit one must have. Even if a man lacks some of the other qualifications, he can often make up for it in fighting spirit.
>
> Brigadier General Robin Olds, USAF

Lag Displacement Rolls

In the lag-pursuit discussion one method was mentioned for achieving a lag position from a point inside the defender's turn at medium AOT (about 30° to 60° AOT), when the range is only slightly greater than that desired for lag. This method involves relaxing the turn and allowing the nose to drift behind the target, remaining essentially in the same maneuver plane as the target until approaching the desired lag position. When he sees this maneuver, the bogey pilot may assume that the attacker cannot match his turn performance and is about to overshoot. Such an assumption may induce the defender to reverse his turn direction to gain a position advantage on the overshooting attacker—but this often presents the attacker with a gun-shot opportunity instead.

Other initial conditions require different tactics for reaching a lag position. For instance, when approaching the target at close range with high overtake and low AOT (less than about 30°), simply relaxing the turn may not slow the closure fast enought to prevent overshooting. Should the defender reverse in this situation, the attacker could be in real trouble. Figure 2-4 illustrates this case, which begins much like that described in Figure 2-3, except at closer range and with less AOT. Here, the attacker's high closure causes him to fly out in front of the target after the reversal. Technically, any time the attacker crosses behind the target an overshoot has occurred; but this is usually not dangerous unless the target is moving at a slower speed or has a tighter turn radius. Such a situation often results when a missed gun shot is pressed to minimum range with high closure.

Position "1" in Figure 2-4 assumes that the attacker cannot pull sufficient lead for a gun shot (or is not gun equipped) and is inside minimum missile range (or is not missile equipped). To avoid a dangerous overshoot in such a situation it is necessary to stop the closure rapidly. This may be accomplished by a speed reduction, by a hard turn away from the target (reducing the component of velocity in the direction of the target), or by an out-of-plane maneuver. A speed reduction may not be desirable since a

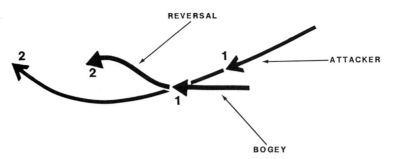

Figure 2-4. Results of an Overshoot

speed advantage often provides a maneuverability advantage (particularly below corner speed), and the attacker may lose maneuvering potential. A hard turn away from the target (pulling toward its extended six o'clock region) in the bogey's plane of turn may cause the attacker to lose sight of the bogey, and also may bleed off valuable energy (speed). Additionally, such a maneuver would make it unlikely that lag pursuit could be reinitiated, and it probably would result in loss of the offensive.

An out-of-plane maneuver is often the best alternative in this situation. Figure 2-5 illustrates one such maneuver, called the lag roll. At point "1" the attacker, in lead pursuit at close range, levels his wings and pulls nose-up out of the defender's plane of turn. The resulting climb reduces speed and the component of velocity in the defender's direction (reducing closure). The attacker continues to pull up, possibly also pulling somewhat toward the bogey's flight path in a rolling-pull maneuver, to ensure

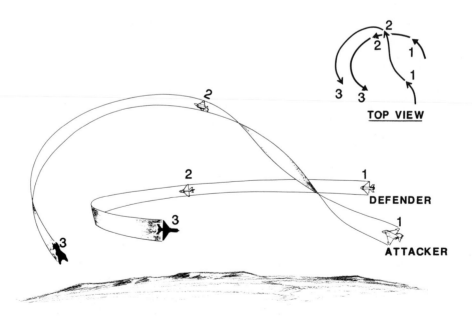

Figure 2-5. Lag-Pursuit Roll

that he passes above and behind the defender as he crosses the bogey's flight path. A slow, continuous roll toward the bogey (here to the right) during this phase of the maneuver enables the attacker to maintain sight throughout, and he passes above and behind the defender essentially inverted, as depicted at point "2." Trading airspeed for altitude in this maneuver allows the attacker to maintain his total energy better than if he had simply pulled more G in a level turn, and low-G conditions once the climb is established may even allow energy addition. From position "2" the attacker benefits from a gravity assist in the nose-low turn, allowing him to pull the bogey closer to the nose and position offensively in lag pursuit.

Should the defender reverse at point "2," the attacker has the options (depending on speed) of performing a second lag roll in the opposite direction or continuing to roll around the bogey's flight path, passing underneath and back into lag on the other side.

The displacement roll is similar to the lag roll, except that it is used in close-range, low-closure situations to reduce AOT and increase range, rather than to prevent an overshoot. This maneuver tends to "displace" the attacker's flight path from inside the bogey's turn toward or to the other side of the defender's flight path. In such nearly co-speed situations lag pursuit is not generally advantageous, so this tactic is primarily of value for positioning the attacker within a missile envelope. It allows the attacker to increase nose-tail separation with the defender (possibly to meet min-range constraints) without reducing speed. After completion of the displacement roll, the attacker will usually be in lag pursuit, requiring him to turn faster than the bogey to point at the target for a boresight missile shot. Essentially the displacement roll trades some angular advantage for increased nose-tail separation and possibly reduced AOT.

After the foregoing description of the lag roll, the following narrative by Colonel Robin Olds, USAF, should have a familiar ring.

> I had another [MiG] in sight at my 10 o'clock, in a left turn . . . I pulled sharp left, turned inside him, pulled my nose up about 30 [degrees] above the horizon, . . . barrel rolled to the right, held my position upside down above and behind the MIG until the proper angular deflection and range parameters were satisfied, completed the rolling maneuver, and fell in behind and below the MIG-21 at his seven o'clock position at about .95 mach. Range was 4500 feet, angle off 15. The MIG obligingly pulled up well above the horizon and exactly down sun. I put the pipper on his tailpipe, received a perfect [missile] growl, squeezed the trigger once, hesitated, then once again. The first Sidewinder leapt in front and within a split second, turned left in a definite and beautiful collision course correction. . . . Suddenly the MIG-21 erupted in a brilliant flash [of] orange flame.[1]

Another variation of the lag roll is known as a barrel-roll attack. This maneuver is useful in making the transition from lead pursuit in the target's beam area or forward hemisphere to a rear-hemisphere position. Such a situation may develop when an attacker is performing lead pursuit against a bogey at fairly long range and the defender turns toward the attacker. At some point the attacker may realize that continued lead pursuit would result in passing the bogey at very high AOT (i.e., in his forward hemisphere). A barrel-roll attack is initiated with a wings-level pull-up and a roll toward the bogey, as with the lag roll. Since the range to the target is considerably greater, however, the climb established is continued for a longer time, resulting in a greater altitude advantage over the defender. Again the rolling pull is timed with the target's motion so the attacker arrives at a position well above the bogey, inverted, before passing slightly behind the defender. As the attacker approaches the overhead position his altitude advantage and gravity assist may provide the opportunity for him to pull hard down toward the target, remaining inside the horizontal boundaries of the bogey's turn, for a "high-side" (i.e., coming down from above and to one side) gun-firing pass. Or, depending on relative aircraft performance, available weapons, or bogey maneuvers, the attacker can delay and moderate his pull-down slightly to arrive at a lag-pursuit position. An illustration of this second option would look much like Figure 2-5, except that, because of the starting conditions, most of the initial phases of the manuever (i.e., the pull-up and roll) would take place in the defender's forward hemisphere. Often there will be a greater heading difference between the fighters at position "2," making lag pursuit impractical. In this case, between times "2" and "3," the attacker may turn steeply nose-low, using lead pursuit to pull inside the bogey's turn. This maneuver keeps nose-tail separation from increasing greatly.

One of the common mistakes made in the employment of lag rolls and barrel-roll attacks is attempting to use them without sufficient initial lead pursuit. Returning to Figure 2-5, note that the attacking and defending aircraft are aligned nearly parallel at time "1." Visualize what would happen if the attacker's nose at time "1" were pointed at, or only slightly ahead of, the bogey. First, as the attacker started his pull-up, the bogey would disappear beneath the nose, requiring the attacker to perform a very quick roll just to maintain sight, and greatly reducing any altitude advantage which may be achieved over the bogey. Without the climb between times "1" and "2," the attacker's forward velocity component may cause him to overshoot the bogey's flight path grossly, or force him to pass too far behind the target, allowing nose-tail separation to increase greatly. The lack of sufficient altitude advantage at time "2" also reduces the gravity assist available to the attacker for pulling his nose back toward the bogey to maintain an angular advantage.

Another common error is beginning the pull-up too late. In order for the attacker to gain the required vertical separation in this case, he must attain a rather high nose attitude. This situation may allow the defender to dive away and gain separation before the attacker can pull back down. Or the bogey may wait until about time "2" and pull sharply up toward the attacker, meeting him on the way down with high AOT, and causing a vertical overshoot.

The attacking fighter may also need a speed advantage over the defender for lag displacement rolls (except for the barrel-roll attack) to work well. If the pull-up is begun in the bogey's rear hemisphere as depicted in Figure 2-5, the attacker must cover considerably more distance than the defender to arrive at position "3" and therefore needs a considerable speed advantage. But if at time "1" the attacker was closer to the target's beam or even slightly into its forward hemisphere, as described for the barrel-roll attack, then the attacker would require less speed to complete the maneuver.

One of the effective defenses against lag displacement rolls and barrel-roll attacks is to dive away in an extension maneuver as the attacker approaches his maximum climb attitude. The defender should simply unload while maintaining his original bank angle, as though he were still turning, during the early part of this extension. Otherwise, the attacker may recognize the tactic and pull back down before sufficient separation can be achieved. The extension may generate enough separation for escape, or it may provide room for a hard turn back into the attacker to negate his position advantage.

Another effective tactic, especially against a barrel-roll attack, is for the defender to execute a simultaneous barrel roll in the opposite direction, i.e., toward the attacker. If he can get his nose higher than the attacker's between times "1" and "2," the defender may be able to reach a rear-hemisphere position on the attacker after completing the roll.

High Yo-Yo

> The Yo-Yo is very difficult to explain. It was first perfected by the well-known Chinese fighter pilot Yo-Yo Noritake. He also found it difficult to explain, being quite devoid of English.
>
> Squadron Leader K. G. Holland, RAF
> Fighter Pilot

Both the lag-roll and the barrel-roll attack may be used to prevent overshooting the flight path of a maneuvering target or to reduce AOT under various conditions. The high yo-yo is also useful for preventing overshoots and reducing AOT, and it is best suited to conditions of moderate AOT (about 30° to 60°), when the attacker is more nearly co-speed with the defender and lacks the excess lead required for lag rolls. As with the various lag displacement rolls, the high yo-yo uses three-dimensional maneuvering rather than increased load factor to reduce horizontal turn radius, thereby allowing the attacker to retain greater energy. Figure 2-6 depicts this maneuver.

At position "1" the attacker is turning in the bogey's plane of maneuver in pure pursuit with rapidly increasing AOT and closure. If this course is continued it could result in an overshoot of the bogey's flight path and loss of the offensive. Therefore, the attacker rolls his wings level (sometimes called a quarter roll or quarter-plane roll) and pulls up, out of the defender's plane of turn. This climb reduces the component of the attacker's velocity which is oriented toward the bogey, eventually stopping the closure, and if it is begun soon enough, it will prevent an overshoot. As the closure slows to nearly zero, the attacker should be high in the defender's rear hemisphere in a nose-high attitude. At point "2" the attacker rolls toward the bogey to place his lift vector ahead of, on, or behind the defender to establish lead, pure, or lag pursuit, respectively. The choice depends pri-

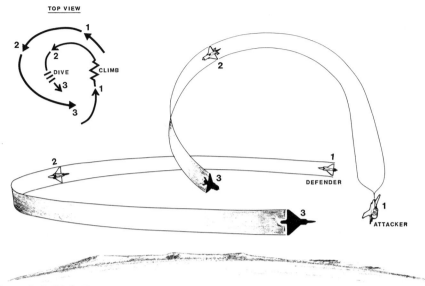

Figure 2-6. High Yo-Yo

marily on the present nose-tail separation and the desired range once the attacker's nose is pointed back toward the defender. In the case depicted the attacker wishes to close the range for a guns pass at point "3," so he pulls for a point ahead of the target's position at point "2" and keeps his nose ahead of the defender throughout the remainder of the rolling, nose-low turn toward point "3."

The lead-pursuit option depicted generally results in the attacker reaching a higher peak altitude, losing more airspeed, and approaching the bogey in a rather steep dive across the circle at point "3." Choosing lag pursuit at point "2" usually will result in the attacker maintaining greater speed but scooping out below the bogey's altitude. The result of this option is usually a hot-side lag-pursuit position looking up at the defender across the circle.

A common error in most out-of-plane offensive maneuvers which have been discussed is to generate excessive pitch attitudes relative to the defender, either nose-up or nose-down. Excessive nose-high pitch may result from beginning a high yo-yo too late. The short range then requires greater pitch attitude to avoid a horizontal overshoot. Once the attacker is very nose-high in the bogey's rear hemisphere, range begins to open very rapidly, affording the defender an opportunity to dive away and gain separation in an extension maneuver.

The excessive nose-down situation usually results from greed on the part of the attacker, when he chooses the lead-pursuit option from the top of a high yo-yo or barrel-roll attack in an attempt for a quick gun shot. If the defender pulls hard up into the plane of this high-side attack after the attacker is committed to being excessively nose-low, the bogey can often generate a vertical overshoot, with the attacker losing the offensive after he passes through the target's altitude. It is important to note that these out-of-plane maneuvers generally will prevent an overshoot and often will improve the attacker's offensive position; but without a significant turn-performance advantage the attacker should not expect an immediate lethal firing position with a boresight weapon.

> The lead *Messerschmitt* suddenly stopped smoking. It was a complete giveaway; I knew that at this instant he'd cut power. I chopped the throttle to prevent overrunning the enemy fighter. I skidded up to my right, half rolled to my left, wings vertical. He turned sharply to the left; perfect! Now—stick hard back, rudder pedals co-ordinating smoothly. The *Thunderbolt* whirled around, slicing inside the *Messerschmitt*. I saw the pilot look up behind him, gasping, as the *Thunderbolt* loomed inside of his turn, both wings flaming with all eight guns. This boy had never seen a *Thunderbolt* really roll; he was convinced I'd turned inside him.[2]

Low Yo-Yo

The out-of-plane maneuvers so far discussed have been designed to slow closure and decrease AOT by pulling the attacker's nose (velocity vector) away from and behind the target in the initial phases. The purpose of the low yo-yo is to increase closure and angular advantage with a lead-pursuit out-of-plane maneuver.

A typical scenario for use of this tactic is represented by a fairly long-range (i.e., probably hot-side) lag-pursuit situation, where the attacker does not have the turn capability to pull his nose to the target quickly for a shot, or where doing so would cause excessive speed loss. Figure 2-7 depicts this situation. Here the attacker would like to pull his nose to the bogey for a gun shot, but he lacks the turn capability to accomplish this rapidly in the horizontal plane. The attacker can increase the horizontal component of his turn rate by pulling the nose down toward the inside of the turn. The gravity assist and the ability to generate a horizontal turning component by rolling the aircraft once it is established in a nose-low attitude allow the attacker to position his nose well in front of, but considerably below, the bogey's position. Ideally, the attacker should generate excess lead at point "2" so that he can level his wings, pull up, and fly essentially a straight path to intercept the bogey at the desired range. At point "3" the attacker approaches the bogey's altitude from below and reestablishes his turn in the defender's plane of maneuver as gun-firing range and lead are reached simultaneously.

Obviously, in practice, it is very difficult to make all these events occur at the same time, at point "3." The greater the nose-tail distance at point "1," the more lead will be necessary at point "2" in order to close the range. But the larger the lead angle, the greater the AOT will be at intercept, so there is obviously a practical limit to the available lead angle. At excessive range the attacker can make up all the distance with one low yo-yo only by flying out in front of the defender. Generally, it is more prudent to close the range a little at a time in several steps. The first low yo-yo can close the range somewhat and can be followed by a high yo-yo or barrel-roll attack from position "2" to reduce excess AOT. This sequence can be repeated as necessary. In general, two small yo-yos (high or low) are safer than one big one.

An attempt to make up too much range in one maneuver leaves the

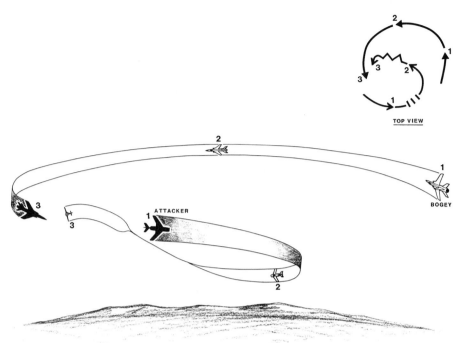

Figure 2-7. Low Yo-Yo

attacker vulnerable to countermoves by the defender. Generally, an attempt to generate large amounts of lead in the low yo-yo results in an excessively nose-low attitude. With sufficient range, greater AOT, and a gravity assist, the defender may be able to pull nose-low down toward the attacker and meet him nearly head-on, neutralizing the attacker's position advantage. Or, if the defender has sufficient energy, he may choose to pull up as the attacker commits his nose too low, and by performing a rolling-pull toward the attacker (essentially a barrel-roll attack) actually achieve a position advantage high in the attacker's rear hemisphere.

> The winner (of an air battle) may have been determined by the amount of time, energy, thought and training an individual has previously accomplished in an effort to increase his ability as a fighter pilot.
>
> Commander Randy "Duke" Cunningham, USN

Lead Turn

The lead turn was discussed in the gun-employment section of Chapter 1 in connection with preparing for a snapshot. In this section "lead" turn is defined as an "early" turn that is started by the attacker before he passes the opponent in a forward-hemisphere approach situation. It does not necessarily connote lead pursuit, and in fact it may be a lag maneuver. Figure 2-8 depicts a lead-turn scenario.

At point "1" the aircraft are converging on opposite headings with offset flight paths. Before the two fighters pass abeam, one of them begins a lead turn toward the flight path of the other (solid tracks), while its opponent

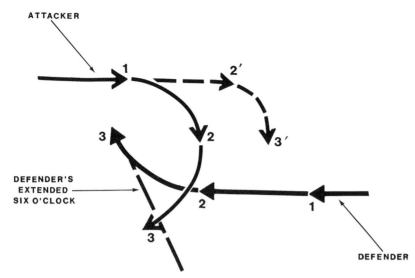

Figure 2-8. Lead Turn

continues straight ahead to point "2." At point "2" the early-turning fighter has a considerable advantage over its opponent. This position may allow a high-angle gun snapshot. At time "2" the defender turns toward the attacker, who then overshoots the defender's six o'clock at time "3" and assumes a temporary lag-pursuit position deep in the defender's rear hemisphere.

For comparison, the broken track shows the result if both pilots wait until they pass abeam before beginning to turn (points "2" and "2'"). At time "3"-"3'," the fighters are still abeam, essentially neutral.

Although the lead turn can be a very effective offensive maneuver, it is not without limitations. The earlier the turn is begun, the greater the potential rewards, but obviously if it is started too soon the attacker will pass in front of the defender's nose. This can be dangerous if the defender is equipped with a short-range, all-aspect weapon such as a gun. It also results in the other blind-lead-turn problems mentioned in the previous chapter. One possible solution to this problem is a slightly out-of-plane lead turn, so that the attacker passes above or below the defender's nose, avoiding a boresight weapons-firing solution.

Another danger of the lead turn is the overshoot potential. In Figure 2-8 the attacker delayed his turn to pass behind the defender, but he overshot the bogey's extended six o'clock position at long range with a track-crossing angle (TCA) of about 90°. TCA is defined as the angular difference in velocity vectors at any instant. As long as turn radii and speed are about equal between the opponents, there is little danger in such an overshoot. If the defender reverses near point "3," he places the attacker on the inside of his turn in lead pursuit and subjects himself to a guns pass. If, however, the defender has a tighter turn-radius capability or slower speed at the time of the overshoot, a reversal may place him inside the attacker's turn, on the offensive, as depicted in Figure 2-4.

The potential danger of an overshoot situation is dependent on many factors, including range, relative turn performance, TCA, and relative speeds. In general, the greatest danger exists for the attacker when overshoots result at close range and low TCAs against a slower bogey with a tighter turn radius, as in Figure 2-4. Against a slower or tighter-turning opponent, the attacker should use caution in employment of the lead turn.

The earlier a lead turn is started, assuming the attacker passes behind the defender, the closer the resulting range and the smaller the TCA at overshoot; both of these conditions can increase the attacker's risk. If the attacker is at a slower speed or has a smaller turn radius, the overshoot risk is reduced and the lead turn may be begun sooner, resulting in greater offensive advantage.

A further consideration in lead turns is a factor called flight-path separation. As shown in Figure 2-9, this is the perpendicular distance from the attacker to the extended flight path of the defender at any moment. In both cases depicted in this figure, the attacker and the defender are co-speed and approaching on opposite courses with each fighter having the same flight-path separation relative to its opponent. In case 1, the attacker's turn radius (R_A) is approximately half the flight-path separation, while in case 2 the attacker's turn radius is doubled, about equalling the flight-path separation. In each case the attacker begins a lead turn (time "1") against the nonmaneuvering defender so as to arrive on his flight path with identical nose-tail separation (time "2"). Note that in case 1 the attacker achieves about a 180° angular advantage, while in case 2 (larger turn radius) he gains only about a 90° advantage. In general, the potential angular advantage of a lead turn against a nonmaneuvering opponent is proportional to the ratio of flight-path separation to attacker turn radius when the turn is commenced. The effect of greater attacker turn rate is to allow the lead turn to be started at closer range, while the attacker still achieves maximum angular advantage. This allows less time for the opponent's defensive counter, which usually involves turning toward the attacker to reduce flight-path separation.

Because of these principles, fighters with tight turn radii stand to benefit most from a given flight-path separation. It therefore behooves less-maneuverable fighters to reduce flight-path separation to a minimum by attempting to pass as closely as possible to an opponent in forward-quarter

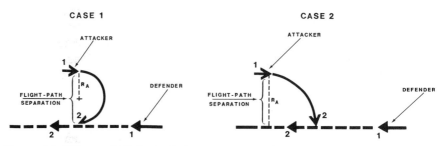

Figure 2-9. Effects of Flight-Path Separation

approach situations. Such flight-path separation may be vertical, lateral, or a combination of both (oblique). This principle is particularly important when one fighter is diving toward a forward-quarter pass with a climbing adversary. The initial portion of the climbing fighter's lead turn will have a gravity assist, giving it a reduced turn radius when compared with the diving fighter, which must oppose gravity in its pull-up. In such situations the pilot of the diving fighter normally should attempt to pass as closely as is feasible above his opponent to preclude an in-plane gravity-assisted lead turn. Unless he is purely vertical, the climbing opponent met with this tactic is forced to turn out-of-plane to receive a gravity assist, to perform a blind lead turn downward, or to complete a purely vertical lead turn, opposing gravity until he is in a vertical attitude.

Although of great benefit, flight-path separation is not essential for a lead turn. A fighter can early-turn its opponent even when the two fighters are meeting head-on on a collision course. In doing so, however, the lead-turning fighter is actually giving its opponent flight-path separation. If the attacker performs a lead turn at too great a range (based on relative speeds and turn performance) the defender may use this separation to gain advantage. Therefore, such a maneuver must be delayed, reducing separation so that the defender will overshoot if he attempts to turn on the attacker. A further consideration of this tactic is the possibility that the attacker may lose sight of the defender, since this is essentially a blind lead turn. Figure 2-10 shows the possible results of this early turn performed properly (case 1) and started too early (case 2). Because of the risks involved, fighters with inferior turn performance (larger radius) or greater speed generally should not attempt this maneuver, since the advantage to be gained seldom justifies the possible consequences. In this case the lead turn should be delayed until the opponent's reaction time does not allow him to counter before the pass has occurred.

Nose-to-Nose and Nose-to-Tail Turns

Nose-to-nose and nose-to-tail turns are two options of fighters meeting in forward-quarter passes. Figure 2-11 graphically defines these maneuvers.

As can be seen from this illustration, the names are fairly descriptive. In the first case, one fighter turns left, across the tail of its opponent, while

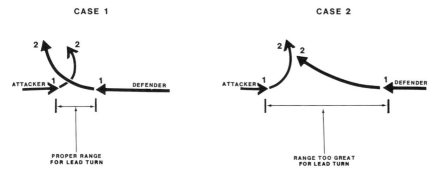

Figure 2-10. Lead Turns without Flight-Path Separation

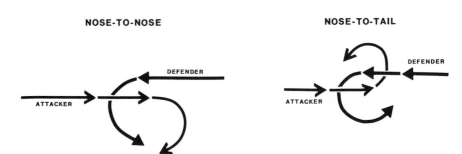

Figure 2-11. Turn Options

the other turns right, away from its adversary, so that the two fighters
again approach in a nose-to-nose fashion. In the second, each pilot chooses
to cross the other's tail, resulting in a nose-to-tail relationship.

In choosing the nose-to-nose turn, one pilot turns away from his opponent at the pass. In nearly parallel approach situations with considerable
flight-path separation, such as that shown in Figure 2-11, this choice may
result in a short blind period when the adversary is out of sight behind and
beneath the attacker's aircraft. Such a situation could lead to loss of sight if
the bogey does something unexpected during this time, but with a fairly
close pass this is unlikely. The nose-to-nose option also tends to keep the
opponents relatively close together throughout the maneuver, so that
maintaining sight is easier. This is to the advantage of the pilot of a larger,
easier-to-see fighter, since reduced separation makes it less likely that he
will lose sight of an opponent in a smaller aircraft.

The pilot choosing to turn nose-to-nose is giving up any flight-path
separation in the plane of his intended maneuver. For this reason, as well as
to decrease the blind period in the initial phase of the turn, the attacker
should attempt to minimize in-plane flight-path separation at the pass, but
some out-of-plane separation may be beneficial. For instance, if he is
planning a level nose-to-nose turn, the attacker may make a fairly close
pass directly beneath or above the bogey. This tactic eliminates all horizontal flight-path separation (useful to the opponent) and also reduces the
blind period.

Figure 2-12 shows the effects of turn-performance variation on nose-to-
nose turns. In case 1 the two fighters have the same turn rates, but the
attacker has a tighter radius and slower speed. This smaller radius allows
the attacker to stay inside the defender's turn, generating flight-path
separation that the defender is unable to take away by pointing his aircraft
at the attacker. The attacker then uses this separation by reversing at point
"3" (lead turn) to arrive at point "4" with good position advantage. Case 2
depicts the same situation, except in this case the fighter with the larger
radius also has a much faster turn rate. This turn-rate advantage, however,
does the defender very little good. The attacker generates nearly the same
flight-path separation, which results in almost the same angular advantage
after the lead turn. In practice, relative turn radius largely determines

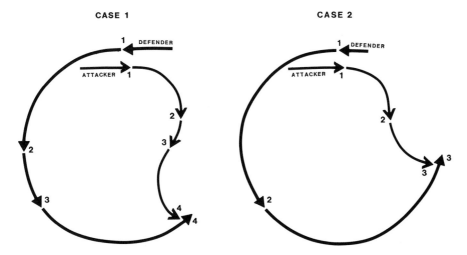

Figure 2-12. Turn-Performance Effects on Nose-to-Nose Turns

potential angular advantage, and turn-rate capability has only a minor effect in nose-to-nose turn situations.

Actually, both turn radius and speed play significant roles in generating advantage in nose-to-nose turns; their relative importance is a function of maximum separation between opponents. This maximum separation occurs as the two fighters reach parallel headings in the maneuver, which in Figure 2-12 (case 1) happens at time "2." Figure 2-13 illustrates the significance of this factor in nose-to-nose geometry.

In each case the attacker (in the fighter nearer the bottom of the figure at time "1") is slower and therefore has a tighter turn radius than the bogey fighter, but about the same turn rate. In case 1 the engagement begins with the fighters side by side and separated by a distance less than the turn radius of either aircraft. Note that very little turning is required by the attacker for him to gain a very good angular advantage at time "3," as the faster bogey essentially just flies out in front of its opponent. When maximum separation (time "1") is less than the larger of the two turn radii, relative speed is the primary factor in determining advantage.

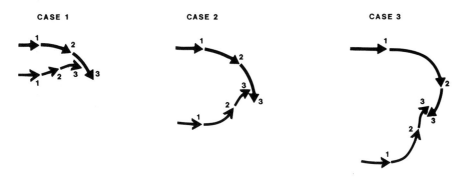

Figure 2-13. Effects of Flight-Path Separation on Nose-to-Nose Turns

In case 2 the fighters again start abeam, but initial separation in this instance is considerably greater than the larger of the two turn radii, and less than the larger turn diameter. (This is also the situation in Figure 2-12.) Here more turning is required, but still the tighter-turning attacker gains a nice bite by time "3." In this situation both radius and relative speeds play a role, but radius is the dominant factor.

Case 3 begins with even greater initial separation, this time exceeding the larger turn diameter. Here the tighter-turning fighter is unable to generate significant flight-path separation and can gain only a very small angular advantage at time "3." Relative speeds contribute essentially nothing in this situation, and a fighter must have a tighter radius to gain any advantage at all.

Figure 2-14 illustrates the effects of turn performance on nose-to-tail maneuvers. In case 1 the two aircraft have identical turn rates, but the attacker has a much smaller radius of turn. From a neutral start at time "1," the fighters maintain their neutrality throughout the maneuver to time "3," and if their paths were continued, the opponents would meet again at their original positions. In this situation a turn-radius advantage did not benefit the attacker, as it did in the nose-to-nose case. The attacker could have gained an advantage, however, if he had chosen to employ a lead turn prior to meeting at time "1," as discussed earlier.

In case 2 the two fighters have the same turn radii, but the attacker has a considerable turn-rate advantage. Note that this situation results in an offensive position advantage by time "3." It is, therefore, primarily turn rate that produces advantage in nose-to-tail maneuvers; however, a radius advantage is also of some benefit as flight-path separation at the pass increases. With greater flight-path separation at the pass, a reduced radius can result in a larger advantage because of lead-turn possibilities.

When planning to use a nose-to-tail turn, the pilot of the better-turning fighter should try to gain some flight-path separation with the bogey, in the

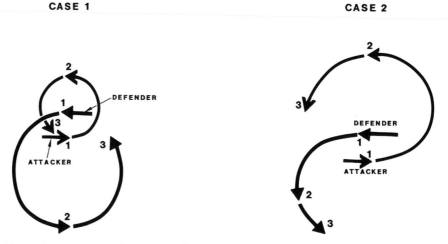

Figure 2-14. Turn-Performance Effects on Nose-to-Tail Turns

plane of the intended turn, before the pass. Generally, this may be achieved by making a small turn away from the bogey before meeting it in forward-quarter approach situations. This separation has considerable impact on the success potential of an early turn, as shown, and it also may reduce or eliminate the blind period occurring at the pass. A very close pass can result in a considerable blind period for the attacker if the bogey crosses the attacker's tail and flies toward his belly-side during the nose-to-tail maneuver. Passing slightly above or below the opponent is not as effective in reducing this blind period as it is with nose-to-nose turns.

Nose-to-tail turns, in general, result in greater separation between opponents during the maneuver, increasing the possibility of losing sight of an opponent in a smaller aircraft, and offering the opponent a better opportunity to escape if he desires. The greater resulting separation may, however, facilitate satisfying weapons minimum-range constraints.

So far this discussion has been limited to nose-to-nose and nose-to-tail turns in the near-horizontal plane. Obviously these maneuvers may occur in any plane, and the near-vertical case is interesting, particularly for nose-to-nose situations. Figure 2-15 illustrates this case. Here the fighters meet essentially head-on and both immediately pull straight up vertically, creating a nose-to-nose condition. Both fighters have similar turn rates, but one has a considerably smaller radius because of less airspeed. From the previous discussion it would be expected that the tighter-turning fighter would gain an advantage from this maneuver, and indeed it does at time "3," where it has generated some flight-path separation.

If the tighter-turning fighter is equipped with a weapon that can be fired effectively from position "3," this may be the end of the story. This generally is not a good gun snapshot opportunity, however, unless the high fighter is very slow and separation is minimal. Likewise, the rather close range and high aspect involved would cause minimum-range problems for most missiles.

If he is unable to fire, the attacker must reverse for a lead turn to

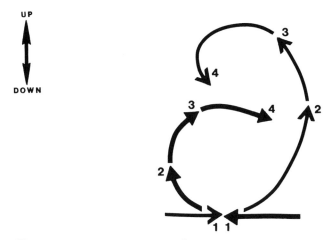

Figure 2-15. Nose-to-Nose in the Vertical Plane

capitalize on his flight-path separation. In this case, however, the aircraft does not have sufficient energy performance to execute a second vertical maneuver at the top of the first. Unable to press his advantage, the pilot of the lower fighter is forced to level off or to dive to regain airspeed. This may allow the high-energy fighter to employ its gravity assist, taking full advantage of the resulting separation to convert to an effective offensive position at time "4." The moral of this story is: Flight-path separation is of little value if it can't be used.

Flat Scissors

The flat scissors is actually a series of nose-to-nose turns and overshoots performed by two fighters essentially in the same maneuver plane, each pilot attempting to get behind the other. Figure 2-16 illustrates a flat-scissors series. In this scenario both fighters have about the same turn-rate capability, but the fighter near the bottom of the figure at time "1" is slower and therefore has a tighter radius of turn. At time "1" the fighters begin side by side, neither having an advantage, and each pilot turns toward the other in an attempt to get behind his opponent. The shorter turn radius of the slower fighter allows it to remain inside its opponent's turn approaching time "2." In this way lateral separation that can be used for a lead turn is created between the two flight paths. This flight-path separation cannot be used by the faster fighter, since it is already turning as hard as possible to the right and would have to turn even harder to perform a lead turn. The slower fighter, however, can reverse its turn direction prior to passing its opponent and gain an angular advantage at the first pass. Although the lead-turning fighter overshoots its opponent's flight path at about time "2," there is little danger because of the opponent's faster speed. Noting this overshoot, the pilot of the faster fighter reverses at time "2" in order to maintain sight of his adversary. This reinitiates a nose-to-nose situation, and by time "3" the slower fighter has a significant angular advantage. At this time another reversal allows the slower fighter to maintain its angular advantage while closing to gun-firing parameters at time "4." The segment of the attacker's turn from time "3" to time "4" is said to be "in phase" with his opponent (i.e., both are turning in the same

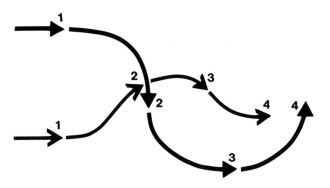

Figure 2-16. Flat Scissors

direction). Although the engagement was determined rather quickly here because of the large disparity in speed, in more evenly matched situations the crisscrossing of the flat scissors may continue for several cycles before one fighter gains a significant advantage.

This maneuver is best analyzed in phases: the nose-to-nose turn, the reversal, and the lead turn. Each of these phases normally is repeated in order during each cycle of the flat scissors.

During the nose-to-nose phase each pilot attempts to get the nose of his aircraft pointed at the opponent first to produce flight-path separation inside the other's turn which cannot be taken away. In general, the slower or tighter-turning fighter will win this phase, as illustrated in Figure 2-13. The flat scissors tends to draw fighters closer and closer together, so speed usually remains the determining factor in the nose-to-nose phase as long as the scissors maneuver continues. To gain advantage during this phase, a fighter should decelerate as quickly as possible.

After one fighter has generated some separation, it must reverse and lead-turn its opponent in order to gain further advantage. Reversal technique and timing are critical to success in the scissors. First, the rolling reversal should be as rapid as possible. This usually involves unloading the aircraft and applying full roll controls, as described in the Appendix. Each fraction of a second during the reversal the aircraft is traveling essentially in a straight line, wasting valuable turning time and decreasing hard-won separation. A significant roll-performance advantage can negate a substantial speed differential.

The timing of the reversal determines the TCA at the overshoot, with an early reversal resulting in lower TCA and subsequently greater angular advantage (lower AOT) later in the maneuver. The reversal point also controls the nose-tail separation at the overshoot, however. The longer the reversal is delayed, the greater the separation will be when the overshoot occurs. Assuming the opponent reverses at the overshoot, setting up another nose-to-nose situation and continuation of the scissors, the nose-tail separation at overshoot is directly related to the range and AOT the next time the attacker's nose is pointed toward the target. Figure 2-17 illustrates this relationship.

In case 1 the two fighters are in the initial nose-to-nose phase of a flat scissors at time "1." Both fighters here have about the same turn rate, but

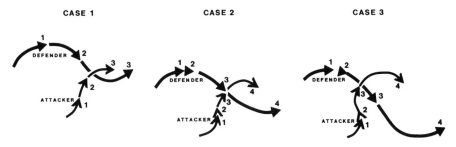

Figure 2-17. Effects of Reversal Timing

one (the attacker) is slower, with a tighter radius, and has gained some advantage. Recognizing this advantage (i.e., recognizing that he can point at his opponent first), the attacker reverses immediately, while his nose is still pointed well ahead of the defender. Turning away from the opponent at this point actually gives away the flight-path separation the attacker has developed, by allowing the defender to point his aircraft at the attacker first. In effect, the attacker has traded this separation for an early lead turn. Realizing the attacker is going to fly across his nose, the defender also reverses at time "2." If the defender is gun equipped he may have a snapshot opportunity here, but in this case his higher speed causes him to overshoot with little nose-tail separation and low TCA, flying out in front of the attacker. At time "3," the attacker has his nose on the defender at very close range and small AOT. Against an opponent with a gun, or a missile with a short min-range, this tactic (passing ahead of the target) is not recommended. Otherwise, as long as the attacker is slower, the early lead turn can result in a very lethal position advantage for him. Up to a point, the earlier the lead turn, the greater the final advantage. The "point," of course, is when the final nose-tail separation is reduced to zero. Any earlier lead turn than this may result in at least a temporary bogey position advantage. The slower the attacker's speed relative to the defender, the earlier he can reverse, and, in general, the greater advantage he can achieve without taking this risk.

In case 2 the same fighters are at the same starting conditions at time "1." This time the attacker delays his reversal until time "2," causing him to pass directly above or below the defender at point "3." At this time the defender reverses, again setting up a nose-to-nose condition, and the attacker brings his nose to bear on the bogey at time "4." The attacker's resulting position is at longer range and greater AOT than that in case 1. Such a position may be preferable if the attacker is not gun equipped, as the greater separation may satisfy missile min-range requirements.

In case 3 the setup, once again, is the same, but the attacker delays his reversal even longer, in this instance until he is pointed at the defender at time "2." This causes the attacker to cross some distance behind the defender at time "3," as the bogey reverses, and results in further increases in range and AOT at time "4."

This sequence of examples serves to highlight the importance of reversal timing in execution of the flat scissors. In general, an early reversal reduces final separation and AOT. The optimum timing depends largely on the range and AOT constraints of the attacker's firing envelope. Relative speeds, turn-radius capabilities, and defender's weapons also play a role. In general, however, the earliest possible reversals lead to the earliest advantage for a gun-equipped fighter.

In such a highly dynamic situation, reversal timing is very subjective. Practice, experience, and an ability to judge relative motion are the determining factors in the outcome of this maneuver, particularly when the aircraft are equally matched.

The lead-turn phase of the flat scissors begins at the attacker's reversal and ends when the defender reverses. The dynamics of this phase are essentially the same as for any lead turn, as previously detailed, and so are not discussed further here. In general, as one fighter begins to gain an advantage in the flat scissors the nose-to-nose phase will become shorter and the lead-turn portion will last longer. In this way the winning fighter begins to get "in phase" with the defender's maneuvers, and eventually the attacker will not overshoot during the lead turn. This event will terminate the scissors.

For obvious reasons, the flat scissors is a very desirable maneuver for fighters that enjoy a low-speed turn-performance advantage (i.e., fighters with lower wing loading, as explained in the Appendix). Less maneuverable, high-speed fighters should avoid this situation like the plague. The scissors is avoided by maintaining sufficient speed for vertical maneuvering and by simply refusing to engage in a co-planar nose-to-nose turn with a slower, better-turning opponent. If a pilot is trapped in such a situation, the sooner he recognizes his disadvantage, the better his chances are for escape. If the defender has an energy advantage, he may be able to pull up at the overshoot and gain separation in the vertical. Figure 2-18 illustrates a means of disengaging in slow-speed situations.

The initial conditions of this setup are the same as those in case 2 of Figure 2-17. This time when the attacker reverses and overshoots at point "2," the defender does not reverse, but continues his hard right nose-to-tail turn until he regains sight of the attacker deep in the rear quarter at time "3." At this point the defender begins an extension maneuver to gain speed and separation, continuing to turn only enough to maintain sight. By time "4" the attacker is beginning to bring his nose around to point at the defender. If the attacker is equipped with only guns or short-range missiles, the extension may already have created enough separation to exceed the attacker's maximum firing range. In this case the defender may continue

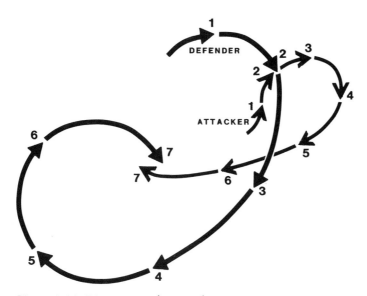

Figure 2-18. Disengaging from a Flat Scissors

his extension to escape, provided he can maintain a speed advantage. If the separation is not sufficient (time "4"), the defender can begin a hard turn back toward the attacker to defend against a possible weapons firing. If he is placed out of firing parameters by this turn, the attacker may be expected to use lead-, pure-, and lag-pursuit techniques to close the range and reattempt to get inside the defender's flight path. The defender's intent should be to get his nose back on the attacker to take out any flight-path separation and to maximize the TCA at the next pass. This he accomplishes at point "7," meeting the attacker with close to a 180° TCA. From this position the defender can engage from a neutral start, or he can repeat his extension maneuver, gain even more separation, and probably escape.

Still another option exists for fighters that have a climb-rate advantage at slow speeds. This involves continuing the flat scissors, but simultaneously climbing at a steeper and steeper angle. A lower-powered opponent will not be able to match this climb angle and must remain in a more horizontal maneuver plane. The defender's greater climb angle reduces the forward component of velocity relative to that of the attacker, possibly leading to a position advantage for the high fighter, assuming speed differential is small.

Vertical and Oblique Turns

The Appendix discusses gravity effects on turn performance. Gravity effects are investigated here to determine how they may be used to advantage in air combat.

Turn performance is dependent on radial acceleration (G_R), which is the vector sum of load factor and gravity. This vector sum is determined by the aircraft's roll and pitch attitude, as shown in the Appendix and in Figures A-18 and A-19. At a given speed, turn performance is directly proportional to G_R, resulting in improved performance when the lift vector is below the horizon, and vice versa. A further consideration is the orientation of the lift vector relative to the gravity (weight) vector. When these two vectors remain in the same plane (i.e., during purely vertical maneuvering) the gravity effect is maximized, both positively and negatively, and the entire lift vector contributes to G_R. From a purely geometrical viewpoint, these relationships mean that for a 360° turn, the vertical plane maximizes turn performance, while a horizontal turn produces the poorest average performance. Performance in oblique turns will vary between these two extremes according to the steepness of the maneuver plane. In a purely vertical maneuver the adverse effects of gravity on turn performance through the bottom half of the loop are offset by the gravity assist over the top, while in a level turn the aircraft must fight gravity throughout.

As a practical matter, however, this phenomenon is of much less importance than average aircraft speed during the maneuver. Turn performance (both radius and rate) is optimized near corner speed; therefore, the maneuver plane that allows the fighter to remain closest to its corner speed for the duration of the maneuver generally will optimize turn performance. If an aircraft is at or below its corner speed, a nose-low vertical or oblique turn may allow a power-limited fighter to remain near optimum speed for maximum performance. Conversely, a nose-high maneuver tends to reduce excess speed.

Since many fighters are unable to maintain corner speed at maximum G (i.e., they are power limited under these conditions), nose-low spirals often maximize turn performance for them. The optimum descent angle depends on many factors, even for the same aircraft with the same power. These factors include weight, configuration, and altitude; greater weight, increased drag, and higher altitude usually require steeper descents.

The fighter pilot is concerned not only with optimizing absolute turn performance, however, but also with his performance relative to that of his opponent. Maximum performance is of little value if the aircraft is turning in the wrong direction. For instance, if a defender wishes only to maximize AOT for an attacker in the rear hemisphere, the defender generally should turn toward the attacker in the plane of the attack, assuming his aircraft is physically able to maneuver in this plane. This usually is accomplished in high-G situations by rolling to place the opponent near the vertical-longitudinal plane (i.e., perpendicular to the wings) so that all the radial acceleration is working in the right direction. If both fighters are using the same technique this results in co-planar maneuvering.

Placement of the radial-acceleration vector, which for simplicity can be called the lift vector, may be compared with placement of the velocity vector in performing lead, pure, or lag pursuit. Since these two vectors define the maneuver plane, the velocity vector will follow where the lift vector pulls it. Placing the lift vector ahead of or behind the target in out-of-plane maneuvers is essentially lead or lag pursuit, respectively, and is used for the same reasons lead or lag pursuit are used, as demonstrated by the lag displacement rolls and yo-yos.

It has been shown that turn radius is important in many maneuvers, such as nose-to-nose turns. The fighter pilot is concerned primarily with the projection of his radius in the maneuver plane of his opponent. Figure 2-19 illustrates this principle.

In this example the opposing fighters meet on opposite headings, and one (the defender) chooses to turn horizontally while the other (the attacker) pulls straight up vertically. At time "2" each has completed about 90° of turn in its respective plane, and neither has any great advantage. At this point the attacker is in a near-vertical attitude and rolls to point his lift vector ahead of his opponent's position in a lead-pursuit maneuver, predicting the bogey's future position across the circle. As the attacker peaks out at the top of his "pitch-back" maneuver, his nose is oriented toward a point almost directly above the defender at time "3." Looking at the top view of this maneuver (i.e., looking straight down from above) reveals that the change of vertical maneuver planes in the nose-high pitch-back has essentially had the effect of reducing the attacker's turn radius in the horizontal plane, which is the plane of the opponent's maneuver. As with other nose-to-nose maneuvers, this smaller radius has given the attacker flight-path separation, this time both vertically and horizontally. He also has an angular advantage, largely because of his tighter horizontal turn radius and the nose-to-nose geometry.

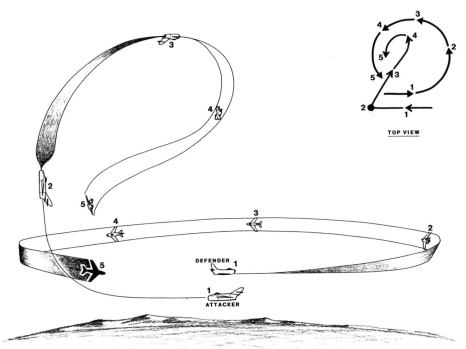

Figure 2-19. Vertical versus Horizontal Maneuvering

At time "3" the attacker could pull down inverted to point at the target for a boresight, forward-hemisphere missile shot, if he is so equipped; but, as was explained, the look-down involved may not be optimum for missile seeker performance. In this case the attacker chooses to fly essentially a straight path along the top of his maneuver, accelerating to improve his turn capability. During this period his nose drifts into a lag position as the defender passes underneath. At time "4" the attacker begins a pull-down, using the increased turn rate and decreased radius provided by the oblique-turn geometry and the gravity assist to gain a very advantageous offensive position in the defender's rear hemisphere at time "5."

A lead-pursuit roll at time "2" usually results in a steeper dive and somewhat greater potential angular advantage for the attacker than do the pure- or lag-pursuit options; but the cautions mentioned in the high yo-yo and barrel-roll attack discussions also apply here.

The effects of vertical and oblique maneuvers on an aircraft's energy state can also influence the outcome of an engagement. Possibly the best way to approach this concept is to determine the fighter's sustained-G capabilities (level, constant speed) at its given conditions of weight, power, configuration, and altitude. If a fighter is in a descending or climbing maneuver, this same load factor cannot be exceeded without loss of energy. For instance, in a nose-low oblique turn the rate of descent is equivalent to negative specific excess power (P_S). (See the energy-maneuverability discussion in the Appendix for an explanation of P_S.) If the pilot adjusts load factor to maintain constant speed, he is losing energy in proportion to his descent rate, but he is also increasing his turn rate. In order to maintain energy in such a maneuver he must reduce G and constantly accelerate, which would result in approximately the same turn rate in this oblique maneuver plane that he could achieve in a level, constant-speed turn at his altitude. However, if speed is allowed to increase to a value higher than that best for sustained maneuvering, allowable G for maintaining energy will decrease further. Likewise, even unloaded dives at speeds higher than maximum level airspeed may reduce total energy, even if the aircraft continues to accelerate.

Rolling Scissors

While a flat scissors often follows a slow-speed, horizontal overshoot, the rolling scissors more often results from a high-speed overshoot or an overshoot resulting from a high-to-low attack. In this situation, the defender pulls up to reduce both speed and the forward component of his velocity, further adding to the attacker's overshoot problems; then he rolls toward his opponent, continuing to pull the nose directly toward the attacker's constantly changing position. If the attacker continues to pull directly toward the defender, the fighters begin to develop twin spiraling flight paths as each performs barrel rolls around the other. Figure 2-20 depicts this scenario.

Here the attacking fighter (MiG-21) overshoots the defender (F-5E) with high TCA in a nose-down attitude at time "2." Recognizing the impending overshoot, the defender rolls 90° away from the direction of the initial attack (quarter rolls away) and begins to pull up into the vertical. As the overshoot occurs the defender rolls to keep his lift vector pointed toward

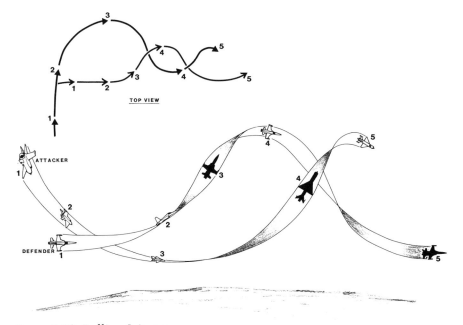

Figure 2-20. Rolling Scissors

the bogey and continues to pull to maximize the overshoot. Simultaneously the attacker is rolling to keep his lift vector on the defender in an attempt to point at his target. The defender's reduced airspeed and higher nose attitude approaching time "3" provide what appears to be a much-improved position at time "4," well above and slightly behind his opponent. The fighters continue to pull toward each other, with the MiG nose-high and the F-5E nose-low until point "5." At this time the advantage appears to have reversed. As long as the scissors is fairly neutral, the fighter at the top of its rolling maneuver will appear to have a position advantage but will lose it again on the bottom.

Success in this maneuver, as in most others, depends on both relative aircraft performance and pilot technique. Unlike the flat scissors, the rolling variety is not a contest determined by which fighter can fly slower. Although the forward component of velocity is still the deciding factor, the helix angle (i.e., the steepness of the climbs and dives) usually has more impact on this velocity component than does absolute speed, assuming speed differentials are not excessive. The rolling scissors is, therefore, a contest of energy management, a trade-off of airspeed and position in which slow-speed sustained turn performance is a critical factor, with slow-speed acceleration and controllability also very important. Figure 2-21 illustrates the techniques involved in winning the rolling scissors.

The initial setup in this scenario is the same as that in the last example. Both aircraft have about equal energy and performance, and the MiG (the

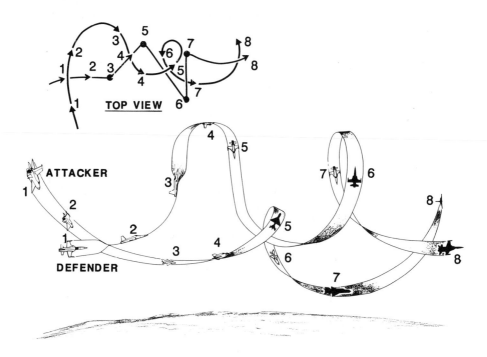

Figure 2-21. Rolling-Scissors Technique

attacker) will use the same tactics as before—that is, continuously pulling toward the defender. But this time, rather than rolling toward the attacker between times "2" and "3," the defender continues to pull straight up into the vertical. Once vertical, this fighter rolls quickly, placing its lift vector ahead of the attacker's position (lead pursuit), just as shown in Figure 2-19. Unlike the example in Figure 2-19, however, the opponent (i.e., the attacker) here is not restricted to horizontal maneuvering, and so he pulls up obliquely toward the high fighter, reducing the flight-path separation generated by the vertical maneuver of the defender.

The direction chosen by the defender to stop his roll at time "3" is calculated so that the inverted, wings-level pull-down will place him at point "4," the peak of the maneuver, with his nose aimed at a point almost directly above the bogey's predicted position at that time. Again returning to Figure 2-19, this situation is analogous to time "3" in that example. The horizontal depictions (i.e., top views) of both these examples show that each is essentially a nose-to-nose maneuver to this point. The high fighter's vertical move has created vertical separation, and pointing its nose directly at the opponent (as viewed from above) as quickly as possible has maximized its angular advantage. The next phase of the high fighter's maneuver will be designed to take advantage of its separation, by use of nose-to-tail geometry and a gravity assist, and to convert to the greatest position advantage.

In Figure 2-21, the F-5E passes directly over the MiG at time "4" and pulls down vertically into the MiG's rear hemisphere. This maneuver causes the MiG pilot to reverse his turn, rolling to the left in order to keep his lift vector on the high fighter and also to help maintain sight. These requirements deny him the opportunity to go purely vertical, and he is forced to keep his flight path in an oblique plane, which increases his forward speed across the ground relative to that of his opponent.

> The important thing in [tactics] is to suppress the enemy's useful actions but allow his useless actions. However, doing this alone is defensive.
> Miyamoto Musashi (1584–1645)
> Japanese *Samurai* and Philosopher
> More Than 60 Victories in Hand-to-Hand Combat

By selecting a lead roll at time "3" and maintaining a constant maneuver plane until time "5," the high fighter has in effect "averaged out" the opponent's position during that time. Lead pursuit is being employed during the first half of the inverted pull-down, and lag pursuit results during the last half, which has nearly the same effect as pure pursuit (i.e., keeping the lift vector on the bogey) throughout the pull-down. This technique maximizes the angular gain as well as the energy efficiency of the high fighter.

Approaching position "5," the F-5E pilot determines that insufficient separation has been generated to avoid an overshoot. Therefore, in a purely vertical dive, he performs another lead roll and pulls wings-level through the bottom of his maneuver, passing as closely as possible behind the bogey. This portion of the maneuver is analogous to the reversal and subsequent overshoot described in the flat scissors. The more aggressive the lead roll at time "5," the smaller the high fighter's nose-tail separation and TCA will be at the overshoot. If this lead is overdone, it is possible to squirt out in front of the bogey at the overshoot and lose the offensive. If insufficient lead is taken, the high fighter will pass well behind the MiG at the bottom of the maneuver, giving away valuable separation that the opponent can use to turn around and bring his nose to bear as the F-5E approaches the top of its next vertical move.

An extremely important further consideration in this phase is the high fighter's airspeed as he begins his pull-out. Since another vertical move is planned after the impending overshoot, the pilot must ensure adequate airspeed at the bottom of the loop to enable him to complete the maneuver with good control over the top. This airspeed should be gained as quickly as possible in an unloaded dive at about time "5." The pull-out can begin as the required airspeed is approached, using a load factor near sustained-G capability for that particular airspeed/altitude condition. With two fighters closely matched in energy performance this will usually result in the diving fighter bottoming out below the altitude of its opponent at the overshoot. This situation is acceptable as long as the altitude differential is not so great as to allow the bogey to pull down for a gun snapshot as the diving fighter passes underneath. On the other hand, it is not advantageous for the pilot of the diving fighter to delay the pull-out after reaching his desired speed, since it is preferable to pass above the bogey if possible.

After the overshoot the F-5E continues to pull to the pure vertical at time "6" and rolls as before to aim at a point calculated to be directly above his opponent's position when the F-5E reaches the top of the loop. Pulling over the top of each vertical maneuver it is important that the pilot of the high fighter not hesitate or "float" in an unloaded condition, but continue to apply G to get his nose back down expeditiously. Any delay coming over the top allows the bogey time to get its nose higher, slowing its forward velocity and also reducing flight-path separation. The proper amount of G to be used across the top of each loop is generally small (in the range of 1 to 2 Gs), since most fighters will be slow and unable to pull much more at this point. (If the fighter is not slow on top, excessive speed was probably attained in the preceding pull-out.) Added to the 1 G of gravity, however, this load factor can produce substantial turn performance at slow speeds. Maximum-attainable G should be used over the top of each loop, unlike in the bottom of the maneuver, when sustained-G levels are appropriate.

One further note about coming over the top of the loop: It is not necessary for the attacker to cross over the bogey's flight path at this point (as shown in Figure 2-21) for the rolling scissors to work. Depending on how hard the bogey turns, it may be necessary to delay the pull-down in order to ensure crossing its flight path. This is not advantageous, as any delay reduces subsequent advantage. In this situation it is better to pull down inside the opponent's horizontal flight path, as illustrated in Figure 2-19. Unless it is determined that an overshoot can be avoided at the bottom of the maneuver, however, care should be taken to ensure that the pull-down is continued to a vertical attitude.

At position "7" in this example the high fighter has the necessary separation to avoid another overshoot, so rather than the lead roll and wings-level pull-out as before, it performs a rolling pull-out to arrive at an offensive lag-pursuit position at time "8."

In case things do not work out quite as smoothly as he would wish, the defender (in the F-5E) may wish to disengage from the rolling scissors and exit the fight. The time to make this decision is during the pull-down to the vertical dives, positions "5" and "7" in this example. If things do not look rosy at such times, the pilot of the high fighter should modify his pull-out to minimize separation and maximize TCA at the next pass. Ideally he would like to pass directly over the bogey on an exactly opposite heading (180° TCA) and dive away in an extension as described in Figure 2-18.

> To get ability you need good training.
>
> Colonel Erich "Bubi" Hartmann, GAF

To recap, the most efficient technique in the rolling scissors limits all turning to vertical planes (i.e., wings-level pull-ups and pull-downs) until purely vertical attitudes are reached. All heading changes (horizontal turns) are performed by rolling in the vertical attitude. Lead rolls are normally employed in both the climbs and the dives. Max-G should be used over the top of each loop, and sustained-G levels are maintained along the bottom. Speed control is very important, particularly in the pull-out.

Returning to Figure 2-21 for a moment, consider that the condition that precipitated the rolling scissors, and the eventual loss of the offensive for the attacker, was the overshoot that occurred between times "1" and "2." If the attacker had recognized the situation earlier he could have rolled his wings level (performed a quarter roll) at time "1," pulled up vertically to minimize his overshoot (as with the high yo-yo), and probably retained the offensive even if a rolling scissors had resulted.

When both fighters are fairly evenly matched in performance and use the tactics outlined here, the rolling scissors often evolves into a co-planar tail-chase in the vertical plane. The same techniques still apply, except that no rolls are required. The successful pilot must control speed, modulate load factor with airspeed for best sustained performance, and pull lead (i.e., use max-G) across the top of the loop and lag (use sustained G) along the bottom.

> The most important thing for a fighter pilot is to get his first victory without too much shock.
>
> Colonel Werner Moelders, Luftwaffe
> 115 Victories, WW-II and Spanish Civil War

Defensive Spiral

The defensive spiral is essentially a very tight rolling scissors going straight down. It quite often results when one fighter has achieved a close-in, rear-hemisphere position against a slow-speed opponent. Figure 2-22 depicts an example of this maneuver.

In order to generate some AOT to spoil a guns-tracking solution, the

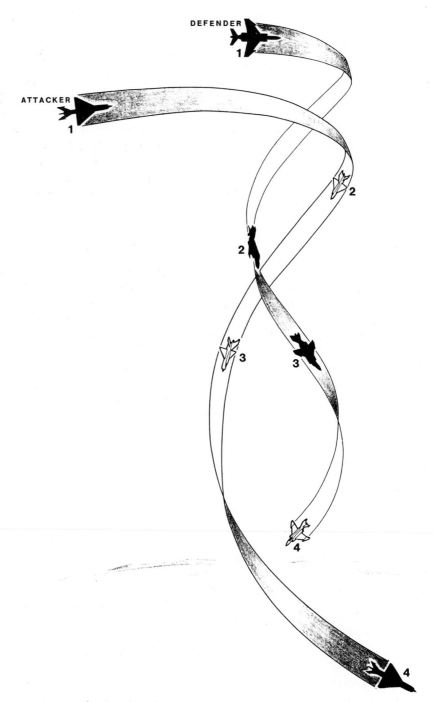

Figure 2-22. Defensive Spiral

slow-speed defender may roll nearly inverted and pull down sharply, using his gravity assist. To maintain his lead for a gun shot, the attacker follows the target into the nose-low spiral, as shown at time "2." At this time both fighters have rolled to place their lift vectors on the other, and they have entered a vertical, descending rolling scissors or defensive spiral. The rolling maneuver is quite effective for spoiling guns-tracking solutions, since the maneuver plane is constantly changing, but obviously there is a very real limit to the duration of this tactic—that is, terra firma.

As with the rolling scissors, success in the defensive spiral depends largely on forward, or in this case downward, velocity. The descent rate is the product of airspeed and steepness of the dive. The typically close range at which this maneuver is performed requires the fighters to roll rapidly to keep the opponent in sight, above the plane of the wings. This continuous roll tends to keep the lift vector horizontal, preventing a pull-out and prolonging the steep descent angle.

Most aircraft tend to accelerate rather rapidly when commencing a dive at a slow airspeed. With the two fighters approximately co-speed in the spiral, it is the relative acceleration that will change nose-tail separation. Minimum acceleration is the desirable factor, so idle power, speed brakes, reverse thrust, drag chutes, or almost any action that reduces forward thrust and increases drag is appropriate. At slow speeds, the largest component of maximum total drag is usually induced drag, which is generally maximized by maintaining the highest controllable angle of attack. (See the Appendix for a discussion of aerodynamic drag.) Normally any configuration that increases maximum lift at a given airspeed, such as extended flaps and slats, also increases induced drag. One exception to this rule may be fighters with swing-wing designs. Although maximum lift is usually attained with wings spread for the greatest wing span, this configuration also tends to make the wing more efficient from a lift-to-drag standpoint, and induced drag may be reduced under these conditions.

Returning to the example in Figure 2-22, the defender has reduced his acceleration to a minimum, allowing the attacker's increasingly greater speed to reduce altitude separation to zero (time "3"); he will be flushed out below by time "4." At this point the original defender is back in the driver's seat and can modulate his power and configuration as necessary to stabilize and maintain the desired nose-tail separation while holding his position in the spiral, waiting for the bogey to begin a pull-out. When this occurs the low fighter should present an excellent, stabilized guns-tracking target. Likewise, "4" would also be a good time for the high fighter to exit the fight if he desires. He can roll to place his lift vector on the bogey, initiate a pull-out, generate maximum TCA crossing over the bogey, and extend for separation.

This decelerating tactic (actually minimum acceleration) can be particularly effective for fighters that are able to generate a great amount of induced drag, as well as for those that are equipped for reverse thrust. One caution is required, however. If the decision is made to press the offensive gained by this technique, the high fighter had better not miss his firing opportunity as the bogey performs a pull-out, since the lower fighter usually will complete its level-off with superior energy, which then may be used to regain the advantage.

As the defensive spiral progresses, most fighters tend to accelerate to some degree. If maximum-controllable AOA is maintained, this increased speed will result in greater load factor and turn-rate capability (below corner speed). At steep dive angles, most of the heading change required to keep the opponent in sight above the plane of the wings is accomplished by roll rate. Greater speed allows more of this heading change to be achieved by turn rate and results in gradually reducing dive angles with increasing airspeed. Although further increases in airspeed would reduce the dive angle even more, at angles steeper than about 40° the added speed usually more than offsets the reduced dive angle attained, resulting in greater descent rate. If, as a result of aerodynamic design, one fighter can maintain an equal or slower speed than its opponent while still generating greater turn rate, it will have a shallower dive angle and a reduced descent rate. Should dive angle decrease to less than about 30°, it will become the dominant factor in descent rate. In this case, maximum power, minimum drag, and maximum-lift configuration should be used to improve turn rate, shallowing the dive angle and reducing descent rate. If speed ever increases to above corner velocity in the spiral, deceleration is in order regardless of descent angle.

Returning for a moment to the beginning of this maneuver, success in the defensive spiral rests largely in the ability to induce the opponent into following the initial nose-down move. This reaction is likely if the attacker is attempting to achieve a guns-tracking solution on the defender by matching his bank angle at position "1" in Figure 2-22. The defensive spiral can, therefore, be a very effective guns-defense tactic, but it may subject the defender to a close-range snapshot as the spiral begins. The defender should generally enter the spiral by rolling just fast enough to stay ahead of the attacker's bank angle. As the attacker attempts to match the target's attitude, he suddenly finds himself in the spiral at position "2," with the defender already having begun deceleration tactics. By easing into the maneuver in this manner, the defender may avoid "scaring off" the attacker. A snap roll into the spiral immediately informs the attacker of the defender's intentions, allowing the attacker to counter effectively by delaying his pull-down. Although this technique (i.e., a snap roll) would remove the target from immediate guns-tracking danger and temporarily increase nose-tail separation, it would leave the defender open to a rear-quarter missile shot, probably cause loss of visual with the attacker, and usually allow the attacker to maintain the offensive.

One of the most effective counters to the defensive spiral, when it is recognized early, is for the attacker to continue his level turn at time "1" to pass directly over the target's position and then begin the pull-down. This tactic makes it extremely difficult for the defender to maintain sight, and generates enough separation to preclude immediate loss of the offensive by a vertical overshoot.

Success flourishes only in perserverance—ceaseless, restless perserverance.
Baron Manfred von Richthofen

When it is performed properly, the defensive spiral may offer a hard-pressed defender an escape opportunity or even a temporary close-in gun shot. Unless the attacker loses sight or blunders badly, however, it is unlikely that this maneuver would produce a good missile-firing opportunity or result in a lasting offensive position for the defender.

If one of the fighters stops its rolling maneuver at any point and begins a wings-level pull-out, the defensive spiral has ended, and deceleration tactics are no longer appropriate. The first fighter to commence a pull-out offers his opponent the opportunity to continue the spiral to a rear-hemisphere or belly-side position and probably will lose sight temporarily. If the opponent has generated a vertical advantage at this point and is gun equipped, he may have a shot opportunity. Otherwise, it is probably prudent for the opponent to use this chance for escape. Escape may be executed by rolling for the bogey's blind spot, then pulling-out directly away from the bogey at full power and max-lift conditions. If the bogey is missile equipped, it probably will be necessary for the escaping opponent to turn slightly back toward the bogey after reaching an approximately level attitude in order to reacquire it visually and watch for a possible missile launch during the extension maneuver.

As long as the spiral is fairly even, exiting the maneuver usually can be accomplished by simply leveling the wings and pulling-out at max-power and max-lift AOA. The first fighter to attempt this exit from a neutral position should bottom-out above an opponent with similar performance and should have greater energy. Although the opponent will probably be in the rear hemisphere, it will take him some time to get his nose back up for a gun shot, if, indeed, he has sufficient energy to accomplish this at all. This delay is often enough for the higher fighter to extend beyond effective guns range or to position offensively above the lower-energy opponent. Extending from a missile-equipped bogey, however, may be hazardous.

You fight like you train.

Motto, U.S. Navy Fighter Weapons School (TOPGUN)

Notes

1. Gordon Nelson et al., eds., *Air War: Vietnam,* p. 245.
2. Robert S. Johnson, *Thunderbolt!* p. 191.

3

One-versus-One Maneuvering, Similar Aircraft

Fight to fly, fly to fight, fight to win.
Motto, U.S. Navy Fighter Weapons School (TOPGUN)

For purposes of this work, *similar aircraft* denotes fighters having essentially equal performance capabilities in all areas. Because of the human influence on the performance of manned fighters, similar aircraft are not necessarily exactly equivalent in performance, since on any given day, even with the same pilot, an aircraft is unlikely to duplicate consistently a given maneuver so that all parameters are within tolerances much closer than 5 or 10 percent. For this reason it is logical to consider performance within 10 percent to be similar in most cases. However, considering the multitude of possible design variations and the influences of each variation on the many performance parameters, obtaining similarity in all performance areas almost requires that the aircraft be of the same type. Even among fighters of the same type, fuel loads and ordnance loads and configurations can alter weight and drag enough to create performance variations well in excess of 10 percent.

In most cases combat endurance plays an important role in the significance of performance variations. The longer the combat endurance of the opposing fighters, the more telling a small performance differential can be. Available combat time for many modern fighters is on the order of five minutes or even less, so larger performance variations may be considered within the bounds of similarity.

In the present world, which contains a limited number of large arms exporters and constantly shifting political loyalties, combat between similar fighters is very likely. The fact is, performance similarity enhances the importance of soundly conceived and executed tactics for a quick and decisive victory. For this reason alone the study of ACM between similar aircraft is exceedingly valuable.

In this, and in most of the following chapters, the discussion of ACM does not consider external environmental factors that may affect tactical decisions. In this "sterile" environment there is no concern for weather, ECM, additional unseen hostile aircraft, groundfire, or anything else that can force profound tactical changes. Except as noted, the effects of such realistic factors are covered in other chapters.

Likewise, there is obviously an infinite number of possible starting conditions for any ACM engagement. Limitations in the scope of this work require that essentially one initial setup—a roughly neutral, co-energy, forward-quarter approach scenario—be covered in detail. The tactics recommended in this chapter and in following chapters cannot be optimized for every conceivable air combat scenario, but they are selected to present a broad range of tactical concepts and principles which may be applied effectively in many commonly encountered situations. This is not to imply that other techniques might not be superior in some cases; but the methods presented here are based on sound tactical principles and should be quite effective within the limitations imposed. Caution: Even minor deviations from the stated assumptions may invalidate an entire tactical concept.

In deriving tactics for use against a similar aircraft, two basic approaches are available: the "angles" fight and the "energy" fight. These labels refer to the first objective of the engagement. In the angles fight the tactician first seeks to gain a position advantage (angles), even at the expense of relative energy, and then he attempts to maintain or improve on this advantage until he achieves his required firing parameters. The purpose of the energy fight is to gain an energy advantage over the opponent while not yielding a decisive position advantage. Once a sufficient energy advantage has been attained, it must be converted to a lethal position advantage, usually without surrendering the entire energy margin. In the case of similar aircraft, each of these tactical theories has benefits and drawbacks, depending in large measure on the weapons involved. Therefore both angles fights and energy fights are discussed.

> The guy who wins is the guy who makes the fewer gross mistakes.
> Lieutenant Jim "Huck" Harris, USN
> U.S. Navy Fighter Weapons School Instructor

Guns Only

As long as a fighter has altitude and flying speed for maneuvering, and its pilot has reasonable tactical knowledge, awareness of his situation, and the will to survive, the pilot can deny a guns-tracking solution to an adversary in a similar aircraft. For this reason it is usually more practical to maneuver for the snapshot envelope; then if the opponent makes a mistake, a tracking opportunity still may be available. A reasonable snapshot envelope, as described in Chapter 1, is located in the target's rear hemisphere at close range, requires excess lead, and is enhanced by the attacker maneuvering in the same plane as the target. Attaining this envelope is the ultimate goal of the tactics described in this section.

Everything I had ever learned about air fighting taught me that the man who is aggressive, who pushes a fight, is the pilot who is successful in combat and who has the best opportunity for surviving battle and coming home.

Major Robert S. Johnson, USAAF

The Angles Fight

In attempting to gain a position advantage against a similar adversary, the angles tactician has essentially two choices: He can turn harder or he can turn smarter. Although the primary objective for the angles fighter is to achieve a position advantage, energy considerations cannot be ignored with impunity. An angles fighter that races around the sky with its pilot pulling on the pole as hard as he can normally will lose energy in the process. Since potential energy (altitude) is limited, this energy loss eventually will mean loss of speed. If the angles fighter becomes too slow, its maneuverability suffers, so that eventually it reaches a point where it has insufficient performance remaining to gain further position advantage, or even to maintain previous gains. The prudent angles tactician must, therefore, achieve his angular gains as efficiently as possible, so that he can defeat his opponent before his own aircraft reaches the point of critical maneuverability loss.

In nearly all cases where machines have been downed, it was during a fight which had been very short, and the successful burst of fire had occurred within the space of a minute after the beginning of actual hostilities.

Lt. Colonel W. A. "Billy" Bishop, RAF

In the last chapter two types of turns were defined: nose-to-tail and nose-to-nose. The discussion there brought out the fact that gaining advantage in nose-to-tail turns requires excess turn rate, while reduced turn radius and slower speed bring success in the nose-to-nose case. Since sustained turn radius is usually more sensitive to speed reduction than is sustained turn rate (see the Appendix discussion of sustained turn performance), nose-to-nose turns generally provide the greatest angular gain per knot of speed loss. In other words, nose-to-nose geometry is more energy efficient. For this reason, the angles tactics recommended here are based primarily on the nose-to-nose turn.

Fly with the head and not with the muscles. That is the way to long life for a fighter pilot. The fighter pilot who is all muscle and no head will never live long enough for a pension.

Colonel Willie Batz, GAF
237 Victories, WW-II

Besides direction of turn, another consideration of the angles fight is plane of turn. Earlier discussions showed how oblique turns reduce a fighter's horizontal turn radius, so, assuming the opponent turns level, the angles fighter can use oblique turns to increase angular gains during nose-to-nose maneuvering. Now this leaves the question, "Should the oblique turn be made nose-high or nose-low?" When two similar fighters meet nearly head-on, the maximum separation that will result from a subsequent immediate nose-to-nose turn is about one turn diameter. As pointed out in the last chapter, at this range turn radius is the primary factor in gaining an angular advantage. Turn radius is minimized, as a rule, by pulling max-G at or below corner speed. Most fighters, however, will decelerate rapidly during such a maneuver, causing the angles fighter to lose excessive energy before a similar opponent can be dispatched with a rear-hemisphere weapon. Allowing the opponent too great an energy advantage can spell big trouble (this is discussed later in this chapter).

One answer to this dilemma is to turn nose-low, trading altitude for angles, rather than bleeding excessive airspeed. Figure 3-1 shows how this might work. At time "1" the two fighters approach head-on at roughly equal altitude and speed. Since energy nearly always seems to be a very precious and hard-to-get commodity during an engagement, both pilots should be trying to grab all they can at this point. The angles tactician has set his best energy-rate climb speed, and he is climbing with full power at that speed to gain energy (altitude) as quickly as possible. (See the discussion of climb performance in the Appendix.) Since the angles tactician would like to engage at corner speed, however, and he is currently faster, he starts a zoom climb at time "1." This zoom reduces airspeed without incurring a loss of total energy, and it also generates vertical flight-path separation, which will be useful for a lead turn.

This zoom-climb tactic is appropriate for most jet fighters at medium to low altitudes, since best climb speed normally exceeds corner speed under these conditions. Prop fighters and subsonic jets at high altitudes, how-

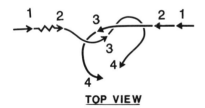

TOP VIEW

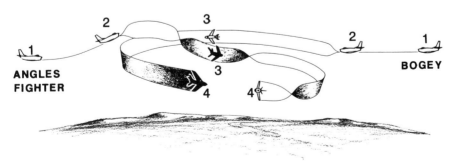

Figure 3-1. Guns-Only Angles Fight: First Phase

ever, usually climb best at speeds below the corner. If this is the case, the angles fighter should accelerate to corner speed, or as close to it as possible, and climb at that speed, even at a reduced rate. When there is no airspeed in excess of corner velocity to dissipate approaching the first pass, the zoom climb is unnecessary.

The angles tactician levels off when he reaches corner speed and turns hard right at time "2" to build additional flight-path separation laterally. As the bogey approaches, the angles fighter pilot reverses his turn and begins an aggressive, nose-low lead turn on the opponent. The objects of this initial turn are to force the bogey pilot's reaction, put him in a defensive frame of mind immediately, and generally see what he's made of. In this case the opponent is made of "the right stuff," because he counters with a hard turn of his own up toward the attack, taking away all the flight-path separation with a close pass at time "3."

> A good fighter pilot must have one outstanding trait—aggressiveness.
> Major John T. Godfrey, USAAF

If he is able to grab substantial angles on the first pass, the angles tactician should take advantage of the gift and continue his nose-low left turn in the nose-to-tail direction. In this case, however, the pilot reverses to set up a nose-to-nose condition. He should still be very near corner speed, and immediately after the reversal he pulls max-G in his nose-low right turn to minimize turn radius. The nose-low turn reduces deceleration at high G and also adds a little benefit from out-of-plane geometry. This max-G turn is normally performed with the lift vector pointed at, or slightly below, the bogey, causing the angles fighter to descend somewhat below the bogey's altitude while maintaining enough airspeed for vertical maneuvering. After a few seconds of this, the G is relaxed a little and the nose is started back up toward a level attitude; the maneuver is timed so that the angles fighter can be climbing up toward the bogey at the next pass.

The initial maximum-performance turn after the reversal (time "3") should place the angles fighter inside the turn radius of a bogey turning in a nearly level plane. Another reversal and a lead turn approaching the next pass (time "4") should convert the resulting flight-path separation into angular advantage. After the initial portion of the nose-to-nose turn, however, G should be relaxed to allow the angles fighter to regain some of its lost altitude and conserve airspeed. As a rule of thumb, the guns-only angles fighter should stay within about one-quarter of a turn radius or one-half of an effective guns range, whichever is less, of the bogey's altitude, and its pilot should not allow airspeed to decrease below that required to get the nose up purely vertical if necessary. These precautions add a measure of safety to angles tactics and still should enable the fighter to gain between 20° and 30° on a similar opponent on the first turn. The angles tactician cannot afford to get too greedy when he is facing a well-flown opponent in a similar aircraft.

Throughout this angles-tactics sequence, except for possibly the initial pass at time "3," the angles fighter should meet the bogey from below coming up at each pass. This tactic encourages the opponent to turn nose-low in response, which allows the angles fighter to continue nose-low on the following turn without losing so much altitude relative to the bogey. Attacking from below also discourages the bogey pilot from making a steep pull-up prior to the pass to make use of his excess energy, since such a pull-up would, at least temporarily, increase the attacker's angular advantage. In addition, overshooting the bogey's flight path from low to high is considerably less dangerous than overshooting from above, which invites the opponent to initiate a rolling scissors. Since the bogey will probably have an energy advantage after the first pass, the angles tactician should avoid participating in a rolling scissors. If the defender pulls up sharply at an overshoot and the angles fighter pilot judges he cannot get his aircraft's nose on the bogey quickly for a gun shot, a diving extension is called for to gain separation for an escape or a return under more favorable circumstances.

Passing the bogey at time "4" with a good bite may offer the attacker a forward-quarter gun snapshot opportunity, which he should take. Being shot at places the opponent more deeply on the psychological defensive and should force a defensive reaction, which will bleed his aircraft's energy and possibly give the angles fighter greater advantage. The shooter may even get lucky and score some hits. An angular advantage at the pass also will likely cause the defender to lose sight temporarily as the angles fighter overshoots at six o'clock and flies toward the bogey's belly-side. In this situation there is a very strong tendency for the bogey pilot to reverse his turn direction to regain sight, which is exactly what the angles tactician would like. Such a reversal reinitiates a nose-to-nose condition in which the tighter turn radius and slower speed of the angles fighter should bring further gains at the next pass.

If the bogey does not reverse at time "4," the angles fighter pilot should continue to press his advantage in the nose-to-tail direction, using alternate low and high yo-yos (Figures 2-7 and 2-6) to make repeated low-to-high gun passes on the bogey, while making small angular gains on each pass. If this sequence continues, the attacker should eventually either score hits or force the defender into a reversal or zoom climb.

> Once at the enemy, you should not aspire just to strike him, but to cling after the attack.
>
> Miyamoto Musashi

In Figure 3-2 (a continuation of the engagement begun in Figure 3-1), the bogey reverses and zooms at time "4" in a climbing oblique right turn. The angles fighter also pulls up sharply inside the opponent's turn and threatens a gun shot as the defender tops out at time "5." Because the angles fighter normally has less energy, it probably will not be able to reach the defender's altitude at time "5," but all that is required for a gun shot is that the shooter draw within effective guns range with lead. Without sufficient energy to zoom out of range, the bogey is forced into a defensive pull back down toward the attacker. Figure 3-3 shows the end-game of this engagement.

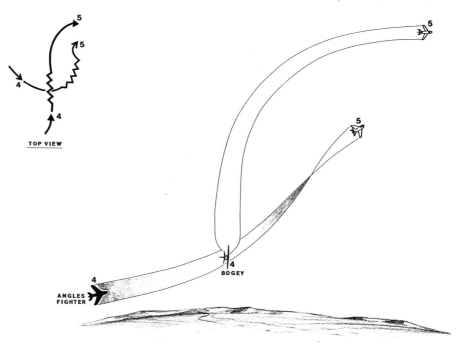

Figure 3-2. Guns-Only Angles Fight: Mid-Game

From his position of advantage below and behind the bogey, the angles tactician at this point puts everything he's got into a lead turn to position for a snapshot as the target dives by at point-blank range and too slow to defend against the shot, time "6." An in-plane, "blind" lead turn is most effective for this purpose, but, as discussed previously, this tactic takes much practice and can be risky. Normally little is lost by turning slightly out-of-plane so that the target can be kept in view over one side of the angles fighter's nose.

In the situation just described at time "6," the bogey should soon be cold meat. If the shot is missed, however, the situation could change rather rapidly. The angles fighter most likely will overshoot vertically at a lower energy level than that of the bogey. This may allow the bogey to escape or to force a rolling scissors, which would be to its advantage. Although there is probably not much that can be done at this point to prevent the bogey's escape, the angles tactician does need to be wary of the rolling scissors. At min-range he should perform a quarter roll away from the bogey and continue his pull-out. After safe separation has been gained, he can either reengage on neutral terms or escape.

There's no kill like a guns kill.

Lt. Commander Joe "Hoser" Satrapa, USN
Gunnery Instructor

The Energy Fight

This tactic involves building an energy advantage and then converting that energy to a snapshot position. Figure 2-15 depicts one method by which an energy advantage may be used to generate vertical separation and a possi-

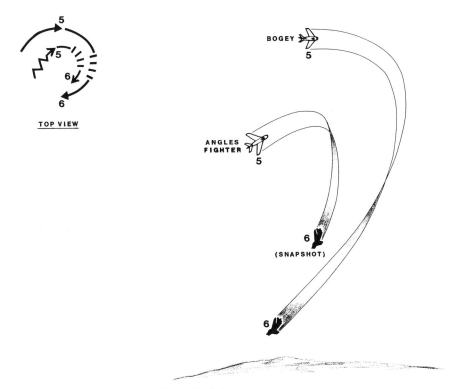

Figure 3-3. Guns-Only Angles Fight: End-Game

ble firing opportunity. Against a similar adversary, however, it may be difficult for the energy tactician to gain enough energy margin over his opponent to avoid being menaced at the top of a zoom climb.

The rolling scissors (also described in Chapter 2) provides another, probably more practical, tactic by which an energy advantage can result in multiple firing opportunities and disengagement opportunities while enabling the energy fighter to remain on the offensive throughout. Because of these advantages, the rolling scissors, as depicted in Figure 2-21, will be the end-game goal of this section. Given a reasonable initial energy advantage and good technique, the rolling scissors should result in a snapshot opportunity against a similar fighter within one or two turns. These firing opportunities are ordinarily achieved at the bottom of the vertical maneuvers, but before he initiates such a guns pass it is important that the pilot of the energy fighter attain the speed his aircraft requires for vertical maneuvering. This ensures the ability to continue the rolling scissors, retain the offensive, and generate further shot opportunities if the first shot is unsuccessful.

The outcome of the rolling scissors with similar fighters is highly dependent on relative energy states at initiation of the maneuver. Figure 3-4 illustrates a method by which the energy tactician can ensure that he has an energy advantage over his opponent before the two fighters begin the scissors. Prior to time "1" the fighters are in a forward-quarter approach situation. A fancy radar may allow some insight into the oppo-

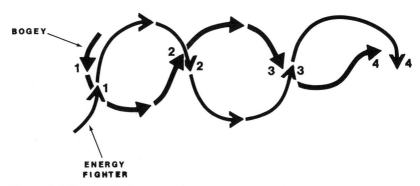

Figure 3-4. Energy Fight: First Phase

nent's speed during this period. As with the angles fight, the energy tactician should not be satisfied with a neutral start. Flight-path separation should be generated prior to the pass for a lead turn, as described in Figure 3-1. In this case, however, the energy fighter pilot is not looking for corner speed at the pass, so the break-away and lead turn will probably be made in a level plane. The energy tactician should also avoid bleeding airspeed during this maneuver to below best sustained-turn-rate speed or vertical-maneuvering speed, whichever is greater. The lead turn, therefore, may not be quite as aggressive as it is with angles tactics. If the bogey allows the energy fighter a good bite on the first pass, the lead turn should be continued in the same direction to press the advantage. The pilot of the energy fighter might consider making the transition to angles tactics in this case, since these methods are usually more effective against a nonaggressive opponent. In this example, however, it is assumed that the bogey turns into the fighter's attack, taking away all flight-path separation and generating a neutral pass at time "1."

> Aggressiveness was fundamental to success in air-to-air combat and if you ever caught a fighter pilot in a defensive mood you had him licked before you started shooting.
>
> Captain David McCampbell, USN
> Leading U.S. Navy Ace, WW-II
> 34 Victories (9 on One Mission)

After determining the bogey's turn direction at the pass, this energy fighter pilot begins a level, sustained turn in the nose-to-nose direction. If speed is greater than that required for vertical-maneuvering potential, the initial turn should be at max-G, and then G should be relaxed to maintain vertical-maneuvering speed. Since the energy tactician plans to maneuver horizontally, any vertical separation he may allow (up to about a quarter of a turn radius) at the pass is of little value to the bogey, so if the energy fighter can gain an altitude advantage at the first pass, this height should be maintained.

Once the series of nose-to-nose turns commences, the energy fighter pilot should monitor his adversary's turn performance carefully, using his own performance as a standard. By maintaining the slowest possible speed consistent with vertical-maneuvering potential, the energy fighter will keep its turn radius tight, minimizing any angular advantage that the bogey may gain in the nose-to-nose turns. Even if the bogey is faster, it may still be able to gain a good bite on the energy fighter during the first turn by using max-G; but further significant improvement in the bogey's position during successive nose-to-nose turns will require its pilot to reduce the bogey's airspeed to below that of the energy fighter.

Once the bogey has gained a position advantage by pulling high G in the nose-to-nose turn, there is a very strong temptation for its pilot to continue this tactic to increase his advantage, resulting in rapid deceleration. The energy tactician can monitor this process by noting the bogey's angular advantage at each pass. In general, the larger the bogey's angular position gain at each pass, the greater the speed differential between the fighters will be. Large bogey gains (20° to 30°) indicate a substantial speed advantage for the energy fighter. Smaller angular gains (10° or less), however, could mean only minimal speed differential. In this case the adversary is displaying sound tactical judgment, hoping eventually to achieve a snapshot position or to force the energy fiighter up with only a small energy advantage, as described in the angles-fight discussion. In such a case the pilot of the energy fighter might consider exiting the fight by use of a nose-to-tail type extension (Figure 2-18) before his opponent has gained too great a position advantage. It doesn't pay to pick on the "Red Baron."

> The smallest amount of vanity is fatal in aeroplane fighting. Self-distrust rather is the quality to which many a pilot owes his protracted existence.
> Captain Edward V. "Eddie" Rickenbacker, USAS
> Leading U.S. Ace, WW-I
> 26 Victories

Assessment of the opponent's angular advantage is a matter of comparing relative nose positions. The easiest time to do this is when the bogey is pointed at the energy fighter. At this time the angle off the bogey's nose (AON) is zero, and its angular advantage is equal to the energy fighter's AON. So if, after the first nose-to-nose turn, the pilot of the energy fighter looks at his one o'clock or eleven o'clock position and sees the bogey's nose pointed directly at him, the opponent has about a 30° advantage. The energy tactician should continue to turn toward his opponent (although not precisely in-plane while the bogey has sufficient snapshot lead) until the bogey approaches the six o'clock region. An earlier reversal gives away flight-path separation, resulting in an increased angular gain for the bogey on the next pass without attendant speed reduction.

Assuming the bogey is improving its position rapidly with each turn, the pilot of the energy fighter should continue the nose-to-nose process until his opponent achieves between 60° and 90° of angular advantage, after which time a wings-level pull-up is initiated as the bogey crosses behind the energy fighter. If the bogey continues in a fairly level maneuver, the energy tactician then can force a rolling scissors with advantage, since his adversary should be well below vertical-maneuvering speed. If the bogey pulls sharply up in response, the energy fighter pilot should continue a zoom climb. In this case his greater energy should allow him to top out higher than his opponent, providing vertical separation for an attack as the bogey pilot is forced to level off or to dive (Figure 2-15).

> When your opponent lunges at you . . . feign weakness. When the opponent has come in quite close, suddenly increase the distance by backing . . . away. Come in forcibly . . . and win as the opponent shows signs of slacking.
>   Miyamoto Musashi

A nose-to-nose turn series was described here because this maneuver makes it easier to keep sight of the opponent. Particularly as the bogey gains more angular advantage, nose-to-tail turns can result in lengthy blind periods after each pass. Another complication with nose-to-tail turns (illustrated in Figure 3-5) is that a faster-turning opponent will complete his turn, time "3" (i.e., point his nose in the general direction of the energy fighter again), at greater range. This separation allows him to accelerate without turning for some time before he is required to begin a lead turn to achieve maximum angular advantage over the energy fighter at the next pass. The period of acceleration and greater aircraft separation distances make it more difficult to judge the bogey's relative energy.

In cases where maintaining sight of the opponent is not considered to be a problem, a nose-to-tail turn series is actually superior to the nose-to-nose technique for the purposes of bleeding the bogey's energy. Once the bogey pilot has reduced his speed and turn radius slightly by making an initial hard nose-to-nose turn, he can attain further angular gains without pulling so hard on subsequent turns—and reduced bogey G results in less energy bleed. Nose-to-tail turns, however, require the bogey to continue at a greater turn rate throughout the maneuver, turning hard and bleeding energy for every degree of advantage. Even if the bogey pulls the same load

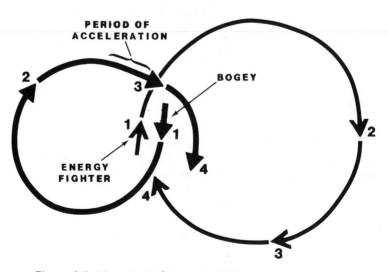

Figure 3-5. Nose-to-Tail Turn Complications

factor in each situation, nose-to-nose dynamics result in its gaining a given angular advantage in about half the time required for it to do so by nose-to-tail turns. Obviously, less time spent at high G means less energy bleed and less speed differential when the pilot of the energy fighter decides to zoom.

The greater time involved in use of the nose-to-tail method raises other points. More time spent in this predictable maneuver subjects both fighters to more danger in a hostile environment. Combat endurance is also a factor. Neither fighter may have the fuel necessary to gain a substantial advantage with nose-to-tail turns. Maintaining visual contact with the opponent, however, is the most important consideration here. If this cannot be done comfortably during a nose-to-tail turn, the energy tactician may be forced to the nose-to-nose technique, and he will just have to accept the inefficiencies involved.

Although a level turn has been specified for this portion of the energy fight, this is certainly not a requirement. In fact, there are some valuable advantages to slightly oblique diving or climbing turns, particularly in the nose-to-tail case. For instance, a diving spiral may allow the energy fighter to maintain speed while pulling its maximum structural-G limit. Since he cannot safely pull higher load factor in a similar aircraft, the bogey pilot can gain angles in a nose-to-tail turn only at a limited rate. If the energy fighter stays near corner speed, the opponent may be completely stalemated as long as altitude allows the descending spiral to continue. This technique can be very valuable, particularly when the energy fighter pilot finds himself at an initial position disadvantage. The bogey might be held outside firing parameters in this manner until its pilot loses interest or runs out of fuel and is forced to disengage. Such a stalemated nose-to-tail turn has come to be called a "Lufbery," after the American ace Raoul Lufbery, who fought with the French Lafayette Escadrille and the U.S. Air Service during World War I.

Although the nose-low method slows the rate of angular gain for the bogey in both nose-to-nose and nose-to-tail situations, a tradeoff is involved. Because of the energy fighter's higher G, the bogey is likely to pull less excess G during the maneuver, resulting in more efficient angular gains. This can mean less speed differential between the fighters when the energy fighter zooms.

The opposite is true, however, for nose-high turns. An energy fighter in a climbing turn must pull less G if it is to maintain a given airspeed. This leaves the opponent more G margin to play with, and he typically will use it to gain angles at a faster rate, bleeding relatively more energy in the process. A nose-high spiral tends to reduce the time necessary to bleed the bogey's energy by a desired amount in a nose-to-tail turn. This is seldom a requirement with nose-to-nose turns, however, and use of the nose-high technique in a nose-to-nose situation may allow the bogey to grab a lethal position advantage before the energy fighter pilot realizes it.

For the energy fight, of equal importance with reducing required engagement time is limiting the number of nose-to-tail turns necessary to bleed the bogey's energy by the desired amount. For example, if in a level or nose-low sustained turn it takes three passes before the bogey gains about 90° of angular advantage, each pass subjects the energy fighter to a possible gun snapshot. Additionally, as the nose-to-tail fight progresses, the bogey typically overshoots at a greater angle, which results in longer blind periods and an increased chance that the pilot of the energy fighter will lose sight. By employing the nose-high-turn technique, the energy tactician may be able to reduce the number of passes required (ideally to one), thereby limiting his exposure to these hazards.

From the standpoint of energy performance, the optimum speed for an energy fighter engaged in nose-to-tail turns is about the speed for maximum sustained turn rate, assuming, of course, that this value is greater than minimum vertical-maneuvering speed. Load factor, however, should be held to only about two-thirds of the maximum sustained-G capability at this speed, and the remaining P_S should be used for climbing. Depending on the rate at which the bogey gains angles early in the first turn, this climb angle and G may need to be modified. For example, if the bogey does not turn aggressively, the energy tactician might reduce G and increase climb angle somewhat so that the bogey will make angles faster and reduce the number of passes required. On the contrary, should the opponent turn very hard, or refuse to follow the energy fighter up in its climb, it may be necessary for the pilot of the energy fighter to increase G and return to a level or even nose-low turn. The bogey cannot be allowed to gain much more than 90°, nor can it be allowed to build excessive vertical separation (such as would occur if it didn't climb while the energy fighter did), since either of these factors facilitates its ability to point at the energy fighter when the zoom occurs.

Another aspect of this energy fight which deserves attention is guns-defense technique. With each pass the energy fighter is subjected to a forward-hemisphere snapshot by the bogey. Because of the high closure involved with the forward-hemisphere approach, the adversary has very little time for careful aiming, but he still may be successful unless the energy fighter performs a good defensive jink. Assuming the attacker is approaching at about co-altitude, the defender can quickly roll wings-level, either upright or inverted, just as the bogey approaches firing range with lead. One quick, hard, out-of-plane pull, followed by a 180° roll and another pull, or a hard negative-G maneuver, is usually sufficient to spoil the shot. On the final pass of the fight, the one after which the energy tactician plans to zoom, a pull-down early in the guns defense may have other benefits. If the attacker pulls down to continue his guns pass, the energy fighter's subsequent pull-up into a zoom may result in a nose-low, vertical overshoot by the bogey, which should give the zooming fighter greater advantage in the ensuing rolling scissors.

Although energy tactics often allow the opponent to gain an angular advantage in return for an energy margin, these tactics do not have to be defensive in nature. If the energy fighter can get a good angular advantage on the opponent (on the order of 90°), lag pursuit may be used in a nose-to-tail turn to bleed the bogey's energy. The energy fighter maintains its best sustained turn rate, forcing the defender to turn harder to maintain sight and to neutralize the attacker's position advantage. Once the bogey has regained angular neutrality, the energy fighter should have generated enough energy margin to begin vertical maneuvering, as depicted in Figures 2-15 and 2-19. This technique is much safer than allowing the opponent an angular advantage.

> In contests of [tactics] it is bad to be led about by the enemy. You must always be able to lead the enemy about.
>
> Miyamoto Musashi

So far the assumption has been made that the opponent will maneuver near horizontally; but what if he instead pulls up steeply after the first pass? By maneuvering out-of-plane, the bogey may be able to make a high-side attack on the level-turning energy fighter, forcing a defensive pull-up and immediate entry into a rolling scissors. If the bogey has an energy advantage at the pass (a factor that may be difficult to determine), a rolling scissors could be to its benefit early in the engagement. When the bogey makes an oblique nose-high turn at the first pass, the energy fighter can counter with a nose-to-tail turn, which should prevent the angles fighter from making gains without incurring an energy penalty. For near-vertical bogey maneuvers, the energy tactician should turn only enough to gain sight of the bogey; then he should continue a climb at optimum-climb airspeed to gain separation. As the bogey approaches the top of its zoom, the energy fighter can begin an oblique turn back toward the bogey in the nose-to-tail direction. During his come-back turn the pilot of the energy fighter should keep his lift vector on or slightly below the bogey to reduce vertical separation to within a quarter of a turn radius by the next pass, and he should pull hard enough to limit the bogey's angular gains to 90° or less. If possible, the energy tactician should not allow his speed to bleed below that required for vertical maneuvering.

> If you are thoroughly conversant with [tactics], you will recognize the enemy's intentions and thus have many opportunities to win.
>
> Miyamoto Musashi

Comparison of Angles and Energy Tactics

In the guns-only scenario, the angles and the energy techniques discussed may both be effective. Angles tactics are inherently more aggressive, placing the opponent in a defensive position early in the engagement, and they can have considerable psychological impact, particularly on an inexperienced adversary. This technique is also generally quicker than energy tactics, an important consideration when a fighter is limited by very short combat endurance.

Energy tactics, on the other hand, require more patience and training. Speed control is very important, as is the ability to judge the bogey's energy state accurately. This technique also demands proficiency in the rolling scissors, which is a difficult maneuver to master. On the positive side, except for the possibility of a forward-hemisphere snapshot, which normally can be defeated by a small jink on each pass, the energy technique discussed here is inherently safer than angles tactics. As long as the bogey's angular advantage is limited to approximately 90°, and a vertical move is not initiated with insufficient energy advantage, separation and termination of the engagement are possible throughout the fight.

By comparison, the angles technique does not afford sufficient opportunity to assess the opponent's energy. Once the vertical move is begun, the pilot of the angles fighter is "betting the farm" on his ability to force the bogey back down first. If he is unable to accomplish this because of insufficient energy or because of adept maneuvering by the adversary, the angles tactician may find himself at the top of his zoom, out of airspeed and ideas with nowhere to go but down, and with an angry enemy above. Some insurance against this condition is provided by the angles fighter maintaining at least enough airspeed for a vertical zoom climb.

With any of the tactics outlined here, whenever the opponent makes a forward-quarter approach, consideration should be given to attempting a short gun burst at the pass. Although this is generally not a high-percentage shot, it is useful in establishing offensive and defensive psychological sets between the opponents, and it may disrupt the adversary's game plan. The pilot should assess the possible value of this shot against its effect on his own maneuvering requirements and ammunition supply.

> Every time your opponent attempts to dive at you or attack you in any way, the best thing to do is to turn on him, pull the nose of your machine up, and fire.
>
> Lt. Colonel W. A. "Billy" Bishop, RAF

Unless a pilot has extensive training in energy methods, the cautious use of angles tactics is probably preferable in this scenario. With similar aircraft, however, it is often necessary to take what the opponent will allow. For instance, if the enemy appears tentative in the first turn, the experienced fighter pilot will generally "go for the throat" with aggressive but controlled angles tactics. On the other hand, faced with an aggressive opponent, the best course might be to "finesse" him with energy tactics.

In the one-versus-one-similar scenario, it quite often becomes advantageous to switch tactics during the engagement. For example, if the fight is begun using aggressive angles tactics and the opponent matches angle-for-angle through one or two turns, odds are very good that the engagement will quickly degenerate into a dangerous slow-speed flat scissors at low altitude. The outcome of such an engagement often rests on which pilot first loses control and crashes or runs out of fuel. Normally the angles tactician should not allow the engagement to reach such a stalemate; he should make the transition to an energy fight instead. This is usually accomplished by converting to a nose-to-tail turn at the next pass and relaxing the G to the minimum value required to keep sight of the bogey. This turn is continued, allowing the aircraft to accelerate toward best sustained-turn-rate speed (or climbing in the low-G turn if the aircraft is above this speed), adjusting G and climb/dive angle so that the enemy gains about 90° by the next pass. At this point excess airspeed is traded for an altitude advantage by the methods detailed previously. If a fighter is very slow when the pilot commences using energy tactics, it may be necessary to dive the aircraft in the turn to pick up minimum vertical-maneuvering speed before starting the zoom. Care must be taken not to delay the transition to energy tactics so long (i.e., until the fight is too low and slow) that insufficient height is available for such a maneuver.

> When reaching a stalemate, win with a technique the enemy does not expect.
> Miyamoto Musashi

The converse case, when the opponent refuses to take the angular advantage offered by the energy fighter, may also arise. This situation should become apparent before completion of the first nose-to-tail turn, and it invites the energy tactician to begin angles tactics, normally by starting a low yo-yo from across the circle.

Recognizing the need for, and making, tactical transitions such as these are signs of great experience in a fighter pilot. Usually, once implementing a tactical plan a less-experienced pilot will continue it to its conclusion.

Rear-Quarter Missiles Only

Rear-quarter (RQ) AAMs, as discussed in the weapons chapter, are most often heat seekers. As with other missiles, they can be expected to have minimum- and maximum-range limits and aiming requirements in addition to their AOT boundaries. Although this firing envelope (min-range, max-range, and AOT) varies greatly with fighter and target speeds, altitudes, maneuvers, and other factors, for simplicity in this section it will be assumed to be fixed and to have constant min- and max-range limits and AOT boundaries of plus or minus 45°. Even though this envelope is usually much larger than that required for a gun snapshot, it is not necessarily easier to satisfy. This is partly because of the relationship between an attacking fighter's nose position (aiming) and its resulting maneuver (position). In order to reach a certain position in space (e.g., the firing envelope) conventional fighters must attain strictly defined nose positions; but the nose position required for the fighter to reach the firing envelope may not satisfy the missile's aiming requirements. The aiming requirements for this section of the discussion are boresight, i.e., the fighter's nose must be pointed directly at the target (AON equals zero).

With guns, maximum range is one of the most severe limitations, but it can often be satisfied by use of lead-pursuit techniques. Fortunately for this weapons system, lead pursuit is compatible with the lead-aiming requirement. In addition, the other envelope constraints, min-range and AOT, are sufficiently nonrestrictive for the snapshot so that they too may be satisfied simultaneously.

For RQ missiles, min-range and AOT are usually the toughest envelope constraints to meet. Unfortunately, pure pursuit, which is compatible with the assumed aiming requirements, results in decreasing range and increasing AOT against a maneuvering target. This is exactly opposite to the desired effect. Lag pursuit, which tends to increase range and decrease AOT, is much more compatible with RQ missile requirements; however, once a firing position is attained, this technique usually leaves the fighter with a large AON that must be reduced to zero in order to satisfy aiming constraints. Before this can be achieved, a target with comparable turn rate will probably have increased AOT beyond firing limits once more. This situation highlights the value of missile off-boresight capability.

A further difficulty arises from the min-range boundary in conjunction with an AOT limit and a maneuvering target. Figure 3-6 illustrates the "envelope rotation effect." This figure depicts a maneuvering target at times "1" and "2" along with the missile-firing envelopes appropriate to its positions at those times. Although depicted here in two dimensions, the envelopes are actually three-dimensional cone segments rather than flat planes. The centers (hearts) of these envelopes are also shown, as well as the track required if the attacker is to maintain position at the center of the firing envelope. Normally an attacker is not required to maintain such a rigid position, but this example serves to illustrate the movement of the RQ missile-firing envelope and the effects of target turn rate and range on that movement. In addition to the velocity of the target itself, the envelope rotates at a speed proportional to target turn rate times range. The faster the target's speed and turn rate, and the greater the missile's min-range limit, the more difficult it is for the attacker to maneuver into, and remain inside of, the firing envelope for any length of time.

Because of the combined effects of the flight path–nose position interrelationship and the envelope rotation effect, tactics designed for the use of RQ missiles against similar aircraft usually focus on reducing target turn-rate capability to a minimum while retaining a performance advantage for the attacker. Energy tactics are uniquely suited to this purpose. Since

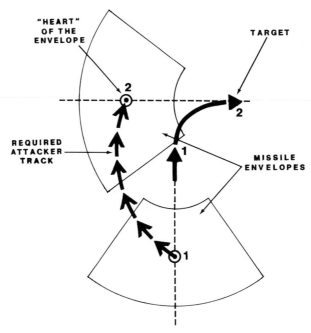

Figure 3-6. Envelope-Rotation Effect

conventional aircraft generate turn-performance capability by maintaining speed within certain limits and by sacrificing altitude to gain a gravity assist, total energy (speed and altitude) must be considered in achieving a turn-performance advantage. Unless one fighter is able to generate a significant energy advantage, the usual loss of energy during the engagement often results in something resembling a slow-speed flat scissors or a stalemated nose-to-tail turn at tree-top level.

> I never went into the air thinking I would lose.
> Commander Randy "Duke" Cunningham, USN

The Angles Fight

The angles tactics outlined for the guns-only scenario are not as well suited for the RQ missiles case, but they may be successful with minor modifications. Referring to Figure 3-1, the angles fighter no longer has the threat of a gun snapshot at time "4" to force the bogey up, out-of-plane, in a nose-high move. This gives the bogey pilot freedom to continue a level or nose-low turn, leaving the angles fighter temporarily in an offensive, rear-hemisphere position; but with an energy deficit, and probably a turn-performance disadvantage, the pilot of the angles fighter may have a difficult time improving on or maintaining his position. In such a case, the angles tactician might perform a low yo-yo after the overshoot to continue pressure on the bogey.

Faced with an overshooting situation at time "4," it is likely that the bogey will attempt to capitalize by reversing nose-high, as shown in Figure 3-7. If so, the angles fighter pilot should pull sharply up to point at the

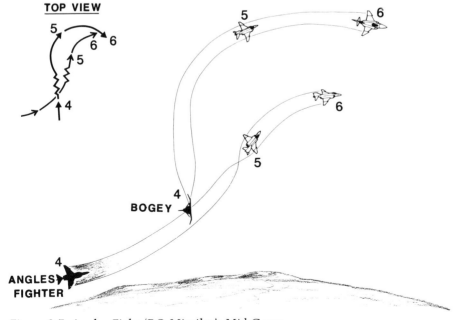

Figure 3-7. Angles Fight (RQ Missiles): Mid-Game

bogey and threaten it as quickly as possible. If he is unable to point at the target and force it back down, the attacker should pull for a position behind and below the bogey, as shown at time "5." The angles fighter should climb as close to the bogey's altitude as possible at time "5," while retaining enough speed for maneuvering. The desired position at time "6" is slightly behind and beneath the bogey, with minimum nose-tail separation and the angles fighter's fuselage aligned as closely as possible with the bogey's.

At time "6" both fighters will be near minimum-controllable airspeed. The angles fighter's position forces the pilot of the high fighter into a steeply banked turn, or a series of turn reversals similar to a flat scissors, in order to maintain sight of his opponent behind and below. The angles tactician should maneuver as necessary to remain out of sight on the bogey's belly-side. Concern over his opponent's position should eventually cause the bogey pilot to pull his aircraft's nose sharply down in order to increase his turn performance. Figure 3-8 depicts the end-game.

After the bogey pilot has committed his nose steeply down, the angles fighter should continue a level turn until the bogey approaches co-altitude. At that point the pilot of the angles fighter can roll inverted and pull his nose sharply down toward vertical (time "7"). After overshooting the altitude of the angles fighter, the bogey pilot will usually begin a pull-out to increase AOT and maintain sight. If his turns are properly timed, the angles fighter pilot may be able to pull his nose to the target and fire (time

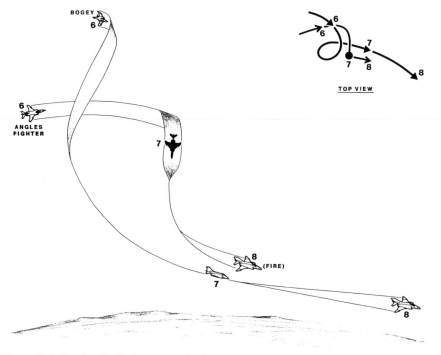

Figure 3-8. Angles Fight (RQ Missiles): End-Game

"8") before AOT increases beyond limits. Should the attacker begin his pull-down too early, he will have insufficient nose-tail separation and probably will induce a defensive spiral. If the pull-down is performed too late, the target may generate enough AOT in its pull-out to preclude a valid shot.

Timing is very critical to this end-game, and the shot opportunity will be missed quite often. When timing the pull-down at point "7," it is usually preferable to err on the late side, rather than be early. Too much nose-tail separation resulting from a late vertical pull normally allows the angles fighter to maintain an offensive position; but too little separation often results in a defensive spiral, from which either fighter may gain advantage.

If it is obvious at about time "7" that a shot will not be forthcoming, the attacker has the option of disengaging or continuing the fight. Disengagement may be accomplished by rolling opposite to the direction shown in Figure 3-8 and extending away from the bogey. When a pilot is separating from a missile fighter, however, it is imperative that it be kept in sight until maximum firing range has been exceeded. Accelerating to maximum speed and diving to low altitude usually aid disengagement by reducing the maximum firing range of a hostile missile.

If the angles tactician chooses to pursue the bogey after a missed shot, he can expect his opponent either to extend for separation or to come back in a nose-high maneuver, which often results in a rolling scissors. Therefore the attacker should be careful to attain his vertical-maneuvering airspeed before pulling out of his dive, even if this requires overshooting the bogey vertically. The threat of the angles fighter deep in his rear hemisphere may induce the bogey pilot to pull out at too slow an airspeed, giving the angles fighter an advantage in the ensuing rolling scissors.

The Energy Fight

The energy tactics described in the guns-only section are almost entirely relevant to the RQ missile scenario. Although this scenario eliminates the threat of a forward-hemisphere gun shot with each pass, there are other dangers inherent in the use of energy tactics with these weapons. For instance, although these missiles are termed "rear quarter," a very slow target with little G capability is unable to present a high LOS rate to the missile in its terminal phase and therefore may be vulnerable at much greater AOT than a highly maneuverable target would be. The energy fighter will be slow and vulnerable at the top of its vertical maneuvers. Going vertical without sufficient energy advantage, allowing the bogey to gain more than 90° of position advantage, or pulling-up substantially before the bogey crosses six o'clock may allow the opponent to get his nose on the energy fighter for a beautiful look-up shot. Although these errors can also cause trouble in the guns-only scenario, they are even more deadly here since increased range of the missile can offset a considerable target height advantage over the shooter.

It can be expected that more turns in the rolling scissors will be required to satisfy RQ missile parameters than to reach the gun snapshot envelope.

As the energy fighter gains advantage in the rolling scissors, it will soon be able to point at its opponent for a short period of time during the bogey's pull-out. The sooner a missile can be pointed at the target, the earlier the bogey pilot will be required to begin his pull-out in order to increase AOT beyond the missile's limits. This threat may induce the defender to start his pull-out before he achieves his desired speed, and it often leads to increased advantage for the energy fighter on the next loop of the scissors. The energy tactician can hasten this process by performing an earlier, more aggressive lead turn over the top of his loop. Each cycle of the scissors will generally result in less AOT as the energy fighter points down at the bogey.

Figure 3-9 shows the end-game of this scenario. At time "1" the energy fighter is in a very advantageous offensive lag-pursuit position at the bottom of its rolling-scissors maneuver. As the bogey continues its oblique loop, the energy fighter pulls up vertically. Approaching the vertical attitude, the pilot of the energy fighter projects the bogey's future flight path and rolls to place the lift vector ahead of the bogey's position (time "2"). He then pulls down smartly toward a nose-down vertical attitude once more, but not before the bogey pilot has committed his nose down. Ideally, as the energy tactician begins to pull down over the top of his loop, he would like to be directly above his opponent. The nose should then be pointed at the target as quickly as possible, and the shot taken (time "3") before the bogey can generate too many angles.

In the guns-only energy fight, a vertical pull-up was prescribed for entry into the rolling scissors. The vertical pull-up is the most energy-efficient method for converting excess airspeed to altitude; but this luxury may not be always available to the pilot of the energy fighter, especially against a missile-equipped opponent. The increased range and relaxed aiming requirements of these weapons may allow the angles fighter to pop its nose up, point, and fire even before the energy fighter can complete its zoom. One technique for preventing this involves substituting a spiral pull-up, illustrated in Figure 3-10, for the wings-level one. After the bogey's energy has been bled, and the decision to trade airspeed for altitude advantage has been made (time "1"), the energy tactician should begin to pull his fighter's nose higher and higher, in a positive manner, while still continuing to turn in the nose-to-tail direction. This forces the angles fighter (bogey) to turn considerably farther to point at its target. The energy fighter pilot must watch the bogey carefully over the inside shoulder, and monitor its nose position closely. Initially the bogey pilot can be expected to attempt to follow the energy fighter up into the spiral, continuously pulling his nose directly upward and around toward his target, and he may appear to be gaining angles. Eventually, though, as the spiral steepens, the bogey's angular gains will slow, and then its climb angle will appear to stabilize (time "2"). This is an indication that the bogey no longer has the airspeed necessary to get its nose up to point at its target, and it is the energy tactician's clue that it is now safe for him to steepen his climb to near vertical, seeking a position above and behind the bogey. This is done by leveling the wings and pulling toward pure vertical. The bogey then can be reacquired over the opposite shoulder, and the roll and flight-path angle can be readjusted to bring the energy fighter to a position above and behind the opponent (time "3"). Such a position makes it extremely difficult for the bogey pilot to maintain sight. Should the bogey hold its nose up and continue to turn during this time, the energy fighter can continue its zoom to achieve maximum height advantage, remaining unloaded as much as

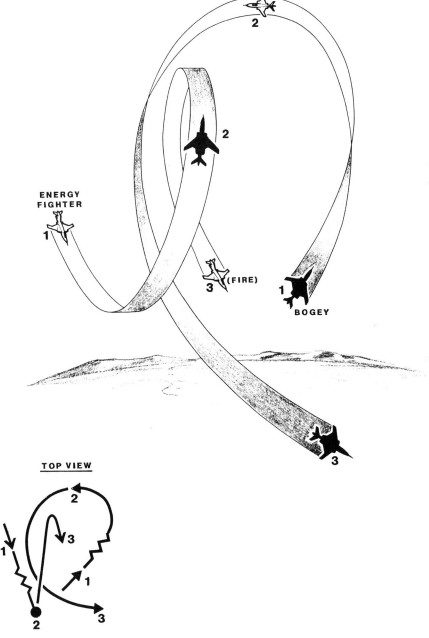

Figure 3-9. Energy Fight: End-Game

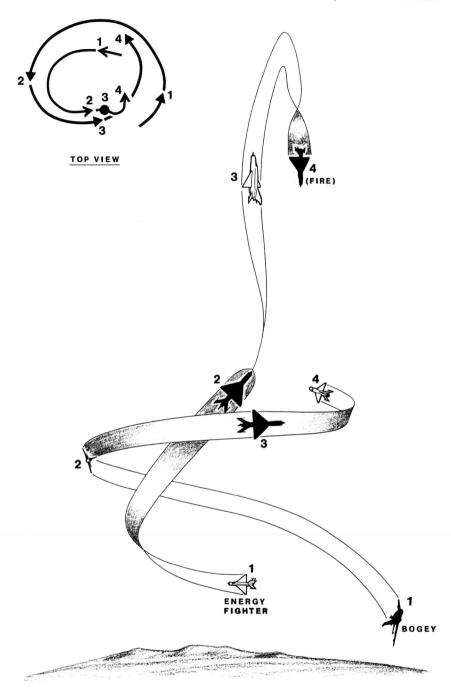

Figure 3-10. Modified-Zoom Maneuver

possible. Approaching the peak of his zoom, the pilot of the energy fighter drops his nose, points at the target, and fires (time "4"). Even if the shot available at this point is a high-angle one, the bogey should be very slow, unable to break upward toward the missile, and too slow to present the missile with a tracking-rate problem, even at 90° off the tail. As long as the missile can acquire the target, probability of a hit is usually high. In any case, the bogey's defensive maneuver undoubtedly will put it in a vulnerable position for a follow-on shot.

The timing of the energy fighter's vertical reversal depends on many factors, including missile min- and max-range, probability of missile target acquisition as angle-off increases, and aircraft turn radius. The last of these factors involves the possibility of a dangerous vertical overshoot in case the target is not destroyed, so at least one minimum-turn-radius separation is desirable before committing the nose down. Should such an overshoot occur, it will be necessary for the energy tactician to perform a nose-to-tail extension to disengage or to recommence energy tactics. If at any time during the zoom the bogey's nose falls, it is often necessary to terminate the zoom, point, and fire quickly before the target exceeds max-range. Vertical-reversal technique is quite dependent on aircraft handling qualities (vertical-reversal technique is covered in greater detail in the next chapter).

This actual combat example of the spiral-zoom technique is found in *Thunderbolt!* by Major Robert S. Johnson.

> Habit brought my head swiveling around to look behind me. I was just in time to see a *Focke-Wulf* bouncing, nose twinkling from the .30-calibers. My left hand slammed forward on the throttle, my right hand hauled back and left on the stick, my heart went to the top of my head and the *Thunderbolt* leaped upward. I racked the Jug into a tight left climbing turn, staying just above and in front of the pursuing *Focke-Wulf*. . . . To get any strikes on me the [German] first had to turn inside me, and then haul his nose up steeply to place his bullets ahead of me. The *Focke-Wulf* just didn't have it. At 8,000 feet he stalled out while the *Thunderbolt* roared smoothly; I kicked over into a roll and locked onto his tail.[1]

Comparison of Angles and Energy Tactics

Again, most of the comments made in the guns-only section apply to this case, except that energy techniques are more dangerous in this environment. Although they are more difficult in this scenario, angles tactics are still effective, and they offer the added advantage of an offensive position throughout the engagement.

> It should not be taken that one must always be the first one to attack regardless of the situation or circumstances, but at the same time, it is generally desirable to be the one to initiate the attack and thereby put the opponent in the defensive position.
>
> Miyamoto Musashi

All-Aspect Missiles Only

As discussed in the chapter on weapons, all-aspect missiles generally employ radar or IR guidance and can be fired at a target from any direction. The performance of both of these guidance systems usually is enhanced when the weapon is looking up at the target with a clear-sky background. Although technically all-aspect capable, most of these weapons are better in some situations than in others, with beam aspects often causing the most difficulty. As with other missiles, these also have maximum- and minimum-range limits and aiming requirements. Although many all-aspect missiles are also off-boresight capable, guidance is usually optimized when the missile is fired within a few degrees of the target LOS (often with a small amount of lead); so for the purposes of this section all-aspect missiles will be assumed to be limited to a boresight launch.

Inherent in all-aspect capability is the opportunity for a forward-quarter shot before the first pass of the engagement, possibly even beyond visual range. Assuming such an opportunity is available, this shot should not be passed up, particularly since a similarly equipped opponent may not hesitate. A missile in the air prior to the pass establishes a psychological set between the combatants, placing the pilot of the target fighter immediately in a defensive frame of mind. Moreover, such a shot must be honored by a defensive maneuver that almost surely disrupts the defender's game plan, and it usually places the firing aircraft in an offensive position and at higher energy than its opponent even before the maneuvering begins. Since maneuvering is the prime concern of this section, however, it will be assumed that neither aircraft has a firing opportunity prior to the first pass.

In a visual engagement with all-aspect missiles, minimum-range and aiming constraints are usually the most difficult to meet. Again, these restrictions oppose each other, since the usual boresight or lead-angle aiming requirement tends to reduce separation.

The Angles Fight

The tactics described for the rear-quarter AAM, simply a less capable version of the weapon in this scenario, are largely applicable and will result in rear-hemisphere firing positions, as before. Improved aspect capability, however, makes the firing envelope much easier to reach and results in fewer missed shot opportunities.

Referring to Figure 3-1, the first phase of the angles fight recommended for both guns and RQ missiles, an all-aspect missile shot may be available between times "3" and "4." Aircraft separation at this point can be expected to be about one fighter turn radius, which might satisfy the min-range requirements of some missiles when they are employed by certain fighters.

The mid-game of this angles fight, as shown in Figure 3-7, may also offer a firing opportunity at time "5." Although the aircraft separation at this point is likely to be less than nominal missile min-range, the typical slow speed and lack of maneuverability of the high fighter in this situation can make it vulnerable.

The end-game of this engagement, Figure 3-8, remains the same as for the RQ missile case, except that greater AOT is allowed for the shot. It should be noted here that the final firing position produced by these tactics is a look-down shot, probably with negative closure (i.e., increasing range). Such parameters can cause problems for many all-aspect missiles, particularly those with radar guidance.

Although these tactics may be effective, they do not take full advantage of all-aspect missile capabilities. Figure 3-11 illustrates a somewhat cleaner approach. Here the nose-to-tail turn is used to generate the aircraft separation necessary to satisfy missile min-range constraints. At time "1" the fighters meet in the standard forward-quarter approach. Minimum lateral separation and an angular advantage at the pass are optimum for this method. As the aircraft pass each other, the angles fighter begins a nose-to-tail turn across the bogey's six o'clock. Between times "1" and "2," the opponent's aspect should be monitored closely, and the angles fighter should turn just hard enough for it to match the bogey's turn rate. On reaching time "2," a neutral position with about 90° of target aspect, the angles fighter pilot begins a maximum-performance turn to point at the target as quickly as possible. The segment of the maneuver between times "2" and "3" may be performed obliquely nose-low to provide a look-up shot at time "3," if such a shot is desired.

At time "2" in this maneuver, the angles fighter requires the airspeed that will maximize its average turn rate (i.e., minimize the time required) between that time and time "3." Although corner velocity yields maximum instantaneous turn rate, many fighters cannot sustain this speed for more than a very few degrees of turn. Usually for this reason a somewhat higher speed is desirable. The typical arc from time "2" to time "3" is about 135°, so the best speed at time "2" can be determined either by engineers or by experimentation as that initial speed which minimizes the time for a level turn of this magnitude. The optimim speed should be known by the fighter pilot for a representative combat weight, configuration, and altitude at full power. Generally, an increase in weight, drag, or altitude requires a higher initial speed.

Arriving at time "2" with optimum airspeed is not a simple matter, since speed at that point is dependent on initial velocity at the pass (time "1") and the maneuver between times "1" and "2." Because fighters can slow down more easily than they can accelerate during heavy maneuvering, it is normally advisable for the angles fighter to carry excess airspeed at the initial pass. If the bogey's turn rate cannot be matched between times "1" and "2" at this higher speed, a power reduction, speedbrakes, or a

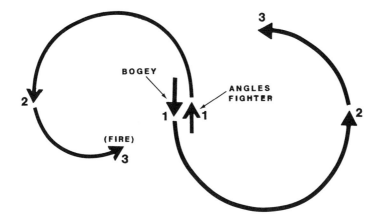

Figure 3-11. All-Aspect-Missile Separation Maneuver

climb can be employed to reduce speed and increase turn performance. It is essential that the angles fighter arrive at time "2" with at least neutral angles.

The choice of maneuver planes from time "2" to time "3" is largely dependent on the fighter's speed at time "2." Any excess speed should have been eliminated by this point, but sometimes hard bogey maneuvering results in the angles fighter arriving at time "2" with less than the desired airspeed. This deficit may be partially offset by a nose-low oblique turn, but a couple of cautions should be recognized. Any altitude differential generated by such a maneuver results in greater turn requirement for placing the nose on the target, delays the shot, and reduces aircraft separation. Another factor is the difficulty in maintaining the plane of maneuver. Just as the shortest distance between two points is a straight line, the shortest turn between times "2" and "3" is a constant-plane maneuver. When his aircraft is turning out of the target's maneuver plane, it is difficult for the pilot to predict the final plane of the attack at time "3," and therefore that maneuver plane cannot be established reliably at time "2." Any miscalculation results in greater required turn and reduced separation at the shot. Because of these complications it is usually best to keep the lift vector on the bogey throughout the maneuver from time "1" to time "3," regardless of the target's maneuver selection. At time "2" a small differential may be established in maneuver planes to compensate for lower than desired speed or to provide a bit of look-up for the shot.

The procedure just described typically provides aircraft separations of about two fighter turn radii. The actual separation at the shot is largely dependent on the level of bogey maneuver, however. If the opponent turns at his maximum capability throughout the engagement, and the angles fighter matches this performance as prescribed, separation will be minimal or nonexistent. Off-boresight capability is valuable for increasing launch separation in this maneuver, since the missile may be fired before the angles fighter completes the turn.

If the missile misses at time "3," the angles fighter could be at a considerable energy disadvantage, depending on the target's defensive maneuver. If the pilot of the angles fighter does not have an offensive position following such a missed shot, he should pass the bogey with minimum flight-path separation and then should commence a nose-to-tail extension maneuver to gain separation for escape. Returning to re-engage a bogey with all-aspect missile capability is not recommended.

Another viable angles tactic for all-aspect missiles involves the nose-to-nose technique described for other weapons scenarios, whereby the angles tactician attempts to gain a small angular advantage with each pass. Along with the angular gain on each turn, aircraft separation at the instant the target is boresighted also tends to increase during the nose-to-nose turn series. Once about 90° angular advantage has been achieved, aircraft separation at boresighting should be equivalent to about one fighter turn radius. This method is generally inferior to the nose-to-tail tactic, since it takes longer and usually generates less separation for the shot. It does, however, facilitate maintaining sight of the opponent, since maximum separation is reduced, and it also makes bogey escape more difficult.

Whichever method is chosen, unless the weapon has a very short min-range requirement or the fighters have very large turn radii, separation for the shot is likely to be pushing min-range limits at the boresight point. If there are weapons system functions that must be accomplished prior to launch (such as radar acquisition, lock, and firing delays), some means must usually be found to complete these functions prior to the boresight point. Any delay after this time may result in a missed firing opportunity. With long min-range limits, small fighter turn radii, or unavoidable weapons-system delays, the angles tactician may be forced to use the more conventional angles tactics recommended for rear-quarter-limited weapons. If so, the full capability of the all-aspect missile may be usable in this scenario only in forward-quarter approach situations (prior to the first pass) or when the angles fighter begins the engagement with a position advantage.

The Energy Fight

The energy techniques described for the previous scenarios offer the opponent a temporary angular position advantage in exchange for a reduction in his airspeed. Although the nose-to-tail turn is ideal for this process, all-aspect missiles may render this tactic unusable because the greater aircraft separations involved may allow the opponent to satisfy his min-range requirements, as shown in Figure 3-11. Therefore, the energy tactician may be forced to use the less efficient nose-to-nose procedure (Figure 3-4). In some cases, even the separation allowed by this method may not be acceptable. While a forward-hemisphere gun shot can usually be defeated with a quick out-of-plane jink of very short duration, an all-aspect missile must be honored with a radical defensive maneuver that must be continued as long as the weapon appears to have even the most remote possibility of guidance. Such a maneuver almost invariably places the energy fighter in a defensive position and makes it highly vulnerable to a second shot by the bogey. In addition, once an adversary has a substantial position advantage (and this advantage must usually be allowed to ensure an adequate speed advantage for the energy fighter), the maximum-range and all-aspect capability of these weapons make escape by use of nose-to-tail extensions almost impossible for a similar fighter.

Assuming that the min-range capabilities of the missiles involved preclude shot opportunities during nose-to-nose turns, energy tactics may be a viable option in this scenario. As in the RQ missile scenario, the energy fighter's zoom maneuver may have to be modified to a climbing spiral, as shown in Figure 3-10. Because of the energy inefficiencies inherent in the nose-to-nose turns and the spiral zoom maneuver, it is difficult to gain sufficient height advantage against a similar fighter to avoid a vertical overshoot in the event of a missed shot. With all-aspect missiles, the pilot of the energy fighter cannot afford the luxury of a rolling scissors after such an overshoot, since the opponent could have a sizable angular advantage.

Instead, the energy tactician normally should attempt to escape after a missed shot by use of a nose-to-tail extension, as depicted in Figure 3-12. This can be done by diving toward the bogey's six o'clock position (time "2"), then beginning a gradual rolling pull-out while turning slightly in the nose-to-tail direction in an attempt to reach a heading approximately 180° from that of the bogey (time "3"). During the pull-out, care should be taken not to cross the bogey's tail, since this would encourage the bogey pilot to reverse his turn direction. If the bogey does reverse, the energy fighter must also reverse to reinitiate the nose-to-tail condition, and then continue the extension. The gradual pull-out is continued until the energy fighter reaches a shallow diving attitude, at which time the pilot should concentrate on accelerating rapidly to gain separation, while he turns only enough to keep the bogey in sight deep in the rear quarter. This diving acceleration should be continued to gain maximum speed at the lowest possible altitude to shrink the opponent's missile envelope. The extending pilot must attempt to keep the opponent in sight as long as possible and only turn back if a missile shot is observed within apparent range limits. This technique forces the bogey pilot to turn greater than 180° (after time "2") to place his aircraft's nose on the energy fighter, often providing sufficient time for separation beyond max-range limits.

Comparison of Angles and Energy Tactics

The firing opportunities offered by energy tactics usually involve look-down conditions. To the contrary, those presented to the opponent are more often look-up shots, more desirable for many weapons. Off-boresight weapons present even greater danger for an energy fighter. Considering all the hazards and disadvantages of energy tactics in this scenario, they are

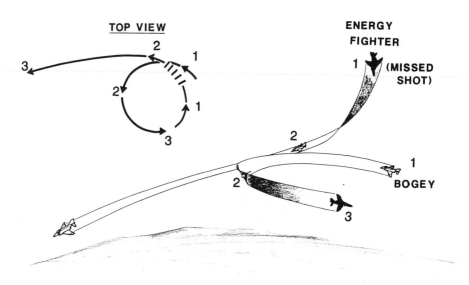

Figure 3-12. Disengagement Maneuver

not recommended, since angles tactics offer a much greater probability of success.

Multiple-Weapons Scenarios

Quite often, modern fighters are equipped with more than one class of weapon, most usually a gun in combination with either RQ or all-aspect missiles. This weapons situation forces the tactician to decide which envelope he wishes to satisfy; that is, which will be his primary weapon.

Guns and Rear-Quarter Missiles

As discussed in the RQ missile section, the gun snapshot envelope is considerably easier to satisfy once a fighter is engaged against a similar opponent. For this reason it is recommended that the gun be considered the primary weapon in this scenario, with the long-range capabilities of the missile serving to preclude the opponent's separation and escape.

Both the angles and the energy methods detailed in the guns-only section can be effective, with angles tactics probably preferable unless the pilot has extensive training in energy techniques. In many cases, relative advantage at the first pass will determine the best choice of tactics. Once the fighter has achieved a reasonable snapshot position, the bogey pilot must be concerned with maneuvering to defeat the opponent's weapon rather than with his aircraft, which usually leads to further offensive gains by the attacking fighter. After the fighter has a substantial position advantage, it becomes very difficult for the bogey to gain enough separation in an escape attempt to preclude a missile shot. Such a shot then forces the bogey pilot to turn hard back toward the attacker to defeat the missile, bringing him back into the attacker's gun range. This process continues until the bogey no longer has the energy to defeat the gun shot or to escape the missile.

Guns and All-Aspect Missiles

In this case the choice of the primary weapon largely depends on the quality of the missile in the maneuvering environment, or its "dogfight compatibility." A dogfight-compatible missile has a short min-range in relation to fighter turn radius (i.e., less than two turn radii against maneuvering targets in the forward quarter), little or no weapons system delay once the envelope is satisfied, and off-boresight capability that is usable in highly dynamic maneuvering situations. Such missiles are usually preferable to guns, primarily because of higher lethality. Unless the missile has at least two of these three qualities, however, the gun snapshot envelope may be easier to satisfy than the missile envelope. In this case the gun should be the primary weapon, and the missile can deter escape, as with the RQ weapon.

When the all-aspect missile is compatible with the maneuvering environment, it becomes the weapon of choice. Angles tactics should be employed in this case, preferably the nose-to-tail procedure illustrated in Figure 3-11. Regardless of whether this method or one of the nose-to-nose techniques is chosen, a missile should be launched at the first opportunity, even if separation is marginal. Such a shot could be successful, but even if it is not, the target's defensive maneuver usually places it in a very vulnerable position for a follow-up gun shot.

Dissimilar Weapons

So far in this chapter it has been assumed that the opposing fighters have identical weapons. Although this is a very likely situation with similar aircraft, it does not always hold true. Supply problems, ordnance expenditure, or weapons system malfunction, for instance, quite conceivably could result in dissimilar weapon capabilities. In this section the more common weapons mixes are investigated.

Guns versus Rear-Quarter Missiles

Since the gun is a close-range weapon and the missile generally a longer-range weapon, it is to the advantage of the pilot of the guns-only fighter to remain as close to his missile-equipped opponent as possible. The angles tactics outlined in the guns-only section serve this purpose better than the energy methods described there. Since gun snapshot parameters are usually easier to satisfy than those of the RQ missile, the guns-only fighter may have some advantage in this scenario. The missile-equipped fighter, however, will have the better chance of safely disengaging from defensive situations. The gunfighter may have a more difficult time with separation, unless it disengages from a position of advantage.

For defensive purposes, on the other hand, the pilot of the missile fighter would like to maintain his speed and separation from the gunfighter. Energy tactics are ideal for this purpose. The pilot of the missile fighter therefore should attempt to deplete his opponent's energy, and then he should initiate a zoom maneuver to gain advantage.

In the case where the missile fighter is also gun equipped, its pilot should still employ energy tactics because of the added measure of safety inherent in greater speed, more separation from the opponent's weapon, and better disengagement opportunities. The gun, however, should be his primary weapon, since its parameters are easier to satisfy. The missile then becomes the means of preventing the opponent's escape.

Guns versus All-Aspect Missiles

Again in this scenario, the gunfighter pilot would like to stay close to his missile-equipped opponent to deny him min-range separation. Angles tactics and nose-to-nose maneuvers should be used exclusively for this purpose. If the missile-equipped fighter reverses at the pass to set up a nose-to-tail situation as depicted in Figure 3-11, the gunfighter pilot must make a rapid decision. His choices are to extend and disengage, continue in the nose-to-tail maneuver, or reverse to reinitiate a nose-to-nose condition. The best choice depends primarily on when the bogey reverses and on the capabilities of its weapons system in the maneuvering environment. The disengagement option is usually available if the pass occurs with high TCA and the gunfighter has good speed. By turning only far enough to keep the bogey in sight, diving to low altitude, and accelerating to maximum speed, the gunfighter pilot usually can exceed missile max-range limits. The direction he happens to be heading at the time may have some bearing, since the pilot of the gunfighter may not wish to risk having to turn around and fly back past the missile fighter to return home.

Continuation of the nose-to-tail turn may also be an option for the gunfighter pilot in this situation. By turning at maximum rate, the gunfighter pilot normally can reduce separation to below min-range limits before the missile fighter can point at him. But when the bogey's weapon is highly compatible with the maneuvering environment (as defined previously), and particularly if it has a usable off-boresight capability, this can be a dangerous option. Even an immediate reversal by the gunfighter, reinitiating a nose-to-nose condition, may allow the opponent a shot with such a weapon. Disengagement may be the preferable option here.

A short delay in the missile fighter's reversal, or a second reversal, alters the situation considerably. Once it is well established in one turn direction, the gunfighter should disengage or continue in that direction, even if this results in a nose-to-tail condition. A delayed nose-to-nose turn by the gunfighter can generate a great amount of separation, allowing the missile fighter to meet its min-range requirements.

As for the missile-fighter tactics in this scenario, either angles or energy tactics are viable. The angles method of Figure 3-11 is probably preferable, since it is quicker, subjects the missile fighter to fewer snapshots by the gunfighter, and makes full use of the available all-aspect capability. Obviously, the missile fighter should shoot the bogey in the face prior to the first pass if possible.

Since the gunfighter pilot is likely to attempt a nose-to-nose maneuver at the pass, allowing him some lateral separation (up to about a quarter of a turn radius) may encourage a nose-to-tail turn instead, since a turn away might give the missile fighter angular advantage. Another ploy that may be useful in this situation is a "feint" turn. The pilot of the missile fighter can bank sharply toward the gunfighter approaching the pass, using top rudder to hold the nose level, but turning very little if at all. On seeing this, the gunfighter pilot is likely to turn away from the missile fighter to set up a nose-to-nose condition. In this case, just as the pass occurs and the missile fighter is out of sight on its opponent's belly-side, its pilot can reverse to establish a nose-to-tail turn, as desired. Quite often this tactic will result in the gunfighter pilot losing sight altogether. In any event, by the time he realizes the situation it is usually too late for the gunfighter pilot to reverse nose-to-nose without increasing separation even farther.

The pilot of the missile fighter may also use energy tactics in this scenario, since his opponent presents a reduced threat without a missile capability. The techniques involved are those described in the sections on guns only and rear-quarter missiles only. In this case, however, the missile fighter has the added possibility of forward-hemisphere shots from opposite positions in the rolling scissors. These are most likely to occur as the missile fighter comes over the top of its vertical maneuvers and points down at the gunfighter just starting up.

The foregoing discussion is relevant to other weapons mixes as well. For instance, if the gunfighter also has RQ missiles, tactics would remain essentially unchanged, but the missiles would tend to restrict the opponent's disengagement possibilities. Likewise, inclusion of guns and RQ missiles in the arsenal of the all-aspect missile fighter probably would not alter its pilot's tactics as long as his all-aspect weapon is dogfight compatible. With a less capable all-aspect missile, however, the gun may be the most effective weapon in this environment. Such a situation would bias optimum tactics in favor of those described in the guns-only section.

Defensive Maneuvering

> If you think "Here is a master of . . . [tactics]," then you will surely lose.
> Miyamoto Musashi

All the scenarios considered to this point have assumed essentially equal starts, both in angles and in energy, for both fighters. Obviously this will not always be the case. When starting with an advantage on the opponent, the course of action is fairly simple: The advantage should be pressed, using either angles or energy tactics as appropriate, until the fight is won, the advantage is lost, or a disengagement is called for, possibly for fuel considerations. When one pilot recognizes he has an advantage and then he loses that advantage, he is losing the fight even though he and his opponent may still be neutral. This is the best time for him to realize that he is overmatched and immediately execute a "bugout" (escape). Once a trend is established in one-versus-one ACM, it is seldom reversed without a serious mistake on the part of the winning pilot. It is not healthy to bet all your marbles on an opponent's future mistakes. It is much wiser to admit that this guy may be the Red Baron, disengage while the opportunity still exists, and return another day, when he can be surprised and shot in the back. The days of white horses and chivalry went out with King Arthur.

> My system was to always attack the [enemy] at his disadvantage if possible, and if I were attacked at my disadvantage I usually broke off the combat, for in my opinion the [Germans] in the air must be beaten at [their] own game, which is cunning. I think that the correct way to wage war is to down as many as possible of the enemy at the least risk, expense and casualties to one's own side. . . . I hate to shoot a [victim] down without him seeing me, for although this method is in accordance with my doctrine, it is against what little sporting instincts I have left. . . . At the same time, when one is taken at his advantage and one has to fight, one always has . . . to fight him like anything, for, as far as fighting the [Germans] in the air is concerned, nothing succeeds like boldness, and the [enemy] is usually taken aback when boldness is displayed.[2]
> Major James T. B. McCudden, RAF
> 57 Victories, WW-I

Although no true fighter pilot will admit it, it is also possible to start a fight at a disadvantage, or to find yourself in such a predicament during an engagement. This is the situation that "separates the men from the boys," and it calls for the greatest possible skill and cunning.

After a pilot recognizes that he is at a disadvantage (and the successful fighter pilot must be able to recognize this situation), he must assess the type and magnitude of that disadvantage. An angular advantage is pretty easy to see: The fighter that has its nose pointed closer to its opponent has the angular advantage. The magnitude of this advantage is simply the difference in the turns required by each fighter to point at the other. As explained earlier, the magnitude of this angular advantage is most easily assessed when one fighter is pointing directly at the other (its AON equals zero), since that leaves only one angle to estimate.

An energy advantage can be much more difficult to recognize and assess than an angular advantage. An energy advantage can be in the form of excess speed, altitude, or both. An altitude advantage is easy to see, but determining a total energy advantage can be difficult because of possible speed differences between fighters. Particularly in slow-speed situations, however, the higher aircraft must be assumed to have an energy margin unless the pilot of the lower fighter has some reason to believe his aircraft is significantly faster. Speed differences can be very difficult to determine. Probably the most effective method of assessment is for the pilot to observe the bogey's maneuvers in relation to his own, as explained in conjunction with energy tactics. With similar aircraft, the one that turns hardest bleeds the most airspeed, etc. When the fighters are below corner speed, instantaneous turn rate can be a good indication, since the faster fighter will generally turn faster. Nose-to-nose turns provide perhaps the best measure of relative speed. In this situation, unless one fighter has a significant angular advantage, a faster opponent will appear to move forward along the horizon, and vice versa. In addition, when similar fighters are maneuvering at near their maximum capabilities, the slower one will normally remain inside the flight path of the faster aircraft in nose-to-nose turns.

Unfortunately, when he is taken by surprise, the pilot may not have the luxury of making a safe, quick energy comparison. Probably the surest method is an immediate zoom climb to zero airspeed. Then, assuming the bogey does likewise, the fighter that tops out highest has the most energy (i.e., all energy is converted to altitude, where differences are readily apparent). A zooming contest is not wise, however, if a pilot is unsure of his relative energy state, since he will be in serious trouble at the top if he falls off first.

A MiG at your six is better than no MiG at all.

Unknown U.S. Fighter Pilot

Maneuvering with an Angular Disadvantage

The first point for a pilot to remember when he is at a disadvantage of any kind is to avoid panicking. It's never too late for a fighter pilot until he's dead, and then he won't care anyway. Very few good moves are generated in panic, so careful, deliberate maneuvering is in order. Secondly, the defensive pilot should not attempt to go directly from the defense to the offense. The first goal should be to regain neutrality without being shot. At that point the pilot can decide to terminate the engagement and escape, or to continue from a neutral position as discussed in detail previously. Too often the overeager pilot will expend excessive energy in a maximum effort to go from angular defensive to angular offensive, only to discover that he is now energy defensive and cannot maintain his angular advantage.

There is wide range in the degree of angular disadvantage, from almost neutral to weapons in the air. The situation needs to be evaluated instantaneously and only the necessary reaction made. A break turn is wasteful when a hard turn will suffice.

Starting with the easiest situation first, when a bogey with an angular advantage is detected in the forward hemisphere, the reaction depends largely on the range and the weapons involved. If the enemy is gun equipped but is outside firing range or lacks proper lead, an in-plane turn is called for. This turn should be hard enough to pull the bogey to the nose by the time maximum effective firing range is reached, so that the defender has an equal firing opportunity. If the bogey has already satisfied snapshot parameters, a guns defense is in order. The techniques involved here have already been discussed in detail. Should the bogey's initial angular advantage be judged too great for the defender to meet the attacker head-on, but guns parameters have not yet been satisfied, the defender can perform an in-plane turn just hard enough to stabilize the angular situation and watch for the opponent's next move. If the attacker begins to satisfy guns parameters (i.e., pulls lead as he closes), the defender can start guns-defense maneuvering. The attacker's other likely responses are to drift toward a lag-pursuit position or to initiate an out-of-plane maneuver, such as a high yo-yo or barrel-roll attack. In either case the immediate danger has passed, and the defender can begin to work toward regaining angular neutrality.

If the attacker chooses lag pursuit, the defender should continue to pull toward him just hard enough to prevent the bogey from reaching the blind spot at six o'clock. In some cases this may require using max-G and a shallow nose-low turn to maintain speed and turn rate. If it becomes obvious, however, that such a nose-low turn must be steeper than 10° to 15° in order to maintain sight, a quick turn reversal is usually the best move. A reversal can be dangerous against a gun-equipped bogey with an angular advantage, as explained previously, but it is normally preferable to losing sight or giving the opponent an excess altitude advantage at this point. If a reversal is executed it should be level or slightly nose-low. A nose-high reversal often results in a zooming contest or a rolling scissors, neither of which is recommended until the defender has had a chance to evaluate the bogey's energy. After the reversal the defender should try to meet the bogey head-on to neutralize its angular advantage. Normally the defender should remain level with or below the opponent, at or below corner speed, during this nose-to-nose turn. Angles tactics are appropriate here since the defender's goal is to gain angles, from defensive to neutral. Altitude differential should be limited to about a quarter-turn-radius equivalent, however, even if several repetitions of this process are required to neutralize the opponent's advantage completely.

Returning to the initial defensive turn, if sight can be maintained in a level or slightly nose-low nose-to-tail turn, this maneuver should be continued as hard as necessary until there is no longer any danger of the bogey reaching the blind spot. At this point the defender might continue a nose-to-tail extension maneuver and escape. If this is not practical, he should initiate a low yo-yo, pulling hard enough to make a definite gain in angles evident (i.e., bogey moves forward along the canopy). This rate of angular gain should be adjusted so that the defender will meet the bogey head-on at the next pass.

If the opponent's response to the initial defensive turn is an out-of-plane maneuver, the immediate pressure is once again taken off the defender. When maneuvering out-of-plane the attacker is no longer gaining angles, so the defensive turn should be terminated quickly and a nose-low unloaded extension commenced. The defender should maintain his original bank angle, however, to avoid revealing his intentions to the opponent. This extension maneuver gains both energy and separation for the defender which can later be traded for angles. Once the attacker's climb angle peaks and he begins to pull in-plane again, the defender needs to decide whether he has enough separation to make a safe escape. If so, this is probably the prudent move. One mistake has already been made in allowing the opponent to gain the initial offensive; another error could easily be fatal. Assuming an escape is not practical, however, the defender should pull back into the attacker in the closest direction, keeping the lift vector on or slightly below the bogey. This technique ensures that the defender will meet the bogey level or slightly below. Once again, altitude differential should be limited to about a quarter of a turn radius. This turn should be just hard enough to take away the opponent's angular advantage in the horizontal plane, and it should be completed with the minimum necessary altitude differential. If this cannot be achieved on the first attempt, the defender can repeat the entire process again, this time probably starting at less angular disadvantage, until neutrality can be achieved.

When an attacker begins with a large angular advantage on the defender, possibly greater than 90°, the initial defensive reaction is again dependent on the enemy's weapons and his range. It might be possible, for instance, to outrun a guns-only bogey in the rear hemisphere, depending on relative speeds and closure. Such a large angular advantage, however, often places the attacker very near his firing parameters, so defense against his weapons is normally first priority. For guns this is a hard in-plane turn toward the bogey until it approaches firing parameters, then some sort of out-of-plane maneuver to spoil the attacker's aim. When the attacker is expected to have missile armament, an in-plane break turn should be started toward the threat (a missile may already be on the way), keeping the lift vector slightly below the bogey. This technique should quickly begin reducing the attacker's angular advantage, possibly holding him outside RQ missile parameters, while generating a look-down situation for the bogey's missile and maintaining speed for a subsequent missile-defense maneuver. If at any point a missile comes off the rail, the defender must immediately begin missile-defense tactics as discussed earlier. Unless a missile is in the air, the initial break turn is usually continued until the bogey's advantage is reduced to about 90°, then it can be relaxed to stabilize the situation while reducing energy bleed. An exception to this rule might arise when an attacker is equipped with all-aspect heat seekers, in which case the break turn might be continued until the bogey penetrates min-range.

Once he is inside missile min-range or outside angular parameters, the gun-equipped attacker can either continue to press for a shot, begin to lag, or start an out-of-plane maneuver, as before. In the first case a guns-defense maneuver should be performed at the appropriate time. An attempt by the attacker at a high-deflection gun shot will usually lead to an overshoot with high closure and little nose-tail separation—the ideal set-up for the defender to perform a nose-to-nose reversal. Again, such a reversal should be made level or slightly nose-low in an attempt to force a flat scissors. This maneuver should be to the defender's advantage, since he is likely to be at slower speed and inside the attacker's turn radius. If the bogey begins a rolling scissors or a zoom after the overshoot, the defender should normally attempt a diving, nose-to-tail extension to escape, unless he is missile equipped and able to meet firing parameters quickly. Going vertical with the bogey is usually not wise, since the attacker is likely to have greater energy.

If the attacker chooses the lag option, a level or slightly nose-low turn should be continued in an attempt to reduce the attacker's advantage to about 90° or less as he crosses six o'clock. With such a high TCA it is unlikely that the defender will be able to maintain sight of the bogey in a continued nose-to-tail turn, however, so a reversal should be started as the attacker crosses six. This hard nose-low, nose-to-nose turn should be made at or below corner speed in an attempt to reduce the bogey's angular advantage as much as possible by the next pass while limiting altitude differential to about a quarter of a turn radius. A guns-defense maneuver may be required at the next meeting, but the attacker should have only a forward-hemisphere snapshot. After the second pass the defender can revert to the techniques outlined earlier in this section for defending against opponents with a smaller angular advantage.

An attacker who selects an out-of-plane repositioning maneuver on the first pass can be countered as though he had less angular advantage, i.e., with an unloaded extension. In this case, however, the attacker's out-of-plane maneuver is likely not to be so radical, allowing less extension time and forcing the defender to come back sooner. The same come-back technique as before is still appropriate; namely, make a hard turn in the closest direction holding the lift vector on or slightly below the bogey. This should reduce the attacker's angular advantage at the next pass, and the cycle can be repeated, depending on the attacker's reaction.

After the first pass, essentially the same defensive techniques apply regardless of the attacker's weapons. Defensive turn reversals, however, are much safer against bogeys without guns, and escape is more difficult from a missile-equipped enemy.

In addition to an initial angular bite, the opponent may also have an energy advantage. In general, the angular disparity should be corrected first, since this is normally the more dangerous of the two. After drawing neutral on angles it is much easier to redress the energy balance.

Maneuvering with an Energy Disadvantage

At the beginning of an engagement the pilot may suspect that the enemy has an energy advantage, with or without an angular advantage. Also, if he has had to regain angular parity, the defender must assume that he is at an energy disadvantage. After all, energy bleed has probably been necessary to nullify the attacker's initial angular advantage. With this in mind, the defender's next goal is either to escape, an option that is often available from a neutral angular position, or to regain energy parity. Even though the trend may have been in the defender's favor, he must recognize that he is still at a disadvantage, so escaping to return another day is certainly an honorable choice. On the other hand, the opponent has failed to capitalize on any initial angular advantage, and the only way to win with an energy advantage alone is to run the opponent into the ground. Therefore, the defender has reason to be positive about his chances of success at this point.

Just as recovery from an angles disadvantage requires angles tactics, correcting an energy deficit calls for energy tactics. The nose-to-nose turn is the defender's primary tool for bleeding the energy of a faster opponent. When two fighters meet essentially head-on and perform co-planar nose-to-nose turns, it is the fighter with the smaller turn radius that gains advantage at the next pass. In order to match turn radius, a faster fighter must pull substantially more G and bleed energy at a much faster rate than a slower opponent. Figure 3-13 illustrates an example of this process.

At time "1" in this example the fighters meet nearly head-on and about co-altitude, but the bogey is substantially faster. At the pass, assuming the defender wants to engage, he checks the bogey's direction of turn and quickly begins a level sustained turn in the nose-to-nose direction. The bogey's greater airspeed results in its having a larger turn radius than that

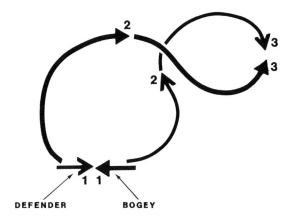

Figure 3-13. Maneuvering with a Speed Deficit

of the defending fighter, so the bogey is forced to pull harder in order to limit the defender's angular gain at the next pass. Meanwhile the defender just maintains his sustained turn and reverses at time "2," taking whatever angular advantage the bogey allows, and possibly attempting a gun snapshot. In this case the bogey has turned hard, taking away most of the defender's angular advantage, but consequently bleeding excess airspeed while the defender has been maintaining speed. After this second pass the bogey pilot reverses to maintain sight, generating another nose-to-nose turn. The defending fighter simply continues its sustained turn. Approaching the third pass, time "3," the defender's angular gain has not increased noticeably since the previous pass. This is an indication that the two aircraft are now approximately co-speed. The defending fighter has succeeded in neutralizing the bogey's energy advantage while maintaining, or possibly even gaining, angles. The defending pilot can now continue with either angles or energy tactics as he chooses, from a neutral start.

Returning to time "2" in the previous example, what if the bogey pilot refused to reverse his turn at this point, but instead continued to the right, nose-to-tail? In this case, because of its angular advantage at the pass, the defending fighter is still at an advantage. First of all there is a good chance that the bogey pilot could lose sight during this turn. Secondly, the bogey must turn farther than the defending fighter to generate a head-on pass at the next meeting, giving the defender another excellent escape opportunity. Because slower speed does not offer the defender an inherent advantage under nose-to-tail conditions, he should take this opportunity to accelerate. The nose-to-tail turn should be continued (assuming the defender chooses to remain engaged), but only hard enough to ensure a head-on meeting at the next pass. In doing so the defender trades his angular advantage at time "2" for additional speed, while the attacker must turn farther, leaving him with little chance to build energy. At the next pass, if the defender is still unsure of his relative energy, the nose-to-nose technique can be tried again. If the defending fighter is able to accelerate up to its best sustained-turn-rate speed, however, it is time to begin offensive angles or energy tactics.

An even more efficient technique for this situation (i.e., continued bogey nose-to-tail turn at time "2") from an energy standpoint is an unloaded acceleration just after the pass (time "2") until the bogey has regained the angles lost in the first nose-to-nose turn. When the bogey reaches a heading exactly opposite that of the defender, the defender can resume his sustained nose-to-tail turn at his new higher airspeed. Either of these techniques can be dangerous against an all-aspect-missile-equipped opponent, however, since he still may be able to bring his nose to bear first, with sufficient separation to satisfy his min-range parameters.

The techniques outlined in conjunction with Figure 3-13 should work well against a bogey that remains roughly co-altitude, but what if it has a substantial altitude advantage at the first pass, or climbs steeply during the engagement? The general rule here is to work below the bogey, make it come down to engage, and try to confine the fight to the horizontal plane. A higher-energy opponent with an altitude advantage can be either faster or slower than the defender, and it may not be readily apparent which is the case. Since the nose-to-nose turn technique just described is predicated on the defender having a smaller turn radius, it may not be effective against a higher, slower opponent. One means of correcting this situation is for the defender to climb up toward the bogey, either approaching the first pass or during the first turn, allowing speed to bleed down to the range for minimum sustained turn radius. For most jet fighters under normal combat conditions this speed will be roughly 1.5 times power-on stall speed for its weight, configuration, power, and altitude (usually somewhat slower for prop fighters). This speed will vary somewhat among different fighter types, and it is often faster at very high altitudes, so performance charts should be consulted. In general, use of any configuration (e.g., flaps, slats) which lowers power-on stall speed is advantageous for this tactic. If they are employed, however, use of any devices that increase unloaded drag or decrease forward thrust should be discontinued before periods of acceleration. By operating in this speed range, the defender can be assured that a similar bogey cannot outperform him in nose-to-nose turns regardless of the opponent's speed. The nose-to-nose turn tactic should then allow the defender to put angular pressure on the attacker, forcing him to expend his energy advantage in response.

It must be cautioned, however, that minimum sustained-turn-radius speed will be well below corner speed for the defender, and this may not be a healthy condition in a hostile combat environment where the possibility of SAMs or additional threat fighters exists. In addition, if after the defender climbs to obtain optimum maneuvering speed the bogey still has a substantial altitude advantage, the attacker may be able to make an overhead attack and force a weapons-defense maneuver. Such a defense may be difficult at slow speed.

As an alternative to this tactic, the defender can maintain speed and altitude and perform a sustained nose-to-tail turn instead. In response to this move the bogey is likely to make a nose-low turn, possibly gaining some angles by the next pass, but expending some of its energy margin in the process. Once the altitude advantage is reduced, the defender can return to the nose-to-nose technique or to the previously described tactics appropriate for opponents with speed or angles advantage.

An opponent who maneuvers vertically or steeply oblique after a head-on pass may be able to use his vertical geometry to offset the defender's smaller turn radius in level nose-to-nose turns. This may enable the bogey pilot to maintain his energy advantage while making repeated attacks on the defender. The response to this tactic is much like that recommended against the high yo-yo; namely, an unloaded acceleration after the pass until the bogey's climb angle peaks, then a hard come-back in the closest direction, keeping the lift vector on or slightly below the bogey. This technique should limit the bogey's angular gains while forcing the attacker to expend his energy advantage. An all-aspect-missile-equipped opponent may be able to satisfy firing parameters with such vertical maneuvers, so the defender may prefer an escape attempt immediately if the bogey zooms. A shot from well above the target, however, may be severely limited by look-down as well as marginal with respect to min-range, and the defender should be well positioned for a defensive maneuver. Whenever meeting the bogey from well below, as may be the case after a maneuver such as that just described, the defender should normally make every effort to reduce the opponent's vertical separation just prior to the pass. A zoom climb to within about a quarter of a turn radius of the bogey's altitude at the pass should limit the attacker's opportunity for a lead turn and an effective overhead attack.

Summary

In the similar-aircraft, one-versus-one environment, pilot ability is the single most critical factor in determining success or failure. Tactics are selected primarily on the basis of the available weapons capabilities of the opponents, and they are designed to optimize aircraft performance to achieve firing parameters before the adversary reaches his parameters. Depending on the initial conditions and weapons mixes, either angles or energy tactics may be preferable. Victory depends on having a tactical plan prior to the engagement and executing that plan aggressively.

> The aggressive spirit, the offensive, is the chief thing everywhere in war, and the air is no exception.
>
> Baron Manfred von Richthofen

Notes

1. Robert S. Johnson, *Thunderbolt!* p. 204.
2. James T. B. McCudden, *Flying Fury*, pp. 264, 280.

4

One-versus-One Maneuvering, Dissimilar Aircraft

Dissimilar fighters are fighters that have some performance characteristics which differ from those of the opponent by more than about 10 percent. The performance measures of most interest are turn performance (both instantaneous and sustained) and energy performance (climb, acceleration, and speed). Of course there are many other ways in which fighters may differ (e.g., roll and pitch performance, size, pilot visibility limits, combat endurance, and radar capabilities). The influence of some of these factors is also discussed when appropriate.

As explained in the Appendix, instantaneous turn performance is determined primarily by the ratio of aerodynamic lift to aircraft weight at low speeds (i.e., below corner velocity) and by the ratio of structural strength to aircraft weight at high speeds. Except in cases of extreme disparity in structural strength between fighters (i.e., on the order of a 50 percent advantage in maximum structural G for one aircraft), this limit is not usually as important in air combat as the aerodynamic limit. When a fighter pilot finds himself in a serious defensive situation, and to some extent when he is very near a lethal offensive position, he will use whatever G is required to save himself or to get the shot. A few popped rivets or some wrinkled skin is a small price to pay for the pilot's life or for a downed enemy aircraft. Since World War I there have been very few instances when a pilot has actually pulled the wings off his own fighter. Limits of structural strength must be adhered to in peacetime, however, since overstresses result in additional maintenance time, expense, and lost training. Therefore, ways must be found of winning within the design limits of the aircraft.

The relative low-speed instantaneous-turn-performance capabilities of two fighters can be determined by comparing their velocity-load factor (V-n) diagrams (see the Appendix). The aircraft with the greatest usable G capability at a given speed has superior instantaneous turn performance (i.e., faster turn rate and smaller radius) at that speed. This G capability reflects the maximum lift-to-weight ratio of the fighter, which depends to a great extent on the ratio of aircraft weight to total wing area, commonly called the "wing loading." As explained in the Appendix, wing loading alone can be misleading in this regard if one fighter has a more efficient wing for producing lift, possibly as a result of maneuvering slats or flaps. The way in which wing loading is calculated provides a further complication, as illustrated in Figure 4-1. The wing loading of the F-14 fighter shown here might be stated conventionally as 97 lbs/sq ft, based on the shaded area in the left-hand silhouette. The very broad fuselage of this aircraft, however, provides a large proportion of the total lift, particularly at very high AOA, so a more realistic value of wing loading (54 lbs/sq ft) might be based on the area shaded in the right-hand silhouette.

Because of these complications it will be necessary to make some assumptions to simplify maneuver discussions. Therefore, the term *low wing loaded* is assumed to denote superior instantaneous turn performance and slower minimum speed.

Sustained turn performance is a little more complex. The Appendix explains that sustained-G capability is the result of a fighter's thrust-to-weight ratio (T/W) in combination with its aerodynamic efficiency, which may be expressed as its lift-to-drag ratio (L/D) at the particular maneuvering conditions. But G alone does not make turn performance, as turn rate and radius are also dependent on airspeed. Lower airspeed at a given G level improves both turn rate and turn radius. All`else being equal, low-wing-loaded aircraft tend to achieve their best sustained G at a lower speed, and therefore they often have a sustained-turn advantage. It is possible, however, for a high-wing-loaded fighter to have better sustained turn rate at a higher airspeed by sustaining much greater G, which, in the case of aerodynamically similar aircraft, could be achieved with greater T/W. Sustained turn radius, however, is such a strong function of airspeed that the low-wing-loaded fighter nearly always has the advantage here, regardless of T/W. In this chapter a low-wing-loaded fighter is assumed, unless other-

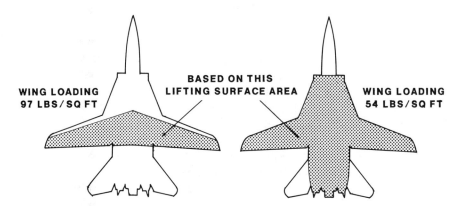

Figure 4-1. Calculation of Wing Loading

wise stated, to have an equal or better sustained turn rate and a tighter sustained turn radius than its high-wing-loaded opponent.

Energy performance reflects a fighter's P_S under specified flight conditions. P_S at a given airspeed is a function of the ratio of excess thrust to aircraft weight, as shown by Equation 4 in the Appendix, and is a measure of the aircraft's ability to climb or accelerate under those conditions. A fighter's T/W is a fairly good indicator of its energy performance. This ratio is usually stated in terms of static sea-level thrust and a representative combat weight. For piston-engine aircraft a parameter known as "power loading," the ratio of aircraft weight to brake horsepower (normally maximum sea-level power), is used rather than T/W. Both these measures may be misleading, however, since operating conditions of altitude and airspeed can affect two fighters in different ways. For example, a fighter with a relatively powerful normally aspirated piston engine may have lower power loading and better performance than a turbocharged fighter at low altitudes; but the turbocharged fighter would retain its power better at altitude and could have superior energy performance at higher levels. Likewise with jet engines, performance can vary greatly with inlet design, therefore a fighter may have higher T/W and better performance at slow speeds but be inferior at faster speeds.

A fighter's aerodynamic efficiency, in particular its lift-to-drag ratio, is also vitally important to energy performance, especially at high G or high speed. In order to simplify this discussion, however, the term *high T/W* infers greater climb rate, faster acceleration, and higher maximum speed capability relative to the opponent.

Obviously fighter performance can be a complex subject, and the numbers alone don't always tell the whole story. Development of effective tactics against dissimilar aircraft is, however, highly dependent on intimate knowledge of all aspects of relative fighter performance and design, as well as total familiarity by the pilot with his own aircraft and weapons system. Comparison testing, in which enemy aircraft are flown against friendly fighters, is undeniably the best method of gathering this crucial information.

> One of our achievements at this period was the "Rosarius Traveling Circus." This was a flight comprised of all air-worthy captured planes we could find. They traveled through the West from unit to unit in order to familiarize our pilots with enemy technique. The leaders could fly these enemy types themselves. In this way we found out that we had usually overrated their performance. The circus proved a great success.
>
> Lt. General Adolph Galland, Luftwaffe

Low Wing Loading versus High Thrust-to-Weight

Encounters between a low-wing-loaded fighter and an enemy fighter with greater T/W are quite common. In this case each fighter has performance advantages and disadvantages relative to its opponent. The engagement strategy is for the pilot to exploit the opponent's most serious weaknesses while taking full advantage of his own fighter's greatest strengths.

The low-wing-loaded fighter's greatest performance advantages are assumed to be good instantaneous turn performance, slow minimum speed, and a tight sustained turn radius. In some cases this aircraft also might have a significant sustained-turn-rate advantage. Its weaknesses include inferior climb and acceleration performance under low-G conditions, and slower "top-end" speed.

These characteristics are ideally suited to the use of angles tactics as described in the last chapter. One of the problems of the pilot of a low-wing-loaded fighter is how to get close to an opponent who has greater speed capability. This may be accomplished with geometry by use of pure and lead pursuit. High and low yo-yos and barrel-roll attacks also may be useful. Since the high-T/W opponent has better climb capability and vertical potential, the pilot of the low-wing-loaded fighter should attempt to constrain the fight to the horizontal plane as much as possible. Nose-to-nose turns make best use of a turn-radius advantage, and lead turns can be devastating because of instantaneous-turn superiority. A flat scissors should be lethal to the high-T/W fighter since it suffers from both a turn-performance and a minimum-speed disadvantage. The low-wing-loaded aircraft might also have some advantage in a rolling scissors because of better slow-speed controllability, but usually not so great an advantage as in the flat scissors. In cases where the high-T/W enemy has a sustained-turn-rate advantage, the rolling scissors generally should be avoided.

On the other hand, the pilot of a high-T/W fighter should concentrate on energy tactics when he is engaging a low-wing-loaded opponent. Lag pursuit and vertical/oblique maneuvers are necessary ingredients. Nose-to-tail geometry is usually preferable because of the assumed disparity in turn radii.

The defensive spiral might be handy if the pilot of the high-T/W fighter finds himself at a serious disadvantage. A high-wing-loaded aircraft often can generate much greater induced drag than a low-wing-loaded adversary, which may lead to a rapid vertical overshoot and subsequent position advantage for the high-T/W fighter. If this advantage cannot be capitalized on quickly, however, the low-wing-loaded bogey may use its superior low-speed turn performance to shallow out its spiral and regain the upper hand as the maneuver continues.

The Angles Fight: Guns Only

The angles tactics recommended in the similar-aircraft guns-only scenario are almost all relevant to the low-wing-loaded fighter in this case. There are a few slight differences in detail, however. For instance, in the similar-aircraft case each fighter attempted to gain an energy advantage over the other by climbing or accelerating before the first pass. In this case the bogey's higher T/W may allow it to win this preengagement race and achieve a speed and/or height advantage. To reduce this factor to a minimum, the pilot of the angles fighter might choose to cruise at an altitude well above that at which bogeys might be expected, so that his initial height advantage may offset the bogey's preengagement performance and provide the low-T/W fighter with an energy advantage, or at least make it nearly equal in energy to the high-T/W fighter at the beginning of the fight. Since the low-wing-loaded fighter is likely to have lower maximum speed capability, some height advantage is desirable at the pass to help ensure energy parity. Practical considerations such as visibility and weapons-system performance, however, may prevent use of this technique.

Another consideration is the performance superiority of the low-wing-loaded fighter at slow speeds. For example, its best climb speed, best sustained-turn speeds, and minimum vertical-maneuvering speed all are probably lower than those of its high-wing-loaded adversary. This slow-speed efficiency improves relative performance in nose-to-nose turn situations. The angles fighter also may have some sustained-turn-rate advantage, which would enable it to make angular gains in nose-to-tail turns with little relative energy sacrifice, but this process would be very slow and is definitely inferior to the nose-to-nose technique.

> On individual combat tactics, aggressiveness is the keynote of success. . . . The enemy on the defensive gives you the advantage, as he is trying to evade you, and not to shoot you down.
>
> Major Thomas B. "Tommy" McGuire, USAAF

In approaching the initial pass, the angles fighter should attempt to generate some flight-path separation for a lead turn, as shown in Figure 3-1. Turn-performance superiority should provide the low-wing-loaded fighter with some angular advantage at the pass. If the bogey continues straight ahead or turns away from the attack to set up a nose-to-nose condition, the angles fighter should continue in the original turn direction. Should the bogey turn toward the attack, however, a turn reversal is called for, as depicted in Figure 3-1. Since the pilot of the low-wing-loaded fighter does not have to optimize his turn performance to gain an advantage on the opponent, best sustained-turn-rate speed, rather than corner velocity, is normally the best engagement airspeed. Because energy is so critical for this fighter, the pilot should maneuver only as hard as necessary. Quite often small angular gains can be made in nose-to-nose situations simply by using level sustained turns.

> This should be an initial attack which on the surface is very forceful and fast, but which leaves you some reserve. Do not spend all your energy on your first attack.
>
> Miyamoto Musashi

The rest of the angles-fight sequence shown in Figures 3-1, 3-2, and 3-3, and the discussion of these figures, applies here, as well. The high-T/W fighter may, however, achieve higher zoom-altitude advantage, preventing the angles fighter from threatening a gun shot at time "5" of Figure 3-2. In this case the tactic of hiding beneath the bogey, as shown in Figure 3-7, may be useful. Instantaneous turn performance should give the pilot of the angles fighter a sweeter snapshot, or even a tracking shot in the end-game (Figure 3-3).

If the shot is missed, the bogey can usually dive away and escape even easier than it could in the similar-aircraft case, since it now has higher acceleration and max-speed performance. If the bogey pilot decides to stay and fight by pulling back up steeply vertical, however, the pilot of the angles fighter should ensure he has minimum vertical-maneuvering speed before following the bogey up. Such a maneuver should result either in a repeat of the sequence of Figure 3-2 or in a rolling scissors. In the latter case the low-wing-loaded fighter normally has an advantage because of better slow-speed controllability.

Throughout the fight, the pilot of the angles fighter can be somewhat less concerned with overshoots than he would be in the case of similar fighters, since the bogey's larger turn radius and higher speed make it more difficult for its pilot to gain advantage after an overshoot by the angles fighter. Gross vertical overshoots still should be avoided, however, since they may allow the bogey at least a temporary advantage, and possibly a snapshot, after one turn of a rolling scissors. Minimum vertical-maneuvering speed should be observed whenever the angles fighter is in close proximity with the bogey to guard against zoom maneuvers. Greed is the angles fighter pilot's greatest enemy. He should avoid trying to grab angles faster than his aircraft's performance permits. Once further angular gains can no longer be made at speeds greater than that required for vertical maneuvering, the high-wing-loaded fighter must have bled its speed down to or below that of the angles fighter, so the bogey should have little vertical potential remaining. In this case the pilot of the angles fighter can safely bleed to slower speeds and finish off his opponent.

> Don't let the [enemy] trick you into pulling up or turning until you lose your speed.
>
> Major Thomas B. "Tommy" McGuire, USAAF

In the case of dissimilar fighters, the high-wing-loaded bogey pilot is less likely to allow the angles fighter the advantages of nose-to-nose geometry. By being uncooperative, the bogey pilot can make things more difficult. For instance, he may choose to reverse his turn direction after the first pass, reinitiating a nose-to-tail condition, as shown in Figure 4-2.

The reaction (reversal) of the pilot of the high-T/W bogey depicted here is likely to occur at some time after the first pass, when he observes the angles fighter's nose-to-nose reversal. A reversal at this time requires the bogey pilot to "kick his opponent across the tail" and usually results in a protracted blind period when the angles fighter is out of sight. Such a maneuver performed well after the pass may cause the bogey pilot to lose sight of the angles fighter altogether, particularly when small, high-speed fighters are involved, so it is not without risk. The pilot of the angles fighter can increase his chances of being lost at this point by making a radical change in his maneuver plane (i.e., zooming or diving). Figure 4-3 shows one possible mid-game approach in this situation.

In this top view the fighters are initially positioned at time "3" as in Figure 4-2. Because of the bogey's late reversal and the low-wing-loaded fighter's better turn performance, the angles fighter already has a signifi-cant angular advantage at this point, but it is probably well outside effec-tive guns range. The task of the angles fighter pilot in this nose-to-tail

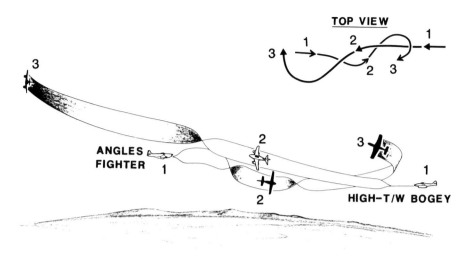

Figure 4-2. First Pass: Case 2

situation is to get inside the bogey's turn, build some flight-path separa-tion, and lead-turn the opponent at the next pass. The farther the angles fighter can get inside the bogey's flight path during the lead turn, the more separation will be attained and the more effective the early turn will be. The pilot of the angles fighter, therefore, should "bend it around" in a tight, high-G turn to aim as quickly as possible at a point estimated to be the center of the bogey's turn, as depicted in Figure 4-3. In this particular illustration, the resultant heading initially places the angles fighter nearly in pure pursuit (i.e., pointed at the bogey); but depending on the geometry, lead pursuit, or in some cases even lag pursuit, may result. A precise visual determination of the bogey's center-of-turn is almost im-possible, but it can be estimated accurately enough by noting that it will lie very nearly along a line perpendicular to the bogey's fuselage axis and at some distance from the bogey itself. Pulling a few degrees of lead on a

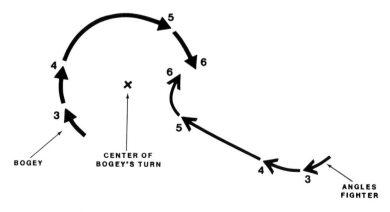

Figure 4-3. Dissimilar-Aircraft Angles Fight: Mid-Game

hard-turning bogey showing its full planform (i.e., 90° aspect) is about optimum.

Once he is established on the proper heading, the pilot of the angles fighter should try to reach his goal (i.e., the early-turn point) as quickly as possible. This generally is accomplished by an unloaded acceleration to retain any speed lost in the first turn. Airspeed should not be increased indiscriminately, however. Once his aircraft reaches the lead-turn point, the pilot should use a minimum-radius turn in order to take full advantage of the available separation. Minimum turn radius, averaged over a short period of time, usually is attained by commencing the turn at about corner speed, pulling maximum available G, and allowing speed to decay as the turn is completed. The pilot of the angles fighter, therefore, should attempt to accelerate between times "4" and "5" until his aircraft reaches corner speed. If the early-turn point has not been reached by this time, a constant-speed climb can be commenced to build additional separation in the vertical and to provide a gravity assist for the subsequent lead turn.

Determination of the early-turn point, time "5," is, as always, a matter of judgment and experience in assessing relative motion. Ideally the lead turn is conducted at near maximum G and results in passing almost directly over, under, or slightly behind the bogey for greatest advantage. This geometry is also ideally suited for a gun snapshot at the pass. Once again, however, care should be taken not to allow speed to bleed too far below that required for vertical maneuvering, just in case the bogey zooms at the overshoot. Nose-to-tail geometry makes judging the bogey's energy level even more difficult.

Figure 4-3 depicts only a very small angular advantage for the angles fighter at the pass (time "6"), and this is often the case in practice. In fact, the geometry and relative turn performance may be such that the bogey is able to achieve another neutral head-on pass. In most cases, however, doing this will require it to expend a great amount of energy, which will eventually lead to trouble for the high-wing-loaded bogey.

Time "6" in Figure 4-3 is essentially the same as time "3" in Figure 3-1 and time "2" in Figure 4-2 (except that both fighters are probably slower), so the angles fighter pilot can repeat the same reversal in an attempt to establish the more advantageous nose-to-nose condition. Depending on the advantage gained at the pass, however, it may be preferable for him just to continue nose-to-tail. Generally speaking, once the angles fighter has gained about 60° to 70° angular advantage, it is probably better for it to continue nose-to-tail. Doing so results in a considerable blind period for the bogey pilot, during which he may lose sight altogether or get nervous and pull harder, further bleeding his aircraft's energy. A reversal under these conditions causes a blind period for the pilot of the angles fighter instead, and because of the time wasted during the reversal, results in little increase in position advantage. As with nose-to-nose tactics, continued nose-to-tail turns may eventually yield a lethal position for the low-wing-loaded fighter, but arriving at this point will almost surely take longer. Once again, the angles fighter should take only what his turn-performance advantage will allow, chipping away a few degrees at a time while maintaining at least vertical-maneuvering speed.

So far in this discussion it has been assumed that the pilot of the high-T/W bogey will maneuver in the near-horizontal. He does, however, have the steeply vertical option. Figure 4-4 shows how the angles fighter pilot can cope with this situation. This illustration begins, as before, with the head-on approach. The angles fighter pilot attempts to gain flight-path separation for a lead turn, as in the previous examples; but this time, rather than taking out this separation with a close head-on pass, the high-T/W bogey immediately pulls up in the vertical. Because of the co-energy assumption of this section, the angles fighter could zoom with the bogey at this point. Even with a co-energy start, however, the greater P_S of the high-T/W bogey during the zoom would ordinarily allow it to reach a higher altitude. In cases where the P_S disparity is not too great, the angles fighter may be able to zoom high enough to threaten a gun shot at the top, forcing the bogey back down for a lead turn. In practice, however, there is usually no assurance of being co-energy at the initial pass. If instead the bogey should have a considerable energy advantage at this point, attempting to zoom with it could be disastrous. If unable to threaten the bogey on top, the pilot of the angles fighter may find himself too slow to defend against the bogey diving from above. Later in the engagement, after the angles fighter pilot has had time to ensure energy parity, zooming with the bogey can be attempted more safely. In that case a maneuver sequence similar to that described by Figures 3-2 and 3-3 might force the bogey back down for a lead turn. If he is too low on energy to threaten a gun shot on top, the pilot of the angles fighter can resort to the tactic illustrated by Figure 3-7 (i.e., hiding beneath the bogey to force it down).

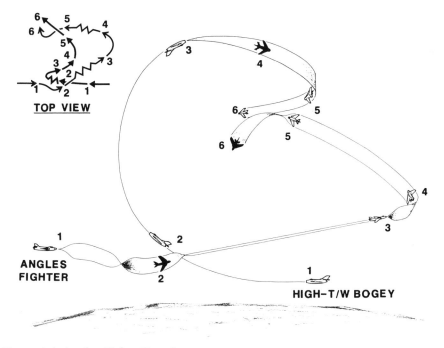

Figure 4-4. Angles Fight: Case 3

Whenever he is engaging in a zooming contest, the angles fighter pilot must take care not to allow his speed to bleed below that required for control in level flight (i.e., power-on stall speed). Once the nose is parked near vertical, it is all too easy to let the airspeed fall below this value, even to zero, in an attempt to get a few more feet of altitude out of the zoom. If this is allowed to happen, the nose of the airplane will soon become an "earth seeker," falling to a near-vertical nose-down attitude. Even if the pilot can maintain control during this maneuver, he will have very little G available with which to fend off an attack by the higher bogey, which now has been placed astutely in the rear quarter.

If it becomes apparent during a zoom that the bogey will top out much higher, the angles fighter pilot should immediately pull the nose back down to near a level attitude in a direction as far from the bogey as possible while he maintains sight of his opponent. This tactic generates separation and provides time for the angles fighter to build up some speed for defensive maneuvering.

The tactic illustrated in Figure 4-4 is more conservative and probably more appropriate early in the engagement than zooming with the bogey on the first pass. Here, on observing the bogey's zoom, the angles fighter pilot simply levels his wings and climbs. An unloaded acceleration might also be appropriate during this segment if his speed is substantially below that required for best climb performance. The climb allows the low-wing-loaded fighter to build energy at near maximum rate, while the high-T/W bogey remains at high G in its vertical pull-up, gaining little or no energy in the process. Simultaneously, the angles fighter is creating horizontal separation and reducing the bogey's altitude advantage.

The angles fighter should continue in a straight line until the bogey approaches the top of its loop. Any horizontal turning during this period merely wastes valuable energy, since the bogey can nullify any such turn simply by rolling while in a near-vertical attitude.

As the bogey approaches the top of the loop (time "3"), the pilot of the angles fighter rolls to place the bogey perpendicular to the wings (i.e., points the lift vector at it), and bends his aircraft around to generate about a 90° AOT (time "4"). At that time he can relax the G but continue to turn obliquely up toward the bogey just hard enough to hold it about 90° off the tail.

This tactic has several positive benefits for the angles fighter. The co-planar turn holding the bogey at 90° AOT presents the bogey with the highest possible horizontal LOS rate, forcing it to turn mainly in the horizontal to gain a position advantage. The bogey's shallow oblique turn at slow airspeed prevents it from gaining any great amount of energy. The angles fighter meanwhile is turning at fairly low G near optimum maneuvering speed and usually can maintain or even add energy during this segment. In addition, by allowing the bogey to remain very near the angular limits of a gun envelope, the angles fighter pilot is encouraging the opponent to continue his maneuver with hopes of success.

This "baiting" tactic is continued until the bogey approaches firing parameters of range and lead. At that point (time "5") the pilot of the angles fighter performs an out-of-plane guns-defense maneuver, nose-down in this case (essentially a high-G barrel roll underneath). Once the bogey's nose is observed to fall behind a proper lead position, the angles fighter pilot can reverse, forcing an overshoot at close range (time "6"). Such an overshoot, with the bogey co-energy or below, should provide the low-wing-loaded angles fighter with a valuable offensive position advantage. It remains only to press this advantage to a lethal position, as discussed earlier.

Now that several likely angles-fight scenarios have been presented, some attention needs to be paid to the end-game. When faced with an impending gun shot by a low-wing-loaded opponent, the pilot of a high-T/W bogey will often attempt to defend in the vertical. If he feels he can out-zoom his opponent, he is likely to try it. As discussed in the last example, when the angles fighter pilot feels he has energy parity, zooming with the bogey might be appropriate. Otherwise, the tactics illustrated by Figure 4-4 are safer.

When he is caught at slow speed with some altitude available, the pilot of a high-wing-loaded bogey is more likely to attempt a defensive spiral. As discussed in Chapter 3, this can be a very effective guns defense, and skillful use of decelerating tactics may even gain an offensive position for the bogey, particularly if the angles fighter pilot attempts to press for a gun shot as the spiral develops. If the angles fighter pilot allows the bogey some initial vertical separation, however, he can maintain an offensive position (above the bogey). The pilot of the angles fighter then simply waits and nails the bogey during its pull-out. Judging when to pull down after the bogey can be a very close call, since following too closely can result in a vertical overshoot, and excessive delay may allow the defender to dive out of range.

Should a vertical overshoot occur, however, and the angles fighter pilot find himself level with or below the bogey in the spiral, decelerating tactics should not be attempted. Instead, the low-wing-loaded fighter pilot can continue the spiral to defeat any guns solution while slowly pulling out of the dive at full power and maximum lift. The turn-performance advantage of the low-wing-loaded fighter should allow the pilot to shallow his dive angle more quickly, causing the high-wing-loaded bogey to overshoot vertically, again becoming defensive.

The Energy Fight: Guns Only

> Everything in the air that is beneath me, especially if it is a one-seater . . . is lost, for it cannot shoot to the rear.
>
> Baron Manfred von Richthofen

The preceding scenarios of angles tactics should make the task of the energy fighter pilot evident. The pilot of the high-T/W fighter must avoid getting shot until he can build a large energy margin, allowing him to zoom well above his opponent and position for a high-to-low gun attack. A steep approach to a high-side gun pass helps the high-wing-loaded fighter compensate for his turn-performance deficiency. Roll rate can be substituted

for turn rate to accomplish much of the heading change required in maneuvering to a gun-firing envelope, and in a steep diving attitude the energy
fighter has to oppose less gravity than it would when performing a level
turn. It should be noted, however, that while the guns approach may be a
steep dive, the firing pass itself usually is more successful if it can be
shallowed somewhat, as discussed later. Even with these advantages,
however, the pilot of the energy fighter should not expect a lengthy tracking gun shot against a well-flown low-wing-loaded fighter with a substantial instantaneous-turn advantage, since this bogey nearly always can
generate enough turn performance to keep the energy fighter out of steady
tracking parameters. The major exceptions to this rule occur when the
bogey pilot loses sight of his attacker or the bogey is near stall speed at
tree-top altitudes. Although the energy fighter pilot can work at creating
these conditions, a lethal snapshot opportunity often will be achieved first.

Obviously, an energy fighter must have a substantial altitude advantage
over its opponent immediately preceding an effective high-side or overhead gun pass. The exact amount of this required advantage depends on
many factors, but in general the altitude advantage should be about equivalent to the minimum instantaneous turn radius of the energy fighter. That
is, a fighter that can generate a minimum horizontal turn radius of 2,000 ft
at engagement altitude and optimum speed (i.e., below corner speed)
would require about a 2,000-ft altitude advantage for an effective overhead
or steep high-side gun attack. A well-flown angles fighter can be expected
to deny such an altitude advantage, if possible, whenever the energy fighter
is near guns range. The bogey pilot may do this by zooming with the energy
fighter or by saving enough airspeed to allow a vertical pull-up, if necessary, to meet the diving attacker nearly head-on.

The pilot of the high-T/W fighter, therefore, needs to build an energy
advantage sufficient to allow him to zoom higher than the low-wing-
loaded bogey by the required amount. Then if the bogey pilot engages in a
zooming contest, the energy fighter pilot simply waits for his opponent to
top out in the climb, and then pounces on him from above before the bogey
can dive and gain sufficient airspeed for effective defensive maneuvering.
This sequence was discussed in conjunction with Figure 2-15.

There are at least two pitfalls in this tactic, however. The most serious
of these is the possibility that the zooming contest will occur before the
high-T/W fighter has a great enough energy advantage. The results of this
error were described under guns-only angles tactics in this and the preceding chapter and are depicted in Figures 3-3 and 3-8. The other possibility is
that the bogey pilot will refuse to join in a zooming contest, but rather will
use his free time during the energy fighter's pull-up to build energy for a
later defensive move or a "baiting" tactic like the one shown in Figure 4-4.
These are just two of the factors that make this energy fight a very difficult one.

Engaging with an Initial Energy Advantage. Depending on relative performance, the energy fighter pilot may be able to assure the desired energy
advantage at the first pass by attaining a speed that is well above the
maximum capability of the low-T/W bogey. This is common when a

supersonic fighter engages a bogey that is limited to subsonic speeds. Just how much excess speed is required can be estimated using an altitude-Mach (H-M) diagram or Equation 3 in the Appendix before the engagement. Assuming an engagement altitude, the bogey's maximum attainable energy level can be located on the chart. Adding the desired energy (altitude) advantage to the bogey's energy level determines the approximate energy level required of the high-T/W fighter. The speed at which this desired energy level intersects the engagement altitude represents the necessary airspeed of the energy fighter.

The speed advantage necessary to provide a given zoom-altitude advantage is highly dependent on the bogey's airspeed. For example, a 2,000-ft zoom advantage over a bogey traveling at 100 knots true airspeed (KTAS) would require the energy fighter to have about 130 knots of excess airspeed (230 KTAS total). But with the bogey at 500 KTAS, the energy fighter would need about 540 KTAS (only a 40-knot advantage). Although faster bogeys require less speed advantage for the energy fighter to attain a given zoom-altitude margin, this phenomenon is offset to a large degree because faster fighters generally need more altitude margin. The figures given here are only gross estimates, since they do not consider possible energy changes during the zoom maneuver.

Assuming this energy advantage can be attained at the first pass, the pilot of the high-T/W fighter may choose to zoom immediately, as shown in Figure 4-5. The major difference between this scenario and that of Figure 4-4 comes from the great energy advantage of the high-T/W fighter in this case, which enables the energy fighter to remain well above its opponent, and facilitates its maneuvering in the vertical plane.

In this scenario the energy fighter has a substantial speed advantage approaching the pass (time "1") as well as slightly greater altitude. Together this speed and altitude advantage form the high-T/W fighter's desired energy margin. The purpose of the height advantage in this case is not only to provide extra energy margin, but also to induce the bogey pilot into a sharply nose-high maneuver. Allowing some vertical separation (i.e., passing almost directly over the bogey) gives the bogey room for a lead turn, but the pilot must turn almost purely in the vertical to take advantage of it. Too much separation here may provide the low-wing-loaded opponent a reasonable snapshot at the pass, while too little vertical advantage offers him little incentive to zoom. An altitude advantage at the pass equal to about one-quarter of the bogey's best turn radius is usually a good compromise.

In Figure 4-5 the angles fighter begins a near-vertical lead turn at time "1," while the energy fighter continues straight ahead for a few seconds. Here the pilot of the energy fighter must assess whether the bogey pilot has timed his pull-up properly to gain lead for a gun snapshot at the pass. If so, a quick out-of-plane (level) jink is in order to spoil the shot before he starts a pull-up of his own. This slight delay in the energy fighter's zoom also helps the pilot keep sight of the bogey underneath. The energy fighter should begin its pull-up, at sustained-G levels, as the bogey begins to approach effective guns range. Turning up and away from the bogey at this point increases the LOS rate seen by the bogey pilot, and consequently increases his lead requirement, forcing him to pull harder and reach a higher climbing attitude. If the bogey pilot keeps pulling for a shot, he should be committd to a very steep climb by the pass (time "2"). Mild jinks left and right during the pull-up complicate the aiming problem of the bogey pilot and may also facilitate keeping sight of the bogey.

During the next segment of this maneuver the energy fighter pilot should continue a wings-level, sustained-G pull-up, and reacquire the

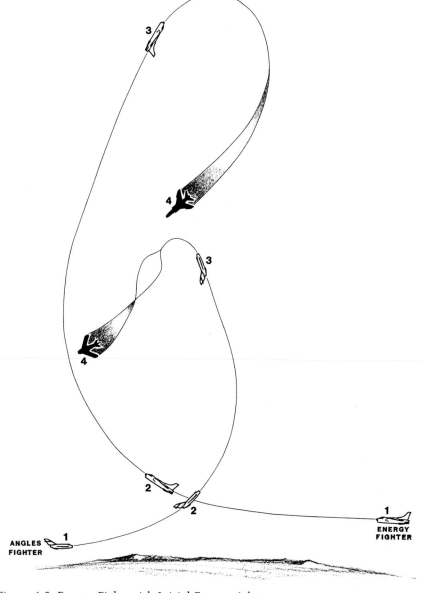

Figure 4-5. Energy Fight with Initial Energy Advantage

bogey visually. Once he reaches a vertical attitude, the pilot of the high-T/W fighter can roll slightly one way or the other if necessary to align his aircraft's wings perpendicular to the bogey's position, then pull slightly past the vertical toward the bogey. During the remainder of the zoom toward time "3," the energy fighter pilot should ease to a zero-G or slightly negative-G condition in order to achieve the highest possible zoom altitude. Simultaneously, he should begin to drift toward a position almost directly above the bogey. Care should be taken, however, not to position directly above and in front of the opponent too early. If altitude separation at time "3" does not exceed the bogey's effective guns range the opponent may squirt out some lead at this point, force a defensive maneuver, and seize the offensive. When its maneuver is timed properly, the energy fighter will drift over the bogey near the top of the zoom, with maximum vertical separation, just as the bogey pilot is becoming more concerned with controlling his aircraft at slow airspeed and less concerned with aiming his guns.

After establishing the proper zoom attitude and beginning the drift toward the bogey, the energy fighter pilot may choose to roll his aircraft in the unloaded condition to point either wingtip at the bogey. This tactic, known as "profiling," reduces the presented area of the energy fighter as viewed by the bogey pilot, making it more likely that the enemy will lose sight. It also may facilitate the task of the energy fighter pilot in watching the bogey, and reduce the possibility of his flying out in front of the opponent's guns.

At time "3" the bogey runs out of airspeed and its nose begins to fall toward the horizon. Allowing the bogey to begin its pull-up first also ensures that it will top out first. Once he reaches a slightly nose-down attitude, the bogey pilot rolls upright to regain sight of the energy fighter above, and begins a nose-low, unloaded acceleration. On seeing the bogey's nose start to fall through, the pilot of the energy fighter needs to assess whether sufficient vertical separation exists for a successful gun attack. If not, the zoom can be continued until the required separation is available. Once this separation has been created, the energy fighter pilot should get his nose pointed down at the bogey very quickly to cut his opponent's acceleration time to a minimum. This may be accomplished by configuring for greatest lift (flaps, slats, etc.) and using maximum available G to drop down into the bogey's rear hemisphere for a diving gun attack.

When flying at very slow airspeeds the energy fighter pilot may choose instead to push over the top or to employ a "rudder reversal" at the peak of his zoom. Also sometimes called a "hammerhead turn," the latter maneuver causes the aircraft to rotate about its vertical axis, pivoting sideways from a nose-high to a nose-low attitude. In most aircraft the rudder reversal is performed in an unloaded condition by applying full rudder in the direction the pilot wishes the nose to fall.

This technique apparently was first used in combat by Max Immelmann, a World War I German flyer who was one of the world's first fighter aces. (He won his fifth victory within a few days of Oswald Boelcke's, another great German air fighter and tactician.) One of Immelmann's favorite tactics was to make a high-speed diving attack on his victim, then pull up vertically, perform a rudder reversal, and dive back down for another attack, and so on, until the target was destroyed. This tactic so confounded his Allied opponents that they dubbed it the "Immelmann Turn" and were convinced it defied the laws of aerodynamics. Once it was figured out, the technique was widely copied by both sides. Today there is a precision aerobatic maneuver known as an "Immelmann," but it varies considerably from the original. The modern Immelmann begins with the first half of a loop to the inverted position, followed by a roll to the upright attitude at the top.

> The Immelmann Turn was very successful. . . . But later, when more power-
> ful engines became available, it was a dangerous move, for the lower pilot
> could climb after the Fokker and attack when it hung almost motionless in
> the vertical position, not under full control, and presenting an easy shot.
> Air Vice-Marshal J. E. "Johnnie" Johnson, RAF

Passing directly over the bogey and then pulling down toward its six o'clock almost ensures that the opponent will lose sight of the energy fighter temporarily. Faced with these tactics, the bogey pilot essentially has only two options. He can begin to turn almost immediately in a level or slightly oblique plane, attempting to regain sight and to hamper the attacker's impending gun shot, or he can continue an unloaded diving acceleration. In the first case his guns defense is not likely to be successful because of low G available at his slow airspeed. In the second option he almost surely will not regain sight of the attacker and will be forced to guess when to perform his guns break. If he guesses correctly the guns defense should be more effective at the resulting higher airspeed. An incorrect guess should terminate the engagement.

In the event that the energy fighter pilot misses the shot at time "4," a vertical overshoot is probable. At min-range the attacker can unload or roll away from the target aircraft (quarter roll away) and continue to dive for separation. Generally his speed advantage in the dive will carry him beyond guns range before the opponent can reverse and threaten a shot. This separation and speed advantage then can be used to exit the fight or to return for another head-on pass. If the vertical overshoot is not great and the energy fighter has attained at least vertical-maneuvering speed at the overshoot, the pilot may choose to pull immediately up into another vertical pitch-back and repeat his overhead attack. However, if the overshoot carries the attacker substantially below the bogey's altitude (i.e., approaching the equivalent of one attacker turn radius), the energy fighter pilot first should climb back up near the bogey's altitude before beginning a second vertical maneuver. Otherwise the altitude advantage on the top of the second pitch-back may be less than required, resulting in an even greater overshoot on the next pass.

Some modification may be required in these tactics if the energy fighter is subject to restrictions against prolonged zero or negative G. The fuel or oil systems of many power plants may cause temporary engine stoppage or even permanent damage when engines are subjected to these operating conditions. However, the pilot of the energy fighter still may be able to make use of this tactic under these conditions by relaxing the G after the initial pull-up to a slightly positive load factor for the duration of the vertical zoom maneuver.

A well-flown bogey can counter these tactics effectively in several ways. One method is not to zoom with the energy fighter at the first pass, but instead to counter with the maneuver described by Figure 4-4. Even after he is committed to a zoom the bogey pilot can complicate matters if he recognizes his situation soon enough. In this case he can break off the zoom early, before he runs out of airspeed, by leveling-off on a heading away from the energy fighter, regaining maneuvering speed, and then coming back again, as in Figure 4-4, or attempting an escape. Normally in this situation it is not advantageous for the energy fighter pilot to continue his zoom to low airspeeds in order to maximize zoom altitude. Instead he should roll as necessary to place the bogey on the lift line and continue to pull over the top of the loop at sustained-G levels. This situation is depicted in Figure 4-6.

In this example both fighters begin a zoom at the pass, as in Figure 4-5. This time, however, the pilot of the low-T/W fighter recognizes his opponent's great energy advantage and terminates the zoom, leveling off to establish a sustainable climb angle at time "3." Once he reaches a vertical zoom attitude at time "3," the energy fighter pilot sees that his opponent is leveling off, and so he continues to pull over the top of the loop at

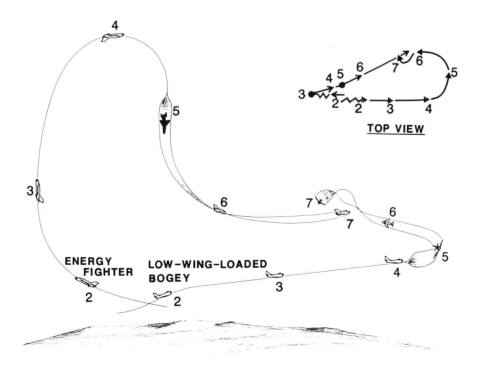

Figure 4-6. Energy Counter When Bogey Refuses to Zoom

sustained-G levels. As the energy fighter comes over the top at time "4," the bogey pilot begins a slightly climbing left turn to reengage. The energy fighter pilot continues to pull his nose down near pure vertical (time "5"), then rolls completely around to reacquire the bogey visually and to point the lift vector ahead of the bogey's current position (i.e., performs a lead roll). Once pointed downward, the energy fighter is unloaded and accelerating while performing the lead roll. The pilot continues this acceleration until approaching vertical-maneuvering speed, adjusting roll angle as necessary so that a wings-level pull-out will result in a close pass with the bogey at the next meeting. At time "6" the energy fighter pilot has begun his sustained-G wings-level pull-out. This pull-out should not be delayed any longer than necessary to achieve vertical-maneuvering speed at the bottom, since any delay can give the bogey vertical separation for a lead turn at the pass. The energy fighter pilot should resist any temptation to perform a rolling pull-out, as this wastes energy.

Approaching the pass at time "6," the bogey pilot decides to pull sharply up for vertical separation and a barrel-roll attack. If the energy fighter's pull-out has been executed properly the bogey pilot will have to do a lot of hard, energy-bleeding maneuvering to gain any substantial position advantage at the pass. In such a case the bogey is unlikely to have any vertical potential remaining. The opponent is merely attempting to intimidate the energy fighter pilot, hoping to bluff him into some energy-bleeding defensive maneuvering.

In response, the pilot of the energy fighter should be aware that his best defense is an altitude sanctuary. Defensive maneuvering should be limited to perhaps one quick out-of-plane jink, appropriately timed, followed by another pull-up (time "7"). Depending on the dynamics of the situation, this second pull-up may not have to be continued to the pure vertical. Once the energy fighter pilot determines that sufficient altitude separation will be generated by the climb and (possibly) the bogey's dive, he should terminate the pull-up immediately with a quick roll and a pull-down for a gun attack.

In the case of Figure 4-6, the energy fighter pilot was unable to avoid pulling out below his opponent at the second pass if vertical-maneuvering speed was to be reached. When possible, however, it is more advantageous to remain above the bogey's altitude throughout, so that the opponent is forced to make his attack nose-high, fighting gravity and losing more airspeed. Bottoming-out below the bogey allows it to attain a greater angular advantage at the pass and makes the enemy's bluff more believable. Except for very gross altitude overshoots by the energy fighter, however, the bogey's attack still can be adequately defeated by a quick out-of-plane jink.

> Defense against [Japanese] fighters is resolved around the superior speed of our fighters. . . . Offensive measures go according to the number of the enemy, but they are always hit-and-run because the [Zeros] can outmaneuver us about two to one.
>
> Major Richard I. "Dick" Bong, USAAF
> Leading U.S. Ace, WW-II
> 40 Victories

Engaging without an Initial Energy Advantage. All the foregoing tactics are predicated on the high-T/W fighter having a significant energy advantage at the first pass. If this cannot be assured, other methods will be required to gain this energy margin during the engagement. In order to accomplish this, it is necessary that energy performance (P_S) be optimized relative to that of the opponent. Higher T/W normally confers a P_S advantage to the energy fighter during low-G conditions, especially during unloaded accelerations and climbs. This is not necessarily so for hard-turning conditions, when the assumed larger wing or greater efficiency of the angles fighter may actually provide this aircraft with better energy performance (i.e., higher P_S for a given load factor, turn rate, or radius). Therefore, in order to optimize relative energy performance, the pilot of the high-T/W fighter needs to minimize turning and maximize low-G accelerations and climbs. Any necessary turning should be done as efficiently as possible from an energy standpoint, which usually means vertical maneuvering. Figure 4-7 illustrates how these generalities can be put into practice.

In this example the opponents approach head-on at time "1." As in previous engagements, the pilot of the low-wing-loaded bogey can be expected to attempt to generate some flight-path separation for a lead turn before the pass. The energy fighter pilot counters by turning toward the bogey to reduce lateral separation and in this way reduce the bogey's potential angular advantage at the pass (time "2").

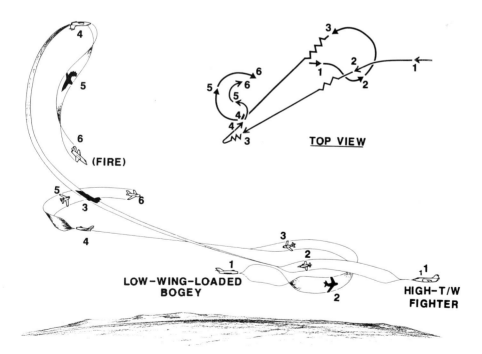

Figure 4-7. Extension/Pitch-Back Tactics

Any angles you give the bogey on the first pass will haunt you for the rest of the fight.

Lieutenant Jim "Huck" Harris, USN

Unlike in the previous example, the fighters here are assumed to have approximately equal energy (co-speed and co-altitude) at the first pass. Because of his aircraft's greater T/W the energy fighter pilot could pull up immediately and out-zoom his adversary, but this generally is not advisable. One reason for this is that the bogey may be faster than assumed. Another is the timing involved in a zooming contest. The first fighter to begin a zoom normally will peak first. Even if the low-T/W fighter cannot quite reach the same altitude, it will be considerably more maneuverable in approaching the top of its climb than the first-zooming energy fighter, which may have already peaked. At this time the energy fighter will be very slow and vulnerable as it begins to accelerate or starts back down. If the angles fighter can get close enough to threaten an attack at this point, the high-wing-loaded fighter could be in serious trouble.

To avoid this situation the energy fighter pilot accelerates to best climb speed (or, if he is faster than that, he slows by climbing steeply) and climbs straight ahead at full power. Turning during this segment should be limited to the minimum required to keep sight of the bogey. In this way the energy fighter gains separation from the bogey to preclude being menaced at the top of a subsequent zoom and also builds an energy advantage while the bogey is turning and most likely bleeding energy.

Once the bogey completes its turn and is pointed back in the general direction of its opponent (time "3"), the energy fighter pilot begins a wings-level, sustained-G pull-up to gain further vertical separation. Before its pilot commences this pull-up, the energy fighter must have at least vertical-maneuvering speed. If this value is faster than best climb speed, the climb between times "2" and "3" may have to be eliminated or cut short to allow for acceleration to the required pull-up speed. As airspeed decays in the zoom, the energy fighter pilot should constantly be reducing G to approximate the sustained-G capability of his aircraft at that speed, otherwise valuable energy will be lost in the vertical maneuver. Approaching the top of the climb (time "4") the energy fighter should be slightly faster than 1-G stall speed and be pulling only about 1 positive G while inverted.

The separation between the fighters at time "3" and the vertical maneuver of the energy fighter give the bogey pilot some breathing room between times "3" and "4." He can be expected to use this period to regain some of his energy deficit by accelerating or climbing. But since it has lower T/W, the angles fighter cannot offset all the energy margin gained by the high-T/W fighter during the earlier climbing extension. Assuming the energy fighter does not bleed energy in the zoom, it should arrive at time "4" with a significant energy advantage.

Approaching the purely vertical attitude in his pull-up between times "3" and "4," the energy fighter pilot needs to study the bogey's position and maneuver. The object is to arrive at the peak of the zoom, time "4," as near directly overhead the bogey as possible. If the bogey is still some distance away horizontally as the energy fighter reaches the vertical, it may be desirable to delay the completion of the pitch-back for a few seconds to allow the bogey to drive closer. This may be done by unloading in a near-vertical attitude and continuing the zoom. This tactic may be accompanied by profiling, as explained earlier. In this way extra altitude and time may be gained by zooming to a very slow airspeed, and then performing a rudder reversal or a pull-down at the appropriate moment.

In the case depicted, however, the bogey is near enough that the pitch-back can be continued. Therefore the pilot of the energy fighter rolls to place the bogey perpendicular to the wings, and continues to pull in an attempt to pass directly over the bogey without any horizontal maneuvering. The bogey pilot may defeat this effort by turning horizontally after the energy fighter's rolling maneuver, but this should have little effect other than further reducing the bogey's energy.

In the engagement depicted in Figure 4-7 the bogey begins a climbing oblique turn to the right at time "4." After crossing above the bogey, the energy fighter pulls steeply down toward its opponent's rear hemisphere. During the first part of this descent (between times "4" and "5") the energy fighter pilot uses lag pursuit, keeping his aircraft's nose pointed slightly behind the bogey, driving toward its extended six o'clock region. This technique results in a spiraling flight path, with most of the required heading changes accomplished by rolling the aircraft. During this period load factor should be minimized to permit greater acceleration.

This lag-pursuit technique should force the bogey pilot to turn hard and climb more steeply in order to keep sight of the diving energy fighter, thereby bleeding even more energy. At time "5" the energy fighter pilot determines that separation and angular advantage are such that an effective high-side gun attack can be initiated. Therefore he begins to turn harder, shallowing the dive angle, and pulling inside the bogey's turn by making the transition to pure, and then lead, pursuit. At time "6" the energy fighter has achieved a fairly high AOT, but it is in an effective firing position against the relatively slow and less maneuverable bogey.

In this example the high-T/W fighter's energy-performance advantage was sufficient to provide an attack opportunity after only one vertical move, but this may not always be the case. Coming over the top of the pitch-back (time "4"), the energy fighter pilot may discover that the bogey has turned early and is already near position "5," offset from directly below and much higher than before. In this situation an attack still may be possible by pulling directly into lead pursuit, turning nose-to-nose with the bogey when the maneuver is viewed from above, and reversing for the shot as firing range is approached. Usually, however, this technique results in a very steep diving approach and a high-AOT firing position that may not be effective. The steep approach also results in a large vertical overshoot after the firing pass, which could cause problems later on. Therefore, this nose-to-nose tactic is most appropriate when the energy fighter pilot intends only to take whatever shot is available at the first opportunity and then exit the fight in a high-speed diving extension.

If instead the pilot of the energy fighter intends to continue to work for an effective firing position, he still should employ lag pursuit, forcing the bogey to turn horizontally while the energy fighter is accelerating to vertical-maneuvering speed for another wings-level pitch-back. Figure 4-8 shows this tactic. In this example the energy fighter pilot comes over the top of the pitch-back at time "4" to find the bogey offset below, performing a climbing lead turn. Realizing that insufficient altitude advantage is available and too many angles have developed for an effective guns attack, the energy fighter pilot pulls vertically downward and rolls into lag pursuit, pointing the lift vector slightly behind the bogey. A rolling pull-out is continued until the aircraft has accelerated to vertical-maneuvering speed, and the roll is timed to place the energy fighter approximately opposite the course of the bogey at level-off. This technique forces the bogey to turn completely around again to pursue, and prevents it from gaining any appreciable energy. At time "5" the energy fighter can go immediately back up into a second extension and pitch-back, this time resulting in greater altitude advantage and better attack possibilities. This process can be repeated until an effective firing position is achieved or disengagement is desired.

In the descent from times "4" to "5" in Figure 4-8, it is desirable to complete the pull-out above the bogey's altitude. This keeps the bogey turning nose-high, keeps it loaded-up, and does not permit it to turn more efficiently nose-down after a vertical overshoot. Of much greater importance, however, is the attainment of vertical-maneuvering speed before the energy fighter pilot begins his next pitch-back. Scooping-out slightly below the bogey's altitude generally does not present a problem. Large vertical separations can, however, allow the bogey pilot to perform a nose-low lead turn and reach a temporary firing position during the pull-out. If forced to pull out quickly to avoid this situation, the energy fighter pilot should perform an unloaded level or diving acceleration after the pull-out to gain vertical-maneuvering speed before he attempts another pitch-back. It may be necessary to lower one wing or turn slightly to keep sight of the bogey during this extension.

One viable alternative to the climbing-extension energy tactics just discussed is the energy technique recommended for similar aircraft in the last chapter, namely, the nose-to-nose turn series at near minimum vertical-maneuvering speed, as depicted in Figure 3-4. In the case of an overly aggressive bogey, or whenever the turn-performance advantage of the angles fighter is not overwhelming, this technique may succeed in bleeding the bogey's airspeed sufficiently to permit the energy fighter to zoom safely and begin high-side guns passes.

One advantage of this method is that it facilitates keeping sight of a smaller opponent, since separations during the engagement are greatly reduced. The major drawback is that it may not be effective in the case of a dissimilar fighter. A low-wing-loaded fighter generally sustains its turn performance at a slower speed than its opponent, resulting in a smaller turn radius. This smaller radius can result in angular gains against the opponent in nose-to-nose maneuvers without bleeding energy. In addition,

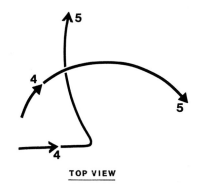

TOP VIEW

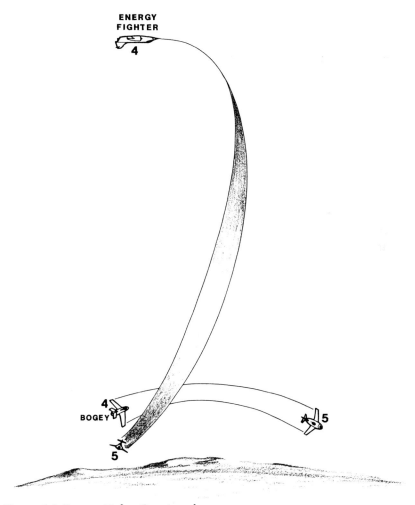

Figure 4-8. Energy Fight: Continued

the low-wing-loaded fighter's vertical-maneuvering speed is generally lower than that of its high-wing-loaded adversary, so a reduced speed can be accepted without total loss of vertical potential. Therefore, if he is patient, the angles fighter pilot can make small angular gains on each nose-to-nose turn until the energy fighter zooms with only a small speed advantage. The angles fighter pilot then may be able to zoom with his opponent and surprise him at the top of the maneuver.

The energy fighter's defense against this technique is careful observation of the bogey's maneuvering during the first few nose-to-nose turns. If after the first two turns in the series the bogey is not approaching a 90° angular advantage, the energy fighter pilot should use his superior speed to execute a nose-to-tail extension to exit the fight or to gain sufficient separation to come back, meet the bogey on neutral terms, and try something else.

Probably a better option for the energy fighter in this scenario is a sustained nose-to-tail turn. This procedure was discussed in the previous chapter; its advantages are even greater in this case. Since the low-T/W fighter seldom has a substantial sustained-turn-rate superiority, such a maneuver forces it to turn harder than sustained-G levels to gain a rapid angular advantage. The energy fighter pilot should maintain best sustained-turn-rate airspeed, or vertical-maneuvering speed, whichever is greater, in a level or climbing turn, and watch the bogey's turn performance. A shallow, climbing turn is usually preferable, since this generally induces the bogey into bleeding energy more rapidly. If it appears that the bogey will gain more than 90° advantage on the first turn, a slightly nose-low turn can be started to maintain speed while limiting the opponent's angular advantage at the pass to about 90°. In this case the energy fighter should have adequate airspeed margin at the overshoot to begin a pitch-back safely. Should the angles fighter gain substantially less than 90° after about two turns, however, the energy fighter's airspeed advantage may be inadequate. In that situation the energy fighter pilot probably should consider disengaging, since it may be better to come back the next day and hope for an easier opponent. Otherwise a nose-to-tail extension may be used to gain enough separation to come back and meet the bogey again on neutral terms. From that point extension/pitch-back tactics can be commenced.

It should be recognized that, as with economics, there is no free lunch in tactics. The tradeoffs for using the more efficient nose-to-tail turn technique, as discussed previously, include added difficulty in judging the bogey's energy and increased problems in maintaining sight. In any case, if the bogey's turn-performance advantage is very great, the energy fighter pilot may find it necessary to employ the modified spiraling pitch-back (Figure 3-10) to avoid being shot during the pull-up.

Actual combat accounts of the successful use of energy tactics are rather rare, but the following example is a beauty. Here John Godfrey's P-51B Mustang has probably 20 percent lower wing loading than the German Focke-Wulf 190D-9 opponent, and Godfrey increases his turn advantage further by skillful use of flaps. The Focke-Wulf, however, may have 20 percent better power loading. Here are two masters at work:

A plane was approaching, and because of its long nose I thought it was a Mustang. Turning into it I received a shock; it was neither a Mustang nor an ME-109, but a new Focke-Wulf; its long nose was the latest improvement of the famed FW. These planes with the longer noses were rumored to have more horsepower than their predecessors, and were capable of giving a Mustang a rough time. We met practically head-on and both of us banked our planes in preparation for a dogfight.

Around and around we went. Sometimes the FW got in close, and other times, when I'd drop my flap to tighten my turn, I was in a position to fire; but the German, sensing my superior position, kept swinging down in his turn, gaining speed and quickly pulling up, and with the advantage in height he would then pour down on my tail. Time was in his favor, he could fight that way for an hour and still have enough fuel to land anywhere below him. I still had 400 miles of enemy territory to fly over before I could land. Something had to be done. Throwing caution to the wind I lifted a flap, dove and pulled up in a steep turn, at the same time dropping a little flap. The G was terrific, but it worked, and I had the Jerry nailed for sure. Pressing the tit I waited, but nothing happened, not a damned thing. My guns weren't firing.

By taking this last gamble I had lost altitude but had been able to bring my guns to bear while flying below the FW. With his advantage of height he came down, pulled up sharp, and was smack-dab on my tail again. The 20 mm. cannons belched and I could see what looked like golf balls streaming by me. A little less deflection and those seemingly harmless golf balls would have exploded instantly upon contact with my plane. "Never turn your back on an enemy" was a byword with us, but I had no choice. Turning the plane over on its back I yanked the stick to my gut. My throttle was wide open and I left it there as I dove. The needle stopped at 600 miles per—that was as far as it could go on the dial. Pulling out I expected at any minute to have the wings rip off, the plane was bucking so much. The last part of my pull-up brought me up into clouds. I was thankful to have evaded the long-nosed FW, for that pilot was undoubtedly the best that I had ever met.[1]

Practical Aspects of the Energy Fight. Although the foregoing tactics are academically sound in a sterile environment, there are some practical considerations which complicate matters in actual combat. One of these is the difficulty of maintaining sight of the opponent. Extension/pitch-back tactics result in great distances being generated between fighter and bogey. Additionally, the pilot of the energy fighter spends much of his time looking over his shoulder at the bogey, making visual tracking even more difficult. A very small bogey may force the energy fighter pilot into reducing his extension times, thereby achieving less energy advantage during each extension. Looking over his shoulder also complicates aircraft control for the pilot of the energy fighter. For example, it is difficult to judge a wings-level attitude for commencing a pitch-back while looking backward. The aircraft's speed and altitude also may have to be judged by feel, since the pilot may not be able to afford to take his eyes off the bogey for a peek at the gauges. This can be especially hazardous during low-altitude engagements, as more than one pilot has extended himself right into the ground while looking back over his shoulder. A second crew member is very useful for these tactics, since workload can be divided between watching the bogey and monitoring aircraft performance.

Aircraft design is another factor which must be considered. Poor rearward visibility, very high vertical-maneuvering speed (i.e., well above best climb speed), poor slow-speed control qualities, or low-G power plant limitations can make these tactics impractical. Even a cloud layer can prevent offensive use of the pitch-back.

Another consideration is the possibility of other hostile fighters in the area, or even a surface-to-air missile threat. The energy fighter is exceedingly vulnerable to such threats while at slow speed near the top of a pitch-back. Also, since pilots tend to concentrate their lookout along the horizon, the pilot of an aircraft maneuvering vertically almost assures he will be seen by nearby fighters in a wide altitude band, making attack by an unseen enemy even more likely.

All these practical considerations present severe limitations to the use of energy tactics and make their employment even in sterile situations very difficult; they require much training for proficiency. The alternatives when a pilot is armed with an aircraft having inferior turn capabilities include "hit-and-run" tactics. These usually involve stalking an unsuspecting bogey, pouncing on it in one high-speed gun attack, and exiting the area. Unlike the low-T/W angles fighter, the high-speed energy fighter usually has the option of engaging and disengaging at will, especially in the guns-only environment. Another possibility is to "gang-up" on the better-turning bogey using multiple-aircraft tactics, which is the subject of later discussions.

> There is a big difference if you are in actual war or if you are playing war.
> Colonel Erich "Bubi" Hartmann, GAF

The Angles Fight: Rear-Quarter Missiles Only

The pilot of a low-wing-loaded fighter equipped only with RQ weapons can employ essentially the same tactics as for the guns-only scenario. As a matter of fact, it may be necessary for this fighter to pass through the gun-firing envelope in order to reach missile parameters, which demonstrates the value of a gun even for a missile fighter. Because of the envelope-rotation effect, as explained in the last chapter, and the superior speed of the high-T/W bogey, the angles fighter generally is unable to drive directly toward the RQ missile envelope of its opponent. As long as the bogey is faster, the angles fighter pilot must employ lead or pure pursuit in order to close the range, but both these options lead to increasing AOT against a defensively maneuvering target. Once the high-wing-loaded bogey has been bled down in energy to the point where the angles fighter is actually as fast or faster, then lag pursuit can be used to reach the missile envelope.

The angles tactics already described are designed to make use of the low-wing-loaded fighter's turn-performance superiority to gain an angular advantage steadily while inducing the bogey to bleed its energy with hard defensive maneuvering. If the pilot of a high-wing-loaded bogey allows this process to continue for too long, the patient angles fighter pilot should eventually reach a lethal missile-firing position unless the opponent makes skillful and timely use of the vertical or exits the fight. Because of its much greater range the missile can create serious limitations for the energy fighter in both vertical maneuvering and disengagement.

As an example, consider the scenario depicted in Figure 4-4, where the energy fighter zooms on the first pass. When his aircraft is equipped with a missile, the pilot of the angles fighter can be much less hesitant to zoom with his opponent. He can pull up behind the bogey and fire before the energy fighter ever reaches the top of its zoom. Just the threat of such a shot usually will cause the bogey pilot to pull too quickly over the top of his maneuver in order to increase AOT before the missile can be fired. Without even firing a missile the pilot of the angles fighter can bleed the bogey's energy and reduce its zoom altitude, forcing it back down for a lead turn. Even if the bogey succeeds in generating AOT in excess of nominal missile-firing parameters, a weapon that has adequate guidance information (usually the target's exhaust heat) still may be successful, since the target will be slow and unable to maneuver effectively in defense.

One probable ploy a high-T/W bogey may use involves climbing toward the sun. By placing his aircraft between the sun and the angles fighter, the bogey pilot may be able to avoid a hostile heat-seeking missile shot, since such a weapon most likely would be decoyed by the sun's heat. It can also become very difficult to keep sight of the opponent when a pilot is forced to look very near the sun. A dark-colored helmet visor is useful in these situations, especially one that can be flipped down into position at critical moments and removed quickly from view when not needed. Generally visors (even "clear" ones) are not recommended in the air-combat environment, since anything extra between the pilot's eyes and his adversary makes visual acquisition and tracking more difficult.

Another useful technique for watching a bogey close to the sun is to close one eye and block out the sun's disc with the palm of the hand, a thumb, or a fingertip. This technique usually is effective unless the bogey pilot positions his aircraft perfectly in the sun, which is quite difficult to accomplish.

> I closed one eye, holding the tip of my little finger up in front of the open orb, blocking out just the fiery ball of the sun in front of my opened eye. I found that it was impossible for an enemy to come down from out of the sun on a moving target without showing up somewhere outside of my fingertip if I continuously kept the fiery part from my vision.
> Colonel Gregory "Pappy" Boyington, USMC

A radar also is quite helpful in these situations for fighters so equipped. As soon as the angles fighter pilot recognizes the opponent's intention to seek sun masking, a radar lock should be established. Then, if the bogey subsequently is lost in the sun, the radar may provide valuable clues as to where to look to reacquire it visually. One dirty, rotten trick to watch for in these cases is a reversal in the sun. For instance, the bogey may appear to fly into the sun from the left side, reverse directly in the sun, when it is not visible, and come out unexpectedly on the left side.

The angles fighter pilot also can maneuver to complicate the bogey's attempts at sun masking. For instance, if the bogey begins a near-vertical zoom toward the sun, the angles fighter pilot can fly left or right, perpendicular to the opponent's flight path. Likewise, if the bogey is well above and approaches the sun from one side, the angles fighter pilot can fly horizontally toward or away from the sun with the same effect, or he can perform steep climbs or dives.

The missile's range greatly complicates the energy fighter pilot's attempts to disengage. When the bogey attempts to run, the angles fighter often can turn hard, point, and shoot before the target can exceed maximum range. This is especially true when the energy fighter pilot is most likely to disengage, that is, when he begins to feel defensive with his speed reduced and his opponent at an angular advantage. Once a missile has been fired the target usually will perform a defensive break turn, further reducing its energy. Continued defensive turning against the missile, or an attempt to preclude a firing by turning to hold the attacker at high AOT, results in arcing. The angles fighter pilot then can use lead pursuit to close the range once more and force continuation of the engagement. Firing a missile "for effect," even when the target is out of range, often will induce a defensive turn and preclude the bogey's escape.

> I started shooting when I was much too far away. That was merely a trick of mine. I did not mean so much to hit him as to frighten him, and I succeeded in catching him. He began flying curves and this enabled me to draw near.
>   Baron Manfred von Richthofen

Once angles tactics have succeeded in placing the low-wing-loaded fighter in gun-firing parameters, it may be too close and at too great an AOT for a RQ missile shot. Figure 4-9 shows how the desired position may be attained. At time "1" in this example, the angles fighter is in pure pursuit inside the bogey's turn and in its rear hemisphere, but it is too far off the target's tail for an effective RQ missile shot. (The nominal firing envelope is shown behind the target at positions "1" and "4.") The geometry of the situation is such that continued pure pursuit on the part of the angles fighter would allow it to close, but it would remain outside angles parameters until it was inside minimum firing range. The bogey is forced to continue its arcing defensive turn, since any relaxation in G allows the attacker to drift deeper into the rear hemisphere.

To begin the transition to RQ missile parameters, the attacker first pulls some lead (time "2") to increase closure. Once he is established in lead pursuit the attacker relaxes his turn, allowing the bogey to drift toward his nose at close range, then continues a lead turn to pass as closely as practical behind the bogey (time "3"). A maximum instantaneous turn is then performed to bring the nose to bear on the target before max-range is exceeded or the envelope rotates away (time "4"). By passing as close to the bogey as practical at time "3," the attacker makes

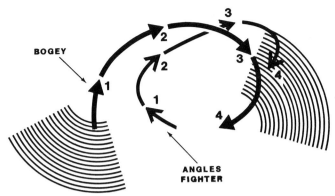

Figure 4-9. Transition to Rear-Quarter Missile Envelope

more time available for the shot before the target can open to max-range. The optimum speed for the angles fighter at time "3" is somewhat above corner speed, as this maximizes its average turn-rate capability during the turn from time "3" to time "4." Time "2" is also a good opportunity for a lag displacement roll, which may be equally effective. Note that the attacker probably passes through an effective gun snapshot envelope between times "2" and "3," and he can take advantage of it should he be so equipped.

At time "3" in this scenario, the bogey pilot may decide to reverse, probably spoiling the shot. This should only delay the inevitable, however, since the attacker can retain the offensive and repeat his transition attempt from the other side. Each time the bogey pilot performs such a hard reversal he further bleeds his energy.

Another option for the bogey at time "3" is a vertical pull-up. In this case the attacker must decide whether his performance will allow him to pull up behind the bogey and get off a shot. Obviously, vertical-maneuvering speed would be desirable at this point, but it may not be required. The angles fighter only has to get its nose high enough to point at the target and fire before running out of airspeed. This is a risky proposition, however, since if the shot is missed for some reason, the angles fighter is left in a very vulnerable position. The safer option is to extend away, as shown in Figure 4-4, and return on better terms.

The Energy Fight: Rear-Quarter Missiles Only

As difficult as the energy fight is in the guns-only environment, the substitution of RQ missiles further complicates matters, both offensively and defensively. Although the energy tactics described offer reasonable prospects of attaining a lethal gun snapshot against a low-wing-loaded adversary, this generally is not the case when the fighters are limited to RQ missile parameters. A more maneuverable fighter nearly always seems to have the turn performance necessary to rotate its lethal cone away from an opponent at just the critical moment. The exception to this is when the low-T/W bogey is very slow and is unable to create a tracking-rate problem for the missile. In such cases "RQ only" missiles can assume all-aspect capabilities. Against a well-flown bogey, however, this situation is quite difficult to generate, and even if it was possible it might take longer than combat endurance or prudence in the combat environment would allow. Against a bogey of known limited combat endurance, however, energy tactics do offer a means of remaining neutrally engaged until the bogey pilot is forced to retire for fuel considerations. At that time he becomes quite vulnerable. Running the opponent out of gas is as good as shooting him.

Because of the constraints of the weapon, the immediate goal of energy tactics in the RQ missile scenario might well be causing the opponent to lose sight. Use of extension/pitch-back tactics, as shown in Figure 4-7, can be quite effective for this purpose, especially against a larger bogey. The extension from time "2" to time "3" in this example presents the bogey pilot with a tail-aspect view of the rapidly retreating energy fighter. This reduced presented area and extended range while the bogey is in a high-G turn (which reduces the pilot's visual acuity by lowering blood pressure to his eyes) enhances the probability that the bogey pilot will lose sight during this segment.

You can't fight what you can't see.

Unknown

Another factor of prime concern to the energy fighter pilot is sun position. Whenever practical, each extension and pitch-back should be made in the direction of the sun, forcing the opponent to look up-sun as much as possible. This is particularly important in the RQ missile scenario, since maintaining sight is more difficult for the bogey pilot in such situations, and the presence of the sun also may preclude a heat-seeking missile shot during the extension or subsequent pitch-back. Both these factors are so critical in this scenario that some preengagement consideration and maneuvering, or even a level nose-to-tail turn after the first pass, may be justified so that the extension and pitch-back can be made toward the sun.

During the pitch-back itself, profiling should be used whenever practical to make visual acquisition even more difficult. Arriving at the top of the pitch-back (time "4" in Figure 4-7), the pilot of the energy fighter should attempt to pass directly over the bogey and use lag pursuit, as depicted, to spiral down toward the firing envelope. Great attention should be paid to remaining in the bogey's hard-to-watch high six o'clock region during this approach so that the energy fighter is more difficult to reacquire if the bogey pilot has lost sight. Although reaching the RQ firing envelope may be difficult, the prospects are greatly enhanced if the bogey pilot has lost sight, since the usual tendency is for him to relax his turn noticeably under these conditions. If this process does not cause the opponent to lose sight, further extension/pitch-back attempts can be made as combat endurance permits.

If during a diving attack it becomes apparent that the bogey pilot has not lost sight, the energy fighter can continue hot-side lag pursuit, forcing the opponent to continue his hard turn and discouraging a reversal. The energy fighter should maintain a respectful distance from its opponent during this maneuver, within missile-firing limits, while building speed. An overshoot and subsequent bogey reversal during this period can place the energy fighter in a hazardous position. Once he regains vertical-maneuvering speed, the pilot of the energy fighter has the option of continuing a level turn in lag pursuit until his nose is pointed toward the sun, which is normally the optimum moment for another extension. Or the energy fighter can employ the nose-to-tail extension maneuver depicted in Figure 3-12.

Along with the techniques already discussed, there are some other practical points worth mentioning about becoming invisible and staying that way during a pitch-back. For instance, the energy fighter pilot should be aware of the contrail level. Depending on air temperature and humidity, the water vapor in the exhaust of both jet and reciprocating engines may condense to form a vapor trail that can turn a small invisible fighter into an airliner, visible for a hundred miles. This is generally a high-altitude phenomenon that can be predicted fairly accurately by meteorologists. A more accurate determination of the contrail level can be made prior to engaging by checking for a contrail during a climb. It should be recognized, however, that the contrail level also is sensitive to exhaust temperature, so this check should be made at combat power when practical. For instance, jet contrails may appear at different altitudes depending on whether or not the fighter is using afterburner. The contrail most often becomes a factor approaching the top of a pitch-back in a high-altitude fight. The contrail level may require completing the vertical maneuver as quickly as possible rather than continuing a zoom to the highest attainable altitude.

Another consideration is known as the "burner puff." Many jet engines will exhaust a considerable amount of unburned fuel whenever afterburner is selected and/or deselected. This fuel may leave a puffy "cloud" or short contrail, calling attention to the fighter's position. If this is known to be a problem, the energy fighter pilot should select afterburner early in the engagement and resist the temptation to change power settings if there is any possibility that the bogey pilot has lost sight. Such changes can be made when the energy fighter is passing close to the opponent, obviously in plain view, or when it is positioned in the bogey's blind zone.

It's the little things that cost you victories.

Captain Reade Tilley, USAAF

"Vortex trails" also may cause problems for the energy fighter. These are condensation trails that are formed when air pressure is suddenly reduced as the air passes over an aerodynamic surface. Particularly prevalent in humid conditions, these condensation trails may stream considerable distances behind wingtips or other high-lift areas of the aircraft, especially when a vortex is present. Under given conditions of humidity, vortex trails may appear at a predictable G level. If the offending load factor is determined before the engagement, the energy fighter pilot might be able to reduce or eliminate vortex trails by holding G below this level during critical portions of vertical maneuvers. Under some conditions, however, vortex trails may be produced at such low G that they are unavoidable.

A natural phenomenon that actually can aid the energy fighter pilot in positioning his aircraft properly between the bogey and the sun is known as the "pilot's halo." This effect, which is caused by diffraction of sunlight around the body of an aircraft, often produces a ring of light which is visible against the terrain or clouds below. In hazy or humid conditions, this circle of light may appear to be suspended in the air and drift along beneath the aircraft that produces it. When the aircraft's shadow is visible, it will appear in the center of the halo. Therefore, when the bogey also appears in the halo its pilot must look directly at the sun to see his opponent. With a little practice the energy fighter pilot can learn to "fly" his halo over the bogey to complicate visual acquisition and tracking.

One further consideration in the energy fighter's attempt to disappear is electromagnetic emission. As mentioned earlier, many fighters are equipped with radar-warning receivers that serve to detect radar signals from enemy aircraft and display the direction of the threat to the pilot. Since the RQ heat-seeking missile generally is not dependent on radar input, the energy fighter might consider turning off his radar transmitter during an engagement with an RWR-equipped adversary. If practical, this procedure might conceal the attacker's position at a critical moment.

Because of the importance of the energy fighter's disappearing act in the RQ missile scenario, extension tactics may be more productive than the nose-to-nose or nose-to-tail options described, particularly when there are great performance differences between the aircraft. When the sun is very high and bright, when performance does not vary too widely between fighters, or when a large energy fighter is engaging a much smaller angles fighter, however, these tactics may be more useful. The greater turn performance of the angles fighter in this scenario almost necessitates use of the modified spiraling pitch-back by the energy fighter, as depicted in Figure 3-10. Special emphasis is required on pitch-back timing and use of the sun. Starting a pitch-back before the bogey is committed to an overshoot, allowing the opponent to gain too much angular advantage, failing to pull up into the sun, or misjudging the bogey's energy can be fatal.

If things do not appear to be going well, the energy fighter pilot should consider disengaging before becoming decidedly defensive. Disengaging from a missile fighter, however, can be more difficult than in the guns-only scenario. The energy fighter pilot should attempt to maintain high speed, and he should pass the bogey with minimum flight-path separation as close to head-on as practical. He can then perform an extension while turning in the nose-to-tail direction only enough to maintain sight of the bogey. It is very important to watch the opponent throughout the disengagement to observe any possible missile firing. The bogey should be held very near the rear visibility limits of the energy fighter to increase the opening velocity component. Maintaining approximately a 90° angle of bank during this extension may allow the energy fighter pilot to keep sight and reduce the requirement for turning. The nose of the aircraft can be allowed to fall, producing a ballistic flight path, which will increase acceleration and decrease altitude, both of which will reduce the bogey's maximum firing range. Viable alternatives include pulling up and extending away toward the sun, as well as ducking into a cloud, either of which should preclude a heat-seeking missile shot.

The retreating energy fighter pilot should not attempt to avoid a missile firing by turning to increase AOT, as this results in arcing, which may allow even a slower opponent to close the range and force reengagement. If a missile is fired at what appears to be near max-range, the target pilot should employ all available defensive countermeasures short of maneuvering (flares, chaff, power reduction, etc.) first, while watching the progress of the missile. A defensive break turn should be made only when the target pilot cannot stand to wait any longer. Even then, such a turn should be continued only as long as absolutely necessary before resuming the extension. If the break is delayed, the missile may run out of poop. The first indication of this is often oscillations of increasing magnitude in the missile's flight path.

The Angles Fight: All-Aspect Missiles Only

Essentially all the comments pertaining to the angles fight between similar fighters equipped with all-aspect missiles are relevant in this dissimilar-fighter scenario. The tactics discussed in relation to Figure 3-11 are particularly effective in this case because of the turn-performance advantage of the low-wing-loaded fighter. One complication might be the loss of energy resulting from the hard prefiring turn (between times "2" and "3" in Figure 3-11). After firing the missile, or if he does not take the shot for some reason at time "3," the pilot of the angles fighter should relax his turn and accelerate to regain some of this lost energy before the next pass. The subsequent maneuvering might resemble that depicted in Figure 3-3, and it could be followed by another nose-to-tail turn attempt.

The Energy Fight: All-Aspect Missiles Only

This is a very unenviable scenario for a high-wing-loaded fighter. The extension/pitch-back technique may be workable against a heat-seeking missile, provided the pitch-back is made into a high sun. The shot provided the energy fighter pilot by this tactic generally will be forward-quarter, looking almost straight down on his target, as he comes over the top of his vertical maneuver. Without proper sun protection, the energy fighter will be vulnerable to the bogey's missile during the pitch-back, as the low-wing-loaded fighter will reach a firing envelope first. Against a radar-missile-equipped opponent, this tactic is probably suicidal. Essentially the same comments apply to engaging with an initial energy advantage, as depicted in Figure 4-5, except that this method may be safer than extension/pitch-back tactics when the sun is extremely high.

Level nose-to-tail turns should be avoided, since these result in precisely the situation shown to be optimum for the angles fighter in this scenario. The nose-to-nose series introduced in the last chapter (Figure 3-4) and amplified in the discussion of energy tactics earlier in this chapter may be viable here. Nose-to-nose geometry keeps aircraft separation to a minimum and may "trap" the angles fighter inside its min-range firing requirements. If the bogey's energy can be bled sufficiently in this manner to deny it any vertical potential, a spiraling pitch-back (Figure 3-10) may result in a shot opportunity for the energy fighter. This may be the only viable tactic against a dogfight-capable radar missile, but it is still exceedingly dangerous. A competent pilot in a low-wing-loaded fighter usually can preserve enough vertical potential to get his nose up for the shot before the energy fighter can complete its pitch-back.

Coming over the top of the vertical pitch-back, the pilot of the energy fighter should attempt to fire at his first opportunity and then assume lag pursuit. Continuing in pure pursuit while diving, such as when the attacker is pressing for a better shot as min-range is approached, may result in an overshoot, with dire consequences. If the bogey is equipped with a heat-seeking all-aspect weapon, skillful use of the sun may allow multiple pitch-backs and diving attacks. Ordinarily, however, a second pitch-back after a lag-pursuit maneuver will be commenced with considerable lateral separation, possibly allowing the bogey to reach firing parameters more easily. If the energy fighter survives one pitch-back in this scenario, the pilot should probably consider himself fortunate and follow his attack with a nose-to-tail extension and disengagement as shown in Figure 3-12.

In this very difficult scenario, probably the best tactic for the high-wing-loaded fighter is to shoot first, head-on, before the first pass, and exit the fight regardless of the results of the shot. An even better alternative, when possible, is to sneak up on the enemy and shoot him in the back—unless points would be deducted for sportsmanship!

Multiple-Weapons Considerations

As discussed in the last chapter, modern fighters often carry a combination of air-to-air weapons, generally guns together with either RQ or all-aspect missiles. This offers the pilot some choice as to which weapons envelope he should attempt to satisfy first.

In the case of the low-wing-loaded fighter, the addition of the RQ missile to his arsenal has little effect on the pilot's tactics in the sterile one-versus-one environment, except to make his task somewhat easier. He should still consider the gun to be his primary weapon, but, as explained in the RQ-missile-angles-fight section of this chapter, the missile serves to deny the high-T/W bogey the option of disengaging at will. The missile also allows the angles fighter pilot to threaten his high-T/W opponent more seriously from a position of greater energy disadvantage and offers a more potent offense against the bogey's energy tactics. The gun and the rear-quarter AAM are very complementary weapons systems for the low-wing-loaded fighter.

For the high-wing-loaded fighter, however, this is not nearly so true. As previously explained, such a fighter has little chance of achieving a RQ missile envelope against a low-wing-loaded opponent who can maintain visual contact. In general, this scenario offers the high-T/W fighter two options. The high-risk option is to employ guns tactics in an effort to achieve a snapshot. More attention must be paid to sun position and pitch-back technique, however, because of the bogey's missile threat. The greatest elements of risk in this option involve the possibility of a missed gun shot and the almost inevitable low-TCA, close-range overshoot, which may allow the bogey to reverse for a missile shot. The more conservative approach is to use RQ missile tactics, firing high-angle shots down at the bogey from above, and concentrating on causing the opponent to lose sight. This approach offers better escape opportunities. A note of caution is in order here, however. Although the second option may be safer in the sterile environment, it may take more time, thereby exposing the energy fighter pilot to greater risk in a hazardous combat arena. Furthermore, the added time may not be available if combat endurance is limited.

When both aircraft are equipped with guns and all-aspect missiles, the pilot of a low-wing-loaded fighter is faced with a similar choice. Here the quick and dirty solution is the nose-to-tail turn and forward-quarter missile tactic depicted in Figure 3-11. The risk here again is that of a missed shot, possibly because of sun position, weapons-system malfunction, or missile misfire, since this tactic leaves the angles fighter open to a retaliatory shot from the bogey. The more conservative option in this case is to employ guns tactics, attempting to stay close to the bogey (by nose-to-nose turns, etc.), trapping its missile inside min-range limits. The angles fighter pilot should exercise caution, however, not to expend so much energy in attempting a gun shot that he cannot get his nose up for a missile shot if the bogey zooms. In this scenario the gun should be used more as a threat than as a primary weapon. Its function is to cause the high-T/W bogey to bleed energy and then to attempt an escape, either by zooming or diving, both of which should be fatal. The angles fighter pilot should employ guns tactics conservatively, taking any shot that is offered, but the all-aspect AAM in most cases still will be the lethal weapon. The greatest disadvantage of guns tactics is the increased time involved. In the case of a small bogey, however, this factor may be outweighed by the reduced separation distances, which facilitate maintaining visual contact.

Unfortunately for the energy fighter, the dismal prospects just described are about as good as they get in this scenario. The combination of the dogfight-capable all-aspect missile and the turn-performance superiority of the low-wing-loaded bogey is extremely dangerous. As discussed in the all-aspect-missile-energy-fight section of this chapter, nose-to-nose turns can be used to bleed the energy of an overly aggressive opponent; but the addition of the gun in this scenario makes this tactic even more hazardous and difficult. An extension and pitch-back into a high sun may be workable in the case of heat-seeking AAMs; lots of luck is required against a radar missile. One possibility, especially against a larger bogey, is a diving, nose-to-tail extension after the first head-on pass. This tactic may cause the bogey pilot to lose sight, allowing the energy fighter to come back for a shot. Even if the opponent maintains visual contact, the extension may exceed his maximum firing range until the energy fighter begins its comeback. A level or nose-low turn by the energy fighter to reengage can place the bogey in a look-down situation, possibly reducing the effectiveness of its missiles, while the energy fighter has optimum look-up. Off-boresight firing capability can be quite valuable here in the attempt to get off the first shot. It may be necessary to reduce power during the reengagement turn to delay the bogey's heat-seeking missile-firing opportunity, if it is so equipped. Full power can be reapplied after the bogey reaches min-range; but even so, this defensive tactic will result in great loss of energy, leaving the high-wing-loaded fighter very vulnerable if the bogey is not destroyed.

Dissimilar Weapons

Just as the performance of the two opposing fighters may be dissimilar, their weapons capabilities also may vary. In addition to the similar-weapons scenarios for the aircraft-performance pair already discussed, there are at least twenty possible combinations of aircraft performance and weapons loads. Obviously, covering all these possibilities would become rather tedious and is probably unnecessary. Instead, only a couple of the more likely combinations are addressed.

Until the 1950s, guns and unguided rockets were essentially the only air-to-air weapons available. At about that time the RQ heat-seeking AAM became operational. Some existing fighters were retrofitted to carry this weapon, and other new fighters were designed for its employment. Many of the new designs stressed high T/W for supersonic speed capability at the expense of wing loading and turn performance. It was theorized that the great speeds of these new fighters would preclude the classic turning dogfight, so turn performance was no longer important. Likewise, the gun would not be an effective weapon in this environment, so it was eliminated from some new designs in favor of missiles. These trends eventually resulted in combat between older, low-wing-loaded fighters equipped only with guns, and newer high-T/W fighters having guns and missiles or only missile armament.

The addition of RQ missiles for the high-T/W fighters has little effect in the sterile one-versus-one guns-only scenario already discussed. In actual combat, however, the AAM provides several important benefits. The most likely time for satisfying RQ missile-firing parameters remains those instances when the low-wing-loaded bogey pilot does not have sight of the attacker, loses sight, or attempts to escape. Under these conditions the missile affords greater lethality than the gun and usually enables a quicker kill since it does not require running the bogey down. Firing the missile also requires less time and concentration than gun shots do. All of these factors combine to make the high-T/W fighter less predictable and less vulnerable in a hostile environment. Whether or not the high-T/W missile fighter has a gun, energy tactics are considerably safer and more workable against a guns-only bogey, as the inherent high speeds and greater aircraft separation common with these methods make the opponent's task more difficult. The missile shot may be more difficult for the energy fighter to obtain, but attempting it is less risky. A missed gun shot against a low-wing-loaded opponent can leave the energy fighter slow and very defensive. For this reason (endurance and environment permitting) it may be more prudent for the energy fighter pilot to wait for the missile shot rather than to attempt a quick guns kill.

Enemy RQ missiles cause two serious problems for the low-wing-loaded gunfighter. Since an attacker can fire at much greater range with these weapons, initial visual detection of an attack is more difficult. In addition, the missile further complicates the chances of this fighter being able to escape once it is engaged. Tactics for the gunfighter would not change appreciably, however, with angles tactics still being appropriate. Maintaining an angular advantage at close range with angles tactics effectively removes the RQ missile threat. When the high-T/W bogey is not also equipped with a gun, the pilot of the low-wing-loaded gunfighter can be even more aggressive. Lack of a short-range, all-aspect weapon leaves the bogey defenseless against radical lead turns, and makes it more difficult for the bogey pilot to capitalize on an overshoot by the gunfighter.

> A fighter without a gun . . . is like an airplane without a wing.
> Brigadier General Robin Olds, USAF

During the early years of the Vietnam conflict the low-wing-loaded, low-T/W MiG-17 Fresco opposed the U.S. F-4 Phantom. With nearly a ten-year technology advantage, a powerful air-to-air radar, semi-active radar-guided Sparrow missiles, RQ heat-seeking Sidewinders, and supersonic speed capability, the Phantom might have been considered more than a match for the subsonic, guns-only MiG-17. Several extenuating circumstances, however, greatly altered the balance. The long-range, all-aspect Sparrow missile, for instance, often could not be used, since it was usually impossible to identify the target as hostile except visually at close range. By that time the MiG-17 was probably inside the weapon's min-range capabilities and tended to remain there during subsequent maneuvering. Since this missile was not "dogfight compatible," and the Phantoms generally lacked gun armament, only the RQ Sidewinder remained viable against the more maneuverable MiG. Even so, energy tactics should have allowed the F-4 to escape or to remain neutrally engaged until the MiG pilot lost sight or had to retire. Unfortunately for the Americans, the Phantom crews often were poorly trained in energy techniques, were faced with a much smaller enemy aircraft that was hard to track visually, and sometimes lacked the combat endurance for extended engagements far from their bases. These circumstances often led to hard-turning engagements, to the advantage of the MiGs. The MiGs also were generally blessed with better ground-based radar control and could spot and identify the Phantoms at long distances because the F-4 engines smoked badly. Therefore, the MiGs often reached a firing position, or at least gained substantial advantage, before being detected. The Vietnamese pilots, however, generally lacked the proficiency necessary to take full advantage of their many opportunities, and they lost somewhat more fighters than they downed in air combat.

Late in the war, U.S. Navy pilots reaped the benefits of improved air combat training provided by the newly formed Navy Fighter Weapons School (TOPGUN) at Miramar Naval Air Station in California. The following excerpt is found in *Fox Two* by Commander Randy "Duke" Cunningham. In this engagement Cunningham and his backseat Radar Intercept Officer, "Willie" Driscoll (sometimes called "Irish"), bagged their fifth victory (third on this mission) to become the first U.S. aces in Vietnam. They were flying a F-4J Phantom with semi-active radar Sparrow and heat-seeking Sidewinder missiles (no guns); their opponent was a battle-wise Vietnamese ace in a MiG-17 Fresco that was probably equipped only with guns (although at the time some were rumored to be carrying heat-seeking Atoll missiles). Under these combat conditions the F-4 is esti-mated to have a T/W advantage of about 20 percent, but a wing loading 80 percent greater than that of the MiG. Cunningham attempted to employ energy tactics in this fight and met with little success against the well-flown bogey. Frustrated, Duke finally pulled a desperate gamble and won. Incidentally, "Fox Two" is a radio call used to warn other friendly aircraft in the area of an impending Sidewinder missile launch.

As we headed for the coast at 10,000 feet, I spotted another airplane on the nose, slightly low, heading straight for us. It was a MiG-17. I told Irish to watch how close we could pass the MiG to take out as much lateral separa-tion as possible so he could not convert as easily to our six o'clock. We used to do the same thing against the A-4s back at Miramar since the two aircraft were virtually identical in performance. This proved to be my first near-fatal mistake. . . . A-4s don't have guns in the nose.

The MiG's entire nose lit up like a Christmas tree! Pumpkin-sized BBs went sailing by our F-4. I pulled sharply into the pure vertical to destroy the [enemy's] tracking solution. As I came out of the six-G pull-up I strained to see the MiG below as my F-4 went straight up. I was sure it would go into a horizontal turn, or just run as most had done in the past. As I looked back over my ejection seat I got the surprise of my life: there was the MiG, canopy to canopy with me, barely 300 feet away! . . . I began to feel numb. My stomach grabbed at me in knots. There was no fear in this guy's eyes as we zoomed some 8,000 feet straight up.

I lit the afterburners and started to outclimb my adversary, but this excess performance placed me above him. As I started to pull over the top, he began shooting. My second near-fatal mistake—I had given him a predictable flight path, and he had taken advantage of it. I was forced to roll and pull to the other side. He pulled in right behind me.

Not wanting to admit this guy was beating me, I blurted to Willie, "That S.O.B. is really lucky! All right, we'll get this guy now!" I pulled down to accelerate with the MiG at my four o'clock. I watched and waited until he committed his nose down, then pulled up into him and rolled over the top, placing me at his five o'clock. Even though I was too close with too much angle-off his tail to fire a missile, the maneuver placed me in an advantageous position. I thought I had outflown him—overconfidence replaced fear.

I pulled down, holding top rudder, to press for a shot, and he pulled up into me, shooting! I thought, "Oh, no maybe this guy isn't just lucky after all!" He used the same maneuver I had attempted, pulling up into me and forcing an overshoot—we were in the classic rolling scissors. As his nose committed I pulled up into him.

In training I had fought in the same situation. I learned if my opponent had his nose too high, I could snap down, using the one G to advantage, then run out to his six o'clock before he could get turned around and get in range.

As we slowed to 200 knots, I knew it was time to bug out. . . . The MiG's superior turn radius, coupled with higher available G at that speed, started giving him a constant advantage. When he raised his nose just a bit too high, I pulled into him. Placing my aircraft nearly 180° to follow, Willie and I were two miles ahead of him, out of his missile range, at 600 knots airspeed.

With our energy back, I made a 60° nose-up vertical turn back into the pressing MiG. He climbed right after us, and, again, with the Phantom's superior climbing ability, I outzoomed him as he squirted BBs in our direction. It was a carbon copy of the first engagement seconds earlier as we went into another rolling scissors.

Again we were forced to disengage as advantage and disadvantage traded sides. As we blasted away to regain energy for the second time, Irish came up on the [intercom], "Hey, Duke, how ya doin' up there? This guy really knows what he's doin'. Maybe we ought to call it a day."

This almost put me into a blind rage. To think some [bogey] had not only stood off my attacks but had gained an advantage on me twice!

"Hang on, Willie. We're gonna get this guy!"

"Go get him, Duke. I'm right behind you!"

Irish was all over the cockpit, straining to keep sight of the MiG as I pitched back toward him for the third time. Man, it felt good to have that second pair of eyes back there, especially with an adversary who knew what air fighting was all about. Very seldom did U.S. fighter pilots find a MiG that fought in the vertical. The enemy liked to fight in the horizontal for the most part, or just to run, if he didn't have the advantage.

Once again I met the MiG-17 head-on, this time with an offset so he couldn't use his guns. As I pulled up into the pure vertical I could again see this determined pilot a few feet away. Winston Churchill once wrote, "In war, if you are not able to beat your enemy at his own game, it is nearly always better to adopt some striking variant." My mind simply came up with a last-ditch idea. I pulled hard toward his aircraft and yanked the throttles back to idle, popping the speed brakes at the same time.

The MiG shot out in front of me for the first time! The Phantom's nose was 60° above the horizon with airspeed down to 150 knots in no time. I had to go to full burner to hold my position. The surprised enemy pilot attempted to roll up on his back above me. Using only rudder to avoid stalling the F-4 with the spoilers on the wings, I rolled to the MiG's blind side. He attempted to reverse his roll, but as his wings banked sharply he must have stalled the aircraft momentarily and his nose fell through, placing me at his six but still too close for a shot. "This is no place to be with a MiG-17," I thought, "at 150 knots . . . this slow, he can take it right away from you."

But he had stayed too long. We later found out that this superb fighter pilot, later identified as "Colonel Tomb" of the North Vietnamese Air Force, had refused to disengage when his GCI [ground-controlled intercept] controller ordered him to return to base. After the war we found out that "Tomb," presumably with 13 American aircraft to his credit, had to run for it if he were going to get down before flaming out.

He pitched over the top and started straight down. I pulled hard over and followed. Though I didn't think a Sidewinder would guide straight down, with the heat of the ground to look at, I called "Fox Two" and squeezed one off. The missile came off the rail and went straight to the MiG. There was just a little flash and I thought it had missed him. As I started to fire my last Sidewinder, there was an abrupt burst of flame. Black smoke erupted from the 17. He didn't seem to go out of control . . . the fighter simply kept descending, crashing into the ground at about a 45° angle.[2]

After the RQ missile, the next revolution in air combat was the development of truly dogfight-compatible all-aspect AAMs. Although all-aspect radar-guided missiles have been operational since the mid-1950s, it was not until the mid-1970s that these weapons had been perfected to the point where they were a factor to be reckoned with after the first pass of a visual dogfight. At about the same time there appeared all-aspect-capable heat-seeking AAMs. By this period most fighters, with or without guns, carried RQ missiles, and the more advanced fighters were sometimes adapted to (or were already compatible with) the new weapons. Thus, encounters between high-T/W fighters armed with all-aspect AAMs and low-wing-loaded aircraft having guns and RQ missiles are now possible.

For the high-T/W, high-wing-loaded fighter, the addition of all-aspect weapons greatly improves offensive potential. It is very difficult to obtain a good RQ shot against a better-turning target using the almost obligatory energy tactics, but these methods do allow a high-T/W fighter to generate high-aspect firing opportunities consistently. Unfortunately, these shots are most often of the look-down variety, which may limit their usefulness under many conditions.

Defensively, the high-T/W fighter pilot's job is made considerably more difficult by the inclusion of RQ missile armament in the opponent's arsenal. Zooms must be timed and performed more precisely, and the usual escape option of the energy fighter may no longer be available.

The pilot of a low-wing-loaded fighter in this case must be more careful of his energy state during the engagement. He can no longer afford the luxury of allowing the energy fighter to zoom with impunity to gain separation. Whenever the bogey zooms, the angles fighter pilot must either put a weapon in the air, even if only for effect, or immediately attempt an escape beyond visual range. It is even more critical in this scenario for the low-wing-loaded fighter pilot to follow the guidelines of angles tactics strictly; he must use nose-to-nose geometry to stay inside the bogey's min-range parameters, and he must remain below the opponent's altitude whenever he is positioned in the opponent's forward hemisphere.

At this time there do not seem to be any valid examples available of actual combat engagements in this scenario, although the potential certainly exists. There have been several conflicts in which these weapons mixes were matched, including the Gulf of Sidra incident (1981), the Falklands Conflict (1982), the Bekaa Valley encounters in Lebanon (1982), and the ongoing Iran-Iraq War. In all these cases, however, the high-T/W fighters equipped with all-aspect weapons also had at least parity in turn performance, if not outright superiority in instantaneous or sustained turn, or even in both. This scenario is covered in the next section.

Single-Dissimilarity Engagements

So far this chapter has discussed situations in which a low-T/W, low-wing-loaded fighter was pitted against a high-T/W, high-wing-loaded aircraft. This pairing might be termed "double dissimilarity," since there are significant differences in both of the critical performance parameters. Another likely situation is that the two fighters will be similar in one of these parameters but one aircraft will have a significant advantage in the other. For instance, both aircraft may have similar T/W, while one fighter has a significant wing-loading advantage; or both may have similar wing loading, but there is T/W disparity. These are examples of "single-dissimilarity" conditions.

Low versus High Wing Loading with Similar T/W

In this situation the low-wing-loaded fighter should enjoy a considerable instantaneous-turn-performance advantage, and also probably a significant sustained-turn superiority. Therefore, the pilot of such a fighter usually should base his tactics on this turn advantage and conduct an angles fight. Although T/W parity makes this an easier fight than that previously described for the low-T/W aircraft, it is not without danger. The low-wing-loaded fighter pilot still must be conscious of energy and not attempt to grab angles faster than his turn-performance advantage will allow. More aggressiveness is allowable because of the T/W similarity, but greed on the part of the angles fighter pilot will permit the opponent to use energy-based countertactics effectively. A good rule of thumb for the angles fighter pilot is to maintain at least vertical-maneuvering speed at each pass as protection against the opponent's possible zoom. Lower speeds are acceptable once the bogey has obviously bled its speed to the point where it lacks any significant vertical potential. Vertical-maneuvering speed for the low-wing-loaded fighter should be somewhat slower than for the high-wing-loaded adversary.

On the other side of this coin, the pilot of the high-wing-loaded fighter has a serious problem; namely, he has no performance advantage to exploit. In this case he usually should choose energy tactics, since there is at least parity in that area. He should recognize, however, that the opponent possesses the superior dogfighter and should win a one-versus-one fight, assuming the skills of the two pilots are equal. With this in mind, the energy fighter pilot should engage with the intention of evaluating the opponent's technique quickly, and then disengaging if he proves to be the Red Baron.

Because of the T/W equivalence, the climbing extension/pitch-back tactics described earlier generally are not viable. This method is based on exploiting a climb-rate superiority, which does not exist in this scenario. In order for the high-wing-loaded fighter pilot to gain an energy advantage where one does not exist initially, he must either increase energy faster than the opponent (which may be done by exploiting superior diving acceleration and high-speed energy addition rate in a diving extension), or induce the bogey to bleed energy at a faster rate (which may be accomplished by sustained-turn techniques). The latter method allows evaluation of the bogey's turn performance based on its known sustained capabilities relative to those of the high-wing-loaded aircraft.

For instance, assume that at optimum speed the high-wing-loaded fighter can sustain a 10°/sec turn rate, so that a 360° turn would require about 36 seconds to complete. If the bogey can sustain 11°/sec at its optimum speed (a 10 percent advantage, which would be considered significant), it could gain about 30° in one nose-to-tail turn without losing a single knot of airspeed relative to the opponent. Grabbing greater angles advantages than this with each turn, however, requires the bogey to pay dearly with energy. Armed with this knowledge, the pilot of the high-wing-loaded energy fighter can assess his opponent's energy management by observing the bogey's angular gains. The energy fighter pilot should set up a nose-to-tail turn at maximum sustained-turn-rate speed (or vertical-maneuvering speed, if that is higher), either level or slightly nose-high. The bogey's nose position is closely monitored, and climb angle is adjusted to allow the bogey about a 90° angular advantage at the completion of one turn. If the bogey appears to be making angles too fast, the energy fighter pilot makes the transition to a nose-low turn, maintaining speed, to slow the opponent's angular gains. When, on the other hand, a bogey appears to be gaining little angular advantage in the turn, the climb angle can be steepened, reducing G to maintain speed, to allow the opponent to gain angles more rapidly.

If the bogey is pulling lead approaching the second pass (i.e., at the end of the first turn), the energy fighter pilot may be required to perform a quick out-of-plane guns-defense maneuver before beginning a vertical pull-up to trade his energy advantage for altitude separation at the overshoot. When an opponent uses lag pursuit approaching the pass, preserving nose-tail separation to minimize his overshoot, the spiral zoom will probably be necessary to deny the bogey a shot during the pull-up.

Against an all-aspect-missile-equipped adversary, the nose-to-tail turn technique may be unusable, since it can allow the bogey to satisfy min-range parameters during the first turn. In this case the energy fighter pilot may have to employ a less efficient nose-to-nose turn instead, using essentially the same procedures but reducing speed to the slowest value consistent with vertical-maneuvering potential. This slower speed keeps turn radius low, forcing the opponent to bleed more energy for angular gains. The nose-to-nose technique should help to hold separation inside the bogey's min-range limits, while bleeding its energy nicely. The pilot of the energy fighter should not allow this maneuver to continue into a repetitive flat scissors, however, since the low-wing-loaded opponent can make further small gains on each turn without bleeding additional energy.

An opponent who refuses to accept a large angular advantage on the first turn either is very nonaggressive or is playing it smart by using his turn-performance superiority to nibble away a few degrees at a time without bleeding energy. It may be difficult for the energy fighter pilot to determine which bogey is which, but "You pays your money and you takes your chances." The nonaggressive bogey can be beaten with angles tactics, so the usual procedure is to put one aggressive move on the bogey and check its reaction. A bogey that counters this move effectively should be left alone, and the pilot of the energy fighter should employ a nose-to-tail extension to separate and disengage. If the bogey's defense is inept, the attacking pilot should jump right into its knickers. Normally a rolling scissors should be avoided against a well-flown bogey, since the opponent will usually be better in this maneuver unless he is at a considerably lower energy state.

High versus Low T/W with Similar Wing Loading

In this scenario the high-T/W fighter should have an acceleration and climb-rate advantage as well as better sustained turn rate and faster top speed. Instantaneous-turn capability, however, should be similar. The pilot of a high-T/W fighter in this case can employ either angles or energy tactics, but angles methods are probably preferable since they are quicker, less complex, and more offensive. The angles fighter pilot can be quite aggressive in such a fight, since his T/W advantage offers insurance against an opponent's possible energy tactics.

If the high-T/W fighter pilot chooses the energy fight, climbing extension/pitch-back tactics are normally very effective, but other methods should also be useful. The energy fighter pilot can try to grab an initial angular advantage, then use lag pursuit and allow his sustained-turn superiority to bleed the bogey's energy in nose-to-tail turns. Once the opponent has neutralized the angular advantage, or gained a small one of his own, the energy fighter pilot can begin vertical maneuvering. The initial vertical move is generally a climbing spiral begun across the circle from the bogey. A wings-level vertical pull-up might also be workable, provided the bogey is equipped with guns only. Otherwise the wide lateral separation at the moment of the pull-up may allow the bogey to pull its nose up, point, and shoot as the energy fighter nears the top of its zoom.

Bleeding the bogey's energy by using offensive lag pursuit may take several turns, since it is up to the low-T/W opponent in this case to decide how fast he wishes to trade energy for angles. The bogey can prolong this fight considerably by turning nose-low, trading altitude for turn rate while maintaining speed. In this case the energy fighter pilot generally should follow the bogey down, maintaining a small altitude advantage, since the opponent can use the vertical separation for a zooming lead turn and a snapshot if the altitude differential is allowed to build too far. Likewise, diving on the bogey from a considerable height advantage tends to give back any energy margin gained, and may result in a vertical overshoot and a rolling scissors. Since the lower bogey has maintained speed and now has energy equivalence, it may gain a temporary advantage in this maneuver. Therefore, it is preferable simply to follow the bogey down from slightly above until it reaches low altitude and is forced to begin trading speed for turn rate. Once the bogey has been bled to a slow speed it will be much easier to handle.

A beautiful example of this process is found in an engagement between Baron Manfred von Richthofen (ten victories at the time) and the first British ace, Major Lanoe Hawker (nine victories), on 23 November 1916. The German was flying an Albatros D-II against the British de Havilland DH-2. The fighters were roughly equivalent in turn performance, but the Albatros had a significant climb and top-speed advantage. This is the way von Richthofen described the fight in his book *The Red Air Fighter*. (No dissenting version is available!)

> The Englishman tried to catch me up in the rear while I tried to get behind him. So we circled round and round like madmen after one another at an altitude of about 10,000 feet.

First we circled twenty times to the left, and then thirty times to the right. Each tried to get behind and above the other.

Soon I discovered that I was not meeting a beginner. He had not the slightest intention to break off the fight. He was travelling in a box which turned beautifully. However, my packing case was better at climbing than his. But I succeeded at last in getting above and beyond my English waltzing partner.

When we had got down to about 6,000 feet without having achieved anything particular, my opponent ought to have discovered that it was time for him to take his leave. The wind was favourable to me, for it drove us more and more towards the German position. At last we were above Bapaume, about half a mile behind the German front. The gallant fellow was full of pluck, and when we had got down to about 3,000 feet he merrily waved to me as if he would say, Well, how do you do?

The circles which we made around one another were so narrow that their diameter was probably no more than 250 or 300 feet. I had time to take a good look at my opponent. I looked down into his carriage and could see every movement of his head. If he had not had his cap on I would have noticed what kind of a face he was making.

My Englishman was a good sportsman, but by and by the thing became a little too hot for him. He had to decide whether he would land on German ground or whether he would fly back to the English lines. Of course he tried the latter, after having endeavoured in vain to escape me by loopings and such tricks. At that time his first bullets were flying around me, for so far neither of us had been able to do any shooting.

When he had come down to about 300 feet he tried to escape by flying in a zig-zag course, which makes it difficult for an observer on the ground to shoot. That was my most favourable moment. I followed him at an altitude of from 250 feet to 150 feet, firing all the time. The Englishman could not help falling. But the jamming of my gun nearly robbed me of my success.[3]

The pilot of a low-T/W fighter in such a scenario has definitely got his hands full, since he really has no performance advantage to exploit. He will have a very difficult time winning an energy fight against a pilot of similar ability, and an angles fight will be no picnic, either. However, his turn-performance equivalence (in instantaneous turns) favors angles tactics. This needs to be a fairly patient angles fight, using nose-to-nose turns and working below the bogey, as explained previously. If the opponent is able to gain too great an altitude advantage in a zoom to be threatened, the angles fighter pilot can attempt to gain separation by diving away and then coming back hard to meet the bogey nearly head-on to begin the fight anew. Escape is generally not available to the pilot of the slower fighter, unless he can cause his opponent to lose sight. Probably the most useful piece of equipment the low-T/W fighter pilot can have in such an engagement is a radio with which to call for help.

Double-Superior and Double-Inferior Conditions

The quality of the box matters little. Success depends upon the man who sits in it.

Baron Manfred von Richthofen

A "double-superior" condition occurs when one fighter has both significantly higher T/W and lower wing loading than its opponent. Obviously the unlucky adversary in this situation is "double inferior."

> Only the spirit of attack borne in a brave heart will bring success to any fighter aircraft, no matter how highly developed it may be.
>   Lt. General Adolph Galland, Luftwaffe

Double superiority is a condition for which a fighter pilot would gladly trade several semi-essential parts of his anatomy. A double-superior fighter has the speed and acceleration to force an opponent to fight, and the maneuverability to win the fight. In such a situation the superior fighter generally should choose angles tactics, for a variety of reasons. This method is generally quicker and easier, it facilitates maintaining sight, and allows the opponent fewer weapons-firing opportunities and less chance of escape. The pilot of the superior fighter can be quite aggressive in this scenario, using his turn performance to gain advantage and relying on his power to keep him out of trouble. Lower minimum vertical-maneuvering speed and higher P_S provide a measure of safety against the bogey's possible energy tactics, but the angles fighter pilot can still lose this fight if he tries hard enough. If he races around with fangs out and hair on fire, with total disregard for energy, he may allow even an inferior opponent to gain a substantial energy advantage and convert this to a temporary but lethal position advantage. This usually can be avoided by allowing the superior aircraft to do the job at its own pace, which normally will be fast enough. Aside from overaggressiveness on the part of the pilot, speed control is the superior fighter's greatest problem. Excess power often results in excess speed and a tendency to overrun or overshoot the adversary. Under the best of circumstances such overshoots prolong the fight, which, particularly when missiles are involved, may be fatal. Judicious use of power is the key here. In the sterile, one-versus-one engagement, the pilot of the superior fighter normally should attempt to keep his speed the same as, or slightly below, that of his opponent.

The pilot of the inferior fighter in this scenario has real problems. He may not be able to avoid engagement, and he may not be able to escape once he is engaged. These problems may be alleviated, however, by a very thorough aircraft preflight inspection, followed by a decision to spend the day in the bar. If this luxury is not available, high-speed hit-and-run tactics or multiple-aircraft engagements may offer some relief; otherwise the pilot of the inferior fighter must be very good and very lucky.

> If he is superior then I would go home, for another day that is better.
>   Colonel Erich "Bubi" Hartmann, GAF

With an inferior aircraft, victory in one-versus-one combat must come through superior tactics and better technique. Because energy tactics are so much more complex than angles tactics, they tend to magnify variations in pilot ability. This is one reason energy tactics are recommended for this scenario. Another factor is the increased time involved. Besides prolonging the agony, energy techniques may allow the pilot of the inferior fighter to hold the opponent off until he loses interest or is forced to withdraw for fuel considerations. The high-G descending nose-to-tail turn is ideal for this purpose. If the opponent is equipped with RQ missiles, this tactic may allow the pilot of the inferior fighter to hold the bogey just far enough off the tail to prevent a weapons firing while he unexpectedly reduces power or uses speedbrakes to slow down and thereby generate rapid closure with the opponent. Then at the critical moment he can make a break turn toward the bogey to produce an overshoot. If the bogey pilot does not recognize this ploy soon enough and immediately quarter roll away and pull up, the inferior fighter may be able to reverse for a cheap shot. If the bogey does pull up nearly vertically, the defender may have a chance to unload and accelerate down and away, generating separation to prolong the fight, or even causing the bogey pilot to lose sight. When the bogey is gun equipped, the defender should expect a snapshot prior to the overshoot and be prepared to defeat it with a sharp, out-of-plane jink.

Climbing extension/pitch-back tactics cannot be expected to work for the inferior fighter in this scenario, since the opponent has a P_S advantage. The other energy tactics discussed, which are intended to bleed the bogey's energy with a nose-to-tail turn (or nose-to-nose in the case of a very small bogey or one equipped with all-aspect missiles), can still be effective against an inexperienced or a careless opponent.

The following episode, found in *Thunderbolt!* by the World War II USAAF ace Robert S. Johnson, is one of the best examples available of the use of energy tactics (diving extension/pitch-back) to defeat a double-superior opponent. The encounter described is a mock combat engagement over England between Johnson (P-47C) and an unidentified RAF pilot in a new Spitfire IX. The Spitfire had about a 25 percent better power loading and nearly a 25 percent lower wing loading. The Thunderbolt's only performance advantages were faster top speed, greater acceleration in a dive (because of the P-47's heavier weight and higher density), and better roll performance. (See the Appendix for a discussion of roll and acceleration performance.) Johnson, undoubtedly one of the greatest natural fighter pilots of all time, used his roll performance defensively to allow himself the chance to build an energy advantage in a diving extension.

> We flew together in formation, and then I decided to see just what this airplane had to its credit.
>
> I opened the throttle full and the Thunderbolt forged ahead. A moment later exhaust smoke poured from the Spit as the pilot came after me. He couldn't make it; the big Jug had a definite speed advantage. I grinned happily; I'd heard so much about this airplane that I really wanted to show off the Thunderbolt to her pilot. The Jug kept pulling away from the Spitfire; suddenly I hauled back on the stick and lifted the nose. The Thunderbolt zoomed upward, soaring into the cloud-flecked sky. I looked out and back; the Spit was straining to match me, and barely able to hold his position.
>
> But my advantage was only the zoom—once in steady climb, he had me. I gaped as smoke poured from the exhausts and the Spitfire shot past me as if I were standing still. Could that plane *climb!* He tore upward in a climb I couldn't match in the Jug. Now it was his turn; the broad elliptical wings rolled, swung around, and the Spit screamed in, hell-bent on chewing me up.

This was going to be fun. I knew he could turn inside the heavy Thunderbolt; if I attempted to hold a tight turn the Spitfire would slip right inside me. I knew, also, that he could easily outclimb my fighter. I stayed out of those sucker traps. First rule in this kind of a fight: don't fight the way your opponent fights best. No sharp turns; don't climb; keep him at your own level.

We were at 5,000 feet, the Spitfire skidding around hard and coming in on my tail. No use turning; he'd whip right inside me as if I were a truck loaded with cement, and snap out in firing position. Well, I had a few tricks, too. The P-47 was faster, and I threw the ship into a roll. Right here I had him. The Jug could outroll any plane in the air, bar none. With my speed, roll was my only advantage, and I made full use of the manner in which the Thunderbolt could whirl. I kicked the Jug into a wicked left roll, horizon spinning crazily, once, twice, into a third. As he turned to the left to follow, I tramped down on the right rudder, banged the stick over to the right. Around and around we went, left, right, left, right. I could whip through better than two rolls before the Spitfire even completed his first. And this killed his ability to turn inside me. I just refused to turn. Every time he tried to follow me in a roll, I flashed away to the opposite side, opening the gap between our two planes.

Then I played the trump. The Spitfire was clawing wildly through the air, trying to follow me in a roll, when I dropped the nose. The Thunderbolt howled and ran for earth. Barely had the Spitfire started to follow—and I was a long way ahead of him by now—when I jerked back on the stick and threw the Jug into a zoom climb. In a straight or turning climb, the British ship had the advantage. But coming out of a dive, there's not a British or a German fighter that can come close to a Thunderbolt rushing upward in a zoom. Before the Spit pilot knew what had happened, I was high above him, the Thunderbolt hammering around. And that was it—for in the next few moments the Spitfire flier was amazed to see a less maneuverable, slower-climbing Thunderbolt rushing straight at him, eight guns pointed ominously at his cockpit.[4]

V/STOL and Helicopter Tactical Considerations

Progress in aviation and weapons technology has begun to result in several types of "unconventional" fighter aircraft. Among these are vertical/short-takeoff and -landing (V/STOL) fighters, and helicopters.

V/STOL versus Conventional Fighters

There are currently two distinct variations in V/STOL design. The first of these to be considered is the thrust-vector type, typified by the British Harrier. This design has four jet exhaust nozzles that can be pivoted to direct the exhaust directly astern, or downward, or even slightly forward. Two nozzles are located behind and two forward of the CG, so that the aircraft can be supported in a hover by the four downward columns of jet exhaust, much like the legs of a four-poster bed. The Harrier has only a single engine, but fighters of this type with multiple engines could follow. While it is at very slow speeds the fighter's attitude is controlled by small reaction jets of engine bleed air located in the nose and/or tail and on the wing tips.

In order to takeoff and land vertically, this fighter must have a T/W of greater than 1. When the aircraft is heavily loaded with fuel and ordnance, however, weight may exceed thrust; in this case the aircraft requires a short horizontal run and assistance from the wings to get airborne or to land safely. Also, since jet thrust is diminished by high altitude or hot temperatures, horizontal takeoff and landing runs may be required under some operating conditions, even at low weights. Still, the short-takeoff and -landing capability allows operations to take place from short, makeshift airfields in forward battle areas, from battle-damaged runways, and from the decks of ships.

The second type of V/STOL fighter is the lift-fan design, such as the Russian Yak-36 Forger. This type incorporates one or more (two in the Forger) lift jets that exhaust only downward; these are used in conjunction with the main engine(s). The primary engine of the Forger has two pivoting exhausts located in the rear, much like the Harrier, to vector the thrust downward or aft. The lift jets support the front of the aircraft and the main engine supports the rear during a hover.

The added capabilities of V/STOL fighters are not achieved without penalties. The primary limitations of these designs are short range and low ordnance-carrying capability in comparison to conventional fighters of similar technological level. The requirement for high thrust and low weight leaves little margin for large structures, great amounts of fuel, or large ordnance loads. Such fighters, therefore, are usually small, lightly armed, and lightly armored, with limited radius of action and combat endurance. Although T/W and wing loading must be compared to those of an opposing aircraft for them to have much relevance to fighter performance, some generalizations can be made. Since improved landing and takeoff performance is provided by a vertical thrust component, large wings are unnecessary. In addition, large wings reduce high-speed performance and add weight, so V/STOL fighters tend to have relatively small wings and high wing loading, which can degrade turn performance. Even so, inherent high T/W generally keeps sustained turn performance rather high. Instantaneous turn performance, however, is likely to suffer because of high wing loading.

Some V/STOL fighters can improve their instantaneous turn performance through a technique known as "VIFFing" (vectoring in forward flight), in which thrust vectoring can be used to assist the wings. By pointing the exhaust downward (relative to the aircraft), thrust vectoring increases instantaneous load factor by about 1 G. Under slow-speed, low-G conditions this feature might double instantaneous turn performance, but at high speed and high G its effect would be minimal. This increased turn performance also must be paid for, however. Since essentially all the thrust is directed downward, there is no forward component to oppose drag, and therefore the aircraft will decelerate even faster than a conventional fighter performing a similar maneuver. The V/STOL fighter operating in this way needs all that good T/W to accelerate out of its energy hole after the turn.

Not all V/STOLs have the option of using thrust vectoring in this manner. In particular, the lift-jet designs often have intake covers that open outwardly to deflect air into the lift fans. These deflectors may have airspeed limitations, and if not, they would certainly act as speedbrakes, further increasing deceleration. Another problem with the lift-fan/lift-jet design is fuel flow. Cranking up those jets for a magic turn can double total fuel flow and greatly decrease combat endurance. The lift jets usually are intended for use during takeoff and landing, and they must be carried as dead weight during the rest of the mission. This feature generally increases aircraft weight and decreases fuel storage space, and it also may result in installation of a smaller main engine. All these handicaps tend to reduce T/W and the combat endurance of the lift-jet V/STOL variety, which is usually inferior to the pure thrust-vector type.

The unique characteristics of the V/STOL fighters make them well suited to energy tactics. Their good sustained turn, acceleration, and zoom capabilities can be capitalized on by energy methods. Some models are able to vector exhaust nozzles well forward for use as airborne thrust reversers. This feature provides very rapid deceleration and, possibly in conjunction with increased instantaneous turn performance, may be useful in preventing or causing overshoots. Rapid deceleration is also invaluable in the early stages of a flat scissors or a defensive spiral. Normally, VIFFing should be reserved for such defensive or terminal-offensive situations.

One glaring exception to this rule, however, is the vertical reversal after a zoom climb. If the rear nozzles can be deflected downward (toward the belly of the aircraft) while the fighter is near vertical in a slow-speed zoom climb, the aircraft can be made to pitch forward and "swap ends" very quickly to point down at the bogey. Alternatively, thrust vectoring may be used to increase G over the top of a more conventional looping maneuver. This capability, as well as the usually fine sustained turn performance and good slow-speed control, also can make this a very mean opponent in a rolling scissors. All these attributes, and small size, often result in a very fine energy fighter; but energy tactics and the added complexity of operating this type of aircraft require highly skilled pilots and extraordinary air-to-air training.

The ability to swivel rear-mounted exhaust nozzles of a fighter upward relative to the aircraft makes a V/STOL or other thrust-vector fighter more compatible with angles tactics. When combined with an airframe that is well behaved at a high angle of attack, VIFFing, much like the thrust-vector control system discussed earlier for missiles, can cause a fighter to pivot about its CG and literally swap ends at virtually any airspeed. The ability to point quickly in any direction can be extremely valuable, particularly when the aircraft is equipped with all-aspect missiles. Again, however, such thrust-vector maneuvers should be used judiciously because of the rapid energy dissipation that results.

The hover capability of the V/STOL is often highly overrated in the air-to-air environment. First of all, most V/STOLs lack hover capability at realistic operating weights and altitudes. Even if these aircraft could stop in midair, attitude control is usually not adequate for aiming boresight weapons at an enemy fighter unless the bogey flies in front of the weapon. Off-boresight weapons may make this tactic slightly more feasible; but still, a motionless aircraft presents an all-aspect heat source and is a sitting duck for nearly any weapon in the enemy's arsenal, either air-to-air or surface-to-air. (The Doppler radar-guided AAM is a notable exception to this rule.)

For a conventional fighter opposing a V/STOL, angles tactics usually will be more appropriate. The angles fighter pilot must be mindful of the V/STOL bogey's ability to generate overshoots and be ready to quarter roll away and pitch off high in case the V/STOL slaps on a "bat-turn." In such a case the bogey pilot has most likely forfeited his vertical capability for increased turn performance, so the angles fighter pilot should find a safe sanctuary at higher altitude, provided he has practiced good energy management himself. If the pilot of the angles fighter allows himself to get well below vertical-maneuvering speed, such an overshoot probably will result in a flat scissors, placing him in deep and serious kimchi. The rolling scissors also should be avoided unless the V/STOL bogey is obviously low on energy, like after a magic turn; and a defensive spiral must be rejected at any cost. In short, the pilot of the conventional fighter often will obtain the best results from the early use of careful angles tactics to keep pressure on the V/STOL bogey and deplete its energy. Then, when the V/STOL pilot decides to use his VIFFing ability for slow fighting, the angles fighter pilot can revert to energy tactics. If the engagement cannot be ended quickly, and the bogey is allowed to regain its energy, it may be necessary for the pilot of the conventional fighter to resume angles tactics once more.

Helicopters versus Conventional Fighters

Although helicopters generally have not been considered air-to-air machines in the past, many current attack helos are heavily armed and can offer some interesting problems to fixed-wing fighters. When compared with conventional jet fighters, helos are so slow they can't get out of their own way, so they simply do not have the capability to seek out and offensively engage faster aircraft. Therefore, engagements are most likely to occur while the helo is out minding its own business, or making life miserable for enemy ground forces. Although the helo probably will be the attackee rather than the attacker at the start of the engagement, a well-flown helicopter is far from defenseless.

> The primitive can also be a weapon.
>
>   Lt. General Adolph Galland, Luftwaffe

One of the helo pilot's first defensive actions when he is faced with a fixed-wing attack is to dive to as low an altitude as possible and accelerate to max-speed while turning toward the attacker. This reaction serves many purposes. Very low altitude operation degrades the bogey's weapons systems by denying its pilot the look-up necessary to optimize radar operation and the guidance capabilities of heat-seeking and radar-guided missiles. Simply flying at low level is sufficient to defeat most pulse-type radars, which cannot distinguish the target from the ground return (clutter). Although sophisticated pulse-Doppler (PD) radars are theoretically capable of detecting and tracking a low-flying target, their operation usually will be degraded by a "jamming" effect inherent to the helicopter rotor. Since the PD radar sees only moving objects, the real target will appear to be surrounded by many other "targets," as each of the rotor blades alternately increases and decreases its speed over the ground with every revolution. A Doppler radar and missile normally will have great difficulty maintaining a steady track on the helo itself with all this distraction, which can result in erratic guidance, increasing miss distance, and possibly missile-ground impact. This phenomenon also plays havoc with most Doppler-rate fuzes, causing early fuzing and warhead detonation. Active fuzes have problems in this environment, too, as they are susceptible to detonation on ground return before detecting the target. When the attacker's primary weapon is known to be a Doppler-type radar missile, the helo pilot may choose to fly at roughly right angles to the bogey's approach, which (as described in Chapter 1) should eliminate the primary radar return completely, or at least hide it in the ground clutter. This tactic leaves only the rotor blades as radar targets and further complicates the missile's task. Hovering motionless would serve the same purpose, but that tends to make the helo highly vulnerable to other weapons.

Flying toward the attacker has other benefits. The increased closure reduces the bogey's firing time for either guns or missiles, and if the attacker attempts to track the helo visually to fire a boresight weapon, the moving target causes the shooter to steepen his dive angle rapidly. This is a very uncomfortable maneuver for the pilot of a high-speed fighter close to the ground, and it often causes the attacker to break off a firing pass before reaching his most effective range. Pointing at the attacker also tends to hide the helo's jet exhaust from a heat-seeking missile.

Low-level flying is the bread and butter of most helo drivers, and they are very comfortable in this environment. Not so with the average fighter jock, who is likely to be quite uncomfortable attempting to bring weapons to bear against a moving, highly maneuverable, low-level target. This factor is of great advantage to the helo. The helo pilot also should be aware of the background he is presenting to his opponent and use any available opportunity to make things as difficult as possible for the bogey. This can be done by positioning over variegated terrain, which blends most closely with the helo's color scheme. Dark camouflage over dark terrain works best, since shadows may tend to highlight the low-flying helo on sunny days over a light-colored surface. Mottled terrain is usually more effective than uniform colors, unless the aircraft camouflage matches the terrain very closely. Trees, shadows, and hills can also be very useful hiding places. Water, tall grass, and dusty areas usually should be avoided because of rotor effects on these surfaces. At best, low-flying aircraft are very difficult to spot and track visually. With a little effort they can be made almost invisible.

The helo pilot should also attempt IR masking when he is faced with a heat-seeking missile threat. Visual masking and IR masking are often mutually exclusive, however, since hot, usually light-colored desert backgrounds offer the greatest problems for IR missiles. Such unlikely surfaces as water and snow can also be quite effective reflectors of IR energy, particularly if the bogey is attacking toward a bright sun.

As a fighter, the helicopter is the very epitome of a low-T/W, low-wing-loaded aircraft, being blessed with exceptional turning capability but very poor energy performance when compared with fixed-wing fighters. Therefore angles tactics, as described earlier in this chapter and in Chapter 3, can be applied by the helo in their purest form. Helo weapons useful in the air-to-air arena most often include flexible guns, manually aimed or turret-mounted; fixed, forward-firing guns; unguided rockets; and heat-seeking AAMs. A helo's gunsights, however, are seldom optimized for the air-to-air arena, so unguided weapons require lots of Kentucky windage for use against high-speed fighters.

Once the immediate priorities of getting to low altitude and turning toward the attacker have been accomplished, the helo is faced with defeating any possible firing attempt made by the bogey prior to the first pass. The attacker's job is made more difficult if the helo is not flown directly toward the bogey, but at an angle of 30° to 45° instead. This tactic forces the attacker to turn in order to establish lead for a gun shot, unguided rockets, or bombs (that's right, bombs!), or to track with a boresight missile. Once the bogey is established on the proper heading for releasing its weapon and is approaching firing range, the helo should turn sharply toward the attacker and pull him across the nose to the opposite side. This forces the bogey to turn in order to reestablish the proper lead or boresight heading. As the attacker approaches the proper heading again, the helo can pull him across the nose once more, keeping the attacker's nose out of phase and spoiling the shot. One or two of these jinks should be all that are required before the bogey reaches minimum firing range. Helos equipped with forward-firing, turret-mounted guns may be able to bring the attacker under fire during much of his approach, even during this jinking process. The opportunity to fire an all-aspect missile head-on should not be passed up either, probably as the bogey crosses the nose during a jink. The helo's look-up angle should provide better target discrimination, making this shot more effective than the similar, but look-down, firing by the attacker. A few dozen unguided rockets thrown up in front of the attacker prior to the pass can also have a startling effect on his marksmanship.

> Being under fire is bad for the nervous system.
> Captain Willy Coppens
> Leading Belgian Air Force Ace, WW-I
> 37 Victories (36 of Which Were Tethered Balloons)

Although no self-respecting fighter pilot would carry a bomb, there is no telling what kind of low-life may be met over a battlefield, so such an attack must be considered. Should some sort of ballistic projectile be seen falling from the enemy aircraft, the helo should immediately turn away from the predicted impact point and make tracks to gain separation as rapidly as possible. The chances of actually being hit by such a bomb are small (especially when it is dropped by a fighter pilot), but the fragments from typical bombs can be lethal more than 2,000 ft from the point of detonation.

Approaching the pass, the helo pilot should try to generate some flight-path separation and lead-turn the bogey, as recommended for the angles fighter in previous scenarios. Because of the helo's very tight turn radius, even minimal lateral separation can be converted to large angular gains at the pass. If the bogey continues straight or pulls up after the pass, the helo driver can continue to pull the nose around for a shot before the target extends out of range. Should a shot at this point be unsuccessful, and the bogey exceeds max-range, the helo pilot might think of making a break for some protected area or hiding place. If such a safe haven is not available, or if the helo driver begins to like playing fighter pilot, he may choose to pursue the bogey, wait for it to turn around, and repeat the head-on pass tactics. Unless the helo pilot has considerable air-to-air experience, however, this is probably a mistake.

If the bogey pulls sharply vertical at the pass and the helo pilot cannot make a shot, he should follow the attacker at low altitude and attempt to get beneath the bogey as it completes the vertical maneuver. This ploy makes a second attack by the bogey more difficult, since it would necessitate a steep dive angle. Pilots usually will avoid steep dives at low altitude for fear of misjudging the pull-out and hitting the ground. As the bogey approaches overhead, the helo can pull up in an oblique climbing turn beneath the attacker for a look-up, RQ weapons firing, or it can at least hide beneath the opponent, forcing him to turn hard to regain sight.

Returning to the first pass for a moment, if the fixed-wing bogey turns hard toward the helo, taking out most of the lateral separation and preventing an effective lead turn, the helo might have trouble turning around fast enough to get a shot. If this happens, the helo can continue the classic angles tactics illustrated by Figure 3-1; that is, reverse nose-to-nose. In this case, however, there is such a large disparity in speed and turn radius that a simple reversal and a level nose-to-nose turn should quickly place the helo inside the opponent's flight path, making it impossible for the pilot of the fixed-wing fighter to get his nose pointed at the helo for another attack. The helo pilot should continue the turn for at least 90°, then straighten out or reverse into a gradual lead turn, maintaining 20°–30° of lead on the bogey. Care should be taken not to turn so hard in the lead turn that the helo flies out in front of the bogey. This situation can be anticipated by watching the bogey's drift against the far horizon, and ensuring that this apparent motion is always forward. Ultimately, if the bogey continues its turn, the helo pilot can play his lead turn to arrive at a close-range gun-firing position or within RQ missile parameters. An all-aspect-missile-firing opportunity may be available soon after completion of the nose-to-nose turn, provided min-range parameters can be met.

Now for the other side of this coin. How does a fixed-wing fighter attack a helo? It has been shown that a helo can be a very difficult opponent, but the fixed-wing fighter does have some advantages that can be exploited. For one thing, odds are the helo driver has very little air-to-air experience, so he may not be as serious a threat as the foregoing discussion might suggest. Still, caution and deviousness form the best policy.

First there is the matter of what weapons to use, given the fighter pilot has a choice. The gun can be very effective against helos, particularly when the attack is unseen; but, as discussed, scoring against an evasive helo can be quite difficult and may subject the fighter to return fire. In addition, most radar lead-computing gunsights are more than worthless in this environment because of ground clutter and rotor-blade effects. The attacker may find a simple fixed sight more effective, especially at low altitudes. Stories are told of an Israeli fighter pilot who made eight gun passes on a helo before switching to a fixed gunsight for the kill. Unguided rockets, fired in large salvos, can be lethal weapons, since greater dispersion increases the probability of a hit, and increased firing range can keep the attacker outside the helo's effective guns range. The helo pilot's not likely to do much shooting anyway once he sees a flock of rockets headed his way! Rockets fired singly, however, offer little chance of success.

Although any real fighter pilot hates to admit it, bombs may be the best low-altitude anti-helo weapon. The kill mechanism here is not necessarily a direct hit, which would be very difficult to achieve against an evasive target, but the rather large fragmentation pattern. With a typical 500-lb bomb, a 500-ft miss would probably be sufficient to do some damage to a low-flying (i.e., below 1,000 ft) helicopter. Even this degree of accuracy is not easy to achieve, however, against a moving, evasive target that must be led considerably when the bomb is released. Retarded bombs are usually best for this purpose. (*Retarded* does not relate to the bomb's intelligence level, but refers to high-drag devices that retard the bomb's speed after its release, allowing the bomber greater separation from the frag pattern before weapon impact.) Retarded weapons allow the bomber to release much lower and closer to the target for improved accuracy, and their shorter time of fall (because of a closer release) allows the target less time for evasive action. Although such close releases may bring the fighter within the target's gun range, the helo pilot is likely to lose all offensive intentions once the bomb is in the air.

One notable exception to this technique occurs when the helo is equipped with all-aspect heat-seeking missiles. In this case a low-altitude bomb run at high speed and power setting may allow the helo a forward-quarter, look-up missile shot before the fighter reaches the bomb-release point. A better method of attack would be to approach the helo at high altitude and low power setting, well above its missile's max-range, then make a steep dive-bombing run at idle power, at least until inside the threat missile's min-range. After release of the bomb or bombs the fighter should make a low-altitude pull-out and extend at high speed and low level out the bogey's extended six o'clock. Afterburners, which increase the fighter's IR signature by an order of magnitude, should not be required after a dive from high altitude and should not be used. Low-drag (unretarded) bombs are generally best for this tactic because of reduced time of fall from a high release. With either retarded or low-drag bombs, fuzes set to explode instantaneously on ground impact, or even slightly before, are optimum because of the resulting frag-pattern increase.

Cluster bombs (bombs that dispense large numbers of small "bomblets" after release) can also be effective against helos, but they are usually inferior to general purpose bombs for this mission because of the greatly reduced frag pattern of the cluster weapon. Although this "shotgun" weapon makes a direct hit more likely, a direct hit would probably be required to destroy the target, and it would still be quite difficult to achieve against an evasive helo. The cluster bomb would be better than general purpose bombs against a helo at high altitude, but other air-to-air weapons would probably be more appropriate in that case.

AAMs may also be viable weapons against the helo. The radar-guided weapons, however, have serious problems, as noted earlier, and probably would be rather ineffective, especially against a low-altitude target. A Doppler-guided missile might have a chance if it was employed in a low-level, head-on attack, so that the helo's closing speed would aid the missile in distinguishing the target from ground clutter. Side-lobe clutter, as described in Chapter 1, is the problem with RQ attacks with this weapon, and it may necessitate a higher-altitude, shoot-down launch.

Heat seekers are much better suited to this scenario, but they still are not without problems. Helicopters often have exhaust shields that reduce their IR signatures, and hot exhaust gases may be dispersed by the rotor wash. In a look-down environment, especially over hot desert terrain, RQ-only heat seekers may be more effective than their all-aspect counterparts because they are less sensitive to background IR radiation. RQ heat-seeking missiles should be fired whenever the target heat source can be detected, regardless of aspect. Even "RQ" AAMs may have all-aspect capabilities against slow aircraft that are unable to generate high speed or a high load factor.

If all else fails, a high-speed pass very low over the top of the helo is very likely to disrupt airflow through the rotor blades sufficiently to cause a loss of control, and can drive a low-altitude helo into the ground.

Probably the best tactic to employ against a helicopter is to sneak up on it and attack with bombs, guns, unguided rockets, or IR missiles. If detected by the target, about the best the pilot of a fixed-wing fighter can hope for is a head-on pass. Turning with a helo is fruitless and can be downright dangerous. If the first attack is not successful and multiple runs are necessary, a variation of extension tactics can be used. On each pass the fighter pilot should turn hard toward the helo to reduce lateral separation to a minimum, then extend at low altitude and high speed, turning in the nose-to-tail direction only as necessary to keep sight of the helo behind. If the helo is missile equipped it is important both to stay low to avoid giving the bogey any look-up and to cease use of afterburners before the bogey can complete its turn and fire. The combination of high fighter speed, low altitude, and the slow speed of the helo all work to reduce the helo missile's max-range to probably half that advertised for fighter engagements at higher altitudes. Against non-missile-equipped helos, a gradual climb may be more comfortable during the extension.

The extension should be continued until the fighter is well outside the helo's missile range, and until the fighter can make a reversal to meet the helo again head-on and still have sufficient separation for gun, missile, or bomb-sight tracking. A power reduction and a nose-high oblique reversal may allow the fighter pilot to tighten his turn and get the nose around quicker. The length of the extension may be reduced by the requirement to keep sight of the helo, and tracking times may be short as a result. If two fighters are available, one can orbit around the fight high, keeping track of the helo and directing the engaged fighter pilot in case he loses sight of the bogey. Or both fighters can engage the helo simultaneously from different directions. Caution is required, however, when the fighters are dropping bombs, as the frag pattern from one bomb must be given time to dissipate before the second fighter enters the area.

In general, except for the comments on rotor-blade effects, the tactics and considerations outlined here are relevant to most low-altitude engagements between fighters with very great disparity in performance.

Notes

1. John T. Godfrey, *The Look of Eagles,* pp. 98–99.
2. Randy Cunningham, *Fox Two,* pp. 104, 106–8.
3. Manfred F. von Richthofen, *The Red Air Fighter,* pp. 84–85.
4. Robert S. Johnson, *Thunderbolt!* pp. 148–49.

Section Tactics, Two-versus-One

Never break your formation into less than two-ship elements. Stay in pairs. A man by himself is a liability, a two-ship team is an asset. If you are separated, join up immediately with other friendly airplanes.

Major Thomas B. "Tommy" McGuire, USAAF

Background

Section is the term used to describe a team of two fighters acting in concert against the adversary. This concept was first employed early in World War I by the Germans Oswald Boelcke and Max Immelmann. Even in the infancy of air combat, it was readily apparent that one-versus-one engagement has serious flaws in practical application. Among these failings is inadequate defense against surprise attack by an unseen opponent. It has been estimated that throughout the history of air combat 80 to 90 percent of downed fighter pilots were unaware of their danger until the moment of the attack. Suprise, then, and, conversely, the avoidance of surprise, must be considered the most vital element in air combat.

> The first rule of all air combat is to see the opponent first. Like the hunter who stalks his prey and maneuvers himself unnoticed into the most favorable position for the kill, the fighter in the opening of a dogfight must detect the opponent as early as possible in order to attain a superior position for the attack.

Lt. General Adolph Galland, Luftwaffe

Most aircraft, and particularly single-seat fighters, have blind spots that cannot be monitored visually on a continuous basis by the pilot. The underside of the aircraft and the rear hemisphere are usually the most troublesome areas. Although these regions can be checked sporadically by rolling and turning the aircraft, this technique may not be adequate against an attacker with high closure. Additionally, one-versus-one combat, and particularly weapons employment during combat, demands that the pilot's full attention be devoted to the opponent he sees, leaving little or no opportunity for him to defend against a second attack.

> There are no eyes for your backside, no eyes for who is coming from below . . . if you are single you have too many blind spots.
>   Colonel Erich "Bubi" Hartmann, GAF

In theory, the operation of two fighters together can alleviate this problem by allowing each of the two pilots to cover the blind zone of the other before an engagement and by allowing one pilot to prosecute an attack confident in the knowledge that his vulnerable areas are being protected by his wingman. A fallout of this strategy is the old military principle of concentration of forces, as greater firepower can be brought to bear on the adversary.

Although this principle of "mutual support" sounds straightforward enough, it has given rise to a multitude of tactical doctrines designed to exploit its advantages. Most of these doctrines have been successful to some degree under certain combat conditions. Three of the most common are discussed here, but it should be recognized that there may be many tactical variations within each broad doctrine, all of which, obviously, cannot be covered in detail.

Fighting Wing

Fighting wing tactics, sometimes called "welded wing," designate a leader and a wingman. The leader's primary responsibilities are navigation, forward-hemisphere search for the enemy, attack planning, and engaged maneuvering, and he has a secondary responsibility of rear-hemisphere visual coverage. The wingman flies a rather loose formation on the leader; his primary task is maintaining a rear-hemisphere defensive lookout, and he has secondary forward-hemisphere duties.

The position flown by the wingman is shown by Figure 5-1. In actuality this is not a rigid position, but rather is a maneuvering area roughly described by a cone-shaped airspace extending aft of about 60° off the leader's tail. Distance from the leader varies with the performance of the aircraft involved. Generally the wingman needs to maintain sufficient separation to preclude any danger of collision with the leader in the event of unexpected heavy maneuvering, but he must be close enough to facilitate the task of remaining behind the leader during maximum-performance turns. This formation task becomes nearly impossible when aircraft separations are allowed to approach the equivalent of about one minimum turn radius for the aircraft involved. Because of the increase in the speeds of fighters and their turn radii since World War I, maximum separations in fighting wing have also increased dramatically. Typical maximum separations have ballooned from about 200 ft in World War I, to 600 ft in World War II, 1,000 ft during the Korean War, and 3,000 ft for the Vietnam conflict. Since turn radius increases with altitude, at high levels, separations up to twice these values might be workable. Minimum comfortable maneuvering distances also have expanded, primarily as a result of the possibility of greater closure between leader and wingman, from 20 to 30 ft during the biplane era to 200 to 300 ft for modern jets.

Fighting wing "formation" is not really a formation at all, but an engaged tactical doctrine. Pre-engagement formations used with fighting wing have varied widely. These sections may cruise in "echelon," with the wingman behind and to the side, as depicted in Figure 5-1 (right echelon when the wingman is on the leader's right side). The wingman might also fly directly abeam the leader in what is known as "line-abreast" or "combat-spread" formation. The fighters could even choose to cruise in "trail," one directly behind the other, a formation also known as "line astern." Separation between aircraft in these cruise formations typically has varied from one extreme to the other, between the minimum and maximum ranges outlined here. The wingman is usually "stepped-down" (i.e., lower in altitude) a few feet, which makes it easier for him to stay out of the way should the leader decide to turn sharply toward the wingman. During the biplane days, stepping-up was common because of better wingman visibility looking forward and down. The merits and shortcomings of each of these pre-engaged tactical formations are discussed in a later chapter. Suffice it to say here that echelon is probably the tactical formation most widely used in conjunction with fighting wing, but that line abreast is probably better, since this arrangement offers each pilot an equal view of the other's rear hemisphere. The difficulty with line abreast is that the wingman is initially forward of the prescribed fighting wing position and may not be able to regain it in the event of unexpected heavy maneuvering.

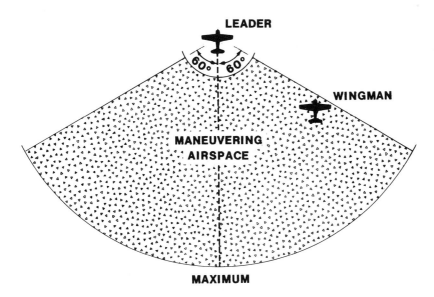

Figure 5-1. Fighting Wing Formation

Engaged Maneuvering

Once the engagement begins, the fighting wing leader essentially fights the opponent one-versus-one, while the wingman hangs on for dear life. The wingman should attempt to maintain a position as far off the leader's tail as practical to give himself the best possible view of the leader's vulnerable rear hemisphere and to afford the leader the chance to check the wingman's six o'clock. Within limits, greater separation between fighters also provides for better visual coverage and quicker support by the wingman should the leader be attacked. In general, however, the greater the aircraft separation and the farther forward the wingman flies, the more difficult the task of maintaining the position. A great deal of practice, therefore, is required to produce an effective fighting wing wingman.

> Mainly it's my wingman's eyes that I want. One man cannot see enough. When attacked I want first for him to warn me, then for him to think. Every situation is different and the wingman must have initiative and ability to size up the situation properly and act accordingly. There is no rule of thumb for a wingman. . . . The wingman's primary duty is protection of his element leader. It takes the leader's entire attention to destroy an enemy aircraft. . . . Good wingmen, smart wingmen, are the answer to a leader's prayers.
>
> Lt. Colonel John C. Meyer, USAAF

In addition to improved defensive coverage, fighting wing tactics have several other advantages as compared with operating as a single aircraft in a combat environment. One of the greatest pluses is that it takes much less training for a pilot to fly fighting wing well enough to stay with his leader than it takes to enable that pilot to survive on his own. Trained fighter pilots are almost always in short supply during wartime, and fighting wing allows inexperienced pilots to engage in combat under the tutelage of a veteran leader at reduced risk. Actual combat is the best teacher, but historically the highest attrition rate for fighter pilots has occurred during their first few combat missions. Fighting wing can get the fresh recruit through this vulnerable period while he is serving the useful function of offering some visual support to the leader. A second set of eyeballs can be invaluable in the combat environment.

> A steadily increasing percentage of the young and inexperienced pilots were shot down before they reached their tenth operational flight—soon it was more than five percent.
>
> Lt. General Adolph Galland, Luftwaffe

The other major advantage of fighting wing is concentration of fire. The lead is essentially maneuvering two firing platforms rather than just one. Under the ground rules of fighting wing it is the wingman's responsibility to stay with and cover his lead, not to engage the bogey. Any attention paid to the opponent detracts from the wingman's defensive potential. Against most maneuvering fighter opponents, when concentration of fire is not critical and shot opportunities are likely to be fleeting, the leader usually will do all the shooting. But quite often an enemy fighter's defensive reaction to the leader's attack sets up a shot for the wingman. Against heavily armored, nonmaneuvering targets, especially bombers, the lead may clear the wingman to fire, either simultaneously or in rapid succession, to make best use of all available firepower. The wingman may also be allowed to finish off a defeated or crippled opponent as an effective means of building confidence and combat weapons-firing experience. In this case the lead clears his wingman to attack and temporarily assumes the duties and position of wingman himself. In the case of a relatively experienced wingman, there may be a pre-engagement agreement between team members that the wingman may attack any bogey he sees first, and assume the temporary lead. As a rule, however, the wingman should attempt to get the leader's eyes on the bogey and let him decide whether and how to attack. Obviously, if the leader is threatened severely by an attacker, it is the wingman's duty to warn the leader and counterattack immediately.

> It is true to say that the first kill can influence the whole future career of a fighter pilot. Many to whom the first victory over the opponent has been long denied either by unfortunate circumstances or by bad luck can suffer from frustration or develop complexes they may never rid themselves of again.
> Lt. General Adolph Galland, Luftwaffe

Another scenario in which fighting wing provides concentration of fire is with multi-crew fighters having rear-hemisphere weapons. The close spacing between aircraft makes it difficult for an attacker to bounce one fighter without coming under fire from both. This also accounts for some of the logic behind close bomber formations.

Analysis of Fighting Wing Doctrine

In addition to its obvious benefits, fighting wing doctrine has some serious flaws. With the exception of the pre-engagement line-abreast formation, the wingman's position behind the leader results in reduced visual coverage of the wingman's six. Moreover, once is he engaged, the lead is likely to be too busy with the bogey to provide adequate support to his wingman in any event. Although the wingman is theoretically burdened only with defensive lookout responsibility, in practice he is so occupied by maintaining position during hard maneuvering that he may be of little defensive value to either the leader or himself. In this case he is literally "hung out to dry." Many a wingman has been lost without the leader even being aware of it.

Lack of offensive efficiency is also a serious problem with this doctrine. The bogey pilot is essentially fighting only one opponent. Having one of his adversaries in sight virtually assures having the other in sight. From an offensive point of view the fighting wing leader must engage the opponent one-versus-one. If his aircraft is superior to the bogey, this may be practical, but he clearly cannot hope to defeat a better fighter that is well flown unless the bogey can be taken by surprise. Even this is more difficult with two aircraft rather than one, since the section is more visible.

Neither is fighting wing compatible with most energy tactics. As detailed previously, most of these methods require the energy fighter to trade position advantage for an energy margin, then convert that energy to a position advantage with a zoom climb. Although the leader of a fighting wing section may be capable of pulling this off safely, the zoom often leaves the wingman behind, below, and very vulnerable. Angles tactics are much more appropriate for fighting wing, but they are not likely to bring success unless the section fighters have a turn-performance advantage over their adversary. If this is not the case, the section may be forced to resort to hit-and-run methods, but under some circumstances (e.g., when the section aircraft have a large energy advantage over a bogey that is not all-aspect missile equipped) extension/pitch-back tactics may be workable. A considerable T/W advantage (or initial energy advantage) usually is required for this method, since the leader is generally restricted to partial power for benefit of the wingman. Otherwise the wingman would have a difficult time keeping up during the extensions and zooms.

> It was my view that no kill was worth the life of a wingman. . . . Pilots in my unit who lost wingmen on this basis were prohibited from leading a [section]. They were made to fly as wingmen, instead.
>
> Colonel Erich "Bubi" Hartmann, GAF

Even with its many failings fighting wing has survived from early World War I right up to the most recent air combats, and it probably will continue to find applications as long as manned fighters exist. In most cases it is still superior to engaging one-versus-one in a hostile combat environment.

Double Attack

Double attack, also known by many other names, is a system by which each aircraft of a pair of fighters can support the other without remaining in the rigid structure prescribed by fighting wing. This doctrine permits the section to split, allowing for coordinated, sequential attacks. There is still a leader and a wingman in this method, but the relationship can change back and forth during an engagement.

Pre-Engagement Considerations

Pre-engagement formations used with double attack doctrine are generally the same as with fighting wing (echelon, line astern, or line abreast), except that aircraft separation can be increased somewhat since there is no longer a requirement for the wingman to remain closely behind his leader once the section is engaged. Greater separation between fighters can provide better visual coverage of the teammate's rear hemisphere, allows the fighters more maneuvering room to counterattack a bogey that may attack the other fighter, and makes it more difficult for a single bogey to see or attack both fighters simultaneously.

The ideal separation between fighters using double attack doctrine depends on several factors, one of which is the turning radius of the aircraft involved. It does little good for the wingman to detect an attack on his partner if something cannot be done about the situation quickly. In addition to warning the threatened pilot to take evasive action, the wingman should be able to bring offensive pressure to bear on the attacker in minimum time. In general, this task is easiest when separation between fighters is on the order of one or two turn radii, since this gives the wingman maneuvering room to turn and point weapons at the attacker. This maneuvering space is often not available in close fighting wing formations. Obviously, optimum lateral spacing will vary with turn radius, as this performance parameter varies with fighter speed and altitude.

Cockpit field of view and enemy weapons are also important considerations. To illustrate the interaction of these seemingly unrelated factors, Figure 5-2 shows two fighters in line-abreast, or combat-spread, formation. This figure depicts typical "blind cones" behind each fighter. At least one of the pilots has an unobstructed view from the cockpit of all airspace around the section, except the cross-hatched region between the aircraft marked "danger zone." Arcs are also drawn to represent the maximum effective firing range of the enemy's weapons in the rear quarter of each fighter. These weapons could be guns, rockets, or missiles. The goal is to space the fighters so that an enemy cannot achieve firing parameters undetected.

Visualize how greater cockpit field of view, and more narrow blind cones, would tend to push the danger zone farther aft. A similar effect is

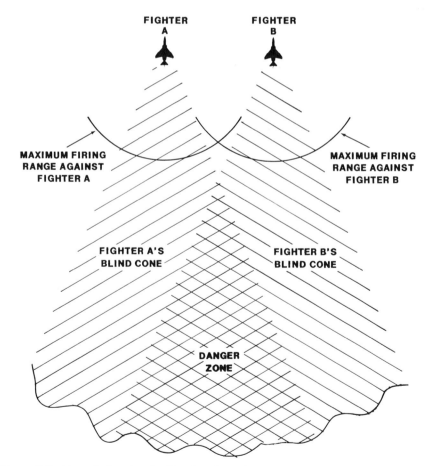

Figure 5-2. Aircraft Spacing in Combat Spread

accomplished by increasing lateral separation between fighters. It can also be seen here that allowing one fighter to fall back behind the other into an echelon formation would cause the danger zone to recede farther from the lead fighter, offering it greater protection, but cause it to approach the trail fighter, which makes it more vulnerable. This illustration should make very clear how the longer max-range of the AAM struck a deathblow to the close aircraft spacing required by fighting wing doctrine, which had been so effective in a guns-only environment.

The maximum firing range of the enemy's weapons, particularly AAMs, can vary substantially depending on altitude, fighter speed, bogey closure, etc. These factors may, therefore, need to be taken into consideration by the defending pilots. Generally speaking, higher altitudes and slower speeds require greater separation between fighters if a bogey is to be denied an AAM firing opportunity within the section's danger zone. Typical separation between fighters in combat spread in a modern AAM environment is on the order of one to two miles.

The physical size of the aircraft involved also plays an important part in determining the optimum section spacing. While minimum separation is largely dependent on turn radius, field of view, and weapons considerations, maximum split is limited by aircraft size and visibility conditions. The fighters need to remain close enough together for there to be little danger of them losing sight of each other under prevailing visibility conditions. When approaching the limits of this range, each pilot must spend more and more time watching his teammate, which leaves less time for offensive or defensive scanning. Unless the enemy fighters are considerably larger than the friendlies, bogey size is often a more restrictive factor than the size of the section's aircraft. As a bogey approaches firing range within the blind cone of one fighter, range from the bogey to the target's wingman may be considerably greater than the separation between fighters. Fighter spacing, therefore, must be restricted to provide reasonable assurance that an enemy approaching firing parameters on one fighter will be detected by the other.

Under many conditions of visibility, bogey size, and weapons ranges, maximum allowable separation between fighters may be less than that required to ensure that the enemy cannot fire within the section's danger zone. Under such circumstances, high speed and low altitude may restrict the bogey's AAM firing envelope sufficiently to solve the problem. Allowing the fighters to weave may also help by effectively reducing the size of the blind cones. Weaving, however, makes fighters more detectable because of the increased probability of sun reflections off various parts of the aircraft catching the enemy's attention. Weaving also slows a section's forward progress, which may allow a slower bogey to close from the rear.

Optimum vertical separation between fighters in section is determined by environmental, performance, and aircraft structural design factors. For instance, the wingman would not want to be stepped-up on the sun side of his leader, since the leader's vision would be impaired as he looked into the sun to check the wingman's rear hemisphere. The wingman would normally step up when he is on the leader's down-sun side and fly below the leader when he is up-sun of the leader.

Large vertical separations between fighters can reduce defensive capability, since the lower aircraft may not be able to climb up quickly to the level of the wingman to render assistance without losing so much airspeed that it becomes ineffective. Higher performance fighters can, therefore, afford larger altitude splits.

Aircraft structural design enters the picture because of its effect on cockpit field of view. A modern low-wing fighter, for instance, often has a more restricted field of view behind and down because of the obstruction of the wing. If one fighter is stepped-up in this case, its wing might obscure a large portion of the wingman's rear hemisphere. When necessary this problem may be alleviated by rolling the aircraft periodically to check the hidden region, but generally it is better to avoid the problem altogether by readjusting relative aircraft altitudes.

In general, within the limits described, larger splits, both horizontally and vertically, provide better offensive potential. This is partially because greater separation affords more maneuvering flexibility and partially because enemy fighters are less likely to see both aircraft simultaneously. However, this improved offensive potential may be gained at the cost of reduced defensive capability, because of visibility and performance factors. Usually the prudent section will opt for splits nearer the minimum limits in high-threat areas, or when the immediate chances of engaging offensively are slim. Wider splits are more appropriate in low-threat conditions and in the final stages of an offensive attack.

Engaged Maneuvering

It is in the engaged phase that double attack departs most dramatically from fighting wing doctrine. For example, when the enemy is spotted by the wingman, no time is wasted getting the leader's eyes on the target. If the wingman is in a favorable position and he considers attack to be advisable, he assumes the lead and attacks. The new wingman positions to cover his teammate, usually high above the fight. Since the wingman is relieved of his close-formation requirement, he can devote full attention to the more important task of providing effective visual coverage. His maneuvering requirements are also reduced, so the wingman can use this opportunity to increase his energy level, making him more effective in case he later becomes engaged.

> It is wonderful how cheered a pilot becomes after he shoots down his first machine; his moral[e] increases by at least 100 per cent.
>
> Captain Ira "Taffy" Jones, RAF
> 40 Victories, WW-I

Once the section has split, there is a subtle shift from the leader/wingman relationship between pilots to an engaged fighter–free fighter relationship. The pilot of the engaged fighter is the one more closely involved with the adversary. In essence, he is the section leader at that moment. The first duty of the engaged fighter in offensive double attack is to press the attack. The result of this attempt will be either destruction of the target or loss of the offensive. At the first sign that the offensive is being lost (i.e., impending overshoot, energy depletion, etc.), the engaged-fighter pilot should disengage immediately and call in the wingman to assume the offensive. The engaged fighter–free fighter roles then reverse, and the new free-fighter pilot assumes the duties of visual coverage and replenishment of his expended energy until he is called once again into the fight by the engaged pilot.

> Only one man can shoot down an opponent. If one airman has tackled his enemy the others cannot assist. They can only look on and protect his back. Otherwise, he might be attacked in the rear.
>
> Baron Manfred von Richthofen

To be most effective, the pilot of the double attack free fighter needs to keep the engaged fighter in sight and stay close enough to offer adequate visual support and quick response to an attack on his teammate without getting in the way. In order for the pilot of the free fighter to provide the quickest defensive reaction potential, he must maintain high energy (preferably higher than that of the engaged fighter), minimize separation from the fight, and avoid letting the fight get too far behind his wing-line. Probably the most effective technique for meeting all these parameters is to maneuver in a plane perpendicular to that of the fight. For instance, if the bogey and the engaged fighter are making essentially level turns, the free-fighter pilot can perform a series of vertical or very steep oblique loops around the fight. He can also use a series of high and low yo-yos. Conversely, if the fight is progressing vertically, the free fighter can arc around the fight in level turns. In this way the free fighter stays close to the fight and can keep the engaged fighter within about 90° of the nose for a quicker defensive response. This is especially important for slow-turning fighters. In addition, the free fighter's turn rate is "decoupled" from the fight in this manner. This means the fight itself may be allowed to go through two or three turns while the free fighter completes just one revolution in a perpendicular plane. The free fighter can therefore hold lower G and build an energy reserve for future offensive or defensive maneuvering.

In most situations involving double attack, there are clearly defined engaged and free fighters, but this is not always the case. For instance, when both pilots have the target in sight prior to the attack, they may take an "offensive split" in an attempt to "bracket," or surround, the bogey. One such scenario is illustrated in Figure 5-3. In this case the section is meeting the bogey head-on (time "1") and takes a wide offensive split, forcing the opponent to choose one fighter or the other to engage (time "2"). This choice gives the other fighter flight-path separation, which its pilot uses to make a lead turn to gain a good advantage at the pass (time "3").

In the case of the offensive split, the bogey pilot is allowed to choose which fighter he will engage. Until that choice is made, both aircraft in the section are, theoretically, engaged fighters. If the bogey continues merrily straight ahead, both fighters could convert to its rear hemisphere. When the bogey pilot chooses to engage one fighter, this should leave the other in a more favorable offensive position. Following the pass, this more offensive fighter usually will assume the engaged-fighter role and commence

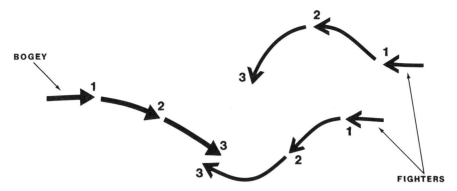

Figure 5-3. The Bracket

double attack maneuvering; or both fighters may choose to disengage from the attack together for a hit-and-run maneuver.

Throughout World War II, fighting wing was the tactical doctrine of the U.S. Army Air Force (USAAF) in the European theater. A few highly experienced teams, however, recognized the limitations of these tactics and developed their own variations, generally along the lines of double attack. Probably the most famous of these teams was made up of Captains John Godfrey (16.33 victories) and Don Gentile (19.83 victories). These pilots' success was so astounding, and their methods so revolutionary, that Luftwaffe Reichsmarschall Herrmann Goering supposedly stated he would trade two of his best squadrons for their capture. The following encounter sounds suspiciously like a double attack bracket. Godfrey and Gentile are flying P-51B Mustangs against the lone Me 109.

> "Break! Break! One coming in at 4 o'clock to you!"
> "Okay, break starboard," said Gentile.
> They broke together and the 109 made a head-on pass.
> "All right, Johnny," said Gentile, "when he comes back around on the next turn you break right and I'll break left."
> They circled and the 109 came boring in for another head-on attack. He looked mean and vicious. He was bold enough to joust with two Mustangs. As the planes bored straight at each other's spinner, Gentile ordered the foxing maneuver:
> "Now!"
> Gentile broke sharply to the left; Godfrey to the right. They honked their sticks back, climbed and came barreling down on the 109's tail.[1]

Defensively, the engaged fighter–free fighter roles also can become somewhat blurred. Whenever one fighter becomes defensive, the other fighter should immediately attack the bogey. In this case there will be two engaged fighters until the bogey can be placed on the defensive, releasing the original defensive fighter to become free. This situation is depicted in Figure 5-4. In this scenario the right-hand fighter is threatened by a bogey detected at its six. The threatened pilot breaks to the right, away from his wingman, to defend against the attacker. If the bogey continues to press

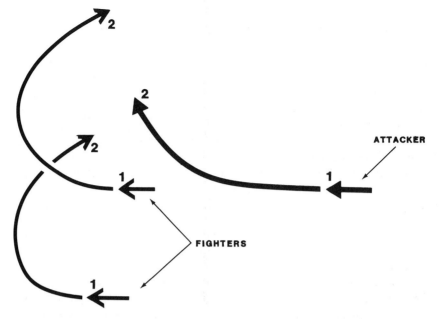

Figure 5-4. The Sandwich

the attack, as shown here, it quickly becomes sandwiched by the second fighter.

The sandwich is an ideal defensive maneuver when the threatened fighter can be identified early in the attack. This identification is made easier by the wider cruise formations available with the double attack doctrine. When the bogey does not commit clearly to one fighter early in its attack, a "defensive split" may be used to force the attacker's hand. This technique is illustrated in Figure 5-5.

In this scenario the fighter section is cruising in combat spread, line abreast, when a bogey is detected closing from six o'clock at time "1." The attacker's position between the fighters, and the relatively long range, makes it difficult to determine which of the fighters the bogey pilot intends to attack. Therefore the fighters take a defensive split north and south, turning away from each other. Assuming the attacker is still beyond the range of his weapons, these turns can be of the energy-sustaining variety rather than break turns. The defensive split quickly forces the attacker to commit to one fighter or the other, and, in pressing the attack on one fighter, the bogey must turn its tail to the other, often causing the attacker to lose sight of the free fighter. In this engagement the northern fighter is engaged more heavily and is definitely defensive. The defender can expect to be fired on around time "2" if the bogey is carrying all-aspect missiles, and he almost certainly will be required to perform a guns defense at about time "3" against a gun-equipped attacker.

The bogey's overshoot between times "3" and "4" leaves the engaged-fighter pilot (assuming he has survived to this point) with the options of either continuing his turn, as shown, or reversing nose-to-nose, setting up a scissors. Against a gun-equipped attacker with a definite angular advantage, reversing at this point subjects the defender to another close-range gun shot, unless the defender is much more maneuverable (i.e., has a tighter turn radius). The reversal option also tends to drag the fight away from the free fighter, delaying any help it may be able to render. Engaging the bogey in a slow-speed, close-range knife fight can even leave the free fighter helpless to assist, since a missile fired at the bogey under these conditions might very easily guide on the friendly fighter instead. This would greatly reduce the popularity of the free-fighter pilot at the bar following the mission.

A better option here is probably to continue to turn in the same direction, as shown at time "4." This action delays any further weapons firing by the attacker and pulls the fight back toward the free fighter. If the bogey continues to press the attack in this case, it will turn belly-up to the free fighter coming in from the south. The free fighter would then be in an excellent position to sandwich the bogey, probably unseen, and achieve either gun- or missile-firing parameters. If the bogey detects the free fighter's attack, a switch may occur, with the bogey releasing the original defender to concentrate on the other fighter. In this case the original free fighter becomes engaged, usually on at least equal terms, and can begin one-versus-one maneuvering or disengage. Meanwhile the original defender is now free to catch his breath, recover some energy, and assume a cover position, usually high above the fight, to await his turn at the opponent while watching for additional ("wild-card") bogeys.

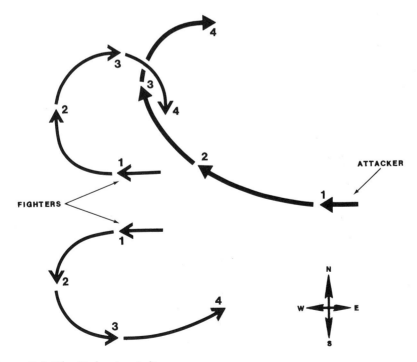

Figure 5-5. The Defensive Split

Again the team of Godfrey and Gentile provides a combat example of the defensive split. The maneuvering following the split is also very representative of offensive double attack doctrine.

> Don was the first to see the ME-109.
> "Johnny, at six o'clock high there's a single bandit."
> I looked back, and there he was high above us. I gazed in disbelief as his nose dropped and he plummeted down on us.
> "Don, the crazy son of a bitch is bouncing us."
> "I know. When I yell, 'Break,' you break right and I'll break left."
> I watched as the 109 dropped closer and closer. "Break, Johnny."
> I pulled sharply to the right, and thought at first I had broken too late as the 109 pulled on my tail. I tightened my turn and met Don halfway around as he tried to fire on the 109 in a head-on attack. I went around twice more, with the Jerry on my tail, before Don could reverse his turn and swing down for a rear attack. But this German pilot was a smart, capable flyer. As Don brought his guns to bear, he split S and dove to the ground. Don and I followed him, our motors roaring in pursuit. He pulled out of his dive and banked left, which brought him close to me. I followed him and fired. He wasn't one to sit still, however, and changed his turn to swing into Don. I followed, firing intermittently. Don, meanwhile, had climbed for altitude, and I kept the Jerry busy in a tight turn. As I fired, I saw flashes on his wing, fuselage and even his motor, but the pilot wouldn't bail out. Turning all the time and losing height, we were now just above the tree tops, and the 109's engine was spewing smoke. I had no forewarning that my ammunition was running out, but as I prepared for the final burst only silence came as I pressed the tit.
> "Finish him, Don. I'm all out of ammunition."
> Don, who had been maneuvering above us waiting for the Jerry to break out of the turn, zoomed down in front of me and made one pass at the courageous German flyer. His shots hit home, and the 109 crashed into the ground.[2]

A common variation on the defensive split is a high/low split. In this case one fighter pulls up steeply (either vertically or obliquely toward the wingman) while the other turns away level or nose-low. This tactic generates both a vertical and a horizontal split and again forces the attacker to make a choice. If he attacks the low fighter, the high fighter can come over the top of its vertical or oblique loop and dive down on the bogey. This can be a very effective tactic when a section is attacked by a low-T/W adversary who does not have the poop to reach the high fighter in its zoom.

The high/low split has some serious limitations, however. One of these is the slow speed resulting from the high fighter's zoom climb which leaves it vulnerable to a second, unseen, attacker. Another is the beautiful look-up shot it presents to a missile-equipped opponent. A third consideration is the relative energy of attacker and defender. If the bogey is closing from the rear quarter at the same altitude or higher, it has an energy advantage over the defending fighters. This energy margin may allow even a low-powered bogey to zoom with the high fighter, catch it at the top of the loop, and cause real problems long before the low fighter can become a factor.

The high/low split was used very effectively by the Chinese and Russian

MiG-15s against U.S. F-86 Sabres in Korea. The MiGs would stay very fast, near the maximum speed of both aircraft types, so the attacking Sabres could not achieve a significant energy advantage. Since the MiG had a substantial T/W advantage over the guns-only Sabres, the MiG splitting high was usually in little danger of being caught in its zoom.

In general, the high/low split should not be attempted against an all-aspect missile threat, or when the section is attacked by a fighter nearly equivalent in zoom capability. The relative merits of the sandwich (fighters turn in the same direction) and the split (fighters turn away from each other horizontally or vertically) depend on several factors. One of these is the range at which the attack is detected. To be effective, the sandwich (Figure 5-4) requires that the attacker be approaching a range approximating the lateral separation between the defending fighters and be firmly committed to one target. If the attack is discovered early, it may be possible to delay defensive maneuvering until just prior to the bogey's open-fire point, to allow the range to close and the target to be determined. A slight miscalculation here, obviously, would be unfortunate. The long range of an attacker's AAM also may preclude this option. Under such circumstances the defensive split (Figure 5-5), either the level or the high/low variety, may be more appropriate.

It is apparent that the sandwich and the high/low split, which place the free fighter in a threatening position within 90° to 180° of turn, are more efficient than the left/right horizontal split, which typically requires 270° to 360° of turn before a firing position can be achieved. Another disadvantage of the level defensive split is the great separation generated between the fighters (several miles at today's speeds), which easily can cause the free-fighter pilot to lose sight of the fight, with disastrous results. The high/low split, when appropriate, reduces this separation significantly.

Another tactic is something of a combination of the sandwich and the split. The "half-split," as illustrated by Figure 5-6, involves one pilot turning hard away from his wingman, who in turn extends straight ahead. In practice the pilot of the extending fighter may need to turn slightly to keep sight of his wingman and the attacker, and he may also choose to climb or dive while extending.

At time "1" the section (in combat spread) detects an attacker behind it closing fast, but still out of range. The pilot of the southern fighter turns left (away from his wingman) using sustained-G levels to conserve energy and separate from his wingman. The pilot of the northern fighter, meanwhile, extends essentially straight ahead and watches the bogey and his wingman. In this case the bogey pilot chooses to attack the southern fighter, a fact that becomes evident before time "2." The defender now tightens his turn to defeat the attack, while the wingman comes back hard to sandwich the attacker. Figure 5-7 illustrates how the section can counter if the bogey attacks the extending fighter.

In this scenario the positions at time "1" are the same as for the previous example, and the section employs the same half-split. This time, however, the bogey follows the extending fighter. When the situation becomes clear, at time "2," the pilot of the southern fighter reverses his turn direction

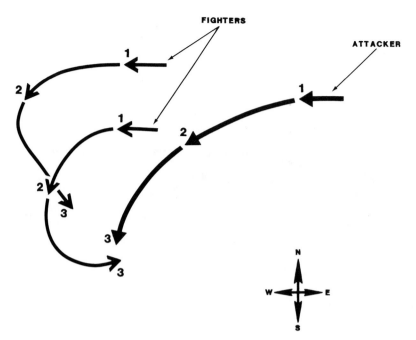

Figure 5-6. The Half-Split (Bogey Attacks Turning Fighter)

back toward his wingman, who continues to extend, turning only to keep sight of the bogey. This extension "drags" the bogey out and assists the wingman in positioning for a shot. At time "3" the attacker has closed the range sufficiently to force the defender to break into his attack; but by this time the free fighter has achieved a sandwich (time "4"). A barrel-roll attack commenced at about time "3" may assist the free fighter in gaining an offensive position.

As with the pure defensive split, the half-split forces the attacker to commit to one fighter or the other, so that the section can clearly define the engaged fighter and the free fighter. Separation is increased to allow maneuvering room for the free fighter, but it is not increased so far that the defenders are likely to lose sight of the attacker or each other. In addition, the sandwich usually can be set more quickly with this method than with the pure defensive split.

One other defensive tactic which deserves mention at this point was developed by the U.S. Navy early in World War II. For some time after America's entry into the war, the Navy found their F4F Wildcat fighters badly overmatched by the Japanese Zero, which could both out-turn and out-climb the Wildcat. The Wildcat's strong points, aside from a slightly faster top speed, were better roll rate, particularly at high speeds, heavier armor, and armament better suited to fighter-versus-fighter engagements (most models had six .50-cal machine guns as opposed to the Zero's two 20-mm cannon and two synchronized .30-cal-class machine guns).

To survive under these conditions, the Navy adopted hit-and-run tac-

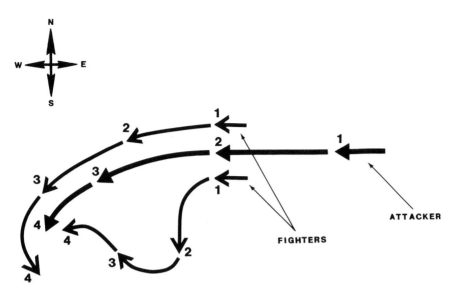

Figure 5-7. The Half-Split (Bogey Attacks Extending Fighter)

tics and relied heavily on teamwork between and among sections of two fighters. The classic defensive tactic of this time was known as the beam defense maneuver or, more commonly, the "Thatch weave," after LCDR John Thatch, who introduced it. Figure 5-8 shows how it worked.

At time "1" the fighters are in a fairly wide (about 1,000 ft for the F4F) combat-spread formation when the northern fighter is attacked. The fighters immediately turn hard toward each other. In the case illustrated the bogey presses its attack on the northern fighter and is met almost head-on at time "2" by the free fighter with all guns blazing. The Wildcat pilots were more than happy to go toe-to-toe with a Zero in this manner because of greater firepower and a more durable aircraft. Navy pilots were also well trained in high-deflection shooting and forward-quarter attacks.

After meeting his wingman (time "2"), the defending pilot uses his superior roll rate to reverse his turn quickly to set up another pass with his wingman, who also reverses. This technique generates repetitive firing passes against the bogey, and it also allows the defender to offer protection to his wingman, should he come under attack by a second bogey. The secrets to this tactic lie in the initial wide line-abreast formation (separation greater than fighter turn radius) and heavy gun firepower. Because of the short-range high-aspect shots provided, this technique would not be appropriate for fighters equipped only with RQ missiles, or even all-aspect missiles, unless they have very good min-range capabilities. In such scenarios, the sandwich or half-split probably would be better. In the situation for which it was developed, however, the Thatch weave was very effective. It could also be considered the forerunner of a new engaged doctrine for fighters known as "loose deuce," which is covered later in this chapter.

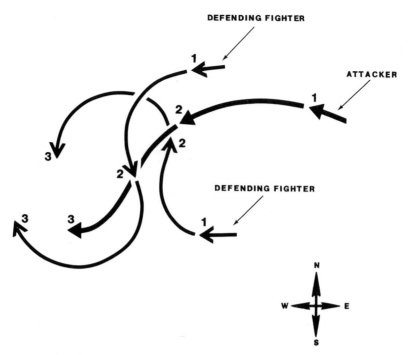

Figure 5-8. Thatch Weave

Analysis of Double Attack Doctrine

Double attack allows two fighters to split for better mutual support. There are still a leader and a wingman, as in fighting wing, but these roles are allowed to change back and forth during an engagement as the situation warrants. After the engagement begins, the leader/wingman relationship becomes one of engaged fighter–free fighter. Offensively, after the initial attack, which can be made by both fighters simultaneously or in rapid succession, the fighter with the greatest offensive potential becomes the engaged fighter and commences one-versus-one maneuvering while the free fighter assumes a cover position. The duties of the free-fighter pilot are to remain in the general area and maintain a visual lookout for other hostile aircraft, but he is not tied rigidly to the engaged fighter, as he is in fighting wing. The engaged-fighter pilot's responsibility is to attack and destroy the target, if possible. If the offensive advantage is endangered, the pilot of the engaged fighter should call in his wingman for help and disengage before becoming truly defensive. The engaged fighter–free fighter roles then reverse, and the engagement continues. Offensively the pilot of the free fighter should attempt to maintain a favorable position from which to attack the bogey if needed, but he should not engage until he is called in by the engaged pilot. The exception to this rule occurs when the engaged fighter becomes defensive. In this case the pilot of the free fighter is obligated to attack the bogey immediately, while the engaged fighter pilot does his best not to get shot. When not in extremis, the defensive engaged fighter may be able to maneuver so as to make it easier for the free fighter to gain an offensive position, as illustrated in Figures 5-4 through 5-8.

The advantages of double attack doctrine over fighting wing doctrine are considerable. Offensively, it is much more efficient and effective to allow the fighters to split. The bracket attack can be absolutely devastating. In an engagement, the division of roles allows the engaged pilot more tactical latitude than he has in fighting wing. He does not have to be concerned with out-maneuvering his wingman and becoming separated. In addition, he is now free to use either angles or energy tactics as appropriate. By using these methods, a pair of fighters can defeat even a more capable adversary. One pilot attacks the bogey, causing it to bleed energy, until he can no longer maintain an offensive advantage. Then the engaged pilot calls his wingman down to assume the attack and the cycle is repeated. The bogey is forced to fight each fighter in rapid succession and is denied an opportunity to regain lost energy. Meanwhile the free fighter is building energy for a fresh attack. Eventually the opponent is worn down in this manner until he no longer can successfully defend himself. His preoccupation with his current partner may also cause him to lose sight of the free fighter, resulting in a more effective unseen attack on the next cycle.

Defensively, double attack is also superior, particularly in a missiles environment. The wider cruise formations allowable provide better visual coverage of the vulnerable rear hemisphere and give the fighters more maneuvering room to support each other when they are attacked. Greater lateral and vertical separation between fighters also makes it less likely that both will be seen by an attacker. Also, since the wingman is not required to stay behind the leader once engaged, he can more comfortably maintain a line-abreast cruise formation, which provides better visual mutual support. Once the leader is engaged, the free-fighter pilot can be much more effective defensively, since less of his attention is required for maintaining position. The section's option to split when attacked makes it very difficult for a bogey to press an attack on one fighter without quickly being threatened by the other.

Double attack is not all roses, however. This doctrine requires more training, experience, and judgment on the part of the wingman than does fighting wing. Communications are also more critical, especially if the section has not fought together extensively. The lack or loss of a radio, or communications jamming, can hinder coordination and greatly reduce double attack effectiveness. Another possibility that must be considered in a hostile environment is the wild-card bogey. Two-versus-one engagements can quickly become two-versus-two or two-versus-many. If the pilot of the free fighter is attacked and forced to defend himself, the engaged fighter may be left without support at a critical moment, resulting in two one-versus-one engagements. Because of the greater separation between the fighters and their widely varying directions of flight in double attack, it is considerably easier for hostile aircraft to split the section, breaking down the mutual support. For the same reasons, double attack carries a higher risk of the fighters becoming separated simply through loss of sight.

Although some double attack principles were used occasionally during World War I, the doctrine is generally considered to have been developed during the Spanish Civil War in the late 1930s by Werner Moelders of the German Condor Legion. The installation of radios in most German fighters, the increased difficulty of defending against high-speed attacks from the rear, and the necessity of engaging more maneuverable opponents led to use of the loose pair, which the Germans called the *rotte*. This doctrine provided the Luftwaffe with a considerable advantage over their foes early in World War II, but eventually it was accepted and employed to some extent by most of the Allied air forces, and it survives today as probably the most common air-to-air doctrine in use.

Loose Deuce

> Why let rank lead, when ability can do it better?
> > Commander Randy "Duke" Cunningham, USN

"Loose deuce" is the popular name of a tactical doctrine developed by the U.S. Navy during the Vietnam conflict. Rather than being an entirely new doctrine, loose deuce is actually a rather minor variation of double attack, but its use today is general enough that a discussion of loose deuce is warranted here.

Similarities with Double Attack

Like double attack, loose deuce is based on a loose, coordinated pair of fighters in mutual support. Pre-engaged philosophy and cruise formations are essentially identical in these two doctrines. Combat spread is probably the most common cruising formation, for all the reasons described earlier. A pre-engagement leader is designated, but once they are engaged the pilots revert to engaged fighter–free fighter roles. Variations on the bracket attack (Figure 5-3) are also the bread and butter of loose deuce. Defensive loose deuce maneuvering is essentially identical to that of double attack, and the techniques illustrated in Figures 5-4 through 5-8 are all relevant.

Engaged Maneuvering

In offensive engaged maneuvering philosophy, however, the two doctrines diverge. The primary responsibility of the loose deuce free-fighter pilot is to position for his own attack on the bogey, rather than simply covering the engaged fighter. While the offensive double attack free-fighter pilot is primarily defensive, and awaits the engaged pilot's call before attacking, the loose deuce free-fighter pilot is not under any such restrictions. Each pilot is responsible for visually clearing his wingman and himself. The engaged pilot devotes most of his attention to offense, however, and the free pilot's duties are split about fifty-fifty between offense and defense.

The pilot of the engaged fighter in double attack doctrine fights the bogey one-versus-one until he destroys the target or he faces imminent loss of the offensive. Ideally, there should never be two fighters offensively engaged at the same time. One fighter pulls off the target before the other engages. This is not the case with loose deuce, as the free-fighter pilot constantly works for a favorable attack position and then strikes on his own. This may result in both fighters attacking the target simultaneously, but sustained offensive maneuvering against the same aircraft is to be avoided. Once the free-fighter pilot launches his attack the original engaged pilot usually should disengage to rebuild energy and position for another attack.

> There is a peculiar gratification in receiving congratulations from one's squadron for a victory in the air. It is worth more to a pilot than the applause of the whole outside world. It means that one has won the confidence of men who share the misgivings, the aspirations, the trials and the dangers of aeroplane fighting.
>
> Captain Edward V. "Eddie" Rickenbacker, USAS

Although the distinction between double attack and loose deuce may seem minor, it results in some major tactical differences. While in double attack doctrine the pilot of the engaged fighter is expected to get the kill while the free-fighter pilot stays out of his way and cheers, it is more often the free fighter that gets the shot in loose deuce. The engaged fighter sets up the kill by forcing or inducing the bogey to maneuver predictably, thereby making it easier for the free fighter to position for a shot. This is exactly the role of the engaged fighter in defensive situations using double attack, as discussed in conjunction with Figures 5-4 through 5-8. Loose deuce carries this philosophy into the offensive also. This is not to say that the engaged-fighter pilot should not attempt to shoot the bogey if the opportunity is presented, but he should not risk loss of the offensive (e.g., by risking a gross overshoot or by depleting energy excessively) to do so. When he is opposing a fighter of equal or superior maneuverability, this quite often means that the engaged pilot must be less aggressive in prosecuting his attack. A classic example of this is illustrated by the situation shown in Figure 5-9.

In this scenario the engaged fighter has attained an offensive position in the bogey's rear hemisphere, but it is still beyond effective guns range (assume guns only). Double attack doctrine would call for pure and lead pursuit to close to guns range with proper lead for a high-deflection snapshot against the hard-turning target at time "2'" (broken flight path). If this attack is unsuccessful, the engaged fighter will most likely overshoot and lose the offensive. The attacker will probably have bled considerable energy in this high-G attack, and he may even be in danger of becoming defensive if the bogey pilot decides to exploit the overshoot by reversing to initiate a flat or a rolling scissors. At the very least the high-angle, close-range overshoot temporarily takes the pressure off the bogey, allowing the defender the option of reversing, unloading for acceleration, or diving away to escape before the free fighter can take up the attack.

Loose deuce doctrine would dictate a less aggressive approach to this situation. Rather than pulling for an immediate but low-percentage shot, the pilot of the engaged fighter employs pure and lag pursuit instead, to

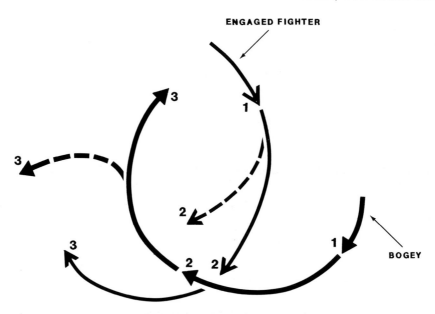

Figure 5-9. Loose Deuce Engaged-Fighter Maneuvering

establish a commanding position deep in the bogey's rear hemisphere (solid flight path). By maintaining increased nose-tail separation with the defender at time "2," the engaged pilot avoids a serious overshoot, preserves his energy, and achieves a temporary lag-pursuit position.

If the bogey pilot reverses after time "2," he subjects himself to a gun attack, as shown by the broken flight path to time "3." He is therefore encouraged to continue turning in the original direction (solid flight path to time "3"), which makes him predictable for a longer period of time. This predictability may allow the free fighter to position for an unseen attack that is more effective and lethal. As a rule of thumb, the engaged fighter needs to force the adversary through about 360° of predictable turn in order to allow the free fighter a reasonable chance of success, especially when only RQ weapons are involved. Having accomplished this task, the engaged fighter has served its purpose; but if the engaged pilot allows the bogey to change its maneuver unpredictably (possibly because of a premature, unsuccessful attack), the free-fighter pilot's attack plan will be spoiled and the fight will be prolonged unnecessarily. The bogey may also be unpredictable if the engaged fighter does not apply sufficient pressure. The target must be threatened to the point where any significant change in its defensive maneuver will get it shot by the engaged fighter. Applying just the right amount of pressure is the engaged pilot's most critical duty. He should plan and execute the attack with the goal of maintaining this pressure as long as possible, and he should take only those shots which will allow him to maintain that pressure.

This technique has a very close analogy in basketball. The offensive ball handler can attempt to charge through the defense, taking whatever shot at the basket becomes available at the risk of throwing the ball up for grabs, or he can prosecute his charge only until his path is blocked, then pass off to his wide-open teammate for an easy basket. In double attack, the team-mate (free fighter) positions for the offensive rebound, while in loose deuce he looks for an open shot. The ball handler (engaged fighter in loose deuce) sets up the shot by forcing the defense to concentrate on his play for the basket.

The pilot of the free fighter in loose deuce doctrine is responsible for positioning as quickly as possible into a lethal firing position. The first step in this process is to predict the bogey's future flight path and the resulting movement of the lethal weapons envelope. The pilot must then decide on the fastest way to reach this envelope, and maneuver accordingly. This process, which is illustrated in Figure 5-10, highlights the importance of bogey predictability.

At time "1" in this scenario the fighters have bracketed the bogey, which is meeting the southern fighter head-on. The wingman, coming in from the north, has performed a lead turn and has a good offensive bite at the pass, forcing the bogey to turn hard left to defend. Since the pilot of the northern fighter is in the best position to apply pressure, he assumes the role of engaged fighter. Rather than attempting an immediate, high-angle attack, however, the engaged fighter avoids overshooting the defender's six o'clock by easing into a lag position at time "2," pushing the bogey around in a predictable left turn. A reversal by the bogey at this point would subject it to a gun attack by the engaged fighter.

Meanwhile the pilot of the free fighter pulls his nose up into a fairly

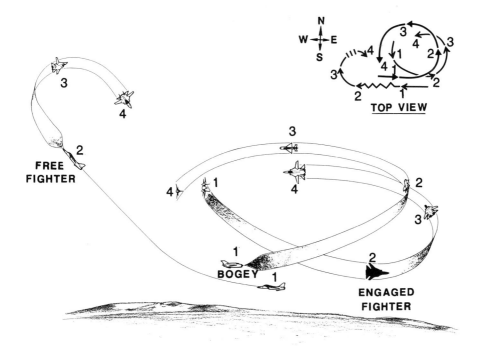

Figure 5-10. Loose Deuce Free-Fighter Maneuvering

steep zoom climb and extends straight ahead. Looking back over his shoulder at time "2," he has a nice view of the fight and can begin to plan his attack. The bogey is in a shallow oblique climbing left turn, and the engaged fighter is pushing it around the circle using lag pursuit in a low yo-yo. If this situation continues the engaged fighter will eventually pull to the inside of the bogey's turn in order to close the range and maintain offensive pressure. If the free-fighter pilot can attack from outside the target's turn, from its belly-side, he will have created a bracket. Therefore, the pilot of the free fighter plays his oblique turn between times "2" and "4" for a high-side gun attack from the bogey's belly-side at time "4." Such a well-planned, unseen attack should have a high probability of success.

Analysis of this engagement shows that the engaged fighter did a good job of maintaining offensive pressure on the bogey, occupying the defender's attention and forcing a predictable turn through about 270°. This gave the free-fighter pilot the necessary time to project the bogey's flight path and position for an effective shot. The free fighter's pull-up at time "1" served several purposes. First of all the straight-ahead extension buys the free fighter some time until the flow of the fight can be determined. If the engaged fighter had overshot at time "2," and the bogey had reversed, the fight could have proceeded to the right instead of to the left as shown. By not committing himself to a left or a right turn immediately at the pass, the pilot of the free fighter has preserved the option of performing an oblique turn either left or right at time "2" to optimize his attack after the engagement has settled into a predictable pattern. The extension also gets the free fighter outside the horizontal bounds of the fight to facilitate a belly-side entry. In addition, extending away from the fight and zooming well up above the plane of the bogey's turn increases the chances that the opponent will lose sight of the free fighter. A small turn one way or the other between times "1" and "2" might be justified if the pilot of the free fighter can take advantage of the sun to mask his attack.

The free pilot's choice of a pull-up at time "1" could also be altered by the weapons available. Positioning above the fight is quite favorable for a gun attack, since the high-side attack offers somewhat greater margin for error and is practiced often. Missile armament, however, leads to other considerations. It might be preferable, for instance, to extend away in a dive at time "1," which would give the free fighter a more desirable look-up shot coming back into the fight, as well as generating more separation from the target for missile min-range considerations. Such a nose-low extension can also hamper the defender's visual problem by removing the free fighter from the bogey's altitude, and possibly by masking the aircraft against the terrain. For a RQ missile attack the free pilot should generally plan to attempt a belly-side entry and a launch as close as possible to 90° off the target's tail on the belly (cold) side. Although this high AOT is not strictly "rear quarter," it may be ideal for missile guidance if acquisition is possible at this aspect. An AAM launched on the target's belly-side tends to stay there through much of its flight, making it unlikely the target pilot will see it. As the target continues to turn away from the missile, more and more of a tail-on aspect is presented, which decreases track-crossing rate and improves fuzing in the end-game. Planning for a 90°

AOT belly-side launch also provides more margin of error, since if the free-fighter pilot is a little late in positioning for the shot he should still have a good RQ firing opportunity.

One other consideration is pertinent in situations where the bogey is all-aspect missile equipped. In the engagement shown in Figure 5-10, the free fighter presents the bogey with a lovely look-up shot at about time "3." The diving-extension option just discussed for the free fighter at time "1" might provide some protection from this situation. Another free-fighter option against an all-aspect missile is to pull up steeply vertical at time "1," loop over the top of the fight, and attack the bogey from high inside its turn, with either guns or all-aspect missiles. This maneuver was depicted in Figure 2-19. Remaining inside the bogey's turn in this way prevents it from pointing at the free fighter for a shot and generates something of a vertical bracket with the engaged fighter coming up from below. It is somewhat easier for the bogey to defend against, however, with a break turn to the left in the general direction of both the antagonists. The free fighter is also more likely to be seen in an attack from the inside (hot side) of the bogey's turn.

At time "2" in Figure 5-10 the pilot of the free fighter chose a right-hand oblique turn as optimum for his attack. This option is known as "counter-flow" because the free fighter is turning in the opposite direction to the general flow of the fight, i.e., free fighter turns right while bogey turns left. This option quite often results in the quickest attack for the free fighter. In this case the free fighter is in position as the bogey completes about 270° of turn. The "in-flow" option, with the free fighter turning left in this case, would have required about 360° of bogey turn for the free fighter to gain a firing position.

Although counter-flow maneuvering is usually quicker, it is also more difficult. During the final stages of the attack (time "3" to time "4"), the fighters approach almost head-on with high closure and rapidly changing target aspect. These conditions make attack timing very critical and lead to a large number of missed shot opportunities. Although the in-flow attack takes longer, things are changing much more slowly in the final phase of the attack, so the approach can be less hurried, with easier timing and greater precision. Generally in-flow maneuvering results in greater separation for missile min-range considerations. Another factor here is maintaining sight of the fight. In this case the counter-flow turn allows the free-fighter pilot to watch the bogey through the entire maneuver. The in-flow option here would have required "kicking the fight across the tail," with added probability that visual contact would be lost, at least temporarily. This is not a general characteristic of in-flow maneuvering, however. In some situations counter-flow turns require pulling the bogey across the tail, so this consideration should be factored into free-fighter attack planning.

Engaged Fighter–Free Fighter Responsibilities

In summary, the primary responsibility of the pilot of the free fighter in loose deuce doctrine is to kill the bogey as quickly as possible, without placing himself in undue danger. Generally this goal is accomplished most effectively by keeping sight of the bogey, using the vertical plane, and maintaining a high energy level while maneuvering to the target's belly-side. When convenient, environmental conditions should be exploited to mask the attack (i.e., sun or terrain masking). The free-fighter pilot's secondary responsibility is to maintain visual defensive coverage for himself and his wingman as protection against additional threat aircraft, SAMs, etc.

The loose deuce engaged-fighter pilot, on the other hand, is primarily responsible for maintaining offensive pressure on the bogey to force it into a predictable flight path for the free fighter. If during this process the bogey presents an opportunity, the engaged pilot should not hesitate to blow it away; but, in general, if the bogey can be forced into a predictable flight path, the free fighter will have the quicker chance to reach a lethal position. The pilot of the engaged fighter should employ lead, pure, and lag pursuit, high and low yo-yos, and barrel-roll attacks as appropriate to remain a serious offensive threat for as long as possible without severely depleting his energy. Although the bogey may be induced into a predict-able flight path from a defensive position (e.g., the drag technique shown in Figure 5-7), this technique is less desirable since the bogey pilot usually has the option of disengaging or switching his attention from one fighter to the other at critical moments, frustrating or delaying the desired outcome of the engagement. The pilot of the engaged fighter, therefore, should maintain a high energy level and exercise sound judgment as to the amount of offensive pressure that can be exerted without increasing the risk of becoming defensive. Once it is trapped in a serious defensive situation, the engaged fighter becomes more of a hindrance than an asset to the free fighter, especially in slow-speed scissoring conditions, in which the bogey is unpredictable and too near the engaged fighter to provide a safe target. Whenever facing imminent loss of the offensive, or when effective offensive pressure cannot be maintained, the engaged pilot should call his wingman back into the fight and assume the role of free fighter if practical. The engaged-fighter pilot's secondary responsibility is to maintain a defensive visual lookout for himself and the free fighter. Practically speaking, since the engaged pilot will have to devote almost all of his attention to the bogey, his defensive lookout is likely to be very marginal, leaving the free fighter with most of the defensive load. Multiple-crew fighters can be much more effective at this, since offensive and defensive duties can be divided among crew members.

Analysis of Loose Deuce Doctrine

Loose deuce has some considerable advantages over other doctrines in the two-versus-one scenario. Use of the fighters in a shooter/shooter relationship, rather than in shooter/cover roles, as with double attack, results in much greater offensive efficiency. When a section is fighting a better-turning opponent, double attack doctrine usually requires considerable time to wear down the bogey's energy before an effective firing position can be achieved. Loose deuce, on the other hand, can provide a shot opportunity much quicker, often within only one turn.

Defensively against a single threat loose deuce and double attack doctrines are essentially identical. In a nonsterile environment, however, loose deuce fighters are more vulnerable to attack since the free-fighter pilot's attention is split between offensive and defensive responsibilities. Referring to Figure 5-10, for instance, note how little support the fighters can render each other at about time "2." A "break" call from the wingman in case of a second bogey attack or a SAM sighting is about all the help that could be offered for a considerable period of time with the fighters so widely separated by distance and direction of flight. A good double attack free-fighter pilot, however, would most likely be high above the fight at time "2," inside the bogey's turn, in a much better position defensively.

The only proper defense is offense.
                                        Air Vice-Marshal J. E. "Johnnie" Johnson, RAF

Although double attack might offer a more effective defense against unexpected threats in the two-versus-one nonsterile environment, in some cases the best offense truly may be the best defense. Lack of offensive efficiency in double attack doctrine, particularly when the fighters are opposing a better-turning bogey, prolongs the engagement unnecessarily, thereby subjecting the section to higher risk of attack. In many cases, especially in low- to medium-threat environments, loose deuce maneuvering allows the section to terminate the engagement quickly and rejoin in a good defensive formation before coming under a second attack. A section using double attack doctrine would run a higher risk of being bounced by another bogey, but it probably would be better able to defend against such an attack. In a very high threat environment, however, when even a loose deuce section can expect to be jumped during a two-versus-one engagement, double attack may be the doctrine of choice. Double attack also becomes more viable against a very inferior bogey aircraft or pilot, since the engagement can be terminated quickly.

Communications between fighters is essential for high effectiveness with either loose deuce or double attack. The engaged-fighter pilot in double attack should give the free-fighter pilot as much warning as possible before calling him in to assume the offensive role. Likewise, the free pilot may need to communicate defensive action to the engaged pilot in case of a second attack.

In loose deuce both fighters have defensive duties that require communications. In addition, the engaged pilot should tell his wingman what he is trying to force the bogey to do and how effective he expects to be at this task. Meanwhile, the free-fighter pilot probably has a better picture of the overall situation and often can make the job easier by directing the engaged pilot to influence the bogey's turn in one direction or the other. Defensively this may mean that the engaged fighter drags the bogey in the best direction for the free fighter's position. Offensively the bogey's maneuver can sometimes be influenced by intentional overshoots and by giving the bogey flight-path separation during a forward-quarter pass to induce a turn in the desired direction. All offensive directions by the free-fighter pilot to the engaged pilot are advisory only, however, and the engaged pilot should not follow any directions that would place him in unacceptable jeopardy.

Another situation calling for rapid communications is when the bogey pilot "switches" his attention from one fighter to the other. Such a switch usually demands a swap in engaged fighter–free fighter roles and should be called out instantly by whichever pilot first sees it. Loose deuce also leads to problems in clearly defining the free fighter–engaged fighter roles, since there are many instances when both fighters are attacking simultaneously. Generally it is the free pilot's responsibility to announce his attack and call for a role switch if he judges himself to be better positioned to assume the duties of engaged fighter. In cases where both fighters remain engaged for any period of time, offensive and defensive efficiency are both impaired. Neither pilot can provide effective defensive lookout in this situation. In addition, the two engaged fighters tend to drift toward the same piece of sky (generally inside the bogey's turn), where they are easy to see and can be fought as one aircraft, much like the situation with fighting wing doctrine. The fighters also tend to get in each other's way, and the danger of midair collisions increases. Double attack doctrine suffers fewer problems in role definition because responsibilities are more clearly divided.

Communications have always been a problem in air combat, and they probably always will be. Much attention is required in training to ensure timely, descriptive, and brief commentary. Personal call signs and standardized brevity codes should be used, and all transmissions by one pilot must be acknowledged by the other. In combat situations there may be hundreds of fighters in the area on the same radio frequency, which can render even essential communications virtually impossible. This situation should be avoided whenever possible by use of several different tactical frequencies (but all fighters in any local engagement area should be on the same frequency), and strict radio discipline must be observed.

Intentional comm-jamming might also be a fact of life in combat, and it is usually accomplished by broadcasting high-power noise on the opponent's tactical frequencies. Jam-resistant radios, very short transmissions, and frequent channel changes may offer some relief. Very low altitude operations may also enhance communications, as terrain may blank the enemy's ground-based jamming transmitters. Quite often two pilots in close proximity will be able to communicate adequately through the noise. This fact, and the somewhat reduced communications requirements of double attack, may favor this doctrine over loose deuce in heavy comm-jamming conditions. Either doctrine is still usable in this environment with practice, but reduced efficiency can be expected of both. Fighting wing doctrine is probably least affected by comm-jamming (intentional or otherwise), but depending on the bogey aircraft, its weapons, and its pilot abilities, fighting wing may not be effective either offensively or defensively.

Some forms of nonverbal communications can also be useful in comm-out or limited-comm conditions. In very close pre-engagement formations, hand signals may be used. In wider formations, coded movements of the leader's aircraft, such as rolls, short repetitive turns, or short climbs and dives, can be employed for signaling. Other visual signals, such as dumping a little fuel, jettisoning external fuel tanks, and creating burner puffs have also been used. During World War I, before installation of radios in fighters, even color-coded flare pistols were widely employed as signaling devices.

> In the air you cannot find a general or a colonel. Who has the most kills, he was the leader. . . . It worked very well in the war.
>
> Colonel Erich "Bubi" Hartmann, GAF

The complexities of both double attack and loose deuce doctrine require a high degree of pilot training and experience to be effective. While the wingman in fighting wing doctrine has few responsibilities other than formation flying and defensive lookout, this is certainly not the case in the more advanced doctrines. Particularly with loose deuce, a high level of responsibility, skill, and judgment are required of both pilots. For greatest efficiency members of the section should constantly train, talk, eat, and sleep together. Each team member must know what the other is thinking, what he will do in various situations, his strengths and weaknesses. This intimate knowledge also serves to reduce some of the communication requirements in combat.

> One has to know one's flying partner.
>
> Baron Manfred von Richthofen

One-versus-Two Maneuvering

The foregoing discussions have demonstrated the power and effectiveness of two fighters operating in mutual support against a single adversary. But what about the other side of the coin? How can a single fighter survive and even prevail when outnumbered two-to-one? The answer is "Very carefully!" First of all the pilot of the singleton must realize when he is engaging two opponents that he has already broken one of the cardinal rules of air warfare: Do not engage without advantage. This sage piece of advice can be ignored only at great risk. In this case the singleton pilot is outnumbered, so he already has one strike against him and can ill afford another. He must weigh all the tactical factors carefully and attempt to optimize them in his favor.

Offensive Maneuvering

> One should force the battle upon the enemy, not have the battle forced upon oneself.
>
> Major Sholto Douglas, RAF
> 6 Victories, WW-I
> (Marshal of the RAF during WW-II)

Surprise and offensive advantage are two of the most important factors to consider. The singleton pilot should stalk his victims carefully and attain a favorable position before committing to the attack. High in the section's rear hemisphere, out of the sun, is a favorite position. From such a perch the fighter may be able to dive on the section unseen, close quickly, and eliminate one of the bogeys before the section knows what hit it. If he has been successful and is still favorably positioned, the attacker may choose to take on the remaining bogey one-versus-one, or simply dive away and disengage at high speed. If the first attack is unsuccessful, the disengagement option is usually called for. Depending on weapons and environmental considerations, other attacks may also be viable or even preferable, but the high, diving approach has been most successful.

> If you have to fight with the eyes only, not with using instruments [such] as radar . . . then the first thing that I do is I go to the sun and I come from the sun as I start my attack. . . . Always with your eyes fly into the sun and never have the sun in your backdoor. . . . That's very dangerous.
>
> Colonel Erich "Bubi" Hartmann, GAF

When preparing to engage a section offensively, the singleton pilot is presented with the choice of which bogey to attack first. Generally the best choice is the more vulnerable bogey, which is usually the one behind in echelon or trail formations. The rear hemisphere of this "sucked" bogey is probably least well guarded visually, making surprise easier. In addition, the "acute" bogey, the one ahead in the formation, will require some time to get turned around and into position to support the wingman. Figure 5-11 depicts the preferred method of attacking an echelon pair.

This figure shows a section of bogeys in echelon formation. At time "1" the singleton closes on the wingman from very nearly six o'clock, probably in a dive to increase closure and take advantage of sun position for surprise, and to provide greater attack speed for possible escape if the attack is detected or is not successful. High six o'clock is a very difficult area to defend, but it may not be optimum for environmental conditions (e.g., high overcast clouds that may highlight the attacker) or weapons, so a climbing

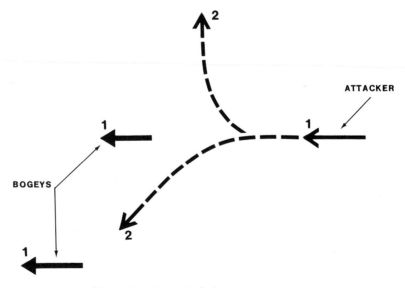

Figure 5-11. Attacking a Section in Echelon

approach may be preferable. One useful compromise is to dive slightly below the bogey's altitude and then attack from low six o'clock in a shallow climb.

Following the initial attack on the wingman, the singleton pilot can assess the situation and decide whether to continue the attack on the leader (track 2) or break away and bolt for home (track 2'). Factors to be considered here are fuel state, the degree of surprise achieved, success of the first attack, and relative performance of the bogey aircraft and their weapons and pilots. Quite often an aggressively flown singleton achieving a surprise attack can so demoralize a hostile section that it completely forgets about its offensive potential and reacts only defensively.

The following engagement describes John Godfrey in his P-47 making an inadvertent solo attack on an unsuspecting pair of German Me 109s which are apparently stalking a formation of American B-17 Flying Fortress bombers ("Big Friends").

> When I saw two ME-109's in back of the Fortresses, I peeled off from formation and dived on them. "Shirt Blue Purple One, this is Shirt Blue Purple Two. Cover me. I'm diving on two 109's attacking the rear box of Big Friends. Over."
>
> There was no answer. Looking to my rear I saw that no one was following me, but it was too late for me to change my mind; I'd committed myself to the attack and had to follow through. There was cloud cover down below, and maybe this influenced my judgment. The two ME-109's flew blissfully along unaware of my approach from 8,000 feet above them. Their Number Two man flew to the rear in much the same fashion as we did. For this reason I chose him for my first target, and when his wings touched both outside circles of my ring sights, I let him have it. Strikes appeared all over the plane and suddenly his engine was smoking. Still flying faster than the leading ME-109, I banked into him and pressed the firing button again. Strikes all around, but still he flew on. I straightened into line astern of him and fired again. Bits of his plane were breaking off. With my finger pressed firmly on the firing button I watched the frantic efforts of the pilot as he stood up in the cockpit and threw himself over the side, his body hurtling by me. I pulled my plane up and slowly my air speed slackened.[3]

As explained, the combat-spread or line-abreast formation normally offers the fighter section the best defensive lookout and maneuvering potential. Attacking a combat-spread section is therefore somewhat more difficult. Again, stalking the prey is in order to reach a favorable position before attacking. In this case there is no trailer to pick on, but some areas are generally more vulnerable than others. For instance, since the wingman's primary duties are to maintain position with his leader and visually cover the leader's rear hemisphere, this area is usually well defended. The leader, on the other hand, is often burdened with navigational and offensive responsibilities and does not have to watch the wingman so closely to maintain position, so the wingman's rear hemisphere is normally less well guarded. Singling out the wingman in a combat-spread formation is not always easy, but, given a little observation time, the attacker can usually determine the wingman's aircraft as the fighter that maneuvers more radically in an apparent effort to scramble back into position after a section change in direction.

Quite often there will be some altitude split between the fighters, and typically the wingman will be the higher of the two, allowing himself some energy margin which can be useful for maintaining position during heavy maneuvering. When performing a diving attack, it is usually preferable to hit the high bogey first, since it will take the low bogey longer to be a threat because of its lower energy level. Diving on the high bogey also allows the momentum of the attack to carry through the first target and down onto the second. Additionally, this technique prevents the attacker from ever being co-altitude with either bogey prior to the attack, which reduces his chances of being seen. Bogey visual lookout is normally best in their altitude band.

As in most aspects of tactics, there is some difference of opinion about whether to attack the leader or the wingman of a section.

> If you attack a formation . . . that is deployed . . . so that the risk in attacking any one aircraft is equal, always take a crack at the one who appears to be leading; he may be a big shot!
>
> Captain Reade Tilley, USAAF

The leader in most cases will be more experienced and more dangerous, and therefore he will be the more valuable target; but he is also likely to be harder to surprise. It is true that once the section leader has been eliminated the wingman should be less effective as a single, making a double score easier to achieve. If this particular leader keeps losing wingmen, however, he will not be a leader very long, and he can be picked off after he has been demoted to wingman.

> The peacetime qualifications for promotion—age and seniority—do not apply in war.
>
> Air Vice-Marshal J. E. "Johnnie" Johnson, RAF

All else being equal, an attack from the right side of an enemy section is often most effective. This is because the usual right-handed cockpit control configuration of most fighter aircraft makes it more difficult for the pilot to twist around to the right than to the left for visual lookout. Defensive break turns to the right are also usually a little slower, for the same reason.

> Always attack a lone enemy fighter from slightly to starboard of dead astern, as 95% of all pilots keep a better lookout to port, as it is natural to turn both the aircraft and body to the left.
>
> Captain Reade Tilley, USAAF

When it is necessary to attack a section from below, the lower bogey is normally the target of choice. It must be recognized, however, that the higher bogey will have greater energy than the target and can become a threat much faster. A climbing attack normally should not be made unless the attacker can maintain a significant speed margin over the bogeys. Even so, the singleton pilot should not plan to stay with the low bogey for more than a quick, slashing attack before turning his attention to the high bogey.

Figure 5-12 illustrates one method of attacking a section in combat spread. In this scenario the bogey section is in combat spread, with the wingman stepped-up on the right flank. At time "1" the fighter dives on the wingman from a position high and slightly outside the section. Aside from the reasons already discussed, an attack from outside the section on the wingman's side was chosen here for several other reasons. First, this area receives less visual attention from the pilot of the target aircraft, since his primary area of responsibility is inward, toward the six o'clock region of the leader and the section as a whole. Second, such an approach increases the range between the attacker and the section leader on the far side of the formation and presents him with a reduced aircraft profile, both of which limit the chances of the attacker being detected by the leader. Third, this angle of approach provides good visibility of both bogeys throughout the attack.

> Always above, seldom on the same level, never underneath.
>   Major Edward "Mick" Mannock, RAF

In this example the attack is detected just as the fighter approaches maximum missile-firing range, and the target breaks. If possible, the attacker should put a missile in the air at this point, even if he is still out of parameters, just to give the target bogey something to think about other than mutual support. Whether the initial attack succeeds or not, the dive will carry the attacker through the section and down toward the next target (or threat). In this case both bogeys break into the attack, allowing the fighter to slide down onto the leader, who has been thrown into trail. This is a very advantageous situation for the attacker, since he can now work on the leader while keeping track of the wingman on the same side of the aircraft. The wingman's position out in front will leave the singleton

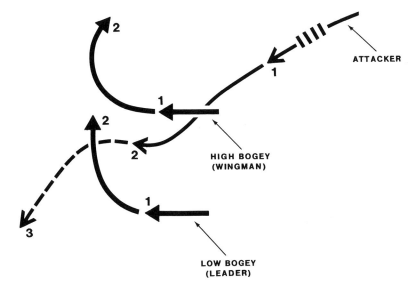

Figure 5-12. Attacking a Section in Combat Spread

pilot with considerable time to hammer the leader before having to worry about the second threat. Time "2" also presents an ideal escape situation in which the attacker can reverse and dive away, out the six o'clock of both bogeys (track to time "3").

> It is well if you are against odds never to stay long after one machine.
> Lt. Colonel W. A. "Billy" Bishop, RAF

Figures 5-6 and 5-7 illustrated the half-split, one of the most effective counters offered by double attack and loose deuce doctrines against such an attack. Figure 5-13 shows one technique the attacker can use in response to the half-split defensive maneuver. Here the initial setup is identical to that of Figure 5-12. Once again the attack is detected at time "1," and the target bogey breaks into the attack. Again the attacker should put a missile in the air at this point, since he has obviously been seen and no longer needs to worry about the missile smoke giving away his location. Even if it is fired for effect at this point, a weapon in the air gives the attacker a great psychological advantage, assuming of course that his weapons load allows such an expenditure. A target under missile attack also is likely to dissipate much more energy in its defensive maneuver, making it less of a threat later on.

The pilot of the southern bogey (the leader in this case), determining that he is not immediately threatened, extends to gain separation from his wingman. Rather than pressing for a gun pass on the original target or breaking away toward the second bogey as in Figure 5-12, the attacker eases into a lag position on the northern bogey while keeping an eye on the

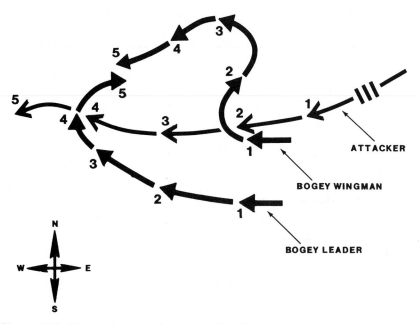

Figure 5-13. Countering a Defensive Half-Split

southern bogey. At time "2" the attacker is still not committed to an overshoot of the original target, and he has created some confusion as to which bogey is being threatened. Is the attacker really pursuing the southern bogey, or is he merely establishing a lag position on the northern one? An unloaded condition, or a slight turn with a steep bank toward the northern bogey, may make this feint more effective, as long as the other bogey can be kept in sight. When the attacker is gun equipped, this lag position can be very threatening to the northern bogey, since a reversal of its turn direction at this point could subject it to a gun attack with the wingman possibly too far away to offer any help. If the attacker is only equipped with missiles, this ploy may be less credible, but it can still be effective.

At time "2" the northern bogey has turned its tail to the wingman and is opening very rapidly. With great separation in both distance and direction of flight, it will be some time before the northern bogey can be of any assistance to the leader. At this point the attacker switches targets and pursues the second bogey, whose pilot continues to drag and calls for his wingman to reverse for a bracket. Unfortunately for the bogeys, the split has generated so much separation by this time that the wingman cannot get back into the fight soon enough. Between times "3" and "4," the attacker makes a gun or missile run on the second bogey and then reverses, exiting the engagement at time "5." The attacker should realize that between times "2" and "4" he will be bracketed and most probably will lose sight of the first target while concentrating on the second. He should, therefore, be aware of his tenuous situation and be careful not to press his second attack too long or turn so much that he is drawn back toward the first bogey, where escape may be doubtful. Note that time "5" has the bogeys meeting almost head-on with their mutual support broken down and the section in general disarray. It will be some time before these bogeys can rejoin in an effective defensive formation to guard against further attacks.

Time "2" in the foregoing engagement is a critical one. The attacker's switch at this point puts maximum strain on the bogeys' coordination. Should the northern bogey not execute a reversal at this time, it would be stranded way out in right field, even farther from the action.

In summary, when the pilot of a single fighter attacks a section he should seek the element of surprise. A rear-hemisphere attack on the more vulnerable bogey is usually optimum. The attack should be planned so that each bogey can be threatened in turn, with minimum threat to the attacker by the other bogey. If the attacker is detected, maximum confusion should be generated by weapons firings and switches at critical moments. Both bogeys should be kept in sight if at all possible, and concentration on any one bogey must be kept to a minimum. If the bogeys remain in welded wing, they might be engaged as a single adversary, with the wingman the more likely target. When the bogeys employ an effective split, however, it is generally not in the singleton's favor to engage in prolonged combat. In this case the attacker should attempt to avoid a bracket by keeping both bogeys on one side of his aircraft, and he should plan to hit and run unless one bogey is destroyed quickly or the singleton has a significant advantage in weapons, performance, or pilot training.

Defensive Maneuvering

Generally speaking, unless the single fighter has a tremendous performance or weapons advantage, prolonged maneuvering with a section of well-coordinated opponents can be very unhealthy and is not recommended. The element of surprise and an offensive advantage should be sought in an effort to reduce the odds quickly to a more manageable one-versus-one situation. If this goal cannot be achieved, the object of the singleton pilot should be to disengage and live to fight another day.

> Speed is life.
>
> Israeli Tactics Manual

The luxuries of surprise and offensive advantage are not always available, however, so the well-dressed fighter pilot should have some techniques in his wardrobe to survive an attack by an adversary section until an escape opportunity can be generated or until help can arrive. The general theory here is to keep both bogeys in sight, or to have one in sight and have a good idea of the other's position and threat potential, and attempt to avoid critically defensive situations. As a rule, energy should be conserved religiously, but there are occasions when energy must be traded for position. The following examples should serve to illustrate some of these techniques.

In Figure 5-14 the single fighter is approached by a hostile section that begins an offensive split north and south at time "1" in an attempt to bracket, as shown in Figure 5-3. The singleton pilot picks one side of the enemy formation and turns sharply (but not depleting energy) in that direction, trying to get outside the bracket (time "2"). In choosing a turn

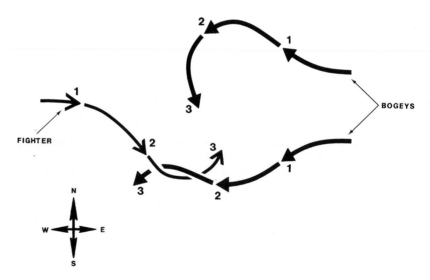

Figure 5-14. Defending against a Bracket: Case 1

direction, the singleton should generally pick the side of the closest hostile fighter, if there is any discernible difference in range. In response to this tactic, the near bogey must continue heading away from its wingman in order to achieve a bracket. The wingman will require some time to react to the situation and begin his turn back into the action. By this time (time "2") the northern bogey has been left somewhat out of the fight as the other bogey drags away from it, so that the singleton will pass the southern bogey long before the wingman can get into a RQ firing position.

As the situation is developing, the pilot of the singleton must watch the northern bogey carefully to observe its reaction. If this bogey pilot reacts quickly, he may be able to gain an effective offensive position before the singleton passes the southern bogey. This may require the singleton to come back left again to negate the attack from the north. In general, switching to the northern bogey should be delayed as long as possible without allowing it to gain too much position advantage. Just how much is too much depends on relative fighter performance and the bogey's weapons. If the singleton pilot can delay until he is passing outside the southern bogey, this bogey is likely to turn south (nose-to-tail with the singleton), placing the bogeys in trail (time "3"). Allowing the first bogey some flight-path separation at the pass may induce its pilot into turning south, as shown. Now the singleton can come hard back left to negate the wingman's attack from the north. If the bogeys have all-aspect missiles, the singleton pilot should be prepared to make a defensive maneuver at about time "3." At this point the singleton is no longer in any immediate danger from the first bogey and can concentrate on defending against the second. If the second bogey has not been allowed a significant offensive position advantage, its attack can be defeated and the singleton should be able to disengage before the first bogey can return to the fight.

Allowing the first bogey a small offensive advantage at the pass induces it to initiate an engagement turn. Subsequently, the pilots of both bogeys are likely to consider their roles to be that of "engaged fighter," causing confusion and reducing the efficiency of either double attack or loose deuce maneuvering. When the bogeys can be induced into turning in the same direction like this, both their offensive and their defensive mutual support is poor.

> A tactic the 109s are very keen on is known as "Boxing." 109s come over top and split into two groups, one on either side of you. Suddenly one group will peel down to attack from the beam. You turn to meet the attack, the other group come in and sit on your tail. If you are leading a section or squadron you can fox them easily by detailing half your force to watch one side and half the other. When you are alone and two box you, it's easy providing you work fast. As the first one starts his dive, chop the throttle, yank the nose around, fire a quick squirt in front of him, then skid into a sloppy half roll, keep the stick well back, and pull out quickly in a skidding turn. The second 109 will have lost sight of you beneath his wing. You should be in a good position to pull up and give him a burst at close range.[4]

A very well coordinated bogey section, however, often can prevent the singleton from getting outside the section at the pass. This can be done when the pilot of the free bogey (northern bogey in this case) reacts quickly to the single fighter's turn away from him. Figure 5-15 shows this situation. As in the previous scenario, the bogey section splits at time "1" and the fighter responds with a turn to the south. This time, however, the northern bogey reacts quickly, turning back to close the singleton and apply immediate pressure. If the defender continues in his attempt to get outside the southern bogey, the northern bogey will achieve a very threatening position. Again the defender delays as long as possible, and then turns hard left to negate the attack of the northern bogey (time "2"). In so doing, the singleton must turn away from the southern bogey, giving it lateral separation and probably some position advantage. In this case the pilot of the southern bogey chooses to take advantage of this lateral separation, turning across the fighter's tail and arriving in a nose-to-nose position at time "3."

The singleton's situation at time "3" is heavily dependent on the weapons involved and the relative performance of the aircraft. When the singleton is faster, it may be able to escape, as shown by the broken flight path to point "4'." If the singleton is slower, the defender may not have the option of escaping, but his fighter's very lack of speed and probable turn-radius advantage can be used to pounce on the engaged bogey (the original southern bogey), which has turned nose-to-nose. The free bogey (original northern bogey) overshot and has been spit out of the fight. This gives the singleton pilot a considerable amount of time to concentrate on the engaged bogey before the free bogey can become a threat again. A gun would be very valuable to the singleton in this situation, since this weapon would probably yield quickest results against the engaged bogey in the flat or rolling scissors that is likely to develop. The singleton's task here is to destroy the engaged bogey quickly, but in so doing it should not get so slow that defense against the free bogey becomes impossible. The pilot of the

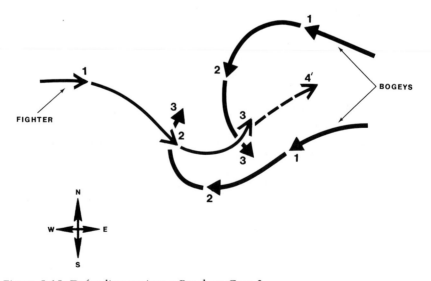

Figure 5-15. Defending against a Bracket: Case 2

single fighter also desperately needs to reacquire and track the free bogey visually. This may be difficult, since sight will most likely be lost temporarily at the overshoot occurring at time "3," but reacquiring sight is important for determining the point at which the singleton must switch off the engaged bogey and defend against the free bogey.

Even if the free bogey is not visually reacquired, however, its pilot's task is not a simple one. He has a long way to go to rejoin the fight, and an engaged bogey pilot who is fighting for his life cannot make the single fighter predictable. The free bogey will also likely have a large speed advantage as it reenters the action, which makes attack timing critical and difficult for its pilot. In addition, guns tracking an aircraft in a scissors, particularly a rolling scissors, is next to impossible, and lobbing a missile into a slow-speed scissors is like flipping a coin to decide which aircraft is the target.

A kill is a kill.

Anonymous

Figure 5-16 shows how the singleton pilot might respond to the free fighter's attack later in this engagement. At time "4" the singleton has gained a good advantage on the engaged bogey in the scissors but has not been able to deliver the coup de grâce. Meanwhile the free bogey is reentering the fight from the south. The pilot of the single fighter sees the free bogey and determines that a reversal to continue the scissors would place the attacker at too great an advantage. Therefore the singleton switches off the engaged bogey to defend against the free bogey, generating an overshoot at time "5." At this point the defender has the option of attempting an escape (the broken flight path to point "6'") or continuing the engagement by reversing as shown by the flight path to point "6." Against much faster bogeys the first option may not be available, and if it is attempted the defender must watch the bogeys carefully to determine whether they have had enough or intend to press their attack. The second option is essentially a repeat of the previous phase of the engagement; namely, hassling one bogey (in this case the one that just overshot) while keeping track of the other.

If all-aspect missiles are carried by the bogey fighters, they can make switches such as that shown in Figure 5-16 very hazardous. In this case close proximity to the engaged bogey may be the singleton's best protection against the free bogey. The engaged bogey might be used as a shield until the free bogey reaches min-range for its missile, and then the singleton can perform a switch more safely.

> The F-4 had a hotter afterburner heat source than the MiGs, and with both MiG and wingman in my sight, it was difficult to fire, lest the missile kill my "wingie."
>
> Commander Randy "Duke" Cunningham, USN

Returning to Figure 5-15 for a moment, and assuming the bogeys are more maneuverable but slower, the singleton simply cannot afford to get tied up one-versus-one with the engaged bogey as just outlined. Success in

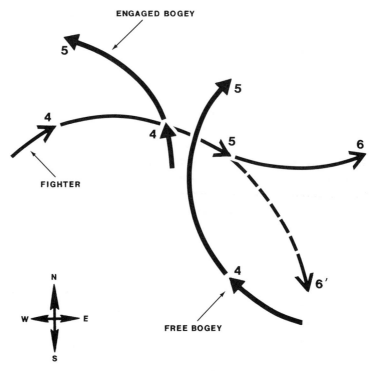

Figure 5-16. One-versus-Two Engaged Maneuvering

such an endeavor requires energy tactics. As described in earier chapters, energy tactics involve a rather protracted process of very predictable turns to deplete the opponent's energy, then some sort of zoom climb at a critical moment to convert an energy margin into a position advantage. Against bogeys using double attack doctrine, this process may be allowed to continue for a while, since the engaged bogey usually will appear to be winning the fight in the early stages. The free bogey in this case can be expected to stay out of the fight, but it will have the opportunity to conserve its energy. Energy tactics require the pilot of the singleton to devote very close attention to the engaged bogey and his own performance, which hinders keeping track of the free bogey. When the proper time for the zoom is reached,the high-energy free bogey may very well be in a position to threaten. Almost superhuman technique and lots of luck would be required for the pilot of the single fighter to time his zoom consistently so as to be immune from both bogeys. Bogey missiles make this process even more hazardous, as the bogeys' look-up shots against a very slow speed target are likely to be superior to the singleton's look-down opportunities. It is also very difficult to mask an aircraft in the sun against two widely separated bogeys.

If the bogeys employ loose deuce techniques, the very predictability and time involved in energy tactics will usually allow a well-flown free bogey to reach an effective offensive position, often undetected. In light of these realities it is not recommended that the high-wing-loaded fighter attempt prolonged engagement with any one aircraft of a bogey section. Instead the singleton pilot should maintain high energy and use his aircraft's superior speed to separate from the fight whenever the opportunity is presented. Time "3" in Figure 5-15 is such a point, following successive forward-quarter passes with both bogeys. The high-T/W singleton may be able to extend away from both bogeys (broken flight path to point "4'"), taking care to watch at least the more threatening opponent, probably the one on the left (original southern bogey) in this case. Against guns-only bogeys, escape may be possible here. When the opponents are missile equipped, however, it soon may be necessary to defend against a weapon, pass through the bogeys once more, and attempt another extension. This process can be repeated (i.e., attempting to get outside a bracket and passing each bogey in turn as nearly head-on as possible) until the singleton can escape . . . at least theoretically. Problems most often arise when the singleton pilot temporarily loses sight of one of the bogeys and then is seriously threatened. Maintaining adequate energy is another problem, especially when a singleton is required to defend against hostile missiles. In addition, limited combat endurance may force an escape attempt under less than optimum conditions.

In a scenario in which the single fighter has a very great T/W advantage over bogeys that are not equipped with all-aspect missiles, the pilot of the single fighter might choose to remain offensively engaged by employing extension/pitch-back tactics as described in the last chapter (Figure 4-7). As long as both bogeys can be kept in sight, the singleton pilot may be able to make repeated passes through the hostile section at high speed, taking forward-quarter gun or missile shots as they become available.

Summary of One-versus-Two Maneuvering

Although one-versus-two is certainly not an attractive scenario, there are numerous examples throughout air combat history in which a single aggressive, well-flown fighter has successfully made a shambles of an enemy formation. The necessary ingredients include attaining an offensive advantage by a surprise hit-and-run attack, maintaining high energy, and knowing when to disengage. When he is caught in neutral or defensive situations, the singleton pilot should maneuver to avoid brackets by keeping both bogeys on the same side of his aircraft, try to keep track of both opponents, maintain high energy, and watch for escape opportunities. Forced to maneuver against two well-flown adversaries, the pilot of a single fighter must be particularly aggressive in an attempt to cut the odds quickly. Engagements prolonged by tentative maneuvering inevitably lead to more serious defensive situations for the singleton.

Notes

1. Grover C. Hall, Jr., *1000 Destroyed,* p. 209.
2. John T. Godfrey, *The Look of Eagles,* pp. 107–8.
3. Ibid., pp. 83–84.
4. Group [sic] Captain Reade Tilley, "Fighter Tactics," *USAF Fighter Weapons Review* (Summer 1981), p. 10.

6

Section Tactics, Two-versus-Two

The advantages of mutual support and the potential effectiveness of section maneuvering were detailed in the last chapter. The recognition of these benefits in air combat has become nearly universal, so that the pair has been a part of the fighter doctrines of the air forces of most nations for some time. Although many doctrines prescribe pre-engagement formations of more than two fighters, most notably divisions of four aircraft, once they are engaged these divisions normally split into elements of two aircraft, and their pilots attempt to coordinate their maneuvering and provide for mutual support. In most cases these pairs also attempt to cooperate with the other section or sections within their original division. This technique is investigated further in the next chapter.

Since the pair has become so widely employed, combat between hostile sections is quite common, and therefore training for this scenario is of great importance. This chapter is devoted to the elements involved in employing one fighter section against another; but before diving into the attack on this subject, a few general comments are in order.

Human Limitations and Task Loading

The guy you don't see will kill you.

Brigadier General Robin Olds, USAF

Although the tactics discussed here are based on many of the same principles that were introduced in the previous chapter, on two-versus-one maneuvering, in practice the addition of one more aircraft to the equation makes a world of difference. The reason for this is human limitations. Most people can handle one job at a time. Many highly skilled and well-trained people (it is hoped that this group includes fighter pilots) can accomplish two tasks concurrently. In air combat this might include maneuvering against a bogey while keeping track of a wingman's position and providing him with some visual defensive coverage. For the two-versus-one free-fighter pilot, depending on doctrine, the tasks include controlling and positioning his own aircraft with respect to either the bogey or the engaged fighter and keeping track of the other aircraft (not to mention checking his own six). To be manageable, this task loading requires extensive training.

The two-versus-two scenario further complicates matters with the addition of a second bogey aircraft that also requires monitoring. This gives each pilot three aircraft to watch during heavy maneuvering while maintaining some facade of a defensive lookout for additional bogeys. Result: Overload! Even in the sterile environment, very few fighter pilots handle this task loading consistently, regardless of the amount of training they receive, a fact that is quite disturbing considering the likelihood of this scenario in combat.

> [Like] nearly all other pilots who come face to face with the [enemy] in the air for the first time, I could hardly realize that these were real live, hostile machines. I was fascinated by them and wanted to circle about and have a good look at them.
>
> Lt. Colonel W. A. "Billy" Bishop, RAF

Human reaction under conditions of task overloading is a well-established phenomenon. First the operator devotes less attention to each task in an attempt to complete them all. At some point, however, this process leads to neglect of one task, which renders the operator ineffective in that area. Depending on the perceived relative importance of each task, the operator then must either concentrate on the completion of one task to the detriment or exclusion of the others, or drop it altogether in favor of a more critical task. The longer this overload condition exists the more tasks are discarded to allow the operator to concentrate on the perceived most critical element, eventually resulting in what might be called "task fixation." Beginning instrument flight students can easily relate this process with the tendency to fixate on one aircraft instrument to the exclusion of all others during hectic moments of blind flying. Add to this situation the stress of air combat, and the predictable result might be described in layman's terms as "Going to hell in a handbasket."

> He who gets excited in fighting is sure to make mistakes.
>
> Baron Manfred von Richthofen

What can be done to reduce the impact of these recognized human limitations? The most obvious route is through constant training and practice, so that the pilot becomes proficient at each task of his mission and can accomplish each one with less attention and effort, thereby leaving more time for the others. Standardized procedures and habit patterns can also play an important part here by allowing the pilot to perform certain portions of the overall mission "automatically" while he devotes brainpower elsewhere. This is where a firm foundation in the basics of aircraft maneuvering and one-versus-one tactics is vital. The pilot simply does not have time to be thinking about optimum techniques of turn and acceleration, or whether the situation calls for a high yo-yo or a barrel-roll attack, if he is to have brainpower remaining for the other elements of his mission. The less concentration the juggler must spend on any one object, the more balls he can keep in the air for a longer period of time. Unlike swimming and bicycle riding, however, the skills required for success in multi-aircraft combat are lost quickly and must constantly be practiced if they are to be retained.

> He must be able to loop, turn his machine over on its back, and do various other flying "stunts"—not that these are actually necessary during a combat, but from the fact that he has done these things several times he gets absolute confidence, and when the fight comes along he is not worrying about how the machine will act. He can devote all his time to fighting the other fellow, the flying part of it coming instinctively.
>
> Lt. Colonel W. A. "Billy" Bishop, RAF

Overloading can also be curtailed by reducing the number of tasks that each pilot must perform to accomplish his mission. To some degree this is the basis on which all the previously discussed mutual-support tactical doctrines are built; namely, division of responsibilities. Using fighting wing doctrine in a two-versus-two encounter, for instance, allows the leader to fight one bogey while keeping track of the other: only two major tasks. The wingman meanwhile must only fly formation and maintain a defensive lookout: again, only two tasks. Tactics, however, are a two-way street, in that the adversary's tasks are also affected. In this case the use of fighting wing by one section reduces the number of aircraft which must be watched by the opposing section, since both fighting wing aircraft remain close enough together to be considered as one unit. This tactic, therefore, makes the job of the opposing fighters easier, and it might be self-defeating. Obviously the choice of tactical doctrine must be based on all known and expected factors, and in many cases on assumptions and conjecture, as well.

A second method of reducing the pilot's task loading is through the use of multi-crew aircraft. A second crewman in each fighter may be able to cover some of the tasks of the pilot during combat, such as keeping track of one bogey aircraft or performing defensive lookout duties for his own fighter or for his wingman. Design and employment of multi-crew fighters does have tradeoffs, however, since these are usually larger, more complex, and more expensive aircraft, and they often have reduced performance relative to single-seat fighters.

Another strategy for minimizing pilot overload is to make each task necessary in air combat as easy as possible. This is largely a function of aircraft and weapons-system design. Every task is composed of a great number of subtasks, each requiring some of the pilot's time and attention. Reducing the number and difficulty of these subtasks makes the whole job quicker and easier, freeing the pilot to "keep more balls in the air." Desirable features in fighter design include good handling qualities in all operating regimes, dependable engines that can take abuse, unrestricted cockpit visibility, and clear, dependable communications. Factors such as these are often overlooked by designers, but they may be every bit as important as the more widely recognized predictors of fighter-aircraft combat effectiveness such as turn, climb, and speed performance. This is especially true for multi-plane engagements. Another very important factor in this environment is relative aircraft size and the effects of camouflage on visual detectability. Obviously the fighter pilot would prefer to be flying the smallest thing in the sky in order to make the opponent's visual acquisition and tracking tasks as difficult as possible.

In the area of weapons systems, effective envelopes and lethality are two of the most important factors. All-aspect capability is desirable, since this can greatly reduce the maneuvering required to attain a firing position. High lethality is necessary because the fighter must be able to destroy the target at the first opportunity. The price of the time and attention necessary for a second attempt may be unacceptably dear in the hostile combat environment. Other, less obvious, factors include weapons-system delays, such as gunsight and radar settling times, which should be minimized; and relaxed aiming requirements (i.e., off-boresight guided missiles). Weapons-system operating switches should be minimized, and design and placement should enable the pilot to manipulate them without looking inside the cockpit or taking his hands or feet off the aircraft controls. In addition, the pilot benefits if all readouts and information necessary for full operation of the aircraft and the weapons system are displayed so that his eyes can remain outside the cockpit constantly during an engagement.

> I will not say that I fought this action ideally, but I led my formation to a fairly favorable firing position. Safety catch off the gun and rocket switches! Already at a great distance we met with considerable defensive fire [from the bombers]. As usual in a dogfight, I was tense and excited: I forgot to release the second safety catch for the rockets. They did not go off. I was in the best firing position, I had aimed accurately and pressed my thumb flat on the release button—with no result. Maddening for any fighter pilot!
>
> Lt. General Adolph Galland, Luftwaffe
> (During his last combat engagement,
> after eight years of combat and 104 victories)

Regardless of training or attempts to minimize the number and difficulty of the fighter pilot's tasks in combat, he is still likely to reach a saturation point if he is exposed to the difficult two-versus-two environment for an extended length of time. Just how long the pilot can keep all the balls in the air depends on all the factors discussed here and many more. This length of time can also change daily, depending on the pilot's physical and mental conditions, weather, etc. Once overload is reached, another length of time will pass before calamity, such as one fighter being attacked by an unseen bogey, results. In recognition of the fact that this result is only a matter of time, tactics should be devised with overload in mind. For example, when the fighter section anticipates it will be overloaded long before the bogeys are (e.g., because of pilot experience level, relative aircraft design, or relative aircraft size), hit-and-run tactics might be adopted to limit exposure to the two-versus-two environment. Or the section may plan to begin the engagement offensively and aggressively, with the hope of quickly reducing the odds, and then make the transition to a more conservative, defensive posture as the anticipated point of overload is approached.

> I scooted for our lines, sticky with fear. I vomited brandy-and-milk and bile all over my instrument panel. Yes, it was very romantic flying, people said later, like a knight errant in the clean blue sky of personal combat.
>
> "W. W. Windstaff," RFC
> Anonymous American WW-I Ace

Conversely, if the bogeys can be expected to reach overload first, tactics can be geared toward extending engagement time and maintaining a constant pressure on the bogeys, at minimum risk, until the opposing section makes a critical mistake. In this case it has been found that the majority of losses can be expected early in a two-versus-two engagement, while the opposing section is likely to have its best situation awareness. As the engagement wears on, the section retaining its situation awareness longer (i.e., the section least likely to overload) should enjoy greater and greater probability of success.

> If you come back from an operation with a kill but without your wingman, you lost your battle.
>
> Lt. Colonel Dietrich Hrabak, Luftwaffe
> 125 Victories, WW-II

In developing a two-versus-two tactical doctrine, overload considerations should be weighed at least equally with aircraft and weapons-system performance comparisons. Training for this scenario should also emphasize the pilot's ability to recognize the signs of impending task overload, so that some allowance can be made (e.g., disengagement or a transition to defensive tactics) before disaster strikes. Recognition of opponent overload is more difficult, and this condition is not normally apparent until it results in an obvious mistake.

Two-versus-Two Tactical Doctrine

All of these factors are important in two-versus-two tactics, which the remainder of this chapter addresses more specifically. These tactics are based on the same doctrines described in the previous chapter on two-versus-one and one-versus-two scenarios.

The viability of fighting wing doctrine in the two-versus-two arena depends largely on the enemy's engaged doctrine, and also on relative pilot, aircraft, and weapons-system performance. If the bogeys also use fighting wing, the two-versus-two scenario essentially becomes one-versus-one. In this case all the tactics discussed in the one-versus-one chapters are relevant, including the modifications made necessary by relative aircraft and weapons-system performance. A discussion of this situation is therefore unnecessary.

When the bogeys are expected to employ a more advanced tactical doctrine (i.e., some form of double attack or loose deuce), the fighting wing section can be considered the singleton as it was described in the one-versus-two discussion in the previous chapter. In actuality the welded wing fighters will probably be somewhat less effective offensively than the singleton because they will be easier to see and they will be less maneuverable. They should be better equipped defensively, however, because of the additional set of eyeballs available. Success under these conditions depends on the same factors outlined for fighting wing in two-versus-one scenarios. The leader conducts the offensive and defensive maneuvering plan while the wingman maintains the fighting wing position and provides defensive lookout and support. Surprise and offensive advantage should be sought whenever possible prior to engagement, normally with the intent to hit and run if the initial attack is not successful. If it is forced to engage in the role of singleton against two bogeys, the fighting wing section must keep track of both bogeys, maintain high energy, employ timely switches, and look for opportunities to escape. In general, without initial advantage and surprise, the probability of success in this scenario is poor for a fighting wing section unless it possesses a tremendous advantage in pilot, aircraft, or weapons-system performance.

In the converse situation, a section of fighters using double attack or loose deuce against welded wing bogeys, two-versus-one tactics can be employed with high probability of success. When the adversary section is expected also to employ one of the more advanced tactical doctrines, the situation becomes much more interesting.

Attack Phase

Figures 5-11, 5-12, and 5-13 illustrated some recommended methods by which a single fighter might attack a bogey section operating in mutual support. These methods are equally applicable to the case of one section attacking another from the rear hemisphere with some element of surprise. The most useful attack formation for this case is usually considered to be a sucked echelon (where the wingman is more than 45° aft of the leader's beam) or trail. This arrangement provides for rapid sequential attacks on each target bogey in turn, while providing some protection for the lead fighter during the attack. It should be recognized, however, that such a formation in general is rather poor defensively, and its use is recommended for only a short duration to improve offensive potential during an actual attack. In order to avoid unpleasant surprises, the fighters generally should maintain a more defensive posture, such as combat spread or an acute echelon (where the wingman is greater than 45° off the leader's tail), until just prior to the actual attack run.

The rules outlined in the previous chapter concerning which bogey to attack first are equally applicable here. In general, the aft bogey in the formation is more vulnerable and should be bounced first. For line-abreast formations the higher bogey is usually more vulnerable, since it will take longer for the lower wingman to offer support. When two combat-spread bogeys are about level with each other, the wingman (when he can be determined) is usually the easier to surprise. It may also be possible in such situations to attack both bogeys simultaneously.

But what if surprise cannot be achieved, and the two sections turn toward each other approaching head-on, essentially neutral? The bracket, as illustrated in Figure 5-3, is still the primary method of attack. In this case each section should normally attempt to bracket the other. The section with the widest initial lateral separation, or the section that commences the bracket first, generally has the advantage. Figure 6-1 illustrates the use of the bracket against the three standard fighter formations: combat spread, echelon, and trail.

In each case the friendly section (bottom of the figure) begins in combat spread, since, as explained earlier, this is normally the most effective pre-engaged formation. At time "1" in the first example a hostile section is detected approaching head-on, also line abreast. Assuming that none of the

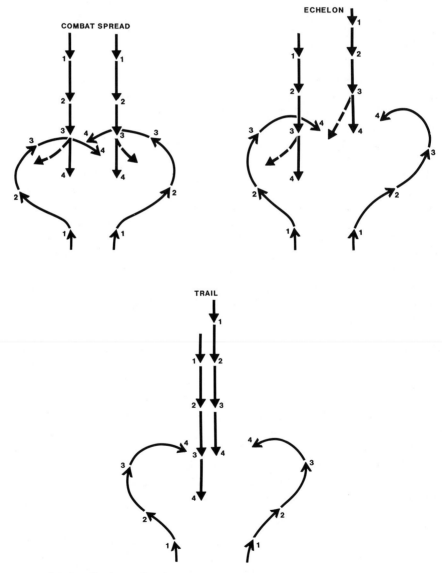

Figure 6-1. Bracketing a Section

fighters has all-aspect missile capability, or that the sections are already inside minimum firing range, the friendly section begins a bracket to convert to a rear-hemisphere position. By time "2" the attackers have successfully bracketed the hostile section and each fighter has generated some lateral separation for a reversal and a lead turn back toward the targets. Note that at time "3" each attacking pilot has a clear view of all aircraft, targets and wingman, on one side of his fighter. The bogey pilots, however, have to look both left and right to get the full picture, greatly adding to their visual acquisition and tracking problems. Odds are, neither defender can keep track of everybody by this point.

In this depiction, between times "3" and "4" the attacking fighters pass behind the bogeys on their respective sides of the formation and attack the one on the opposite side. Although the attackers may have built enough lateral separation to gain substantial advantage against the nearest bogey, especially if the bogeys continue straight ahead as shown, there will be even more separation with the opposite target. In addition, the bogeys are likely to feel most threatened by the attacking fighter on their side of the formation and will probably turn toward this attacker in defense (i.e., each bogey is likely to turn away from its wingman), as shown by the broken flight paths from time "3." Such defensive moves turn the tail of each bogey at the other attacking fighter, which may very well be unseen by the target in any case. For all these reasons the attacking fighters are more likely to have better rear-hemisphere shot opportunities against the bogey on the far side of the enemy formation. If this turns out not to be the case, they have the option of choosing either bogey at the last instant, since they have a clear view of the entire situation throughout the attack.

It should be noted here that although both bogeys may be brought under attack, double attack doctrine does not, in general, allow engaging both bogeys simultaneously. If at least one kill is not obtained in the initial attack, the pilot of the more offensive fighter will normally continue to press his attack while the other pilot assumes the role of free fighter.

Another name for this bracket tactic is the "heart attack." This name might come from the heart-shaped figure inscribed by the flight paths of the attacking fighters; but it may also derive from the near-midair-collisions that often occur between the attackers at about time "4" in this illustration. The danger of a collision may be lessened if the attackers also take an altitude split, one going high and the other low at time "1." An added benefit of this procedure is to produce both vertical and horizontal brackets simultaneously, further compounding the bogeys' problems.

Moving now to the second example of Figure 6-1, the same approach scenario is seen, except that the bogeys are in echelon. Depending on the altitude differences between the opposing sections, the change in bogey formation may not be readily apparent to the attackers at time "1," but this is not critical. They simply begin their bracket as before, and at time "2" it becomes apparent to the pilot on the left that he should begin his counter-turn to pass behind the bogey on his side of the formation. The attacker on the right, however, since his bogey is more distant, must delay or ease his counterturn or risk crossing ahead of the bogey on his side. This delay allows him to build more lateral separation and results in a greater angular advantage against this bogey at the pass, assuming the bogey does not turn into the attack. So the attacker on the right usually will have a better shot on the trailing bogey than on the leader. The left-hand attacker can press the far-side bogey (the trailer in this case) as before, resulting in both fighters converging on the more vulnerable trail bogey, with the enemy leader in a poor position to offer support. The bracket in this case is self-adjusting, and whether the trail bogey continues straight ahead, turns right (as shown by the broken flight path), or turns left, it is probably in a heap of trouble.

The third example in Figure 6-1 shows the bogey section in trail or in a very sucked echelon formation. In this case it should be obvious to each attacker by time "2" that he is facing a trail formation (all these examples assume, of course, that the attacking section has both bogeys in sight), which makes the trailer the most likely target for both. This situation is also probably the most dangerous to the attackers from a midair collision standpoint, and at about time "3" some radio coordination may be called for to clarify which fighter has the lead on the attack.

Obviously the attackers would like to destroy both bogeys, either simultaneously or in rapid succession in the initial attack. The bracket, or "pincer," attacks are designed with this goal in mind; however, if only one bogey can be eliminated, the attacking fighters should still be in an offensive position and can use the two-versus-one tactics already described to engage the remaining bogey. On those occasions when both bogeys survive the initial attack, the considerations outlined previously govern whether the section should attempt to engage two-versus-two or disengage. Mission objectives also play an important part in this decision. Merely disrupting and delaying the enemy formation, or forcing fighter-bombers to jettison their air-to-ground ordnance to defend themselves, may accomplish the attackers' purpose. In other cases only bogey destruction may be acceptable. Some of these considerations are addressed further in Chapter 9, which discusses fighter missions.

The advanced tactical doctrines, when employed in the two-versus-two environment, usually attempt to isolate one bogey from its wingman, and then eliminate each bogey in turn using two-versus-one techniques. Examples of this procedure can be seen in the Figure 6-1 echelon and trail scenarios. In each case the trail bogey is isolated and attacked by both fighters. Ideally this target can be destroyed before the bogey leader, temporarily neutralized by his position, can return and provide support to his wingman.

Figure 6-1 gives examples of how this "divide and conquer" approach might be pursued through use of an offensive bracket. Figure 6-2 illustrates another technique, sometimes called a "drag tactic." In this example the opposing sections, both in combat spread, approach head-on, as in the first scenario of Figure 6-1. Here, however, the attackers (bottom of figure) split only one fighter in an apparent bracket attempt. The other fighter continues merrily along toward a head-on pass with the bogey on its side of the enemy formation. At time "2" the bracketing fighter begins a counterturn back toward the near bogey, which is forced to defend by turning into the attack, while the fighter on the right turns away from its bogey. This turn-away is intended to induce the right-hand bogey into turning away from its wingman by allowing it lateral separation and some offensive advantage. The bogey pilot sees a lot of fighter belly, the "Blue Max" flashes before his eyes, and he goes for what appears to be an easy kill against an enemy who apparently does not see him. The dragging pilot must time his turn-away very carefully so as not to give the bogey a decent shot at the pass (time "3"), considering its weapons capabilities. Meanwhile the bracketing pilot passes outside his bogey at time "3," then essentially ignores it and heads straight for the other bogey. Between times "4" and "5," the pilot of the dragging fighter continues to tempt the bogey pilot by holding him near, but preferably just outside, an effective firing envelope. Against a slower bogey, arcing is useful for this purpose because it allows the bogey to stay fairly close so that its pilot does not get disinterested and start looking around at what is going on. By time "5" the bogey has been suckered into a sandwich, with its wingman way off in left field and unable to render assistance. Following destruction of this bogey, the fighters can rejoin in a good defensive formation and either exit the fight or return to engage the remaining bogey.

Although the drag can be a very useful device, it is in general more risky, and therefore less desirable, than the bracket. Intentional drags place one fighter at an unnecessary disadvantage while it serves as the "bait." This pilot could be in serious danger if his supporting wingman comes under attack and must defend himself or just becomes distracted and loses sight of the dragging fighter. There is also the possibility that the bogeys may not

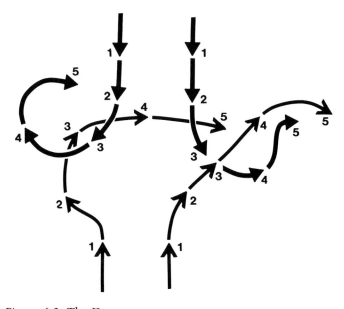

Figure 6-2. The Drag

fall for the ruse, and both of them might pounce on the bracketing fighter. In this case the dragger is often positioned poorly to offer immediate support. Good communications and coordination are required for this tactic, since it would be a disaster if both fighters decided to drag at the same time!

Engaged Maneuvering

Assuming no bogeys are eliminated in the initial attack and two-versus-two maneuvering is indicated, there remains the question of which tactical doctrine to employ. For the reasons stated earlier in this chapter, fighting wing doctrine holds little promise of success unless the bogeys can also be expected to use this tactic (or to operate as single, uncoordinated fighters) and can be beaten in a turning fight, considering opposing weapons, pilots, engagement conditions, etc. Either double attack or loose deuce can be employed in this scenario, but both require some modification. The question of which doctrine is the better of these two is guaranteed to generate some spirited discussions around the bar.

In the last chapter a comparison between these two doctrines in the two-versus-one environment concluded that loose deuce was probably more effective in this scenario because of greater offensive efficiency. Such advantage, however, is not gained without costs, which in this case include increased training requirements, reduced defensive capability, and greater dependency on communications (and therefore greater vulnerability in comm-jam environments). In low- to medium-threat two-versus-one scenarios, the greatly enhanced offensive efficiency of loose deuce probably offsets these disadvantages. The two-versus-two scenario, however, might be considered merely a very high threat two-versus-one environment. It is unlikely, for example, that one bogey can be isolated and engaged in the classic loose deuce manner (as illustrated by Figure 5-10 in the last chapter) without interference from the free bogey. The same statement applies to double attack doctrine to an even greater extent (because it will probably take longer to destroy the engaged bogey), but at least the free fighter can be assigned to defend against any attack.

Following an unsuccessful initial attack using double attack doctrine, the fighter with the better offensive advantage should engage one of the bogeys. The free-fighter pilot then assumes the responsibility of keeping visual track of the free bogey and covering the engaged fighter in the event of attacks from this or other (wild-card) bogeys. The pilot of the free fighter should avoid engagement if at all possible, but of course he must defend himself if he is attacked. In this case he must notify the engaged pilot of the situation and should try to disengage as quickly as possible to resume his covering responsibility. If the engaged fighter is threatened, the free-fighter pilot issues a warning and attacks the offending bogey. This attack, however, is not for the purpose of engaging, but rather for removing the threat to the engaged fighter. Rapid destruction of the attacking bogey is the goal, but simply causing its pilot to break off his attack is usually sufficient. Once this has been accomplished the free-fighter pilot should not press his attack further; doing so would usually be to the detriment of his defensive duties.

The pilot of the free fighter in double attack must exercise a great amount of discipline if he is to fulfill his defensive responsibilities fully in the two-versus-two environment. There is an almost insurmountable urge for both fighters to become entangled in separate one-versus-one engagements. This situation is very dangerous in hostile environments, where either fighter may be jumped by wild-card bogeys. Fighters engaged one-versus-one are also quite vulnerable to attack by the other member of the bogey pair, which may be able to coordinate a switch at a critical moment.

In order for double attack doctrine to be practical in the two-versus-two scenario, the fighters should have turn performance at least as good as that of the bogey aircraft. The fighters should be able to handle themselves one-on-one with the bogeys, since this situation is so likely to occur. Better turn performance also enables the free fighter to frustrate attacks by the free bogey without having to become involved in prolonged offensive or defensive maneuvering. The engaged fighter will also benefit from greater turn performance, since the angles tactics best used with such an advantage place more pressure on the engaged bogey, making it more difficult for this aircraft to escape or break away temporarily for an unsuspected attack on the free fighter.

It is ideal if, once engaged, the pilot of the engaged fighter can prosecute his attack until the bogey is defeated. Switching engaged fighter–free fighter roles is hazardous in the two-versus-two environment and should be avoided when possible. There are two good reasons for this. First, the pilot of the engaged fighter will probably lose track of the free bogey and will require some radio assistance from the free-fighter pilot to locate this bogey during any role switch. Even if the free bogey can be located, the new free fighter (original engaged fighter) is likely to be low on energy and out of position at the time of a role switch, poorly prepared to defend against either the free bogey or a wild card.

A role switch is quite often necessary, however, when either fighter becomes defensive. If the engaged fighter gets into trouble or is threatened by a second bogey, the free fighter should attack in order to relieve the threat. Once he is out of immediate danger, the engaged-fighter pilot should normally assume the role of free fighter while the new engaged-fighter pilot continues to press his attack. Likewise, if the free fighter becomes defensively engaged, the engaged-fighter pilot should terminate his individual engagement as quickly as possible and offer assistance to his wingman as the new free-fighter pilot.

When the bogeys have a maneuverability, weapons, or training advantage that would likely make one-versus-one engagement a losing proposition, both double attack and loose deuce doctrines incur serious problems. With some modifications, however, they may still be viable in the two-versus-two environment. As mentioned previously, it is unlikely that one bogey can be isolated long enough for the attackers to engage it in classic engaged fighter–free fighter maneuvering without interference by the free bogey. This opportunity is even less likely when a section is engaged with superior bogeys.

In such situations double attack and loose deuce might evolve into a series of offensive attacks such as the brackets and drags illustrated in

Figures 6-1 and 6-2. At the conclusion of each attack, whether it was successful or not, the section can quickly rejoin in an effective defensive formation (usually combat spread), then either disengage or maneuver to return for another attack. If tapped during this defensive interval, the section can employ one of the techniques illustrated by Figures 5-4 through 5-8 (defensive splits, sandwich, etc.).

The purpose of this method is to place the greatest possible offensive pressure on the bogeys while minimizing the risks of becoming separated into probably fatal one-versus-one engagements. If an attempt is made to remain offensively engaged for an extended period with multiple bogeys, particularly with smaller and more maneuverable bogeys, there is a very high risk of an unseen attack on one fighter at a vulnerable moment. By striking quickly and then rejoining for defensive mutual support, the section reduces the probability of separation, and it is better able to defend against unexpected attacks.

One of the disadvantages of this method, however, is that in reforming for better defense, the attackers usually place the bogey (or bogeys) in an offensive position behind the section, and in many cases the enemy will be lost from sight. This is certainly an undesirable situation, and, depending on the bogeys' weapons, disengagement may be the best choice at this point, particularly if the fighters have a speed advantage. Returning to face an all-aspect missile threat from multiple unseen bogeys is generally not conducive to reaching retirement age.

Section Reversal Techniques. Against less formidable opposition, such as when one bogey has been eliminated and the remaining opponent is not equipped with all-aspect missiles, a reattack may be much less hazardous. At this point a technique is needed for reversing the course of a section in formation. The prime consideration in development of this tactic should be defensive mutual support. Figure 6-3 illustrates some common methods.

With the in-place turn both fighters turn in the same direction simultaneously. In this example the fighters begin at time "1" in combat spread, either co-altitude or with an altitude split. The pilot on the left turns away from his wingman and will usually lose sight of him between times "1" and "2," regaining sight between times "2" and "3," after the wingman crosses behind and pulls to the inside of the turn. This reversal offers reasonable visual cover to the fighter originally on the side of the turn, but it places the other fighter in trail and out of sight during most of the reversal. An attack on the trailing fighter at time "2," for instance, could be disastrous.

The next example is the cross turn, in which each fighter turns inward, toward its wingman. The fighters meet nose-to-nose just prior to time "2" and continue their turns until they are reestablished line abreast at time "3." This turn provides better visual coverage for the fighters throughout the reversal, since each pilot can see the other aircraft except for possibly a few seconds after they cross. Neither fighter is well positioned for the pilots to offer other than visual and moral support, however, at any time between when the fighters cross and then regain combat spread at about

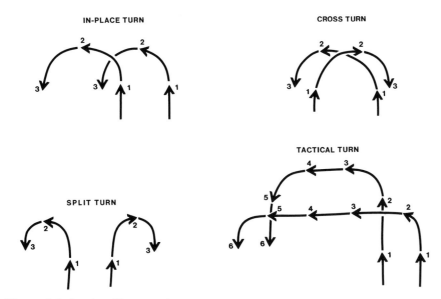

Figure 6-3. Section Maneuvering

time "3." Another problem is the separation that may occur at the conclusion of the reversal. If the fighters begin the turn at time "1" separated by less than one turn diameter and make level turns, their separation will increase at time "3," possibly causing loss of sight and generally reducing defensive capability. Such a wide split may, however, facilitate a bracket attack against bogeys detected at long range in the rear hemisphere. The cross turn can also be used to reduce separation when the section is originally split by more than one turn diameter.

Some of the problems associated with increased separation in the cross turn may be alleviated by split-plane maneuvering. Both fighters can turn obliquely nose-high, or one can turn nose-high and the other level or nose-low. Both these methods tend to reduce final lateral separation, but the latter has some valuable fringe benefits. One is that the low fighter has improved coverage from its higher wingman. Also, the fact that the fighters do not pass so close to one another during the turn makes it more difficult for a bogey pilot to see and track both fighters during the maneuver. This effect is enhanced if the higher fighter at time "1" goes high while the other stays low.

The third maneuver depicted in Figure 6-3 is the split turn, where each fighter turns away from the other. This method is useful as a means of allowing closely spaced fighters to achieve a wide bracket against bogeys detected in the rear hemisphere, but it is undoubtedly the poorest reversal so far considered from a defensive standpoint. Each pilot is out of sight of his wingman for most of the turn, and the extended separations generated are conducive to losing sight completely. Modern high-speed fighters could easily be six to eight miles apart at time "3." At such ranges one pilot is not likely to find his wingman until a fireball marks the spot! This maneuver is therefore not recommended except for very tight turning aircraft, possibly as an offensive or defensive tactic against a threat that is well defined and in sight of both fighters. (The defensive split was discussed in Chapter 5.)

All the reversals discussed to this point have the common problem of exposing both fighters to attacks from one direction while they are turning to meet a threat from the other direction. Referring to Figure 6-3, bogeys approaching from the top of the page (i.e., the forward hemisphere at time "1") could be big trouble if they tapped the fighters from their belly-side during any of these reversals. Since little protection is available from such an attack, these turns can all be quite dangerous in a hostile environment, and they are better suited to conditions when the threat sector can be well defined.

The last illustration in Figure 6-3 depicts the tactical, or "tac," turn. Also known as the delayed turn or cross-over turn, this turn is referred to here as tactical, tac, or delayed to avoid confusion with the cross turn. The tactical turn accomplishes the reversal in two segments of 90° each. At time "1" in this example a "tac turn left" is called, whereupon the fighter on the right begins an immediate left turn. The pilot of the left-hand fighter delays his turn for a few seconds and continues straight ahead to time "2," when he, too, turns left. At time "3" both fighters complete 90° of turn and regain a line-abreast formation. They can then continue in this new direction for some time, as shown, to provide them an opportunity to search the area thoroughly in all directions, or they can immediately commence another "tac ninety left" to complete the reversal. As with the other turns described, split-plane maneuvering is also useful with the delayed turn. Generally the inside fighter turns nose-high during the first stage (time "1" to time "3") while the outside fighter stays level or nose-low. At time "4" the fighter high on the outside (right in this case) can dive toward the inside of the turn while the inside fighter completes a climbing left turn from time "5" to time "6."

There are several advantages to this method over the others described. The periods when one fighter is in a poor defensive position, or out of sight, are kept to a minimum (here a short period between times "2" and "3," and again between times "5" and "6"). In cases when the threat sector is not well defined, the tac turn provides for visual coverage of the section's belly-side throughout the turn. Since only one fighter is doing any serious turning at any given time, the other pilot is free to clear the vulnerable belly-side of his wingman. In addition, dividing the reversal into two 90° segments with a straight-line segment (time "3" to time "4") in between tends to place a rear-hemisphere threat on one side of the section, inside the turn. In this case a bogey trailing the section at some distance at time "1" will normally be caught on the inside (left side) of the section's turn by time "6." Narrowing the threat sector to one side of the section greatly facilitates visual acquisition of an attacking bogey. The drawback here, however, is that the large effective radius of the section's turn is much like arcing in the one-versus-one case, and it allows the bogey to cut across the circle and gain an angular advantage on the section.

The tac turn can also be very useful when the section wishes to disengage from slower bogeys in the rear hemisphere but must go either around or through the bogeys to get home. This situation is illustrated in Figure 6-4. In this scenario the section is line abreast and headed away from home, and it suspects a slower bogey is somewhere behind it out of range. Perhaps the bogey has all-aspect weapons and superior maneuverability, and the section would like to avoid tangling with it on the way back to the barn. One possibility is a 90° tac turn right or left, followed by a long extension. The bogey is likely to counter by trying to cut the section off using lead pursuit (time "2"). Eventually, however, the slower bogey must drift back into a long trail once more (time "3"). At some point the section then performs a second tac ninety in the same direction and streaks for home (time "4"). The bogey attempts to close by again using lead pursuit, but it still can't get close enough for a shot.

Although it is effective, this technique may not be practical in all cases. The straight-line extension between turns must be lengthy or the bogey may still manage an intercept. Constraints on the section's combat fuel endurance or area restrictions (e.g., there may be hostile SAM sites on either side of the engagement area) may force the section into a tighter reversal, requiring it to fight its way back to the bar.

One further reversal method is worth mentioning for its usefulness in select situations. This is the section vertical pitch-back, where both fighters perform simultaneous half Cuban-8s (i.e., a vertical pull-up to the top of a loop, then a roll to an upright attitude and a dive back down to near the original altitude). When a lower-energy bogey that is not equipped with all-aspect missiles is behind the section, this method allows the section to remain line abreast throughout the reversal and either meet the bogey head-on with minimum flight-path separation or pass overhead at an unreachable altitude. Against a guns-only bogey a section Immelmann might be better. The Immelmann (described in Chapter 4) is a vertical pull-up to the top of a loop, followed by a roll to the upright attitude and acceleration while remaining roughly level. This method keeps the sec-

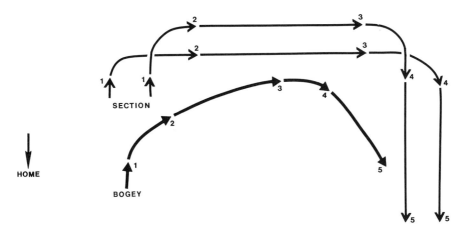

Figure 6-4. Tac-Turn Disengagement

tion high above the low-energy bogey, out of guns range. Another possibility is the section vertical reversal, where both fighters pull up into a near-vertical zoom, perform a rudder reversal or some other end-swapping stunt at very slow speed at the peak of the zoom, and accelerate steeply back downhill for a simultaneous pull-out.

While these maneuvers can be very valuable in certain situations, they do have severe limitations. High-energy bogeys may catch the fighters at slow speed near the top of their pitch-backs, with disastrous results, and all-aspect missiles just love those high, slow targets. These techniques can also be dangerous in high-threat environments, where the section may be jumped by wild-card bogeys or fired at by SAMs while the aircraft are at slow speed.

Strike-Rejoin-Strike.

> The best approach to a battle . . . is surprise, make your attack and disappear and start a new attack. Don't get engaged and make it a dogfight.
>
> > Lt. General Adolph Galland, Luftwaffe

The study of one hypothetical engagement using the "strike-rejoin-strike" technique may best serve to illustrate most of the key elements involved in the employment of a section in the two-versus-two environment. In Figure 6-5 the fighters are in combat spread on patrol headed north when the pilots spot a hostile section approaching head-on. A split is called at time "1" to bracket the bogeys, but shortly after the split is commenced,

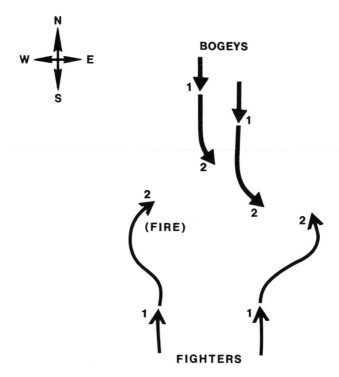

Figure 6-5. Two-versus-Two Engagement

the bogey leader spots the eastern fighter and turns toward it. As the bogey wingman begins to follow his leader, the pilot of the western fighter sees a shot opportunity coming, reverses hard, and fires a heat-seeking missile at the trailing bogey from its belly-side. The shot is unobserved, and the missile appears to begin tracking toward the target.

Figure 6-6 shows that, between the missile firing at time "2" and impact at time "3," the eastern fighter and the lead bogey approach a close head-on pass. The shooter is hypnotized by the sight of his missile's smoke, the fireball, and the subsequent ejection of the bogey pilot, and he temporarily loses track of the other aircraft. Meanwhile the pilot of the eastern fighter has to jink to avoid the debris, sees his wingman cross in front, and (after the shooter's victory whoop) calls him to come left to join in combat spread (time "4"). During all the excitement the pilots of both fighters lose sight of the bogey leader, and neither of them knows whether he disengaged or not.

In Figure 6-7 the victors close up their formation for a better defensive posture, make sure they have sight of each other, and quickly check the area visually. Having been successful to this point, the section is eager to return and engage the remaining bogey, so the leader calls a tac left at time "5," and then immediately calls another to complete the reversal at time "6." The bogey pilot, meanwhile, has both fighters in sight and, being somewhat annoyed, has been stalking the section from a distance. At time "7" he is able to convert to a rear-quarter firing position on the nearest fighter and cuts loose with a heat-seeking missile.

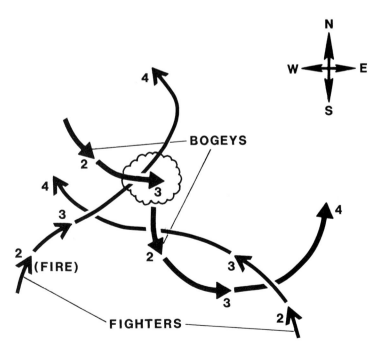

Figure 6-6. Two-versus-Two Engagement (Continued)

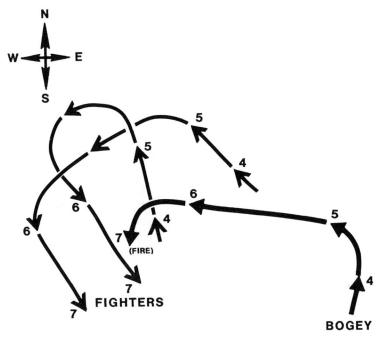

Figure 6-7. Two-versus-Two Engagement (Continued)

At that moment (Figure 6-8, time "7") the pilot of the western fighter sees the smoke as the missile leaves the rail and calls the target pilot to break left against the missile. Simultaneously the western fighter turns hard left toward the bogey to set up a sandwich. The wily bogey, however, has other ideas and switches to the western fighter (time "8"). Meanwhile the early warning has allowed the target fighter to defeat the missile through a combination of hard maneuvering, power reduction, and flares. The engaged pilot (in the western fighter) sees his wingman has survived the missile, calls the bogey switch, and directs the free-fighter pilot to reverse in order to get himself back into the fight as quickly as possible. As the bogey overshoots after time "8," the engaged-fighter pilot reverses nose-to-nose to keep it in sight and draw it away from the free fighter (for AOT and min-range considerations). At time "9" the bogey overshoots again, and the engaged fighter reverses, keeping the enemy interested but not allowing him to reach firing parameters. The bogey pilot continues to pursue his victim, unaware of the free fighter's position. By time "10" the bogey has been dragged in front of the free fighter, and its pilot launches an unobserved missile to end the engagement. The fighters then rejoin in defensive spread and head for the champagne.

> I always thought to go around in circles, slower and slower, was a ridiculous thing. . . . It's not the way to fight. The best tactic is to make a pass, then break off and come back. If you don't do this you'll lose people; one can't be greedy.
>
> Brigadier General Robin Olds, USAF

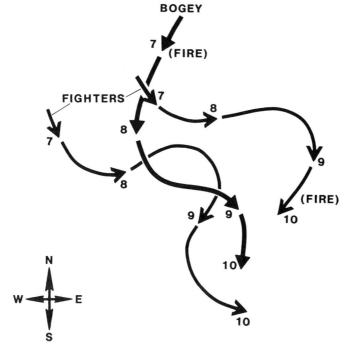

Figure 6-8. Two-versus-Two Engagement (Conclusion)

In analyzing this engagement, the value of the first visual contact with the enemy, which takes place in Figure 6-5, is evident. This early "tallyho" gave the friendly section the initiative to begin an offensive bracket of the hostile section before the reverse situation could occur. As discussed previously, the bracket attack, or offensive split, is one of the tactics associated with both double attack and loose deuce doctrines. The enemy section's response to this attack indicates that its leader probably has only one fighter in sight, and the fact that the wingman followed his leader with no apparent attempt to split or bracket the eastern attacker could mean that he does not have either fighter visually, or the bogey section might intend to employ fighting wing tactics.

Once the bogey section begins its turn to the east, the pilot of the western fighter must cut short his bracket maneuver and reverse quickly to avoid being placed outside missile range. Note that he fires at high angle-off on the target's belly-side, not waiting for the dead-six shot. As discussed previously, the belly-side shot can be deadly with a nominally rear-quarter AAM at medium range. Following the shot, the shooter makes a very common mistake in watching the weapon all the way to the target and then watching the bogey explode. This practice tends to give the shooter tunnel vision, leading to his loss of situational awareness. A better technique might be a quick unloaded roll to the left immediately following the shot to get a visual check of his own belly-side just in case a third, unobserved, bogey or a hostile missile is threatening. After this quick "belly-check" the shooter can reverse back to the right to check on the fate of the target and locate the other aircraft.

See, decide, attack, reverse.

Major Erich "Bubi" Hartmann, Luftwaffe

Luckily the pilot of the eastern fighter has a little better handle on the situation and is able to talk the shooter off cloud nine and back into line-abreast formation in Figure 6-6. Reforming the section here is probably a good move, since the eastern fighter had no advantage on the bogey leader at the pass, lost him completely soon after, and realized the section was operating in a hostile environment with poor defensive mutual support. Had either pilot maintained visual contact with the bogey leader, immediate re-engagement using two-versus-one techniques would probably have been preferable.

When the enemy starts to collapse you must pursue him without letting the chance go. If you fail to take advantage of your enemy's collapse, he may recover.

Miyamoto Musashi

In Figure 6-7 the attackers close up into a good defensive spread formation, take a couple of deep breaths, and execute a tac-turn reversal. Had they been trying an end-run around the bogey to disengage, they could have delayed the second turn, as shown in Figure 6-4. In this case, however, the pilots intend to re-engage, so they complete the reversal as quickly as possible. The tac turn was chosen here because it offers better protection against the remaining bogey, which is unseen, and also against wild cards in a hostile environment. This technique does, however, produce a large radius of turn for the section, which may allow a bogey originally located directly behind to gain greater angular advantage. Had the opponent been in sight directly astern in a relatively sterile situation, a cross turn or a split turn might have offered better offensive capabilities, provided the target range was sufficient to allow completion of the reversal before the adversary could close on one of the fighters. An in-place turn might be more effective against a bogey that is in sight in the rear hemisphere but is not directly astern. The object when the bogey is in visual contact is to reduce its flight-path separation with the center of the section to a minimum (i.e., meet it head-on) and generate a bracket if possible.

The section completes the reversal at time "6" in good defensive condition; but even with supposedly the optimum formation for visual coverage, the bogey remains undetected until it actually launches a missile. This is not an unusual occurrence, particularly when small, well-camouflaged bogeys and poor visibility conditions are involved, since the range from bogey to target fighter at time "7" might be well over a mile, and from the far fighter (the one whose pilot is more likely to see the attacker), several miles. The fact that visual detection of the missile launch itself enabled the target to avoid destruction highlights the value of defensive visual support. Undetected AAMs are almost invariably fatal.

The decision of whether to return and engage an unseen adversary is dependent on many factors. Among the most important of these is the opponent's weapons system. Under the conditions described here (i.e., with an unseen bogey) the section can expect to engage defensively, which may be unacceptable against an adversary equipped with all-aspect AAMs, smokeless missiles, or an extremely lethal weapon (defined as one that probably cannot be evaded once it is fired) of any kind. Such weapons make re-engagement under defensive conditions a very risky proposition and call for a great deal of discretion.

On sighting the hostile missile, the pilot of the far fighter (the one to the southwest in Figure 6-8) calls his wingman to break, and he simultaneously turns to engage the attacker. To this point in the scenario the section could have been employing either loose deuce or double attack doctrine, as all the tactics used so far (i.e., line-abreast formation, pincer attack, tac turns, sandwich) are elements of both tactical doctrines. At time "8," however, double attack would ordinarily call for the southwestern fighter (engaged fighter) to engage the bogey in one-on-one maneuvering while the free fighter (having defeated the missile attack) regains its energy and assumes a covering role. Loose deuce doctrine allows the engaged-fighter pilot to employ a drag technique, whereby he permits the attacker to gain a nonlethal offensive advantage in order to tie him up, giving the pilot of the free fighter time to position for a shot. While this method probably provides for a much quicker kill of the bogey, it is a calculated risk, particularly in a hostile environment. Any number of things could go wrong. For instance, the bogey might get off a lucky shot on the engaged fighter, or the pilot of the free fighter might lose sight of the fight or be jumped by a wild-card bogey (or even a SAM), which could result in both fighters being engaged defensively in separate one-versus-ones. In choosing their tactics here the pilots must weigh the odds and then throw the dice. Does the improved offensive efficiency and quicker kill provided by loose deuce offset the greater defensive vulnerability? If successful, the pilots are brilliant tacticians; if not, they are foolish and probably dead.

Prolonged Engagement. In the foregoing hypothetical engagement, the initial attack was successful, reducing the scenario to two-versus-one against an unseen adversary. The attackers chose to reform defensively before continuing the engagement, which provided some protection until they could regain the offensive. Had both bogeys survived the first attack and been lost from sight, disengagement might have been in order, at least until the opponents could be located and re-engaged on favorable terms.

Another likely possibility is the destruction of one bogey, with the other opponent remaining in sight of one or both of the friendly pilots. In this case immediate re-engagement is usually preferable to reforming defensively, except in very hostile environments. Immediate re-engagement keeps pressure on the bogey pilot and takes advantage of his temporary confusion and fright resulting from the loss of his wingman in the initial attack. Delaying the attack on the remaining bogey generally gives its pilot greater advantage, and it quite often results in loss of contact and subsequent bogey escape, or re-engagement on less than optimum terms for the fighters (as illustrated by the previous example). When both pilots have the bogey in sight, both double attack and loose deuce doctrines provide for an immediate bracket attack if the fighters are positioned favorably. Otherwise the fighter with the greater offensive potential attacks while the wingman assumes the free-fighter role. When only one pilot has sight of the bogey, he may attack and engage the opponent under cover of his wingman until the free-fighter pilot can gain visual contact. At that point the free pilot can position for a shot (loose deuce) or continue his cover duties (double attack) and await his turn with the bogey.

In the event that both bogeys survive the first attack but are still in sight, the decision of whether to re-engage immediately depends on such factors as the hostility of the environment, whether both pilots have sight of the bogeys, and the confidence the pilots have in their ability to handle the threat. If any of these factors is negative, disengagement might be the prudent option. Otherwise a bracket or drag attack might be preferable. When the situation does not provide for such coordinated attacks, double attack doctrine calls for one fighter to attack the more vulnerable bogey while the wingman holds the free bogey at bay. This method can be quite effective if the fighters have significant performance and/or weapons advantages over the bogeys, or if the friendly pilots are better trained than the bogey pilots; otherwise loose deuce techniques are probably preferable.

Loose deuce doctrine in prolonged two-versus-two engagements calls for each fighter to operate semi-autonomously, much as in the one-versus-two engagements described in the previous chapter. The tactic involves neutralizing the more threatening bogey (by causing it to overshoot), then attacking the other bogey. The second bogey is likely to be involved with the other fighter and be vulnerable to attack. This attack cannot safely be prolonged, however, because of the threat of the free bogey. Each fighter switches from one bogey to the other in this manner until one opponent can be caught looking the wrong way.

This is a complex and difficult to master tactic, primarily because of the difficulties involved in keeping track of both opponents. The task is made easier when the adversary is flying larger and/or less maneuverable aircraft and when the fighters are equipped with all-aspect missiles while the bogeys are not. Larger bogeys are less difficult to see, and greater maneuverability makes neutralizing an attacker easier and reduces the time required to reach firing parameters against a target bogey. All-aspect AAMs provide many quick shot opportunities with a minimum of maneuvering. When bogeys cannot be eliminated quickly, the factors discussed earlier in this chapter concerning task overloading must be considered in making the decision between continuing and terminating the engagement. Disengagements are better begun too early than too late, when fuel considerations or critical defensive situations might complicate escape.

Defensive mutual support during prolonged loose deuce maneuvering is by chance and opportunity rather than by design. Each pilot is primarily responsible for keeping himself out of trouble by keeping track of both bogeys, maintaining high energy, and not getting tangled up with one bogey for any length of time. It is difficult enough to maintain visual contact with two separate bogeys without also having to clear the wingman's six, but the fact that both fighters are engaged in close proximity, and are trading bogeys back and forth, inevitably leads to chance sightings of the wingman. When these opportunities arise, the pilot should quickly check the airspace around the wingman visually, announce any bogeys in a threatening position, and attack them if possible. The mere presence of two fighters alternately threatening each opponent keeps an adversary from concentrating on either fighter for any length of time. Knowing that a second fighter is in the area also tends to make an individual bogey less aggressive against any one fighter. This condition is sometimes referred to as "mutual support by presence."

Again, a hypothetical sample engagement should serve to clarify some of the techniques involved in this method. Figure 6-9 depicts the same initial head-on approach situation shown in Figure 6-5, except that this time the bogey pilots see both fighters and split, denying the attackers a quick kill opportunity. Each friendly pilot continues his pincer maneuver in an attempt to get outside the hostile section and keep both bogeys in sight on the same side of the aircraft. This tends to draw the adversaries apart, making it unlikely they will be able to keep track of the other half of the fight.

Figure 6-10 shows that each pilot passes his bogey close aboard on the side away from the second bogey, and continues to turn in the same

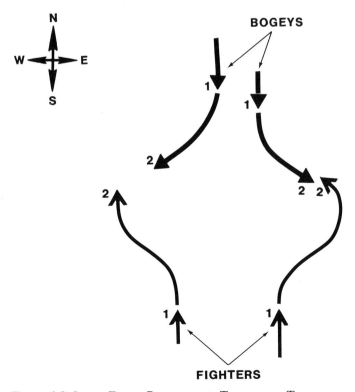

Figure 6-9. Loose Deuce Engagement, Two-versus-Two

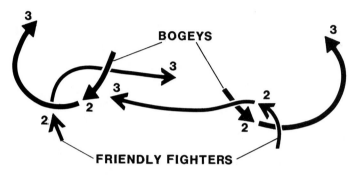

BOGEYS

FRIENDLY FIGHTERS

Figure 6-10. Loose Deuce Engagement, Two-versus-Two (Continued)

direction toward the second bogey. Immediately after the pass each pilot should watch his own bogey long enough to determine which direction it will turn before switching his attention to the next bogey. Observing the bogey's move at the pass is valuable in estimating the time available before it again could become a threat, in planning the attack on the second bogey, and in forming a "mental plot" of where the first bogey should reappear after the pilot concentrates on the other bogey for a few seconds. Approaching time "3" the fighters meet almost head-on and have a chance to clear each other's six as they press on toward bogeys on the opposite sides of the fight.

At time "3" the pilot of the eastern bogey sees the nearest fighter's attack and turns hard to negate it, as shown in Figure 6-11. The pilot of the eastern fighter saw the first bogey he passed turn to the north; therefore he plans to attack the eastern bogey from the south side to keep both opponents on the same side (north). After the pass at time "4" the pilot of the eastern fighter continues his left turn toward the perceived threat sector and observes that the bogey he just passed turned south. Then he begins to look for the other bogey again.

Meanwhile the pilot of the western fighter is pursuing the bogey to the north and has not yet been detected at time "4." He has a good offensive position at this point but is still outside RQ missile parameters. The pilot of the northern bogey has all along been watching the first fighter he passed (now the eastern fighter), and he pulls inside its turn for lateral separation at time "4." The pilot of the eastern fighter gets a "tally" on this bogey and

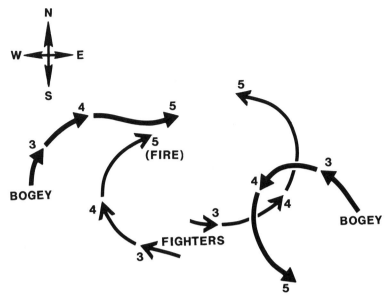

Figure 6-11. Loose Deuce Engagement, Two-versus-Two (Conclusion)

maneuvers to negate its attack and keep it on the left side (i.e., to keep both bogeys to the south). Just as the bogey pilot reverses for a lead turn (time "5") he points his tail to the unseen western fighter, which obliges by blowing him away. Both pilots can then turn either north, to leave the area, or south, to find and engage the second bogey.

The techniques of loose deuce in two-versus-two engagements can be summarized this way: first each pilot negates any attack, keeping both bogeys on the same side of the aircraft if at all possible. Once the threat has been neutralized and the turn direction of the nearest bogey noted, an attack is made on the other bogey. This attack should be planned so that the final turn can be made in the direction of the first bogey, i.e., toward the anticipated threat sector. If an offensive advantage can be gained the target may be pursued, but only as long as both bogeys can be kept on one side of the aircraft or the free bogey is known to be no threat because of range, heading, etc. The attacking pilot should break off any attack and switch bogeys before allowing himself to be sandwiched.

In studying this sample engagement, it should be quite apparent that success hinges on having sight of both bogeys at critical times. In single-seat fighters this normally requires that the pilot shift attention from one bogey to the other as each becomes a threat or the object of pursuit. Multi-seat fighters have a distinct advantage in this environment since, with proper coordination, responsibility for watching each bogey can be shifted back and forth between crew members. This technique can reduce the chances of losing track of one opponent while concentrating on the other. The results of focusing full attention on one opponent to the exclusion of all else (known as "padlocking") are demonstrated by the fate of the unlucky bogey in this example. Although more eyeballs can improve a

fighter's efficiency in a multi-bogey environment, this advantage is sometimes offset, and even reversed, if the additional crew members are gained
at the expense of larger aircraft size and/or degraded maneuverability and
performance. Field of view from each crew station is also critical.

The value of all-aspect AAMs in this environment can be appreciated in
Figure 6-10. With all-aspect missiles, both bogeys probably could be taken
under fire at about time "3" in this example, thereby terminating the
engagement much quicker and reducing the fighters' exposure in this
hazardous environment. These weapons also have implications prior to
the first merge (Figure 6-9) which are covered in a following chapter.

The defensive capabilities of fighters involved in protracted loose deuce
maneuvering can be quite poor because of the inherent wide separations
between fighters in both range and heading and the very high task loading
placed on the pilots. Even with two-seater fighters, little time is available
for purely defensive lookout duties, and advantage should be taken of any
such opportunity presented. Defensive mutual support by presence can be
effective, however, especially in low- to medium-threat environments. In
such scenarios the quicker kill provided by greater offensive efficiency
often compensates for a diminished defense. In very hostile scenarios the
alternating offensive-defensive-offensive (i.e., strike-rejoin-strike) technique may be more effective.

Another problem inherent to prolonged loose deuce is the prospect that
the engagement will break down into two separate one-versus-ones.
Although this situation may be manageable by superior fighters, it does
increase vulnerability to bogey loose deuce techniques and to additional
wild-card attacks. One-versus-one engagements most often occur because
of a lack of disciplined offensive switching or because a pilot loses sight of
one bogey until he becomes critically defensive. Maintaining a good lookout and high energy reduce the chances of such a situation occurring.

Returning to the example illustrated by Figures 6-9 through 6-11 for a
moment, note that the fighters made all turns in the nose-to-tail direction
(i.e., turned across the bogey's tail) at each pass. This occurred because
both bogeys were to one side of the fighter on each pass, so that by turning
across the near bogey's tail the fighter was also turning toward the other
bogey (i.e., toward the threat sector). Turning toward the threat sector is
one of the keys to loose deuce maneuvering. After a head-on pass, a pilot is
more likely to turn nose-to-tail because of greater ease in maintaining
sight of the opponent he just met. By meeting each bogey on the side away
from his wingman, the loose deuce pilot can turn nose-to-tail toward the
threat sector while observing the near bogey's turn for future reference,
and probably induce this bogey pilot into turning away from his own threat
sector.

When a pilot is unable to pass a bogey on the desired side, he may have to
execute a nose-to-nose turn to confront the threat sector. This situation is
depicted in Figure 6-12, which is much the same as the scenario of Figure
6-10, except that in this case the western bogey has managed to get outside
the western fighter at time "2." The pilot of the western fighter performs a
nose-to-nose turn toward the eastern threat, while the bogey continues
across the fighter's tail in a left turn. Since this bogey pilot has been

induced into turning back to the east (the direction of his threat sector), the possibility that the eastern fighter will be presented with an easy RQ kill is greatly reduced. Also, depending on the bogey's turn performance and weapons range, the pilot of the northern fighter (at time "3") may be forced to turn back south to defend against a missile launch by the western bogey. Such a defensive move may cause the northern fighter to turn in front of the eastern bogey and into a dangerous sandwich. This technique is therefore generally undesirable against bogeys that are more maneuverable and have long-range missiles. In this case, particularly against lower-energy bogeys, a vertical pull-up may be preferable at time "2," followed by a pitch-back toward the near bogey, a close pass (on the proper side this time), and another turn toward the threat sector. When the bogeys are equipped with all-aspect missiles, or when they have equal or better energy performance, however, vertical maneuvering can be quite dangerous and normally should be avoided.

In general, nose-to-nose maneuvering tends to keep aircraft closer together during an engagement, which is usually beneficial to the larger fighters. In addition, tight fights may limit the use of an enemy's all-aspect missiles because of minimum-range constraints. This is of particular value when only the enemy is so equipped.

Summary

The two-versus-two scenario can be very complex, and the outcomes of engagements often hinge more on such factors as section coordination, aircraft size, and number of crew members than on the more widely accepted measures of fighter performance. Aircraft performance and weapons-system performance remain as important players, but the impact

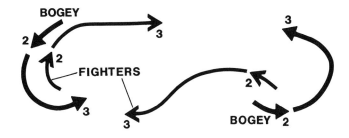

Figure 6-12. Nose-to-Nose Turns during Loose Deuce Maneuvering

of these factors may more easily be overshadowed by the more obscure parameters of fighter design, and by chance, in the multi-bogey environment. Fighters, weapons systems, and tactics must be designed to reduce crew task loading. The vast majority of fighter pilots lost have been unaware of their attacker until it was too late. Reducing crew task loading, designing fighters for improved aircrew field of view and minimum detectability, and employing tactical doctrines that incorporate mutual support must, therefore, be of prime concern.

Four tactical doctrines have been examined so far: fighting wing, double attack, loose deuce, and one-versus-one engagement techniques. Fighting wing has been shown to be generally ineffective in the two-versus-two environment except against opponents with inferior pilot training, aircraft, or weapons. Engaging the bogey pair in two separate one-versus-one fights can be effective, provided the fighters have a weapons, pilot proficiency, or performance superiority. The lack of mutual support provided by this approach, however, may reduce offensive efficiency and leave the fighters vulnerable to coordinated bogey attacks as well as to attacks by additional wild-card enemy fighters.

Double attack and loose deuce doctrines employ essentially identical initial attacks (i.e., brackets and drags) in an attempt to eliminate one or both bogeys. If necessary, a single remaining opponent can be engaged with greater safety and effectiveness than an enemy pair can be engaged. (The comparative attributes of these two doctrines in two-versus-one situations were covered in the preceding chapter.)

The decision to re-engage or disengage is particularly critical if both opponents survive an initial attack, since prolonged two-versus-two maneuvering is a difficult and chancy undertaking. This decision can usually be made by the flight leader before the fighters ever take off; the decision is based on such considerations as mission objective, likely opponents, comparative pilot experience, relative aircraft and weapons-system design, and environmental conditions. Disengagements are most effective with minimum hesitation.

Once the fighters are committed to two-versus-two, double attack doctrine calls for the fighter with the greatest offensive potential to engage the more vulnerable adversary one-on-one (offensive), or to engage the greatest threat (defensive), while the free fighter protects the engaged fighter from attacks by the free bogey or by wild cards. If either fighter becomes defensive, the other comes immediately to its aid in any way possible. This method can be quite effective, particularly when the friendly fighters have superiority in pilot proficiency, performance, or weapons. Double attack can become easily saturated by additional bogeys (more than two), however, and mutual support between fighters can be effectively destroyed by determined attacks against the free fighter. In such situations the fight tends to divide into two separate engagements, often with undesirable results. The free fighter (and therefore the entire tactical doctrine) is especially vulnerable to hostile all-aspect missiles.

Loose deuce doctrine during prolonged two-versus-two engagements dictates that each fighter pilot operate semi-autonomously, alternately countering and attacking each bogey in turn until one succumbs to an unseen attack. Defensive mutual support is generally by presence only, unless one fighter becomes defensive, at which time the wingman attempts to relieve the threat as quickly as possible. This method is potentially superior to double attack offensively, since both fighters are allowed to assume the offense at the same time. In addition, since it does not rely totally on the ability to outmaneuver the enemy aircraft, loose deuce can be successfully employed against superior enemy fighters and weapons.

The relative defensive merits of loose deuce and double attack are more open to question. The fact that the double attack free-fighter pilot is tasked only with defensive responsibility seems to argue for the superiority of this doctrine over the less structured mutual support "by presence" available during loose deuce maneuvering. The double attack free fighter, however, can effectively counter only one free bogey at a time, and even this ability is questionable when the friendlies are opposing superior fighters or all-aspect missiles. Once the free fighter is neutralized, double attack offers essentially no mutual support at all.

Loose deuce, on the other hand, because of its greater offensive efficiency, provides quicker kills and therefore subjects the section to less chance of interference by additional bogeys in a hostile environment. There is also less tendency for loose deuce fighters to become separated one-versus-one. These advantages, however, do not come cheaply. Loose deuce imposes an increased task loading on the aircrew which must be overcome by extensive training and the maintenance of high proficiency. Although pilot proficiency is of vital importance to any tactical doctrine, loose deuce is generally more sensitive to an incremental improvement in pilot performance than to a similar gain in aircraft performance. In addition, fighter design features such as aircraft size and pilot field of view may have greater impact than thrust-to-weight ratio or wing loading.

In conclusion, loose deuce appears to be the superior tactical doctrine in the two-versus-two scenario, provided aircrew proficiency is high. A notable exception to this generalization might be found when the friendly fighters have a significant performance or weapons advantage in a sterile environment against an enemy that is not equipped with all-aspect missiles. Caution, however, is necessary, because loose deuce is a relatively new tactical doctrine and has not been subjected to the test of time under actual combat conditions. Until they have been proven in many theaters of action under widely varying combat scenarios (and probably long afterward), the merits of this doctrine will remain hotly disputed.

7

Division Tactics

The essence of leadership . . . was, and is, that every leader from flight commander to group commander should know and fly his airplanes.
Air Vice-Marshal J. E. "Johnnie" Johnson, RAF

Background

During World War I it was recognized that the operation of two fighters together offered improved survivability and increased firepower. If two fighters are good, then why shouldn't three, four, or more be even better? Inevitably this philosophy was tested as the war ground on, and it met with some success. Greater numbers of aircraft, properly arranged, theoretically offered increased defensive lookout. More firepower could be brought to bear on the enemy in an initial attack, and the chances of being engaged by superior numbers of the enemy were diminished.

We were too busy fighting to worry about the business of clever tactics.
Harold Balfour, RAF
WW-I Fighter Pilot
(Later British Under-Secretary of State for Air)

Increasing the size of fighter formations also has disadvantages, however. The larger the formation, the easier it is to see, and the more difficult is the formation's task of achieving a surprise attack. Large formations are also less maneuverable. Turning can become an exercise in avoiding a midair collision, a situation that greatly decreases defensive lookout. The formation leader must carefully plan and execute each maneuver at considerably less than maximum-performance capability, allowing the other formation members to maintain position. Stragglers are very vulnerable, and their numbers must be minimized. Communications between and control of large numbers of aircraft can also be difficult. Hand signals may be given and relayed from fighter to fighter if aircraft spacing is close, such as in the "wild-goose Vs" of many fighters which were popular with both sides late in World War I; but tight formations have been shown to reduce greatly a formation's defensive capability, especially against modern AAMs. Colored signal flares (fired from Very pistols) were sometimes used for signals during World War I, but they are generally impractical, particularly for modern fighters. The advent of radio in fighters in the 1930s greatly aided the communications and control task, but radios cannot always be relied on because of the possibility of malfunction, jamming, or interference. Movements of the leader's aircraft (e.g., wing rocking and porpoising) have generally proven to be the most effective means of nonverbal communication, but are by no means infallible.

Once they are engaged it is extremely difficult, if not impossible, to keep a large number of fighters together. A battle between large fighter forces most often degrades into a "fur ball," with each pilot fighting for his life independently and giving mutual support only by presence. Although such a condition may be positive from an offensive standpoint, defensively it leaves much to be desired. For instance, disengagement from such a fight is extremely hazardous for a lone fighter. For this reason many flight leaders in World War I attempted to reform their formations before disengaging. They would often have their aircraft painted in bright, distinctive colors or carry a banner streaming from some part of the aircraft for recognition purposes. In theory, any pilot who became separated in a melee could find and rejoin his leader. The enemy, however, seldom allowed such luxuries.

The German Air Service seems to have initiated the trend toward larger and larger fighter formations during World War I. The probable reason for this, besides the natural inclination toward tactical innovation by such great leaders as Boelcke and von Richthofen, is the fact that they were generally outnumbered by the Allied fighters on the western front. Flying in large formations often allowed the Germans to achieve local superiority in numbers at selected locations whenever they chose. Naturally, however, the Allies countered with larger formations of their own, leading to some really interesting engagements of as many as fifty fighters on each side.

> One of the guiding principles of fighting with an air force is the assembling of weight, by numbers, of a numerical concentration at decisive spots.
>
> Lt. General Adolph Galland, Luftwaffe

Between the world wars the advancements in aircraft technology, namely increased speed and reduced maneuverability, led most world powers to conclude that the day of the dogfight had passed. In future conflicts the role of the fighter was seen to be interception of strategic bomber forces. Bombers were much in favor at this time and were thought to be capable of defending themselves against fighter attack because of the effectiveness of the heavy, massed firepower of large bomber formations and the armor protection they could carry. Therefore, they would not require fighter escort protection, and there was little chance for fighter-to-fighter engagement. Consequently, the lessons of fighter tactics learned in World War I were largely forgotten, and training (what little there was) revolved around the interception and destruction of bombers. Fighter design began to stress aircraft speed and heavy armament and armor and to neglect maneuverability and cockpit field of view.

> With no war, we forgot about building airplanes we could see out of.
> Colonel Erich "Bubi" Hartmann, GAF

The fighter formation almost universally accepted during this period was the three-plane vee, or "vic," with the aircraft positioned almost wingtip-to-wingtip for concentration of firepower. This formation (see Figure 7-1) allowed the leader to maneuver fairly well and to fly through clouds with little chance of losing his wingmen. He was able to hit quickly to limit exposure to bomber defensive fire, and all fighters could fire at once at the same target for maximum concentration of destructive power.

The vic had some drawbacks, however: only one bomber could be targeted at a time, and the close formation allowed defensive fire to be concentrated on all fighters simultaneously. The leader was also the only one likely to have a good shot, since the wingmen had to be more concerned with not running into somebody than with aiming their guns. Firing range for the wingmen was also increased, since they had to cease fire when the leader reached minimum range and broke off his attack.

Several of these vics could operate together and coordinate their attacks to bring additional targets under fire and to spread the defensive fire. These additional vics also offered each other some visual mutual support, since the defensive effectiveness of individual divisions was very limited because of formation requirements. One favorite arrangement of vics on patrol was for several vics to form a larger vic spaced at wider intervals than the individual elements. This was a fairly effective formation for visual cross-cover, but it was difficult to maneuver, so the elements often dropped into trail on each other when substantial maneuvering was required. This arrangement still offered good defensive coverage for all elements except "Tail-end Charlie."

This, then, was the thinking of most of the air powers of the world in the 1920s and 1930s. Some were able to test this doctrine during conflicts in the late 1930s, notably the Spanish Civil War and the Sino-Japanese War. These conflicts revealed that the relative superiority of bombers over fighters of the period was greatly exaggerated. Whenever bombers were met by determined fighter resistance, the bombers nearly always suffered

Figure 7-1. The Vic

unacceptably high loss rates. It was found that only air superiority supplied by fighter escort could provide the bombers with the protection necessary for the successful completion of their mission. Fighter-versus-fighter combat had returned!

This revelation, however, was not readily apparent to those nations which did not participate actively in these pre–World War II conflicts. Even the Russians, who took an active part in both wars, seemed to have missed the point. They, in addition to the British and the French, continued to retain the rigid vic doctrine into World War II. The Germans seem to have made best use of their experience, emerging from the Spanish Civil War employing the loose pair (*rotte*) and the division of four fighters composed of two pair (*schwarm*). The Japanese generally retained the division of three fighters, known as a *shotai*, and arranged them in vics, in echelons, or in a loose, staggered trail formation. This last formation (illustrated in Figure 7-2) provided better visual defense by allowing the wingmen to maintain looser positions on the leader; often they would weave back and forth to check the rear quarter. Once they were engaged, the aircraft in the *shotai* stayed together, falling into trail for hit-and-run attacks, or broke apart, with each aircraft fighting independently.

The German *schwärme* normally deployed in a "finger-four" formation,

LEADER

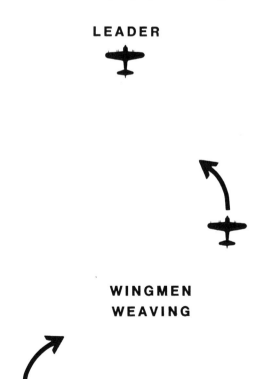

WINGMEN
WEAVING

Figure 7-2. Japanese *Shotai*

so called because of its similarity to the positions of the finger tips on the hand (see Figure 7-3). Spacing between aircraft in this formation was on the order of 600 ft, roughly the equivalent of the fighters' turn radius, which provided ample maneuver room and good visual cross-cover. The *schwarm* typically separated into two *rotten* for coordinated attacks and engagements. Several *schwärme* were often combined and coordinated for massed air strength.

The finger-four arrangement proved to be vastly superior to the tighter formations of the Allies, and it gave the Luftwaffe a considerable advantage early in the war. It was soon copied, however, by nearly all the combatants. The Germans then decided that a line-abreast arrangement might provide even better defensive coverage and, typically, jumped another step ahead of their adversaries. Late in the war the line-abreast, or "wall," formation (shown in Figure 7-4) was generally favored by the Luftwaffe, with the Allies retaining the finger four.

Interestingly, however, near the end of the war the Germans often employed their new Me 262 jet fighters, the only jets to see significant combat, in the old tight vic (which they called *ketten*). Jet fighters were used primarily as bomber interceptors rather than as dogfighters, and the *ketten* provided more concentrated firepower as well as a greater number of divisions with limited aircraft assets than would have resulted from four-plane flights. Since each of the divisions (*ketten*) normally attacked only one bomber on each pass, more divisions allowed a greater number of bombers to be attacked in a shorter time. Defensive protection against fighter attack in this tight formation was supplemented by a tremendous speed advantage over Allied aircraft (about 100 kts), which made rear-quarter intercept very unlikely at combat speeds.

Pre-Engaged Division Maneuvering

With fighters widely spaced and nearly line abreast as in the finger-four and wall formations, maintaining position in turns requires some ingenuity. Probably the most effective method is based on the cross-over turn, or tac turn, as discussed for two aircraft in the last chapter. Figure 7-5 illustrates

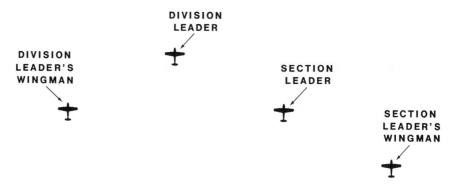

Figure 7-3. German *Schwarm* in Finger Four

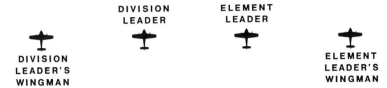

Figure 7-4. Line-Abreast or Wall Formation

how this concept is applied to a division of four fighters in finger four. A line-abreast division would turn almost identically.

In this case the division leader (sometimes called the flight leader) wants to turn the flight 90° to the right, toward the second section (element) of two fighters. He does this by simply turning right at time "1." The division leader's wingman, on the left in this case, immediately turns hard right to pass behind the leader. The wingman's turn needs to be a little tighter than that of the leader, and the wingman may have to dive slightly in his turn, crossing below and behind the leader, in order to maintain speed and regain the proper position quickly at time "2." Meanwhile the element leader generally pulls up to cross over the flight leader, and he will be almost directly overhead at time "2," having turned considerably less. After passing over the flight leader, the element leader tightens his turn and drops back down to regain his speed and position at time "3." The element leader's wingman pulls up with his leader between times "1" and "2," crosses above the flight leader, then begins a very gradual turn, generally crossing over his element leader between times "2" and "3" to assume his proper position on the opposite side of the formation at time

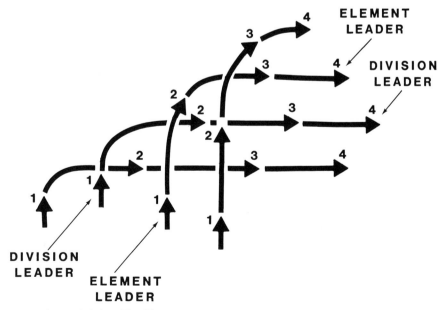

Figure 7-5. Division Tac Turn

"4." At time "4" the division is again in finger four, but it is reversed; that is, the element is now on the flight leader's left rather than on his right.

Although this drill may look very complex on paper it is really quite simple with a little practice. The element leader simply does a tac turn on the division leader, and the wingmen do what is necessary to maintain position on their respective leaders. Essentially, each element does a tac turn, with a delay between. The individual aircraft, however, must travel different distances from start to finish of the turn. The fighters originally on the outside of the turn will fly farthest. Since all the fighters are likely to be at or near maximum power, speed is adjusted as necessary by climbing or diving relative to the other aircraft to maintain the desired positions.

As with the two-aircraft tac turn, two of these maneuvers can be performed in the same direction to effect a complete reversal. The advantages and disadvantages of tac turns were discussed in the previous chapter and remain the same here. A reversal of this type takes a lot of time and space, but it provides good visual cross-cover throughout.

Along with the tac turn, many of the other turn techniques described in the last chapter for use by fighter pairs, such as the cross turn and the in-place turn, can be adapted to most division formations, although some can become rather complex with large numbers of aircraft. In some cases, however, the increased number of fighters in the division and the required staggering of the turns of individual aircraft can provide improved visual coverage for the division over that of a two-plane section performing the same maneuver.

> The commanding officer is responsible [for seeing] that neither he nor any of his pilots are surprised by the enemy. If he cannot see to that, he is no good as a leader.
>
> Baron Manfred von Richthofen

Other Division Formations

To this point little has been said about trail formations, largely because of their inherent defensive weakness. Trail, or sucked-echelon formations, can, however, be very effective offensively, since they are well suited to sequential attacks by the trailing elements. When more than two fighters are involved, trail formations can also be devised to offer a reasonable defensive posture. One example is the "battle box," an arrangement of sections in trail as shown in Figure 7-6.

In this formation the defensive function is provided by visual cross-cover within each section, which may be arranged in spread, as shown, or in acute echelon. The trailing section also covers the leading section and provides improved offensive potential. This and similar arrangements have been used by nearly all air forces at one time or another from World War I to the present day. Additional sections can be added to the string ad infinitum, each stepped up or down as desired to enhance visibility or to reduce detection. The maneuverability of trail formations is greatly simplified, since each element has only to "follow the leader," and cross-overs involve only two aircraft at a time. The defensive capability of trail formations, although greatly improved by two-plane elements, is still inferior to

Figure 7-6.
Sections in Trail

the more line-abreast arrangements, since with trail formations leading elements are poorly placed for rapid support of trailing elements.

When the division is composed of only three aircraft, a modification of the old vic can be useful. This formation, depicted in Figure 7-7, places a section in loose trail on the lead fighter. This arrangement is particularly well suited to the use of decoy tactics. The lead fighter can "stooge" around looking helpless until it is attacked by the enemy, at which time the trailing section, often stacked high, can swoop in and pull off a rather rude surprise party. Separation between lead and trail elements of this formation normally should be such that a bogey cannot slip into its weapons parameters behind the lead fighter without entering the trailing element's firing envelope.

> The [German] is a master at using stooge decoys who would probably be as helpless as they look, if half the Luftwaffe were not keeping a jealous eye on them from the sun.
>
> Captain Reade Tilley, USAAF

The reverse of the vic is the "section-and-stinger" formation depicted in Figure 7-8. In this case the single fighter (the "stinger") trails the lead

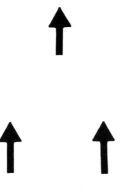

Figure 7-7. Modified Vic

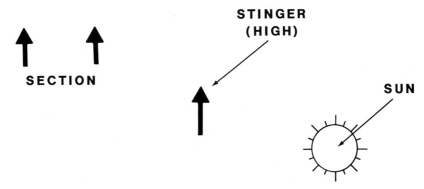

Figure 7-8. Section and Stinger

section to offer the element of surprise. This was one of the favorite tactics of the Flying Tigers during World War II. The Japanese, since they normally flew in three-plane divisions, could more easily be enticed into battle against a section of two. The stinger could then have his pick. Although beautiful when it works, this tactic has obvious defensive weaknesses, as the stinger is quite vulnerable. It is probably best suited as an occasional variation to standard two-plane section doctrine rather than as a steady diet. The best position for the stinger is usually high above the section on the sun side, and only slightly in trail. If he is attacked, the stinger should normally attempt to dive and drag his attackers down toward the support of the section. In a radar environment, a stinger positioned very low "in the weeds" may be able to avoid enemy detection.

Tactics are much like plays in any team sport. Each tactic has weak and strong points and can be anticipated and defeated by the opponents if the fighters "go to the well" too often with the same routine. Probably the most effective system is to employ a basic fighting unit, the two-plane section, for example, so aircrews can become highly proficient in its use. Then, depending on the number of aircraft available, the mission, and the expected opposition, these units can be combined with others in trail or stacked high or low according to environmental conditions. This technique varies the look presented to the enemy and always leaves him guessing as to whether he has everyone in sight before he attacks. Enemy pilots tend to get rather paranoid after they have attacked a leading or low element a few times.

Engaged Division Maneuvering

"DICTA BOELCKE"

1. Try to secure advantages before attacking. If possible, keep the sun behind you.
2. Always carry through an attack when you have started it.
3. Fire only at close range and only when your opponent is properly in your sights.
4. Always keep your eye on your opponent, and never let yourself be deceived by ruses.

5. In any form of attack it is essential to assail your opponent from behind.
6. If your opponent dives on you, do not try to evade his onslaught, but fly to meet it.
7. When over the enemy's lines never forget your own line of retreat.
8. Attack on principle in groups of four or six. When the fight breaks up into a series of single combats, take care that several do not go for one opponent.[1]

(Note: Captain Oswald Boelcke, who drew up this list, was killed in a midair collision with his wingman while both were attacking the same aircraft.)

> Captain Oswald Boelcke
> German Air Service, 1916
> 40 Victories

As discussed earlier, engaged maneuvering with many fighters in a rigid formation (i.e., the equivalent of division fighting wing doctrine) has serious limitations and generally has proved effective only against unescorted, poorly maneuvering aircraft such as bombers and transports. Something more flexible is required when fighter-versus-fighter engagement is anticipated.

Fluid Four

The most effective doctrines generally build the division by combining two or more elements of two fighters. Pilots in the division attempt to stay together during the pre-engagement phase and, when it is practical, to exit together from hostile airspace. During an offensive attack the elements of the division may remain together or they may split for coordinated attacks, but the pilots in each section attempt to stay together. Once the division has been split up, each element of it may operate according to any of the section doctrines detailed in the previous two chapters. Mutual support can also be provided between the elements using double attack or loose deuce tactics, and there is no requirement that the doctrine employed between the elements be the same as that used within each section.

As a case in point, consider the example of a four-plane division composed of two sections. Each section might fly welded wing, but the two elements can cooperate as in double attack. For instance, one section could attack an enemy formation while the other section provided defensive "top cover." This combination of fighting wing and double attack doctrines is commonly known today as "fluid four," and it has been widely used by many air services from the time it was first introduced by Werner Moelders during the Spanish Civil War, right up to the present.

In fluid four doctrine each two-plane section essentially replaces one fighter of the double attack pair. Instead of an engaged fighter and a free fighter, fluid four uses an engaged section and a free section, each flying fighting wing. With this substitution, virtually everything said about double attack to this point applies to fluid four, including the offensive attacks, defensive counters, and engaged maneuvering. Fluid four offers the obvious advantage over double attack of increased numbers. The greater firepower available is especially valuable during an initial attack.

The effectiveness of this fluid four doctrine is probably best demonstrated by a four-plane division of U.S. Navy F6F Hellcat fighters led by

Lieutenant Eugene Valencia (23 victories) during World War II. His division, nicknamed "Valencia's Mowing Machine," accounted for the destruction of fifty Japanese aircraft without a loss (or even a hit). This team developed fluid four tactics, which were by no means universally accepted by the Navy at that time, to a fine art. The name "Mowing Machine" was derived from the alternating attacks by the two elements of the division, which traded roles as engaged element and free element (top cover), producing action resembling that of the blades of a lawn mower.

By combining fighting wing with double attack, fluid four gains more offensive potential than either two-ship doctrine makes available. Defensively there are pluses, also. More eyeballs positioned properly afford better lookout in the pre-engagement phase, and the wingmen in each element can provide additional insurance for their leaders which is not available in double attack. The wingmen can be very effective defensive factors once the division is engaged, particularly when the enemy is equipped only with guns. The longer firing ranges of AAMs and the close spacing of the wingmen in fighting wing greatly reduce the defensive value of the wingmen against missile-equipped bogeys, but a wingman can still at least provide valuable moral support. Most of the defensive potential when engaging missile-equipped bogeys is derived from the free element.

With this last fact in mind, modifications have been made to fluid four doctrine to improve it both offensively and defensively. These involve more extensive use of double attack and even loose deuce techniques within the fluid four framework. During a fight, for instance, the engaged section can vastly increase its offensive effectiveness by employing loose deuce methods, while defense, the major shortcoming of loose deuce, is supplemented by the free section. If the scenario requires less offensive power and greater defensive capability, the engaged section may use double attack instead of loose deuce. This substitution provides two layers of defense: the free section protects the engaged section, and the free fighter of the engaged element protects the engaged fighter. In most cases, however, this redundancy amounts to overkill and unnecessarily sacrifices offensive potential.

Particularly in an AAM environment, additional defensive effectiveness can be attained by relaxing the fighting wing restraints on the free element. During engagements the free section generally is more vulnerable to surprise attack, since a large portion of the pilots' attention must be devoted to guarding the engaged section. Allowing the wingman in the free element to maintain a flexible position, as nearly line abreast as possible, provides better defensive mutual support within the free section. The leader of the free element should continue to hawk the fight in the double attack manner, but the looser position of his wingman allows each pilot in the section to divide his attention about equally between defending his own formation and guarding the engaged element.

When modified as described, fluid four is an extremely powerful offensive doctrine and a very tough nut to crack. It suffers, however, from the same problems associated with double attack, namely, the tendency for the division to break down in the face of superior numbers, and difficulties when the division opposes an all-aspect missile threat. Division integrity is most likely to be broken by a determined attack on the free element during an engagement. The free section is then forced to defend itself and can no longer provide direct support to the other element of the division. This situation is considerably less critical than when it occurs in double attack, however, because mutual support can still be maintained within each section of the division. Each element should employ double attack or loose deuce techniques to maintain section integrity and defeat or drive off the opponents quickly. As soon as the opportunity arises, each section should attempt to rejoin and support the other.

When facing overwhelming numbers, even section integrity is very difficult to maintain during an engagement. It is generally futile under these conditions to attempt close support on a division level after the division has made an initial coordinated attack. Section integrity might still be maintained, however, and the strike-rejoin-strike technique described in the last chapter offers perhaps the most workable plan. Every effort should be made under these circumstances to avoid extended section maneuvering, either offensive or defensive, since the chances are very high that the aircraft of the section will become separated, leaving each fighter vulnerable to attack by multiple bogeys. An offensive attack should be broken off if success is not achieved immediately. Likewise in defensive situations, every opportunity to disengage should be seized and the section reformed for best mutual support.

An interesting divisional defensive tactic that was devised by Raoul Lufbery during World War I has survived into the modern era. Known as the "Lufbery circle" or the "wheel," this tactic calls for all fighters to fall into trail and follow each other around in a circle. When there was a large number of evenly spaced fighters, each fighter could effectively cover the tail of the one ahead and discourage any attacks. The wheel was continued until the enemy gave up and went home, or until the division leader could slowly work his fighters back to friendly airspace.

The advent of all-aspect missiles pretty much destroyed the effectiveness of this tactic, since it was no longer necessary for attackers to enter the wheel to shoot. Even RQ missiles can usually be fired from well outside the confines of the circle on the target's belly-side. The Lufbery circle can be quite effective in a guns-only environment, however. Techniques used to counter it successfully include simply waiting out the defenders' combat endurance until they are forced to abandon the circle and break for home. High-speed hit-and-run attacks using steep diving and climbing reattacks and high-deflection gun passes can also effectively counter the wheel. Use of the vertical plane and high-angle approaches minimizes the attackers' exposure to the defensive fire of other aircraft in the circle.

Engaging multiple bogeys armed with all-aspect missiles is tough. The free element in a fluid four engagement is quite vulnerable to attack in this case. Once the division is engaged by such bogeys the free element is almost obligated to maintain close contact in order to deny the enemy min-range parameters for his weapons. Ordinarily when bogeys extend away, the free element should break off its pursuit so that defensive support can be maintained for the engaged element. When all-aspect AAMs are involved, however, allowing the enemy a free extension invites him to turn around and shoot. This complication greatly reduces the free element's value in division defense. Section strike-rejoin-strike techniques result in a similar dilemma. Releasing a bogey from attack to rejoin in a defensive formation almost guarantees that the section will be greeted by missiles in the face if re-engagement is attempted. Section hit-and-run tactics may prove to be the prudent course in this scenario.

Gaggle Doctrine

Occasions invariably arise when the fighters do not have the luxury of using hit-and-run tactics, regardless of how necessary they might be. The mission objectives might require extended engagement of the enemy to avoid losses to friendly bombers, transports, reconnaissance aircraft, high-value ground targets, etc.; or the division may be attacked and forced to defend itself until escape is possible. When a division is faced with roughly equal numbers of the enemy whose fighters, pilots, and weapons are not clearly superior, using modified fluid four is normally very effective. In general, however, a fighter force cannot be expected to prevail over a well-flown opposing force composed of a greater number of independent elements. For instance, three fighters operating independently (i.e., three separate elements) often will wreak havoc with four fighters operating in two fighting wing sections (i.e., two independent elements). A greater number of independent elements allows the superior force to achieve a two-on-one situation against some hostile elements, while one-on-one holding actions are maintained elsewhere. This is the primary reason for the increased offensive power of loose deuce over fighting wing. The other advantage enjoyed by numerically superior forces is that all elements are not likely to be engaged simultaneously, which gives free elements more opportunities to attack from unseen positions while maintaining more energy and, therefore, better maneuvering potential. This is the primary offensive advantage of double attack over fighting wing.

When one fighter force is faced with engaging a numerically superior enemy force, or a force of roughly equal numbers but better aircraft or weapons, its offensive potential can be greatly expanded if the friendly force breaks up into smaller elements. In many cases this means allowing each aircraft to operate independently. As with loose deuce, defense in this scenario is not normally organized, but generally is provided through presence only. The more friendly fighters involved, generally speaking, the more effective will be mutual support by presence, and this type of support can be effective long after any organized support has broken down. Unfortunately, organized mutual support most often disintegrates when each supporting element becomes defensive, in which case the elements can be of little assistance to each other and mutual support by presence is largely ineffective. This situation too often degrades into several one-versus-one fights with no support among elements. For best results, mutual support by presence should be preplanned, and independent action should be initiated while the division is still offensive or neutral.

"Gaggle" doctrine applies loose deuce techniques to groups of three or more fighters. According to this doctrine, patrol and attack normally are coordinated on the division level, or with several divisions, as described for fluid four. Once the battle is joined, however, individual pilots are permitted to operate independently. The techniques involved in such engagements are essentially identical to those discussed in conjunction with the loose deuce engagement described by Figures 6-9 through 6-11, but on a greater scale. Basically, each pilot attempts to define the threat sector, neutralize any attack in such a way that a final turn can be made comfortably toward the threat sector, and be alert for "shots of opportunity" on unwary bogeys. As in loose deuce, classic one-versus-one engagement is discouraged by this doctrine. Pilots should turn only as necessary to neutralize an attack, or to position for a slashing attack of their own. In general, a turn should not be continued past 90° in any one direction without a reversal, or at least a roll reversal and a visual check of the belly-side. This means that if a bogey is sighted which cannot be shot within about 90° of turn, the pilot had better look for another target. Some of the basics of gaggle tactics can be illustrated by the sample engagement begun in Figure 7-9.

At time "1" in this example the intrepid fighter pilot approaches the "bogey cloud" from the east. This bogey cloud represents a volume of airspace which appears to contain the greatest number of enemy fighters. At this time the pilot picks out one bogey in a vulnerable position on the edge of the cloud and decides to attack it. Unfortunately, his attack is discovered and the target turns hard left in defense. By time "2" it has become quite obvious that a quick kill is not going to be available, so the attacker breaks off his attack before he is committed to a critical overshoot and continues to watch the bogey until he is certain it will be no immediate threat (time "3"). Recognizing that the threat sector (i.e., the bogey

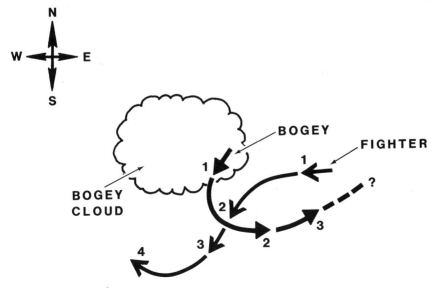

Figure 7-9. Gaggle Engagement

cloud) is now on his right side, the pilot of the fighter reverses hard right to negate any attack which might be coming from that direction.

At time "4" in Figure 7-10 the fighter has completed a turn of about 90° to the right. Since the pilot is not certain all the bogeys are localized inside the bogey cloud, he decides a belly-check is called for at this point, and he rolls left to clear his south side. Seeing nothing, he rolls quickly back to the right just in time to discover an attack from the north (time "5"). This attack requires a break turn into the bogey, which overshoots at time "6." The defensive maneuver now leaves the fighter pilot in a difficult position. Having already turned about 90° he would like to reverse, or at least roll left for a belly-check. A reversal, however, would likely place him in jeopardy with the overshooting bogey, probably resulting in a slow-speed scissors (not a healthy place to be in a bogey-rich environment), or, at best, forcing the pilot to turn his aircraft's tail to the bogey cloud. If the pilot even pauses for a belly-check at this point he could present the bogey with a RQ missile shot, and he would also most likely penetrate the bogey cloud. Once inside the bogey cloud, the pilot would be in great danger because he would no longer have a well-defined threat sector and he could easily be attacked from several directions at once.

In Figure 7-11 the fighter pilot makes the decision that at the moment seems to be the least hazardous, to continue his defensive turn toward the southeast until the threat sector is placed on the left side. At time "7" he then reverses into a gentle left turn, overbanked to get a good visual check deep in his left rear quarter, and accelerates to regain some of the energy he lost in the recent defensive break. At time "8" he notices a friendly fighter just to the left of the nose, its pilot apparently unaware of a bogey attacking from his right.

The pilot immediately gives his threatened wingman a radio call: "Break right." Then, as shown in Figure 7-12, the free-fighter pilot quickly

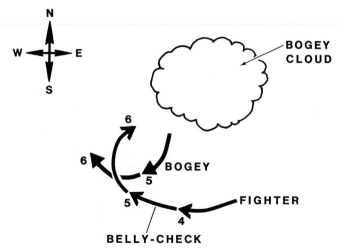

Figure 7-10. Gaggle Engagement (Continued)

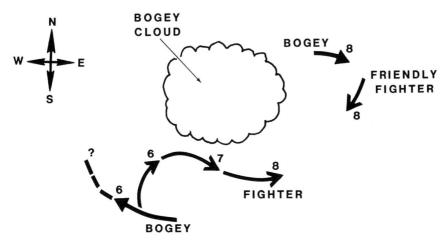

Figure 7-11. Gaggle Engagement (Continued)

rolls right to check his south side and, finding himself clear, reverses back left to bracket the attacking bogey.

The bogey pilot, who has not seen the second fighter, continues to press his attack to time "10" in Figure 7-13, when the unseen fighter reaches a near "dead-six" position and squeezes off a missile. As the weapon leaves the rail, the shooter rolls right to check his belly-side (to the east in this case), then rolls back to assess the results of his shot.

At time "11" in Figure 7-14, the bogey explodes. At about the same time, the much-relieved defensive pilot announces he is low on fuel and is "bugging out." That sounds good to the other pilot at this point also, so he comes hard right to join in combat spread, and the section departs together to the southeast (time "12").

In summary, gaggle doctrine is loose deuce tactics applied to more than two fighters, with each pilot operating autonomously once the engagement begins. Each pilot attempts to define a bogey cloud that encompasses

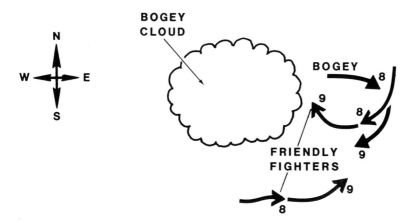

Figure 7-12. Gaggle Engagement (Continued)

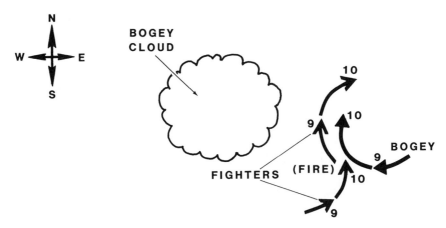

Figure 7-13. Gaggle Engagement (Continued)

the majority of the enemy aircraft, and cruises the perimeter of this hostile region in an attempt to pick off unsuspecting victims around its edges. Attacks are generally made only on those bogeys which offer an easy shot requiring a minimum of maneuvering. If the attack is discovered, it should normally be broken off and the hunt resumed. A useful rule of thumb is to turn no more than 90° in one direction at any time without a reversal or a belly-check. When attacked, counter as necessary with the goal of escaping as quickly as possible, and avoid prolonged one-versus-one maneuvering. Normally, enemy fighter pilots are just as cautious as the friendlies in this scenario, and they are reluctant to press an attack against a fighter that is maneuvering defensively.

As a rule, level or nose-low turns should be made to maintain adequate speed for effective defensive maneuvering. Steeply nose-high moves should be avoided, unless the friendlies are opposing guns-only bogeys of much inferior energy performance and there is a well-defined bogey cloud. Likewise, hard turns should be avoided in order to maintain energy. If at all possible, only sustained-G levels should be used, and speed for optimum sustained maneuvering should be maintained.

Penetration of the bogey cloud should be avoided if at all possible. If he enters the cloud inadvertently, the fighter pilot should extricate himself as quickly as possible, using repeated belly-checks in both directions.

> By this time, there were fifteen Camels and twenty or more Fokkers in the "Scrap," and it had become a question of luck more than good judgement, as Camels and Fokkers alike twisted, half-rolled, turned and dove, the tracer bullets flying in every direction. The [Germans] knew that they were good fliers and, being brave men, they tried to bring down their opponents singly. This more than any one thing proved their undoing, as the pilots of the "148th" watched their chances and wherever a pilot was in trouble, two or more would help him out by shooting the Fokker down. One after another the Fokkers went down, seven in all.[2]

Mutual support in gaggle doctrine is by presence only. Each pilot is primarily responsible for guarding himself, but he must remain constantly on the lookout for threats to friendly fighters. Whenever a wingman is sighted, the airspace all around his aircraft should be scanned visually to determine if he is under attack or is pursuing a bogey that might make an easy target. Egress from the hostile area should be made with other friendlies if at all practical. When a pilot is leaving the area, he should make a "bugout" call on the fighter frequency so that the remaining friendly pilots can assess the changing numerical odds.

> If you have a lot of pilots flying around you, many to fly with, then you are not very keen to look around. A lot of people are not looking at all.
> Colonel Erich "Bubi" Hartmann, GAF

The problems associated with gaggle tactics are the same as for loose deuce, with the added difficulties arising from increased numbers of fighters and bogeys. With more bogeys comes greater difficulty in defining the threat sector, since some of the enemy are almost always unaccounted for at any one time. Some degree of task overloading is generally present throughout the engagement. As the battle continues the bogey cloud tends to expand and it becomes more difficult to define. When he is unsure of the threat sector the pilot might be well advised to extend a considerable distance from the fight, though preferably he should remain within visual range of some participant, and then return in an attempt to redefine the "fur ball" from a distance. Extending away in the direction of the sun or climbing or diving to highlight the fight against low or high clouds are effective techniques. Due care must be exercised during these maneuvers, however, since enemy pilots may be using the same methods. The pilot cannot afford to padlock some aircraft in the distant fight and neglect his

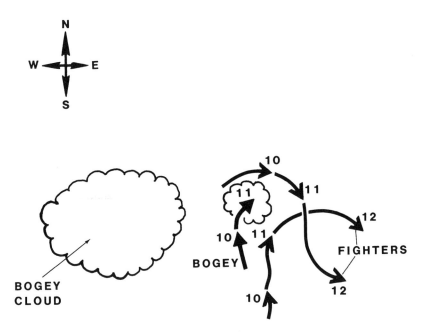

Figure 7-14. Gaggle Engagement (Conclusion)

defensive lookout. Defensive mutual support by presence is sacrificed when a fighter leaves the immediate engagement area.

If the decision is made to return to the fight after extending away, there are two points to keep in mind. First of all the fighter should approach the fur ball from well above or below the general engagement altitude to highlight the fight against favorable background, to minimize the chances of being detected, and to provide greater flight-path separation for attacking an unsuspecting target. This technique can also provide look-up to enhance missile shots, and it tends to limit the vertical threat sector, improving lookout efficiency. The second point is to avoid pointing the aircraft directly at the bogey cloud during the return, especially in the final stages of approach. Positioning the fight in the left or right forward quarter again allows concentration of lookout in one quadrant by defining the threat sector. This procedure also enhances offensive effectiveness by allowing the pilot to pick his time to point and shoot into the fur ball as he cruises the boundary, rather than making him dependent on the shot geometry provided at the moment he arrives within firing range. In addition, keeping the fight off to one side reduces the chances of accidental penetration of an ill-defined bogey cloud.

Comparison of Fluid Four and Gaggle Doctrines

The choice between the two divisional tactical doctrines presented here is often not clear-cut, as each doctrine has both strong and weak points. Both, however, recognize the advantages that may accrue from numbers, mutual support, and coordination in the pre-engagement, attack, and disengagement phases. Fluid four, particularly when it is modified to allow the engaged element to employ loose deuce techniques, offers credible offensive power while providing effective defensive potential. When engaging an inferior or roughly equivalent number of independent fighting elements, or an enemy of inferior or roughly equal capabilities, this admirable balance between offense and defense often tips the balance in favor of fluid four.

Regardless of the name, fluid four techniques are not necessarily limited to groups of four fighters. When only three fighters are available a single can serve as the free element, although with degraded capability. If more than four fighters comprise the force, it should generally be divided into groups of four or two for maneuverability, lookout, and control reasons; but once it is time to fight, the group leader usually decides which divisions or elements will engage and which will provide cover. The general rule for this decision is to ensure that the engaged fighters enjoy at least parity in numbers (of individual elements, but not necessarily of individual aircraft) with the enemy force, but at least one element is held in reserve to guard against additional bogeys or to join in the fight should the engaged element or elements get into trouble.

> When attacking an inferior force we use only the strength necessary and always maintain a flight or an element as top cover.
> Lt. Colonel Gerald R. Johnson, USAAF

It is when a force is opposed by a larger enemy force, or by one equipped with superior aircraft or weapons, that gaggle tactics are most useful. A hypothetical scenario has a force committing to engage with two-plane elements against a superior enemy force, waiting for the almost inevitable breakdown in section integrity, and then trying to salvage the situation by fighting as individual fighters; but gaggle doctrine permits each fighter to operate as a single from the outset. This tactic multiplies the offensive potential of the force by greatly increasing the number of independent elements, and it relies on defensive mutual support by presence when it is most effective, namely, while the friendly force is offensive or neutral. As with loose deuce, the object is to shoot targets of opportunity whose pilots are unaware of their immediate danger. If a bogey is not positioned to provide a quick kill, or if it shows some effective defensive reaction, it should not be pursued, but neutralized. The hunt then continues for an easier victim. Extended one-versus-one combat is to be avoided in this doctrine. If an aircraft is engaged defensively, its pilot's goal is to terminate the engagement as quickly as possible. Usually this means escape from the attacker, but sometimes it may be necessary to fight until the offensive can be regained and the bogey destroyed. When neither is possible, the defender calls for help and does his best to survive until some nearby team member can lend support.

Because of the multiplication of independent elements, increased ability to maintain the offensive, and the effectiveness of mutual support by presence under such conditions, gaggle tactics are normally more productive than fluid four when a force is opposing an enemy of equal or greater numbers. For example, assume that two four-plane divisions engage with similar aircraft, weapons, and pilot capabilities. One division employs modified fluid four, allowing its engaged section to split (two independent elements) for loose deuce maneuvering, while retaining a free element in fighting wing (one element) for cover. This arrangement effectively yields a total of three separate elements. Meanwhile, the opposing division uses gaggle tactics, splitting into single fighters (four independent elements). By using this method the gaggle division effectively outnumbers the fluid four division and can be expected to have the better day. This is the same principle which gives a double attack or loose deuce section dominance over opponents in fighting wing.

In situations where the friendly force outnumbers the enemy, the added offensive power of gaggle doctrine may not justify the reduced defensive capability. Inefficiency results when an overwhelming number of fighters are involved on any one side. These pilots are likely to spend much time staying out of each other's way and reacting offensively or defensively, at the expense of combat effectiveness, to unidentified aircraft that are later found to be friendly. Under such circumstances, holding free elements out of the engagement in the fluid four manner can pay dividends. The number of engaged elements maintained should equal or slightly exceed the number of the enemy. When modified fluid four is used with more than four fighters, the result is a combination of the two doctrines, with the engaged fighters employing gaggle tactics and the free fighters fluid four.

In a dog-fight such as this, when the odds are heavily on your side, there is a great temptation to lower your guard, to get in close, and hammer your enemy until he falls. Too many pilots concentrate on one target and forget to keep a sharp lookout for friend or foe; too many airplanes converge, in a dangerous funnel-like movement, on the single quarry, and the risk of mid-air collision is high.

Air Vice-Marshal J. E. "Johnnie" Johnson, RAF

Dissimilar-Aircraft Divisions

Quite often employment of different fighter types within the same division becomes necessary or desirable. This situation can result from shortages of any one aircraft type or from complementary capabilities. For instance, one aircraft type may have better navigation, communications, radar, or weapons capability, and another may have superior performance as a clear-weather, daylight dogfighter. Combining these two types might provide greater flexibility and increased mission capability.

Obviously there are almost unlimited possible combinations for such dissimilar divisions, and all of them cannot be covered here. In general, however, the most likely scenarios involve small numbers of larger, more expensive, heavily armed, or high-capability aircraft in combination with larger numbers of smaller, cheaper, highly maneuverable day fighters. For instance, a single sophisticated fighter might provide navigational or radar capability to position the division favorably for an attack, and maybe supply first-shot, long-range weapons capability, while a section of simpler day fighters provides improved close-in offensive and defensive power.

Likely formations for such a combination include line abreast, with the sophisticated fighter in the center flanked by the day-fighter section, or the loose modified vic as depicted in Figure 7-7, with the day fighters in trail. In either case the day fighters, as the defensive members of the team prior to engagement, are normally stepped-up to provide quicker defensive response to attacks on the single and to furnish them with greater energy when an engagement begins.

The modified vic generally offers greater protection against attack, particularly by long-range RQ missiles, and may also allow small day fighters to fly closer together to facilitate keeping each other in sight. Another possible advantage of this formation arises when the day fighters are equipped with all-aspect missiles, but visual identification (VID) must be made on any target before firing. This VID might be accomplished by the pilot of the lead fighter, who could then clear the trailing day fighters to fire before the target penetrates their min-range boundary. The modified vic is also conducive to "baiting" tactics. Enemy fighters might be overeager to pounce on a single, poorly maneuvering lead fighter, and be bounced in turn by trailing day fighters.

The more nearly line-abreast arrangement of fighters is useful when all of them are equipped with all-aspect missiles and are likely to be cleared to fire well outside min-range parameters. In this case all fighters can fire in unison for maximum firepower, much like a battleship broadside. This formation also contributes to the effective use of the bracket or pincer attack by the day fighters. As illustrated in Figure 7-15, in the final stages of approach the day fighters can use their altitude advantage to dive and accelerate ahead of the leader to bracket the target at the merge.

Once they are engaged in a close-in visual fight, the day fighters are in their element and generally should carry the load. This may be an ideal scenario for modified fluid four tactics; the sophisticated single provides cover by sanitizing the area visually and/or electronically, while the day fighters engage using loose deuce methods. Large, poorly maneuvering fighters should, in general, be kept out of such hassles, since this is not their arena and they are likely to do poorly in it. Aircraft that are large relative to others in a fight attract bogeys like a flame draws moths. If such a fighter becomes engaged, the day fighters will be forced to spend most of their effort in support. When one fighter goes defensive, the effectiveness of the entire division suffers.

Generally speaking, it is important in mixed-bag divisions for formations to be designed, and missions assigned, so that each fighter type can concentrate on what it does best. Some fighters are better in a dogfight, some are more heavily armed, and some operate better than others at high altitude. Whenever possible, advantage should be taken of these qualities.

A couple of historical examples may serve to illustrate this point. The Luftwaffe in World War II often used twin-engined Me 110s, Ju 88s, and Me 410s, heavily armed with cannon and unguided rockets, to attack Allied bombers, while the more maneuverable Me 109s and Fw 190s kept the escort fighters occupied. Early in the same war in the South Pacific the

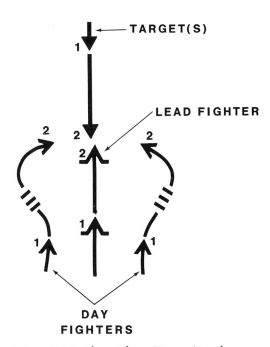

Figure 7-15. Three-Plane Pincer Attack

Americans employed turbocharged P-38 fighters as top cover in combination with P-39s and P-40s (equipped with simple, medium-altitude superchargers) on fighter sweeps against the Japanese. P-39s and P-40s stayed at low levels where they could retain decent performance, while the P-38s tackled any high-altitude threat.

Operating mixed-bag sections or divisions is not without its problems. Quite often the optimum cruise speed of one type is significantly below that of the other, requiring some fighters to operate at less than ideal speeds in order to keep a formation together. This condition may result in reduced range, endurance, or defensive effectiveness for one or both types of fighters. The faster fighters in such situations often weave from side to side so that average forward progress can be slowed while they maintain high airspeed for maneuverability considerations. This technique allows the mixed formation to remain together, but it usually still reduces the range and endurance of the faster aircraft, as well as making them more vulnerable to attack from the rear. Weaving formations are also more easily spotted visually.

The attack phase can be complicated by aircraft performance variations. For instance, when supersonic and subsonic fighters operate together, attack timing can be difficult. The requirement that each fighter type enter a fight at a given time at near its respective best engagement speed can affect formations and usable tactics. The timing for a pincer attack (Figure 7-15), for example, would be difficult with subsonic day fighters accompanying a supersonic single. For all aircraft to arrive at the target at nearly the same time, either the day fighters would have to begin their attack from well in front of the single (section-and-stinger formation), or the single would have to enter the fight subsonic. If neither of these situations is satisfactory, the day-fighter pilots may just have to accept the fact that they will engage at some time after the initial pass between the enemy and the supersonic fighter or fighters. In any case, this situation calls for careful consideration.

The engaged phase of mixed-bag operations is more complex also. The relative performance capabilities of different fighter types can change depending on altitude. For instance, subsonic jets (and non-turbocharged prop fighters) generally have poor combat performance at high altitudes, but they may be superior at low levels. There are two schools of thought on vertical deployment of high-performance and low-performance fighters. One school recommends deploying the low-performance fighters level with or above the high-performance wingmen. The altitude margin adds to the low-performance fighters' energy level at the start of an engagement and allows them to provide better support to the other fighters at lower altitudes. If the aircraft in the higher element are engaged, they can drag the fight downhill, while the high-performance fighters should be able to climb up to support rather quickly. One problem with this philosophy, however, is that both aircraft types may be forced to fight, at least for some time, at less than ideal altitudes for their performance; that is, poor high-altitude fighters may be engaged at high altitudes, and vice versa. This makes the entire division more vulnerable to hit-and-run attacks. Placing low-performance fighters at higher altitudes also leaves the division more vulnerable to high-to-low attacks, which can be very dangerous because of the high closure typically involved in this kind of attack.

The second philosophy calls for stacking the high-performance fighters above the lower-performing aircraft. A division deployed in this manner is stronger against attacks from above, and each fighter type will be closer to its ideal regime if attacked. The high element in this arrangement can still support the low fighters, but the low-performance fighters may not be able to climb up to a high-altitude fight. This situation is not usually a great disadvantage, however, since such fighters likely would not fare well in a high-altitude fight anyway, and the high-performance fighters can drag the fight down to low altitude to gain support if necessary. During high-altitude engagements, the low-performance fighters should generally remain below the fight, providing defensive lookout and waiting to pounce like hungry alligators on any bogey that falls out the bottom of the fight.

Disengagement from mixed-bag fights also deserves some close attention. Typically, high-performance fighters will be forced to withdraw first for fuel considerations. If it is considered prudent for all friendly fighters to exit the combat arena together, this may effectively limit the combat endurance of the low-performance fighters. In addition, high-speed fighters may not have the luxury of a simple "red-line" bugout if they are forced to remain with their slower wingmen. Disengagement may have to begin even earlier if these fighters are to have enough fuel reserves to fight their way back home. Complications such as these quite often offset any advantage gained through mixed-bag fighter operations.

Notes

1. Johannes Werner, *Knight of Germany*, pp. 183–84.
2. W. P. Taylor and F. L. Irvine, *History of the 148th Aero Squadron*, p. 39.

8

Unlimited-Aircraft Tactics

Of course, with the increasing number of aeroplanes one gets increased opportunities for shooting down one's enemies, but at the same time, the opportunity increases of being shot down one's-self.

Baron Manfred von Richthofen

In previous chapters there has been at least an implied assumption that the number of hostile fighters involved in the action was known to the friendly forces, although frequent references have been made to additional, unseen, wild-card bogeys. Assumptions such as this are necessary in order to allow investigation of some of the fine points of ACM; but anyone who has ever been involved in actual combat will realize that total confidence in one's perception of a given situation is rarely, if ever, achieved. The great Prussian strategist Karl von Clausewitz referred to this phenomenon as the "fog of war," a fog that obscures reality from the combatants. In the air-to-air arena this can mean imperfect knowledge of an opponent's energy state, or uncertainty as to the type of weapons or tactics he might employ. It can also mean that friendly fighters can almost never be absolutely sure of the number of enemy aircraft they will face, either prior to or during engagement. Is that enemy section really alone, or is the entire enemy air force lurking undetected in the sun?

Any soldier knows that during a war it is not always the ponderables that count, but that a great deal depends on luck.

Lt. General Adolph Galland, Luftwaffe

Obviously, if the friendly fighters always chose to assume the worst case, they probably would never engage and therefore be of little use. So the standard procedure adopted by most combatants is to gather and analyze all the information available about the tactical situation from every possible source, and then employ tactics accordingly. In the early days of air warfare, knowledge was limited to that supplied by intelligence reports on the numbers and types of enemy aircraft and ground defenses in the area, previous enemy tactics, and whatever could actually be seen by the pilots in the air. World War II saw the first large-scale use of ground-based radar stations, IR sensors, data link, and radios for passing information to and among airborne forces. Airborne radars also came into use during this conflict, but they were useful primarily for night interceptors and in poor visibility conditions. Inevitably, the advances in sensor and communications technology were closely followed by techniques for neutralizing or limiting their value, such as jamming and deception. All this electronic technology is intended to increase the situational awareness of friendly forces in battle and to deny such valuable information to the enemy. The incredible attention electronics technology has received in recent years is a clear indication of the importance of situational awareness in air combat.

The task of the fighter pilot is to obtain as much tactical information as possible from every available source and then to filter and analyze this information based on knowledge of its source and his best estimates of its timeliness, accuracy, and reliability. Some of the information received may be conflicting, and pilot judgment is required to separate the wheat from the chaff. The necessity of making such judgments is one reason training and experience on the part of the fighter pilot are so important. Many of these information-gathering and -analyzing functions may be performed by the flight leader in multi-plane scenarios, but individual pilot experience and ability in this area contribute greatly to overall success, as tactical judgments must be made, on a larger or smaller scale, by each pilot during combat. The ability of each member of a flight to gather and analyze electronic and visual information, and to pass critical information to other members of his flight, plays a significant role in overall flight efficiency and mission success.

Overreliance on any one source of tactical information is a common problem and often leads to disaster. This condition can be the result of actual lack of available informational sources, loss of some sources (through jamming, for example), or simply ignoring available inputs. The disregard of some available information can be fostered by a tactical doctrine that relies heavily on one source to the exclusion of others, or it may be caused by sensory overload resulting from too much information being fed to the pilot at critical moments. This latter condition can be likened to drinking water from a fire hose. Strict radio discipline, practiced by controllers as well as pilots, is vital to avoid sensory overload. It is normally impossible for every participant involved in a mission to relay everything he knows, sees, or thinks to everyone else. Each individual must analyze his information and assess its importance at that moment before adding to the "water pressure in the fire hose." The ability to perform these tasks effectively requires considerable training and experience at every level.

One-versus-Many

Good airplanes are more important than superiority in numbers.
                              Air Vice-Marshal J. E. "Johnnie" Johnson, RAF

Previous chapters in this text have expounded the virtues and benefits offered by employment of multiple fighters, usually pairs or flights of several pairs, in air combat scenarios. The many advantages provided by tactical doctrines that rely on mutual support have been sufficiently detailed and will not be repeated here, but the tradeoffs involved deserve additional attention. Remember, there is no free lunch in either economics or air combat.

> The fighter pilot is an independent character. He doesn't like too many people around him. He is an individualist.
>
>   Colonel Erich "Bubi" Hartmann, GAF

For example, it is more difficult to hide multiple fighters than it is to hide a single aircraft, both from visual detection and from electronic sensors. This is a critical factor, since surprise has been shown to be roughly nine-tenths of air combat success, both offensively and defensively. Coordinated tactics also force the pilots involved to divide their attention. Considerable time can be required to keep track of wingmen and to maintain a proper formation. This is time that is not available for visual lookout, monitoring radars, analyzing tactical situations, making plans, etc. The attention required for this purpose will also contribute to earlier task overloading and breakdown in situational awareness.

> It is difficult for large numbers of men to change position, so their movements can be easily predicted. An individual can easily change his mind, so his movements are difficult to predict.
>
>   Miyamoto Musashi

In addition, formation tactics usually result in reduced effective aircraft performance relative to a single fighter. Leaders cannot use maximum speed, power, or maneuvering potential because of the probability that wingmen will be unable to maintain position. Small individual variations in performance, even among aircraft of the same type, contribute to this problem, as does the normal reaction time of a wingman who is maneuvering in response to his leader's actions. Maintaining position will usually require excess maneuvering by the wingmen, which reduces their energy potential, decreases combat fuel endurance, and makes them easier to spot visually because of "wing flashes" and the inability to use profiling effectively. Coordination of multiple fighters also requires increased communications, with the attendant task loading and greater probability of electronic detection.

The following excerpt from *Full Circle* by Air Vice-Marshal "Johnnie" Johnson, RAF, describes the tactical thinking of Captain Albert Ball, RFC (47 victories in World War I). These are some of the reasons Ball preferred his famous solo "lone-wolf" methods to leading a division of fighters (scouts) in combat. Ball disappeared mysteriously in May 1917; Lothar von Richthofen, brother of the "Red Baron," was credited with shooting him down, but most historians believe he was the victim of ground fire.

> A formation of four or five airplanes was far harder to hide against earth, cloud, or sun than a solitary machine, and therefore surprise, the essence of a successful attack, would be more difficult. He would have to wait for stragglers and inexperienced pilots who could not hold a steady formation; when

attacking from a diving turn or a wide curve of pursuit he would have to throttle back so that his flankers would have sufficient power in hand to keep abreast. This meant that a team attack would take far more time than the flat-out, stooping dive of a single scout. More time usually meant less surprise. . . . The bigger the [German] formation, the better as far as he was concerned. Such tactics would concentrate the [enemy] into large, unwieldy, conspicuous gaggles, and they would be so busy watching each other that a man could be in and away before they knew what had hit them![1]

With these factors, as well as the advantages of mutual support, in mind it is not difficult to develop scenarios for which single-ship, autonomous fighter operations might be optimum. One of the most obvious of these operations takes place at night or under poor visibility conditions, when it may be impossible to maintain an effective formation or to provide useful visual mutual support. The tactics applicable to such operations are highly aircraft and weapons-system dependent and do not lend themselves readily to generalization; therefore, they are beyond the scope of this text.

Another factor that reduces the importance of mutual support and makes autonomous operation more practical is a highly effective and dependable system of internal or external surveillance and control. This capability might be provided internally by sophisticated electronic means such as radar, IR sensors, and/or RWR systems, which can be depended on to give adequate warning of attack from any direction. Such internal systems may be supplemented or replaced by external sensors and control networks like ground-controlled-intercept (GCI) stations or airborne-intercept-control (AIC) aircraft, which can provide defensive warning to the single fighter while assisting in locating and identifying the enemy for attack purposes. In effect, the visual mutual support function of a wingman can be replaced electronically. Factors to be considered here include the reliability and effectiveness of such systems under the expected environmental and EW conditions, possible enemy countertactics, and the relative capabilities of friendly and enemy surveillance and control systems.

The strong man is mightiest alone.

German Proverb

Weapons capabilities also have significant bearing on the practicality of single-fighter operations. Friendly all-aspect weapons capability, and the absence of it in enemy fighters, greatly enhances the prospects of success for a single. The reduced maneuvering required to satisfy all-aspect-missile-firing parameters limits the single's exposure to detection and its vulnerability to threat weapons. Conversely, the lack of all-aspect missile capability by the enemy makes surprise attack on the single fighter more difficult and increases the single's attack and escape options. Particularly when both sides are all-aspect capable, missile maximum range and guidance type can be critical. If the single is able to fire at the enemy while remaining outside his firing range, obviously the single's survivability is enhanced. Active or passive guidance, which enable the single to "launch and leave" or to fire and then defend against an enemy weapon, may offset the longer range that may be provided by weapons that have more restrictive semi-active guidance. A means of identifying a target as hostile at long range, either optically or electronically, is another valuable aid in providing first-shot capability. Long-range target identification is essential when a pilot is facing an all-aspect-capable threat, or it must be replaced by very permissive rules of engagement (ROE) which allow the fighter to fire on targets beyond visual range (BVR). Such ROE are often easier to implement when the single fighter is known to be the only friendly aircraft in the combat arena, but they may not be possible when several fighters are operating autonomously in the same area.

> In aerial warfare the factor of quality is relatively more decisive than the factor of quantity.
> Major Alexander P. de Seversky, USAAF
> 13 Victories with Russian Imperial Naval Air Service, WW-I

A significant performance advantage by the single fighter over enemy aircraft is another factor that favors autonomous operations. A substantial speed advantage and the ability to use this speed when it is required and still complete the mission (combat endurance) are probably the most valuable qualities for the single fighter. This speed improves the chance of surprise by reducing attack time, greatly decreases the likelihood of being caught from behind by the enemy, shrinks the enemy's rear-hemisphere missile-firing envelope, and greatly facilitates the friendly fighter's escape from disadvantageous situations. A significant speed advantage can allow the pilot of a single fighter to establish a sanctuary from which he can attack and withdraw at will without fear of attack from the rear. Obviously, the greater the range of enemy rear-hemisphere weapons the greater the friendly's speed advantage must be to provide this sanctuary. Enemy all-aspect missiles, off-boresight capability, and very high turn rate may also offset the defensive value of a single fighter's speed advantage.

> Speed is the cushion of sloppiness.
> Commander William P. "Willie" Driscoll, USNR
> 5 Victories as Radar Intercept Officer, Vietnam Conflict

A maximum-altitude advantage can also be valuable to a single, especially against an enemy equipped only with guns or short-range missiles. This altitude sanctuary may allow the single fighter to choose his attack opportunities carefully and then fire at the enemy with long-range lookdown, shoot-down weapons, or dive down for a surprise high-speed attack followed by a zoom climb to a safe altitude. The altitude margin provides the single with adequate defense and allows the pilot to concentrate on offensive matters. Important considerations here include weapons-system capabilities (Can the target be detected and attacked from above?), environmental conditions (Will the attack be highlighted by a higher cloud layer or contrails?), and possible threats other than enemy aircraft (e.g., SAMs).

> Take up an attitude with the sun behind you. . . . You must look down on the enemy, and take up your attitude on slightly higher places.
> Miyamoto Musashi

Other design factors that contribute to single-fighter survivability include small aircraft size, reduced aircraft detectability, and multiple crew members with wide fields of view. A significant maneuverability and/or weapons advantage over the enemy is also of some value, since these factors improve the single's defensive capability and reduce the time required for it to reach a firing position.

Another factor that may favor single-ship operations is the existence of an extremely lethal enemy weapon that is not likely to be defeated once it is fired within parameters. Defense against such a weapon depends on avoidance of the firing envelope rather than post-launch maneuvering, etc. The reduced probability of detection, higher possible speeds, and decreased maneuvering requirements inherent to autonomous fighters all contribute to avoiding the enemy's firing envelope, while the increased visual mutual support of a wingman probably would not be sufficient to overcome the disadvantages of multiple-aircraft flights.

A severe comm-jam environment can also detract from the advantages of mutual support. The inability to communicate freely increases the attention necessary to maintain formation integrity and decreases the ability of one pilot to provide support to another. Such conditions quite often lead to inadvertent single-aircraft operation because of a breakdown in mutual support, a situation that is usually more hazardous than preplanned autonomous operation.

Preplanned single-plane operation may be desirable whenever its advantages, as enumerated above, outweigh the benefits of mutual support. The number of hostile fighters should also be factored into the equation, with greater numbers generally working to the disadvantage of autonomous operation. Single-ship operation may be required even under less than optimum conditions if only one fighter is available for a critical mission. Whenever there is a choice, however, mission priority and the chances of the mission's successful completion should be weighed against the probability of single-plane survival. It may be wiser to wait for reinforcements than to "hog" all the bogeys alone. Preparation for multi-plane combat should include contingency planning for inadvertent single-plane operation in case the wingman is shot down or the fighters in the formation become separated and mutual support is lost. It is much easier to decide before takeoff whether a particular mission and the prevailing conditions warrant continuing as a single ship or calling for an abort.

Offensive One-versus-Many

> In my opinion the aggressive spirit is everything.
> Baron Manfred von Richthofen

Once the decision has been made to continue operation under one-versus-many conditions, the pilot of the single fighter should plan his tactics to make use of every advantage available to him. In order to be successful offensively, however, the singleton must avoid becoming defensive. Defense, therefore, should be the primary concern. To take advantage of a speed sanctuary, the single should normally maintain near maximum speed in hostile airspace. The lowest possible altitude is often optimum because of its "shrinking" effects on threat missile envelopes. Against bogeys carrying only guns or very short range AAMs, higher altitudes may offer a greater speed margin. This is particularly likely when a single supersonic fighter opposes subsonic bogeys. High altitude allows the supersonic fighter to attain higher Mach than, and therefore greater speed advantage over, a bogey restricted to subsonic speeds. This greater speed advantage may offset increased threat missile range at high altitude. Combat endurance is another consideration when choosing an operating altitude. Low-altitude high-speed flight is very inefficient, particularly for jet fighters, and high fuel consumption may reduce the chances of completing the mission. Operation at higher altitudes normally results in increased range and endurance at near maximum speed. Other considerations include the threat of hostile ground fire; effectiveness of the single's weapons system at low altitude and in look-down situations; effectiveness of the enemy's weapons and sensors in look-up, and in look-down, situations; and whether the single is likely to be harder to see looking up or looking down. This last factor varies with cloud conditions, sun position, and aircraft coloring. The possible effects of altitude on friendly and enemy GCI is a further point to consider. Very low altitude operation can enable the single to avoid enemy detection, but it may also deny the pilot the valuable offensive and defensive support of friendly controllers.

> The effect of superior numbers in a decision to attack is small. The tactical advantage of position—altitude—sun—and direction of attack are the influencing factors. With these factors in my favor the number of enemy aircraft is irrelevant.
>
> Lt. Colonel John C. Meyer, USAAF

Quite often when he is selecting an operating altitude the pilot is faced with conflicting choices. These most often involve the interaction of radar and other factors, as in the GCI conflict above. Another example is the choice between staying high to take advantage of the sun or a speed/altitude sanctuary or a low undercast, and degrading the fighter's radar capability by placing it in a look-down condition. Going in at lower altitude in this case probably would enhance the fighter's offensive potential by optimizing its radar operation, but it would leave the singleton more vulnerable to detection and attack. Such choices can be tough to call, and they require careful analysis. Just how much is the radar likely to be degraded looking down? Can GCI supplement the fighter's own radar? How likely is it that the single will be detected at low altitude? If it is attacked at low altitude, what are the chances of escape, considering bogey numbers and relative aircraft and weapons-system performance? Questions like these must be answered as accurately as possible in order to weigh the probability of mission success against chances of survival. Except for very critical missions, where success is absolutely essential, it is usually wiser in one-versus-many scenarios to opt for the safest approach. The pilot who saves his hide today can return tomorrow under more favorable circumstances, unless of course his heart is set on the Medal of Honor.

We never flew on top of clouds because we were all silhouetted against them;
we flew underneath them.

Air Vice-Marshal J. E. "Johnnie" Johnson, RAF

The choice between optimizing offensive or defensive potential can
often be reconciled by assessing the likely results of being attacked. If the
pilot is confident that he can detect and neutralize a hostile attack and
either escape or defeat the enemy quickly, before he is overwhelmed by
numbers, then optimizing offensive potential might be a reasonable
choice. Otherwise it is probably prudent to assume a more defensive
posture.

Chapter 5 ("Section Tactics, Two-versus-One") included a section on
one-versus-two offensive attacks and maneuvering. Many of the techniques described in that section are relevant to the one-versus-many scenario and would be worth reviewing at this point. There are also some
significant differences, however.

When faced with a known one-versus-two situation, an undetected
fighter pilot can stalk his victims and position for an optimum attack at his
own discretion. This luxury is not generally available in the one-versus-
unknown environment, since prolonged time in the combat arena and the
attention that must be devoted to the intended targets leave the single
fighter vulnerable to attack by other hostile forces. The single fighter
must, therefore, operate primarily in a defensive mode, devoting only the
attention and time which are absolutely necessary to prosecute attacks of
opportunity.

I attempt to attack out of the sun. If the enemy aircraft is surprised, he's duck
soup, but time is an important factor and it should not be wasted in securing
position.

Lt. Colonel John C. Meyer, USAAF

Forward-hemisphere gun and missile attacks are often ideal for this
scenario, since high target closure limits the time required to complete the
attack and therefore reduces the time that must be devoted to offensive
functions. Such attacks also tend to reduce the amount of maneuvering
required of the attacker, which contributes to higher energy levels and
makes it more difficult for undetected enemy fighters to overhaul the
single from behind. As is discussed later in this chapter in regard to
defensive maneuvering, a single is often most vulnerable to attack during
protracted turns. As a general rule, the pilot should plan his attack so that
turns of more than about 90° are not required without an opportunity for a
roll reversal and a belly-check. Targets that cannot be attacked while
adhering to this rule should whenever possible be abandoned in favor of
more vulnerable victims. The sooner this decision can be made the better,
since attacks aborted in the last moments are more likely to be detected.
When disengaging from a position in a bogey's rear hemisphere, a lag-
pursuit heading and a slight turn in the nose-to-tail direction allows the
single fighter to gain the most separation before the bogey pilot can bring
his aircraft's nose to bear. (This nose-to-tail extension technique was
introduced in Chapter 2.)

I decided to make a run on this [Japanese Zero]. He never changed his course much, but started an ever-so-gentle turn. My Corsair gradually closed the gap between us. I was thinking: "As long as he is turning, he knows he isn't safe. It looks too easy."

Then I happened to recall something I had experienced in Burma with the Flying Tigers, so I violently reversed my course. And sure enough, there was his little pal coming along behind. He was just waiting for the sucker, me, to commence my pass on his mate.

Colonel Gregory "Pappy" Boyington, USMC

The fighter's internal radar and GCI/AIC support should be used to identify likely victims at long range and to aid in early positioning to optimize the final attack geometry. Defensive procedures (i.e., high air-speed, optimum defensive altitudes, etc.) are usually employed early in the attack phase, with a transition to a more offensive posture, if necessary, delayed until the last practical moment. Search modes of airborne radars are usually optimum during preliminary attack positioning to sort out the hostile formation and to clear the area of other bogeys. Once the fighter takes a radar lock on a single target, which may be necessary for final attack maneuvering, visual acquisition, or weapons guidance, the attacker is likely to lose track of the big picture, such as enemy formation changes, and he is also more susceptible to detection by the bogey's RWR equipment. The point at which this radar lock is taken normally corresponds to the fighter's shift from a defensive to an offensive posture, and taking it likewise should be delayed as long as practicable. Somewhere around one minute to the point of merging with the hostile formation is generally a useful reference for planning this transition. An even longer delay is desirable if weapons-system performance and maneuver requirements allow. "Track-while-scan" radars, which allow search for and track of multiple targets to be performed simultaneously, can be very valuable in this environment.

When the single fighter's weapons require conversion to a stern attack, radar and GCI should be used to position the fighter with ample lateral and vertical separation to allow the final conversion turn to be limited to approximately 90° or less. Figure 8-1 is an example of this technique.

In this example the single fighter detects a possible hostile formation approaching nearly head-on at time "1." The fighter quickly assesses the situation, determines that there is sufficient range to position for a stern attack, and takes a cut to one side to build lateral separation. Altitude and speed are maintained at this point consistent with best defense against attack by other enemy threats. The direction of the offset should be based on environmental conditions to optimize either the attack or the escape following the attack, whichever appears to be the more critical phase. This could mean offsetting toward the sun side to mask the attack, or toward the opposite side to facilitate a retreat toward the sun after a hit-and-run attack. An offset toward friendly airspace makes escape easier should the fighter be detected at long range and the bogeys begin to react offensively, while a cut to the opposite side provides a shorter route of escape following

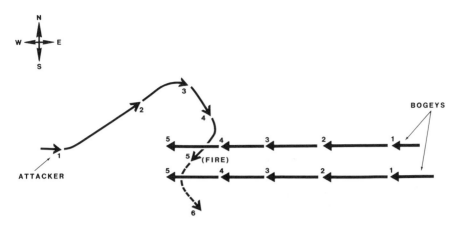

Figure 8-1. Stern Conversion in a Hostile Environment

an attack. These factors and many others affect probability of mission success as well as survival, and they should be considered carefully.

Concealment and swiftness are the two principal elements of closing.
Colonel V. Dubrov, Soviet Air Force

The number of degrees of offset taken by the pilot at time "1" depends largely on the target range and the fighter's radar limitations. At long range adequate lateral separation can be obtained with smaller cuts. If the fighter is radar equipped it is usually desirable that the displacement turn not be so radical that the targets are placed outside the radar antenna gimbal limits. Generally, the smallest offset that will generate the desired lateral separation is optimum, since this reduces maneuver requirements throughout the intercept.

From time "1" to time "2" the fighter should be concentrating on defense while monitoring the developing situation for changes in intercept geometry, bogey formation, other aircraft in the area, etc. Defensive techniques useful during this phase are discussed later in this chapter. Between times "2" and "3" the fighter determines that sufficient lateral separation exists for an optimum stern conversion. This is also a good point to decide whether to commit to the attack or to abort and escape. The desired amount of lateral separation at this point is a function of target range, offset angle, fighter turn radius, and other factors and should be determined by experimentation. It is seldom less than three or four fighter turn radii, however.

At point "3" the fighter has committed to the attack and performed a recovery turn to a pure-pursuit or lead-pursuit heading. If this turn must be greater than 90° it should be performed in two stages interrupted by a belly-check. In any event, one or more belly-checks should be performed between times "3" and "4." Shortly before or after point "3" is often an optimum time to make the transition from a defensive to an offensive posture by taking a radar lock, repositioning to optimum attack altitude, attempting to acquire the targets visually, etc. The heading selected at time "3" should be chosen to place the attacker near the target's beam position at time "4," from which a final conversion turn of 90° or less will result in arrival within the lethal firing envelope.

At time "4" the fighter must choose which bogey to attack. The geometry of this particular intercept favors an attack on the far (southern) bogey because of a less radical conversion turn, although slight variations in heading between times "3" and "4" could reverse this situation. Optimum target selection often becomes apparent only at the last moment, and the choice often must be delayed until then. Hard conversion turns can deplete energy and reduce the fighter's chances of escape, but protracted easy turns take longer and leave the fighter more vulnerable to undetected attacks during the conversion. Something in the maximum sustained-G region is usually the best compromise.

Notice that, assuming he is equipped with a RQ weapon, the attacker takes his shot at the first opportunity, on the edge of the envelope (time "5"). A very hostile environment does not allow the luxury of "sweetening" shots by driving to the heart of the envelope. This pilot has been concentrating almost exclusively on offense since time "4" and is very vulnerable at this point to attack from the belly-side (i.e., from the east). After taking the shot, a rapid reversal and turn to the left serves as defense against a possible enemy missile approaching from the belly-side, temporarily foils an impending enemy gun shot, allows the pilot to clear his most vulnerable area visually, and quickly puts distance between the attacker and the known enemy fighters. After clearing his six, the attacker can reverse quickly to assess the results of his shot and to check on the bogeys' reaction. Delaying the defensive turn reversal until after missile impact is a common mistake, and often a fatal one. For this reason semi-active missile guidance, which may restrict the shooter's maneuvers after launch, is an undesirable burden.

> When actually firing at an enemy aircraft you are most vulnerable to attack. When you break away from an attack always break with a violent skid just as though you were being fired at from behind. Because you probably are.
>
> Captain Reade Tilley, USAAF

Another difference in attack procedures between sterile one-versus-two and unknown scenarios involves target selection and post-attack planning. In the former situation the recommended approach carried the attacker from one bogey to the other for sequential firing passes and possible engagement of the second bogey one-versus-one in case the first was destroyed. The hostile environment often makes sequential attacks too risky and almost certainly precludes one-on-one maneuvering if it can possibly be avoided. In addition, although only two bogeys are indicated here, these procedures are intended to be applicable to formations of any size. The recommended technique for such situations is to pick a target that will not draw the attacker deeply into the bogey formation, and the far-side rear bogey often fills this requirement. Another point that should be mentioned is the increased probability of detection inherent to a weapons firing. It is very desirable for the single fighter to be well positioned for escape at the moment of attack.

> Every day kill just one, rather than today five, tomorrow ten . . . that is enough for you. Then your nerves are calm and you can sleep good, you have your drink in the evening and the next morning you are fit again.
>
> Colonel Erich "Bubi" Hartmann, GAF

When attacking bombers it may be necessary to destroy as many as possible during each intercept. In this case the sequential attacks discussed in the one-versus-two section of Chapter 5 may be justified. Consideration, however, should be given to the effects of an attack on even one member of an enemy formation. Such an attack, even if it is unsuccessful, may accomplish the attacker's purpose by breaking up the bomber formation, inducing the enemy pilots to jettison their bombs or abort their mission, etc. When attacking hostile fighters, the single pilot generally should try to control his greed, settle for one victim per pass, and leave some bogeys for his buddies.

Bogeys detected at short range in the forward hemisphere can be attacked if the target appears not to be aware of the fighter's presence, and if the attack can be made without continuous turns of greater than about 90°. The singleton pilot should continuously plan for and assess his chances of escape during an attack. The attack should be broken off as soon as escape avenues appear to be closing or if the target performs an effective defensive maneuver. Prolonged offensive engagement should be avoided.

> Turn to kill, not to engage.
>
> Commander William P. "Willie" Driscoll, USNR

Enemy fighters that appear to be maneuvering offensively or defensively against the single are candidates only for all-aspect missiles or gun snapshots. The pilot of the single fighter should neutralize any forward-hemisphere threat by turning hard into the attack to create a head-on pass with minimum flight-path separation. Depending on the bogeys' speed, weapons, and turn rate, the singleton may then be able simply to continue straight ahead and leave the threat in the dust. Extension distances can be increased if necessary by turning slightly in the nose-to-tail direction after the pass. If the bogey is missile equipped, a dive to low altitude is generally called for to reduce the enemy's maximum firing range. Faster bogeys should be watched carefully during an extension to observe their reaction. The fighter pilot must still consider himself defensive when he is being pursued by faster aircraft.

Fuel state is extremely critical to single-plane operations. Sufficient reserve must be retained for a maximum-speed bugout to friendly airspace at whatever altitude is likely to be required. The pilot of the single fighter must also allow for the possibility of having to fight his way out by defending against hostile fighters, SAMs, etc. Afterburning jet fighters at low altitude can consume an incredible amount of fuel, so prudent penetrations of hostile airspace can be severely limited. In fact, under many combat conditions, a single fighter may literally be pushing bugout fuel state at takeoff.

Once committed to a bugout, the pilot must again assume a defensive posture. Engagement should be avoided if possible. Only those bogeys in the line of retreat should be engaged offensively, and then only if engaging them does not put escape in jeopardy. The only difference between running out of fuel and being shot down is that some hard-working enemy pilot is denied a well-earned score.

Under most conditions the pilot of the single fighter should not consider returning to the combat arena after committing to a withdrawal. Once he is very close to friendly airspace, however, much of the uncertainty of fuel requirements has diminished, and the singleton pilot may find that sufficient fuel remains for an attack on a known, nearby bogey. Care must be exercised in this case to ensure such an attack does not carry the fighter far from friendly airspace or result in a defensive situation.

Another situation which may call for a return to the fray is when another friendly pilot finds himself in a serious defensive position nearby. If fuel is available, even one high-speed pass through the fight, and a shot of opportunity if it becomes available, often can relieve enough pressure from a hard-pressed defender to enable him to escape. Such assistance would, no doubt, be appreciated, and would probably be worth a beer on return to the pub.

> It is a code of honour to help out any comrade who is in distress, and no matter how serious the consequences may seem, there is only one thing to do—dash straight in, and at least lend moral support to him.
> Lt. Colonel W. A. "Billy" Bishop, RAF

Defensive One-versus-Many

In a hostile environment, the pilot of a single fighter should consider himself to be defensive whenever he is not actively engaged in an offensive attack. This ordinarily means that the singleton pilot spends the vast majority of his time in a defensive posture, although, hopefully, not actively defensive. The Chapter 5 discussion of defensive one-versus-two techniques stressed the importance of keeping track of both opponents so that one bogey can be engaged until the other becomes a threat. A switch can then be performed and the process continued until an escape opportunity is presented or until one bogey is destroyed. By definition, in the one-versus-many scenario all the enemy fighters cannot be located or tracked. It must always be assumed that additional bogeys could appear at any moment from essentially any direction. This unknown element normally precludes the prudent fighter pilot in a single aircraft from choosing to engage any number of known bogeys in an extended dogfight. This does not, of course, mean that the single fighter should not attempt to be offensive; but such offense generally must be limited to surprise hit-and-run attacks, as described in the previous section, if the single is to have much chance of survival. For most fighter pilots survival is fairly high on the list of priorities.

Quite often in the heat of battle fighter pilots come up with some fairly novel survival techniques. One of the more bizarre is recalled in *The First and the Last* by Adolph Galland.

> With the first bursts from four Mustangs—I sobered up . . . I simply fled. Diving with open throttle I tried to escape the pursuing Mustangs, which were firing wildly. . . . The tracer bullets came closer and closer. As my FW-190 threatened to disintegrate and as I had only a small choice of those possibilities which the rules of the game allow in such embarrassing situations, I did something which had already saved my life twice during the Battle of Britain: I fired everything I had simply into the blue in front of me. It had the desired effect on my pursuers. Suddenly they saw the smoke which the shells had left behind coming toward them. They probably thought they had met the first fighter to fire backward or that a second attacking German fighter arm was behind them. My trick succeeded; they did a right-hand climbing turn and disappeared.[2]

Defense in the unknown one-versus-many environment becomes a statistical problem of how to reduce the probability of being shot by an undetected enemy. This is a major and obviously very difficult dilemma, as evidenced by the fact that about 90 percent of air-to-air combat losses in all wars have been the result of undetected attacks. Some of the techniques that have proven useful to single fighters in this scenario have already been mentioned. These include maintenance of high airspeed, selection of favorable operating altitudes, use of "hit-and-split" attacks, etc. This section goes into a little more detail on the art and science of staying alive in the one-versus-many environment.

> The logic of the theory of probabilities showed us incontestably that one's number was up after a certain amount of sorties. For some it was sooner, for some later.
>
> Lt. General Adolph Galland, Luftwaffe

Probably the greatest amount of time a single fighter spends in this environment will be devoted to cruising, patrolling, or transiting hostile airspace. This includes both pre-engagement positioning and the disengagement, or bugout, phase. The fighter pilot's task at such times is to get from one place to another without being shot. Obviously, maintaining the highest possible speed in these situations, consistent with fuel availability, will limit the fighter's exposure time. An added benefit of speed is the increased difficulty that enemy fighters attempting to reach a rear-hemisphere firing position will experience. Such an attack is generally the most likely to be lethal and is usually the most difficult to detect. A substantial speed advantage for the single fighter can make a rear-hemisphere intercept essentially impossible. In any case, greater speed by the single fighter requires the attacker to employ more lead heading to effect an intercept from a starting position to one side of the fighter's flight path, placing the attacker farther forward relative to the defending fighter during the approach and making the attack easier to detect. Rear-hemisphere attacks also take longer against a faster target, increasing the possibility that such attacks will be detected. In addition, as has been emphasized before, the size of a target's vulnerable rear-hemisphere missile envelope is reduced by greater speed. Taken together, these factors probably make speed the most important defensive tool for the single fighter in the unknown environment.

Altitude selection is also important. It may be possible for the single fighter to cruise above the altitude capability or normal operating ceiling of enemy fighters. Such an altitude advantage may have to be substantial, however, if the enemy has AAMs, especially since high altitudes give these weapons increased range capability. Whenever there is a possibility of being attacked by either an AAM or a SAM, the fighter should not be so high that it is incapable of achieving at least corner velocity for defensive maneuvering purposes. In addition, if the singleton pilot wishes to avoid visual detection, he should remain clear of the contrail level. Cruising above the contrail layer, however, can aid in detecting an enemy attack from below, while taking a position slightly below the con level can highlight attacks from above.

Very low altitudes can also have advantages in this scenario. Chief among these are greatly reduced range for enemy missiles and, often, decreased enemy radar detection capabilities from both airborne and surface platforms. It should be remembered, however, that a diving enemy fighter may be able to catch even a faster aircraft cruising at low altitude. Generally speaking, depending on the circumstances, either very high or very low altitudes are preferable to medium levels. If nothing else, choosing one of these extremes decreases the probable threat sector by half. Factors that favor high-altitude operation include the need for improved friendly radar coverage, control, navigation, and communications; a high sun; a medium to low cloud layer or light-colored terrain to highlight other aircraft visually; greater required operating range; heavy hostile low-altitude ground defenses, such as AAA and low-altitude SAMs; dependable look-down, shoot-down weapons capability; and enemy fighters equipped only with guns or short-range missiles.

> When flying low over water or desert, adjust your height so that you can see your shadow on the surface; then, in addition to your routine gentle weave, look out, watching the water for other shadows sneaking up behind yours; these may represent unfriendly aircraft.
>
> Captain Reade Tilley, USAAF

The converse of most of these factors favors low-altitude operation. In addition, low-level tactics may be preferable when the enemy has better radar coverage of the area than does friendly GCI; when the enemy has long-range SAMs; when bogey fighters do not have look-down, shoot-down capability; and when medium to high cloud layers are present. A high dynamic-pressure (Q)-limit advantage (essentially greater indicated airspeed capability) can also be better exploited at low altitude, but a Mach-limit advantage is generally more useful at high altitudes. High-to-low attacks are usually safer because of faster closing and probably greater speed available for escape after the attack. A further consideration with many fighter radars is decreased effectiveness at very low altitudes, as explained in the first chapter. Many of these considerations often conflict, and it is necessary for the pilot to weigh the importance of each to his survival and to mission success.

> When attacked by much superior numbers I get the hell out of there using speed, or clouds . . . and only as a last resort by diving to the deck. . . . I do not like the deck. . . . The danger from small arms ground fire . . . is great. . . . Two-thirds of our Squadron losses have been from enemy small arms fire.
>
> Lt. Colonel John C. Meyer, USAAF

Once speed and altitude have been selected to optimize the single fighter's survival prospects under a given set of conditions, there remains a choice of technique in transiting from one point to another. This choice is between flying in a straight line and weaving. When the singleton pilot is fortunate enough to have what he believes to be an effective speed or altitude sanctuary, when he is essentially immune from rear-hemisphere attacks, straight-line flight is often preferable. This method maximizes speed over the ground, limiting exposure time, increasing combat radius, and making it more difficult for slower aircraft to close from the rear. When he is at high altitude and worried about attacks from below, the pilot can alternately roll one way and then the other, turning as little as possible, to check blind spots below his aircraft. This technique will, however, increase the likelihood of wing flashes alerting the enemy to the fighter's presence.

> The [MiG-] 21 was so small that each time it ran straight away from us, we lost sight of it. . . . Each time he turned, we regained sight of his planform.
>
> Commander Randy "Duke" Cunningham, USN

In most situations, however, enemy rear-hemisphere attacks will be a possibility, even when flying at high speed in a straight line. In this case it is usually better to improve the ability to detect such an attack, even at the risk of some increase in attack probability. Weaving does just this. It makes the fighter easier to see and to catch, but it usually improves the chances of successfully defending against an attack. An exception to this generalization might be that "magic missile," mentioned previously, which cannot be defeated once it is launched.

The purpose of weaving is primarily to allow the pilot of a single fighter to cover his rear quarter more easily. The usual blind areas near dead astern, especially the low six o'clock region, can be visually checked intermittently by banking and turning alternately in each direction. On any given heading a fighter will have a blind cone behind and/or below. For most aircraft a turn of 60° to 90° is required to clear this area adequately. The new heading then generates a new blind region, and a turn of like magnitude in the opposite direction can be used to clear six again, and so on. Turns of less than 60° to 90° generally are not effective for this purpose, and turns of greater than about 90° in one direction tend to make a fighter predictable for too long, which aids an unseen bogey in gaining a firing position. If turns of greater than 90° are required, they should be made in segments of less than 90°, interrupted by a roll reversal and a visual check of the belly-side.

> If it is necessary to fly down sun, do so in a series of 45-degree tacks.
> Group Captain Reade Tilley, RAF

The timing of the turns in a weave can be quite important. The object is to check blind areas for attacking fighters or airborne missiles so that they can be detected before they reach a lethal position. In a guns-only environment an attacking fighter must be detected somewhere between the maximum range at which it is likely to be seen under the prevailing visibility conditions from a nose-on aspect, and the range at which its guns become effective. The difference between these two distances, in conjunction with the bogey's probable closing speed, yields the time interval during which all vulnerable areas should be checked.

As an example, consider what might be a typical scenario during the World War II time frame. Assume that visibility on a given day is such that a bogey closing from the rear should be seen at a range of about half a mile (3,000 ft), and it can be expected to open fire at about 1,200 ft. This leaves the defending fighter with about an 1,800-ft detection band. Now assume that the bogey may gain a small speed advantage in a diving attack, and with a little help from geometry could be expected to close at about 60 kts (100 ft/sec). This works out to about eighteen seconds available to the defender to discover the attack. Therefore the weave should be performed so that the blind area is covered every eighteen seconds. If a turn of 60° to 90° is made during each eighteen-second interval, the fighter will be turning at the rate of 3° to 5°/sec. This is a fairly gentle "guns weave" of something less than 2 Gs at typical speeds of the assumed period.

> Check belly because 50 percent of your aircraft is below you.
> Lieutenant Jim "Huck" Harris, USN

Now consider a more modern example, of supersonic jet fighters and RQ AAMs. Because of the range of typical missiles, it is quite likely that a rear-hemisphere attack will not be discovered before the weapon is launched, at which time the missile smoke trail, hopefully, will alert the defender. The task, therefore, is to see the missile sometime between launch and impact. Assuming a typical launch range of 6,000 ft, considering the fighter's speed and altitude, and an expected missile closure averaging about 800 ft/sec, the defender's available reaction time (assuming the missile is detected at launch) would be on the order of seven seconds. (To make matters worse, effective detection time may be even less, since a couple of seconds are required for an effective defensive maneuver.) A turn rate of 9° to 13°/sec would be necessary to complete a 60° to 90° turn during this period, requiring 6 or 7 Gs from a fighter at low supersonic speeds. This essentially amounts to continuous break turns for the defending fighter, which would likely result in loss of energy, vastly increasing the chances of being caught from behind, and would be so physically taxing for the pilot that both his offensive and his defensive efficiency would suffer greatly. It is highly probable, therefore, that such radical maneuvering performed on a continuous and routine basis would be counterproductive.

Obviously, some modification of this procedure is necessary in this scenario. In cases where the single fighter can assume a substantial speed advantage over the bogeys, it may be preferable to rely on this speed to clear the aircraft's tail, as only those enemy fighters with near-perfect position and excellent conversion technique would have a chance to reach a firing envelope. To provide additional peace of mind and insurance against this possibility, the pilot can make short, gentle turns back and forth every few seconds, or simply roll alternately in each direction and possibly kick the tail around with excess rudder. Either of these techniques greatly increases RQ visual coverage without substantially reducing speed over the ground.

A compromise technique that may be useful against faster bogeys or those with long-range missiles, which make a RQ attack more likely, is a combination of the hard turn and the rolling belly-check. The pilot begins this procedure with a hard turn (approximately maximum sustained G) for the usual 60° to 90°, followed immediately by a roll reversal to check for threats approaching from the belly-side. This sequence is followed by straight-line flight for about the same time required for the hard turn, then the turn-and-belly-check sequence is repeated, either in the same or in the opposite direction. The pilot should choose his turn directions for each sequence so that he makes progress toward his objective but does not become too predictable. There are two advantages to this technique. One is that the hard turns may provide an effective defense even against unseen missiles. Another is that an attacker, seeing a hard turn from his intended victim, may assume that the attack has been discovered and break off rather than risk becoming involved in a prolonged fight with an actively defending opponent.

> An aggressive act in the initial phases of the attack will very often give you a breather and a head start home. . . . Showing a willingness to fight often discourages the enemy even when he outnumbers us, while on the other hand I have, by immediately breaking for the deck on other occasions, given the enemy a "shot in the arm," turning his half-hearted attack into an aggressive one.
>
> Lt. Colonel John C. Meyer, USAAF

Whenever an enemy aircraft is detected in a threatening position, the singleton pilot must quickly assess the potential threat and decide on the best course of action. A slower bogey detected near maximum weapons range in the rear hemisphere might be left far behind by turning away, placing the bogey near the fighter's aft visibility limit, and extending away at high speed. Faster bogeys, or those well positioned for a lead turn in the forward hemisphere, generally call for a hard turn to meet the threat as nearly head-on as possible with minimum flight-path separation before attempting an extension and escape. If weapons can be brought to bear during this process, they should be fired. Even with a marginal chance of success, such weapons use can place the bogey in a defensive posture and may aid the singleton pilot in making good his escape. Remember that in the hostile one-versus-many environment, maneuvering is reserved for defensive purposes and for attack; it is not used for prolonged offensive engagement.

> Fokkers can dive as fast as we can. First you must turn, bank ninety degrees and keep turning. They can't keep their sights on you. Watch the sun for direction. Now there's one on your right—shoot at him. Don't try to hit him—just spray him—for if you try to hold your sight on him you'll have to fly straight and give the others a crack at you. But you put the wind up him anyway and he turns. Quick, turn in the opposite direction. He's out of it for a moment. Now there's another one near you. Try it on him—it works! Turn again, you are between them and the line. Now go for it, engine full on, nose down.[3]

If he is forced into maneuvering defensively, the pilot of a single fighter must react like a cornered animal and attack with all the ferocity and aggressiveness he can muster. Survival at this point depends on how quickly the singleton pilot can destroy his attacker or draw neutral and escape. Time is of the utmost importance here, as every second increases the likelihood of more hostile fighters entering the fight. Fighter pilots generally consider a single aircraft to be easy meat, and the tendency is for them to become careless. This lack of aggressiveness on the part of the enemy can quickly lead to offensive situations for a well-flown and determined defender. Even while fighting with abandon, however, the singleton pilot should watch for an escape opportunity, and if one develops he should seize it rather than prolong the engagement. Air-to-air dogfights tend to draw a crowd very quickly with their wheeling fighters, tracers, missile smoke, flares, explosions, etc. (During World War II the Japanese were notorious for staging mock dogfights just to attract enemy fighters.) This is no place for a singleton pilot in hostile airspace, and he should get as far out of Dodge as possible at the first opportunity. Until that point the singleton should engage in aggressive maneuvering based on the one-versus-one or one-versus-two techniques discussed in previous chapters. During this process the pilot must fight the bogeys he sees, while remaining aware of the possibility of additional, unseen, threats.

> The best individual defensive tactic is a hard and fast offensive, regardless of the odds.
>
>   Major William D. "Dinghy" Dunham, USAAF
>   16 Victories, WW-II

Whenever he is trapped in defensive situations, the singleton pilot should yell for help from other friendly fighters that may be closeby. GCI/AIC can be invaluable in directing other friendly forces into the fight.

In past guns-only engagements of this sort, defenders have exploited a dive-speed advantage to separate from enemy fighters. Out-of-control flight has also been useful. The defender enters a spin of some sort at high altitude, then recovers and runs close to the ground. Attackers may assume the defender has been hit and is about to crash, relax their pressure for a moment, and give the desperate loner a chance to escape. Spins are very effective guns-defense maneuvers, but they offer little protection against AAMs because of low G and low airspeed.

> Cloud . . . is of most use to a fighter pilot who is in trouble. . . . It's great stuff to hide in; layer cloud is most useful, as you can pop in, or dive out below for a look, and at the same time maintain a more or less steady course towards home and friends. . . . If you are being pursued, turn 90 degrees in every cloud you pop into.
>
> Captain Reade Tilley, USAAF

Clouds can also be lifesavers for a defensive single. Ducking into a cloud is a very effective defense against both guns and heat-seeking missiles. In a radar-missile environment, however, whether AAMs or SAMs, prolonged flight in clouds is exceedingly dangerous. Radar can see through clouds, except possibly those containing heavy rain, but the target pilot cannot see the missile to defend against it. When hostile radar weapons are anticipated, the pilot of a single fighter still can jump into a cloud, change direction about 90°, and pop out again for a look. As long as the threat of radar missiles exists, the defender should not remain for long in clouds. Likewise, flying for any period of time close to a cloud layer between the fighter and the radar-missile threat is not wise, since a missile popping out of a cloud layer may not leave adequate time for defensive reaction.

> Clouds are very effective for evasive action. . . . They're a good way to get home when you're alone.
>
> Lt. Colonel John C. Meyer, USAAF

Very low altitude flight tends to complicate an attacker's guns or missiles employment problems. This may allow the defender to drag bogeys toward friendly fighters or friendly airspace. In desperation a defender might even drag his antagonists over hostile surface defenses, as a bogey is not likely to continue an attack through heavy AAA or SAM launches, even if these weapons are fired by his side. The single defender, on the other hand, may prefer defending against surface fire than against threatening fighters.

Few-versus-Many

> Superior technical achievements—used correctly both strategically and tactically—can beat any quantity numerically many times stronger yet technically inferior.
>
> Lt. General Adolph Galland, Luftwaffe

Under most combat conditions the advantages of mutual support will outweigh the advantages of single fighters. This is particularly the case when friendly and threat aircraft and weapons capabilities are such that there is no reliable speed or altitude sanctuary for the singleton. The section of two fighters is considered by most doctrines to be the ideal mutually supporting element. If it is desirable to combine greater numbers in one mission, they can form divisions of several two-plane elements under the overall control of the leader of one section. Once engaged, however, divisions usually attempt to maintain only two-ship section

integrity, since this has been found to be about the maximum number of
aircraft which can be closely coordinated at the high speeds and large
turning radii of modern fighters. This segment addresses the techniques
used by a section of fighters operating in a highly outnumbered hostile
environment.

> Fighter pilots don't think of not coming back. They are invincible, or think
> they are, and they have to be that way. Down in our hearts we may figure that
> some accident will get us some day, when we are old and gray, when our
> beards get in the way of the controls, or we get to where we don't see well or
> react fast—but we know that no enemy fighter is good enough to shoot us
> down. If that happens it's just an accident.
>
> These thoughts are the "chips" that we carry on our shoulders, and they
> have to be there—arrogant, egotistical chips mellowed by flying technique
> and experience and fortified by the motto, "Attack!" Never be on the defen-
> sive. Shoot the enemy down before he can shoot you down. You are better
> than he is, but don't give him a chance. He may get in a lucky shot but you're
> invincible. Move toward any dot in the sky that remotely resembles an
> airplane. Move to attack, with switches on and the sight ready. If it's not a
> ship or if it's a friendly one you'll be ready anyway, and your arrogant luck
> will last longer.[4]
>
>   Colonel Robert L. Scott, Jr., USAAF
>   10 Victories, WW-II

Chapter 6 ("Section Tactics, Two-versus-Two") discussed the merits of
various tactical doctrines in the two-versus-two environment and stated
that double attack and loose deuce doctrines are probably best suited to
this scenario. The strike-rejoin-strike technique described there can be
employed with either doctrine, providing credible offensive potential with
good mutual support. Like the single fighter in the one-versus-many scenario, the section operating in the few-versus-many environment must be
primarily concerned with defense. Prolonged turning engagements should
be avoided like the plague, as they tend to attract other hostile fighters,
lead to breakdown of mutual support, and foster task overloading, which
leaves the fighters vulnerable to unseen attacks. The strike-rejoin-strike
system, exemplified by Figures 6-5 through 6-8, allows the section to
maintain an effective defensive posture except during brief attack se-
quences, and discourages prolonged engagement. These qualities are ideal
for the unknown few-versus-many scenario.

> In Africa we were outnumbered twenty to one, so it was impossible to get any
> real success. To get out with your neck, to get home in one piece—that was
> success.
>
>   Major Hartmann Grasser, Luftwaffe
>   103 Victories, WW-II

As in the one-versus-many situation, the section in the hostile unknown scenario spends most of its time transiting hostile airspace during
the ingress, patrol, pre-engaged maneuvering, and egress phases of a mission. Combat-spread formation has been shown to be most effective for
section defensive mutual support and is recommended. Small divisions
operate best in line abreast, or in loose vics (3 fighters) or finger-four

arrangements. High speed and optimum altitude selection, as discussed earlier in this chapter, are again critical elements in the survival equation.

> Surprise is always to be aimed for. . . . It is easier to surprise a formation of four or six than it is to surprise one or two. This is probably because the greater number feel more confident in their ability to protect themselves, and also are probably counting upon each other to do a certain amount of looking out. When flying alone or with just one other, it is always a case of constantly turning around in your seat, turning your machine to right or left, looking above and around or below you all the time. It is a very tiring piece of work, so it is but natural that when you have three or four other men behind you, you spend more time looking in the direction where you hope the enemy machines are, if you want to attack them, and to looking at any interesting sights which are on the ground.[5]

In the previous segment on one-versus-many, there was considerable discussion on the merits of weaving. The purpose of this tactic is to allow the pilot of a single fighter better opportunity to cover visually his vulnerable rear quarter. With an effective defensive formation this function is performed more efficiently by visual cross-cover of the wingmen. If the pilots weave in formation, either individually or in unison, their wingman's rear hemisphere will be periodically out of sight and unprotected by mutual support. Considering this fact and the other disadvantages of weaving, it appears that this technique is counterproductive. In most cases it is more effective for the fighters to fly straight and level from one point to the next, maintain strict position and spacing within the formation, and rely on the wingmen to provide visual protection of individual fighter blind areas. An exception to this rule might be when, because of field of view, visibility, threat weapons, etc., the defensive formation is not considered adequate to cover vulnerable areas. The inability to communicate between fighters, because of comm-jamming or radio malfunction, for example, is another possible exception. Obviously this method requires absolute trust in the wingmen.

The tac turn (described in Chapter 6) is an ideal method for maneuvering a section in the hostile unknown environment, and it can also be adapted for use by small divisions (as depicted in Figure 7-5). As recommended for the single plane, section turns should be limited to a maximum of 90°, and smaller turns should be made if possible. A straight-line period should be provided between each heading change to ensure adequate coverage of the rear. Although tac turns offer better visual mutual support than the other methods discussed, there is still some degradation of coverage during the maneuver as compared to straight-line flight in combat spread. Tac turns are also more flexible than other methods, as they can easily be adapted to directional changes of less than 90° with good mutual support throughout, as long as all fighter pilots know the planned duration of the turn at commencement.

> The sun is a most effective offensive weapon and the enemy loves to use it. Whenever possible I try to make all turns into the sun and try never to fly with it at my back.
>
> Lt. Colonel John C. Meyer, USAAF

A good defensive formation should be maintained for as long as practical during the pre-engaged maneuvering phase; the fighters can make a transition to a more offensive arrangement in the final stages of attack. When meeting bogeys in their forward hemisphere, bracket and drag attacks, as described in Chapter 6, are useful in this scenario. Because of better mutual support during and after an attack, however, the bracket is probably preferable in the unknown scenario. Whenever possible, missiles and guns should be fired from the target's forward hemisphere during the bracket or pincer attacks, as conversion to RQ firing parameters normally requires turns in excess of 90°. Such turns leave the fighters predictable for too long and vulnerable to attack by unseen bogeys. Figure 8-2 illustrates the recommended bracket attack technique in the unknown scenario.

At time "1" in this example the fighter section, patrolling in defensive combat spread, spots what may be a hostile formation approaching head-on. If the contact can be identified as hostile at this time, and the fighters are equipped with all-aspect missiles, the weapons should be fired at maximum relative range. In this case, however, the bogeys cannot be identified as hostile, so the fighters begin a bracket maneuver to gain more offensive positions. At time "2" each fighter has completed a counterturn to a pure-pursuit or lead-pursuit heading on the nearest bogey. During the turns between times "1" and "2," the attackers should visually clear the

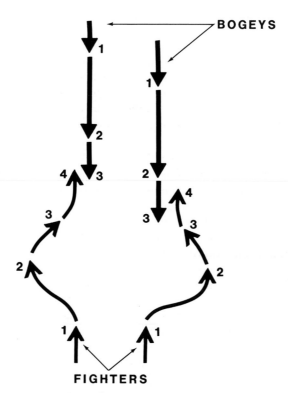

Figure 8-2. Bracket or Pincer Attack, Unknown
Scenario

area inside their turns for attacks by other hostile fighters or missiles. At closer range, and with a greater-aspect view of the bogeys, visual identification is more likely. The first pilot to identify the hostile bogeys calls the VID to his wingman, and both pilots are then cleared to fire if they are all-aspect missile equipped. At time "3" both fighters press ahead for forward-hemisphere gun snapshot passes. After prosecuting their attacks, being careful not to turn more than 90° during the pass, each pilot should reverse and break away to check for threats on his belly-side. At time "4" the fighters are again well positioned to rejoin in spread formation and continue their patrol or bugout.

Again, when attacking a hostile formation from the rear hemisphere, a good defensive formation and posture should be maintained until the last practical moment. Then the fighters can shift into a more offensive echelon or trail formation for simultaneous or sequential attacks. Simultaneous attacks on multiple targets are usually preferable, since one pass is all that should be expected or planned in the hostile unknown environment. As in single-plane attacks, each pilot should choose a target that limits the probability of him being drawn deeply into the enemy formation, possibly complicating the prospects of escape. The break-away direction should be established by the formation leader prior to the attack to facilitate rejoining the section as quickly as possible.

> If your attack is sudden and aggressive, the enemy will be at a disadvantage regardless of his numbers and position.
>
> Lt. Colonel Gerald R. Johnson, USAAF

As a rule in the few-versus-many scenario, attacks should not be made without offensive advantage and the prospect of getting off the first shot. The prospects for escape are also critical in the decision to attack. Remember, the object is to attack, not to engage. Escape beyond visual range is often possible even for slower fighters following forward-quarter attacks. If escape is not likely after an attack because of bogey performance or weapons, the fighter section must choose its victims very carefully with a view toward destroying as many as possible in the initial attack and engaging the rest on at least equal terms. Even this prospect, however, is not an attractive one in this scenario because of the probability of intervention by additional enemy fighters during the engagement. Avoiding combat with superior numbers of such bogeys is usually preferable. In the target-rich few-versus-many environment, easier pickings are normally not hard to find.

Ordinarily, extended engagement in this scenario is only justified when mission objectives dictate such engagement, or when the fighters are attacked and are forced to defend themselves. In the latter situation the pilots should employ one of the defenses described in Chapter 5, namely the sandwich or one of the various defensive splits, to neutralize or destroy the attacker as quickly as possible. When a smaller number of fighters are engaged by multiple bogeys, loose deuce doctrine (or gaggle tactics for more than two fighters) seems to offer the best prospects of maintaining mutual support (by presence). By virtue of its high offensive efficiency, this doctrine also generally provides the quickest kills, which are critical in the hostile arena. When the fighters are committed to engage bogeys of superior speed, it is usually preferable to continue the engagement to its conclusion rather than attempt to escape and risk being caught and re-engaged defensively. The difficulty of escape must be given careful consideration when deciding whether to use strike-rejoin-strike methods against large numbers of superior bogeys.

Although the elements of a section or a division should generally plan to remain together for mutual support in the few-versus-many environment, a high probability exists that breakdowns will occur and pilots will find themselves in a one-versus-many situation. Therefore, this contingency should be preplanned for, and the critical decision of whether to continue the mission under those conditions should be made before takeoff. For the same reason, pilots should be well trained in single-plane attack and survival techniques. GCI/AIC control and prearranged rendezvous points are valuable aids in reforming separated elements.

Many-versus-Many

The many-versus-many scenario denotes large and roughly equivalent numbers of friendly and hostile fighters in the combat area. These fighters may be on coordinated missions or simply be in the same arena by chance. Because large numbers of fighters are difficult to control, they are generally operated in sections or small divisions that are able to coordinate their efforts to achieve a given objective. Each element can therefore operate just as in the few-versus-many case. All pilots should be trained in the same techniques so that they can join with other friendly fighters and operate with undiminished efficiency should they become separated from their own wingmen in the heat of battle. All pilots should monitor the same radio frequency for better coordination, but strict radio discipline is absolutely essential if there is to be any hope of pilots receiving life-or-death transmissions.

> In fighter flying, a panic message is the greatest of all crimes. Practice on the ground the exact words you will use to cover any situation in the air. Say it over and over again until it becomes automatic.
>
> Captain Reade Tilley, USAAF

Although strike-rejoin-strike methods are still preferable in most many-versus-many scenarios, the presence of more friendly fighters in the general area makes engagement somewhat less risky. In addition, enemy fighters are likely to be less aggressive and less eager for extended engagement than they are under previously discussed conditions. Loose deuce and gaggle tactics continue to be most effective in this environment. Additional elements should refrain from joining a mature engagement of roughly equal opposing forces in which friendly fighters appear to be holding their own. A more effective tactic is to cruise outside the periphery of such a fur ball, remain in a defensive posture, and be alert for bogeys exiting the fight and the arrival of additional hostile forces.

The man who enters combat encased in solid armor plate, but lacking the essential of self-confidence, is far more exposed and naked to death than the individual who subjects himself to battle shorn of any protection but his own skill, his own belief in himself and in his wingmen. Righteousness is necessary for one's peace of mind, perhaps, but it is a poor substitute for agility . . . and a resolution to meet the enemy under any conditions and against any odds.

Major Robert S. Johnson, USAAF

Notes

1. J. E. Johnson, *Full Circle*, p. 54.
2. Adolph Galland, *The First and the Last*, p. 213.
3. Elliot White Springs, *War Birds: Diary of an Unknown Aviator*, pp. 235–36 (attributed to 1/Lt. John Grider, USAS, serving with 85 Squadron, RAF, 1918).
4. Robert L. Scott, Jr., *God Is My Co-Pilot*, pp. 178–79.
5. William A. Bishop, *Winged Warfare*, pp. 177–78.

9

Fighter Missions

To use a fighter as a fighter-bomber when the strength of the fighter arm is inadequate to achieve air superiority is putting the cart before the horse.

Lt. General Adolph Galland, Luftwaffe

The primary mission of fighters is air superiority; that is, ensuring use by friendly aircraft of the airspace over critical surface areas, and denying use of that airspace to the enemy. Control of the high ground has always been one of the fundamentals of warfare. Airspace control allows strategic and tactical bombing, close air support of troops and armor, airborne or surface reinforcement and supply, reconnaissance, and other missions vital to the success of any military operation. Although no war so far has been won solely on the basis of air power, the advent of nuclear weapons certainly lends credence to this possibility for future conflicts.

The value of air power became evident in World War I, when airplanes were in their infancy. The airplane did not play a pivotal role in the outcome of that conflict, but by the early days of World War II it was inconceivable that any major military operation could succeed without first achieving air superiority. This evolution was brought about primarily by the quantum increases in firepower and destructive capabilities of the aircraft that were developed between the wars.

The most important branch of aviation is pursuit, which fights for and gains control of the air.

Brig. General William "Billy" Mitchell, USAS

During World War II, the devastating tactical bombing and close air support by the German Luftwaffe during the blitzkrieg attacks on Poland, the Low Countries, and France provided early evidence of the effectiveness of air power. The importance placed on air superiority is obvious in the German decision to cancel the invasion of England after the RAF could not be defeated during the Battle of Britain. The value of air superiority was shown again by the ability of the American bombers to prosecute daylight strategic bombardment of Germany and Japan late in the war. Since that conflict, air superiority has continued to play the decisive role in conventional warfare. Only guerilla conflicts seem to be resistant to the crushing weight of air power, which may be one of the primary reasons behind the recent popularity of guerilla strategies.

> A soldier who is familiar with his weapon can only achieve a maximum effect with it when he believes in the way it is tactically employed.
>
> Lt. General Adolph Galland, Luftwaffe

The major military attributes of the airplane, namely, speed and freedom of movement, are best suited to offensive action, as it is very difficult to defend against an attack that can come at any time, with very little warning, from essentially any direction. These same attributes, however, make the airplane one of the most effective defensive weapons against airborne attack. Paradoxically, the fighter is an offensive weapon used primarily for defensive missions. Regardless of how offensive the fighter pilot may feel when he is attacking another aircraft, his role in the final analysis is usually defensive. He is defending a target against enemy attack or defending friendly bombers from hostile fighters. Only once in a great while is he assigned the tasks of interdicting enemy airborne supply and transport aircraft not directly involved in hostile action or simply ranging over hostile territory in search of targets of opportunity. Missions such as these, however, are best suited to the military advantages of the fighter, and they are covered first in this chapter.

The Fighter Sweep

> The fighter pilots have to rove in the area allotted to them in any way they like, and when they spot an enemy they attack and shoot him down; anything else is rubbish.
>
> Baron Manfred von Richthofen

A fighter sweep is a mission flown generally over hostile or contested territory for the purpose of engaging and destroying enemy fighters or other airborne targets of opportunity. The fighter sweep is designed to establish air superiority by denying the enemy use of the airspace for his purposes, and to make the airspace safer for use by friendly forces. Thus, the fighter sweep can be carried out for either offensive or defensive purposes, but because the conduct of this mission allows the fighter pilot to seek out and attack other aircraft from a position of advantage, it is offensive in nature and is well suited to the inherent offensive character of the fighter. The sweep, therefore, is the preferred fighter mission, and fighter tacticians should employ sweep techniques whenever possible in conjunction with other missions. This concept is explored in greater depth throughout this chapter.

> An air force is, according to its intrinsic laws, by nature an offensive weapon. Air supremacy is of course essential for this. If this has been lost then the fighter force has to be strengthened first of all. Because only the fighter force can achieve this essential supremacy so that the bomber and with it the entire air force can go over to the offensive once more.
>
> Lt. General Adolph Galland, Luftwaffe

Scenarios

Since the usual objective of the fighter sweep is to engage enemy fighters, it is logical for such sweeps to be conducted in areas expected to have a high concentration of hostile aircraft. From World War I to the latest conflicts, the favorite target for fighter sweeps has probably been enemy fighter bases. A surprise fighter attack on an unsuspecting airfield conducting routine flight operations can be utterly devastating. Some aircraft are taking off, often in tight formations, and are climbing at low altitudes and slow speeds; others are circling to land, in dirty configuration, low on fuel and ammo, with exhausted pilots. The enemy pilots are over friendly, familiar ground, and they are generally less vigilant.

> An airplane on the ground, full of fuel and ammunition and unable to evade or shoot back, was a sitting duck and one of the most vulnerable of all military targets, and . . . most of its life was spent in this position.
> Air Vice-Marshal J. E. "Johnnie" Johnson, RAF

In addition, aircraft are quite often caught on the ground, where they are "sitting ducks," taxiing or being refueled and rearmed between missions. Undoubtedly it is best to attack an enemy aircraft when it is on the ground. Unfortunately, many modern air-to-air weapons are ineffective against surface targets. For this type of mission, therefore, even the true fighter pilot might consider hauling some token air-to-ground ordnance. (If everybody does it, it doesn't look so bad.) An alternative is to take along some fighter-bombers, which can concentrate on the surface targets but have the ability to defend themselves credibly or even to join in the air-to-air fun after unloading their other baggage. This is not the time, however, to saddle the fighters with escort duty.

Ability to attack surface targets is an essential element of a fighter sweep against an enemy airfield. Otherwise any aircraft on the ground, and those that can get there quickly, have an effective sanctuary. Recognizing their disadvantage in the air, the enemy pilots have little inducement to come out and play, but for some reason, fighter pilots seem to prefer even the short end of a one-sided air battle to eating mud with bombs falling around their ears. A single bomb on the local pub often turns the trick. The fighter pilots who survive this attack should be blinded by rage and make for easy airborne targets.

Aircraft on the ground are not always easy scores, however, as they can be dispersed, camouflaged, and stored in hardened bunkers. In addition, because of the value of airfields and the likelihood that they will be attacked, these installations are often among the most heavily defended by surface-to-air weapons. Against such defenses, fighter sweeps are best limited to one quick pass with the intent of taking out easy targets and retiring before the ground defenses have time to react. Hit-and-run attacks can be repeated often, generally with better results than are obtained by a smaller number of sustained attacks.

> A squadron commander who sits in his tent and gives orders and does not fly, though he may have the brains of Solomon, will never get the results that a

man will, who, day in and day out, leads his patrols over the line and infuses
into his pilots the "espirit de corps."

Brig. General William "Billy" Mitchell, USAS

Another likely opportunity for a fighter sweep is over a surface battle,
which is often accompanied by ground-attack aircraft that make tasty
targets as they go about their revolting chores. Enemy transport, reconnaissance, and liaison aircraft can also be expected to be in this area. These
are all very lucrative targets because of their vulnerability and their direct
participation in a surface battle. Under such circumstances enemy fighters
should be avoided as long as more favorable targets are available, unless
these fighters are a menace to friendly aircraft.

Enemy fighter sweeps can be expected in these areas for the same
reasons. It is usually good policy, whenever hostile fighters may be encountered, to split the friendly forces into low- and high-level elements.
The majority can work at a low level, where more of the high-value targets
are likely to be found. Low-altitude flight often makes these targets easier
to see, as they are silhouetted against a light-colored horizon.

The duties of the high-level element in this scenario are largely defensive. These aircraft should remain in a comfortable supporting cover position, guarding against attack by enemy fighters on the low-level element or
on other friendly aircraft in the area. In general, they should avoid contact
with nonthreatening aircraft. A radio warning should be issued to any
threatened friendly; this may suffice, and it is generally preferable to actual
engagement with the hostile fighters. If it is required to leave its defensive
station, the covering element should notify the low element of the situation and solicit help if necessary.

The greater altitude of the high element may allow it to serve as a radio
relay from friendly GCI or command-and-control centers. This element
can also usually make better use of on-board radar equipment. These
advantages, plus a better overall view of the battlefield, may allow the high
element to direct the low element to target opportunities. Because of these
factors, when more than one type of fighter is available, the type with the
more sophisticated radar and communications equipment is normally
assigned high-cover duties. This aircraft should, however, have good air
combat capabilities, since it is more likely to engage hostile fighters. These
two qualities may call for a mixture of fighter types to be employed on
high-cover assignment.

In general in this scenario, as in many others, either very high or very
low is the place to be, although the high element may be limited in altitude
if it is to provide effective visual support for the low element. Low, middle,
and high elements might be preferable in this case, depending on available
numbers and surface defenses. Aircraft at medium altitudes are usually
very easily detected and engaged by both surface-to-air and air-to-air
weapons. Battlefields are notorious for heavy low-altitude air defense.
Aircraft recognition has never been one of the soldier's strong suits, and
low-flying aircraft are regularly fired on by both sides. It may be more
practical under these conditions to keep the entire fighter force at high

altitude, detaching small elements as necessary to descend for slashing attacks on low-level targets and then return to the fold.

The purpose of some fighter sweeps is simply to find and engage enemy fighters in a given airspace. Generally these missions are conducted over hostile or contested territory, so the tactics developed for the few-versus-many and many-versus-many scenarios are usually applicable. Quite often the enemy's GCI and command-and-control networks will be superior to friendly capabilities in these areas, so the unexpected attack should be guarded against. The basics include high speeds and very high or very low altitudes, depending on surface defenses, environmental conditions, and relative aircraft and weapons-system performance. Friendly fighter pilots must use every means at their disposal to achieve surprise, and they must approach an engagement with the intent of attaining the first shot opportunity. Whether engaging in sustained maneuvering or employing hit-and-run tactics is called for depends on the factors discussed in the previous chapter. "Slash-and-dash" methods are often preferable when friendlies are facing enemy forces superior in number or quality. The size of the friendly force should be tailored, when possible, to be equivalent to or larger than the expected hostile formations. Dividing the force into engaged and covering elements is usually most efficient when the enemy is greatly outnumbered in any engagement. If friendlies are forced to engage against superior numbers, loose deuce or gaggle tactics tend to even the odds.

Fuel state is often a critical factor in a fighter sweep. The aircraft are often deep into hostile airspace, and they can be very vulnerable if the pilots are unable to avoid extended engagement or if the aircraft are attacked on the way home. One effective technique used to alleviate this problem is multiple, independent sweeps in the same area, with entry into the combat zone staggered by several minutes. This ensures a supply of fresh fighters in the area to assist in the retreat of other friendlies and to take advantage of retiring enemy forces. The last flight to enter the arena in this scheme is devoted to defense. These aircraft should make one pass through the area, avoiding contact with the enemy if possible, make sure that all friendlies are headed for home, and then depart as rear guard at a high fuel state.

One notable example of the use of this tactic was the staggered (usually every five minutes) fighter sweeps by U.S. F-86s to the Yalu River area during the Korean conflict. These missions stretched the range of these aircraft to the limit, and dead-stick, flamed-out approaches were almost routine on return to base.

A possible complication with the use of this tactic arises when the friendly fighters have beyond-visual-range weapons capability. In order to make full use of this capability, and possibly to avoid allowing the enemy to achieve the first shot should they be similarly equipped, it is necessary to identify BVR targets as hostile at the maximum range of the available weapons. If targets cannot be reliably identified at such ranges, either visually or electronically, then it may be necessary to "sanitize" the combat arena of all friendly forces. This means making sure that no other friendly aircraft can be in the combat zone during the sweep, so that any target detected can be assumed to be hostile. Sanitizing can be very difficult in practice, requiring coordination not only within the friendlies' own air forces, but also, possibly, with other combatant forces and neutrals. Such coordination may be impractical from a time or a security standpoint. Even if this ideal condition can be achieved, only the first wave of attacking fighters can take advantage of it, limiting the desirability of multiple, staggered waves in a fighter sweep.

> Two of *Kitty Hawk's* [U.S. Navy carrier] fighters were making a sweep somewhere out there and the Air Force had fighters just north striking Yen Bai. We were obliged to see the bogey aircraft before shooting, virtually eliminating the head-on potential of the *Sparrow* missile system.
> Commander Randy "Duke" Cunningham, USN

One of the most effective fighter-sweep tactics involves staging a simulated air strike against a high-value surface target. Fighters armed strictly for air-to-air engagement can imitate bombers by employing typical bomber formations, altitudes, and airspeeds while following expected attack routes toward an enemy target. The ruse can be as simple or as elaborate as necessary, even including deceptive communications, EW, and supporting aircraft. Once the enemy fighters have been confirmed (usually by a supporting source) to be airborne in defense against the false strike, the friendly forces can redeploy for more aggressive, offensive capability and spring the nasty surprise. Good electronic surveillance of the combat arena and adequate command-and-control are desirable, if not required, for this tactic, however, to avoid an equally nasty surprise by the enemy prior to redeployment.

Control of Fighter Sweeps

Command, control, and communications (C^3) are critical elements in the success of a fighter sweep. Often the combat arena is very large and contains many aircraft, both hostile and friendly. The ability of friendly fighter pilots to find, identify, and engage high-value hostile targets while avoiding potential threats, or at least engaging these threats from a position of advantage, rests in great measure on relative C^3 capabilities.

> Now [in the Battle of Britain] fighter squadrons could be used economically, so that the cathode tube [radar] had the effect of multiplying the fighter strength several times.
> Air Vice-Marshal J. E. "Johnnie" Johnson, RAF

Supporting radar surveillance may be provided by surface-based GCI or airborne AIC controllers. Depending on tactical philosophy, these "controlling" agencies may have absolute authority to dictate every action of friendly fighters, including headings, altitudes, speeds, attack and firing clearances, and bugouts, or they may act merely as an advisory service, passing along real-time intelligence information and monitoring the progress of the battle. Something of a middle-ground approach seems to be more successful, depending on the relative capabilities of the controlling agency and the fighters themselves. It should be kept in mind that the "controllers" support the fighters, and not vice versa. All parties should recognize that, although the controllers often have a better grasp of the big picture, overall success and failure are decided by many small engagements. Generally the fighter crews themselves are in the best position to judge the critical factors and rapidly changing events in close proximity to the enemy.

There are essentially only two types of radar control: close and broadcast. Under close control the duty of the controller usually is to direct the pilots into a tactically advantageous position to attack or identify a target. In order to accomplish this task, the controller generally must monitor the positions of the fighters and the target. He then transmits relative range and bearing of the target to the fighters, and he may dictate or recommend (depending on philosophy) intercept headings, speeds, altitudes, etc. The primary purpose of the controller in this scenario is to position the fighters favorably so that the pilots can acquire the target, either visually or with their own self-contained sensors, facilitating identification or attack. If identification of an unknown contact is the purpose, the pilots may be required to perform either a visual identification or an electronic identification (EID), using onboard equipment. Depending on the outcome of the identification, the fighters may then be cleared by the controller (or by prearrangement) to attack a hostile target, but final attack procedures should be left to the pilots. During the close-control intercept process, the controller is also responsible for advising the pilots of any additional contacts that might pose a threat or that might be of higher attack priority than the original target.

In broadcast control the controller generally gives the position, and other relevant information as available, of any hostile or unknown targets in a given area, relative to one or more geographical or navigational fixes within that area. The reference point is known to the friendlies, as is their own position relative to that point. As the controller calls target positions and movement relative to the reference, the pilots can calculate their own position relative to the target, and they may be assigned by the controller to conduct their own intercepts based on this information. Unlike with close control, no group of fighters gets individual attention, but all pilots in the area get the same information and can react to it offensively or defensively. Specific fighter formations are generally assigned by the controller in real time to investigate a given contact, or each fighter element may be prebriefed to prosecute any contact in a given region.

Close control is usually preferable for fighter-sweep operations, since it offers the fighters the greatest offensive capability. Once the pilots have their own visual or radar contacts, the close controller should generally revert to providing an advisory service. His function then is to monitor the progress of the intercept and the ensuing engagement, warn of additional hostile or unknown contacts that may be a factor, give rejoin assistance to pilots who become separated from their wingmen, recommend egress headings, etc. During this period it is critical that only essential or requested information be passed over voice radio frequencies; the pilots must have those limited frequencies for their coordination purposes.

Regardless of its advantages, close control may not always be possible or practical. Limitations on controllers or control frequencies may lead to saturation of a close-control system with large numbers of separate enemy and friendly formations. Broadcast control may be better suited to such situations. A combination of these two systems may also be useful. For instance, broadcast control can be given over a common fighter frequency, while selected fighter formations may be switched to a separate close-control frequency during intercepts and engagements as controllers and frequencies become available.

Because of their dependence on communications, command and control are very vulnerable to comm-jamming. Aircrews and controllers should both practice communications brevity, and they should be briefed on alternate control frequencies. Data link and jam-resistant radios can be very valuable. In addition, the tactics employed must not be so dependent on external control that pilots are helpless without it. Just such a condition contributed greatly to the Syrian debacle over Lebanon's Bekaa Valley in 1982. "Spoofing," or intrusion, is another C^3 consideration. This is the tactic by which an enemy controller operates on friendly control frequencies and attempts to "steal," divert, or confuse pilots by issuing false instructions. Coded authentication procedures offer some protection against this trick, but they can be cumbersome and are not foolproof. A better defense against intrusions, when practical, is for the fighter crews to be intimately familiar with the controller's voice.

For fighter aircrews and controllers to work most effectively together as a team, each must know the tasks, problems, and limitations of the other. When this is not the case, friction is likely to develop when aircrews do not receive the information they believe is necessary and controllers believe their instructions are not properly followed. Probably the only solution to this problem is for aircrews and controllers to work, live, eat, and play together, so that they know each other well enough to work out these inevitable differences. Even better, fighter crews should be cross-trained as controllers, and each crewman should take his turn in the barrel on a periodic basis, maybe daily or weekly. Unfortunately, most fighter pilots will resist this idea, even with their last breath, whispering something about the high wing loading of a radar console! Threat of transfer to a bomber outfit will usually induce compliance, however.

Point/Area Defense

Orders to protect fixed objects are very much disliked by fighter pilots. Their element is to attack, to track, to hunt, and to destroy the enemy. Only in this way can the eager and skillful fighter pilot display his abilities to the full. Tie him to a narrow and confined task, rob him of his initiative, and you take away from him the best and most valuable qualities he possesses: aggressive spirit, joy of action, and the passion of the hunter.

Lt. General Adolph Galland, Luftwaffe

As previously discussed, the aircraft is primarily an offensive weapon. Its speed and freedom of movement make defense against airborne attack a very difficult task, and these qualities of an airplane usually confer advantage to the offensive forces. The same qualities, however, make the fighter one of the most effective defensive systems for countering airborne strikes. In conjunction with high-quality C^3 networks and strong surface defenses, fighter/interceptors can make life very difficult for attacking aircraft; but it is not possible, in general, to seal the airspace around a given point completely. Skilled, determined attack by state-of-the-art equipment will normally succeed in penetrating even the most ardent defense.

> Space in which to maneuver in the air, unlike fighting on land or sea, is practically unlimited, and . . . any number of airplanes operating defensively would seldom stop a determined enemy from getting through. Therefore the airplane was, and is, essentially an instrument of attack, not defense.
> Air Vice-Marshal J. E. "Johnnie" Johnson, RAF

When faced with attack by conventional (i.e., non-nuclear) forces, the goal of the defenders is usually to make an attack so costly for the enemy that he is either unable or unwilling to strike again. Although some attackers may get through, the assumption is that target damage will not justify the heavy loss rate of enemy aircraft and crews. Obviously, if the one that gets in is armed with a "silver bullet," this strategy may not be effective. Fortunately, as the weapons become more lethal, they and the aircraft that deliver them become more complex and expensive, so that the number of attackers involved in a nuclear strike is likely to be reduced. This factor gives the defense a better chance to stop all the attackers, but it would still be poor headwork to pitch one's tent on ground zero.

> "He who wants to protect everything, protects nothing," is one of the fundamental rules of defense.
> Lt. General Adolph Galland, Luftwaffe

Two distinct types of air attack are considered here: the penetration strike and the massed attack. The penetration strike involves one or more attacking aircraft which normally fly singly or in small formations and attempt to penetrate the defense network undetected, strike the target, and depart from hostile airspace before they can be caught. Quite often many penetrators will follow individual tracks to the same target, maintaining very rigid time schedules so as to arrive on target nearly simultaneously from different directions to saturate the defenses, and then retire again by separate routes. Normally the penetrating aircraft are small fighter-bombers, which fly at very high speeds at low altitudes to avoid radar detection. Conventional strikes of this type may involve large numbers of penetrators, while nuclear attacks are generally limited to one bomber per target. In either case this can be a very difficult tactic to defend against.

> It is not possible to seal an air space hermetically by defensive tactics.
> Air Vice-Marshall J. E. "Johnnie" Johnson, RAF

The massed attack is much more straightforward, usually comprising a formation of bombers flying close together, World War II–style. The attackers' intent is usually not to evade detection, but to rely on high speed and/or high altitude to limit their exposure to defensive weapons. Quite often they plan to fight their way to the target and back home with the aid of ECM, the concentrated power of their own defensive armament, and possibly heavy fighter escort. This is a brute-force attack and is almost invariably conventional.

Defending fighters, in general, can employ one of two concepts: the combat air patrol (CAP) or the ground-alert interceptor (GAI). The CAP is an airborne standing patrol positioned so as to facilitate interception of possible inbound or outbound raids; the GAI waits on the ground until attackers are detected and reported by the C^3 network, then "scrambles" to intercept. A third concept is actually an offensive approach to a defensive problem: the defenders make a fighter sweep of the enemy's airfield which is timed to coincide with the departure or the return of his strike force. Any of these three concepts can be employed singly or in conjunction to form the fighter defenses. Together with the surface defenses and the C^3 network, the defensive fighters form what is termed an integrated air-defense system (IADS).

> It has been demonstrated recently beyond a doubt that the best antiaircraft defense is pursuit aviation.
>
> General H. H. "Hap" Arnold, USAAF

The fighter's primary assets in air defense are its range and flexibility. Fighters can usually engage the enemy farther from the target than the surface defenses can—the fighter sweep is the extreme example of this capability. Fighter defenses, unlike fixed surface weapons, can also be shifted from one sector to another very rapidly as needed. This flexibility is invaluable when the defenders are faced with an attacking force that has the speed and freedom of movement inherent to aircraft.

> Only air power can defeat air power. The actual elimination or even stalemating of an attacking air force can be achieved only by a superior air force.
>
> Major Alexander P. de Seversky, USAAF

Combat Air Patrol

Whether the CAP or the GAI is preferable in a given situation depends on many factors, including the type of raid expected, the number of targets that must be protected, the degree of certainty as to the attacker's approach route, the amount of warning anticipated, and the numbers and capabilities of the defending fighters. One advantage of a CAP is the probability of interception at greater distances from the target, with presumably more time to inflict damage before the raiders reach their objective. This defensive concept may be necessary if the warning of an attack is expected to be insufficient to allow GAI launch and interception at useful ranges. A prime example of this can be found in attacks by aircraft armed with long-range, stand-off weapons that can be launched many miles from their targets (e.g., cruise missiles). It is usually preferable in such cases to engage the attacking aircraft before it reaches launch range, rather than to attempt to find and destroy multiple weapons inbound to the target.

Aside from the time factor, the CAP is best suited to situations when the direction of approach or the route of the attackers is known with some degree of certainty. The volume of airspace which must be covered by one CAP increases exponentially with the distance it is stationed from the target. Since it is unlikely that there will be enough defending fighters to guard all the approaches to a target at a reasonable range, CAPs must be positioned strategically to make the most efficient use of available assets. Likely stations are located directly between enemy bases and anticipated targets; near natural "choke points," such as mountain passes or restricted passages between heavily defended surface points; along likely ingress and egress routes for low-level penetrators, such as in valleys and along mountain ridgelines, coastlines, and rivers; and over natural low-level navigation landmarks, such as coastal inlets and points, lakes, river bends, crossroads, towns, or the end of a ridgeline.

The practical distance from target to CAP station depends largely on the number of defending fighters and the area that must be covered. As the possible threat sector expands, and as the enemy's speed and stand-off weapons range increase, greater numbers of fighters are required to defend a target adequately. Near-, medium-, and long-range CAPs are usually optimum if the numbers of defending fighters are adequate, as this gives depth to the defenses. Surface defenses or GAI often can be substituted for near- and medium-range CAP. Defense is generally more effective when the CAP stations are compressed enough to allow each CAP to cover its entire assigned area reasonably; this is preferable to overextending the defenses just to reach greater distance. The luxury of compressing CAP stations may not be available, however, depending on fighter assets, the extent of the threat sector, and the possibility of stand-off weapons. The effectiveness of the C^3 system and the fighter's own sensors and weapons, as well as environmental conditions, affect the size of the area that can be defended practically by any one CAP.

> I was of the opinion that with the existing shortage of fighter aircraft only a central defense rather than an outer defense ring could promise any success. Squadrons and wings of fighter planes in the inner circle was my idea, rather than a few flights in the outer circle.
>
> Lt. General Adolph Galland, Luftwaffe

The practical range of a far CAP is also affected by the aircraft's useful time on station. As distance from base to CAP station increases, station time decreases because of fuel considerations. Airborne refueling capability can be critical to the ability to maintain a CAP at useful distances. Much valuable time is lost when the CAP must return to base for refueling. A refueling requirement also greatly increases the number of fighters necessary to maintain a constant defensive posture.

CAP requirements can be supplemented by the coordinated use of surface defenses. The necessity for near-CAP stations may be eliminated by installation of heavy surface-to-air defenses around the high-value targets. When they are available, surface defenses can also replace the CAP at likely ingress and egress points. Close coordination is essential between such surface defenses and the fighters, however. "Free-fire zones," in which anything that moves is fair game for surface-to-air weapons, are popular around the surface defenses. The fighters must know where these areas are and avoid them. Another possibility is the use of altitude blocks; in this system, the fighters are free to operate above a given level, and surface-to-air defenses are responsible for low-altitude coverage.

Another consideration for the CAP is altitude. This is usually chosen according to the expected altitude of the threat, but weapons and environmental conditions also play important roles. An altitude advantage over the enemy provides for the diving attack most useful with short-range weapons, while look-up is usually best for all-aspect AAMs and for target detection with most radars. Very low altitude penetrators are often best spotted visually at equally low levels, where they can be highlighted against the light background of the horizon. Fighter endurance performance, which can be critical to maintaining a continuous defensive presence, can also be a factor. In general, prop-driven aircraft achieve maximum endurance at low altitudes, while jets perform better at high levels. Communications and tracking may also be factors in the determination of the CAP's altitude. Controllers must maintain radar contact with the fighters if close control is to be provided, and very low altitudes for the CAP may hamper both controller tracking and communications ability.

The most important factor in selecting the CAP's altitude is usually the optimization of target detection, without which the other tasks of the CAP are meaningless. This objective is usually best achieved by optimizing C^3, onboard sensors, or visual factors, depending on the methods considered to be most effective in detecting the enemy under the prevailing conditions.

Once the CAP's position and altitude have been selected, there remains the question of patrol technique. It is usually necessary for the CAP to stay in a fairly small area and guard against intruders. The considerations involved here include endurance, optimization of sensor and visual coverage, and defense against attack by enemy fighter sweeps or fighter escort.

Conventional aircraft cannot remain motionless over one point, so they must constantly move around in some manner. Remaining in the same general area normally means turning regularly, which complicates employment of directional on-board sensor systems, as these should ideally be continuously pointed in the direction of the threat sector. Fighters with hover capability may be able to accomplish this, but the penalty is greatly reduced endurance. An orbit around the CAP station is the usual compromise. Two fighters on the opposite sides of a race-track-shaped pattern, oriented as shown in Figure 9-1, can provide almost continuous radar coverage of any threat axis. With greater numbers of fighters on a given CAP station, a Lufbery circle, with fighters spaced about equally around the circle, can provide good sensor coverage in any direction as well as visual defensive mutual support. A single fighter on a CAP station has a difficult problem with a directional sensor system. Usually the race-track pattern gives the best sensor coverage of the threat sector, but coverage in this pattern generally averages less than 50 percent of total station time. Coverage may be increased somewhat by flying more slowly on the outbound leg and faster on the inbound leg, but endurance will suffer with this technique. The lengths of the straight-line segments should be maximized and turning minimized in the pattern, as hard or frequent turns reduce endurance. Probably a better technique, when the enemy must be detected visually, is to fly a "figure-8" pattern oriented perpendicular to the threat axis. If all turns are made toward the threat, the defending fighter can stay in one area and never have its tail turned directly toward the enemy. This technique should provide the pilot with continuous visual coverage in the threat direction.

Patrol speed for fighters on CAP station is optimally near max-endurance speed for the given conditions of weight, configuration, etc. This guideline may have to be modified, however, if surprise enemy fighter attack is a probability. Higher airspeeds may be prudent, even with reduced endurance, for defensive maneuvering potential. It is also advisable under these conditions to vary the pattern regularly so that enemy fighter attacks are not aided by the predictability of the CAP.

There are seldom enough aircraft to maintain what the defense would consider an adequate number of CAPs. In order to stretch the available assets as far as possible, the number of fighters assigned to any CAP station is usually small. Two per station, however, should be considered minimal if enemy fighter resistance is expected. The numbers factor is one of the weak points in the CAP defense concept, as small isolated CAPs can easily be neutralized or destroyed by more powerful enemy fighter sweeps or fighter escort. Small CAPs are also usually inadequate to oppose strong massed attacks. Greater numbers are normally required to spread the

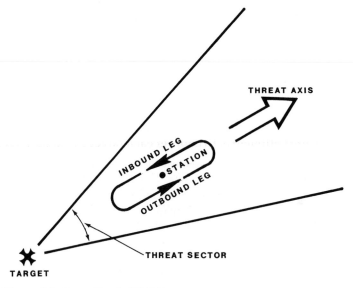

Figure 9-1. Race-Track CAP Pattern

bombers' defensive fire and to deal effectively with the often heavy force of escorting fighters. CAPs are better suited to defending against penetration raids, which are generally composed of small attacking elements that are not accompanied by fighters.

The C^3 network for a CAP defense system can be very complex. Its duties normally include long-range target detection, target identification assistance, assignment of individual CAPs to each raid, long-range intercept control, obtaining from higher authority the clearance to fire on a given target (if clearance is required), and keeping all participants apprised of the current overall defensive situation. When CAPs are committed to various targets, the C^3 system has the responsibility of shifting CAPs from one place to another, committing GAIs, etc., to maintain the integrity of the system and to ensure coverage of the most critical CAP stations. More mundane C^3 tasks include tracking fighter fuel states, allocating airborne tanker assets, and even assisting CAPs in maintaining their assigned stations. When stations are over open ocean or large expanses of trackless desert, etc., the fighters may not have the navigational capability to maintain the prescribed stations, as electronic aids to navigation may be beyond useful range, or they may be jammed, destroyed, or silenced to deny their use to the enemy. A self-contained, jam-resistant navigation capability for each fighter, such as that provided by inertial navigation systems (INS), is invaluable under these circumstances for reduction of C^3 workload. Datalink capability between fighters and controllers provides further workload reduction and increased resistance to enemy jamming. Multiple fighter radios can also aid in reducing frequency congestion.

The best control techniques vary greatly with the defensive situation, but quite often a combination of broadcast and close control provides good results. Broadcast control can be issued on a continuous basis to keep all CAPs updated on the big picture. This information aids the pilots in obtaining their own target contacts, maintaining their defensive posture, and planning for necessary gaps in coverage, such as for refueling. Controllers usually have a better picture of the overall defensive situation than do individual pilots; therefore, under ideal circumstances, pilots should not initiate their own intercepts on contacts which will cause them to leave their assigned station unguarded. When the defense coordinator decides to assign a CAP to a particular target, he should, when it is practical, pass the CAP to another controller and control frequency for close control. It is the coordinator's responsibility to allocate his defensive assets (i.e., CAP, GAI, SAMs, etc.) most efficiently to counter each target track. Individual initiative on the part of the pilots can make this task much more difficult or impossible. Pilots should, however, retain the authority to attack any hostile aircraft penetrating their assigned airspace and to report any sightings or contacts which are apparently unknown to the C^3 system, as determined from monitoring the broadcast-control transmissions.

Contingency plans are necessary for situations in which the C^3 network becomes saturated or communications are jammed. Quite often under jamming conditions the defending pilots can communicate with nearby CAPs, but not with central control. Under these conditions the pilots may have to coordinate among themselves or even operate independently. To be successful under such conditions, the pilots must be prebriefed and have intimate understanding of the rules of engagement, return-to-base procedures, and the total defensive structure and philosophy.

> One of the most important requirements for an active air defense is air intelligence.
>
> Lt. General Adolph Galland, Luftwaffe

The C^3 network is a critical, and often the weakest, link in air defense. As such, its problems are under constant intense study by all major air powers. Some of the more recent advances are effective airborne C^3 platforms and the integration of satellites into the system as communications relay and sensor platforms. C^3 aircraft and AIC have the advantages of flexibility, extended radar horizons, and longer line-of-sight communications capability. They can be deployed quickly to remote battle sites, and they usually can operate well outside the actual combat arena, making them less susceptible to attack.

In general, the CAP concept of air defense is complex and inefficient, and quite often it is ineffective. In some cases, however, there is no viable alternative, and CAPs can be very effective under the right conditions. These conditions are a reasonably sized defended area for the number and capabilities of the fighters available, a limited threat sector, and small penetration raids without fighter escort. CAPs may be required when raids must be countered at long distances from the operating bases of defending fighters or when warning of an attack is insufficient to allow for GAI defense.

Ground-Alert Interceptors

Under other conditions the GAI usually provides much more efficient and flexible air defense. When interceptors can be based close to the high-value targets, they are capable of countering attacks from any direction with equal ease. More fighters can be kept armed, fueled, and ready for action on the ground. Communications and control are much more reliable, and the formation of large fighter forces to oppose massed attacks is more practical. The fighters required to perform the GAI mission can be less sophisticated. Whereas the ideal fighter for the CAP needs long range and endurance; sophisticated sensor, communications, and navigation equipment; and air-refueling capability, the GAIs can be simple, small, and cheap, further increasing the numbers of aircraft likely to be available and serviceable. High speed and climb rate (to oppose high-altitude attacks) are important attributes for GAI fighters.

> You never make a big truck and tomorrow make it a race car. And you never can make a big bomber and the next day a . . . fighter. The physical law means that you need another airplane. . . . You should do one job and should do this job good.
>
> Colonel Erich "Bubi" Hartmann, GAF

The GAI concept is not without its limitations, however. The defense must be assured of its ability to detect incoming raids at sufficient range to allow for launch, formation, intercept, and attack by GAIs on favorable terms. If defending fighters are caught on the ground, surprise attacks can be disastrous, not only for the high-value targets, but for the fighters themselves, which qualify as valuable targets in their own right. The fighter bases must also be located very near the defended targets to be effective in countering attacks from any direction. This basing requirement can greatly degrade the flexibility of the GAI system. A further limitation is the speed at which GAI can be launched. The number of available runways and their vulnerability to battle damage can limit the capacity of the system. A system of many dispersed bases, located throughout the defended area, is ideal for this concept.

Again, close control from GCI or AIC is advantageous for the employment of GAI; but once the system becomes saturated, effective close control of multiple intercepts becomes impossible, and broadcast control can be an effective alternative.

Attack Considerations

The primary mission of either CAP or GAI is protection of the target. Although destruction of incoming enemy bombers is ideal, this is certainly not the only way to accomplish the goal. Merely threatening a bomber or bomber formation is often sufficient to cause it to jettison ordnance off-target in order to increase maneuverability and speed for defensive purposes. Once a bomber has been forced to drop its weapons off-target, the fighters have achieved a "mission kill." Even forcing the pilot of a penetrating aircraft into an extended defensive maneuver is often sufficient to foul up his timing over the target, resulting in an aborted mission (mission kill) or increased vulnerability in the target area. Unfortunately, if the bomber pilot escapes, he can return again the next day, smarter, when the defending pilots may not be so lucky. It may take much less time to achieve a mission kill than an aircraft kill, however, allowing the fighter to intercept more bombers on a given raid. This tradeoff should be considered.

> What does not destroy me makes me stronger.
>
> Prussian Military Axiom

An attack on an individual bomber or on small formations of unescorted low-level penetrators is much like any of the other attacks already described, with a few exceptions. Low-altitude flying and navigation take a good deal of concentration on the part of the bomber pilot, leaving little time for effective defensive lookout. In addition, most low-level penetrators are small fighter-bombers without rear-hemisphere defensive ordnance, and they are designed with limited field of view in the rear quarter. Surprise attacks from the rear quarter can, therefore, be very effective, time and weapons capabilities permitting. Once he has sighted a target visually, the fighter pilot should consider turning off any radar transmitters to avoid being detected by the enemy's RWR equipment while he conducts the actual attack. If they are required for attack, these transmitters possibly can be turned back on just prior to weapons firing. The advantages and limitations of various weapons in the low-altitude environment were discussed in previous chapters.

> We carried out many trials to try to find the answer to the fast, low-level intruder, but there is no adequate defense.
>
> Air Vice-Marshal J. E. "Johnnie" Johnson, RAF

A fighter pilot attacking a low-level penetrator from the rear hemisphere should be especially cautious of a particularly nasty countertactic. Bomber pilots, when they are threatened from the rear, will often drop a retarded bomb that is intended to explode right in the face of the pursuing fighter. A retarded bomb is fitted with a high-drag device that slows its forward speed after release, allowing the bomber to gain safe separation before weapon impact. A pursuing aircraft, however, may well be caught in the weapon's fragmentation pattern. At the first hint of something falling off a bomber ahead, the attacker should break as hard as possible left or right to avoid the frag pattern. A quick pull-up may also work, but it usually provides less separation than a hard turn and makes rejoining the chase more difficult.

> If at all possible the enemy fighters should be avoided completely and strict attention given to attacking the enemy bombers. With a high-speed airplane of the P-38 type this is entirely possible. . . . If the attack is delivered swiftly and the breakaway completed the enemy fighters can be avoided easily. The initial attack should be designed to break up the bomber formation. If this plan is successful the squadron can then break down to flights and proceed to pick off stray bombers. If the formation is not broken the squadron attack should be delivered a second time.[1]
>
> Captain Thomas J. "Tommy" Lynch, USAAF
> 20 Victories, WW-II

Low-level penetrators are usually not escorted closely by defending fighters, since their presence is more likely to give away the position of the penetrator. Massed attacks, however, are a different matter, and fighter escort is a probability. One of the first considerations when attacking massed bombers, therefore, is how to deal with the escort. If the escort is poorly positioned and can be avoided, it is generally best to do so and make hit-and-run attacks on the bombers, then separate before the escort can react. Otherwise the escort usually must be neutralized if the fighters are to stand much chance of inflicting serious losses on the bombers without incurring heavy attrition themselves.

> The first and most important requisite for the destruction of the bombers was the achievement of air superiority against the American escort fighters.
>
> Lt. General Adolph Galland, Luftwaffe

One of the most effective means of neutralizing the fighter escort is to devote some defending fighters to the task of attacking and engaging the escort. When forced to defend themselves, the escorts quickly become separated from their strike group. Fighters are typically much more short-legged than bombers, and they often must carry external fuel "drop-tanks" to provide the necessary escort range. Because of this the escort should be attacked just as early in the mission as possible. If the escort is forced to jettison its partially used drop-tanks and use extra fuel (such as by lighting afterburners) to defend against an early attack, its bombers may be required to abort their mission or to complete much of it unescorted and vulnerable to attack by other defenders. Even a feint attack or a "gun and run" by a very few fighters may effectively "strip the escort" from the strike package.

> To fight the bombers before the escort fighters would mean in the long run to take the second step before the first. But if instead of fighters, the bombers got the priority in combat, then the peripheral defense . . . was absolutely wrong. The continuous demand to attack the bombers as soon as possible could only be successfully fulfilled if the attacks were made in groups. This meant that each of our fighter groups . . . would attack a greatly superior enemy force. In an action like this the results were naturally small, our own losses on the other hand considerable. Instead of attacking the bombers when they were as far as possible out of range of their fighter escort, our fighters had to attack the enemy just when he was strongest.[2]

If the defense is unable to strip the escort at long range, some of the fighters of the main assault force should be assigned to engage and occupy the escort while the remaining interceptors concentrate on the bombers. When different types of fighters are involved, the best dogfighters are generally assigned to the escort while the less maneuverable, but, hopefully, heavier-armed, aircraft attack the bombers. When practical, the number of interceptors assigned to engage the escort should be roughly equivalent to the number of fighters in the escort, and the remaining interceptors will tackle the bombers.

> In air fights it is absolutely essential to fly in such a way that your adversary cannot shoot at you, if you can manage it.
> Captain Oswald Boelcke, German Air Service

Attacking heavy bombers can be a tricky proposition, as they are often well protected by defensive armament, particularly in the rear hemisphere, and usually are well equipped with electronic- and infrared-countermeasures gear. In a heavy ECM/IRCM environment, guns and unguided rockets are often the most effective weapons, but since these have fairly short ranges, the direction of approach to a heavy bomber must be carefully calculated to minimize exposure to defensive fire. Saddling-up at close range on a bomber with rear-firing weapons, particularly in a large enemy formation, is a very unhealthy approach. Bombers are almost always less well defended in some directions than in others, and these weak points should be found and exploited. Often head-on or forward-quarter passes through an enemy formation, using gun or rocket snapshots, prove to be the best tactics. In general, just as with most other military strategies, the approach is to concentrate the greatest offensive firepower against the enemy's most weakly defended point. Few bombers can match a fighter's forward-firing weapons from all directions.

> If you see enemy aircraft, it is not necessary for you to go straight to them and attack. Wait and look and use your reason. See what kind of formation and tactics they are using. See if there is a straggler or an uncertain pilot among

the enemy. Such a pilot will always stand out. Shoot *him* down. It is more important to send one down in flames—so that all the enemy pilots can see the loss and experience its psychological effect—than to wade into a twenty-minute dogfight in which nothing happens.

Colonel Erich "Bubi" Hartmann, GAF

Generally speaking, a massed attack should be met as far from the target as possible. Long-range CAPs are often in position for first intercept, but unfortunately its strength is seldom sufficient for a CAP to have great success in destroying large numbers of enemy aircraft or in breaking up a large massed attack, particularly if fighter escort is present. A long-range CAP, therefore, might best be used in an attempt to strip the formation of its escort.

There are several advantages of early interception of massed attacks. Obviously, the longer the fighters can maintain contact, the more damage can be done to the attackers. Quite often determined attacks will result in damaged bombers and stragglers which provide easy pickings later in the battle. Early attacks may also slow the progress of a massed attack, allowing more defending fighters to make an intercept. In many cases fighter-bombers planning low-level penetration attacks will proceed in massed formation, possibly with fighter escort, to some point short of the target, and then split up for individual penetrations by different routes. These raids are usually more vulnerable to serious damage if they are intercepted before the break-up point.

> The demand of the hour was quantity against quantity. The massing of our fighters was impossible at the periphery and could only be done in the center.
>
> Lt. General Adolph Galland, Luftwaffe

Regardless of its advantages, however, early interception of a massed attack is not always possible; attack may have to be delayed to provide for greater numbers in the attacking force. Multiple small, uncoordinated attacks are more easily defended against by the bombers and fighter escorts than are larger, more concentrated assaults. Depending on the number of escorts, distance remaining to the target, and the likelihood of reinforcements, the first interceptors to arrive on scene might best "shadow" the formation from a good attack position and call for help. Once the fighter force is as large as it is likely to get, or is considered strong enough to take on the escorts on roughly equal terms, the attack can begin.

> The ballistic rocket struck the death knell of the fighter-interceptor.
>
> Air Vice-Marshal J. E. "Johnnie" Johnson, RAF

Integrated Air Defense

A fact that brings the air defense picture into perspective is that, in nearly all conflicts since and including World War I, more aircraft have been lost as a result of surface-to-air defenses than have been victims of fighter action. This is primarily because of the sheer volume of AAA, SAMs, etc., and the great number of firing opportunities encountered. Surface defenses alone, however, have rarely been sufficient to prevent destruction or heavy damage to high-value targets. Only determined fighter defenses have proven consistently capable of inflicting enough casualties on any single raid to turn back the attack or to prevent repeated assaults. Surface defenses are, however, an important component of any IADS. High-value targets particularly should be heavily fortified by surface weapons for terminal defense. Accurate air-to-ground ordnance delivery requires extreme concentration on the part of the bomber crew, even with the aid of the most sophisticated weapons systems. In addition, most air-to-ground deliveries require the bomber to fly a fairly predictable flight path for at least a few seconds prior to weapons release. This predictability and crew preoccupation make the bomber most vulnerable during the weapons-delivery phase of its attack. Simply causing the bomber pilot to break concentration or to maneuver to avoid ground fire may contribute to the defense by reducing the pilot's weapons accuracy.

As mentioned previously, when surface defenses and fighters are integrated into the IADS, there should be a free-fire zone established for surface-to-air weapons which should be known and avoided by the defending fighters. When adequate surface defenses are not available for a high-value target, a CAP orbiting overhead or near the point might substitute for terminal defense. The fighters in this CAP can be very unsophisticated, since their station-keeping is usually visual and they are not required to intercept targets at long range. Their pilots can simply monitor broadcast control and wait for the enemy to come to them. Great speed is not required for this mission, but exceptional maneuverability and having all-aspect weapons that are effective at low altitude are great aids (assuming low-altitude penetrators) in providing quick shot opportunities on short-range contacts. Good endurance and airborne refueling capability are also important attributes for such aircraft.

Offensive fighter sweeps against enemy airfields and rendezvous areas can be extremely effective defensive tactics. The timing of these sweeps is critical if the enemy is to be caught when he is most vulnerable. One ploy which has been used very successfully is following the bombers back to their base and striking during their landing approaches.

Strike Escort

> The fighter, even when tackling a purely defensive task, must never lose the initiative to his opponent.
>
> Lt. General Adolph Galland, Luftwaffe

Escort has historically been one of the most difficult and most frustrating missions assigned to fighters. The escort is often cast in a defensive role, which tends to place it at a disadvantage with respect to enemy fighters. Once a strike has been discovered and intercepted by defending fighters, they enjoy the offensive advantage of the aircraft. History has shown that it is effectively impossible to seal completely the airspace around a strike group, and casualties can be expected when the strike group is opposed by determined fighter attack. It has also been shown, however, that fighter escort holds the greatest hope for limiting losses to acceptable levels during massed attacks in the face of such opposition. Of course "acceptable" losses are zero for fighter crews charged with the protection of strike aircraft, and the unrealistic nature of this goal adds to the frustration of the mission.

> Bomber air power cannot develop where enemy fighters have an air supe-riority.
>
> Air Vice-Marshal Raymond Collishaw, RAF
> 62 Victories, WW-I and Bolshevik Revolution

One bright spot in this picture is that the days of massed-formation attacks appear to be numbered. Many factors have contributed to this trend, including the reduced size of bomber fleets (making any losses more significant), the advent of more lethal surface-to-air weapons (especially SAMs), increased bomber speed, and greatly increased lethality of air-to-ground ordnance (requiring fewer bombers to destroy a given target). These trends have led to a preference for low-level penetration raids, for which close fighter escort may be more a liability (because of greater detection probability) than an asset.

> A fighter can only carry out this purely defensive task by taking the initiative in the offensive. He must never wait until he is attacked because he then loses the chance of acting. The fighter must seek battle in the air, must find his opponent, attack him, and shoot him down.
>
> Lt. General Adolph Galland, Luftwaffe

The fighter sweep provides probably the most effective means of participation for fighter aircraft in a penetration attack. A sweep before the strike, closely timed with the penetration attacks, can be conducted to hinder or prevent launch and formation of GAIs. Sweeps can also assist by engaging and occupying CAP fighters (particularly those near the target area) to prevent them from harassing the bombers during the actual attack or along the bombers' ingress and egress routes. Much of the success of such fighter sweeps depends heavily on the relative capabilities of friendly and enemy C^3 networks in the battle arena. Often the defenders have an advantage here which can be exploited to avoid contact with the sweeps and allow concentration on the bomber aircraft.

Sometimes, however, even penetration strikes proceed as massed formations until they approach the target area. This fact, and the possible necessity of protecting other types of aircraft, such as transports, in a hostile environment, require that the principles of escort be understood.

Fighter escort is essentially point defense of a moving target, so many of the principles already discussed are applicable with certain modifications. Since air strikes are presumably conducted over hostile territory at some distance from friendly airfields, the GAI concept is generally not applicable. An analogous concept, that of the "parasite fighter," has been the subject of some experimentation since World War I. This idea involved carrying a small fighter aboard a large bomber; the fighter could be released for defense if the bomber came under air attack, and then it could be recovered aboard the bomber again after the fight. Probably because of the payload penalties and operational complexities, however, this concept has never been put into practice.

The use of independent fighter sweeps for defensive purposes has already been considered; this discussion focuses on other fighter-escort concepts. In general, there are four types of escorts which have evolved and been proven useful for the strike-escort mission. Here they are called reception escort, remote escort, detached escort, and close escort. The reception escort has the task of meeting the strike force as it returns from the target and guarding its retreat from pursuing enemy fighters. The remote escort may take the form of a fighter sweep ahead of, or along the flanks of, the strike group, proceeding along with the main body, but generally not within visual range. Remote escorts may also be stationed over a fixed geographical point along a line between the strike group and enemy airfields, or between the intended target and enemy bases, in the more conventional CAP role. The detached escort is positioned closer to the main body, normally within visual range. Its duty is to intercept and engage hostile fighters at the most likely points of attack. The close escort, as the name implies, is tied closely to the strike force for terminal defense, analogous to the overhead CAP in point defense. Any or all these concepts of escort, as well as independent fighter sweeps, may be employed, depending on the available assets and the expected opposition.

Reception Escort

The reception escort is intended to provide defensive reinforcements at a time when they are likely to be needed badly. Heavy opposition tends to deplete and scatter escorting fighters, reducing their effectiveness. The main body is also likely to be more spread out because of damaged aircraft and stragglers, making it more difficult to defend. In addition, many of the original escorts may be low on fuel or ammo, or they may be damaged themselves, resulting in reduced effectiveness. A reception escort can also furnish protection for penetration bombers on their withdrawal, often by conducting a sweep of the egress corridors. Even though the strike mission is essentially complete at this point, the enemy may still achieve his objective if he can inflict severe enough casualties during this vulnerable period to prevent further strikes. The reception escort provides a fresh defense, added protection for damaged and straggling aircraft, and discouragement for enemy intruders that may be shadowing the returning strike force. This mission is often assigned to GAIs that have been retained during the strike as part of the home-field defenses. The range and sophistication of these aircraft can be considerably inferior to those of the primary escort fighters.

> We introduced "Fighter reception": fighter squadrons or wings were sometimes sent right up to the English coast to meet the often broken-up and battered formations on their return journey, to protect them from pursuing enemy fighters.
>
> Lt. General Adolph Galland, Luftwaffe

Remote Escort

The remote escort quite often begins as a fighter sweep that is timed to proceed some distance in advance of the main body. Its route of flight generally follows that of the strike group, but it may be diverted at some point for a diversionary attack on another target. (This type of feint attack was discussed in some detail earlier in this chapter in conjunction with fighter-sweep tactics.) The usual mission of the remote escort is to clear the intended strike route of enemy fighters, generally all the way to the target. This escort is usually positioned directly ahead of or on the forward quarters of the main body, and it is intended to surprise hostile interceptors in transit to, or forming up for, an attack on the strike group. Because their intention is to surprise, these escorts often ingress at low altitude to avoid detection by enemy radar, but their altitude should be consistent with the expected threat. If it is assigned the duty of engaging enemy air defense in the target area, the remote escort should plan to reach the target near enough to the intended strike time so that combat endurance will allow it to remain engaged until the strike is complete and the bombers have withdrawn.

Another likely mission of the remote escort is to establish a CAP to block the probable intercept route of enemy fighters launching from hostile airfields. Often the remote escort will proceed along the intended strike route for some time as a sweep, then depart from the primary ingress route to set up a blocking position. This break-away is often a good opportunity to make a feint attack on the enemy airfield to confuse the defense network.

> We fighter pilots certainly preferred the "free chase during the approach and over the target area." This in fact gives the greatest relief and the best protection for the bomber force, although not perhaps a direct sense of security.
>
> Lt. General Adolph Galland, Luftwaffe

Detached Escort

Next in the defensive screen come the detached escorts, which are positioned strategically around the main body to engage enemy interceptors early in their approach for attack. The optimum positions for detached escorts are dependent on the capabilities of both friendly and hostile weapons and on the nature of the anticipated attacks. Ideally a detached escort is located where it can detect and engage any hostile fighter before it can fire at the aircraft of the strike force. Considerations include the enemy's probable intercept geometry and maximum effective firing range, and escort maneuverability, reaction time, and weapons limitations.

Figure 9-2, which depicts a strike-force formation with various friendly and enemy weapons envelopes superimposed, illustrates how some of these factors interrelate. The figure also shows likely enemy attack geometry and representative detached-escort positions to counter these attacks. To oppose a forward-quarter (FQ) missile attack, escorts are stationed on the left and right forward quarters of the strike force, far enough ahead of the bombers so that hostile interceptors can be engaged by the escorts' FQ weapons before the enemy reaches firing range against the bombers. The forward escorts' lateral separation on the strike force also allows maneuvering room to engage interceptors making head-on or FQ attacks with short-range weapons. For this purpose lateral separation between the two forward escorts should be on the order of two to four fighter turn radii, but this distance may need to be modified for visibility considerations. They should be positioned ahead of the lead bomber at least as far as the enemy's short-range weapons-firing distance. This distance may have to be increased to provide coverage of threat FQ long-range missiles, as shown. Obviously the strike force will be extremely vulnerable to FQ missile attack if the escort is not similarly equipped. Denying such a threat would probably be the responsibility of remote escorts. Altitude for the forward escort is typically close to that of the strike force, maybe a little higher to give quicker response to short-range gun or rocket attacks, or possibly a little lower to provide look-up for better radar detection and FQ weapons guidance.

> A compromise between [free chase and close escort] was the "extended protection," in which fighters still flew in visible contact with the bomber force but were allowed to attack any enemy fighter which drew near to the main force.
>
> Lt. General Adolph Galland, Luftwaffe

Similarly, rear escorts are positioned behind the strike force to guard against RQ attacks. These elements are generally stationed near the enemy's maximum RQ weapons range relative to the trailing bombers of the strike force. When each side is equipped with similar weapons, this should allow detection and engagement of RQ attacks before they can

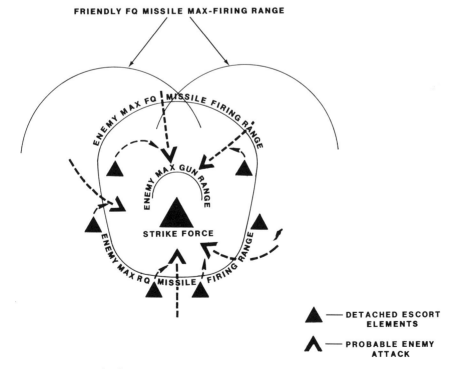

Figure 9-2. Detached-Escort Positioning

become major threats to the strike group. If this maximum weapons range is considerable, however, or if the enemy's weapons have greater range than those of the escort, rear protection may require additional rear-escort elements positioned closer to the strike force. Otherwise the enemy may be able to slip in from the side of the strike group for a close-range attack while remaining out of the rear escort's effective firing range. Whenever it is engaging hostile fighters, the rear escort especially must be certain that a guided weapon is not locked onto a friendly aircraft.

Lateral separation for the rear escorts can generally be somewhat less than that for the forward elements, since the rear escort is not likely to be required to turn more than about 90° to engage a threat to the strike group. Separation of one to two fighter turn radii should be adequate between the rear elements. Rear-element altitude is typically somewhat higher than that of the strike group to provide greater potential energy for quick reaction. Since this scenario assumes fighter opposition, and the trailing aircraft in any formation are most vulnerable to attack, additional trailing elements are often added to the escort for rear-hemisphere protection of the fighters themselves. Such additional elements, sometimes called "rear guard" or "top cover," generally trail the rear element depicted in Figure 9-2 at a comfortable visual range and stepped-up higher. If more rear-guard elements are available they may be added in trail of the last, each stacked higher or lower than the preceding element, ad infinitum. The rear guard can also act as a reserve, moving up to fill holes in the defense created by escort engagement of hostile attacks.

The other escort elements depicted in Figure 9-2 are the flankers to either side of the strike group. These are essentially gap-fillers between the forward- and rear-escort elements, and their mission is to guard against attacks that attempt to split the defenses. Depending on the size of the overall formation and the weapons involved, several flanking elements could be required, or none at all. These elements are sometimes stepped-up considerably higher than the strike group and moved in laterally to guard against near-vertical diving attacks from above.

Whenever the assets are available, each of the detached-escort elements described should be composed of at least two fighters for mutual protection. The detached escort serves as the first line of defense against a fighter attack, and it is most likely to be engaged by the enemy. The speed of the escorting fighters is also important, both for offensive and defensive maneuvering potential. Since the speed of a strike group, particularly when it is heavily loaded inbound to a target, can be considerably slower than the escorts' desired maneuvering speed, weaving is often employed. The escort fighters can weave back and forth to retard their forward progress while they maintain a high airspeed. Care should be taken that the weaving does not degrade visual lookout within an element or take the element far out of position.

Discipline is a key factor in success of the detached escort. Unlike a fighter sweep or a remote escort, the detached escort is tied to the strike group and must avoid engagement with any enemy fighters that are not directly threatening the strike force. The enemy can be expected to use decoys and feint attacks to draw off the escort fighters. Hostile fighters that appear to be approaching an attack position should be offensively engaged by the detached escort. Whenever an attack turns away from the strike group, however, pursuing escorts should immediately return to their assigned positions.

> In escorting bombers it is a good idea to range out on the sides, front and rear and hit enemy fighters before they can get to the bomber formation, but do not run off on a wild-goose chase and leave the bombers unprotected.
>
> Major George Preddy, Jr., USAAF

Close Escort

Close escort doctrine stations fighters over, under, around, and among the aircraft of the strike group itself. In a guns-only environment the close escort and the detached escort may be one and the same because of the short weapons ranges involved. Otherwise, the purposes of the close escort are analogous to those of the overhead CAP in point defense; that is, to provide a response to attacks from any direction, and to harass an enemy in the final stages of his attack. Heavily armed bombers may assume this task themselves.

The detached escort normally serves as a tripwire for this system, detecting incoming raids and calling them out for the close escort. The nearest fighters in close escort then leave the strike group to assist the detached escort with an "inside-out" attack on the enemy aircraft. Exceptional maneuverability and all-aspect weapons (which may include guns and unguided rockets) are valuable attributes for the close escort mission. Great speed and sophistication are not requirements, since all attacks are visual, with the enemy coming to the close escort. The close escort doctrine is usually not very effective unless it is combined with a detached escort for advance warning of incoming raids. Without such warning the attackers are often into the strike group before they can be detected and engaged.

> For each [bomber] group we provided one squadron of P-38s for close and one squadron for top cover. The other two P-38 squadrons made a fighter sweep three to five minutes ahead of the bombers. . . . We were generally able to contact the major concentration of [Japanese] fighters and keep them too busy to make anything like a coordinated attack on the bombers.
>
> Colonel Charles W. King, USAF

Integrated Fighter Escort

A hypothetical strike-escort mission may clarify how all the various tactics outlined in this section can play together. Figure 9-3 sets the stage for the mission. The strike group intends to follow the indicated ingress and egress routes for a feint attack on the northeastern enemy airfield, turn left just short of this airfield to attack the real target, then head directly for home. To add credibility to the ruse, an independent fighter sweep is sent by an entirely different route to harass the northeastern enemy airfield, a tactic that might be expected as part of a prestrike softening-up process.

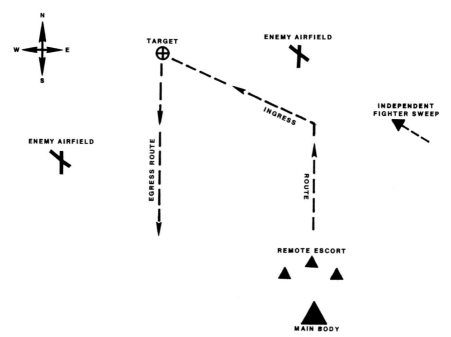

Figure 9-3. Fighter-Escort Mission

This sweep is designed to draw enemy GAIs into battle, causing an expenditure of defensive assets. The hope is that, by the time the real strike force passes through the area, most of the hostile fighters from this airfield will be engaged, destroyed, or out of fuel.

Meanwhile the main body, consisting of the strike force itself, the detached escort and the close escort, proceeds along the ingress route. Preceding this force by a few minutes is the remote escort, composed of three elements, whose task is to clear the route of enemy interceptors or CAPs which may be lying in wait.

In Figure 9-4 the strike force has made the turn toward the intended target and is passing the embattled northeastern airfield. The elements of the remote escort have split and are proceeding on different missions. The center element continues straight for the target area to engage any hostile fighters which might be in that vicinity, or (heaven forbid) to suppress surface defenses. The left and right elements of the remote escort head for CAP stations assigned to block possible interference from either of the two enemy airfields.

Figure 9-5 shows the target under attack by the strike force and the two blocking CAPs in position. Once the strike force arrives on target the remote escort already there is relieved by the detached and close escorts and is free to resume a sweep to clear the egress route. The independent fighter sweep assigned to the northeastern airfield has already reached its disengagement fuel state and is also heading for home. Meanwhile, a reception escort is inbound for a sweep of the enemy's southwestern airfield.

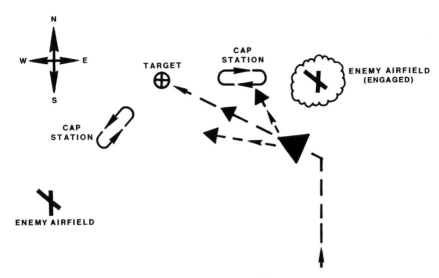

Figure 9-4. Fighter-Escort Mission (Continued)

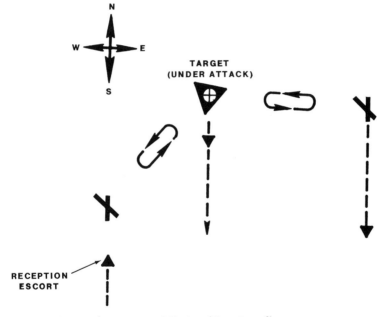

Figure 9-5. Fighter-Escort Mission (Continued)

Finally, Figure 9-6 depicts the strike force, having completed its attack, exiting the area accompanied by its close and detached escorts. The remote escorts, meanwhile, have terminated their stationary CAPs and are also leaving the area. Their exit times have been specified relative to the time of target attack so that they provide something of a moving screen for the strike force, shielding the main body from the hostile airfields. Since the remote escort probably does not have visual contact with the main body

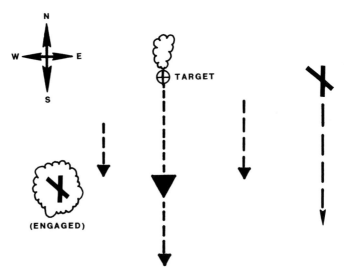

Figure 9-6. Fighter-Escort Mission (Conclusion)

through most of the mission, strict adherence to strike timing is critical for maximum effectiveness. The reception escort has also timed its sweep of the southwestern airfield to coincide with the approach of the retreating bomber formation. After passage of the main body, the reception escort retires along the general exit route of the bombers.

> At the start the American escort also made tactical mistakes. Instead of operating offensively against our fighter units, they limited themselves to a close direct escort. They tried to repulse our attacks in the close vicinity of the bombers. In doing this they went through the same negative experiences as we had done over England and Malta: the fighter pilot who is not at all times and at any place offensive loses the initiative of action. The American fighters learned and readjusted themselves. After January, 1944, they went over to aggressive free-for-all fights in the approach sector.[3]

This example demonstrates, without even getting into the fine points about how each element would carry out its mission in the face of opposition, that strike-escort planning and coordination can be a very complex affair. It should also be apparent that a large number of escort assets might be required for such a mission. If adequate assets are not available (and they seldom are), some priorities must be assigned. Normally the most effective element in defense of the strike group is the remote escort, closely followed by independent (but coordinated) fighter sweeps. Some fighters should usually be assigned to these missions before consideration is given to other escort concepts. Detached escorts have proven to be next in effectiveness. If additional aircraft are available, they can be assigned as close escort or reception escort according to the anticipated requirements and effectiveness of these tactics. Although the overall role of the fighter escort is defensive, greater effectiveness can be achieved by maintaining an offensive attitude through aggressive employment of fighter sweeps and remote escorts. Detached escorts should also seek to be offensive through early detection and engagement of enemy fighters, but their aggression must be tempered by considerable discipline if escort integrity is to be maintained.

Notes

1. Martin Caidin, *Fork-Tailed Devil: The P-38*, p. 282.
2. Adolph Galland, *The First and the Last*, p. 198.
3. Ibid., p. 201.

10

Tactical Intercepts

Confront the enemy with the tip of your sword against his face.

Miyamoto Musashi

Since the introduction of radar to the air combat scenario in World War II, its advantages have been widely recognized and accepted. These advantages include long-range warning of the approach of hostile aircraft, improved efficiency in the interception of these aircraft, and the ability to provide friendly fighters with an initial advantage over the enemy. At night or in poor visibility, radar may provide the only practical means of employing fighter aircraft; but even in good visibility and in the daytime, radar's advantages can be critical to the success of any fighter mission. One prominent example is the use of radar by the British in the Battle of Britain. Early warning of German attacks allowed the British to use the more efficient GAI defense concept to make the most effective use of limited fighter resources, to intercept incoming raids at the greatest distance from their target, to avoid German fighter sweeps, and, usually, to gain first sight of the enemy.

The operational theory of radar and some of the techniques and limitations involved in the employment of radar were covered in detail in the first chapter of this book. Radars can be classified by their use for early warning, acquisition, or guidance. Early-warning radars are generally low-frequency, long-wavelength sets requiring large antennas. Their size usually precludes their installation in fighters, so they are primarily used for GCI/AIC control. They are characterized by relatively long range and poor resolution. A single-aircraft target on an early-warning radar may be displayed on the controller's scope as a "blip" of light representing several miles in width, and many closely spaced aircraft may appear as a single target. Control by use of such equipment is limited to bringing the fighters close enough to the target for them to take over, either with their own higher-resolution equipment or visually.

Fighter radars are generally of the acquisition type, which have higher frequency, smaller antennas, shorter range, and better resolution. They often have the capability to "track" a target in order to gain more detailed information on its relative position, speed, altitude, etc. Often such radars are also capable of guiding air-to-air weapons to the target; that is, they may also serve as guidance radars. Advances in radar and microprocessors make it feasible now even to identify a target directly through its radar signature. The return from so-called "millimeter-wave" radars, rather than displaying only a target blip, may actually depict a recognizable target shape. This capability is not generally available to current fighters, however, so other means of identification are employed. Visual identification is most common, but there are also several electronic identification systems. Each system has its limitations: VIDs are dependent on visibility and have relatively short ranges, while EIDs are sometimes unreliable and are subject to deception and jamming.

This chapter is designed to provide insight into some of the considerations involved with tactical radar intercepts by describing a few of the most common intercept tactics. The scope of this discussion is generally limited to daylight visual conditions. All possible intercept tactics obviously cannot be included here, but an attempt has been made to present a representative sample that can furnish options to cover most tactical situations.

> No one can tell another what to do in a future air-to-air fight. . . . In this game, there is a great demand for the individual who can "play by ear."
> Major Frederick C. "Boots" Blesse, USAF

Intercept Terminology

Before proceeding with the discussion of specific intercept tactics, it is necessary to define some terminology. Figure 10-1, which shows a target and an interceptor on convergent courses, illustrates some frequently used terms. The solid line between the two aircraft represents the radar line of sight (LOS). The angle between the LOS and the target's course is known as the target-aspect angle (TAA), target aspect, or simply "aspect." This aspect may be computed automatically by a sophisticated tracking radar, or it may be calculated mentally by the interceptor pilot based on target bearing (the orientation of the LOS with respect to magnetic north) and GCI's estimate of the target's magnetic heading. Lateral separation is the perpendicular distance from the interceptor to the bogey's flight path. This quantity is usually estimated by the pilot and is a function of target range and aspect. Lateral separation is important if the interceptor plans to make a "conversion turn" to the target's rear hemisphere, since allowance must be made for the interceptor's turn radius. The amount of lateral separation, or "displacement," required is a function of the interceptor's intended turn radius and the amount of turn necessary to complete the intercept. This conversion turn is often described by the number of degrees the interceptor must turn to parallel the target's course and is called "degrees to go" (DTG). DTG is determined by calculating the difference between interceptor heading and the estimated bogey heading.

At given target and interceptor speeds, the interceptor can use heading changes to control displacement. Assume that if both aircraft continue on their present courses in this example they will eventually collide. In that

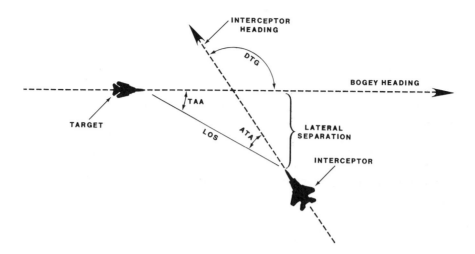

Figure 10-1. Intercept Terminology

case the interceptor is said to be on "collision heading." The angle between the interceptor's nose (heading) and the target LOS is known as the antenna-train angle (ATA), the target relative bearing, or the lead angle (lag angle if the interceptor is pointed behind the target). When the interceptor is on collision heading, the lead angle and target bearing remain constant and target range decreases. This constant target bearing is called "collision bearing," and the lead angle (or ATA) approximates target aspect when fighter and interceptor are roughly co-speed. As long as the interceptor maintains collision heading, target bearing, ATA, and target aspect will remain constant. If the interceptor turns a few degrees to the right in this case, and then flies straight, ATA will continue to increase and target aspect will decrease until the interceptor crosses in front of the target. Conversely, if the interceptor turns a few degrees to the left of collision heading (toward the target), and then flies straight, the target will appear to continue to "drift" toward the interceptor's nose (lead angle will decrease) until the target crosses in front of the interceptor. All the while target aspect will be increasing. A radical left turn by the interceptor placing it on a reciprocal course to that of the target, parallel to the target's course, maintains constant lateral separation, while both ATA and target aspect increase.

Forward Quarter

Description

As the name implies, the forward-quarter (FQ) intercept is one in which the interceptor approaches from the target's forward quarter. A special case of the FQ intercept is the head-on approach, where the interceptor reduces displacement to zero and the two aircraft converge "beak-to-beak." Figure 10-2 illustrates the more general case.

The goal of the FQ intercept is to approach the target from a specified angle off its nose (TAA) in the target's forward quarter. At time "1" in this example the interceptor makes radar contact (or receives a GCI call) which indicates a target slightly right of the nose at fairly long range. An estimate of the target's heading reveals that the two aircraft are on roughly reciprocal courses, and that the interceptor is displaced slightly right of the target's nose (right aspect). The interceptor pilot in this case would like to increase this aspect at intercept, so he turns left, taking a small cut away from the target's flight path. The pilot could have turned right instead, eventually crossing the target's nose and gaining aspect on the other side of the bogey's flight path, but since there was initially some right aspect it was faster to increase aspect in that direction.

Once on the new heading, the pilot of the interceptor monitors the decreasing range and the target's magnetic bearing as it continues to drift to the right. Target aspect is constantly computed to ensure that it is indeed increasing. When target aspect reaches the desired value, another interceptor course change will be required to stop and maintain this aspect. This is accomplished at time "2" by making a turn to collision heading. This heading can be estimated, in the case of co-speed target and interceptor, by turning until the lead angle approximates the desired target aspect (i.e., collision ATA equals desired TAA). Once the interceptor is steady on the new heading, ATA and target bearing should remain constant. If this is not the case small heading adjustments can be made to stop the target's drift. Adjustments can also be made from collision heading in case the desired target aspect has not been attained. Once they are established on a collision course, time "3," the aircraft should pass very close to each other in the horizontal plane.

Relative altitude is another consideration in this or any other intercept. The interceptor may receive an estimate of bogey altitude from GCI, or relative altitude may be computed automatically by the weapons system or mentally by the pilot based on radar antenna elevation and target range, in the same manner that lateral displacement is estimated. This calculation should be made as early as possible in the intercept so that the fighter will have sufficient time to climb or dive as necessary to achieve the

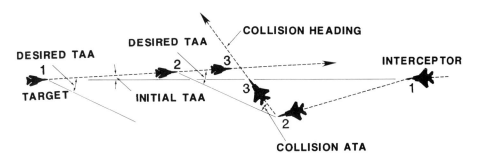

Figure 10-2. Forward-Quarter Intercept

desired altitude separation at intercept. Target altitude should also be monitored throughout the intercept to detect any changes.

Advantages and Disadvantages

The FQ intercept is useful for establishing an initial attack direction for the existing environmental conditions (coming out of the sun, etc.), or for some other purpose. Many all-aspect missiles (notably all-aspect heat seekers) have better capability from FQ firing positions than from directly head-on. Some target aspect during an intercept can also increase the range of a probable VID, since a profile view of the target is larger and usually more recognizable than a strictly head-on view.

Increasing or decreasing TAA does take time, however, allowing the bogey to gain further penetration toward its target. In addition, the method described does not ensure any particular target range once the desired aspect has been achieved; therefore the final approach course may be established well inside maximum weapons-firing range, and displacement might be insufficient for a stern-conversion option. This drawback can be alleviated by controlling displacement and aspect concurrently, a technique that is discussed in the next example. The FQ intercept is also relatively easy for the bogey to counter. In this example, for instance, the bogey could make a substantial turn (jink) away from the interceptor between times "1" and "2," generating so much displacement that the fighter pilot would be hard-pressed even to complete the intercept, much less to control the target aspect. The bogey could later turn back on course and possibly complete an "end run" around the interceptor, which may be thrown well back in trail of the target, out of range. Early detection of a target jink can be difficult for the interceptor between times "1" and "2," depending on the sophistication of its weapons system and GCI capability. Once the target is on collision bearing, jinks are more easily detected as a simple drift rate and a change in closure.

If the restriction of a specified target aspect is removed, the dangers of a target jink can be alleviated by turning the interceptor immediately to collision heading at time "1" and accepting whatever aspect is initially available. This method also minimizes bogey penetration and time to intercept.

Stern Conversion

Description

The stern-conversion intercept "converts" an initial FQ setup into a final rear-hemisphere position for the interceptor. Figure 10-3 depicts an example of a stern conversion.

The initial setup at time "1" is the same as in the previous example. This time, however, the interceptor intends a stern conversion. To accomplish this conversion requires a certain amount of displacement from the bogey's flight path, an amount dependent on how hard the interceptor pilot wants to turn during the final conversion and his true airspeed (i.e., the interceptor's turn radius). The conversion is often planned so that the interceptor's nose is pointed directly at the target through most of the turn to minimize the area of the fighter that is visible to the bogey pilot. The interceptor pilot needs a rough idea of the amount of displacement that is required. Having gained this displacement, the interceptor pilot must know at what target range, or conversion range, the intended conversion turn will bring the interceptor behind the bogey at the desired trail position. Taken together, the desired displacement and the conversion range define the "conversion point," which is the interceptor pilot's initial goal.

Assume for this example that the conversion range is 8 nautical miles (8 NM) with 20,000 ft displacement. At time "1" the target is 30 NM away and the interceptor's radar weapons system computes about 2° of target aspect. With a little mental gymnastics the interceptor pilot can estimate his displacement using the formula:

100 × TAA (degrees) × Range (NM) = Displacement (ft).

In this case, 100 × 2° × 30 NM = 6,000 ft, so more displacement is required. (Some weapons systems also compute this displacement for the pilot.) The interceptor pilot, therefore, takes a cut away from the bogey's flight path, being careful not to turn so far that his radar antenna gimbal limits are exceeded. The actual magnitude of this displacement turn should be great enough to generate the required displacement prior to the conversion range.

Between times "1" and "2" the interceptor pilot continuously monitors range, TAA, and displacement. At 20 NM range, aspect is determined to be about 10°, yielding the desired 20,000 ft displacement. Now the interceptor must maintain that displacement until conversion range (8 NM). To achieve this the interceptor turns to parallel the bogey's course at time "2," and simply drives in to 8 NM range, time "3." At this point the conversion turn is commenced and results in the interceptor rolling out at the desired distance behind the target. This distance is generally planned to be in the heart of the interceptor's RQ weapons-firing envelope. When this weapons range is short, such as for guns, much care must be exercised in the final stages of the conversion turn to avoid overshooting the bogey's flight path at close range.

The conversion range for this intercept is predicated primarily on the time required for the interceptor to complete its conversion turn. This time determines the interceptor's final roll-out distance behind the target.

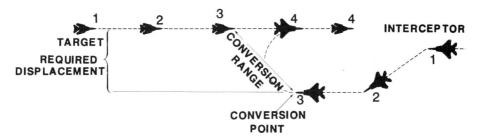

Figure 10-3. Stern-Conversion Intercept

If the turn is completed too quickly, the fighter may arrive in front of the target. Too slow a turn can result in excessive distance behind the bogey at roll-out. Since the rate of turn is linked to the turn radius at a given speed, adjusting turn rate during the conversion will also affect turn radius, on which the required displacement was based. Conversion range with the proper displacement usually assumes the interceptor arrives at the conversion point on a reciprocal heading relative to the bogey (i.e., 180 DTG), as in Figure 10-3. If this is not the case, an adjustment must be made if the conversion geometry is to work out properly. For example, if the conversion point is approached with the interceptor headed somewhat away from the bogey's flight path (DTG greater than 180), the normal conversion turn should be started a little early (i.e., range slightly greater than 8 NM) so that the reciprocal heading is reached at the conversion point. Conversely, if the conversion point is reached with the fighter heading somewhat toward the target's flight path (DTG less than 180), the conversion turn can be delayed slightly to avoid terminating too close to the bogey. In this case, since displacement will be decreasing during the delay, a somewhat harder turn may also have to be made to avoid overshooting the target's flight path.

Adjustments are also available for other than optimum displacement. With too much displacement the fighter pilot should begin his turn a little early (i.e., at greater than standard conversion range) and make an easier turn than usual. If too little displacement is available, the turn should be delayed somewhat and then made tighter than normal. Altitude differential with the target can greatly alter the required lateral displacement. Stern conversions can be made even with zero lateral displacement from below (Immelmann) or above (split-S) if vertical displacement is adequate.

If the interceptor is equipped with long-range FQ weapons and sufficient displacement can be generated, the FQ intercept and the stern conversion can be combined into what is called an attack-reattack. The interceptor pilot attains the necessary displacement, then turns in and fires the weapon at the proper FQ range. He then makes a turn back toward the reciprocal of the target's course until he closes to conversion range, at which time he completes a stern conversion and makes a rear attack.

Advantages and Disadvantages

Probably the primary advantage of the stern-conversion intercept is that it is completed behind the bogey in a tactically advantageous position. The rear-hemisphere position is also optimal for employment of many air-to-air weapons.

This technique does, however, take considerably more fuel and time than the "collision-all-the-way" or the FQ methods, and it allows the bogey to penetrate closer to its target. The stern conversion is also easy for the bogey to counter by jinking. A small bogey turn toward the interceptor early in this intercept will remove the displacement, forcing the fighter pilot to settle for a FQ intercept. Likewise, a jink away from the interceptor can allow the bogey to evade interception altogether and end-run around the fighter. Such jinks may be difficult to detect, since the target bearing and closing speed are changing continuously during this procedure. Another danger is presented by the conversion turn itself, which is a long, blind turn in close proximity to the target. The pilot is exposing the interceptor's belly to the whole world and daring someone to shoot. If there are other undetected bogeys in the area, the fighter pilot may never complete this intercept. It is usually good practice in any event to pause for a belly-check about halfway through the conversion turn. Generally stern conversions are not recommended in an unknown environment.

Although fighter speed is not critical to the conduct of a FQ intercept, an interceptor speed advantage over the target is highly desirable for the stern conversion. In general, the greater the interceptor's speed advantage, the more room there is for error in the conversion process. At co-speed, or with an interceptor speed disadvantage, timing and geometry must be nearly perfect or the fighter pilot is likely to complete the conversion too far behind the target for a successful attack.

Another drawback of the stern-conversion technique is the interceptor's vulnerability to chaff while it is in the target's beam region. It is difficult for most radars to discriminate between chaff and the real target when they are viewed from the target's flank, since closing velocity is so nearly identical. This situation often results in the interceptor pilot losing contact with the target at a critical time or completing an intercept on the chaff. Doppler-type radars are also susceptible to losing track of targets with beam aspects.

The FQ and stern-conversion intercepts comprise the basics of almost all tactical intercepts. The tactics presented in the remainder of this chapter apply these fundamentals to multiple-fighter scenarios. Although the examples depicted here usually show two fighters opposing two bogeys, each aircraft of either formation can be considered to be an element of any desired number, and the tactics can be applied to an encounter of essentially any size.

> Today it is even more important to dominate the . . . highly sophisticated weapon systems, perhaps even more important than being a good pilot; to make the best use of this system.
> Lt. General Adolph Galland, Luftwaffe

Single-Side Offset

Description

The single-side offset places all interceptors on one side of the target formation, and the fighter leader performs either a FQ intercept or a stern conversion, as shown in Figure 10-4.

In this example the fighter section detects the bogey formation roughly head-on, and the leader offsets to the north beginning at time "1," possibly to take advantage of prevailing environmental conditions. Ideally the first pilot with radar contact becomes the tactical leader throughout the intercept. The wingman, initially located on the south side, dives below the leader to increase speed, and then crosses the leader's flight path to emerge

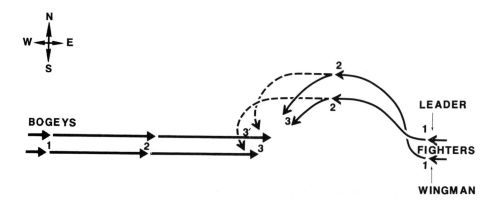

Figure 10-4. Single-Side Offset

on the other side in a good defensive-spread position. This maneuver enables the wingman to "look through" the leader's aircraft toward the bogeys, increasing the wingman's confidence that the threat sector is to the left of his nose. This limits the wingman's primary visual and radar-search sector and improves his safety later in the intercept.

At time "2" the fighter leader determines that he has sufficient displacement for his desired attack, and he continues with either a FQ intercept (point "3") or a stern conversion (point "3' "). The preferable tactic depends on the availability of reliable forward-hemisphere weapons, the amount of offset which can be generated, the time available for the intercept, the degree of certainty as to the enemy numbers and formation, etc. Most of the advantages and disadvantages of these two options have been discussed, but there are a few more. The FQ option is more appropriate for hit-and-run attacks against fighters, particularly in an unknown, hostile environment. It may also be useful against bombers that are heavily defended in the rear. The stern conversion facilitates repeated attacks on numerous targets and places the fighters in a more advantageous position to begin an engagement with enemy fighters. The stern conversion can be fatal, however, if there is an undetected trailing enemy element.

If the stern conversion is selected, or if a significant turn is required for a FQ attack, the wingman normally crosses beneath the lead once more between times "2" and "3." This allows the wingman to keep the leader and the threat sector on the same side of his nose and positions the wingman abeam the leader in a more defensible combat spread. The wingman should be very alert during this turn for bogeys appearing from the section's belly-side.

Advantages and Disadvantages

When the bogeys are deployed in a significant trail formation, there is often some difference of opinion as to which element should be attacked first. The initial choice is usually the trail element, of course, since it is more vulnerable. This may not be the best choice, however, particularly when the interceptors have forward-hemisphere weapons capability. Attacking the lead bogey element first, with a FQ intercept or head-on, may allow sequential attacks on trailing elements. Especially if the bogeys are bombers, it may not be wise to allow the lead element through unscathed.

When the interceptors are equipped only with rear-hemisphere weapons against trailing fighters and the trail element can be identified with some certainty, a stern conversion might be employed against this element. One situation which may develop, particularly against radar-equipped bogeys or those under close GCI control, is illustrated by Figure 10-5.

At time "1" in this example the fighter pilots have their desired offset from the bogeys' flight path and plan a stern conversion on the trail bogey. At time "2" the fighters have reached conversion range against the trailer, and the pilots are beginning their turns. Unfortunately, contact with the lead bogey has been lost because of the fighters' radar antenna gimbal limitations. Being closer, this lead bogey has already begun its own stern conversion against the fighters. At time "3," just when the fighter pilots are feeling confident of a kill, the lead bogey is slipping into firing position and the fighters are sandwiched. This situation can be particularly dangerous against a more maneuverable bogey, which can profit more from the available displacement than can the fighters.

Because of this danger, a single-side offset to a stern conversion is not recommended against fighters in trail. The alternatives are sequential FQ attacks with all-aspect missiles, guns, or rockets on each bogey in turn, or use of a more suitable intercept tactic (one of the tactics that follow).

Even with these limitations the single-side offset offers some advantages. Positively placing the bogeys on one side of the formation isolates the threat sector and reduces the chances of being bracketed by the enemy, as well as allowing the fighter pilots to choose the direction of their approach for environmental reasons. This tactic also provides reasonably good mutual support, since the fighters can remain fairly close together and are not required to venture far from a good defensive-spread formation. In general, however, the single-side offset is a rather defensive tactic, since it offers the fighters few significant advantages that are not also given to the enemy.

Trail

Description

A trail intercept is any intercept in which the fighters are arranged in a trail formation at the merge. Figure 10-6 depicts an example in which the two sections are approaching with some offset at time "1." The fighter leader turns immediately to collision heading for a FQ intercept. Meanwhile, the wingman repositions behind the leader in trail. The trailing distance is normally as great as visual conditions allow; the wingman must keep sight of his lead, and he cannot be so far behind that he cannot offer some support to the leader in case a bogey attacks the lead fighter from behind (i.e., trailer nose-tail distance should not greatly exceed weapons max-range). If the trailer intends to fire a head-on missile on the leader's VID, separation between leader and trailer should exceed missile min-range parameters.

In this case the leader's intent is to make a VID on the bogey aircraft before firing. Sometimes target aspect, bogey size, and visibility do not allow a positive VID to be made within the firing envelope of a fighter's all-aspect weapons. The trail formation is useful in this situation, since the leader can make and relay the VID to the trailing wingman, who then can

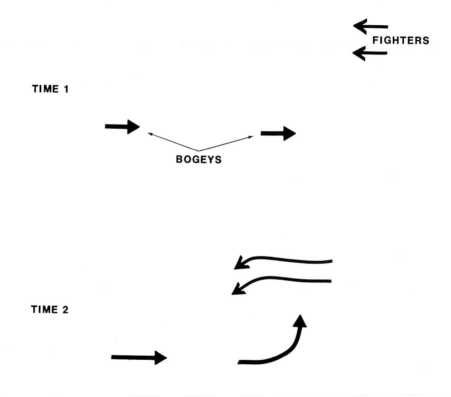

Figure 10-5. Stern-Conversion Hazard against Trail Fighters

shoot before penetrating his min-range limit. The shooter must be certain that his weapon is indeed locked on and guiding on a target, and not on his leader!

Once he gains sight of the bogeys, the leader should usually attempt to make a visual attack, forcing them into a defensive maneuver. The enemy may not have sight of the trailer, and such maneuvering will often present the trailing wingman with easy shot opportunities. Another, generally less desirable, option is to bait the bogeys by allowing considerable lateral separation at the pass. The enemy may be tempted into turning for an attack on the leader, again turning in front of the trailer. The trailing wingman should maintain considerable vertical separation with the leader to reduce the chances of being detected. A low trailer is often the most difficult to detect because of radar clutter and visual masking against the ground. The resulting look-up angle should also optimize all-aspect weapons performance.

Advantages and Disadvantages

The trail intercept, or actually an intercept in the trail formation, can be very effective offensively. The VID/forward-hemisphere advantage has already been mentioned. In addition, a bogey engaging the lead fighter is a grape for the trailing wingman, while a bogey not turning on the leader is likely to be attacked by him. In short, the bogey is caught between a rock and a hard place.

Although the trail arrangement is good offensively, it is rather poor on the defensive side, particularly for the trailer. His position and distance from the leader make it impossible for the leader to cover the trailer visually, and it would be very difficult for him even to lend support if the trailer was attacked. For these reasons trail tactics are extremely hazardous in an uncontrolled, hostile environment, and very high speeds should be maintained to help guard the trailer's rear hemisphere. This danger can be reduced significantly with the addition of more fighters, however. For example, placing two sections, each in combat spread, one behind the other, offers the advantages of the trail formation while retaining mutual support within each section. This is commonly called a "box" formation. A single with a trailing pair (vic) is another option.

Should the trail formation be employed in an uncontrolled environ-

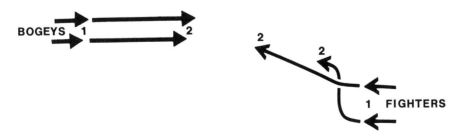

Figure 10-6. Trail Intercept

ment, and the fighters be lucky enough to complete the intercept, it is imperative that they reform as quickly as possible in a more defensive arrangement. A turn of about 90° in either direction by the leader after the pass, and then a reversal, should allow the trailer to close to a good spread position.

The trail formation can be a good defensive tactic against bogeys known also to be arranged in trail. This can allow the leader to perform a single-side offset for attack on the trail bogey with less fear of being attacked by the lead bogey (as he was in Figure 10-5). This is still a relatively defensive tactic, however.

Sweep

Description

The sweep intercept is essentially a stern conversion in a trail formation, as illustrated by Figure 10-7. At time "1" the fighters, in spread formation, are approaching the conversion point for a stern conversion against the bogey section. As the leader begins his conversion turn, the wingman, on the outside of the formation, delays his turn to gain nose-tail separation (time "2"). At time "3" the leader is approaching stern firing parameters with his wingman covering from behind.

Advantages and Disadvantages

This tactic can result in an effective offensive start for the fighters if they can remain undetected until about time "3." They are well set up for sequential attacks and have a good chance of hiding the trailer, especially if he has a good altitude split. The hidden trailer gives the fighters better offensive potential should the bogeys discover the attack and turn to negate it. Defensively, the sweep allows good mutual support until commencing the conversion turn. Against bogey trail formations, the fighter wingman can also provide some protection against the lead bogey as the lead fighter attacks the bogey wingman.

It is quite obvious, however, that the poor wingman is really hanging it out during the conversion turn. Assigning two fighters to the trailing

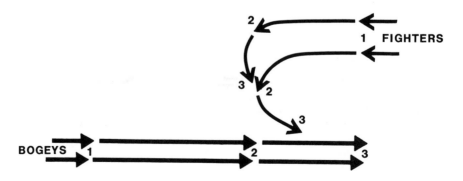

Figure 10-7. The Sweep

element, as explained earlier, offers added safety in an uncontrolled environment. With just two fighters, only a leader with designs on his wingman's wife or his stereo would call for this tactic under most combat conditions.

> During the course of this increasingly difficult fight it was proved that the leader of the fighter squadron only received full recognition if he asked nothing from his men that he was not prepared to do himself.
>
> Lt. General Adolph Galland, Luftwaffe

Pincer

Description

The pincer is a two-pronged, bracketing attack, also sometimes called a "heart-attack," which is analogous to the visual bracket attack. Figure 10-8 illustrates the pincer.

At time "1" the fighters, initially positioned with near-zero aspect, begin displacement turns in opposite directions for independent stern conversions or FQ attacks. Approaching time "2" the enemy fighters detect the attack and turn toward the northern fighter. As soon as such a bogey turn is noticed, the southern fighter must immediately turn to collision course to avoid being left out of the action. The northern fighter pilot continues his attempt to get outside the enemy section without giving away an angular advantage. At time "3" the northern fighter passes the bogeys nearly head-on, while the southern fighter has gained an offensive advantage.

Had the bogeys continued straight ahead, both fighters might have achieved offensive positions from opposite sides. Once again, the chance of escaping visual or radar detection is enhanced when the fighters split high and low to bracket the enemy in altitude during the attack.

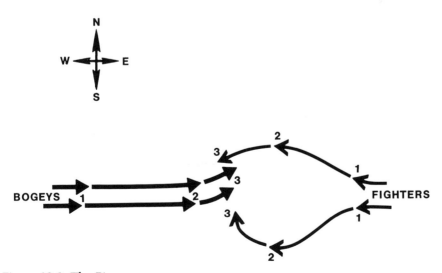

Figure 10-8. The Pincer

Advantages and Disadvantages

The pincer is an extremely effective offensive tactic, but pilots must have considerable training in its use for it to be consistently effective. The fighters are likely to be separated by several miles at time "2" and can provide little mutual support, so these are truly autonomous intercepts. When the pincer is performed at very high speeds and is limited to FQ attacks with all-aspect weapons, this temporary loss of mutual support may be justified, even in the hostile environment, to gain greater offensive potential. The fighter pilots should generally plan to rejoin after the attack, however, for better defense, and stern conversions should be avoided except in well-controlled situations. Again, the pincer is not recommended against bogeys in a significant trail formation.

A further complication with the pincer is the requirement that each fighter have radar contact with the bogeys, or at least have dual GCI close control, prior to the split. All the other tactics described to this point could be performed reasonably with only one operable radar in the section, or with close control only for the leader.

Another limitation for this tactic is the ability of the individual fighters either to defeat the bogeys one-on-one or to escape from a bogey after meeting from neutral positions. This is because the pincer invites the bogeys to split up also, which can easily result in two one-versus-one encounters. If the fighter pilots do not feel confident engaging the enemy one-on-one in the given situation, they can attempt to isolate and attack one bogey, as shown in Figure 10-9.

In this example the bogeys split (time "2") in response to the fighters' bracket attempt. Each fighter pilot continues to run his intercept against the nearest bogey, while at the same time discussing a plan via radio with the other pilot. The two pilots decide to neutralize the southern bogey and attack the northern one. At time "3" each fighter passes its respective

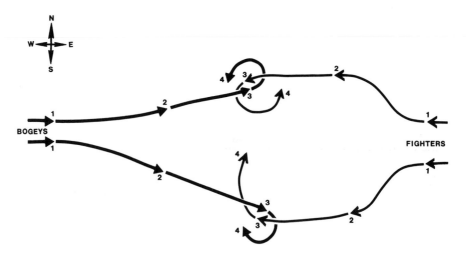

Figure 10-9. Pincer Isolation Tactic

bogey neutrally, on the side away from the other aircraft. The pilot of the southern fighter may want to give his bogey a little extra flight-path separation, if this can be done safely, to induce it to turn away from its wingman. After the pass, the pilot to the south heads for his wingman's position at max speed, leaving the southern bogey in the dust, time "4." By controller vector, by radar, visually, or by any other means available, the free pilot of the southern fighter must now locate the engagement to the north, attempt to pick off the northern bogey, and rejoin with the wingman before the southern bogey can re-enter the fight.

Obviously there are a lot of things that can go wrong in such a scenario; thus the recommended limitation on relative individual fighter perform-ance. Comm-jamming, degraded radar and visual environments, and addi-tional, unknown, bogeys are some of the greatest potential hazards. In addition, the geometry for this attack is difficult when there is consider-able aspect early in the intercept.

Drag

Description

As with the visual drag attack described in an earlier chapter, this tactic involves baiting an enemy, inducing him to pursue one fighter while he presents a shot opportunity to another. Figure 10-10 illustrates one exam-ple of a drag intercept.

At time "1" the fighters contact bogeys on the nose and begin to shift into a trail or very sucked echelon formation. The idea is to ensure that the bogeys have radar contact with the lead fighter and to try to hide the trailer. Against bogeys with pulse-type radars and/or GCI control, this can usually be accomplished by having the trailer dive to very low altitude during the shift. Turning at right angles to the bogeys and dropping chaff is another effective tactic against both enemy fighter radars and controller radars. When the enemy fighters are expected to have Doppler radars, the same right-angle turn by the trailer, who passes fairly close to the lead aircraft if practical and then makes a significant altitude change before turning back on course, is generally sufficient to cause loss of contact with the trail fighter. In either case the leader can change altitude in the opposite direc-tion, usually higher to enhance his chances of being detected, creating a large altitude differential between fighters which makes tracking both of them very difficult.

Nose-tail distance between the two fighters after the shift to trail (time "2") is generally near maximum visual range or 1.5 to 2.0 times the trailer's maximum RQ weapons range, whichever is less.

At some predesignated point, usually at about maximum visual range or approaching the bogeys' maximum head-on firing range (should they be equipped with all-aspect missiles), the leader makes a sharp turn away, preferably toward the trailer if he is in echelon formation. This turn usually places the bogeys near the lead fighter's radar antenna gimbal limits, but care should be taken not to let the bogeys exceed these limits, at least until the leader gains sight of the enemy. The turn-away from the

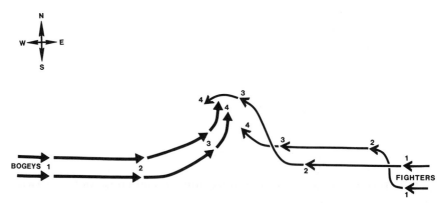

Figure 10-10. The Drag

bogeys serves three major purposes. It increases the enemy's chances of seeing, and therefore the likelihood of them pursuing, the lead fighter. It delays the bogeys' all-aspect-missile-firing opportunities by decreasing their maximum firing range, while simultaneously placing the lead fighter in a good position to defend against such a shot if it is forthcoming. Finally, it tempts the enemy to chase the leader and thereby turn in front of the trailer and provide an easy shot.

The trailer's task is to maintain visual contact with his leader while gaining radar contact with the bogeys. He is usually in the best position to detect whether the enemy is taking the bait, and he should pass this info to the leader. If the enemy continues for the trailer, the leader should turn back in for a FQ attack or a stern conversion with good advantage. This scenario transforms the drag into a lead-around tactic, which is discussed next.

Advantages and Disadvantages

The drag can be a devastating tactic, but, like any complex procedure, it requires much practice and many things can go wrong. As with other trail tactics, it is long on offense and rather short on defense, making it more appropriate for permissive situations. When undetected hostile fighters could be around, extremely high speeds should be used. Even so, the considerable maneuvering required by the lead fighter leaves it vulnerable to surprise attack.

The drag can be performed with only one operable radar in the section or with close control only for the leader, since the trailer can maintain position visually, but two radars are preferable. This tactic is normally not advisable in an all-aspect missile environment, since the enemy is usually afforded the first shot opportunity.

Drag tactics can be very effective against bogeys in trail. When the lead bogey takes the bait, it can usually be picked off by the trailing fighter before the second bogey becomes a factor. The threat of the second bogey must be kept in mind, however, and the pilot of the trailing fighter should be careful not to expose himself to this threat while he attacks the lead bogey. It is usually advisable for the lead fighter (dragger) to maintain a radar lock on the trail bogey and rely on the wingman for protection against the lead bogey, so that the position of the trailer can be determined at the merge. Two radars in the fighter section are therefore highly desirable for conducting a drag attack against an enemy trail formation.

Lead-Around

Description

The lead-around (shown in Figure 10-11) is similar to the drag in that it is begun from a trail or sucked-echelon formation. The distance between the fighters in trail is usually close to maximum visual range, or about twice maximum RQ weapons range, whichever is less. As with other trail tactics, speed should be kept high to help clear the trailer's six o'clock. On reaching a predetermined range during a nearly head-on intercept (time "1"), the lead fighter breaks away to one side to build displacement for a FQ attack or a stern conversion. At time "2" the enemy section is faced with choosing which fighter to engage. If they turn on the leader, the bogeys present the trailer with an easy shot, but if they continue for the trailer the lead fighter will probably gain an effective offensive position.

The displacement turn for the lead-around is usually made away from a wingman if he is in echelon, as shown, in order to generate a wider bracket. This maneuver essentially creates a bracket attack from a trail formation, with both fighters reaching the bogeys at about the same time for best effect. Although it is still desirable to hide the trailing fighter, this is not essential for success of the lead-around. A good altitude split between the fighters, preferably bracketing the enemy vertically, is still recommended, however.

Advantages and Disadvantages

Again, this is a very good offensive tactic, but it is rather poor from a defensive standpoint because of the trail formation and the wide split between fighters. In a permissive environment, and using very high speeds, the offensive potential may well outweigh the risks. In most combat conditions, however, a stern conversion by the leader against enemy fighters is hazardous, and a FQ attack is preferable. The fighters should usually attempt to regain mutual support at the merge.

This intercept can be performed with one radar or with GCI control only for the lead fighter, since the trailer can generally maintain sight of the

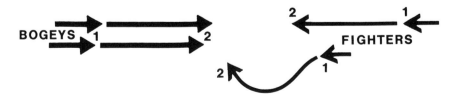

Figure 10-11. The Lead-Around

leader throughout; but two radars are better. The lead-around is generally less complex than the drag, since the fighters are not required to alter their attack significantly in response to bogey reactions. Chances of success are therefore materially improved. As with the drag, however, the lead-around may offer the first shot opportunity to an all-aspect-equipped enemy, limiting its application in some scenarios.

The lead-around is perhaps one of the best offensive tactics against bogeys arranged in trail. The fighter leader should take a radar lock on the trail bogey and run his attack on that aircraft while the fighter wingman guards against interference from the lead bogey. Two radars are still preferable for this situation, but generally the trailing fighter can perform his duties visually.

Hook

Description

The hook is an effective offensive tactic, well suited to the VID of very small bogeys. It has many of the attributes of the trail, in that one fighter (leader) performs the VID while the other (shooter) positions for the shot, but it is probably superior to the trail defensively. Figure 10-12 illustrates the hook.

At time "1" the fighters, in combat spread, detect unidentified radar contacts slightly right of the nose and closing. The leader (northern fighter) adjusts course slightly to place the contacts on collision bearing. At time "2" the wingman takes greater lateral separation from his leader and a large altitude split. Separation should be on the order of one turn diameter both vertically and laterally. If the bogeys are roughly co-altitude the wingman can split either high or low. Often environmental conditions (i.e., high or low cloud decks, sun position, etc.) will determine the better altitude for hiding the wingman. At high altitudes, aircraft performance may not permit the wingman to gain sufficient additional altitude in time

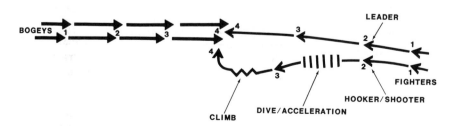

Figure 10-12. The Hook

for the intercept, so a dive may be preferable. Conversely, when intercepting low-level bogeys there may not be enough airspace below the targets, necessitating a climbing separation. If there is a significant altitude differential between the fighter lead and the bogeys, the leader will need to work off this altitude before the merge so that he meets the enemy approximately co-altitude. In this case the wingman may be able to stay at about his original level and allow the leader to create the desired separation during the intercept process.

There generally will be an obvious preference for a high or a low split by the wingman, but all else being equal a low split is often more effective because it usually makes radar detection of the wingman less likely and it allows the wingman to accelerate somewhat ahead of the leader, as shown at time "3," for a better offensive position at the pass. When he is required to climb well above the leader, the wingman must usually settle for a sucked position, slightly behind the leader. In this case the bogey can pass the leader head-on and then turn up toward the wingman, denying him an offensive advantage.

At time "3" in this example, the wingman (shooter or hooker) begins a programmed turn (based on range calls from the leader) timed for him to point at the lead fighter at the merge with the bogeys. During this time the leader is attempting to remove all lateral and vertical separation with one of the bogeys for a close pass. Usually the leader will be able to VID the bogey first and call the aircraft type to the shooter, who is then cleared to fire at an enemy. Sometimes, however, the "hooker's" greater aspect will allow him the earlier VID. In either case both fighters have all-aspect-missile-firing opportunities at the moment of the VID, but with a very small bogey the leader may already have penetrated min-range for his weapons. The hooker should have an all-aspect missile shot at the pass or be in good position to convert to a rear-hemisphere envelope. He should be careful, however, to ensure separation between his leader and the target from weapons launch to impact.

Against a single bogey, or closely spaced multiple bogeys, the lead fighter generally will attempt to place the enemy between himself and the hooker at the pass. This diverts the enemy's attention away from the shooter and often induces the bogeys to turn away from the hooker after the pass, providing him with a sweet belly-side or RQ shot. With widely separated bogeys, such as in this example, the leader will usually try to bracket the enemy closest to the shooter while informing the hooker of the position of any other hostile fighters. This technique helps prevent the shooter from inadvertently turning in front of an enemy and being bagged from the belly-side. The leader should pass the intended victim closely (time "4") and call out the exact instant of the pass to help the shooter get sight (tally) of the target.

Advantages and Disadvantages

The hook has a great many positive attributes. When properly executed it can provide the fighters with an offensive advantage at the pass and, quite often, the quick elimination of one bogey. When the fighters are equipped only with guns or RQ missiles, however, the bogey can often escape an immediate lethal situation by turning hard toward the hooker at the pass, providing the bogey pilot knows (or guesses) the threat sector. This is a very tough tactic to beat, however, when the fighters are armed with all-aspect ordnance and the enemy is not.

Unlike the trail, the hook does not require the fighter wingman to sacrifice all hope of mutual support for a firing opportunity at the pass. The fact that the hooker probably will be more widely separated from his leader, and possibly somewhat acute or sucked, reduces defensive mutual support potential to some extent, but this arrangement is still much superior defensively to a trail formation. This tactic can be performed quite adequately with only one operable radar in the section, but some increased measure of safety can be provided by the wingman also having a radar to check for trail bogeys. Normally the tactical leader of the section is determined by which fighter has a radar contact and is closer to the bogeys' flight path when reaching the point at which the hooker must take his separation, time "2" in this example. Should radar contact be lost subsequent to this split, the fighters should try to return expeditiously to a more defensive spread formation.

When combined with a straight collision-bearing intercept, as in this example, the hook minimizes the enemy's penetration into friendly airspace, which can be an important consideration. The hook is most effective, however, against single bogeys or fairly tight formations. When the bogeys are widely separated either vertically or laterally, it may be impossible for the fighter lead to pass one bogey with the prescribed minimum separation without allowing another enemy to become a serious threat at the pass. In other words, this tactic may allow the bogeys to run a hook of their own.

A trail formation also poses a difficult problem for the hook. This situation usually requires the fighter leader to pass each hostile element with minimum separation with the intent of hooking the last bogey. Achieving this close pass with each bogey is necessary to deny the bogey leader a lead-turn opportunity and to "mark" the trail bogey for the hooker; but such close passes normally require the leader to have sight of the bogey aircraft at some distance before the pass. The necessity of an early tally, in turn, usually requires the leader to have a radar lock on the lead bogey. Most weapons systems provide the pilot with an indication of the radar line of sight when they are locked on a target, which narrows the visual search area enormously and greatly increases the chances of an early tally. Unfortunately, most fighter radars can lock only one target at a time, so while the system is locked on the bogey leader the trial bogey cannot be monitored. After passing the lead bogey element the leader seldom has sufficient time to acquire the trailer and maneuver for a close pass. Even sophisticated track-while-scan radars, which can track more than one target at a time, usually can provide only one LOS cue for the pilot, so these offer little additional help. Therefore, for a hook to be very effective against a trail formation the fighter section needs two radars so the leader can lock the lead bogey while the hooker locks the trailer.

In an uncontrolled scenario the hook can be dangerous for the shooter, since additional, undetected, bogeys may take advantage of the hooker's turn for a belly-side attack. If a shot is not forthcoming within about 90° of turn in this environment, the hooker should break off the attack, perform a rapid turn reversal to clear his belly, and rejoin in a good supporting position with the leader. In such unknown situations the shooter generally should avoid the acute position, since this requires greater than 90° of turn to point at the bogey at the merge with the fighter lead. An abeam or slightly sucked position necessitates less turning but also results in less angular advantage for the hooker at the pass. With the resulting beam or FQ geometry at the pass, the shooter's hopes for a quick kill may be dependent on an all-aspect weapon or a bogey turning away from the hooker's position.

Under the right circumstances the hook can be a very effective intercept tactic, but it does require a well-trained fighter section for optimum results.

Option

Description

The option intercept is essentially the single-side offset tactic described earlier, with the added "option" of making a transition to a bracket attack. Figure 10-13 illustrates an example of this tactic.

At time "1" the fighters detect the bogeys nearly head-on at long range. The pilot with the first radar contact generally should assume the lead and maneuver as necessary to generate displacement for a stern conversion or FQ attack. In this case the wingman is already positioned on the side away from the threat, so he stays on that side. The displacement turn into the wingman may throw him a little acute, as shown at time "2," but this is a temporary state of affairs, as the lead will soon be turning away to place the formation back into combat spread. In a relatively controlled situation the wingman may choose to accept the temporary acute position, but in a very hostile or unknown situation he should maneuver as necessary (normally zoom high in this case) to regain a more optimum defensive position abeam the leader.

At time "2" the fighter lead determines that adequate displacement has been generated for his desired intercept. Choosing between a stern conversion and a FQ attack has been discussed previously, and the decision usually depends on the tactical situation (degree of confidence in situation

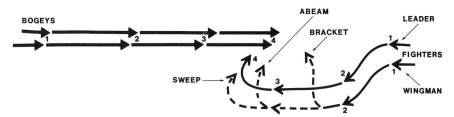

Figure 10-13. The Option

awareness), weapons available, displacement available, etc. For the FQ intercept the lead will normally turn to collision heading once the desired aspect has been generated. In this case, however, the stern conversion is selected, which calls for paralleling the bogey's flight path to maintain lateral separation. The leader's altitude should be adjusted as necessary for environmental or weapons considerations. The wingman will want a good altitude split on the leader at the point of attack to make himself harder for the bogeys to see, so he should be planning the direction of this vertical split and how it can best be achieved.

It is the leader's responsibility during the intercept to inform the wingman of the planned intercept geometry, bogey numbers, formation, altitudes, etc., as available. Wingman positioning during the attack is best left to the wingman, since he is better able to assess his own capabilities as to positioning, radar status, situational awareness, etc. The wingman has three options with this tactic. He can take an early cut to the inside of the leader's turn in an attempt to bracket the enemy, he can perform a tac turn with the leader to maintain an abeam position for the attack, or he can make the transition to a trail position during the conversion turn for a sweep option. Whichever option he chooses, the wingman should inform the leader of his intentions.

For the bracket option the wingman may be required to dive below the leader at high speed in order to reach a position on or across the bogey's flight path at the intercept. If this maneuver is performed within possible visual range of the bogeys, the wingman should try not to pass too close to the leader, since this could give the enemy a chance for a tally on both fighters. Unlike the classic pincer attack, this bracket option is performed visually by the wingman with reference to the leader, so it is not necessary for the wingman to have a radar contact with the bogeys. The bracket option can be a good choice when the fighters are all-aspect capable and the enemy is not. When this option is properly performed, both fighters should have shots by the time the leader can VID the bogeys. Wingman positioning in this case should provide for satisfying his weapon's min-range constraints as the leader terminates the intercept.

The abeam option is simply a section stern conversion or FQ intercept with the wingman holding an abeam position in defensive spread throughout. This option can provide optimum defensive potential in a hostile environment while giving the fighters some tactical advantage at the intercept. It can be very effective offensively when both the fighters and the enemy have all-aspect weapons. The bogeys can easily counter this tactic, however, if the fighters have only RQ weapons, by turning hard into the attack. The fighters may still achieve some tactical advantage if detection of the attack can be delayed until late in the game.

The sweep option is essentially the sweep tactic already described. This option is less well suited to all-aspect weapons than are the previous choices, because normally only the leader is in firing parameters at the moment of the VID. The sweep can be very effective with less capable weapons, however, especially when extended maneuvering is anticipated with enemy fighters, as the trail formation provides good offensive potential, particularly when the leader has an initial angular advantage on the enemy. The pressure applied by the leader in this case often results in bogeys turning in front of the trailer. The trail formation is also good for sequential attacks against bombers, transports, etc. As discussed earlier, however, this is not a healthy option in an uncontrolled, multi-bogey environment because of the poor defensive position of the trailer, particularly if the leader conducts a stern conversion.

Advantages and Disadvantages

The primary advantage of the option intercept is its flexibility. The leader does essentially the same thing regardless of the option, and the wingman positions as the situation dictates. Offensive options are available for both controlled conditions (sweep) and more hostile environments (bracket), and the more defensive option (abeam) can be chosen for highly uncontrolled conditions. The option is compatible with either FQ or stern conversion intercept geometry. The choice here often depends on weapons available and the permissiveness of the environment. The stern conversion is more applicable to controlled situations with RQ weapons, while the FQ geometry may be preferable in poorly defined scenarios and when the fighters have all-aspect missiles.

Against bogeys in a significant trail formation, the bracket is generally the option of choice. The fighter leader in this case should normally lock and attack the trailing bogey, while the fighter wingman's position inside the conversion turn provides protection from the lead bogey. It is highly desirable for the wingman to have radar contact with the lead bogey in this situation to aid in visual detection. The fighter wingman will usually take his split for the bracket earlier against a trail formation so that he can be in position and avoid being detected visually by the bogey leader, which may be considerably closer at this time than is the trail bogey, which is being attacked by the lead fighter.

All three options offered by this tactic allow the fighters to remain close enough together and near abeam to facilitate lead changes in the initial stages of the intercept, which may be required if the leader loses contact with the bogeys or suffers a radar malfunction, etc. Even in the latter stages of a sweep or bracket option the fighters should not be so far apart that they cannot rejoin expeditiously for defensive purposes or a bugout. When the fighters are arranged in trail (sweep option), a 90° turn in either direction by the leader allows the trailer to rejoin in spread. Following a bracket attack the fighters should pass fairly close to each other with high track-crossing angles. In this case nose-to-nose turns by both fighters put them back abeam.

There are some problems with the option, however. It places a lot of responsibility on the wingman to select the best option for the tactical situation and position accordingly. The bracket option, particularly, requires the kind of timing that is gained only through extensive training. Because of the many options available to the wingman, the fighter leader may enter a fight without sight of his teammate or even knowledge of his position, especially in limited-comm conditions. The wide offensive splits and positioning of the sweep and bracket options gain tactical advantage at the expense of defensive mutual support. In addition, the FQ or stern-conversion geometry allows greater enemy raid penetration than head-on or collision geometry. The intercept mechanics for this geometry are also more difficult and complex, and they are more vulnerable to bogey jinks at long range. Late bogey jinks tend to confuse the attack geometry and timing, but an attack might still be salvaged by fancy fighter footwork, provided the jink can be detected quickly.

Break-Away

> With an inferior weapon system you cannot fight a superior one. You can have surprise success but not success for a long time.
>
> Lt. General Adolph Galland, Luftwaffe

Description

In the game of air combat, the break-away is what might be called a "stunt" or a "trick" tactic. Its purpose is to deceive and confuse enemy fighter and GCI radars, to degrade the bogey's situational awareness at the merge, and to get at least one fighter into the merge unobserved. One variation of this tactic is depicted in Figure 10-14.

At time "1" the fighters are in a fairly tight formation so that, on the enemy's airborne and GCI radars, they appear as only one target outside visual range of the bogeys. The maximum allowable separation may be only a few feet, or it may be many hundreds of feet, depending on the characteristics of the specific threat radars. This tactic should induce some doubt in the enemy as to just how many fighters they will be engaging.

Once the bogeys are detected, the fighters turn as necessary to establish collision geometry. If there is sufficient range, either head-on or FQ intercept techniques may be employed instead. At time "2" the fighters are still outside the bogeys' visual range, but they are approaching the final stages of the intercept, where the enemy can be expected to be taking radar locks for their attack. This typically occurs by the time the fighters are within one minute to intercept, but the timing can vary widely. The fighters'

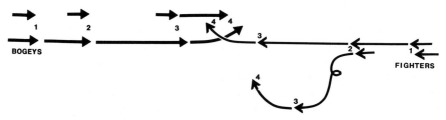

Figure 10-14. The Break-Away

RWR equipment may be of assistance in determining when the bogeys are locked.

At this point the fighter wingman rolls over and pulls hard into a split-S until the aircraft is pointing vertically downward. When the bogeys are equipped with Doppler-type radar systems, this maneuver should place the enemy at 90° to the wingman's aircraft so quickly that the aircraft will be invisible to the bogeys' radar before fighter separation is wide enough to allow both aircraft to be displayed separately. By the time the wingman pulls out of his dive, time "3," he will probably be out of the bogeys' radar scan volume. In addition, the bogeys' look-down angle caused by the wingman's dive will result in clutter problems for enemy pulse radar systems. A hard break-away is essential at time "2," especially against Doppler radars. If the fighters can be in the vicinity of corner speed at this point, a max-G break produces the 90° turn as quickly as possible with the least separation between fighters. Chaff deployment by the wingman just as he approaches the vertical attitude is also very effective against pulse radars, and can even produce false targets on a Doppler radar in high-wind conditions. Paradoxically, the better the enemy's radar performs against targets with a beam aspect, the more vulnerable it is to chaff. Chaff is also useful in confusing enemy GCI controllers, who now probably detect a veritable explosion of targets and may have insufficient time remaining to determine which are real fighters. When it is performed at medium altitudes, the wingman's split-S may also place him too low for the enemy's GCI coverage.

Once his aircraft is purely vertical the wingman does a 180° roll and a wings-level pull-out on the original collision heading at high speed. At this point he should regain visual contact with the leader, who should now be slightly ahead and very much higher, and if time permits he can gain radar contact with the bogeys. The leader should resist changing heading between the wingman's break and his "visual" call, since the wingman may never regain sight if he does. If a heading change must be made, the new course should be relayed to the wingman immediately.

Approaching the merge the leader should call ranges frequently so the wingman can time his pull-up so he is pointing at the leader at the pass. The wingman is essentially performing a vertical hook, so the leader desires a close pass with the bogeys to help the wingman (shooter) get a tally. In this case the leader should try to pass slightly above the bogeys, possibly in a climb, to draw attention away from the low shooter, and possibly tempt the bogey into a pull-up right in front of the hooker.

Advantages and Disadvantages

When it works, this tactic will cause lots of laughing and scratching back at the bar; but when it doesn't, there will no doubt be much incredulous head shaking. The break-away throws caution to the winds for the advantages of deception and surprise. The only positive defensive point that can be made in its favor is the adage "A good offense is the best defense." The fighters are in a poor defensive posture throughout the intercept. They are usually too close for good mutual support before the break-away, and the low, trailing wingman is vulnerable after the split. A well-controlled situation is a prerequisite for this tactic, since an unexpected attack by enemy fighters before the break-away would probably be disastrous.

> As a fighter pilot I knew from my own experiences how decisive surprise and luck can be for a success, which in the long run only comes to the one who combines daring with cool thinking.
>
> Lt. General Adolph Galland, Luftwaffe

The situations in which the advantages outweigh the risks of this tactic include a permissive environment in which the enemy's radar system and aircraft performance are decidedly superior to those of the friendly fighters. When facing a definite mismatch, good execution of sound tactics may not be enough. In boxing terminology, "A good big man will beat a good little man most of the time." In this case a good offense may be the *only* defense, and some exotic stunts may be justified if they result in enemy confusion and degraded awareness at the pass. Obviously, however, such tactics require considerable pilot training and a high level of proficiency before they can be relied on in combat; even then they cannot be expected to work as a steady diet, since the enemy will soon figure them out.

There are many variations on the break-away tactic, but most begin with an initial close formation and employ a radical formation change at close range to sow confusion among the enemy. As with most hook and bracket-type attacks, the break-away is not recommended against an enemy in a significant trail formation.

Cross-Block

Description

The cross-block, also called the weave, is another stunt tactic that is often successful against superior fighters that have a propensity for independent attacks. Figure 10-15 shows this tactic.

At time "1" the fighters and bogeys detect each other about head-on, and the bogeys commence a pincer attack in an attempt to bracket the fighters. The fighter pilots detect this move and continue straight ahead in combat spread until they reach a point at which the bogeys can be expected to have individual radar locks on the fighters on their respective sides of the formation for the terminal phase of attack. Once again, this usually occurs by one minute to go in the intercept, and the fighters' RWR gear may provide further clues.

At this point, time "2," the fighter pilots also take individual locks, but on the bogey on the opposite side of the enemy formation. This process is known as "cross-locking." The fighters then turn toward each other, crossing flight paths, in an effort to get outside the bogey each has locked, time "3." If the bogeys continue their intercepts on their originally intended victims, they too can be expected to turn inward in response to the fighters' maneuvers. The geometry of the situation tends to draw the bogeys together as they approach the merge (time "4"), making it easier for each fighter pilot to tally both bogeys, and dragging each bogey in front of

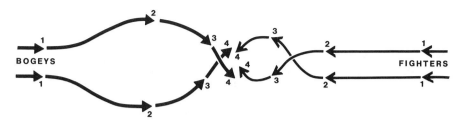

Figure 10-15. The Cross-Block

an unseen fighter. Each fighter should have an unobserved belly-side or RQ shot on its target while meeting the other bogey nearly head-on. The bogeys, on the other hand, are bracketed at the pass; neither enemy pilot is likely to have sight of his wingman, and each probably does have a tally on one fighter—but not the fighter posing the greater threat. Obviously this is a very favorable situation for the friendly fighters!

Advantages and Disadvantages

The cross-block, like most other stunt tactics, is a complex intercept requiring highly proficient aircrews and a good deal of luck. In addition, this procedure depends on two operable radars. Offensively the cross-block can be very effective against a pincer attack. Defensively it is not as poor as many other tactics. The fighters can stay in a defensive spread formation until late in the intercept, and although they are essentially independent during the terminal phase of the maneuver, they usually are not so far separated that they are unable to offer mutual support quickly if it is needed. A serious problem can occur, however, if one fighter loses contact with its bogey in the terminal phase. If this happens, the other pilot should continue his intercept while the pilot without contact attempts to regain a visual cover position for his wingman.

The cross-block offers an effective offensive response to a pincer attack by superior bogeys, even in a hostile environment. With superior fighters in a more controlled environment the pincer isolation tactic shown in Figure 10-9 might be a preferable alternative, since dealing with one bogey at a time is generally less hazardous. A simpler, more defensive option might be a single-side offset to either side in an attempt to get outside the enemy's bracket. This alternative, however, offers little offensive potential and likely will not be highly effective against superior bogeys; but it can be executed with only one radar.

Division Intercepts

As stated previously, any of the intercept tactics described so far in this chapter for use by one or two fighters can be employed by greater numbers. Some major advantages are provided by more fighters, including improved mutual support for fighters in trail formations and for fighters using intercepts that rely on wide offensive splits. This can allow the fighters to choose more offensive tactics without incurring unacceptable degradation

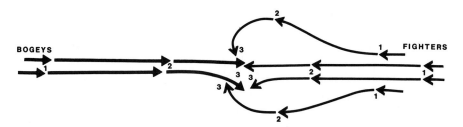

Figure 10-16. Double Lead-Around or Pincer and Trail

of defensive potential. Figures 10-16 and 10-17 are examples of lead-around and pincer attacks adapted to divisions of four fighters.

Visual Considerations in Air Combat

> One of the secrets of air fighting was to see the other man first. Seeing airplanes from great distances was a question of experience and training, of knowing where to look and what to look for. Experienced pilots always saw more than the newcomers, because the latter were more concerned with flying than fighting. . . . The novice had little idea of the situation, because his brain was bewildered by the shock and ferocity of the fight.
>
> Air Vice-Marshal J. E. "Johnnie" Johnson, RAF

The importance of surprise in air combat is illustrated by the fact that about nine out of ten air-to-air victims are not aware of their imminent danger until they are actually fired on. It stands to reason, then, that considerable thought and planning should be devoted to achieving and maintaining sight of the enemy in a visual air combat arena and, conversely, to avoiding visual detection by the opponents. Some attention has been devoted to this topic throughout this book. This section re-emphasizes some of the aforementioned techniques for maintaining and avoiding visual contact and introduces a few others. Although they are presented here in the context of radar intercepts, most of these considerations and techniques are equally relevant to all phases of air combat.

The visual scan is the system used by a fighter pilot to search for and find other aircraft. The sky can be an amazingly big place, and airplanes incredibly small and elusive targets. A fighter pilot just cannot expect to look out and see enemy aircraft at useful distances consistently without a great deal of training, practice, and discipline. In addition, although bogeys are probably the most important things he can see, the fighter pilot has other visual responsibilities, such as keeping track of wingmen, navigating, monitoring aircraft performance, etc. To accomplish all these tasks effectively requires a method or scan pattern.

> It is always the one you don't see that gets you.
>
> Major Thomas B. "Tommy" McGuire, USAAF

First of all, these tasks must be made as simple as possible, so that they can be accomplished quickly and efficiently. The spacing and arrangement of fighters in defensive formations should be such that each pilot can comfortably keep sight of his wingmen and their vulnerable areas. If a wingman is too far away or is arranged high in the sun, maintaining visual contact can take too great a percentage of the pilot's available scanning time, detracting from his lookout. When a high, bright sun is a significant factor, the highest element of a defensive formation should normally be positioned down-sun (i.e., on the side of the formation away from the sun).

The pilot's flight equipment and the aircraft design and maintenance are also important factors. A pilot's flight clothing should be as lightweight and nonrestricting as possible so that movement in the cockpit is not hindered. It is often necessary to turn almost completely around in the seat in either direction to look directly behind, no easy task in a full pressure suit. Restraining straps must also be designed and adjusted to allow this freedom of movement.

The Japanese early in World War II considered this cockpit freedom so important that their fighter pilots generally did not even wear parachutes. Another factor in this personal decision was the fact that they generally fought over enemy territory, and their code of *Bushido* (the *Samurai* code) did not permit them to be captured. This policy was self-defeating, however, since, in combination with the general lack of armor protection and self-sealing fuel tanks, it led to high attrition of experienced pilots and caused great problems for the Japanese later in the war.

Flight controls should be designed for use by either hand, so the pilot can rotate his body completely in either direction and still fly the airplane. The helmet is one of the pilot's most critical flight-gear items. It must be as lightweight as possible, otherwise it can get pretty unwieldy and be hard on the neck under 9 Gs. Neither should it restrict the pilot's vision. This means no part of the helmet should be visible to the pilot wearing it. It must also be fitted and secured so that it doesn't rotate out of place under high G or with pilot movement. The helmet should be fitted with a dark visor that can be quickly flipped into position if it becomes necessary for the pilot to follow a bogey very near the sun. In general, however, visors should not be used in combat, since anything between the pilot's eyes and the bogey, even a "clear" visor, degrades vision to some extent. Dark visors

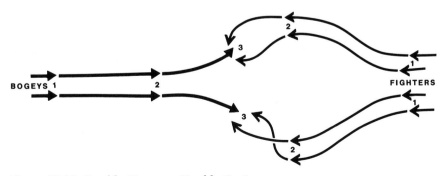

Figure 10-17. Double Pincer or Double Option

also have the effect of reducing the pilot's visual depth of field. All flight gear, and anything else inside the cockpit, should be dark colored and nonreflective. Otherwise, they will cast light-colored images on the canopy, severely restricting visibility. Canopies must be kept spotless and free of scratches. Touching a canopy is a hanging offense. A hard helmet should be covered with some soft material to avoid canopy scratches.

> Whenever you're over the lines you have to keep twisting your neck in all directions every minute, or you're sure to be surprised.
> Captain Edward V. "Eddie" Rickenbacker, USAS

Rear-view mirrors have been used on many fighters for some time now, generally with good success. When properly placed they can significantly expand the pilots' rearward field of view. This is the purpose to which they should be put, however; they should not be used as an excuse for not turning the entire head and body to cover those areas that can be seen without the aid of the mirrors. Mirror placement is quite important; mirrors must be located outside the canopy or their effectiveness will be nullified by canopy glare and reflections. Aircraft designers resist this placement because external mirrors mess up the nice, clean lines of the aircraft and increase drag. This is the same mentality that results in fighters being designed with low-drag canopies faired into the fuselage rather than with bubble-type canopies, which provide a much better field of view.

Monitoring aircraft performance can also be facilitated by design. At the very least, airspeed and altitude instruments should be large, easy to interpret, and located as high as possible in the cockpit. A better idea is to display this and other critical information on some sort of "head-up display" (HUD) that is focused at infinity, so that the pilot is not required to look inside the cockpit at critical moments. Coming inside means refocusing and adjusting to cockpit lighting conditions, and then refocusing and readjusting when returning the scan to the outside. HUDs are usually incorporated in the fighter's gunsight, but they can also be part of the pilot's helmet, with the display projected on the visor. Each method has limitations: the pilot must be looking forward to use the gunsight, and he requires a visor for the helmet unit.

Since much of a fighter's combat time is likely to be spent at high G, the effect of this acceleration on the pilot's vision is an important consideration. As G increases the heart must work against higher gravity forces to pump blood to the pilot's head. The greater the height of the pilot's head above the level of his heart, the lower the blood pressure to his eyes and brain will be under these conditions. Under protracted high-G conditions, blood tends to pool in the pilot's lower extremities and abdomen area, denying an adequate blood supply to the head, which affects both vision and brain function. The first noticeable effect is normally "tunnel vision," which is a gradual reduction of the pilot's field of peripheral vision down to a very few degrees directly along his line of sight. Eventually this "tunnel" can close completely, totally blinding the pilot in what is called a "gray-out." This condition is often accompanied by the "seeing of stars." Under these conditions, the pilot will see nothing until G is relaxed, but he is still fully conscious and aware of what is happening to him, and he can still fly the airplane by feel. If the G is maintained, however, or if load factor is increased still further, reduced blood pressure to the brain will eventually result in "blackout," or total loss of consciousness, during which the pilot loses complete control and is unaware of his condition. Generally at this point the pilot collapses and relaxes completely, releasing the aircraft to return to a low-G condition, which allows him to recover consciousness. Recovery from a blackout can be a fairly slow process, during which the pilot may be disoriented, suffer from convulsions, and even be unaware that he is in an aircraft for some time after vision returns. Obviously this is a very unhealthy condition for a pilot, particularly in combat.

G tolerance is an individual thing, heavily dependent on the pilot's physical health and fitness, height, fatigue, smoking habits, drug intake, etc. Most fighter pilots, with training, can learn to sustain about 5 Gs for a considerable time without ill effects. In addition to training shorter fighter pilots (a personal favorite), there are certain techniques and equipment which can increase G tolerance. In the area of equipment, the G suit is the most common. This is usually a trouserlike garment that incorporates inflatable bladders in the abdominal area and along the legs. These bladders are usually inflated by high-pressure air from the aircraft by an automatic valve in proportion to the G level at any moment. The G suit squeezes the pilot's lower extremities, and this tends to restrict the pooling of blood in these areas, thereby leaving more blood available for the upper body and head. A properly fitted G suit can typically increase a pilot's tolerance by about 1 G. Semireclining seats are another anti-G device that has recently come into vogue (notably in the General Dynamics F-16 fighter). These are also apparently effective to some degree by reducing the vertical heart-to-head distance and raising the legs. Someday a prone pilot position (lying either on his back or on his stomach) may prove to be the answer to high-G tolerance in fighters, if the problems of lookout in all directions under G can be solved.

Techniques that the pilot can use to increase G tolerance include a constant or repetitive straining or "grunting" routine that tenses the body, increasing blood pressure and reducing blood pooling in the abdomen. Another useful technique is to lean sharply forward in the seat against the full extension of the shoulder harness. If the harness restraint system allows, this method can reduce heart-head elevation distance much like a reclining seat. Another practice that can aid in G tolerance is the use of a moderate G-increase rate when beginning turns. Snapping on the G very rapidly, aside from being conducive to aircraft overstresses, may not allow the pilot or other crew members to tense their bodies in anticipation of the increased G loads. Lack of preparation can reduce G tolerance, result in awkward body positions (i.e., faces buried in laps, etc.), or even cause injuries.

Visual Scan Techniques

The best technique a pilot can use in searching for enemy aircraft is the object of considerable dispute. Some schools teach that the sky should be divided into many small segments, say 30° by 30° sectors, and each sector should be searched thoroughly for several seconds to ensure it is clear of targets before shifting to the next sector, and so on. Other schools suggest that the eyes should be moved constantly, never being allowed to stop unless something requires closer investigation. As might be anticipated, each of these techniques has strong and weak points.

The brain cannot interpret visual images when the eyes are moving. When a person scans a wide area quickly, the eyes actually move in many small jerks, pausing repeatedly for a fraction of a second to allow the brain to interpret what is seen. In order to search a sector as thoroughly as possible, the eyes must be focused at the proper distance. Unfortunately, the eye does not provide us with a reliable indication of focal distance. This distance can only be determined by estimating the range to an object in focus. When the eyes have nothing on which to focus, such as when a person is staring into blue sky, they tend to focus at just a few feet away. This focal range is closer to the canopy than to the bogey, so spots, smudges, and scratches on this surface tend to attract the focus of the eyes.

> [Inexperienced] pilots are really blind in the air for the first couple of months.
> Colonel Erich "Bubi" Hartmann, GAF

The problem of focus can seriously degrade visual effectiveness in the air. The usual technique is to focus on a distant object, such as a cloud or a surface feature on the horizon, and then quickly shift the scan to the area of interest. The eyes can usually be held in focus at long range in this manner for a few seconds before the procedure must be repeated. Experienced pilots normally do this continuously and even subconsciously as they shift their scan from place to place. Their lack of a technique for focusing at a distance is probably the primary reason inexperienced pilots see very little in the air.

> Look around—what you see won't hurt you. Keep your head out and use it.
> Captain Thomas J. "Tommy" Lynch, USAAF

In daylight, maximum visual acuity is found in the very center of the scan, in an area that covers only a fraction of a degree of arc around the midpoint. Any object outside this very small central area is generally detected by peripheral vision only if it contrasts markedly with the background, is very large, or shows relative motion. (It is primarily motion that catches the attention of peripheral vision.) This explains the value of a radar LOS indication for obtaining the earliest possible tally on a bogey. The LOS cue normally indicates the position of the bogey, quite often in relation to some point on the gunsight, usually within less than 1° of its actual position. The pilot can then search carefully near the indicated point in space (sometimes called "spot scanning"), generally with the aid of gunsight images focused at infinity to help in finding and holding proper focal range, and can detect very distant and low-contrast targets.

One peek is worth a thousand [radar] sweeps.

Unknown

In some cases pilots have been provided with telescopic devices to allow more distant visual acquisition and VID of airborne targets. Some means of extending VID range is often required if full use is to be made of the head-on capability of all-aspect missiles. Such devices can be as simple as a hand-held telescope or binoculars, or as exotic as a high-powered video telescope slaved to the fighter radar's LOS. In general, even the simpler devices can be effective, but hand-held equipment presents problems of loose gear flying around in cockpits, and hands that are busy performing other required functions in a complex cockpit may not be available for its operation. Usually a better solution is to fasten these devices securely to the aircraft and point them straight ahead. The radar can then be used to point the aircraft, and the telescope, directly at an unidentified target for closer examination. Obviously the telescope's field of view must be compatible with the accuracy of the radar LOS-indicating system.

He who sees first, lives longest.

Unknown

The smallness of the area of maximum visual acuity limits the effectiveness of detailed sector search unless the target's LOS can be limited substantially. It can take several seconds to scan thoroughly an area extending even 1° about a given point. Therefore, dividing the entire world into sectors for consecutive detailed inspection becomes ludicrous. Even if each individual search was limited to only one second, it would literally take all day to complete even one cycle of this process. Based on such realities, it just isn't practical to rely on a detailed sector-search scan technique to produce acceptable results for defensive purposes. Offensively, however, careful inspection of narrow sectors is usually the method that yields tallyhos of the longest range.

The alternative is to devise a scan technique based on peripheral vision, which allows coverage of a very large area in a relatively short time. This method involves moving the eyes (and the head) back and forth across the entire field of view at a fairly rapid rate. Although the head may appear to move smoothly during these sweeps, the eyes will actually make rapid jerks of several degrees at a time, and a fairly large area can be searched by peripheral vision at each pause. This technique is somewhat analogous to speed-reading methods, as opposed to focusing on individual words on a printed page. The actual speed of the scan is dependent on proficiency, as the eyes must be trained to make these movements faster for greater scan speed. If the eyes are not allowed to pause repeatedly, very little will be seen.

There should be a regular pattern to these visual sweeps; both above and below the horizon and from forward to aft visibility limits on both sides of the aircraft should be searched. These visibility limits can usually be extended by rolling, turning, or skidding the aircraft in conjunction with the scan pattern. The scan should be allowed to sweep distant objects periodically (every few seconds) to provide adjustment of focal range.

Likely threat sectors should be limited when practical, possibly by flying very high or low, or by offsetting the threat sector to one side, and the most threatening area should receive the most attention. No sector, however, should be completely ignored for extended periods. Flying in pairs allows each pilot to concentrate his search toward his wingman, and multi-crew fighters can divide visual search areas of responsibility for maximum efficiency.

> What you find with your eyes is the movement, because the country is quiet. Then, all at once you see—movement; an aircraft.
>   Colonel Erich "Bubi" Hartmann, GAF

Another useful technique is to move the head forward and back, and from side to side during the scan process. This helps clear areas hidden behind canopy rails, etc., and also aids in reducing the distraction of canopy scratches, bugs, and spots. Anything on a canopy will appear to move opposite to the direction of head movement, and the brain can use this motion to "filter out" these objects from external targets, which do not react to pilot head movement. There are two categories of fighter pilots: those who have performed, and those who someday will perform, a magnificent defensive break turn toward a bug on the canopy.

Although use of peripheral vision as the primary scanning mode does not generally result in tallyhos as distant as those provided by the sector-search method, the chances of seeing the bogey at all are greatly enhanced, and defensively this is the more important objective.

Camouflage

The value of camouflage as a means of hiding a military target is well recognized. Fighters, however, have a particular problem when camouflage is considered. Their mission makes it likely that they will be viewed from any direction: from above with a surface background, or from below with a blue-sky background. Additionally, since the range of aircraft is so great, surface coloration is likely to vary widely on each mission. The maneuvering requirements for fighters add to the problem, since from any direction the enemy might just as easily be presented with top, side, or bottom views of the aircraft as it rolls and turns in different planes.

Lighting conditions have a dramatic effect on the appearance of an aircraft. In front-lighted situations (viewed object fully illuminated) the actual shade and color of the aircraft are apparent, but when it is back lighted (viewed object in shadow) the presented surface appears to be a shade of gray and darker than its actual color. Since airplanes are generally very angular machines, the many appendages cast shadows on various parts of the aircraft, and these shadows move around as the fighter banks and turns. Regardless of whether an aircraft is up-sun or down-sun from the viewer, large portions of its body may appear to be in shadow, depending on its heading or pitch and bank attitudes. The greatest portions of the aircraft will be in shadow, and therefore will appear darker than they actually are, whenever the viewer and the sun are on opposite sides of the aircraft's nose (vertically or horizontally) or the plane of its wings. In general, these shadow patterns can change very rapidly and would be very difficult to predict accurately under real-time operational conditions, but if a camouflage scheme is to be effective, it must make allowance for these shadow effects.

One means of achieving this objective is to use fairly light colors overall, since a large portion of the aircraft is likely to appear darker anyway because of shadows. If the remainder of the surface is a lighter color, there is greater chance that either the light or the dark portions will blend well with the background at a given instant, which reduces the apparent size of the aircraft. If the entire aircraft is a darker shade it may be very difficult to see against a dark background, but it will stick out like a sore thumb when it is viewed against lighter areas. Lighter colors overall tend to offer a better compromise.

The actual color is not nearly as important as the shade. Bright colors should be avoided, however, since they rarely occur in nature and tend to attract attention. Dull, flat, pastel grays, blues, tans, and greens, although not highly inspirational, are much more effective for camouflage purposes. The actual colors are usually chosen to blend with the normal surface tones for better effect while the aircraft is on the ground or at low altitudes. High-gloss paint and shiny bare metal have no place on combat aircraft because of their tendency to reflect sun flashes. The actual colors chosen are not so important for two reasons. First, a large portion of the aircraft is likely to be in shadow and appear gray regardless of its real color. Second, colors cannot be distinguished at great distances. Even with the rather large size of many of today's fighters, it is usually impossible to distinguish between aircraft painted in muted pastel colors of the same reflectance (shade) at distances greater than two or three miles under optimum lighting and aspect conditions. (This is not very far in today's terms, since fighter turn diameters may exceed one mile, and even "short-range" missiles can be lethal from several miles.) Very bright colors, however, might be recognizable under the same conditions at distances greater than ten miles. The general rule is to avoid the use of colors that are distinguishable at normal visual ranges.

> Weapons should be hardy rather than decorative.
>
> Miyamoto Musashi

The most effective camouflage technique for fighter aircraft seems to involve the use of two or three different shades of paint of either the same or different colors (but all flat, light pastels). The camouflage scheme should be designed so that each view of the aircraft is composed of approximately equal percentages of each shade. The intent of this method is for one of the various shades to blend well with a given background, making that portion of the aircraft difficult to see and effectively reducing the apparent size of the fighter. A greater variety of paint shades increases the probability that one will blend well with the background but reduces the percentage of total area covered by each shade, and therefore the effect of blending is also reduced. This factor leads to a tradeoff in determining the optimum number of shades. Generally speaking, two shades seem to be best for smaller fighters, since a relatively large apparent-size reduction is necessary to make a substantial difference in likely visual range. Three shades may be better for larger fighters, as even a small percentage reduction in the apparent size of these aircraft can decrease visual range a great amount in real terms.

The camouflage pattern should appear to be random, much like shadows cutting across various parts of the aircraft, to break up the recognizable shape of the fighter. Whether straight lines or curves are used does not seem to make a great deal of difference.

Aside from making the aircraft harder to see, there is another important purpose of camouflage for a fighter, namely, disguising its attitude and maneuver. For this reason there should be no significant variation in the camouflage patterns or colors on the top and bottom of the aircraft. On fairly large fighters, even painting a mock canopy on the belly and simulated weapons rails on the top of the wings (to simulate whatever would be carried in a combat situation) can be extremely effective. Such camouflage patterns make it difficult to determine whether the fighter is turning toward or away from the enemy at medium ranges. The direction of this turn may be critical to the enemy's maneuver selection and also to his weapons envelope (is this a forward- or rear-hemisphere shot?). A good paint job can cause the enemy a few valuable seconds of confusion until relative motion clears up the ambiguity, and any delay or confusion in combat can be crucial.

The fighter pilot should be aware of his paint scheme and try to make best use of it during an intercept. Tactical advantage, however, must not be sacrificed for environmental considerations, as the enemy may detect the attack anyway and place the fighter at a severe disadvantage. The importance of avoiding light-colored clouds that could silhouette the fighter has been discussed before. An aircraft of essentially any color when viewed against a cloud background will stand out like a bug on a sheet. Approaching from out of the sun is also a well-known tactic from the earliest days, since a bright, high sun tends to restrict the enemy's vision. Other factors to consider are the shades (lightness or darkness) of the surface and sky backgrounds. Generally the pilot should look for a background that matches the average shade of his aircraft most closely. When in doubt, the darker background is usually better because of the darkening effects of shadows on the aircraft. Particularly when approaching from high or on the sun side, the fighter is more likely to appear much darker than when it is low or down-sun, where its presented surfaces are more likely to be fully illuminated and its real colors more prominent. It should also be recognized that the shade of the sky usually darkens looking upward from the horizon. Approaching a target at co-altitude is usually not a good plan, since pilots tend to spend most of their time looking level. In addition, the lighter background near the horizon often provides better conditions for visual detection, much like clouds. The pilot should be especially cautious about approaching out of a low sun that lacks brilliance. The combination of a light pastel background and the dark shadows on the back-lit fighter, with no visual degradation as with a bright sun, can lead to 30-mile tallys. Varied backgrounds, such as scattered clouds against a dark surface, or a variegated landscape, are often good for hiding against, since a high-contrast object is less noticeable with them. About the only uniform background that makes for a good approach is clear blue sky, since this presents the enemy with a focusing problem. Of course, whenever practical, the fighter's nose can be pointed directly toward the bogey to present the smallest possible profile view when the fighter is within visual range. Alternatively, collision-course intercept geometry can be used to reduce relative motion with the target, making detection by the enemy's peripheral vision less likely.

One condition that can effectively destroy the effects of even the best camouflage is low-level flight over a light-colored homogeneous surface on a sunny day. Even an aircraft as high as 2,000 or 3,000 ft may leave a nice black shadow on such a surface to attract the enemy's attention. Once alerted, the enemy can use spot-scanning techniques to pick up the actual aircraft in the near vicinity of the shadow. Darker or variegated surfaces generally do not present this problem. If he is forced to fly under these conditions, however, the pilot should carefully watch the surface for hostile shadows. It works both ways. This can be a useful defensive technique.

Other visual considerations in the approach are contrails and engine smoke. Little needs to be said about the effect of contrails on visual detection range, since probably everyone has seen airliners a hundred miles away. The contrail level simply must be avoided. Smoke can also be a very serious problem, as heavy smoke trails can be seen for twenty to thirty miles under some conditions, especially against light backgrounds. In addition to selecting a darker background and engine operating conditions that minimize smoke (discussed in a previous chapter), avoiding collision-course intercept geometry can also help. A fighter on a collision course tends to remain in one spot in the sky when viewed by the enemy, so the smoke trail appears to be concentrated behind the fighter and becomes darker and more noticeable. An early displacement turn away from the bogey's flight path, and stern-conversion geometry, can make the trail appear thinner and make it more difficult to see against lighter backgrounds.

Summary

The purpose for presenting many sample intercepts here is to acquaint the tactician with the various intercept concepts currently in use and to provide a selection of tactics from which to choose in a given tactical scenario. The first quality of any intercept tactic which must be considered is controllability: the reasonable assurance that the intercept can be completed in some manner. The factors involved here are both geometry and complexity. Stern-conversion and FQ intercepts, for instance, may be missed altogether if the bogey jinks away. The stern conversion is also generally more difficult to perform effectively than some others, and it may require a speed advantage over the target. Probably the easiest intercept to run is a pure-pursuit course, where the fighter simply holds the target on the nose. Unfortunately this technique provides little control over intercept geometry. When it is started near the bogey's flight path, pure pursuit usually results in a very high angle-off at the intercept with little fighter advantage. When it is begun with lots of target aspect, it generally ends in a tail chase, possibly well out of firing range. A pure-collision intercept is also fairly simple, offers minimum raid penetration, and probably provides the best chance of completing the intercept. Again, however, the geometry may not be optimum for a VID or weapons employment. The choices of intercept tactics should be limited by the capabilities of the aircrews, weapons systems, and air controllers. If proficiency is not high enough to ensure completion of a stern conversion, for instance, then tactics that employ simpler techniques, such as pure-collision geometry, should be chosen.

Probably the next most important factor to consider in selection of intercept tactics for use against fighters, or in a hostile environment, is defensive potential. Formation, separation, and flexibility are the keys to defensive potential. Many tactics require extended portions of the intercept to be run in trail formation or with very wide, offensive splits. Such conditions are not conducive to defensive mutual support. Flexibility becomes important when something unexpected happens, such as a radical bogey jink, attack by an undetected enemy, or perhaps the leader's radar shooting craps late in the intercept. A flexible tactic permits ease of adjustment to such circumstances by quick maneuvering, immediate defensive support, lead changes, etc. Flexibility is degraded by great distances between fighters, and particularly by nose-tail separation. Tactics that require an early shift into such configurations may be asking for trouble, particularly in poorly controlled situations.

The third most important factor in selection of intercept tactics is offensive potential. When the fighters are intercepting bombers or are in a permissive scenario, this factor may even be more critical than defensive potential. Offensive potential implies that the fighters will have a tactical advantage over the enemy at the completion of the intercept. This generally means arriving in a firing envelope before the enemy does, or at least being closer to this firing position than the enemy. Relative weapons capabilities are therefore essential to evaluating the offensive potential of any intercept. A head-on approach is offensive if the fighters have all-aspect weapons and the enemy does not. A stern conversion is offensive in most cases. The rules of engagement must also be considered, especially the requirement for a VID. Optimum offensive capability provides for the earliest possible VID, which generally implies some displacement from the bogey's flight path to generate a planform or profile view for enhanced recognition. Offensive potential is further improved if the VID occurs in the fighter's weapons envelope. Another desirable offensive feature is surprise: increased probability of an unseen attack by one or more fighters.

Unfortunately, there is usually a tradeoff between offensive and defensive potential, since the offense is normally enhanced by large splits, trail formations, etc. The general rule is to select the most offensive tactic available within the capabilities of the fighter crews which allows what is considered to be adequate defensive potential under the tactical conditions at the time. Obviously there is a considerable amount of judgment, experience, and tactical knowledge involved here. Usually two or three different intercepts are chosen, each of which is considered optimal in one likely combat scenario, and these tactics are practiced constantly under the most realistic conditions possible to develop and maintain proficiency. Then, when the pilots get their chance for real, they select the most appropriate tactic and go for it.

Appendix

Fighter Performance

Performance means initiative—the most valuable moral and practical asset in any form of war.

Major Sholto Douglas, RAF

The purpose of this Appendix is to provide a basic understanding of the fundamentals of aircraft performance which allow one fighter to maneuver relative to another and gain a position advantage in air combat. Although the word *performance* encompasses every aspect of aircraft operation, certain capabilities are more germane than others to the subject of air combat maneuvering and fighter tactics. These aircraft maneuvers (i.e., turns, accelerations, climbs, etc.) are covered here in sufficient depth to familiarize the reader with their application to the science of air combat and with the techniques by which their performance is optimized. Other aspects of aircraft performance, such as takeoff, landing, range, and endurance, although possibly critical to the success of any given fighter mission, are more concerned with how the fighter gets to and from the combat arena than with how it performs within that environment, and therefore they are not covered here.

Instantaneous Turn Performance

Turn performance is the ability of an aircraft to change the direction of its motion in flight. This direction is defined by the velocity vector, which may be visualized as an arrow pointing in the direction of aircraft motion and having a length proportional to the speed of that motion. *Maneuverability* is defined in this text as the ability of a fighter to change the direction of its velocity vector. The terms *maneuverability* and *turn performance*, therefore, may be considered synonymous.

[The Luftwaffe High Command] were stuck on the idea that maneuverability in banking was primarily the determining factor in air combat. . . . They could not or simply would not see that for modern fighter aircraft the tight turn as a form of aerial combat represented the exception.

Lt. General Adolph Galland, Luftwaffe

Maximum-performance turns may be classified as one of two types: instantaneous or sustained. *Instantaneous* refers to the aircraft's maximum turn capabilities at any given moment under the existing flight conditions (e.g., speed and altitude). A particular capability may last for only an instant before flight conditions change, resulting in a change in instantaneous-turn capability. *Sustained* turns are those which the aircraft is able to maintain for an extended length of time under a given set of flight conditions. Sustained turns are discussed later in this Appendix.

Any turn may be measured in three ways. One convenient measure of aircraft turn performance is load factor (n), which is actually a component of the centrifugal acceleration generated by the turn. This acceleration is usually expressed in terms of Gs, with one G unit being the equivalent of the nominal acceleration of gravity, 32.2 ft/sec^2. Therefore, in a "3-G turn" the pilot would feel as though he weighed three times his normal weight. Turn rate (TR) is another important performance measure. This is the angular rate of change of the velocity vector, usually expressed in degrees/second, and in a level turn it would equate to the rate of change in the aircraft's course. Turn radius (R_T), the third important measure of turn performance, is generally expressed in feet or in miles.

> Tight turns were more a defensive than an offensive tactic and did not win air battles.
>
> Air Vice-Marshal J. E. "Johnnie" Johnson, RAF

Instantaneous turn performance is the product of the aerodynamic design of the fighter and its flight conditions. The lift-producing capacity of the aircraft is one of the primary factors in this performance. Lift (L) is the aerodynamic force generated by the aircraft perpendicular to its direction of motion (i.e., perpendicular to the relative wind). This force, most of which is usually produced by the wings, may also be visualized as a vector oriented perpendicular to both the velocity vector and the wings and having a length proportional to the amount of lift. The lift that can be produced by a given wing is dependent on the speed and altitude of the aircraft. Since the wing interacts with air to create lift, the density of the air is crucial. Air density decreases with altitude in the atmosphere, resulting in reduced lift capability. The faster a wing moves through the air, the greater the weight of air influenced during a given length of time will be, resulting in increased lift capability. The amount of lift which may be produced by a wing at a given altitude is roughly proportional to the square of aircraft velocity (V).

One of the most common and useful tools for the study of instantaneous turn performance is known as a "V-n diagram," a graphical plot of load-factor capability versus airspeed. Figure A-1 is an example of such a plot.

The V-n diagram for a fighter contains a great deal of information in a compact, efficient, and visually accessible form. The vertical axis is load factor in G units; when he is operating in the upper (positive) half of the

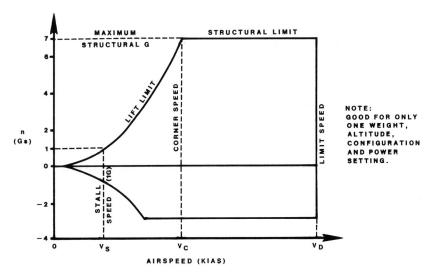

Figure A-1. V-n Diagram

diagram, the pilot is pushed down into his seat, and in the lower (negative) half, he is pulled away from his seat. The horizontal axis is airspeed, specifically in this example knots indicated airspeed (KIAS). This is the speed shown on the pilot's airspeed indicator and is based on the impact pressure of the air hitting the aircraft. This impact pressure, also known as dynamic pressure, is a function of air density as well as aircraft speed and may generally be equated to true airspeed only when the aircraft is operating at sea level. For a given indicated airspeed, true aircraft velocity increases with higher altitude.

The left side of the V-n diagram, labelled "lift limit," indicates the maximum load factor this fighter can generate at a specified airspeed. The curvature of this boundary primarily reflects the variation of lift capability with the square of the airspeed value. Along this line the aircraft is operating at maximum positive lift (pulling upward relative to the aircraft) in the upper half of the diagram and maximum negative lift (pushing downward relative to the aircraft) in the lower half. One important speed which may be identified along this boundary is the minimum 1-G flight speed, known as the unaccelerated stall speed (V_S). If airspeed is reduced below this value in level flight, lift may be lost suddenly (known as a "stall"), resulting in loss of control or at least loss of altitude. Conventional aircraft are physically unable to operate to the left of this aerodynamic boundary.

The upper and lower boundaries of the V-n diagram depict the structural-strength limits of the aircraft in the positive and negative directions, respectively. The more important of these boundaries is the upper (positive) one, which indicates maximum structural-G capability: in this case, +7 Gs. Greater load factor requires the wings to support more weight (in this instance, seven times the actual aircraft weight), so obviously there must be a limit. Usually this limit is independent of airspeed, as indicated by the straight lines. The maximum structural limit is specified by the manufacturer, based on calculations indicating that the aircraft structure will not break or deform permanently during its service life (also calculated by the manufacturer) at that load factor. This does not mean that the aircraft will disintegrate at 7.1 Gs, however, since there is usually a design safety factor of about 50 percent. This safety factor is included because of the likelihood of inadvertent overstresses, and also to increase the service life of the airframe, which is highly dependent on the weakening effects of metal fatigue.

The intersection of the positive aerodynamic boundary (lift limit) and structural limit defines a speed that is crucial in fighter performance. This is known appropriately as the corner speed (V_C) or maneuvering speed. At this airspeed a fighter attains maximum instantaneous turn performance (this is discussed more fully later). As the note accompanying this figure states, the boundaries of the V-n diagram are dependent on the fighter's weight, configuration, power, and altitude. As these parameters change, so will the V-n limits and therefore V_C, but the variations in corner speed are usually insignificant in air combat when V_C is expressed in terms of indicated airspeed.

The fourth boundary of the V-n diagram is the right side, which indicates the aircraft's maximum speed limit, or dive speed (V_D). This limit, set by the manufacturer, may be the result of structural, aircraft-control, engine-operation, or some other considerations. Here too there is usually a safety factor, but in this case probably on the order of 15 percent. With the usual exception of weight, those factors mentioned in the figure note can also have considerable influence on V_D. This boundary of the V-n diagram is a limitation, and it says nothing of the fighter's ability to attain such a speed. The aircraft may be able to exceed this speed in level flight, or V_D may not be attainable even in a power dive, depending on the particular design.

There are very well defined physical relationships between the parameters of turn performance: n, TR, R_T, and V. Figure A-2 graphically depicts these relationships for level (constant-altitude) turns. These charts are applicable to any aircraft. Note that for a given turn, if any two of the four variables are known, the other two are fixed. For example, if a fighter pulls 6 Gs at 400 knots, its turn radius will be about 2,400 ft and the corresponding rate of turn will be about 16°/sec. The airspeed scale in these charts is "true airspeed" in knots (KTAS), which may vary considerably from indicated airspeed, depending on altitude.

For fairly high load factors, the level turn relationships depicted in Figure A-2 may be simplified and expressed mathematically as:

$$R_T \sim V^2/n \tag{1}$$

and

$$TR \sim n/V. \tag{2}$$

From these proportionalities and Figure A-2 it can easily be seen that turn radius is minimized by high G at slow speed. Likewise, turn rate is

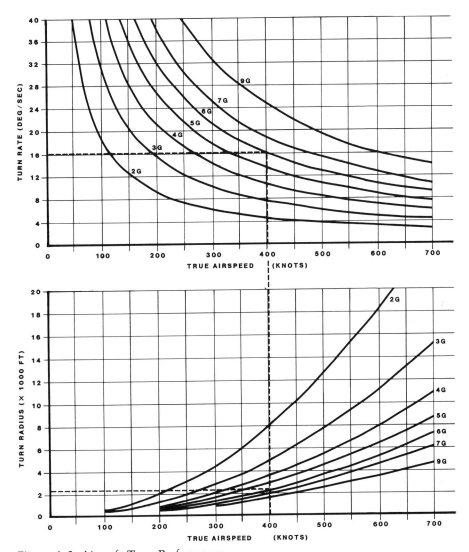

Figure A-2. Aircraft Turn Performance

maximized by high G at slow speed. Since the V-n diagram of a fighter specifies its G capabilities at various speeds, it is possible to determine turn-rate and -radius performance throughout the aircraft's speed range. Figure A-3 is a depiction of the way typical fighter turn-performance varies with airspeed.

In the case of turn rate, the rapid rise in G capability as speed increases above V_S (as shown by the lift boundary in the V-n diagram) leads to improved instantaneous-turn-rate performance, culminating at V_C. Since load factor is limited by structural considerations, however, further increases in airspeed above V_C result in reduced turn rate. Typical fighter turn-radius performance also is degraded (i.e., R_T increases) at speeds above V_C. Although absolute minimum instantaneous turn radius is usually found at speeds considerably below V_C, little change can be expected in R_T

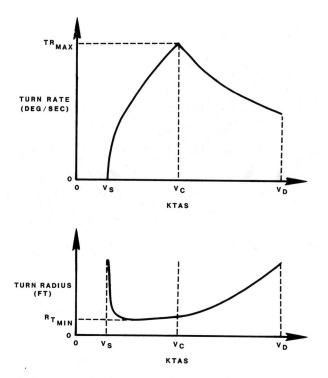

Figure A-3. Level Instantaneous Turn Rate and Radius
Performance

at any speed between V_C and slightly greater than V_S. Very slow airspeeds, however, cause dramatic rises in level turn radius. The importance of corner speed in optimizing instantaneous turn performance is highlighted in Figure A-3.

Altitude also has a significant influence on instantaneous turn performance. Figure A-4 depicts the variations for a typical jet fighter. At speeds below V_C, both rate and radius performance are usually degraded (i.e., larger radii and slower turn rates) with increasing altitude, because of reduced lift capability. At speeds above the corner, instantaneous turn performance is generally limited only by structural strength, and so is usually independent of altitude. Since the plots in Figure A-4 use true airspeed for the horizontal scale, V_C is seen to increase with altitude. As explained previously, however, V_C is normally nearly constant with altitude when it is expressed in terms of indicated airspeed.

Energy Maneuverability

Beware the lessons of a fighter pilot who would rather fly a slide rule than kick your ass!

Commander Ron "Mugs" McKeown, USN
Commander, U.S. Navy Fighter Weapons School
2 Victories, Vietnam Conflict

Energy comes in many forms: heat, light, electromagnetism, etc. In fighter performance the concern is primarily with mechanical energy,

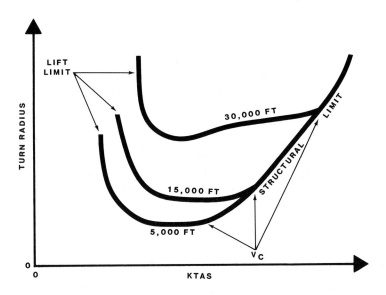

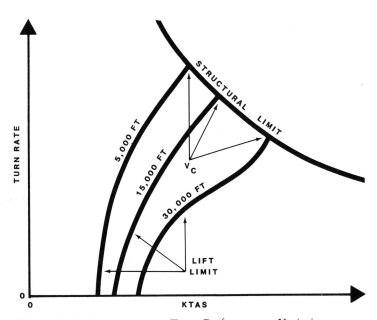

Figure A-4. Instantaneous Turn Performance Variation
with Altitude

which is classified as either kinetic or potential. "Kinetic energy" is the energy of speed. An aircraft in flight possesses kinetic energy that is proportional to its weight (or, more correctly, its mass) and speed. Under the influence of gravity, it can increase its speed, and its kinetic energy, by falling. Altitude, therefore, may be thought of as "potential energy," since it can be readily transformed into kinetic energy. Potential energy is proportional to the weight of the aircraft and the distance through which it may fall. In the case of airplanes, any combination of speed and altitude may be described by an "energy state." In comparing the energy states of two different fighters it is convenient to eliminate aircraft weight from the energy-state calculations to arrive at a better picture of relative speeds and altitudes. The result is a quantity known as "specific energy" (E_S). E_S is expressed mathematically as:

$$E_S \text{ (ft)} = H + V^2/2g, \tag{3}$$

where H = altitude above some reference, usually sea level (ft); V = true airspeed (ft/sec); and g = acceleration of gravity (32.2 ft/sec^2).

From Equation 3 it is apparent that many combinations of speed and altitude will yield the same specific energy. Figure A-5 plots lines of constant E_S on an altitude-velocity grid. These lines describe speed-altitude combinations that yield the same energy state.

The plot of Figure A-5 is valid for any aircraft—or any rock, for that matter. The "ideal zoom" depicted illustrates how kinetic and potential energy may be traded back and forth while total energy remains constant. Theoretically a powerless aircraft in a vacuum with the speed-altitude combination depicted at the start of this ideal zoom could trade its speed for additional altitude as shown. If the pilot was willing to allow his speed to bleed all the way to zero, this aircraft would top out at about 50,000 ft. Then the aircraft falls, accelerating back to its initial condition. Such ideal zooms seldom occur in practice because of the drag of air resistance and the effects of aircraft thrust, but this example does serve to illustrate the concept of total energy.

Energy state can be changed through the application of power. In the case of aircraft, this power is generally the result of thrust (which tends to increase energy state) and drag (which tends to decrease energy). The rate of change in E_S is known as "specific excess power" (P_S) and is given by the equation

$$P_S \text{ (ft/sec)} = \frac{(T-D)}{W} V, \tag{4}$$

where T = total engine thrust (lbs), D = total aircraft drag (lbs), W = aircraft weight (lbs), and V = true airspeed (ft/sec).

Equation 4 reveals that whenever thrust is greater than drag, P_S will be a positive quantity resulting in increasing energy (i.e., climb or acceleration). Conversely, if drag exceeds thrust at any time, energy will decrease. The P_S of a fighter under given conditions of weight, configuration, engine thrust, speed, altitude, and load factor determines the available performance, or "energy maneuverability," under those conditions. Energy maneuverability may be defined as the ability to change energy state, i.e., to climb and/or to accelerate.

Returning to Equation 3 for a moment, note that aircraft weight has been eliminated and does not enter into ideal-zoom calculations, as shown in Figure A-5. In reality, however, this is not quite the case. Since a zoom takes a finite length of time to complete, the fighter is subject to the effects of weight, thrust, and drag (i.e., P_S) during the maneuver. The amount of energy gained or lost in the zoom depends on the average value of P_S during this period. To illustrate this concept, assume two fighters are identical in all respects, except one is heavier (maybe it is carrying more internal fuel). If they begin zooms at the same speed and altitude (i.e., same E_S), Equation 4 shows that the lighter fighter will have greater P_S, will therefore add more energy during the zoom, and will ultimately zoom higher than the heavy fighter. P_S as well as energy state must, therefore, be taken into account when calculating the zoom capability, or "true energy height," of a fighter.

Thrust Variations

The effect of altitude on both piston and jet engines is usually to reduce their performance. "Normally aspirated" piston engines tend to lose power with increasing altitude approximately in proportion to the reduction in atmospheric air pressure. This results in such an engine producing

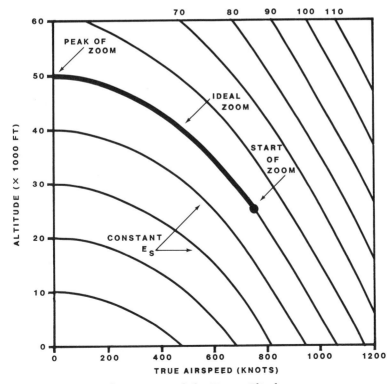

Figure A-5. Specific Energy and the Zoom Climb

only about half its sea-level power at 18,000 ft above mean sea level (MSL). Since the 1930s, however, most first-line fighters have been equipped with superchargers or turbochargers which can allow the engine to maintain its rated power to near 30,000 ft MSL. Jet engines, on the other hand, suffer a loss in thrust which is slightly less than the rate of air density reduction with altitude, and significantly less than that for normally aspirated piston engines. Jets typically lose about half their thrust by 25,000 ft. However, there is no common device similar to the turbocharger for maintaining jet-engine performance at altitude. Figure A-6 shows the typical thrust variations.

The altitude labelled "tropopause" in this plot denotes the level at which atmospheric air temperature ceases to fall. Above this height, typically about 36,000 ft MSL, air temperature is constant. Jet engines in particular benefit from lower air temperatures as altitude increases. Above the tropopause this benefit no longer exists, resulting in a faster rate of jet-thrust decay. Consequently the tropopause is an important altitude in jet-fighter performance. "Critical altitude" is of great significance for turbocharged fighters. This is the highest level at which the turbocharger can maintain full-rated engine power.

The effect of speed on engine thrust is illustrated in Figure A-7. Propeller thrust is usually greatest in the static condition (i.e., zero airspeed) and falls rather rapidly with increasing airspeed. Jet thrust also may be expected to diminish slightly as speed increases above the static condition. As airspeed rises farther, however, ram compression in the engine inlet generally results in significant increases in thrust until engine and inlet design limits are approached. It is quite obvious from this plot why jet fighters exhibit superior high-speed performance.

Drag

As shown by Equation 4, engine thrust is only part of the energy-maneuverability story; aircraft drag characteristics are equally important. Many phenomena contribute to total aircraft drag, some of which can be

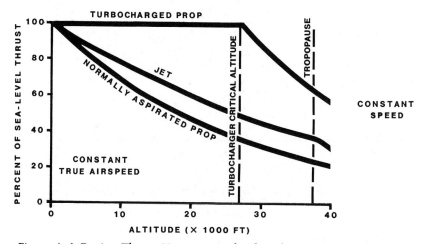

Figure A-6. Engine Thrust Variation with Altitude

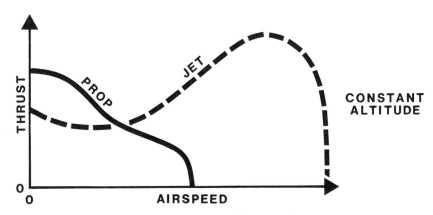

Figure A-7. Engine Thrust Variation with Airspeed

very complex. The most important types of drag are discussed briefly here, but no attempt will be made to qualify the reader as an aeronautical engineer.

"Parasite drag" has many causes, but the most significant forms are skin friction and pressure drag. Skin friction results from air molecules moving across the surfaces of the aircraft. These molecules tend to stick to the aircraft, and much air must be pulled along, adding resistance to the aircraft's motion. Skin-friction drag is reduced by minimizing aircraft surface area and maintaining the smoothest possible surfaces, and by other, more esoteric, methods. Pressure drag results when high-impact air pressure on the leading edges of the aircraft combine with reduced pressure on trailing edges to produce a net rearward force. This form of drag is reduced primarily by minimizing aircraft frontal area, and also by streamlining, which tends to reduce air turbulence and decrease the size of the low-pressure region that forms behind the moving aircraft.

Another type of drag, known as "induced drag," is actually a result of lift. When a wing begins to produce lift, the actual resultant force is not perfectly perpendicular to the relative wind, as lift is defined, but tends to tilt backward somewhat. As illustrated in Figure A-8, this resultant force (F_R) has components both perpendicular to (lift) and parallel with (drag) the relative wind.

In general, for a wing of a given size and shape, the greater the lift produced under given conditions, the greater the induced drag will be. Although this relationship is important for any aircraft, it is especially critical for fighters, since their mission often involves high-load factors requiring a great amount of lift. Induced drag is minimized by designing wings of large area with long, thin planforms. The actual shape of the wing is also very important. For subsonic flight an elliptical planform, made famous by the Spitfire fighter of World War II, is theoretically optimum. Other shapes, however, may be nearly as efficient from an induced-drag standpoint and have other overriding advantages.

Reducing aircraft weight is another critical factor in minimizing induced drag. Less weight requires less lift for a given turn performance, resulting in less induced drag. The aircraft's center of gravity (CG) also has

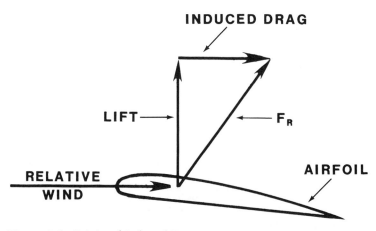

Figure A-8. Origin of Induced Drag

an effect by altering the fighter's apparent weight. Figure A-9 shows how this occurs.

This figure depicts a fighter of a given weight (W) in steady-state flight supported by its lift (L). In this condition the vertical forces must balance each other as well as the pitching moments (torques), which tend to cause the aircraft to rotate ("pitch") nose-up or nose-down. Since weight acts through the CG and lift through the "aerodynamic center" (AC), these two forces cause a nose-down pitching moment with the CG forward as shown. In order to maintain a level flight attitude under these conditions, the tail must produce a downward lift (L_t) large enough to offset the nose-down moment of the wings (i.e., $X_w L = X_t L_t$). This download on the tail, however, must also be supported by the wings, just like dead weight, so induced drag will increase for a given load factor. This additional induced drag is known as "trim drag."

If the CG was moved rearward (by fuel distribution, ordnance loading, etc.) until it coincided with the AC, the tail lift requirement and resulting trim drag would be eliminated. Further rearward movement in the CG would require an upward lift from the tail, which essentially adds additional wing area to the aircraft, thereby reducing induced drag. In practice, however, there is a limit to rearward CG location because of aircraft controllability considerations.

Conventional fighters (i.e., those with rear-mounted pitch-control surfaces) benefit from aft CGs. Canard-configured fighters (i.e., those with pitch controls located forward of the wings), however, normally benefit from forward CG location.

As the speeds of fighters increased through the years, the phenomenon of "compressibility" was encountered. As aircraft move through the air, pressure disturbances are created which propagate outward in all directions at the speed of sound. Those pressure waves that move ahead of the aircraft tend to provide an "advance warning" to the air that the aircraft is approaching, thus giving the air molecules time to begin moving out of the way. The air then begins to part even before the aircraft arrives, which tends to reduce pressure drag. But once a fighter reaches the speed of sound, it begins to outrun its pressure waves and collides with the air molecules with no warning. The air then must be pushed aside almost instantaneously in a process that creates a "shock wave." Shock waves are a relatively inefficient method of changing the flow direction of air, and they create added drag, known as "wave drag," "compressibility drag," or "Mach drag."

Air tends to speed up when flowing over convex curved surfaces, so there may be supersonic flow and shock waves which form at various places on a fighter, even though the aircraft itself is still subsonic. The speed at which the first shock wave appears on a fighter is called its "critical Mach," where Mach number is the ratio of aircraft speed to the speed of sound through the air. Critical Mach (M_{CR}) for modern fighters is usually in the range of 80 to 90 percent of the speed of sound, or .8 to .9 M. At high subsonic and low supersonic speeds it is possible to have a mixture of subsonic and supersonic flow on the aircraft surfaces in a condition termed "transonic."

In addition to increasing pressure drag, shock waves tend to create turbulence and increase skin-friction drag as well. Fundamental changes in the way wings produce lift in supersonic flight also tend to increase trim drag by causing the AC of the wing to move rearward. Because of these combined effects, wave drag is often the most significant form of drag at speeds above M_{CR}.

Fighters began to encounter compressibility problems in the 1930s, usually in the form of large drops in propeller efficiency as the combined aircraft and propeller rotational speeds caused the prop tips to reach their M_{CR}. By the 1940s the aircraft themselves were reaching compressibility limits, usually in prolonged dives from high altitude, which in addition to wave drag also often caused severe control problems. Techniques de-

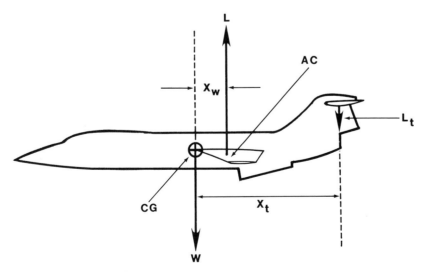

Figure A-9. Origin of Trim Drag

veloped to lessen the effects of wave drag and increase M_{CR} include reducing aircraft cross-sectional area, sharpening leading edges, and sweeping wings. The familiar "Coke-bottle" shape of many jet-fighter fuselages also helps by smoothing out the changes in total aircraft cross-sectional area from nose to tail.

Figure A-10 shows how the various types of drag vary with airspeed and combine to produce total aircraft drag (D). Note that parasite drag (D_p) is insignificant at slow speeds but rises very rapidly as airspeed increases. Conversely, induced drag (D_i) is greatest at very slow speeds and diminishes quickly as the aircraft becomes faster. It should be understood, however, that this plot is representative of an aircraft in straight and level flight (i.e., load factor = 1). Since D_i is proportional to the square of the load factor, this drag component could still predominate in the total drag picture of a high-G fighter even at high airspeeds. Trim drag is not shown explicitly in this figure, but it can be considered as part of the induced-drag component. Wave drag (D_M) can be seen to begin at about M_{CR}; it rises very rapidly in the transonic regime and increases at a slower rate thereafter.

The effects of altitude on drag can be quite complex. Both parasite drag and wave drag usually decrease with higher altitude, but induced drag normally increases. Whether this results in more total drag or less generally depends on aircraft speed and load factor. At low speeds or high G, total drag tends to increase with altitude, but under high-speed, low-G conditions, drag often decreases with increasing altitude.

H-M Diagrams

It should be obvious, considering all the variations in thrust and drag with speed, altitude, etc., that the P_S capabilities of a fighter can be complex. These capabilities are usually determined by flight tests and displayed in graphical formats for pilot study. One such common format is called the H-M (altitude-Mach) diagram. Figure A-11 is an example of this plot for a typical supersonic jet fighter.

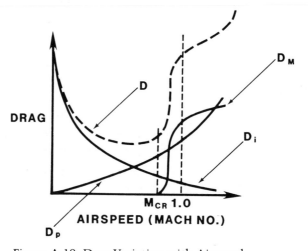

Figure A-10. Drag Variation with Airspeed

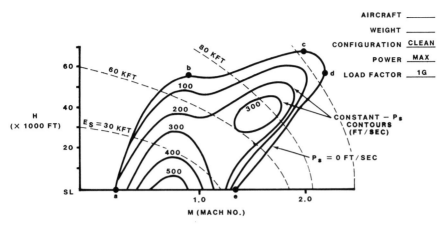

Figure A-11. Typical H-M Diagram

The H-M diagram shows a fighter's P_S capability on a grid of altitude (H) versus Mach number (M). Often lines of constant E_S are also provided for additional reference. Specific excess power is depicted by lines of constant P_S, in this case using ft/sec as the unit of measurement. For the given conditions (weight, configuration, power, load factor), P_S can be related directly with climb rate. For instance, at about 35,000 ft MSL and 1.0 M, this aircraft shows a P_S of about 200 ft/sec. Therefore, under these conditions its climb rate would be 200 ft/sec.

The $P_S = 0$ line on this diagram (the outermost contour) shows the fighter's maximum 1-G steady-state performance. When operating at a speed-altitude combination (energy state) which places it on this line, the fighter cannot climb without losing airspeed and cannot accelerate without losing altitude. Inside this "operating envelope" (region of positive P_S values) the aircraft is free to climb and/or accelerate at will, subject to the rate limitations specified by the P_S contours. Outside this steady-state envelope is a region of negative P_S, where the fighter may operate for short periods of time by giving up energy (i.e., decelerating and/or diving).

Many important operating capabilities of a fighter may be found along the $P_S = 0$ line. Assuming this plot is representative of a 1-G condition, some of these capabilities are:

point *a*: minimum sustained Mach number at any altitude (.3 M at sea level)

point *b*: maximum sustained subsonic altitude (56,000 ft at .9 M)

point *c*: maximum sustained altitude at any speed (67,000 ft at 1.95 M)

point *d*: maximum sustained Mach at any altitude (2.2 M at 55,000 ft)

point *e*: maximum sustained Mach at sea level (1.35 M)

Although this fighter may be capable of the performance depicted from a strictly thrust-versus-drag standpoint, other factors, such as those illustrated by the V-n diagram, may limit performance capabilities. Figure A-12 illustrates the possible impact of such limitations.

The H-M plots presented in Figures A-11 and A-12 have been representative of H-M plots for supersonic fighters. Subsonic jets and prop-driven

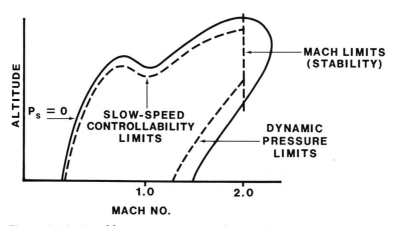

Figure A-12. Possible Limitations to Fighter Performance

fighters can be expected to exhibit fundamentally different operating envelopes. Figure A-13 shows some typical comparisons. Piston-powered fighters suffer from rapid loss of engine performance above critical altitude, thrust decay with increasing airspeed, and possibly prop-compressibility losses at moderate subsonic Mach. These effects can be seen to limit severely the operating envelopes of such aircraft. By contrast, the better high-altitude performance of the jet engine, the typically cleaner aerodynamics of the airframe, and the usually increasing thrust with speed provide the jet fighter with a greater range of operating speed and altitude. The subsonic fighter, however, typically lacks sufficient thrust to overcome the dramatic rise in wave drag above critical Mach, so its performance degenerates badly above that speed. Since the rise in wave drag is usually greater than the corresponding increase in jet thrust with speed, even the supersonic fighter generally exhibits a loss of performance in the transonic region. This aircraft, however, has sufficient excess thrust to carry it through the transonic range so that it may take advantage of the slower rate of drag rise at higher Mach, particularly at high altitude.

As stated in the note to Figure A-11, the performance capabilities depicted in the H-M plot are good for only one condition of weight, configuration, power setting, and load factor. A change in any of these parameters affects the P_S contours and the sustained operating envelope ($P_S = 0$ line), as shown in Figure A-14. To illustrate this effect, assume a fighter is operating at the energy state represented by point f. In the first plot (assume 1 G) the fighter is in an area of positive P_S (inside the steady-state envelope) and can therefore climb or accelerate under these conditions. But if load factor (for example) is increased substantially, as depicted in the second plot, the $P_S = 0$ contour shrinks, placing the fighter outside the steady-state envelope and into a region of negative P_S. This negative P_S, which is probably the result of increased induced drag and wave drag at the higher load factor, will cause the aircraft to lose speed and/or altitude. Obviously there must be some load factor that would cause the $P_S = 0$ line to run exactly through point f. This load factor is defined as the "sustained-G" capability of the fighter at the speed/altitude conditions represented by point f. Sustained G at a given speed defines sustained turn performance in terms of radius and rate. Although H-M diagrams for various load factors may be used to display fighter turn-performance capabilities, other display formats are much better suited to this purpose, as they directly show turn rate and radius values. H-M plots are more convenient for the study of fighter climb performance.

Climb Performance

> Throughout the story of air fighting runs the quest for height, for the fighter on top had control of the air battle.
>
> Air Vice-Marshal J. E. "Johnnie" Johnson, RAF

As explained previously, the climb-rate capability of a fighter under any given flight conditions can be equated to its P_S. The H-M diagram therefore provides an excellent vehicle for the determination of climb rates and optimum climb techniques. At any altitude there is usually one speed that offers the maximum climb rate for a given fighter. The H-M diagram plainly shows this speed as the peak of the P_S contours at that altitude, since any other speed at that altitude would yield a lower P_S value and therefore a lower climb rate. Connecting the P_S peaks with a continuous line generates a "climb profile," which defines the speeds required to maximize climb rate at any point in the climb.

Aircraft, however, can trade altitude for airspeed, and vice versa, almost at will (by zoom climbs and diving accelerations), so an increase in airspeed is essentially the same as an increase in altitude. This fact complicates climb optimization somewhat, since it becomes necessary to maximize

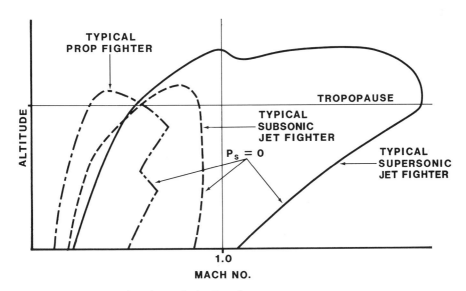

Figure A-13. Typical Fighter Flight Envelopes

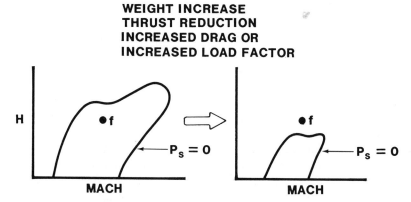

Figure A-14. Effect of Weight, Thrust, Drag, and Load Factor on P_S Contours

the rate of total energy gain rather than just the rate of climb. Such a "maximum energy-rate" climb profile can also be constructed with an H-M diagram, as demonstrated by the example of a supersonic fighter in Figure A-15.

The maximum energy-rate profile is constructed by connecting the points of tangency between the P_S contours and the lines of constant E_S. For the sample fighter at low altitudes this profile, labelled the "subsonic path," differs little from that generated by the P_S peaks. Only slightly faster speeds result, yielding a climb profile of nearly constant Mach between .92 M at sea level and 1.0 M at the climb ceiling of 51,000 ft. Above about 25,000 ft, however, this chart exhibits the characteristic double peaks of the supersonic fighter. As the climb progresses to about 30,000 ft along the subsonic climb path (E_S = 44,000 ft), equal or greater climb rates are available in the supersonic regime at the same energy level. Above this level the faster "supersonic path" becomes the optimum energy-rate profile. This situation becomes quite apparent at higher levels. If, for example, the climb is continued along the subsonic path until it intersects the E_S = 60 KFT (i.e., 60,000 ft) line, climb rate will have dropped to about 50 ft/sec. At the same energy level along the supersonic path the corresponding climb rate still exceeds 200 ft/sec.

Optimum climb techniques for this fighter are best demonstrated through an example. Assume the aircraft is at point A (10 KFT, .6 M) and a climb is to be made to point F (45 KFT, 1.75 M). Theoretically the optimum climb profile would begin with a diving acceleration at constant energy (i.e., parallel to the lines of constant E_S) to intersect the subsonic path at point B (1 KFT, .92 M). The climb would then be continued along the subsonic path until the aircraft reached point C (about 30 KFT), at which time another diving acceleration would be performed to reach the supersonic path at point D (21 KFT, 1.17 M). The supersonic path would be followed to point E (38 KFT, 1.88 M), which represents the final desired energy state (E_S = 90 KFT), and finally a constant-energy zoom climb would be used to reach the goal at point F.

In theory the energy transfers beginning at points *A, C,* and *E* in this example are instantaneous. In practice, however, the aircraft attitude changes necessary to make the transition from climbs to dives, and vice versa, are made slowly and result in a rounding-off of the corners in the climb profile, as shown by the broken lines in these areas. Also because of the finite times involved in such energy transfers, climbs of fairly short duration can sometimes be made more quickly by following "non-optimum" paths, which avoid these time-consuming techniques.

Because of the difficulty of following optimum climb profiles precisely, approximations are usually made. A typical rule of thumb for the fighter in this example might be: climb at .92 M to 25 KFT, then accelerate to and climb at 600 KIAS. Optimum climb profiles for subsonic jet fighters usually begin with a slowly decreasing indicated airspeed until the jet reaches approximately critical Mach, and thereafter a constant Mach number is maintained.

The advantage of using this best energy-rate climb profile as opposed to opting for the nominal best climb-rate path (approximated by the "subsonic path") is quite apparent in the ultimate energy levels attainable. Along the subsonic path this fighter can reach about 51 KFT, and from there it could zoom to about 66 KFT (E_S = 66 KFT), while the supersonic path provides energy levels (and therefore zoom capabilities) in excess of 100 KFT.

Acceleration Performance

> The important thing in aeroplanes is that they shall be speedy.
> Baron Manfred von Richthofen

Aircraft accelerate most quickly by maximizing thrust while minimizing drag. Equation 4 shows that this condition also tends to maximize P_S, so an H-M diagram can give a good indication of the relative acceleration capabilities of a fighter throughout its flight envelope. At any given altitude a fighter tends to accelerate fastest at a speed just slightly below that at which P_S peaks (subsonic peak for supersonic fighters).

Techniques to optimize acceleration include using the highest possible forward thrust and reducing weight and drag as much as practicable. Jettisoning external fuel tanks and nonessential ordnance is useful, since this action reduces both weight and drag.

One of the most effective methods for improving the acceleration performance of fighters is known as "unloading." This involves pushing forward on the pitch controls to reduce load factor, lift, and induced drag. For most fighters induced drag is minimized at a zero-G condition, which may be recognized either by cockpit G-meter readings or by "seat-of-the-pants" indications such as the pilot's feet floating off the rudder pedals, loss by the pilot of any sensation of pressure against the seat, or loose articles and dirt floating around in the cockpit. This last indicator can be hazardous, resulting in jammed controls or dirt in the pilot's eyes, and should be avoided by securing loose articles and maintaining a clean cockpit.

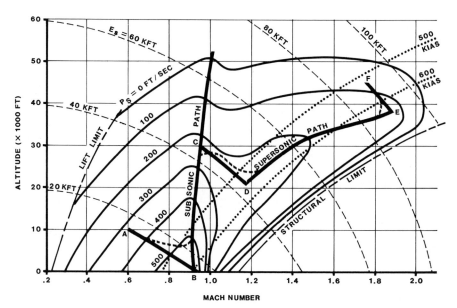

Figure A-15. Sample Climb Profile

Unloading to a full zero-G condition may be limited in some fighters because of engine design. Piston engines with float-type carburetors are notorious for "cutting out" under zero G, which, although usually a temporary condition, obviously would not help acceleration. During World War II fuel-injected German aircraft often used steep unloaded climbs and dives to escape from carbureted Allied fighters. The fuel and oil systems of many other power plants, including quite a few jets, are also restricted or time limited in this maneuver. In such cases unloading may have to be performed at a slightly positive G or be limited in its duration. It is also possible that minimum induced drag will be achieved with some fighters at other than zero G. The fighter pilot should be aware of the characteristics of his particular aircraft and operate accordingly. Figure A-16 illustrates the effects of unloading from 1 G to zero G on the acceleration performance of a typical jet fighter.

This figure is a plot of percentage improvement in acceleration (Δ Acceleration) versus Mach number at various altitudes from sea level to 30 KFT. Note the very large improvement in acceleration at slower speeds, particularly at high altitudes, which can be attributed to the fact that induced drag is the major contributor to total aircraft drag under these conditions. At medium speeds, where induced drag is not as great, its elimination by unloading is seen to have less effect.

Acceleration is of key importance and often overlooked.
                                                Lt. General Adolph Galland, Luftwaffe

Aside from induced-drag reduction, unloading may have other benefits. Parasite drag also may be lowered because of the reduction in frontal area presented to the airstream and a lessening of airflow turbulence over the aircraft surfaces. In the high-subsonic speed range, critical Mach number is usually increased substantially by unloading, which delays the sharp rise in wave drag until the fighter reaches higher speeds. Unloading also tends to reduce the severity of this wave drag once the aircraft accelerates past M_{CR}. These high-speed effects are quite evident in the example of Figure A-16. The impact of unloading on the acceleration performance of a fighter is, however, highly dependent on the fighter's aerodynamic design.

One further method of increasing fighter acceleration is by the use of gravity; a steep dive will often multiply acceleration many times. Such a dive may follow unloading, which causes the aircraft to fly a ballistic trajectory resulting in gradually steepening dive angles. If altitude is available, however, a sharp pull-down to a steep dive attitude, followed by unloading, produces the most rapid long-term acceleration. Discounting the effects of thrust, the acceleration of an aircraft in a dive is a function of its "density," that is, its ratio of weight (actually its mass) to drag. When two fighters are similar in all respects except that one is heavier, the heavier aircraft will accelerate faster in a dive and, assuming structural considerations allow, will have a faster terminal velocity. Likewise, with two fighters of the same weight, the cleaner one (i.e., the one with less drag) will dive better. (This is why a brick falls faster than a feather in air.)

Sustained Turn Performance

In order for a fighter to make a level (constant-altitude) turn, load factor must be increased above 1 G. As load factor is increased at a given airspeed,

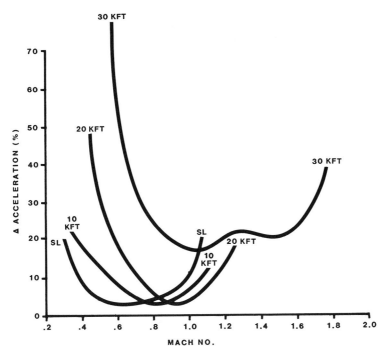

Figure A-16. Effects of Unloading on Acceleration

turn performance (i.e., rate and radius) improves, but total aircraft drag also increases. Eventually a load factor is reached at which the entire thrust of the engines is needed just to offset this drag, leaving no excess power for a simultaneous climb or for acceleration. Equation 4 indicates that when thrust equals drag, P_S is zero. Figure A-14 shows how the zero-P_S line reacts by shrinking and deforming under increased G. This process is further illustrated by Figure A-17.

This figure consists of H-M plots of the same supersonic jet fighter at load factors of 3 Gs and 5 Gs. The outer curve in each case is the 1-G $P_s = 0$ line for reference. Within this 1-G envelope are specific-excess-power values (in ft/sec) for the two sample load factors. Note that the zero-P_S envelope shrinks considerably in the 3-G plot, and even farther under 5 Gs.

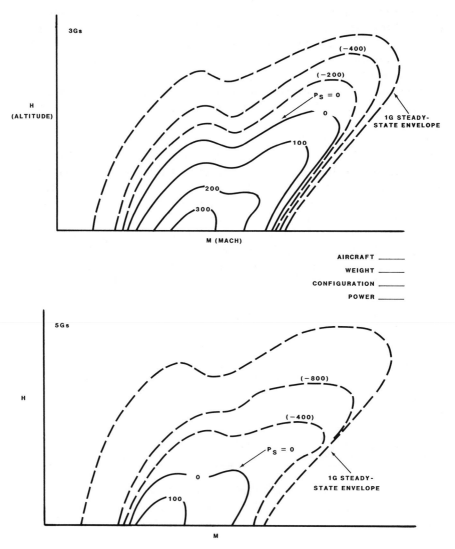

Figure A-17. H-M Diagrams for 3 Gs and 5 Gs

Outside the zero-P_S lines are negative P_S values, which indicate the rate at which energy (altitude and/or airspeed) will be lost while pulling that load factor at a given combination of speed and altitude. Inside the zero-P_S envelope are positive P_S values, which give the rate at which energy may be gained (by a climb and/or acceleration) under those conditions. The conditions under which the given load factor can just be sustained are those which lie directly on the respective zero-P_S lines. Once the sustained-G capability of a fighter is known at a given speed, its sustained turn rate and radius under those conditions may be determined mathematically or by Figure A-2.

Note that for this supersonic fighter the zero-P_S curve has two peaks. At high altitudes and fairly low G levels (less than about 5 G for this aircraft), the highest peak, and consequently the greatest sustained G, is found in the supersonic speed range. At low altitudes, where sustained-G levels are higher, however, the maximum sustained G is usually achieved at speeds near the subsonic peak. Obviously, subsonic fighters would generate greatest sustained G in the subsonic region at all altitudes.

Sustained G, however, is generally of less value in air combat than the corresponding turn rate and radius are. Because of the interaction of airspeed and G, best sustained turn rate is generally achieved at a speed slightly below that for maximum sustained G at a given altitude. For supersonic fighters this speed is almost always near the subsonic-P_S peak, even at high-altitude/low-G conditions, since supersonic speeds greatly reduce turn rate. Because of the very great sensitivity of turn radius to airspeed, minimum sustained turn radius is normally achieved at fairly slow airspeed (generally 1.4 to 1.5 times power-on stall speed for jets), considerably slower than for best sustained turn rate.

Speed control is quite important for prolonged sustained turn performance. Pulling too great a load factor will cause speed to bleed off below the optimum value, resulting in reduced sustained turn. This lost speed can be regained only by relaxing G (further reducing turn performance) until the aircraft accelerates back to the desired speed, or by diving, which allows gravity to provide the needed acceleration.

The sustained-G capability of a fighter is proportional to its ratio of thrust to weight (T/W) at its particular altitude and airspeed. High T/W is analogous to low "power loading" (weight/horsepower) for prop-powered fighters. Just as important for sustained-G performance, however, is the lifting efficiency of the wing-airframe combination of the fighter, which is measured by the lift-to-drag ratio (L/D) at sustained-G levels. Therefore a relatively low-powered fighter with high L/D may possess a greater sustained-G capability. For two fighters with roughly the same sustained-G performance, the one that achieves its optimum sustained turn capability at the lower airspeed will have better sustained turn rate and radius. This superior low-airspeed performance is generally achieved by designing a larger wing for a given aircraft weight, which results in lower "wing loading" (aircraft weight/wing area), or by providing greater L/D for the wing by use of slots, slats, flaps, etc.

The fighter pilot can optimize his sustained turn performance by controlling airspeed, keeping weight and drag to a minimum, and configuring his aircraft to provide maximum L/D for the high-G condition. Still another technique is to maintain the aircraft CG at the rearmost position practicable (assuming a tail-configured fighter) in order to minimize trim drag, as explained earlier.

A feature that is less well known among fighter pilots is a phenomenon known as "gyroscopic precession," which may cause a fighter's turn performance to vary depending on the direction of its turn. High-speed rotational components, such as propellers or jet compressor and turbine rotors, behave as large gyroscopes when the aircraft turns. Gyroscopic precession generates a torque about an axis that is perpendicular to both the rotational axis of the gyroscope (generally near the fuselage axis of the aircraft) and the axis about which the fighter is turning (i.e., the vertical axis for a level turn). For a level turn this results in a gyroscopic nose-up or nose-down moment (relative to the earth) which must be compensated for by increased upward or downward lift from the pitch-control surfaces, and by use of the rudder. Whenever this gyroscopic moment must be offset largely by the pitch controls, there will be an increase or decrease in trim drag, depending on the turn direction. This phenomenon affects both sustained and instantaneous turn performance in a manner that is similar to the effect of an actual weight change in the aircraft.

The significance of the gyroscopic effect is increased by large, heavy rotating parts (high moment of inertia) in relation to total aircraft weight, and by faster rotational speeds. Faster turn rates, slower speeds, level skidding turns, lower G, and shorter distances between the CG and the pitch-control surface also increase the impact of the gyroscopic effect on turn performance.

As fighters have developed over the years they have generally become larger, heavier, faster, and capable of developing more G but less turn rate. All these factors have served to reduce the impact of the gyroscopic effect to the point where it may be insignificant to a modern fighter. This was certainly not the case, however, during World War I, when many fighters of both sides, including some Sopwiths, Nieuports, and Fokkers, were powered by rotary engines. The rotary engine was an air-cooled design with cylinders arranged radially around a central crankshaft. The prop was connected directly to the cylinders, and the cylinders and prop rotated as a unit around the fixed crankshaft. With more than one-quarter of their total weight comprised of rotating parts, some of these fighters earned reputations for being extremely maneuverable—at least in one direction. This same characteristic, however, made these fighters very tricky to handle, and they probably killed nearly as many of their own pilots as they did those of the enemy.

Torque may also have an effect on turn performance, particularly with high-powered prop fighters at slow speed. The effects of engine torque must generally be offset by rudder power to maintain balanced flight. Normally under these conditions considerable right rudder will be required to balance the torque of a prop turning clockwise (when viewed from behind), and vice versa. Another consideration here is called "P-factor," which is the tendency of a propeller to produce more thrust from one side of its disc than from the other. P-factor usually affects the aircraft in the same manner as torque, and it is exacerbated by slow speeds and hard turning. Since even more rudder is usually required in the direction of a turn to maintain balanced flight, there may be conditions under which sufficient rudder power is just not available. The resulting unbalanced flight (slip) may cause loss of aircraft control. Generally the high wing (i.e., the outside wing in a turn) will stall, causing the aircraft to "depart" controlled flight with a rapid roll toward the stalled wing.

This phenomenon has been used to good effect in combat, since it is more pronounced in some fighters than in others, and because prop-rotation direction may be reversed between combatants. The following World War II combat example of this tactic involves the P-38J Lightning versus the German Fw 190. The P-38 is a twin-engine fighter with counter-rotating props and essentially no net torque or P-factor.

> My flight of four P-38s was bounced by twenty-five to thirty FW-190s of the yellow-nose variety from Abbeville. A string of six or more of them got in behind me before I noticed them, and just as No. 1 began to fire, I rolled into a right climbing turn and went to war emergency of 60 inches manifold pressure. As we went round and round in our corkscrew climb, I could see over my right shoulder the various FW-190 pilots booting right rudder attempting to control their torque at 150 mph and full throttle, but one by one they flipped over to the left and spun out.[1]

Gravity Effects on Turn Performance

The acceleration of gravity has a very significant effect on turn perform-ance. Figure A-18 illustrates the influence of gravity on a level turn. In this example the aircraft is flying out of the page in a level left turn. The acceleration of gravity tends to pull downward on the aircraft, and for level flight gravity must be balanced by lift, which is represented by the load-factor vector. Load factor, however, is oriented perpendicular to the fighter's wings, so only the vertical component of this acceleration can oppose gravity. This leaves only the horizontal component of load factor, labelled "radial G," to turn the aircraft. Because load factor must offset

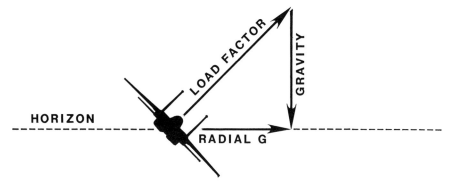

Figure A-18. Level-Turn Accelerations

gravity, radial G will be smaller than the full load factor experienced by the aircraft, and turn performance will suffer.

Gravity also affects vertical maneuvers, such as the loop illustrated in Figure A-19. In this case the fighter is executing a loop at a constant speed and a load factor of 4 Gs. At the bottom of the loop the downward pull of gravity reduces radial G to only 3 Gs, causing a large turn radius and a low turn (in this case "pitch") rate. At the top of the loop, when the fighter is inverted, gravity adds to load factor, producing a 5-G turn, smaller radius, and faster rate. When the aircraft is vertical, both nose-high and nose-low, there is no component of gravity in the direction of lift, so load factor becomes radial G, resulting in intermediate turn performance. The effect of gravity on turn radius during vertical maneuvers causes the flight path to be noncircular, giving rise to the term "tactical egg." In practice the fighter's airspeed is usually very much slower at the top of the maneuver than along the bottom, which serves to accentuate the variation in turn radius even more.

The two maneuver planes discussed (horizontal and vertical) are only two of an infinite number available to the fighter pilot. All other maneuver planes are called "oblique turns." Gravity affects these turns in the same manner, depending on the steepness of the maneuver plane. Whenever the fighter's lift vector is oriented above the horizon, gravity detracts from turn performance; conversely, gravity enhances turn performance when the lift vector is pointing below the horizon.

Roll Performance

The foregoing discussions of fighter performance concerned the aircraft's ability to change the orientation of its velocity vector and its energy state, that is, to turn, accelerate, or climb. This ability is "maneuverability" or "energy maneuverability." There are other important measures of fighter performance which do not fit this definition.

Roll performance, for example, is the ability of an aircraft to change the lateral direction of its lift vector. Since the lift force is primarily responsible for turning an aircraft, roll performance indicates the ability of a fighter to change its plane of maneuver. Therefore, although roll performance is not, in a strict sense, maneuverability, it does have a direct relationship with maneuverability. Roll performance may be defined as a measure of the aircraft's "agility."

A big aerial barge is too clumsy for fighting. Agility is needed.
Baron Manfred von Richthofen

The rolling motion of an aircraft is produced by the action of its lateral control system. These systems vary from fighter to fighter, but presently the most common controls are ailerons, spoilers, and differential tails. Since all control systems are more effective in some situations than in others, many modern fighters are designed with more than one type control to avoid problems throughout the flight envelope of the aircraft.

Aerodynamic roll controls operate by increasing lift on one side of the aircraft relative to that on the other, producing a rolling moment. When this condition occurs, a roll will commence, accelerate to a maximum value, and then stabilize at that rate. A stabilized roll rate is attained when a balancing, or "damping," moment is generated which offsets the torque of the roll controls. This damping moment is produced primarily by lift differences between the two wings caused by one wing moving upward and the other downward, and is proportional to the roll stability of the aircraft. In general, the more stable a fighter is about the roll axis, the slower its roll rate will be.

Figure A-20 graphically illustrates the effects of speed on steady roll performance. The charts in the figure discount both compressibility, which may reduce the effectiveness of roll controls or even cause rolls opposite to the intended direction (called "roll reversal"), and "aeroelastic effects," which may cause similar problems as a result of the wings twisting under the torque of the roll-control deflections. Note that as speed increases, the force (F_r) required from the pilot to maintain full control deflection (δ_r) increases until reaching the limits of his physical ability, after which further speed increases result in reduced control deflection. In the range of maximum-control deflection, roll rate increases almost linearly with speed, reaching a maximum at the highest speed at which full control deflection (δ_{rMAX}) can be maintained. Roll-rate capability then decreases with further speed increase, possibly to very low values at high speeds. To maintain roll performance at high speeds, power-boosted or fully powered controls are often employed to enable the pilot to attain full control deflection. With powered controls the pilot's control inputs usually position valves that allow hydraulic fluid pressure to move the control surfaces. The effects of such systems are shown by the dashed lines. For supersonic fighters it is also desirable to make these controls irreversible, so that variations in airloads on the control surfaces are not transmitted back to the pilot. Shock waves moving around on these surfaces can lead to some very distracting and misleading feel cues, making aircraft control difficult. With such controls, artificial-feel systems are usually provided so that control forces vary as the pilot would expect.

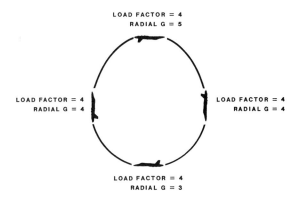

Figure A-19. Load Factor versus Radial G in Vertical Maneuvering

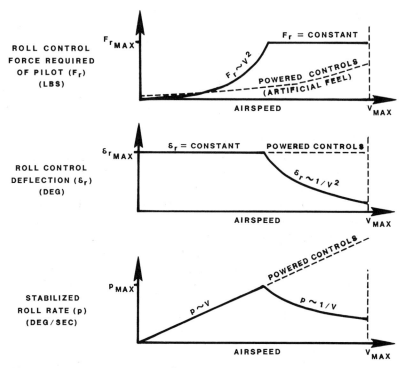

Figure A-20. Variations in Roll Rate with Airspeed

In air combat, continuous rolls of more than 180° are seldom required. Because a certain length of time is necessary to accelerate the roll rate from zero to its maximum value, maximum stabilized roll rate may not be reached during such short periods of roll. Therefore, roll acceleration is often the controlling factor in combat performance.

In addition to roll-control power, roll acceleration is a function of the "moment of inertia" of the aircraft. This moment of inertia about the roll axis depends on the aircraft weight and its distribution. The greater the total weight, and the farther it is distributed away from the fuselage axis, the greater the inertia. Large wingspan, tip-tank fuel, and wing-mounted ordnance or engines, for example, would contribute to increased roll inertia and reduced roll acceleration. In addition, roll performance may vary between left and right depending on the design of the aircraft. Prop-driven fighters, for instance, generally have better roll acceleration in the direction opposite to that of prop rotation because of engine torque effects. Cockpit configuration may also be a factor, particularly with unboosted control systems at high speeds. The pilot's ability to push the stick to the left harder than he can pull it to the right may result in a noticeable difference in roll performance.

Stabilized roll rate is also affected by wingspan. For geometrically similar fighters, shorter wingspan results in higher stabilized roll rate for the same speed and control deflection.

Roll performance is highly dependent on pilot technique as well as on speed control. Many of the effectiveness problems of roll-control devices occur at slow speeds or with high load factors (i.e., when the wings are generating close to their maximum lift). Therefore, if a pilot wishes to achieve maximum roll performance from his aircraft he should whenever possible unload before beginning the roll. Load factor can be reapplied once the lift vector is pointing in the desired direction. Efficient rudder technique can also improve roll performance. Rudder may even be the most effective roll-control device available for some fighters (especially those with sharply swept wings), particularly under high-lift conditions.

A roll-performance superiority has historically been exploited as an effective tool in guns-defense maneuvers. Since for steady guns tracking of a maneuvering target the shooter must have his aircraft's wings closely aligned with those of his victim, such tracking can be rendered practically impossible by an uncooperative defender who can change his plane of maneuver more rapidly than the attacker. Poor roll performance at high speed was one of the few characteristics of the Japanese Zero which could be exploited by the generally inferior American fighters early in World War II. Similarly, hydraulically boosted ailerons improved the agility of the American F-86 Sabre jets relative to their Russian MiG-15 adversaries in Korea. Lack of hydraulic assist continued to plague the later MiG-17 in Vietnam and the Middle East.

Pitch Performance

Pitch performance is the ability of a fighter to rotate about an axis that is parallel to its wings (i.e., the "lateral" axis). In level flight this would mean rotating the nose of the aircraft upward or downward, but the upward direction is generally the more important. Like roll performance, pitch rate is a measure of the fighter's agility.

When pitch controls are applied in a nose-up direction the aircraft begins to rotate, which causes an increase in "angle of attack," as defined in Figure A-21. Angle of attack (AOA) is the angle between the "chord line" of the wing (an imaginary line that connects the wing's leading and trailing edges) and the "relative wind," which is equal in speed to, and opposite in direction to, the aircraft's motion through the air. As AOA increases, so generally do the lift produced by the wing, and load factor, which causes the aircraft to turn (i.e., change the direction of the velocity vector). The motion that is observed is therefore partially turn and partially increasing

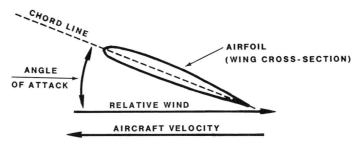

Figure A-21. Angle of Attack

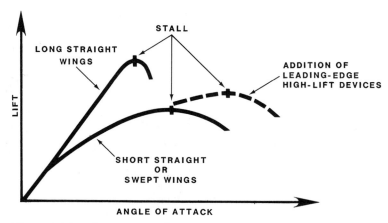

Figure A-22. Lift versus Angle of Attack

AOA. It is difficult to separate these two motions visually, so both are generally included in "pitch rate." Once AOA has stabilized, pitch rate and turn rate in a given maneuver plane are the same.

Pitch rate is important to fighters for several reasons. One of them is that the faster AOA can be increased, the more quickly a turn can begin. This can have a great effect on the early stages of maximum turn-performance maneuvers. A second reason is the influence of pitch rate on gunsight tracking. The ability simply to point the aircraft in a given direction, regardless of its direction of motion, is quite valuable. A third factor has to do with the difficulty of visually differentiating pitch rate from turn rate. Since fighter pilots must rely on visual information to assess the performance of an opponent's aircraft, large changes in AOA easily may be mistaken for increased turn performance. Such a misinterpretation often leads to mistakes in maneuver selection to counter the perceived maneuver of an adversary.

The pitch performance of a fighter, i.e., pitch rate and pitch acceleration, is a function of the effectiveness of the pitch controls and the resistance the aircraft presents to a pitching motion. The AOA contribution to pitch is limited by the maximum usable AOA (stall AOA or limits of controllability) at low speeds and by load-factor limits above corner speed. Since the range of usable AOA is rather small (about 20° to 30°) for most fighters, AOA's contribution to pitching motion is completed quickly. Therefore, as in the case of roll performance, it is pitch acceleration rather than pitch rate which is of greater importance in fighter maneuvering when the discussion is limited to AOA changes only.

Since the rate of AOA increase is on the same order of magnitude as the turn rate and is additive in producing total pitch performance, the greater the range of usable AOA, the greater its contribution will be during the early phases of a turn. Greatest pitch performance is often found near corner speed, which provides the highest instantaneous turn rate and represents the fastest possible speed (for maximum pitch-control authority) at which the full range of AOA is available. Design features such as short or swept wings and leading-edge high-lift devices can increase maximum usable AOA by increasing the stall AOA, as shown in Figure A-22.

Pitch acceleration is dependent on control power and on the aircraft's pitch stability and its inertia. The moment of inertia about the pitch axis is a function of the fighter's weight and its distribution fore and aft about the CG. Increasing total aircraft weight or moving some of this weight farther from the CG either forward or aft tends to increase pitch inertia and reduce pitch acceleration. The position of the CG also has an effect. Aft CG positions usually increase pitch performance by reducing aircraft stability.

> Know and use all the capabilities in your airplane. If you don't, sooner or later, some guy who does use them all will kick your ass.
> Lieutenant Dave "Preacher" Pace, USN
> U.S. Navy Fighter Weapons School Instructor

Note

1. Robin Higham and Abigail T. Siddal, eds., *Flying Combat Aircraft of the USAAF-USAF,* p. 136.

Bibliography

Air Force Flight Test Center. *Performance*. Vol. 1, *Aerodynamic Theory* (AD-A011 992). Springfield, VA: National Technical Information Service, 1973.

Bishop, William A. *Winged Warfare*. Garden City, NY: Doubleday, 1967.

Boyington, Gregory. *Baa Baa Black Sheep*. Fresno, CA: Wilson Press, 1958.

Brickhill, Paul. *Reach for the Sky*. New York: Ballantine Books, 1967.

Brown, David; Shores, Christopher; and Macksey, Kenneth. *The Guinness History of Air Warfare*. Enfield, Great Britain: Guinness Superlatives, 1976.

Caidin, Martin. *Fork-Tailed Devil: The P-38*. New York: Ballantine Books, 1971.

———. *The Ragged, Rugged Warriors*. New York: Ballantine Books, 1967.

Chant, Chris. *The Pictorial History of Air Warfare*. London: Octopus Books, 1979.

Chinn, George M. *The Machine Gun*. Vol. 1. Washington, D.C.: U.S. Government Printing Office, 1951.

Cunningham, Randy, with Ethell, Jeff. *Fox Two*. Mesa, AZ: Champlin Fighter Museum, 1984.

Deere, Alan C. *Nine Lives*. London: Hodder and Stoughton, 1959.

Douglas, Sholto. *Combat and Command*. New York: Simon and Schuster, 1963.

Galland, Adolph. *The First and the Last*. New York: Bantam Books, 1978.

Gibbons, Floyd. *The Red Knight of Germany*. New York: Bantam Books, 1964.

Godfrey, John T. *The Look of Eagles*. New York: Random House, 1958.

Green, William, and Swanborough, Gordon, eds. *The World's Great Fighter Aircraft*. New York: Crescent Books, 1981.

Gunston, Bill, ed. *The Illustrated History of Fighters*. New York: Exeter Books, 1983.

Gurney, Gene. *Five Down and Glory*. New York: Ballantine Books, 1958.

Hall, Grover C., Jr. *1000 Destroyed*. Fallbrook, CA: Aero Publishers, 1978.

Haugland, Vern. *The Eagle Squadrons*. New York: Ziff-Davis Flying Books, 1979.

Higham, Robin, and Siddall, Abigail T., eds. *Flying Combat Aircraft of the USAAF-USAF*. Manhattan, KS: Air Force Historical Foundation.

Hurt, H. H., Jr. *Aerodynamics for Naval Aviators*. (NAVWEPS 00-80T-80). Washington, D.C.: U.S. Government Printing Office, 1960.

Johnson, J. E. *Full Circle*. New York: Bantam Books, 1980.

———. *Wing Leader*. New York: Ballantine Books, 1957.

Johnson, Robert S., with Caidin, Martin. *Thunderbolt!* New York: Ballantine Books, 1959.

Longstreet, Stephen. *The Canvas Falcons.* New York: Ballantine Books, 1972.

Luukkanen, Eino. *Fighter over Finland.* London: Macdonald, 1963.

McCudden, James T. B. *Flying Fury.* New York: Ace Publishing, 1968.

Meyer, John C. "The Long Reach." *Tac Attack* (June 1970), pp. 8–10.

Musashi, Miyamoto. *A Book of Five Rings.* Trans. Victor Harris. Woodstock, NY: The Overlook Press, 1974.

Navy Fighter Weapons School Journal. (numerous unclassified articles, 1977–1984).

Nelson, Gordon, et al., eds. *Air War: Vietnam.* New York: Arno Press, 1978.

Olmsted, Merle. *Aircraft Armament.* New York: Sports Car Press, 1970.

Reynolds, Quintin. *They Fought for the Sky.* New York: Bantam Books, 1972.

von Richthofen, Manfred F. *The Red Air Fighter.* New York: Arno Press, 1972.

Rickenbacker, Eddie V. *Fighting the Flying Circus.* Garden City, NY: Doubleday, 1965.

Sakai, Saburo, with Caidin, Martin, and Saito, Fred. *Samurai!* Garden City, NY: Nelson Doubleday, 1978.

Scott, Robert L., Jr. *God Is My Co-Pilot.* New York: Ballantine Books, 1956.

De Seversky, Alexander P. *Victory through Air Power.* New York: Simon and Schuster, 1942.

Shores, Christopher. *Fighter Aces.* London: The Hamlyn Publishing Group, 1975.

Sims, Edward H. *Fighter Tactics and Strategy, 1914–1970.* Fallbrook, CA: Aero Publishers, 1980.

———. *The Greatest Aces.* New York: Ballantine Books, 1967.

Spick, Mike. *Fighter Pilot Tactics.* New York: Stein and Day, 1983.

Springs, Elliot White. *War Birds: Diary of an Unknown Aviator.* New York: Grosset and Dunlap, 1926.

Stewart, James T., ed. *Airpower: The Decisive Force in Korea.* Princeton, NJ: D. Van Nostrand, 1957.

Taylor, W. P., and Irvine, F. L. *History of the 148th Aero Squadron.* Lancaster, SC: Tri-County Publishing, 1957.

Thyng, Harrison R. "Air-to-Air Combat in Korea." *Air University Quarterly Review* 6, no. 2 (1953).

Toliver, Raymond F., and Constable, Trevor J. *Fighter Aces of the U.S.A.* Fallbrook, CA: Aero Publishers, 1979.

———. *Horrido! Fighter Aces of the Luftwaffe.* New York: Bantam Books, 1979.

Treager, Irwin E. *Jet Aircraft Engines.* Blue Ridge Summit, PA: TAB Books, 1974.

USAF Fighter Weapons Review. (numerous articles, 1978–1984).

Wagner, Ray. *American Combat Planes.* Garden City, NY: Doubleday, 1968.

Werner, Johannes. *Knight of Germany.* New York: Arno Press, 1972.

Ziegler, Mano. *Rocket Fighter.* New York: Bantam Books, 1984.

Index